GW00982734

Recent Advances in
Canine and Feline Nutrition
Volume II

1998 Iams Nutrition Symposium
Proceedings

RECENT ADVANCES IN CANINE AND FELINE NUTRITION

VOLUME II

1998 Iams Nutrition Symposium Proceedings

Edited by

Gregory A. Reinhart, PhD
Director of Strategic Research
Research and Development, The Iams Company

Daniel P. Carey, DVM
Director of Technical Communications
Research and Development, The Iams Company

ORANGE FRAZER PRESS
Wilmington, Ohio, USA

Developmental Editor: Susan M. Yaeger
Section Editors: Michael G. Hayek, PhD
                    Allan J. Lepine, PhD
                    Gregory D. Sunvold, PhD

ISBN 1-882203-21-6
Printed on recycled paper.
Printed in the USA.

Published by
ORANGE FRAZER PRESS
37½ West Main Street
Wilmington, Ohio 45177
USA

Dedicated to Clay Mathile . . .

*who encourages personal and scientific excellence
in the pursuit of new nutritional truths and
boldly submits innovative research concepts
to the rigorous scrutiny of the scientific community.
Without his commitment and support to
advance the well-being of dogs and cats worldwide,
many of the research programs presented in this publication
would not have been possible.*

Mission Statement

***Our mission is to
enhance the well-being
of dogs and cats
by providing world-class quality foods.***

Table of Contents

GROWTH AND DEVELOPMENT

Diabetes Management

Obesity

NEONATAL HEALTH

PHYSICAL STRESS NUTRITION

GERIATRIC NUTRITION

RENAL HEALTH

GASTROINTESTINAL HEALTH

IMMUNOLOGY

Recent Advances in Canine and Feline Nutrition
Volume II

Preface

The roots of the nutritional philosophy that guides The Iams Company today started more than 50 years ago in the entrepreneurial mind of Paul F. Iams. A self-taught animal nutritionist, Mr. Iams was not satisfied with the nutritional value of existing pet foods, so he set a goal to make a perfectly balanced food for dogs that would provide optimal nutrition.

A serendipitous discovery while visiting mink farms was made when Paul noticed that guard dogs at the mink farms were in remarkable condition. Upon investigation, he found that the dogs ate the same food as the mink and that they were thriving — in spite of the fact that the high protein, high fat diet being fed was in opposition to the conventional industry standards that said dogs should eat a low protein, low fat diet.

Paul Iams continued to focus on improving the nutritional matrix of formulas until his retirement when Clay Mathile became sole owner of the small but growing company and infused another brand of leadership and innovation into The Iams Company. As the company continued to expand, Clay boldly developed a plan for building a team of science professionals and a research facility, a major investment made well before company sales could justify such an expenditure. The Paul F. Iams Technical Center represents the company's commitment to scientific excellence and long term quality standards.

The Iams Research and Development team not only provides the technology to develop new diets, but it also directs continuous improvements to existing products to ensure optimal nutrition. This record of development and introduction of new products is unequaled by any other company in the industry.

Driven By A Mission. The mission of The Iams Company is to enhance the well-being of dogs and cats by providing world-class quality foods. This singularity of purpose allows Iams to focus on conducting active research to further understand the nutritional needs of dogs and cats in different life stages, life styles, and life conditions.

In healthy animals this can mean complete and balanced formulas that provide unsurpassed levels of nutritional support to help dogs and cats develop to their fullest potential. In addition, revolutionary concepts in nutrition can help manage normal life progressions, such as obesity, and perhaps delay or offset the evolution of typical geriatric problems.

For compromised animals, the nutritional philosophy of the company is to address the underlying cause of the disease, not just focus on the signs. This must be done in an overall nutritional matrix that provides for optimal nutrition for the entire animal as well as organ specific nutrition for the compromised system(s).

During the early years, formulations were based on controlled observational studies in dogs and cats. Stool quality, skin and hair coat, alertness and general attitude were closely monitored. Establishing the technical center allowed dietary formulation decisions to be based on more in-depth scientific methods. This created many marketplace challenges as traditional viewpoints being espoused by the pet food industry were not supported by scientific studies. Iams studies proved that low protein, high fiber diets were not the best nutritional choice for the natural carnivore, the dog and the cat. Iams formulations for different life styles and life stages were developed based on results of long term feeding studies and university research.

In the early 1990's, the company made an additional commitment to provide veterinarians with nutritional tools to manage compromised dogs and cats. This entailed developing a sophisticated, international research program to truly define the nutritional needs of dogs and cats in various disease states.

Led By A Vision. The vision of The Iams Company is to be recognized as the world leader in dog and cat nutrition. Dedicated to achieving this goal, the company has consistently devoted a higher percentage of sales dollars to research than any other pet food company.

Iams researchers work in partnership with leading universities around the world to conduct independent studies. The knowledge generated from these collaborative studies have allowed Iams to achieve scientific breakthroughs in canine and feline nutrition. Aggressive publication of these research studies in quality, peer-reviewed scientific journals, as well as presentation of data at scientific forums, is a priority. Many of these studies have led to scientific breakthroughs that include the following:

- optimal balance of omega-6 and omega-3 fatty acids for a healthy skin and coat
- moderately fermentable fiber for a healthy gastrointestinal tract
- dietary fructooligosaccharides (FOS) to favorably modulate intestinal bacteria
- normal fiber weight loss products
- fermentable fibers to provide an alternative nitrogen excretion route for renal patients
- puppy foods formulated for breed size

- feline urinary tract products for both struvite and oxalate conditions
- nutrient dense formulas for physically stressed animals
- milk replacer formulas that match growth rates of nursing puppies and kittens
- optimal levels of protein and fat for geriatric animals
- dietary chromium to improve glucose metabolism
- dietary carotenoids to enhance canine and feline immune function

For more than 50 years, The Iams Company has pioneered the implementation of new nutritional concepts and will continue to pursue innovative research into the future.

Author Profiles

Guy Bouchard, DMV, MS, Diplomate ACT

Dr. Bouchard received a DMV from the Université de Montréal, an MS and certificate of residency training in theriogenology from the University of Missouri, and also a second MS in Laboratory Animal Science from the University of Missouri. Dr. Bouchard is board certified in theriogenology and is currently the director of Sinclair Research Center, a biomedical research facility with emphasis on animal modeling and production of miniature swine and cats dedicated to research.

William R. Brawner, Jr., DVM, PhD, Diplomate ACVR

Dr. Brawner received BS and MS degrees in Animal Science and Nutrition from the University of Florida, and a DVM degree from Auburn University. He completed a PhD after research in nuclear medicine at the Medical and Health Sciences Division of Oak Ridge Associated Universities. He is currently Associate Professor, Radiology in the Department of Radiology at Auburn University, College of Veterinary Medicine. His research interests include development of non-invasive diagnostic imaging techniques for assessment of disease process with emphasis on neoplasia and developmental bone disease.

Scott A. Brown, VMD, PhD, Diplomate ACVIM (Internal Medicine)

Dr. Brown received a VMD from the University of Pennsylvania and board certification in Internal Medicine at the University of Georgia. He was a post-doctoral research fellow at the University of Alabama School of Medicine and received a PhD in Renal Pathophysiology from the University of Georgia. He is currently Associate Professor with a joint appointment in the Departments of Physiology and Small Animal Medicine at the University of Georgia. His research interests include progression of chronic renal disease, systemic hypertension, and the impact of nutritional modifications on animals with renal failure.

Geza G. Bruckner, PhD

Dr. Bruckner received a PhD from the University of Kentucky in Animal Nutrition/Toxicology and conducted postdoctoral research at Cornell University on the effects of trans and omega-3 fatty acids on cardiovascular disease. Dr. Bruckner is a Professor in the Department of Clinical Nutrition at the University of Kentucky. His research interests continue to focus on lipid metabolism in cardiovascular disease. During a recent sabbatical at George Washington University, he studied lipid metabolism in the feline using isotopomer analysis.

Randal K. Buddington, PhD

Dr. Buddington received a BS in Biology from the University of California at Riverside, an MS in Zoology from Arizona State University, and a PhD in Ecology from the University of California at Davis. He received further training in gastrointestinal physiology as a post-doctoral fellow at the UCLA Medical Center. Dr. Buddington is now Associate Professor in Biological Sciences at Mississippi State University, College of Veterinary Medicine. His current research program uses a multidisciplinary approach to investigate the interrelations that occur between diet, intestinal structure, functions, and the resident microflora during development, and the health of animals.

Daniel P. Carey, DVM

Dr. Carey received a BA in Biology from Illinois Wesleyan University and a DVM from the University of Missouri-Columbia. He has been in private and clinical practice, including three years in the United States Air Force as Base Veterinarian. Dr. Carey is currently Director of Technical Communications for the Research and Development Division of The Iams Company. Dr. Carey has been directly involved in nutrition research on a wide variety of animals and has experience in clinical, surgical, diagnostic, and nutritional research.

Sharon A. Center, DVM, Diplomate ACVIM

Dr. Center obtained a DVM from the University of California at Davis, then completed a small animal internship at Cornell University. After working for several years in private practice in California, she returned to Cornell to complete a residency in small animal internal medicine. Dr. Center joined the clinical faculty at Cornell where her responsibilities include co-management of the Internal Medicine Referral Service in the Companion Animal Hospital, didactic teaching of veterinary students, and conducting focused research. She is currently a Professor of Internal Medicine at Cornell where she actively pursues research focused in the area of hepatobiliary disease.

Boon P. Chew, PhD

Dr. Chew is an alumnus of Purdue University where he received an MS in Animal Sciences and a PhD in Animal Science and Biochemistry. He received a BS degree in Animal Sciences from Louisiana State University and was a Ford Foundation Postdoctoral Fellow in Reproductive Physiology at the University of Illinois. Dr. Chew is currently Full Professor in Animal Sciences at Washington State University in the area of nutritional physiology. His research focus is on the importance of natural carotenoids on immune modulation, reproduction, and cancer.

Thomas D. Crenshaw, PhD

Dr. Crenshaw received a BS in Animal Science from the University of Tennessee at Martin, and MS and PhD degrees in Animal Science from the University of Nebraska. He is currently Director of the University of Wisconsin-Madison Swine Research Center and has affiliate appointments in the Interdepartmental Graduate Nutrition Program, the Medical Sciences Department in the School of Veterinary Medicine, and the Anatomy Department in the Medical College. Dr. Crenshaw's research interests include inter-relationships of dietary minerals and skeletal integrity, optimization of dietary lysine use by growing swine, and nutritional factors affecting baby pig growth and survival.

Gary M. Davenport, PhD

Dr. Davenport is an alumnus of the University of Kentucky where he received a BS in Animal Science, an MS in Ruminant Nutrition, and a PhD in Nutritional Biochemistry. He was a faculty member at Auburn University in the Department of Animal and Dairy Sciences where his teaching and research programs focused on animal nutrition and the relationship between nutrient availability and the hormonal regulation of growth. Dr. Davenport is currently Research Nutritionist in the Research and Development Division of The Iams Company where his research efforts focus on the protein requirements of dogs and cats during different life stages.

James K. Drackley, PhD

Dr. Drackley received a BS in Dairy Production and an MS in Dairy Science from South Dakota State University, and a PhD in Nutritional Physiology from Iowa State University. He joined the faculty of the University of Illinois at Urbana-Champaign in 1989 and is currently Associate Professor of Animal Sciences and a member of the Division of Nutritional Sciences. Dr. Drackley's research program centers on lipid utilization and metabolism in domestic animals, metabolic changes in the transition from pregnancy to lactation, neonatal nutrition and metabolism, and energy utilization in the intestines.

Jan Elnif, MS

Mr. Elnif received an MS in Comparative Physiology from the August Krogh Institute at the University of Copenhagen. He is currently Associate Professor at the Department of Animal Science and Animal Health, Division of Fur Animal Science at the Royal Veterinary and Agricultural University, Copenhagen. His main research interests are in the development of the gastrointestinal tract in carnivorous species. Mr. Elnif was a sabbatical professor at Mississippi State University in 1996.

Catherine J. Field, PhD, RD

Dr. Field received an MSc in Nutrition from the University of Toronto and a PhD in Nutrition and Metabolism from the University of Alberta. After postdoctoral work in Medicine at McGill University she accepted a faculty position at the University of Alberta in Edmonton, Canada where she is currently an Associate Professor in Nutrition in the Department of Agricultural, Food and Nutritional Science with a cross-appointment in Medicine. Dr. Field's research program centers on the effect of nutrition on the immune system.

Delmar R. Finco, DVM, PhD, Diplomate ACVIM

Dr. Finco received a DVM and a PhD from the University of Minnesota and served on the faculty before joining The University of Georgia faculty in 1970. He is currently Professor in the Department of Physiology and Pharmacology where he has taught and conducted research on diseases of the urinary system. Dr. Finco's recent research is focused on mechanisms of progression of renal failure and the role of nutrients in progression of renal failure. He is co-editor of *Canine and Feline Nephrology and Urology* published in 1995.

T. J. Gruffydd-Jones, BVetMed, PhD, MRCVS

Dr. Gruffydd-Jones graduated from the Royal Veterinary College, London and spent two years in practice before joining the University of Bristol as the Feline Advisory Bureau Clinical Scholar in Feline Medicine. He was awarded a Wellcome Foundation Scholarship and received a PhD. He is currently a Reader in Small Animal Medicine and Director of The Feline Centre, Division of Companion Animals, University of Bristol. Dr Gruffydd-Jones is Chairman of the Feline Advisory Bureau and a founding member of the European Society for Feline Medicine. His interest is in feline medicine, in particular, infectious diseases and gastrointestinal disorders.

Michael G. Hayek, PhD

Dr. Hayek received a BS in Biology from Villanova University, an MS in Animal Science and a PhD in Nutritional Science from the University of Kentucky. He was a Research Associate at the Nutritional Immunology Laboratory at the Jean Mayer USDA Human Nutrition Research Center on Aging at Tufts University where his research emphasis was the interaction between nutrition and the aging immune system. Dr. Hayek is currently Research Nutritionist in the Research and Development Division of The Iams Company where his research interests include geriatric nutrition, longevity, and the interaction between nutrition and the immune response.

Herman A.W. Hazewinkel, DVM, PhD, Diplomate ECVS

Dr. Hazewinkel graduated from the Veterinary Faculty of Utrecht University where he also became a member of the orthopedic group and received a PhD following research on the influence of nutrition in skeletal development. This interesting subject is now extended to investigating dietary influences on calcium metabolism and orthopedic diseases. Dr. Hazewinkel is currently Head, Section of Orthopedics and Neurosurgery. He is a member of the national Hip Dysplasia committee, the Elbow Dysplasia committee, AO-Vet International, the board of the European Society for Veterinary Orthopedics and Traumatology, and is diplomate of the Dutch and the European Society of Veterinary Surgeons.

Kenneth W. Hinchcliff, BVSc, MS, PhD, Diplomate ACVIM (Large Animal)

Dr. Hinchcliff received a BVSc from the University of Melbourne, completed an internship at Louisiana State University, as well as completing a residency in large animal internal and earning an MS in Veterinary Science from the University of Wisconsin. He completed a PhD at The Ohio State University. Dr. Hinchcliff is currently Associate Professor of Equine Medicine at The Ohio State University and is director of the exercise physiology laboratory. His research interests focus on the physiological responses of dogs and horses to exercise, in particular, the cardiovascular and metabolic responses to training and exercise. He is a board member of the International Sled Dog Veterinary Medical Association and chair of the research committee.

Robert J. Kearns, PhD

Dr. Kearns received a PhD in Microbiology from Washington State University and completed a two year post-doctoral fellowship at National Jewish Hospital and Research Center in Denver. He is currently an Associate Professor in the Biology Department at the University of Dayton where his primary area of teaching is microbiology and immunology. Dr. Kearns' research interests have focused specifically on the role of the immune system in prevention of infectious disease and he is currently evaluating the relationship that exists between diet and its impact on the development of intestinal microbial flora and immune function in companion animals.

Susan D. Lauten, MAg, PhD Candidate

Ms. Lauten received a BSBA in Accounting from Mississippi College, completed an MAg in nutrition at Auburn University, and is currently a PhD candidate in canine nutrition at Scott-Ritchey Research Center, Auburn University She completed research projects in omega-3 and omega-6 lipid metabolism prior to becoming involved in large breed growth projects. Current research interests include skeletal development of growing dogs, and development of dual energy x-ray absorptiometry for use in veterinary research and medicine.

Allan J. Lepine, PhD

Dr. Lepine received a BS in Animal Science and a PhD in Non-Ruminant Nutrition from Cornell University, and an MS in Non-Ruminant Nutrition from Virginia Polytechnic Institute and State University. He was Assistant Professor in the Department of Animal Science at The Ohio State University with teaching and research emphasis in non-ruminant nutrition. Dr. Lepine is currently Research Nutritionist in the Research and Development Division of The Iams Company where his current research interests include neonatal nutrition, growth and development, and the effects of nutrition on reproduction in companion animals.

Glenna E. Mauldin, DVM, MS, Diplomate ACVIM (Oncology)

Dr. Mauldin received BS and DVM degrees from the University of Saskatchewan in Saskatoon, Canada and an MS from Cornell University. She was accorded diplomate status by the American College of Veterinary Internal Medicine, Specialty of Oncology and served as Senior Staff Oncologist at The Animal Medical Center in New York and was also Director of AMC's Nutritional Support Service. Dr. Mauldin is currently Assistant Professor of Veterinary Oncology, Department of Veterinary Clinical Sciences at the Louisiana State University School of Veterinary Medicine. Her specific areas of interest include cancer cachexia and critical care nutrition.

Michael I. McBurney, PhD, FACN

Dr. McBurney received a BSc in Biology from Carleton University in Ottawa, Canada and MSc and PhD degrees in Nutrition from Cornell University. He also completed a post-doctoral fellowship at the University of Toronto and a sabbatical at the University of North Carolina. He was a Professor of Nutrition in the Department of Agricultural, Food and Nutritional Science at the University of Alberta with a cross-appointment in the Division of Gastroenterology, Department of Medicine and was a member of the Muttart Diabetes and Research Training Centre. Dr. McBurney is currently Principal Nutrition Scientist at the W. K. Kellogg Institute of the Kellogg Company.

Simin Nikbin Meydani, DVM, PhD

Dr. Meydani is Professor of Nutrition and Immunology at Tufts University and Chief of the Nutritional Immunology Laboratory at the Jean Mayer USDA Human Nutrition Research Center on Aging at Tufts University where she directs studies related to the impact of nutritional factors on the immune response in the elderly. Dr. Meydani was a member of the organizing committee for the first International Aging and Immunology meeting, as well as chair and member of the organizing committee for International Life Sciences Institute 1997 conference on Nutrition and Immunity. Her research interests focus on the effect of nutrients on immune response of the young and the aged with a special emphasis on the role of arachidonic acid metabolites.

Ronald R. Minor, VMD, PhD

Dr. Minor received VMD and PhD degrees from the University of Pennsylvania where he pursued a study of the regulation of chondrocyte differentiation during embryonic development. He was Assistant Professor of Pathology in the School of Veterinary Medicine, and Assistant Professor of Anatomy in the School of Medicine at the University of Pennsylvania. Dr. Minor is currently Professor of Pathology in the College of Veterinary Medicine at Cornell University where his research interests include genetic diseases of collagen in domestic animals and bone turnover in the dog.

R. D. Montgomery, DVM, MS, Diplomate ACVS

Dr. Montgomery received DVM and MS degrees from Auburn University and was accorded diplomate status by the American College of Veterinary Surgeons. He held academic appointments at Mississippi State University, College of Veterinary Medicine, and was also Director of Surgical Research at the College of Medicine, UAB. Dr. Montgomery is currently with the Department of Small Animal Medicine and Surgery at Auburn University College of Veterinary Medicine where his research interest is primarily related to veterinary orthopedics.

Phillip D. Nelson, DVM, PhD

Dr. Nelson received a DVM from Tuskegee Institute and a PhD in Veterinary Sciences with an emphasis in immunology from North Carolina State University. Academic appointments have included Instructor and Assistant Professor at Mississippi State University, Assistant and Associate Professor at Tuskegee University, and Associate Professor at Mississippi State University. Dr. Nelson is currently Associate Dean of the College of Veterinary Medicine and is a faculty member in the Research Program.

Richard W. Nelson, DVM, Diplomate ACVIM

Dr. Nelson received a DVM from the University of Minnesota, was an intern and resident in small animal internal medicine at Washington State University, and is board certified in internal medicine. He was Associate Professor at the Department of Veterinary Clinical Sciences, School of Veterinary Medicine, Purdue University. He is currently a Professor in the Department of Medicine and Epidemiology, School of Veterinary Medicine, University of California at Davis. Dr. Nelson's research interests are in the area of small animal clinical endocrinology, most notably the endocrine pancreas, thyroid gland, and adrenal gland. A primary research focus has involved evaluating the role of dietary fiber in treating diabetes mellitus in dogs and cats.

Jacquie Rand, BVSc, DVSc, Diplomate ACVIM

Dr. Rand received a BVSc from Melbourne University, Australia and worked in private practice before completing a residency and doctorate at the University of Guelph, Canada. She worked at the University of Zurich, Switzerland before returning to Australia where she is currently a Reader in the School of Veterinary Science at the University of Queensland. Dr. Rand is a Diplomate of the American College of Veterinary Internal Medicine and leads a team of five postgraduate students in diabetes research.

Gregory A. Reinhart, PhD

Dr. Reinhart received a BS in Animal Science, an MS in Non-Ruminant Nutrition, and a PhD in Nutritional Biochemistry from The Ohio State University. He was a Clinical Research Associate at Ross Laboratories' Medical Nutrition Department before joining the Research and Development Division of The Iams Company. Dr. Reinhart is currently Director of Strategic Research with active research interests in fatty acid metabolism, fiber nutrition, mineral metabolism, and geriatric nutrition of dogs and cats. He is also actively involved in investigating the nutritional needs and exercise-induced physiological changes in Alaskan sled dogs.

Arleigh J. Reynolds, DVM, PhD, DACVN

Dr. Reynolds received BS and DVM degrees from Cornell University and continued graduate study on the relationship between diet and performance in sled dogs. He completed a PhD at Cornell and served as an instructor in the Department of Clinical Sciences. Dr. Reynolds is currently Assistant Professor of Clinical Nutrition, Department and Section of Clinical Sciences at Cornell University, College of Veterinary Medicine. He divides his time between teaching, clinical service, and research on his colony of Alaskan Huskies.

Paul F. Rumph, DVM, MS

Dr. Rumph received DVM and MS degrees from Auburn University and served as a Captain in the U.S. Air Force Veterinary Corps before joining the College of Veterinary Medicine faculty at Auburn University. He is currently Professor of Veterinary Anatomy, Department of Anatomy, Physiology, and Pharmacology where his primary research interest is kinetic and kinematic analysis of animal locomotion. Dr. Rumph's gait analysis laboratory includes a floor mounted force platform for analysis of ground reaction forces and 2-dimensional kinematic equipment for the study of joint motion.

Jerry W. Spears, PhD

Dr. Spears received BS and MS degrees in Animal Science from the University of Kentucky, and a PhD in Animal Nutrition from the University of Illinois. He was a faculty member in the Department of Animal Sciences at the University of Arkansas before joining the faculty in the Department of Animal Science at North Carolina State University where he is currently Professor with active research programs in mineral metabolism and nutritional immunology.

Gregory D. Sunvold, PhD

Dr. Sunvold received a BS in Animal Science from South Dakota State University, an MS in Ruminant Nutrition from Kansas State University, and a PhD in Nutritional Sciences from the University of Illinois. He is currently Research Nutritionist in the Research and Development Division of The Iams Company where his research focus includes programs in gastrointestinal health, obesity, and diabetes. Special research interests include studying the role of dietary fiber in maintaining and enhancing the health of the dog and cat.

Mark A. Tetrick, DVM, PhD

Dr. Mark Tetrick received his BS in Meat and Animal Science and DVM from the University of Wisconsin-Madison. After a year in large/companion animal practice, he returned to the University of Wisconsin-Madison and received his PhD in Nutritional Sciences. Dr. Tetrick is currently Research Nutritionist in the Research and Development division of The Iams Company. His research interests include the clinical impact of nutrition, with emphasis on the influence of nutrition on urinary tract health.

John J. Turek, PhD

Dr. Turek received a BS in Biology and MS and PhD degrees in Veterinary Microbiology/ Immunology from the University of Illinois. He joined the faculty at Purdue University where he has held several academic appointments and is currently Associate Professor in the Department of Basic Medical Sciences, School of Veterinary Medicine. He is also an Adjunct Associate Professor with Indiana University School of Medicine. Dr. Turek's research is focused on how dietary lipids modulate the immune system in infectious diseases and in tissue injury and repair with further interest in the use of electron microscopic and image analytical methods to study cell structure and function

David A. Williams, MA, VetMB, PhD, Diplomate ACVIM

Dr. Williams received a VetMB from the University of Cambridge and a PhD from the University of Liverpool. He has held faculty positions at the University of Florida, Kansas State University, and Purdue University. Dr. Williams is currently Professor and Head of the Department of Small Animal Medicine and Surgery at Texas A&M University. His research is focused on the development and application of new tests for gastrointestinal and other diseases in animals. He is a co-author of the third edition of Strombeck's *Small Animal Gastroenterology* textbook.

Growth & Development

Serial Orthopaedic Examinations of Growing Great Dane Puppies Fed Three Diets Varying in Calcium and Phosphorous

S.A. Goodman, MS, DVM[a]; R.D. Montgomery, DVM, MS, DACVS[b];
R.B. Fitch, DVM, MS, DACVS[c]; J.T. Hathcock, DVM, MS, DARS[d];
S.D. Lauten, MS[a]; N.R. Cox, DVM, PhD[a]; S.A. Kincaid, DVM, PhD[e];
P.F. Rumph, DVM[e]; W.R. Brawner, Jr., DVM, PhD, DACVR[d];
H.J. Baker, DVM[a]; A.J. Lepine, PhD[f]; G.A. Reinhart, PhD[f]

[a] Scott Ritchey Research Center,
[b]Department of Small Animal Medicine and Surgery,
College of Veterinary Medicine, Auburn University, Alabama, USA;
[c]Department of Veterinary Clinical Services, School of Veterinary Medicine,
Louisiana State University, Baton Rouge, Louisiana, USA;
[d]Department of Radiology,
[e]Department of Anatomy and Histology,
College of Veterinary Medicine, Auburn University, Alabama, USA;
[f]Research and Development, The Iams Company, Lewisburg, Ohio, USA

Introduction

Puppies of the large and giant breeds are over-represented in juvenile orthopaedic diseases such as osteochondrosis, panosteitis, hypertrophic osteodystrophy, hip dysplasia, and others. Orthopaedic examination should identify the areas with pain and structural or biomechanical problems of the musculoskeletal system; when combined with history and signalment, the summation should yield a diagnosis, tentative diagnosis, or a short list of "rule-outs." Subsequent radiographic analysis may confirm the diagnoses. Although seldom fatal, the most serious forms of these diseases can result in pain that can be seriously debilitating.

Nutrition plays an important role in the development of growing dogs and their risk of developing juvenile bone and joint diseases. Dogs will reach the same adult size whether they grow at a normal rate or at a rate accelerated by a special diet.[1] However, juvenile dogs growing at a faster than average rate are at much greater risk for developing juvenile bone and joint diseases.[2] Dietary factors clearly identified as increasing risk for juvenile bone and joint diseases are high calories, high absolute calcium, and *ad libitum* feeding.[3] The Association of American Feed Control Officials (AAFCO) has determined special requirements for "growth" diets, including an increase in the percentage of calcium above that of "maintenance" diet requirements (1% for growth, 0.6 % for maintenance).[4] It is interesting to note that although a minimum amount of calcium is defined, a maximum of up to 2.5% is allowable.

Giant breeds of dogs may have unique dietary requirements for optimal growth. The accelerated growth rate of these dogs allows them to progress rapidly from a birth weight of about 1 kg to a weight of greater than 50 kg in less than a year. A rapidly growing and maturing skeleton has a high demand for calcium and phosphorous. Sixty-five percent of the weight of fully mineralized bone (which contains only 1.8–6% water) is composed of hydroxyapatite $[Ca_{10}(PO_4)_6(OH)_2]$.[5] It might seem reasonable to increase the percentage of certain dietary components, such as calcium and phosphorous, to enhance the growth and skeletal development of giant dogs. To a point, feeding higher calcium and phosphorous does permit more rapid growth. However, recent evidence indicates that although higher calcium levels may initially speed growth, the increased supplementation can ultimately be detrimental. Rapid growth is a major factor for orthopaedic lesions in giant breed dogs, and it is more desirable to slow growth, especially since it does not compromise the overall adult stature of the dog.

The present study was designed to evaluate the effects of varying levels of dietary calcium and phosphorous on the orthopaedic development of the Great Dane. Previous investigations such as the study of overnutrition in Great Danes by Hedhammer[6] and manipulation of dietary calcium by Hazewinkel[7] served as a points of reference for this study.

The details of the orthopaedic examination techniques used and the results of those examinations follow. Some of the major developmental skeletal diseases that were encountered in this study will be discussed briefly, particularly relating their pathogensis to dietary calcium concentration. Other aspects of this study, including a non-invasive total body densitometric analysis (by Dual Energy X-ray Absorptiometry), skeletal radiographic evaluations, and force plate analysis, will be summarized in other chapters of this proceedings.

Materials and Methods

The study involved 36 Great Dane puppies (23 males, 13 females) from 5 separate litters (5 different dams, 3 different stud dogs) born over a 6 month period. The dams were fed the same diet (designed for optimal nutrition for pregnancy and lactation) *ad libitum* during the final month of gestation and through weaning of the puppies. Puppies were whelped in an isolated indoor whelping facility where they were housed until weaning. The dam of the fifth litter was agalactic, and the puppies were hand raised on milk replacer until being weaned to individual diets at 4 weeks of age.

Puppies from each litter were divided randomly into three diet groups at weaning (4–5 weeks of age). The three test diets were isocaloric, varying only in levels of calcium and phosphorous. Diets were designated as Low (0.48% Ca: 0.40% P), Medium (0.80% Ca: 0.67% P), or High (2.70% Ca: 2.20% P) based on the calcium content. The ratio of these minerals was consistent at 1.2:1.0 (calcium:phosphorous). Pups were allowed a 30 minute food consumption twice daily with water available *ad libitum*. After weaning, they were housed in large kennels with indoor and outdoor access. A large, grassy yard was available for additional exercise. Orthopaedic examinations were performed at defined intervals throughout the study evaluating stance, conformation, standing joint angles, range of joint motion, carpus valga, height, certain bone lengths, and muscle mass. Stance was specifically evaluated for "pointing" which would be indicative of decreased weight-bearing on a limb. Conformation was evaluated subjectively with regard to valgus, varus or other deformity (e.g., carpal hyperextension, asynchronous growth of the radius/ulna). Joint angles were measured with a goniometer in both standing as well as maximum flexion and extension of the major appendicular joints (shoulder, elbow, carpus, hip, stifle, and tarsus) and to determine carpa valga.[8] The extension and flexion angles can be combined (extension minus flexion) to give the total range of motion for a joint. Height measurements were made from the floor vertically to the point of the shoulder and the greater trochanter of the femur. Length of the humerus, radius, femur, and tibia were measured. Body length was measured from the point of the shoulder to the tuber ishii. Thigh circumference was determined with a cloth tape measure at 1 cm distal to the greater trochanter. Radial circumference was measured 1 cm distal to the elbow. Circumference readings measure muscle mass (technically muscle, bone, subcutaneous fat, and skin) and can serve as an indicator of growth and weight gain. In addition, decreased weight bearing on a limb results in decreased muscle mass which would lead to a limb with a smaller circumference. Skeletal radiographs for serial orthopaedic evaluations were taken at bimonthly intervals beginning at 2 months of age through 18 months of age. Sites radiographed included the cervical spine, bilateral scapulohumeral joints, left antebrachium, left stifle, and pelvis. Radiographs were also used for length measurements of the radius, ulna, and femur. Additional radiographs were made to evaluate cases of clinical lameness. Photographs (frontal, lateral, and rear views) were taken on a bimonthly basis. Also, force plate analysis of gait and total body densitometric analysis were made at regular intervals.

Results

An increased incidence of poor conformation occurred in the High diet dogs. This was not attributable to any specific lesion observed, but a common feature was a pronounced crouched rear limb stance (**Figure 1**).

Joint angle measurements were performed with a goniometer. Decreased standing angles at the hip, stifle, and tarsus reflected a crouched stance. With the use of the goniometer,[8] numerical values could be assigned to more objectively describe the conformation. If an animal was suffering from a joint disease, the range of motion was decreased. There is reduced flexion of hip, shoulder, elbow, and stifle joints in the more highly muscled animals.

Individual bone length measurements of the femur, humerus, radius, and tibia using bony protruberences as landmarks gave quite variable results. Bone length measurements from the radiographs were a reliable method of determining serial bone lengths. Radiographic measurements also allowed for specific evaluation of diaphyseal lengths as well as total bone lengths. Overall, the measurements of

Figure 1. Lateral and rear view comparisons of what was considered to be the normal conformation of a Medium diet dog (B5) with two High diet dogs (B6 and B7) from the same litter at 6 months of age.

bone lengths reinforced the clinical impression that the dogs on the High and Medium diets initially grew more rapidly than the dogs on the Low diet, but after 4 months of age the growth rate of the High diet dogs fell below that of the Medium diet dogs (*Figure 2*).

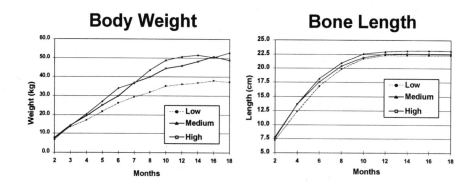

Figure 2. Feed group differences in body weights and bone lengths. The bone length differences were slight.

As described in a previous section, bilateral circumference measurements were made of the radius and thigh. Again, mean measurements of dogs on the Medium diet exceed those of the Low and High diet dogs. *Figure 3* demonstrates the average radius and thigh circumferences per feed group at 6, 12, and 18 months of age.

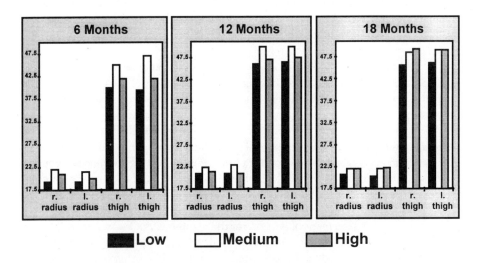

Low　**Medium**　**High**

Figure 3. Medium diet dogs surpassed the dogs on the other two diets in radius and thigh circumference (cm) at 6 and 12 months of age. By 18 months the differences were less discernible.

Comparison of the bilateral measurements of thigh circumference on a per dog basis was reliable in determining muscle atrophy as an indicator of a chronic (i.e., greater than 2–3 weeks) orthopaedic problem. Circumference measures were +/– 0.5 cm of the contralateral limb in an animal with balanced weight distribution. *Table 1* demonstrates representative bilateral circumference measurements.

Table 1. Assymetry of bilateral thigh circumference measurements (cm) may indicate a problem of decreased weight-bearing due to pain. A8 had no clinical lameness. B4 had equal thigh circumferences at 4 months of age, but by 6 months there was a dramatic asymmetry attributed to patellar luxations. C1 exhibited pain of the right stifle during the 12 and 18 month orthopaedic exams. E3 was clinically normal.

	6 months		12 months		18 months	
	right	left	right	left	right	left
A8	46	46	49	49	49	49
B4	46	50	*	*	*	*
C1	34	34	42	43	43	45
E3	42	42	44	44	47	47

* Data not available.

7

Several examples of developmental orthopaedic diseases were observed in this study. Characteristic sites of joint pain confirmed with history and signalment can give a tentative diagnosis of osteochondrosis or osteochondritis dissecans. Evidence of osteochondrosis without osteochondritis dissecans was often discernible radiographically, sometimes without any accompanying clinical signs. Osteochondrosis lesions were also detected through magnetic resonance imaging (MRI). Radiography and MRI are two valuable modalities which provided non-invasive evaluations of joints of interest.

Although clinical lameness was attributable to panosteitis in relatively few dogs, radiographic signs of panosteitis were observed in most of the dogs in our study beyond 8 months of age. A treatment association with panosteitis was not observed.

Hypertophic osteodystrophy (HOD) was the earliest skeletal disease detected. Animals with HOD began to show clinical signs by 6 months of age. Affected animals responded well (return to standing and eating) to subcutaneous prednisone injections and a gruel diet, which was syringe-fed if necessary. Symptoms often recurred. One dog with intense pain on opening the jaw had radiographic signs characteristic of HOD in the antebrachium, as well as an increased radiodensity and enlargement of portions of the mandible. All 5 cases of HOD in the study were seen in the High diet group. Additionally, cases of HOD occurred only in 2 litters, both sired by the same stud, and he sired no other litters in the study.

Discussion

The etiologies of all the juvenile bone and joint diseases are not completely understood. At the outset of this study, the developmental disease of most interest was osteochondrosis, the systemic disease of abnormal cartilage maturation. Osteochondrosis is assumed to have a multifactorial cause, with contributions from genetics, hormones, diet, and trauma.[9] Investigations into the nutritional aspect of skeletal development have resulted in some interesting findings pertinent to osteochondrosis. In the dog, it has been shown that feeding diets containing elevated calcium levels exacerbates effects of defects in endochondral ossification, resulting in skeletal lesions like those seen in osteochondrosis.[10] High calcium availability directly, or indirectly through an increase in calcitonin, promotes a delay of endochondral ossification. Delayed conversion of cartilage to bone causes the sites of cartilage deposition to become thickened.[10] Thickened cartilage is more susceptible to shearing from daily weight-bearing activities, especially in the giant breeds. The interface of articular cartilage and subchondral bone can be especially susceptible to stress by nature of the differences in the elasticity of cartilage and bone.[5] Also, cartilage deformation at certain critical sites, such as the distal ulnar physis, may result in an angular limb deformity. If the development of osteochondrosis is affected by dietary excesses of calcium, feeding a diet lower in calcium could prevent the disease or allow a subclinical case to resolve. If there is not a break in the integrity of the articular cartilage nor development of a cartilage flap ("joint mouse"), the syndrome may never become clinical. If osteochondrosis does progress to a cartilage separation, the condition becomes known as osteochondritis dissecans (OCD). Interruption of the smooth surfaces and release of inflammatory mediators causes irritation, inflammation, and pain, and progresses to degenerative joint disease. Although osteochondritis dissecans often presents as an acute lameness, it is an endpoint of a process that takes place over an extended period of time.

Early and thorough orthopaedic exams may reveal an otherwise inapparent painful foci. Radiographic evidence of osteochondrosis may be present at an early, reversible stage. An animal with only mild clinical signs may be conservatively managed with rest and restricted activity. Conservative management is recommended as a primary option in animals under 6 months of age.[9] Since epiphyseal cartilage has osteogenic potential, a non-displaced osteochondrosis lesion may heal in situ.[5] There is some evidence that a low calcium diet could also be helpful in the conservative management or prevention of OCD. If an effort is not made to prevent the lesion from becoming worse, a complete OCD lesion is more likely to develop. The "cure" generally requires surgical intervention, which has a high percentage of clinical success if done before degenerative joint disease develops.[11] If the patient is being fed a high calcium diet, converting to a diet lower in calcium might be beneficial even postoperatively if the animal is under a year of age.

Panosteitis is considered a developmental bone disease although symptoms can occur long after the closure of the growth plates. The disease is not generally seen beyond 18 months of age. The clinical presentation of shifting pain in the long bones is more commonly seen in the large and giant breed dogs. The frequency of subclinical panosteitis is unknown, but this study suggests that it may be common. Radiographically, panosteitis appears as an intramedullary density that typically begins at the site of the nutrient foramina. One theory to its occurrence is related to decreased endosteal osteoclastic resorption and increased new periosteal bone formation at the nutrient foramina of the bones, which is proposed to occur in dogs fed high calcium diets.[12,13] The resulting edema and medullary fibrosis gives the characteristic radiographic sign of increased intramedullary opacities in long bones (*Figure 4*). Although a reasonable and interesting theory, we did not find a unique association of panosteitis with a diet high in calcium.

Of the developmental bone diseases, hypertrophic osteodystrophy (HOD) is probably the least understood and probably has the potential for serious long term effects. Usually the metaphyses of the long bones are affected, especially in the radius and ulna but also later and less severely in the tibia. The mandible may be affected as well;[14] if so, the change in the thickness of the body of the mandible is easily palpable when compared to the narrow blade of the mandible of a normal dog. Osteogenic proliferation is usually obvious appearing as a bulging of the antebrachium just above the carpus (*Figure 5*). Substantial pain on palpation of the area is a consistent clinical finding, as is hyperthermia. Radiographic changes are characteristic and are presented in the imaging article associated with this study.[15]

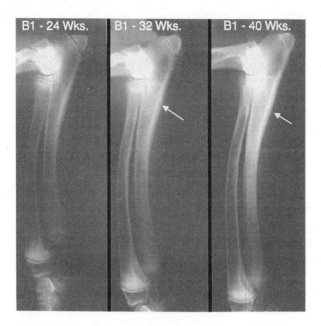

Figure 4. Radiographic composite demonstrating the progression of panosteitis in the antebrachium. In the first panel, at 24 weeks there is no radiographic evidence of panosteitis. In the second panel, at 32 weeks a small area of increased intramedullary density is seen in the mid-proximal ulna (arrow). At 40 weeks the area of increased intramedullary density in the ulna has expanded. This animal presented with pain in the right front limb at the 48 week orthopaedic exam. At the 56 week exam there was pain in both rear limbs and the left front. At the end of the study (72 weeks) there was still radiographic evidence of panosteitis.

A   **B**

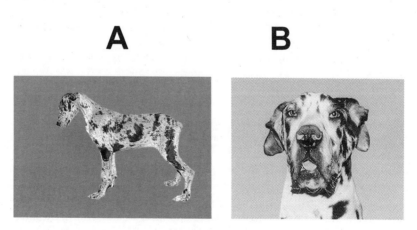

Figure 5. (A) Osteogenic proliferation of the distal metaphyses of the radius and ulna may be apparent in some cases of HOD. (B) Less commonly, the mandible may be affected, with unilateral or bilateral involvement. This dog had a prominent osseous proliferation of the left mandible.

Patients with HOD are febrile (>103°F), often lethargic, consistently in pain, and often unwilling to eat. Anorexia should be distinguished from prehensile inability due to inflammation and osteogenic proliferation of the mandible. Craniomandibular osteopathy (CMO) is a bone disease of mandibular osteogenic proliferation and has been described in Great Danes.[14] More commonly, CMO ("lion jaw") is found in West Highland White terriers. A retrospective pedigree analysis was performed in a kindred of West Highland White terriers which indicated the disease was inherited by an autosomal recessive trait.[16] However, the mandible has also been described as a potential site for HOD. To determine how the mandibular afflictions observed in this study should be classified, it would be necessary to have histopathological comparisons for both abnormalities. This information is currently being sought.

Inadequate nutritional vitamin C has been ruled out as a cause of HOD.[17,18,19] Vitamin C is synthesized in sufficient amounts in the liver and kidneys of dogs by the action of glucurono reductase and gulono oxidase on hexose sugars.[18] Inappropriate metabolism of vitamin C does remain a potential etiology of HOD.[18] Nutritional supplementation with vitamin C is contraindicated in the treatment of this disease. There have been suggestions lately that HOD may be a vaccine-related disease, specifically as a reaction to the distemper vaccine.[19] The timing of vaccine administrations did not seem to be related to the appearance of HOD in our study; however, affected bones were not evaluated for presence of virus. Although an exact explanation has not been elucidated, the fact that HOD only occurred in High diet dogs and only in dogs from one stud, makes a tempting suggestion that not only may the propensity to manifest clinical HOD be heritable, but also that there may a mechanism in place (or a metabolic defect) which could somehow be influenced by feeding a high calcium diet. High dietary calcium will cause a transient hypercalcemia, which subsequently triggers the release of calcitonin, which does have a variety of metabolic effects.[20] If immune compromise can result from high calcium intake,[21] this could be a mechanism for an infectious basis for HOD.[22,23]

References

1. Riser WH. A half century of canine hip dysplasia. *Seminars Vet Med Surg (Small Animal)* 1987; 2:87-91.

2. Fox SM, Walker AM. The etiopathogensis of osteochondrosis. *Vet Med* 1993; 2:116-122.

3. Richardson DC. Nutritional and developmental orthopaedic diseases. *Amer Coll Vet Surg 7th Ann Symp Proceed* 1997; 162-164.

4. Association of American Feed Control Officials. *Official Publication*.1994.

5. Kincaid SA, Van Sickle DC. Bone morphology and postnatal osteogenesis - potential for disease. *Vet Clin N Am Sm Anim Pract* 1983; 13:3-17.

6. Hedhammar A, Wu FM, Krook L, Schryver HF, De Lahunta A, Whalen JP, Kallfelz FA, Nunez EA, Hintz HF, Sheffy BE, Ryan GD. Overnutrition and skeletal disease: an experimental study in growing Great Dane dogs. *Cornell Vet* 1974; 64(Suppl.):1-160.

7. Hazewinkel HAW, Goedegebuure SA, Poulos PW, Wolvekamp WThC. Influences of chronic calcium excess on the skeletal development of growing Great Danes. *JAAHA* 1985; 21:377-391.

8. Mann FA, Wagner-Mann C, Tangner CH. Manual goniometric measurement of the canine pelvic limb. *JAAHA* 1988; 24:189-194.

9. Milton JL. Osteochondritis dissecans in the dog. *Vet Clin N Am Sm Anim Pract* 1983; 13:117-134.

10. Goedegebuure SA, Hazewinkel HAW. Morphological findings in young dogs chronically fed diet containing excess calcium. *Vet Pathol* 1986; 23:594-605.

11. Whitehair JG, Rudd RG. Osteochondritis dissecans of the humeral head in dogs. *Compendium* 1990; 12:195-203.

12. Hazewinkel HAW. Skeletal disease. In: Wills JM, Simpson KW, eds. *Waltham Book of Clinical Nutrition of the Dog and Cat.* Pergamon 1994; 395-423.

13. Hazewinkel HAW. Calciotropic hormones and bone metabolism. In: Rijnberk A, ed. *Clinical Endocrinology of the Dog and Cat.* Dordrecht: Kluwer Academic Publishers, 1996; 190-191.

14. Alexander JW. Selected skeletal dysplasias: craniomandibular osteopathy, multiple cartilagenous exostoses, and hypertrophic osteodystrophy. *Vet Clin N Am Sm Anim Pract* 1983; 13:55-70.

15. Brawner Jr WR, Hathcock JT, Lauten SD, Goodman SA, Cox NR, Baker HJ, Lepine AJ, Reinhart GA. Imaging techniques evaluating skeletal development of the large breed puppy. In: Reinhart GA, Carey DP, eds. *Recent Advances in Canine and Feline Nutrition, Vol. II: 1998 Iams Nutrition Symposium Proceedings.* Wilmington: Orange Frazer Press, 1998; 13-28.

16. Padgett GA, Mostosky UV. Animal model: the mode of inheritance of craniomandibular osteopathy in West Highland White terrier dogs. *Amer J Med Genetics* 1986; 25:9-13.

17. Woodard JC. Canine hypertophic osteodystrophy, a study of the spontaneous disease in littermates. *Vet Pathol* 1982; 19:337-354.

18. Swenson MJ, ed. *Duke's Physiology of Domestic Animals.* London: Cornell University Press, Ltd., 1984; 445.

19. Muir P, Dubielzig RR, Johnson KA, Shelton GD. Hypertophic osteodystrophy and calvarial hyperostosis. *Compendium* 1996; 18:143-151.

20. Nap RC, Hazewinkel HAW. Growth and skeletal development in the dog in relation to nutrition: a review. *Vet Quarterly* 1994; 16:50-59.

21. Hand MS, Lewis LD, Morris ML. Feeding puppies: common errors, their effects, and prevention. *Compendium* 1987; 9:41-44.

22. Clarke RE. Hypertrophic osteodystrophy in the canine associated with a lowered resistance to infection - an unusual case history. *Austral Vet Practit* 1978; 8:39-43.

23. Schulz KS, Payne JT, Aronson E. *Escherichia coli* bacteremia associated with hypertrophic osteodystrophy in a dog. *JAVMA* 1991; 199:1170-1173.

The Role of Diagnostic Imaging in Assessment of Canine Skeletal Development

William R. Brawner, Jr., DVM, PhD, DACVR
Associate Professor, Radiology, Department of Radiology
College of Veterinary Medicine, Auburn University, Alabama, USA

John T. Hathcock, DVM, MS[a]; Susan D. Lauten, BS, MS[a];
Susan A. Goodman, DVM[a]; Nancy R. Cox, DVM, PhD[a];
Henry J. Baker, DVM, PhD[a]; Allan J. Lepine, PhD[b]; Gregory A. Reinhart, PhD[b]
[a]College of Veterinary Medicine, Auburn University, Alabama, USA
[b]Research and Development, The Iams Company, Lewisburg, Ohio, USA

Introduction

Diagnostic radiology was recognized as an important tool for evaluation of the internal structure of the body almost immediately after the discovery of x-rays in 1895. The earliest diagnostic use of x-rays was the assessment of skeletal abnormalities, a natural application because of the marked differential absorption of x-rays by bone and soft tissue. In the intervening 100 years, radiology has been refined and expanded to produce detailed anatomic images of almost all organs and tissues. In recent decades, rapid advances in electronic and digital technology have allowed the development of a large number of new imaging techniques, many of which do not rely on x-rays or other ionizing radiation. As a result, the traditional role of radiology in diagnosis and research has been broadly expanded. Even the term "radiology" is now often replaced with "diagnostic imaging". The new imaging systems use a variety of technological approaches, but they are connected by the basic principles of image interpretation and the need for appropriate selection and application of imaging techniques to accurately and efficiently provide needed information about the internal structure of the body. Although the first radiographic images of the skeleton were made over 100 years ago, many aspects of the development, function, and pathology of the skeletal system remain incompletely understood. Diagnostic imaging techniques are among the essential tools needed to further that understanding. This is certainly true when the study and clinical assessment of growth and skeletal disorders of growing puppies are considered.

Dogs experience rapid growth and development from birth to skeletal maturity in the first 12–18 months of life. There is a wide range of size and conformation among breeds of dogs. The stages of development are similar among different breeds but the rate of development and incidence of developmental abnormalities vary. The process of skeletal development and factors affecting that process have been studied in only a few breeds and even in those breeds, many questions remain. Giant breed dogs have been studied most often because they seem particularly susceptible to developmental and orthopedic abnormalities such as osteochondrosis, hypertrophic osteodystrophy, hip dysplasia, and others.[1-4] Developmental skeletal diseases are relatively uncommon in small breed dogs, common in large breeds, and even more common in the giant breeds.

Intuitively, the rapid growth of giant breed dogs should place stress on the development of the skeletal system. It is interesting to compare the development of giant breed dogs to humans. A person, born at 5–10 pounds, develops to skeletal maturity at a weight of 100–150 pounds in 16–18 years. A giant breed dog, born at less than 2 pounds, develops to skeletal maturity at a weight of 100–150 pounds in 12–18 months. Consequently, it should not be surprising that giant breed dogs are susceptible to skeletal abnormalities and that the adverse effects of poor nutrition, metabolic disease or other illnesses can be magnified in the skeletal development of these dogs and even in the smaller breeds. Because of the rapid growth of dogs and the potential deleterious effects of abnormal skeletal development, it is important that continued effort be made to more fully understand the process of canine growth and the effects of diet, husbandry, and health maintenance on that process.

The investigation of growth and development in dogs requires study of animals over a period of months.[5] Physical examination and observation of size, conformation, and locomotion are often complemented by biochemical analysis of circulating enzymes, electrolytes, and hormones.[6] Ultimately, the bones themselves must be studied. Detailed assessment of cellular growth patterns can be obtained by histopathologic examination, but diagnostic material for that assessment usually can be obtained only from post mortem specimens.[1,2] Modern diagnostic imaging methods provide the opportunity for non-invasive evaluation of the skeletal system with no effect on growth and development and little risk to the subject. Conventional radiography (x-ray film imaging) and newer computer-assisted imaging techniques are commonly used by veterinarians in clinical practice for evaluation of young dogs with skeletal abnormalities and by researchers for study of normal skeletal development and the effects of diet and other extrinsic factors on the developmental process.

Diagnostic imaging techniques provide a number of distinct advantages for investigations of growth and development that require multiple examinations over a period of months. Diagnostic imaging techniques typically do not affect the growth process in any way and may be repeated many times in the same animal. While the information generated by these techniques does not allow assessment of growth at the cellular or molecular level, the array of methods now available does allow portrayal of the morphology of musculoskeletal structures with excellent resolution. A list of currently available diagnostic imaging systems is presented in *Table 1*. Many of these systems are expensive to purchase and maintain and therefore may be available only at universities, other research centers or large specialty practices. It is important to realize that no one system produces images that provide optimal information in every situation. Each imaging system has its own unique characteristics and it is important to be aware of the relative strengths and weaknesses of each

Table 1. Imaging systems available for evaluation of the skeletal system.

Imaging System	Application
Conventional X-ray Machines	Direct x-ray film imaging including contrast radiography such as myelography and arthrography
Digital X-ray Systems	Conventional x-ray tube with digital image receptors
Cabinet X-ray Systems	Specimen radiography and microangiography of excised thin sections only
Computed Tomography (CT) Systems	Cross-section x-ray imaging, including quantitative computed tomography (QCT) for assessment of bone density
Magnetic Resonance Imaging (MRI) Systems	Cross-section imaging using a strong magnetic field and radiofrequency waves
Gamma Scintillation Cameras	Scintigraphy (radionuclide imaging) using injected radiopharmaceuticals
Diagnostic Ultrasound Machines	Reflected sound waves useful for soft tissues and surface features of bones – infrequently employed in orthopedics
Dual Energy X-ray Absorptiometers (DEXA)	Quantitative assessment of bone mineral density and body composition (fat, lean tissue, bone mineral)

in order to select the most appropriate system or combination of systems in a given clinical or research situation. Diagnostic imaging techniques should not be compared on an either/or basis, but should be evaluated with regard to the additional information that can be gained by taking advantage of their complementary strengths.[7,8]

Radiography

Conventional x-ray machines and x-ray film remain the most useful and cost-effective imaging system for most applications. X-ray film images provide excellent resolution of bone detail and usually allow visualization of an entire bone or group of bones on one image. Survey radiographs allow excellent assessment of the size, shape, contour, and opacity of bone and the relationship of adjacent and articulating bones.[7,9] Limitations include the fact that the images are two-dimensional and that superimposition of structures often inhibits clear visualization. For this reason, it is essential that at least two radiographic projections (at 90° angles) be made as part of every examination. Oblique radiographic projections and other special techniques also can be used to overcome the difficulties of superimposition. A second limitation of conventional radiography is that cartilagenous tissues and other soft tissue structures of joints cannot be seen directly. This difficulty can be overcome by introduction of iodinated radiopaque contrast material in procedures such as arthrography and myelography. Arthrography is particularly useful in evaluation for loose cartilage flaps or cartilage fissures in canine joints affected with osteochondrosis. These findings can be used to determine appropriate treatment and prognosis in clinically affected dogs. Myelography is necessary for evaluation of spinal cord compression and other soft tissue abnormalities associated with vertebral disease. It is particularly useful in assessment of dogs with caudal cervical spondylomyelopathy or "wobbler" syndrome.[10] *Figure 1* is an example of a survey (non-contrast) radiograph of the scapulohumeral joint in a dog with osteochondrosis of the humeral head.

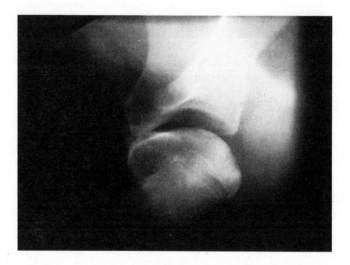

Figure 1. Conventional survey radiograph of the shoulder of a dog. This mediolateral projection shows characteristic signs of osteochondrosis of the humeral head. There is sclerosis and flattening of the subchondral bone at the caudal aspect of the articular surface.

Digital radiography uses a conventional x-ray beam but with digital image receptors instead of x-ray film. This method has the same advantages and disadvantages as conventional radiography except that there is greater opportunity for manipulation of the image once it is captured in digital format. Digital enhancement can allow improved visualization of fine osseous detail. This type of image recording also provides greater potential for quantitative assessment of bone density than does direct film recording.

Cabinet x-ray systems (such as Faxitron units) are designed for high detail radiography of thin specimens of bone. Low milliamperage, low kilovoltage, long exposure time, and special high detail, non-screen film are used to allow resolution of fine osseous elements. These units do not allow *in vivo* imaging; they can only be used to image bones that have been removed and cut into thin sections. They do provide exceptional detail of the trabeculae, subchondral bone plate, and other fine structure of bone. *Figure 2* is an example of a specimen radiograph of a thin section of humeral head from a dog with osteochondrosis. Microangiography can be performed by injecting radiopaque material into the blood vessels of specimens and making radiographs in these cabinet units. This technique allows assessment of the blood supply and vascular pathology to the level of arterioles and capillaries.

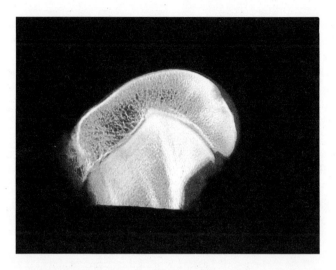

Figure 2. Specimen radiograph of a thin sagittal section of the proximal humerus of a dog. There is an ostechondral defect in the caudal aspect of the articular surface. Specimen radiographs allow resolution of the fine structure of bone. There is excellent visualization of the trabecular pattern, subchondral bone, and the articular cartilage. A lytic defect in the subchondral bone, sclerosis of surrounding subchondral bone, and thickening of the articular cartilage are clearly defined on this image.

Computed Tomography (CT)

Computed tomography (CT) is a cross-sectional imaging technique based on x-ray absorption. Narrow, pencil beams of x-ray are passed through the body as the x-ray tube circles the patient and x-ray detectors on the opposite side of the patient determine the percentage of the x-ray beam that was absorbed. The information from these detectors is manipulated by a computer in a process called back projection that results in formation of a video cross-section image.[11-13] Multiple sequential images ("slices") are made through the anatomic region of interest. A major advantage of CT is that the cross-section images allow visualization of anatomic structures without the superimposition found in planar radiographic images. CT images are also extremely sensitive to small changes in tissue density and thereby allow differentiation of more subtle density differences than can be seen with conventional radiography. Disadvantages include the cost of equipment and its maintenance, the space required, and the relatively long time required to perform a complete diagnostic study. Also, CT examination usually requires general anesthesia of animals to allow restraint and the precise positioning required for examination.

CT units with appropriate software for quantitative computed tomography (QCT) examination have been used to measure bone density of specific bones or regions of the body.[14,15] QCT techniques have been demonstrated to allow precise and accurate measurement of bone mineral density (BMD) in dogs.[16] The application reported was for evaluation of BMD in healing bone after osteotomy. The QCT technique allowed determination of BMD in selected regions of interest at the osteotomy sites.

Specially designed micro computed tomography units have been used to generate tomographic images of small, excised bone specimens. These specialized units produce cross-sectional images of bone at the trabecular level and allow measurements of very small changes in bone structure such as the thickness of the subchondral plate. This equipment moves diagnostic x-ray imaging into the microscopic realm for research applications.[17]

Computed tomography is currently being employed in clinical evaluation of joint disease in animals,[7] but standard protocols or generally accepted indications for CT imaging of canine joints have not been established. The personal experiences of the authors indicate that CT may be particularly useful in evaluation of the elbow for the presence of osteochondrosis of the medial humeral condyle and fragmented coronoid process. These abnormalities can be difficult to diagnose with conventional radiography. CT also allows excellent evaluation of the spine and has been shown useful in the evaluation of caudal cervical spondylomyelopathy. CT myelography allows more detailed assessment of the nature of spinal cord compression and associated soft tissue abnormalities than does myelography using planar radiographs alone.[10,18] The cross-sectional nature of CT offers a distinct advantage in evaluation of spinal lesions. *Figure 3* is an example of a CT image of the shoulder of a dog with osteochondrosis.

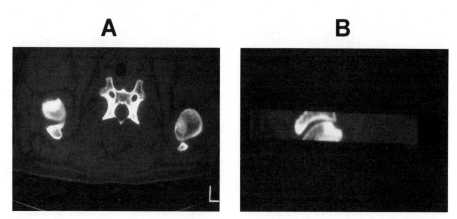

Figure 3. (Panel A) Transverse plane computed tomography (CT) image through the scapulohumeral joints of a dog. The dog was positioned in dorsal recumbancy with the forelimbs extended cranially. A caudal cervical vertebra can be seen in the center of the image between the humeral heads. This dog was affected with osteochondrosis of the right humerus. Notice the irregularity and sclerosis at the caudal aspect of the right humeral head. The left humeral head is within normal limits. (Panel B) Sagittal CT image of the right scapulohumeral joint reconstructed from a series of transverse images, one of which is shown in panel A. The ostochondral defect in the caudal humeral head is clearly visualized. Computed tomography images reconstructed in different plans have poorer resolution and the region that can be reconstructed is limited by the number and thickness of sequential images ("slices") made in the original plane.

Magnetic resonance imaging (MRI) is a cross-sectional imaging system that has been developed since the advent of CT. The patient is placed in a strong magnetic field to align the magnetic vectors of the atoms in the body. Radiofrequency waves are then passed into the body where they are absorbed by atoms and deflect the magnetic vectors. Depending on the characteristics of the atoms in a given tissue, the vectors return to alignment with the magnetic field at different rates. As the vectors realign, the atoms resonate, reemitting radiofrequency waves that are detected by a receiving coil. This information is relayed to computers that use the data to generate cross-sectional images.[13,19,20] A major advantage of MRI is its ability to differentiate soft tissue structures. In orthopedics, this allows visualization of cartilage, ligaments, tendons, and subchondral bone. Another advantage of MRI is that the images can be displayed in multiple planes allowing better interpretation of the three dimensional nature of the involved structures. Displaying MR images in multiple planes does not cause the loss of detail that can occur with reconstruction of CT images in different planes. The major disadvantages of MRI are the high cost of equipment and specialized facility, time required for imaging, and necessity to anesthetize animals for examination. Also, dense bone generates almost no signal and appears as a signal void or negative image on MR images. Computed tomography is superior to MRI for visualization of osseous structures.

Magnetic Resonance Imaging (MRI)

MRI has been used extensively in human medicine to assess joint injury as well as developmental joint abnormalities. Early experience with MRI in dogs indicates that excellent images of joint structure can be obtained, but the images are somewhat more difficult to acquire because of the small size of canine joints. MRI has been shown useful in evaluation of osteochondrosis lesions affecting the scapulohumeral joints of dogs.[21] While conventional radiographs allow accurate diagnosis of osteochondrosis, magnetic resonance images provide additional information regarding the extent of bone abnormality, as well as changes in the articular cartilage and associated soft tissues. MRI arthrography made after injection of gadolinium-DTPA into the shoulder joint was less accurate in demonstrating cartilage defects than MRI without contrast or with intravenous injection of gadolinium agents.[22] MRI has also been evaluated for imaging canine stifles with experimental osteoarthritis.[8] It was found to be useful in determination of cartilage thickness, osteophyte formation, and the presence of loose bodies within the joints. It has also been suggested that MRI may be useful in studying the pathophysiology of juvenile bone diseases such as panosteitis, hypertrophic osteodystophy, fragmented coronoid process, and osteochondrosis as well as cervical spondylomyelopathy.[19] An MR image of the shoulder of a dog with osteochondrosis is presented in *Figure 4*.

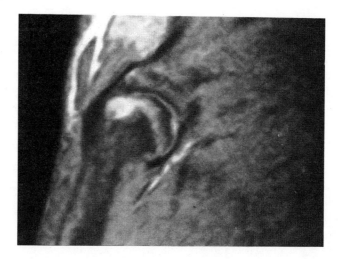

Figure 4. T1-weighted, sagittal plane, magnetic resonance image of the scapulohumeral joint of a young dog showing joint abnormalities characteristic of osteochondrosis. Articular cartilage appears as a thin white line at the articular surface. There is irregular and thickened cartilage at the caudal aspect of the joint. There is sclerosis of subchondral bone beneath the thickened cartilage seen as an area of decreased signal (dark) on the image. Notice that soft tissue structures around the joint are more clearly defined than on radiographic or CT images.

Gamma Scintillation Imaging

Nuclear medicine procedures provide visual images based on biologic distribution of injected radioactive compounds called radiopharmaceuticals.[23] For bone scans, a phosphate compound, methylene diphosphonate (MDP), is labeled with the gamma emitter, technetium 99m (^{99m} Tc). The labeled MDP is incorporated in bone wherever there is turnover of bone mineral.[24] Increased bone activity results in increased accumulation of the labeled MDP. Wherever there is more MDP, more gamma rays are emitted and the increased radioactivity can be seen on the resultant image. Sites of increased accumulation of radioactivity called "hot spots" indicate regions of increased bone activity. The scintigraphic images are very sensitive but they are not specific because any process causing bone turnover will cause increased accumulation of MDP. It is important to realize that in young, growing dogs the metaphyses are active sites of mineral deposition and as a result, all metaphyseal regions will appear quite intense, even in normal animals. **Figure 5** is an example of a scintigram of the normal forelimb of a young dog with increased activity in the metaphyses. The primary advantage of scintigraphy is that it is extremely sensitive; lytic or proliferative bone activity can be seen on scintigrams much earlier than on radiographs. Scintigraphy is also well adapted to whole body scanning, facilitating survey examination of the entire skeleton. The disadvantage of bone scintigraphy is that it does not provide nearly the anatomic detail of other imaging methods and that increased activity shows only the site and extent of a lesion and does not define its etiology. A practical disadvantage is that animals must be held in isolation for 24–48 hours after the scan to allow for decay and excretion of the radioisotope.

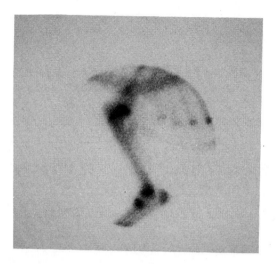

Figure 5. Scintigraphic image of the left fore limb of an immature dog. This image was made three hours after intravenous administration of methylene diphosphonate labelled with technetium 99m ([99m]TcMDP). There is increased accumulation of MDP at the metaphyses. This pattern of metaphyseal activity is characteristic of growing dogs with rapid turnover of bone mineral in the metaphyses. No abnormality is seen on this image. Radionuclide accumulation reflecting osteoblastic activity can be quantitatively assessed from computerized scintigraphic images.

Diagnostic Ultrasound

Ultrasound machines are currently in use in many veterinary practices and most veterinary research facilities. Ultrasound is most applicable for imaging the heart and organs in the abdominal cavity but has been applied to the examination of musculoskeletal abnormalities. In orthopedics, ultrasound is most useful in assessment of muscle, tendons, and other soft tissue. Ultrasound waves do not penetrate bone and therefore do not allow imaging of hard tissues. Surface features of bone such as small sequestra can sometimes be detected, however. Ultrasound has been applied to evaluate epiphyses when they are still in the cartilagenous state. Initial attempts have been made at early assessment of coxofemoral joint conformation using ultrasound, but this application has not been uniformly successful or generally accepted.

Dual Energy X-ray Absorptiometry (DEXA)

In recent years, whole body x-ray absorptiometry scanners have been developed and are now commonly used for assessment of bone density in humans. These machines use a pencil-thin, scanning x-ray beam with receptors which measure absorption of the beam by the patient. Dual energy beams allow differentiation of bone, fat, and lean tissue so that body composition analysis can be made.[15,25,26] The images produced by DEXA units are designed to identify regions of interest for quantitative assessment, not for radiographic diagnosis. Image quality varies but is quite good on the newest systems. DEXA scanning units offer a number of software options so that scans can be made of the whole body or of specific anatomic regions. The software systems are tailored to human use so that some adaptation is necessary for scanning veterinary patients. Early experience with DEXA in dogs indicates that it is a reliable method for noninvasive assessment of bone mineral density, total bone mineral, and body composition. DEXA has been used in research to study bone metabolism, osseous reponse to exercise, and treatments to prevent or reverse loss of bone mass.[27] This technology offers a remarkable tool for study of skeletal growth and development in relation to diet and other extrinsic factors because repeat studies can be made on the same animal without the necessity of harvesting tissues for analysis.[25] With further study, it is possible that DEXA may be used as a clinical screening test in growing animals to determine the adequacy of their diet and in older animals to assess for developing osteoporosis. A great deal of research will be necessary to determine the normal bone density and bone mineral content for dogs of different age, breed, and sex. Absorptiometry is discussed in greater detail in a related chapter in this proceedings.

Application of Diagnostic Imaging Techniques

Too often, radiography and other diagnostic imaging techniques are thought of only as a method to make a diagnosis of clinical abnormality. In many instances, diagnostic imaging does not allow a specific etiologic diagnosis but does provide valuable information about the site, extent, and nature of an abnormality. It is also important to realize that skeletal growth and development is a dynamic process and that diagnostic images represent the state of tissues at only a single point in time; they are a "snapshot" of an ongoing process. Serial radiographs made over weeks or months can provide much more comprehensive information than any single examination. It is also evident that diagnostic imaging techniques can be used to collect information not only from dogs with clinical signs of skeletal abnormality, but also from normal growing dogs to further document the process of skeletal development[5] and to assess for subtle or early stage abnormalities in dogs that do not show overt clinical signs.[28] Screening programs can be developed to detect preclinical signs of disease and allow remedial intervention before irreversible changes occur. A list of the possible applications of diagnostic imaging techniques for the assessment of growing dogs is presented in **Table 2**.

It is certainly not practical to employ the full array of diagnostic imaging techniques on any given animal. Clinicians must choose the appropriate imaging method or methods to most efficiently and effectively arrive at a diagnosis and treatment plan. Likewise, researchers must determine the best method(s) to collect sufficient imaging data to prove or disprove a hypothesis. It is the challenge of imaging specialists to determine the appropriate applications of the many imaging techniques available and to develop algorithms for their appropriate use.[7] Radiography remains the most inexpensive method of skeletal imaging and is appropriate for initial survey of most developmental processes and developmental disorders. The radiographic appearance of various juvenile bone diseases has been well documented.[3,4,6,9,29] Determination of standard protocols for skeletal imaging with CT, MRI, and DEXA and interpretation of those images is ongoing in veterinary medicine.

Table 2. Applications of diagnostic imaging techniques in skeletal evaluation of growing dogs.

Examination of dogs with clinical signs of lameness and/or skeletal pain or deformity
- Provide information to aid in determination of an accurate diagnosis
- Provide information to aid in determination of appropriate medical, surgical and/or nutritional treatment
- Determine the anatomic location of the abnormality
- Determine the morphologic nature of the osseous abnormality (i.e., lysis or osseous proliferation)
- Determine the extent and severity of the abnormality
- Determine whether the abnormality is unilateral, bilateral or multifocal
- Determine, by serial examinations, the progression, resolution, or response to treatment of the abnormality

Examination of growing dogs with no clinical signs of skeletal abnormality
- Screening examinations for early (preclinical) signs of developmental abnormality
  - Assessment of joint conformation (i.e., coxofemoral joints and elbows)
  - Assessment for known heritable diseases such chondrodysplasia or dwarfism
  - Assessment of physeal closure and skeletal maturity
  - Assessment of bone density and body composition
- Serial screening examinations to collect research data on normal skeletal development and incidence of preclinical abnormalities
  - Document appearance and development of secondary ossification centers
  - Document longitudinal and appositional bone growth
  - Document shape, curvature, and alignment of bones
  - Document appearance and progression or resolution of subclinical skeletal abnormalities
  - Document physeal closures
  - Document progressive changes in body composition and bone mineral density

---

A report on chronic long digital extensor avulsion in a dog demonstrated the complementary nature of radiography, CT, and MRI.[7] Radiographs of the stifle allowed initial identification of joint abnormality in the stifle and indicated probable involvement of the region of the extensor fossa of the lateral femoral condyle. CT examination provided excellent osseous detail showing irregularity and deep bone sclerosis at the extensor fossa as well as small calcific opacities in the soft tissue near the origin of the extensor tendon. MRI showed increased signal intensity in the soft tissues around the avulsed tendon origin and also showed increased synovial fluid and changes in the muscle belly of the long digital extensor.

A study of radiography, scintigraphy, and MRI in human patients with osteochondritis dissecans of the knee[30] showed that bone scintigraphy was the most sensitive method for identifying instability of the cartilage flap. The size of the lesion and the thickness of the sclerotic margin as seen on plane radiographs were also good parameters for predicting cartilage loosening. MRI allowed direct visualization of the cartilage fragment which permitted differentiation between loosening and displacement of the fragment. Because they are noninvasive, both scintigraphy and MRI were considered superior to arthrography for further evaluation of OCD lesions seen on radiographs. A list of developmental disorders is presented in *Table 3*, along with techniques which have been shown useful or may potentially be useful in assessment of those disorders. For most conditions, further investigation will be necessary to determine which imaging techniques other than radiography will be most appropriate for diagnosis or routine screening.

Table 3. Development disorders affecting the bones and joints of growing dogs.

Skeletal Disorders	Useful Imaging Tecniques	Potentially Useful Imaging Techniques
Osteochondrosis (OD)	rad, ct, mr, arth	scint
Elbow dysplasia		
Ununited anconeal process (UAP)	rad	ct
Fragmented coronoid process (FCP)	rad, ct	scint, arth
OD of medial humeral condyle	rad, ct	mr, scint
Elbow incongruity	rad	ct, mr
Retained cartilage core	rad	mr
Hyperthrophic osteodystrophy (HOD) (Metaphyseal osteodystrophy)	rad	mr
Panosteitis (enostosis)	rad, scint	mr
Canine hip dysplasia	rad	ct, mr, scint
Asynchronous growth of radius and ulna	rad	
Patellar luxation	rad	
Cervical vertebral malformation/ malarticulation (CVMM) (Wobbler syndrome)	rad, myelo, ct, mr	dexa
Generalized increase or decrease in skeletal mineralization (hormonal, aging)	rad, dexa	qct
Primary hyperparathyroidism	dexa	qct
2° nutritional or renal hyperparthyroidism (fibrous osteodystrophy)	rad, dexa	qct, ct, mr (spine)
Rickets	rad, dexa	qct
Avascular necrosis of the femoral head (Legg-Perthes)	rad, ct	mr
Craniomandibular osteopathy (CMO)	rad	ct, dexa
Multiple cartilagenous exostosis (MCE)	rad	scint
Multiple epiphyseal dysplasia (MED)	rad	mr
Chondrodysplasia / dwarfism	rad	

Rad = radiology, ct = computed tomography, mr = magnetic resonance imaging, scint = scintigraphy, qct = quantitative computed tomography, dexa =x-ray absorptiometry, arth=arthrography, myelo = myelography

At Auburn University, a number of faculty members are currently completing a long term cooperative project to evaluate the effects of various dietary levels of calcium and phosphorus on the growth and development of Great Dane puppies. [25,27,31,32] The puppies were divided into three groups fed different diets described below:

Low calcium diet	0.48% Ca	0.40% P	Ca/P ratio 1.2:1.0
Medium calcium diet	0.80% Ca	0.67% P	Ca/P ratio 1.2:1.0
High calcium diet	2.70% Ca	2.20% P	Ca/P ratio 1.2:1.0

All three diets were isocaloric and the nutrient composition was constant other than the percentage of calcium and phosphorus. The puppies were bred specifically for this study and were randomly assigned to the three groups at birth. The dogs were maintained on the three diets for 18 months and were periodically evaluated by orthopedic examination, force plate analysis of gait, dual energy x-ray absorptiometry, radiographs of the cervical spine, scapulohumeral joints, antebrachium, stifle and pelvis, and by magnetic resonance imaging of the carpus and scapulohumeral joint.

The results of the study showed differences in bone mineral density among the groups. Puppies fed the high calcium diet exhibited significantly higher bone mineral density. Puppies fed the medium diet were somewhat heavier and taller than others at 4–6 months, but by 12–18 months there was little difference in the size of the dogs fed the three different diets. A number of developmental bone abnormalities were seen on radiographs and magnetic resonance images even though many were not associated with clinical signs of lameness.[28] The abnormalities most commonly identified were:

- Osteochondrosis of the humeral head
- Retained cartilage core
- Hypertrophic osteodystrophy
- Panosteitis
- Hip dysplasia
- Cervical spinal abnormality
- Craniomandibular osteopathy

By 6 months of age, 7 of 32 puppies had shown evidence of clinical lameness. Six of the 7 puppies that exhibited clinical lameness were fed the high calcium diet. Preliminary assessment of the results of this study indicates that puppies fed the high calcium diet did not grow faster or taller than puppies on diets with lower calcium content, and that puppies on the high calcium diet seemed to have poorer conformation and a higher incidence of clinical lameness than puppies on the medium or low calcium diets. The differences observed by radiography, MRI, and DEXA were most prominent during the first 6 months of life in these puppies. Clinical lameness and conformational abnormalities were also much more apparent in puppies less than 6 months of age than in older, maturing puppies.[32] These observations suggest that excess calcium in the diet and extra calcium supplementation should be avoided in rapid growing, giant breed dogs, especially in the first 6 months of life.

Other studies have also shown the deleterious effect of excess dietary calcium especially in growing puppies.[1-4] Not only is the developing skeleton more susceptible to alteration than the mature skeleton, growing puppies have a high energy demand and therefore may eat several times the amount of food consumed by an adult dog when adjustments are made for body weight. As a result of this increased consumption, a puppy's intake of calcium can be much higher than anticipated.[33] It is also believed that excess mineral in the diet can contribute to abnormalities of organ systems other than the skeleton.[34] Despite this evidence, many people in the dog industry recommend calcium and other mineral supplements for growing dogs. Unfortunately, such supplements may even be recommended for dogs with skeletal abnormalities who are already suffering from mineral excess. Recent research supports previous work indicating that rapidly growing puppies have the greatest opportunity for normal skeletal development when fed a complete and balanced diet that avoids excess protein, calories, and calcium. Mineral supplementation may actually be counterproductive for the dog owner who is hoping to produce a larger puppy at an earlier age. Studies have shown that puppies fed high calcium diets actually have shorter legs than those fed diets lower in calcium content.[5] The dogs on the high calcium diet in this recent study not only exhibited a high incidence of hypertrophic dystrophy and cervical spinal abnormalities, but also had poorer conformation with more angular limb deformities than the group of dogs fed the medium or low calcium diets. A case report of hypertrophic dystrophy indicated that the condition may be associated with "knock knees" or valgus deformity of the rear limbs.[35] Conformational abnormality would certainly be considered an adverse effect by dog owners even if the affected dogs did not develop clinical lameness.

Experience also indicates that DEXA scanning techniques can be adapted to provide accurate and reproducible information regarding bone mineral density and body composition in dogs.[25] Reliable scanning requires general anesthesia of dogs with careful attention to symmetrical and reproducible positioning on the scanning bed. Evaluation of the serial radiographs showed that there was a high incidence of subclinical skeletal abnormality in these young Great Danes. The magnetic resonance images are currently being evaluated to determine how well they correlate with the radiographic images.

References

1. Dammrich K. Relationship between nutrition and bone growth in large and giant dogs. *J Nutr* 1991; 121:S114-S121.

2. Goedegebuure SA, Hazewinkel HAW. Morphological findings in young dogs chronically fed a diet containing excess calcium. *Vet Pathol* 1986; 23:594-605.

3. Hedhammar A. Nutrition related orthopaedic diseases. In: Kelly N, Wills J,

eds. *Manual of Companion Animal Nutrition & Feeding, Ed.1.* Ames: Iowa State University Press, 1996; 198-206.

4. Kallfelz FA. Skeletal and neuromuscular diseases. In: Lewis LD, Morris ML, Hand MS, eds. *Small Animal Clinical Nutrition III.* Topeka: Mark Morris Associates, 1990; 12.1-12.15.

5. Voorhout G, Hazewinkel HAW. A radiographic study on the development of the antebrachium in Great Dane pups on different calcium intakes. *Vet Rad* 1987; 28:152-157.

6. Hazewinkel HAW. Calciotropic hormones and bone metabolism. In: Rijnberk A, ed. *Clinical Endocrinology of Dogs and Cats.* The Netherlands: Kluwer Acad Publishers, 1996; 177-195.

7. Fitch RB, Wilson ER, Hathcock JR, Montgomery RD. Radiographic, computed tomographic and magnetic resonance imaging evaluation of a chronic long digital extensor tendon avulsion in a dog. *Vet Rad & Ultrasound* 1997; 38:177-181.

8. Widmer WR, Buckwalter KA, Braunstein EM, Hill MA, O'Connor BL, Visco DM. Radiographic and magnetic resonance imaging of the stifle joint in experimental osteoarthritis of dogs. *Vet Rad & Ultrasound* 1994; 35:371-383.

9. Riser WH. Radiographic differential diagnosis of skeletal diseases of young dogs. *J Amer Vet Rad Soc* 1964; 5:15-27.

10. Sharp NJH, Wheeler SJ, Cofone M. Radiological evaluation of "wobbler" syndrome-caudal cervical spondylomyelopathy. *J Sm Anim Pract* 1992; 33:491-499.

11. Hathcock JT, Stickle RL. Principles and concepts of computed tomography. *Vet Clin N Amer* 1993; 23:399-435.

12. Stickle RL, Hathcock JT. Interpretation of computed tomographic images. *Vet Clin N Amer* 1993; 23:417-435.

13. Curry TS III, Dowdey JE, Murry RC. *Christensen's Physics of Diagnostic Radiology, Ed. 4.* Philadelphia: Lea & Febiger, 1990.

14. Cann CE. Quantitative CT for determination of bone mineral density: a review. *Radiology* 1988; 166:509-522.

15. Jergas M, Genant HK. Quantitative bone mineral analysis. In: Resnick D, ed. *Diagnosis of Bone and Joint Disorders, Ed.3.* Philabdlphia: W.B. Saunders Co, 1995; 1854-1882.

16. Markel MD, Morin RL, Wikenheiser MR, Robb RA, Chao EY. Multiplanar quantitative computed tomography for bone mineral analysis in dogs. *Amer J Vet Res* 1991; 52:1479-1483.

17. Dedrick DK, Goldstein KDB, Brandt KD, O'Connor BL, Goulet RW, Albrecht M. A longitudinal study of subchondral plate and trabecular bone in cruciate-deficient dogs with osteoarthritis followed up for 54 months. *Arthritis & Rheumatism* 1993; 36:1460-1467.

18. Sharp NJH, Cofone M, Robertson ID, et al. Computed tomography in the evaluation of caudal cervical spondylomyelopathy of the doberman pinscher. *Vet Rad & Ultrasound* 1995; 36:100-108.

19. Widmer WR, Buckwalter KA, Braunstein EM, Visco DM, O'Connor BLI. Principles of magnetic resonance imaging and application to the stifle joint in dogs. *J Amer Vet Med Assoc* 1991; 198:1914-1922.

20. Shores A. Magnetic resonance imaging. *Vet Clin N Amer* 1993; 23:437-459.

21. Van Bree H, Degryse H, Van Ryssen B, Ramon F, Desmidt M. Pathologic correlations with magnetic resonance images of osteochondrosis lesions in canine shoulders. *J Amer Vet Med Assoc* 1993; 202:1099-1105.

22. Van Bree H, Van Ryssen B, Degryse H, Ramon F. Magnetic resonance arthrography of the scapulohumeral joint in dogs, using gadopentetate dimeglumine. *Amer J Vet Res* 1995; 56:286-288.

23. Brawner Jr WR, Daniel GB. Nuclear imaging. *Vet Clin N Amer* 1993; 23:379-398.

24. Chambers MD. Bone imaging: the diphosphonates. In: Berry DR, Daniel GB, eds. *Handbook of Vet Nuc Med*. Raleigh: North Carolina State University, 1996; 49-59.

25. Lauten SD, Brawner Jr WR, Goodman SA, Lepine AJ, Reinhart GA, Vaughn DM, Baker HJ. Body composition of growing Great Dane puppies fed diets varying in calcium and phosphorus concentration evaluated by dual energy x-ray absorptiometry. *Proc Amer College of Vet Rad*, 1996; 1.8.

26. Slosman DO, Casez JP, Pichard C, Rochat T, Fery F, Rizzoli R, Bonjour JP, Morabia A, Donath A. Assessment of whole-body composition with dual-energy x-ray absorptiometry. *Radiology* 1992; 185:593-598.

27. Grier SJ, Turner AS, Alvis MR. The use of dual-energy x-ray absorptiometry in animals. *Invest Radiol* 1996; 31:50-62.

28. Brawner Jr WR, Hathcock JT, Goodman SA, Lauten SD, Cox NR, Kincaid SA, Baker HJ, Reinhart GA, Lepine AJ. Radiographic lesions observed in growing Great Dane puppies fed diets varying in mineral content: a preliminary report. *Proc Amer College Vet Rad* 1996; 1.9.

29. Wind AP. Elbow Dysplasia. In: Slatter D, ed. *Textbook of Small Animal Surgery 2nd Ed.*, Philadelphia: W.B. Saunders, 1993; 1966-1977.

30. Mesgarzadeh M, Sapega AA, Bonakdarpour A, Revesz G, Moyer RA, Maurer AH, Alburger PD. Osteochondritis dissecans: analysis of mechanical stability with radiography, scintigraphy, and MR imaging. *Radiology* 1987; 165:775-780.

31. Brawner Jr WR, Hathcock JT, Lauten SD, Goodman SA, Cox NR, Kincaid SA, Lepine AJ, Baker HJ, Reinhart GA. Effect of dietary mineral content on the occurrence of juvenile bone disease in Great Danes. *Proc Auburn Univ Annual Conference for Veterinarians*, 1997.

32. Goodman SA, Lauten SD, Baker HJ, Brawner Jr WR, Cox NR, Hathcock JT, Kincaid SA, Montgomery RD, Rumph PF, Lepine AJ, Reinhart GA. Feeding large and giant breed puppies: are we feeding too much calcium? *Proc Auburn Univ Annual Conference for Veterinarians*, 1997.

33. Hedhammer AA. Nutrition as it relates to skeletal diseases. *Proc 4th Kal Kan Symp* 1980; 41-44.

34. Hand MS, Lewis LD, Morris Jr ML. Feeding puppies: common errors, their effects, and prevention. *Compend Cont Ed* 1987; 9:41-44.

35. Milton JL. What is your diagnosis? Hypertrophic osteodystrophy. *Auburn Veterinarian* 1978; 26:29-30.

Nutritional Effects on Bone Strength in the Growing Canine

Thomas D. Crenshaw, PhD
Director, University of Wisconsin Swine Research Center
Animal Sciences Department
University of Wisconsin, Madison, Wisconsin, USA

Rachel A. Budde, DVM[a];
Susan D. Lauten, MAg, PhD Candidate[b]; Allan J. Lepine, PhD[c]
[a]Animal Sciences Department, University of Wisconsin, Madison, Wisconsin, USA;
[b]Scott-Ritchey Research Center, Auburn University, Alabama, USA;
[c]Research and Development, The Iams Company, Lewisburg, Ohio, USA

Introduction

Lameness continues to be problematic in dogs despite ample fortification of diets with minerals and vitamins. Problems are especially evident in large breed dogs. While diet will not prevent all lameness problems, improper fortification contributes to problems and confounds diagnosis of non-nutritional lameness. Considerable disagreement exists about recommended dietary strategies to reduce the incidence of lameness. Lack of a simple technique to evaluate skeletal responses of animals to nutrient inputs also contributes to the disagreements about proper nutritional strategies to reduce the incidence of lameness.

Two common nutritional approaches used in attempts to reduce lameness include growth restriction and varying dietary mineral levels. Rapid growth, especially in large breed dogs, is highly associated with skeletal unsoundness.[1,2,3] Apparent success in alleviating skeletal problems is achieved by nutritional strategies that restrict growth, but a significant growth restriction is generally not acceptable for dog breeders or owners. Similar associations between lameness and growth rate are observed in other companion animals and in production animals such as swine and poultry. Likewise, approaches that restrict growth are rejected in these species. Since dietary calcium and phosphorus concentrations are associated with skeletal tissue development, requirements of these nutrients are often questioned.

Dietary calcium and phosphorus fortification in diets for dogs range from marginal deficiencies to dramatic over-supplementation of diets. Compared with data available for swine or poultry, limited data are available for large breed dogs from which to establish sound recommendations for calcium and phosphorus fortification.

Conclusions about mineral requirements of animals is influenced by the response criteria selected. Maximum growth responses are observed at much lower mineral intake than amounts required for maximum mineralization. The amount of bone mineral is not directly related to bone strength properties,[4-7] although within narrow limits direct relationships have been reported. For these and other reasons such as safety margins, diets are often formulated with excessive levels of minerals in an attempt to insure that skeleton integrity is not compromised. However, over-supplementation may compromise skeleton integrity just as readily as under-supplementation.

This presentation will include an explanation of inferences derived from mechanical testing of bone and limitations of these tests compared with alternate methods used to evaluate mineral requirements. Results from work with swine and preliminary work with dogs will be used to illustrate contributions of mechanical test data in evaluating mineral requirements.

Background: Techniques to Evaluate Bone Response to Nutrient Inputs

Bone Growth. Bone is a dynamic tissue with constant turnover. Two processes, modeling and remodeling, are involved in bone turnover to re-distribute the mineral matrix. Understanding how modeling and remodeling alter bone integrity and the principles of bone mechanical properties will enable our selection of nutritionally adequate diets to enhance animal well-being. In young animals, both modeling and remodeling processes are involved to allow growth in length and diameter.[8] Modeling involves accretion of bone mineral on the ends and periosteal surface with resorption on the endosteal surface. Modeling allows adaptive responses to loads imposed by changes in weight-bearing and muscle attachments. In adults, animal bone turnover occurs mainly by remodeling, a process involving resorption of existing bone coupled with formation of new bone. Remodeling is an important process to repair and strengthen bone in growing animals. Adaptive responses are involved that allow local rather than systemic control of remodeling. The primary bone turnover process in growing animals is modeling.
Figure 1 illustrates modeling and remodeling responses of bone in growing animals.

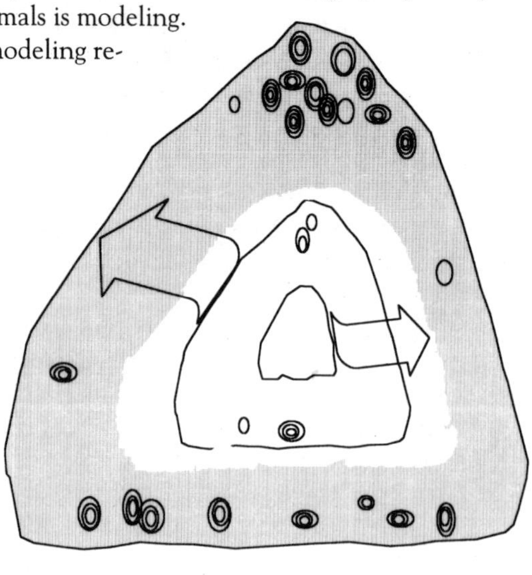

Figure 1. The relationship between modeling and remodeling of mid-diaphyseal bone. Smaller (younger) bones grow via modeling through periosteal expansion and endosteal reabsorption to produce larger (older) bone that has approximately the same shape. Remodeling is illustrated by the increased number of Haversian canals (concentric circles) present in selected regions of larger compared with smaller bone.

The impact of modeling and remodeling processes on bone integrity is often not fully appreciated in evaluation of nutrient requirements. For example, canine bone turnover varied from 20 to 120% per year depending on which bone and which site was sampled.[9] The amount of bone undergoing active modeling and remodeling also changes with age. Bone activity was greatest in growing Beagles at 3 months, then declined from 6 through 24 months.[10] No relationship was established between growth rate (body weight) and bone turnover leading the authors to conclude that weight was not an important factor in predicting variation in bone modeling and remodeling. However, relationships between bone turnover and growth rate have been reported.[1] Ad *libitum*-fed and restricted-fed Great Dane dogs differed in periosteal growth and cortex remodeling by 9 weeks of age. The differences persisted through a 48 week study. In *ad libitum*-fed dogs, lamellar bone on the periosteal surface was a greater part of total cortical area and was widely separated, creating a sponge-like architecture with larger resorption cavities than mid-diaphyseal bone from restricted-fed dogs. *Ad libitum*-fed dogs apparently had lower rates of endosteal resorption and thicker bones. In the later study, quantative histomorphometric data were not provided and the consequences of these changes on mechanical properties of bone were not evaluated. While histomorphometric techniques can quantitate modeling and remodeling responses, these techniques do not provide an assessment of mineralized matrix integrity.

Bone Mechanical Test. The mineralization of bone matrix (i.e., measures of the amount of bone mineral) is often used to assess adequacy of dietary supplements on bone integrity. Most methods used to evaluate mineralization fail to assess fundamental mechanical principles that affect the contribution of bone mineral to structural support and locomotion. These principles are not new and were recognized by Galileo.[11] The following discussion is offered as a simple description of fundamental principles involved in mechanical tests and to outline the fallacies of assessing mineral requirements based solely on measurements of mineralization.

Various degrees of sophistication in test procedures exist for determining the mechanical properties of bone.[12] Procedures range from compression, torsion, and fatigue tests of small sections of machined, cortical bone to a simple bending test of entire excised bone. More elaborate tests are required to generate information needed for design of fixation support[13] while simple tests of entire bone provide a cumulative evaluation of modeling and remodeling processes. In this paper the simple three-point bending test will be used to illustrate the relative importance of mechanical properties as a descriptor of bone integrity in contrast to estimates based only on measurement of bone mineralization.

A three-point bending test involves measurement of the resistance of bone supported by two fulcra to load applied at a constant rate by the third point positioned midway between the two supports. The load-deformation curve generated during the test is exemplified in *Figure 2*. Initially resistance is directly proportional to applied load (i.e., slope is constant) until a yield point is obtained. With application of loads below the yield point, bone is not permanently damaged. Removal of

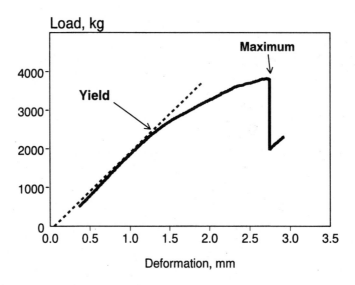

Figure 2. A typical load-deformation curve generated from a three-point bending test of bone.

load would allow bone to return to the original position and shape. As load increases beyond the yield point, permanent damage is inflicted and the bone fractures. An increase in load beyond the yield point is met by continued resistance to load, but at a decreasing rate. Bone fractures at the point of maximum load. Several traits with different inferences can be calculated from the load-deformation curve. These traits are described briefly below. More detailed description are offered in earlier reviews.[12,14]

Bending moment or **force** withstood by bone during mechanical tests describes the quantity of bone. Force is influenced primarily by the amount of mineral and length between the fulcra. **Yield force** is determined at the inflection point of the load-deformation curve (***Figure 2***) and **Maximum force** is determined at the maximum load where failure occurs.

Stress is calculated to describe the force per unit area of bone. Stress describes the quality of the mineralized matrix. Stress can be calculated at the yield (**Yield stress**) and maximum (**Maximum stress**) load points. Critical in determination of stress is a measurement of **moment of inertia** (i.e., distribution of area about the centroid). Moment of inertia takes into consideration both size and shape of an object. Not only is this measurement important because of the mathematical impact on the calculation of stress, but also biological inferences derived are consistent with adaptive responses by animals to mineral deficiencies or excesses. A re-distribution of bone mineral by modeling and remodeling processes has dramatic impact on bone integrity. Both total force and force per unit area (stress) are affected. Examples in ***Figure 3*** illustrate how shape affects moment of inertia and its relationships with area, force, and stress. Objects with the same area (i.e., a rectangle versus a circle) have different moments of inertia. If the same force is applied to the two objects, circular objects generate less stress than rectangles.

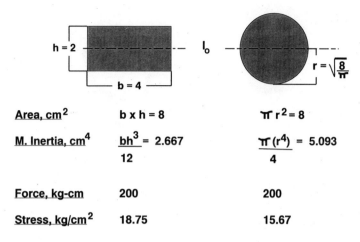

Area, cm^2	b x h = 8	$\pi r^2 = 8$
M. Inertia, cm^4	$\dfrac{bh^3}{12}$ = 2.667	$\dfrac{\pi (r^4)}{4}$ = 5.093
Force, kg-cm	200	200
Stress, kg/cm^2	18.75	15.67

Figure 3. The effect of size and shape on moment of inertia. Two objects of similar area differ in shape and moment of inertia. Thus, if a constant force is applied, the rectangle will resist with a greater force per unit area (i.e., a greater stress).

Distribution of bone mineral via modeling processes have dramatic impact on moment of inertia. *Figure 4* shows the impact that a small re-distribution of mineral mass from the endosteal surface to the periosteal surface has on the amount of force withstood by a cylinder during a mechanical test. Cylinders A, B, and C have the same cortical area but differ in amounts of force withstood, assuming the cylinders are all composed of material with the same stress properties. Doubling the internal radius (cylinder A *v* B) with the same cortical area distributed on the outer surface (i.e., the outer radius increases from 6.0 to 6.245 mm) results in only a 16% increase in moment of inertia and a 12% increase in force. However, if the same area (cylinder A *v* C) were distributed completely on the outer surface (inside radius = 6.0 mm) the outer radius would increase by 40% and moment of inertia by approximately 190%. The amount of force, assuming a constant stress, would increase by 106%. Doubling the cortical area (cylinder D *v* A) with an outside radius of 8.426 mm, results in a 289% increase in moment of inertia and a 177% increase in force.

One overall assumption made with cylinders described in *Figure 4* may not be valid with bone. In the above discussion, the amount of material re-distributed was assumed to have the same stress properties as the original material. A unit of newly deposited bone will not necessarily have the same stress properties as older bone. Factors such as remodeling and the orientation of Haversian canals,[15] collagen fiber orientation,[16] and perhaps even mineral crystal size[17] are factors that influence stress properties in bone. The re-distributed mineral matrix in bone is not the same as assumed for simple cylinders. Thus, direct measurement of mechanical properties is important.

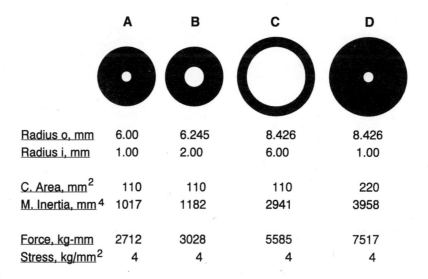

	A	B	C	D
Radius o, mm	6.00	6.245	8.426	8.426
Radius i, mm	1.00	2.00	6.00	1.00
C. Area, mm^2	110	110	110	220
M. Inertia, mm^4	1017	1182	2941	3958
Force, kg-mm	2712	3028	5585	7517
Stress, kg/mm^2	4	4	4	4

Figure 4. The effects of re-distribution of area on the outer diameter of a cylinder. Distribution of area from the inner core to the outer surface will have minor impact on the outside radius but will dramatically increase moment of inertia. Distributing the same area on the inner core would have minimum impact on the force withstood.

A final calculation from mechanical tests, **Modulus of elasticity**, provides a measure of rigidity or stiffness. Modulus of elasticity is simply the stress to strain ratio and is determined at the yield point on the load-deformation curve. In addition to considering size and shape of the object tested, calculation of modulus of elasticity includes a correction for the amount of strain (or deformation per unit of length). Thus, modulus of elasticity describes the amount of force per unit area per unit of deformation.

Results of mechanical tests of bones from growing swine have been used to assess mineral requirements.[6] An increase in dietary calcium concentration from 0.4 to 1.2% increased metatarsal stress by 80 kg/cm^2, approximately the same as the increase observed (60 kg/cm^2) over a 5 week period of growth. These results confirmed the value of bone mechanical properties in evaluation of mineral requirements. Typically, in growing pigs the outside diameter of bone did not change in response to dietary mineral levels, but differences in cortical wall thickness were observed as the endosteal cavity differed in diameter.[14]

Experimental Methods for Tests of Dog Bones

Care and feeding programs for dogs used in this project have been described in another paper.[18] Data presented in this paper are based on samples collected from 18-month-old Great Dane dogs fed diets from weaning to provide either Low (0.48%, 0.40%), Medium (0.80%, 0.67%) or High (2.70%, 2.20%) calcium and phosphorus concentrations, respectively. All diets were isonitrogenous and isocaloric.

Four bones from right front and hind limbs of 18 Great Danes were evaluated by three-point bending tests using methods previously described.[14] Bones evaluated included femur, humerus, and third metatarsal and third metacarpal bones. After mechanical tests a cross section of the mid-diaphysis from each bone was cut for image analysis to determine moment of inertia. Moment of inertia was determined in the direction of applied force using the SLICE program[19] to analyze the digitized image. In addition to moment of inertia, output from the SLICE program provided data on bone area and diameter characteristics of the bone section.

Data presented in the current report are based on an average of four bones from six 18-month-old dogs. Average values from each animal were analyzed using analysis of variance procedures to detect differences among dietary treatments. Inferences of diet differences are based on orthogonal contrasts. Regression analysis revealed that variation due to sex could be removed by use of final body weight as a covariable. Significant variation due to weight could not be removed by including only sex in the analysis. Thus, variation due to final weight includes variation in addition to that due just to sex. The impact of final body weight on bone traits were evaluated using weight as a covariable in regression analysis. Unless otherwise stated, values reported are averages of six animals per dietary treatment group, without adjustment for differences in final dog weight.

Results

Dogs fed Medium and High diets were heavier at 18 months than dogs fed Low diets (**Table 1**). Based on work with swine, dietary calcium concentrations within relative ranges involved in the current study would not cause differences in growth.[6] A marginal deficiency of dietary phosphorus provided in Low diets probably contributed to differences observed in animal growth.

Table 1. Dietary calcium and phosphorus levels alter dog weight and bone size.

Response[b]	Dietary Treatments[a]			
	Low	Medium	High	SEM
Weight, kg[c]	44.2	52.8	48.7	2.37
Total Area, mm^2[c]	228	288	271	13.8
Cortical Area, mm^2[c]	106	123	120	5.4
Medullary Area, mm^2[c]	122	165	151	10.2

[a] Treatments included calcium and phosphorus concentrations (g/100 g dry diet) of 0.48 and 0.40 (Low), 0.80 and 0.67 (Medium); and 2.70 and 2.20 (High) in isocaloric diets formulated to provide 26% crude protein and 14% fat.
[b] Responses based on the average of four bones (femur, third metatarsal, humerus, and third metacarpal bones) from six 18-month-old dogs.
[c] Low treatment group differs from Medium and High groups (P<0.05).

Differences in body size were evaluated for impact on size and strength differences in bone. Total, cortical, and medullary areas of bone from dogs fed Medium and High diets were greater than areas of bone from dogs fed Low diets. Since cortical area increased, dogs fed Medium and High diets simply deposited more bone in proportion to increased growth rates. However, similar trends in treatment differences were noted after removal of final body weight differences by covariable analysis. These observations are consistent with an increase in the amount of bone deposited as dietary mineral concentrations increased. The increased amount of bone is independent of body weight gain. Observation that dietary mineral concentrations increased size and total diameter of bone differs from earlier work with swine.[14] The impact of size differences on mechanical properties of bone are illustrated in **Table 2**. Additional bone deposited in response to increased dietary mineral concentration in both Medium and High diet groups was not the same quality as bone deposited in animals fed Low diets.

Table 2. Dietary calcium and phosphorus levels alter mechanical properties of dog bones.

| Response[b] | Dietary Treatments[a] | | | |
	Low	Medium	High	SEM
Moment of Inertia, mm^{4} [c]	3617	5479	5107	439
Yield Force, kg-mm	1799	1860	1684	116
Yield Stress, $kg \cdot mm^{-2}$ [c]	6.44	5.10	4.56	0.43
Modulus of Elasticity, $kg \cdot mm^{-2}$ [c]	528	412	406	35
Maximum Force, kg-mm	4042	4534	4652	290
Maximum Stress, $kg \cdot mm^{-2}$ [c]	13.39	11.40	11.65	0.60

[a] Treatments included calcium and phosphorus concentrations (g/100 g dry diet) of 0.48 and 0.40 (Low), 0.80 and 0.67 (Medium); and 2.70 and 2.20 (High) in isocaloric diets formulated to provide 26% crude protein and 14% fat.
[b] Responses based on the average of four bones (femur, third metatarsal, humerus, and third metacarpal bones) from six 18-month-old dogs.
[c] Low treatment group differs from Medium and High groups (P<0.05).

Cortical areas of bone from dogs fed Medium and High diets were 1.16 and 1.13 times greater than cortical area of dogs fed Low diets. This increase in area resulted in a 1.51 and 1.41 times larger moment of inertia (**Table 2**). As discussed previously (**Figure 4**), the impact of a 1.5 times greater moment of inertia would suggest that force should increase 1.36 times if the same stress was maintained in the additional bone deposited. However, the force withstood by bones of dogs fed Medium and High diets was not significantly greater than that of dogs fed Low diets and only numerically increased by 1.12 and 1.15 times. Bone stress actually decreased (P<0.05) in dogs fed Medium and High diets with Yield stress and Maximum stress values of only 70 to 80% of the strength of bones from dogs fed Low diets. Observations of an approximately equal force but lower stress values suggests the additional bone deposited in dogs fed the Medium and High diets was not equal to bones of dogs fed the Low diet. The dogs compensated for the lower quality by depositing more bone. However, long term effects of additional bone are not clear from these results. If remodeling of the new bone occurs, the long term benefit of additional bone might be recognized. The potential for bone matrix to initially demonstrate a lower stress and sebsequently compensate by remodeling to make a stronger bone is supported by observations in growing pigs.[20] Pigs fed diets with marginal calcium and phosphorus fortification had bones with less stress at 3 months of age compared with a 1-month-old group, but bone force, moment of inertia, and cortical bone thickness were greater in the 3-month-old group. By 7 months of age, the pigs had compensated and bone stress values had returned to initial values, even in animals fed marginally deficient diets. Thus, lower stress values of dogs fed the Medium and High diets compared with the Low diet need to be evaluated for long term effects.

Modulus of elasticity of bones from 18-month-old dogs differed among dietary treatment groups (**Table 2**). Dogs fed Low diets had bones that were stiffer (P<0.05) than dogs fed Medium or High diets. Differences in modulus of elasticity reflect differences in Yield stress as no differences were detected in the amount of strain withstood by bones. Strain data are not presented.

Removal of variation due to differences in final dog weight resulted in a lower probability of differences due to dietary treatments in bone traits not corrected for size (i.e., force and diameter measurements). However, traits such as stress and modulus of elasticity were not altered by adjustments due to differences in body weight.

Discussion

Lameness problems in large breed, rapidly growing dogs grossly appears to be attributed to osteochondrosis and not mineralization. Yet underlying mechanisms that predispose failure of articular cartilage may be related to inadequate mineralization of subchondral bone. Differences based on subjective evaluation have been reported in subchondral bone of Great Dane puppies raised on *ad libitum* versus restricted (70 to 80% of *ad libitum*) feed intake.[2] Cartilage failure was attributed to inadequate support of subchondral spongiosa, but no quantitative assessments of strength were reported.

Observations of improper bone mineralization and associated lameness have been reported in growing dogs. Great Dane pups fed diets with low calcium (0.55%) and low (0.50%) or normal (0.90%) phosphorus levels had pathological fractures in all but 15% of the animals, leading the authors to conclude that higher calcium levels are required for growing dogs.[21] However, negative consequences in subchondral bone and growth plates of dogs subject to over-supplementation have also been reported.[2]

Limited data are available to establish mineral requirements of large breed dogs. Some of the results available are confounded with nutritional strategies designed to restrict growth rate and the methods used to assess bone integrity.

The importance of growth rate on bone mineralization has been demonstrated in other animal models. For example, rats maintained on a restricted growth program had more total body calcium but equal femur volumes at equal body weights than control non-restricted animals.[22] Femur cortical thickness at the midshafts were thicker at equal body weights supporting conclusions that bone quality was improved in animals that grow slower. These results are consistent with conclusions that "maximum growth may be incompatible with optimal skeletal characteristics".

The type of nutritional strategy used to restrict growth of dogs appears to be important in skeletal response. No differences were detected in skeletal development of Great Dane pups fed diets with 32, 23, or 15% protein from 7 weeks until 20 weeks of age.[23] Growth was reduced in pups fed the 15% protein diets. Dietary protein intake did not affect calcium kinetics nor histomorphometric measurements made in rib biopsies. Pups did exhibit evidence of disturbed bone development, but radiographic and histological indicators were distributed equally among dogs fed the three protein levels. Mild protein restriction did not appear critical in skeletal development.

Control of growth by food restriction does impact on skeletal development. Energy restriction increased the bone length to body weight ratio and increased the ratio of diaphyseal cross sectional area to body weight.[2] These results are consistent with a compromised mineralization in the non-restricted animals and contributes to the propensity to add additional supplemental calcium and phosphorus to diets for large breed dogs.

Failure to assess the integrity of bone mineralization may mislead decisions on optimum mineral fortification for reduction of lameness in dogs. However, mechanical tests to assess bone strength require terminal experiments and are not desirable for studies with client-owned dogs, yet bone strength is the ultimate concern in assessment of skeletal integrity. Non-invasive measures of bone, such as procedures based on single-beam photon absorptiometry, have not proven to be reliable predictors of bone strength.[5,6] Newer methods such as Dual Energy X-ray Absorptiometry (DEXA) have not been extensively studied. Urine and serum markers of bone formation and resorption are qualitative at best and have limited usefulness in prediction of skeleton status because of tremendous variation among various bones. Animals compensate by shifting bone mineral reserves among bones and even within bone by local regulatory mechanisms. Local regulatory signals allow resorption to occur in areas with minimum mechanical loading, but areas influenced by load-bearing demonstrate increased mineral apposition rates.[24,25] The evaluation of small sections of bone may be misleading in evaluation of nutritional responses.[26] Thus, direct measurement of bone mechanical properties remain as the only alternative at this time.

Modeling and remodeling processes affect mineralization of bone. Mechanical tests are useful in detecting changes induced via these processes in response to nutritional programs. Development of nutritional strategies to reduce the incidence of lameness in dogs needs to include assessments of bone mechanical properties.

Based on mechanical assessment of bones from 18-month-old dogs in the current study, Medium diets (0.80% calcium and 0.67% phosphorus) appear to be sufficient. Optimum growth was achieved in dogs fed the Medium diets and no apparent lameness problems were observed. Long term consequences of the reduced stress properties need to be considered. No beneficial effects were attributed to over-supplementation of dietary calcium and phosphorus.

References

1. Hedhammer A, Wu F, Krook L, Schryver HF, De Lahunta A, Whalen JP, Kallfelz FA, Nunez EA, Hintz HF, Sheffy BE, Ryan GD. Overnutrition and skeletal disease. An experimental study in growing Great Dane dogs. *Cornell Vet* 1974; 64(Suppl 5):1-160.

2. Dammrich K. Relationship between nutrition and bone growth in large and giant dogs. *J Nutr* 1991; 121:S114-S121.

3. Meyer H, Zentek J. Energy requirements of growing Great Danes. *J Nutr* 1991; 121:S35-S36.

4. Currey JD. The mechanical consequences of variation in the mineral content of bone. *J Biomech* 1969; 2:1-11.

5. Martin RB, Burr DB. Non-invasive measurement of long bone cross-sectional moment of inertia by photon absorptiometry. *J Biomech* 1984; 17:195-201.

6. Crenshaw TD. Reliability of dietary Ca and P levels and bone mineral content as predictors of bone mechanical properties at various time periods in growing swine. *J Nutr* 1986; 116:2155-2170.

7. Carter DR, Bouxsein ML, Marcus R. New approaches for interpreting projected bone densitometry data. *J Bone Mineral Res* 1992; 7:137-145.

8. Frost HM. Remodeling as a determinant of envelope physiology. In: *Bone Remodeling and Its Relationship to Metabolic Bone Disease*. Springfield: Charles C. Thomas, 1989; 28-53.

9. Kimmel DB, Jee WSS. A quantitative histologic study of bone turnover in young adult beagles. *Anal Rec* 1982; 203:31-45.

10. Fukuda S, Iida H. Changes in histomorphometric values of iliac trabecular bone and serum biochemical constituents related to bone metabolism in Beagle dogs during growth. *Exp Anim* 1994; 43:159-165.

11. Ascenzi A. Biomechanics and Galileo Galilei. *J Biomech* 1993; 26:95-100.

12. Nordin M, Frankel VH. Biomechanics of bone. In: Nordin M, Frankel VH, eds. *Basic Biomechanics of the Musculoskeletal System*, 2nd Edition. Philadelphia: Lea and Febiger, 1989; 3-29.

13. Markel MD, Sielman E, Rapoff AJ, Kohles SS. Mechanical properties of long bones in dogs. *Am J Vet Res* 1994; 55:1178-1184.

14. Crenshaw TD, Peo ER, Lewis AJ, Moser BD. Bone strength as a trait for assessing mineralization in swine: A critical review. *J Anim Sci* 1981; 53:827-835.

15. Martin RB. On the significance of remodeling space and activation rate changes in bone remodeling. *Bone* 1991; 12:391-400.

16. Martin RB, Boardman DL. The effects of collagen fiber orientation, porosity, density, and mineralization on bovine cortical bone bending properties. *J Biomech* 1993; 26:1047-1054.

17. Matsushima N, Hikichi K. Age changes in the crystallinity of bone mineral and in the disorder of its crystal. *Biochem et Biophys Acta* 1989; 992:155-159.

18. Lauten SD, Lepine AJ, Goodman SA, Brawner Jr WR, Cox NR, Hathcock JT, Jungst SB, Kincaid SA, Montgomery RA, Rumph PF, Baker HJ, Reinhart GA. Growth and body composition of the large breed puppy as affected by diet. In: Reinhart GA, Carey DP, eds. *Recent Advances in Canine and Feline Nutrition, Vol. II: 1998 Iams Nutrition Symposium Proceedings.* Wilmington: Orange Frazer Press, 1998; 63-70.

19. Nagurka ML, Hayes WC. An interactive graphics package for calculating cross-sectional properties of complex shapes. *J Biomech* 1980; 13:59-64.

20. Crenshaw TD, Peo ER, Lewis AJ, Moser BD, Olson D. Influence of age, sex and calcium and phosphorus levels on the mechanical properties of various bones in swine. *J Anim Sci* 1981; 52:1319-1329.

21. Hazewinkel HAW, Van Den Brom WE, Van'T Klooster AT, Voorhout G, Wees AV. Calcium metabolism in Great Dane dogs fed diets with various calcium and phosphorus levels. *J Nutr* 1991; 121:S99-S106.

22. Saville PD, Lieber CS. Increases in skeletal calcium and femur cortex thickness produced by undernutrition. *J Nutr* 1969; 99:141-144.

23. Nap RC, Hazewinkel HAW, Voorhout G, Van Den Brom WE, Goedegebuure SA, Van T Klooster AT. Growth and skeletal development in Great Dane pups fed different levels of protein intake. *J Nutr* 1991; 121:S107-S113.

24. Raab DM, Crenshaw TD, Kimmel DB, Smith EL. A histomorphometric study of cortical bone activity during increased weight-bearing exercise. *J Bone Miner Res* 1991; 6:741-749.

25. Tommerup LJ, Raab DM, Crenshaw TD, Smith EL. Does weight-bearing exercise affect non-weight-bearing bone? *J Bone Miner Res* 1993; 8:1053-1058.

26. Iwaniec UT, Crenshaw TD. Predicting femoral mid-diaphyseal dynamic bone activity using subsections of total cross-sectional area. *Anatom Rec* 1998; (accepted for publication).

Studies of Bone Turnover in the Dog

Ronald R. Minor, VMD, PhD
Professor, Department of Pathology
College of Veterinary Medicine, Cornell University, Ithaca, New York, USA

Joyce A.M. Wootton, PhD[a]; Arleigh J. Reynolds, DVM, PhD[b];
Hollis N. Erb, DVM, PhD[b]; Allan J. Lepine, PhD[c]; David Eyre, PhD[d]
[a]Department of Pathology
[b]Department of Clinical Science
College of Veterinary Medicine, Cornell University, Ithaca, New York, USA
[c]Research and Development, The Iams Company, Lewisburg, Ohio, USA
[d]Department of Orthopaedics, School of Medicine,
University of Washington, Seattle, Washington, USA

Introduction

Bone growth, modeling, remodeling, and repair all result in the degradation of collagen and release of mineral. Collectively, these degradative processes are referred to as bone turnover, and they are essential for normal bone growth and remodeling. However, abnormal increases in bone turnover may result from incorrect diets, dietary supplements or disease conditions that stimulate bone remodeling or loss.

Most of the amino acids released by bone turnover are reutilized for protein synthesis, but the amino acids hydroxyproline and hydroxylysine, as well as a number of cross-linked collagen fragments, are not reutilized. Instead, these products of collagen breakdown are all excreted in urine. Urinary hydroxyproline has been used as an indicator of collagen breakdown, but there are many sources of urinary hydroxyproline besides bone breakdown. These include diet, turnover of collagens in cartilage and fibrous tissues, degradation of the serum protein C1q, and the collagenous region of the N-terminal propeptide that is cleaved when procollagen is processed to collagen. Furthermore, hydroxyproline oxidation in the liver also decreases its value as a urinary marker of bone turnover. In contrast, recent studies have shown that collagen in bone and dentin contains fluorescent, lysinopyridinoline (LP), and hydroxylysinopyridinoline (HP) cross-links,[1-3] which are released by osteoclast degradation of bone and are excreted in urine as free cross-links and as cross-linked peptide fragments from the N-terminus of type I collagen of bone.[4-6]

A monoclonal antibody against the N-terminal, cross-linked fragments of bone collagen (NTX) in human urine was recently developed to quantify the excretion of these cross-linked peptides.[6,7] Because of its specificity for the cross-linked fragments for bone collagen, this antibody is now widely used in an ELISA (Osteomark®, Ostex International Inc.) to measure changes in bone turnover in humans.[8,9] Consequently, the question was asked whether this Osteomark ELISA can be used as a non-invasive assay of bone turnover in growing dogs and dogs on different diets. In addition, chemical analysis was used to quantify the total HP and LP excretion in urine of growing and mature dogs on different diets and characterized the collagen cross-links in canine bone, cartilage, tendon, and skin.

Collagen Cross-links in Canine Tissues

HP and LP are naturally fluorescent, are separable by reversed phase HPLC, and are easily quantified at pmole concentrations.[2,3,5,10] As in human beings, HP and LP cross-links were both present in canine bone collagen, but LP cross-linked collagens were not present in the other canine tissues (*Figure 1*). Amino acid analysis of acid hydrolysates of weighed aliquots of delipidized, powdered, and lyophilized diaphyseal bone of two adult dogs showed that collagen constituted ~23% of the dry weight and represented 94±2% of the total protein. HPLC analysis of HP and LP in these hydrolysates indicated that the molar ratio of HP to collagen was 0.207 and the molar ratio of LP/collagen was 0.028 in this mature canine bone. Thus, each nanomole of LP represented ~35.7 nmoles of collagen, or ~44.2 mg of dried bone. Further studies are needed to learn if there is an age, breed, sex or size

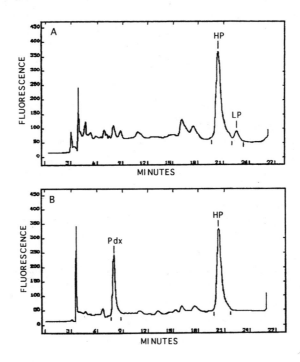

Figure 1. Reversed phase HPLC separation of the fluorescent collagen cross-links, HP and LP, in a hydrolysate of canine bone (A) and hyaline articular cartilage (B). Elution was with a gradient of 17.5 to 22.5% acetonitrile. In B, 50 pmoles of pyridoxamine (Pdx) was added as a standard for quantification of HP and LP. Note the absence of a fluorescent LP peak in the cartilage hydrolysate.

related change in collagen content or in moles of either cross-link per mole of canine bone collagen.

Since free HP and LP, as well as the HP and LP cross-linked collagen fragments, are voided in urine, the chemical analysis of HP and LP in urine hydrolysates is a sensitive method to determine the concentrations of HP and LP, without distinguishing between free and peptide bound cross-links[4,10] (**Figure 2**). Due to the fluorescence of these cross-links, as little as 1 ml of canine urine is required for acid hydrolysis and reversed phase separation of the total urinary HP and LP. These chemical assays are more time consuming than an ELISA, but the cost difference is rather small. To date, the results suggest that the ELISA and chemical assays are each an important non-invasive method of analyzing canine bone turnover.

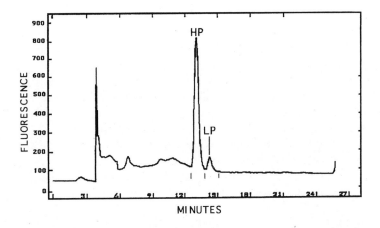

Figure 2. HPLC separation of HP and LP in a hydrolysate of urine of a 4-month-old Alaskan Husky pup. Elution was with a gradient of 19.5 to 22.5% acetonitrile. Note that with this shallow acetonitrile gradient the HP and LP peaks eluted ~6 minutes earlier and had good baseline separation.

To determine the amount of temporal variation in the excretion of HP and LP in dogs, the total urine was collected at 8 successive six hour intervals from four, 14-week-old, Alaskan Husky pups. An aliquot of each sample was hydrolyzed for HPLC analysis of total HP and LP, and the concentrations of these cross-links were normalized to the concentration of urine creatinine (CR). A duplicate aliquot of urine was analyzed with the Osteomark ELISA to measure the bone collagen equivalents (BCE) of N-terminal fragments of bone collagen. Unfortunately, as in human beings,[4,8,11,12] there was a marked temporal variation in the concentration of BCE, HP, and LP, as well as in the ratio of these cross-links to CR in canine urine. These variations were sufficient to suggest that studies of canine bone turnover require analysis of pooled aliquots representing at least the total 24 hour urine output.

When the four dogs were placed in metabolic cages for 48 hours, the BCE/CR and LP/CR increased steadily during their time in a metabolic cage. This increased bone turnover may result from a stress response in dogs that are not accustomed to being caged. This suggestion results from the change in the urinary BCE/CR and LP/CR in one dog that escaped from the metabolic cage after the sixth six hour collection. This escapee's urinary LP/CR increased 28% during the first 36 hours in the metabolic cage, and then decreased by 33% during the six hours after his escape. In contrast, the urinary LP/CR continued to increase gradually in the other three dogs in metabolic cages for 48 hours. Though this was only one observation, the data suggest that experiments should be conducted to ask if urinary BCE/CR or LP/CR can used for studies of factors causing rapid changes in the rates or amounts of canine bone turnover. Because of these results, in all subsequent studies, urine was collected at four successive six hour intervals from dogs in metabolic cages.

Age Related Changes in Bone Turnover in Alaskan Huskies

Age related changes in bone turnover in the growing dog were initially studied in four clinically normal Alaskan Husky pups. Analysis of four successive 6 hour urine collections confirmed that there is considerable temporal variation in urinary LP and CR excretion, so pooled aliquots representing the 24 hour urine output were routinely analyzed to determine the concentrations of BCE, HP, LP, and CR. The BCE/CR ratio was used as an estimate of the excretion of bone collagen fragments, and the LP/CR represented a quantitative estimate of the rate of total bone turnover (*Figure 3*). Results of both the ELISA and chemical assays indicated that there was a direct association between the decreasing rate of skeletal growth and a decreasing rate of urinary excretion of bone collagen cross-links in these pups.

The Osteomark ELISA was developed as an assay of cross-linked bone collagen fragments in human urine, and the amounts of immunoreactive NTX in collagenase digests of human and canine bone are likely to differ. Consequently, at this time BCE values are not being used as a quantitative estimate of the total amount of canine bone turnover. Nevertheless, this ELISA proved to be a very sensitive measure of bone collagen fragments in canine urine, and the rate of decrease in the BCE/CR was similar to the rate of decrease in the LP/CR. The excretion of BCE ranged from ~3,000 to ~4,000 pmoles/μmole of CR at 4 months, from 700 to 1,200 pmoles/μmole at 7 months, and from 300 to 400 pmoles of BCE per μmole of CR in the urine of the 12-month-old pups (*Figure 3*). At 4 months of age, LP excretion ranged from 24 to 44 pmoles of LP per μmole of CR, and this decreased to a range of 11 to 18 pmoles/μmole at 7 months and to 4 to 9 pmoles of LP per μmole of CR in the 12-month-old pups (*Figure 3*). The percentage change per month of the BCE/CR ratio was similar to that of the LP/CR ratio in the urine of these Alaskan Husky pups (*Table 1*). If each nanomole of LP represented 44.2 mg of bone in these pups, as it did in the adult dogs, 6 to 10 gm of bone was degraded per day in the 4-month-old pups, while the daily loss of bone was 4 to 9 gm/day at 7 months and 1 to 6 gm/day at 12 months.

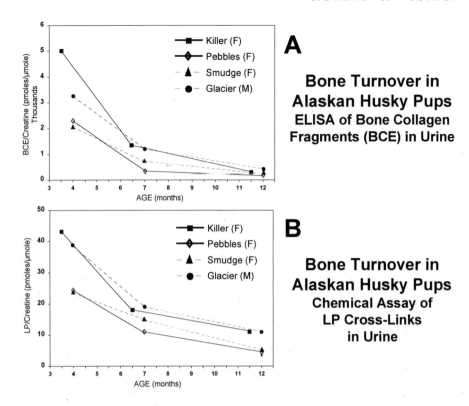

A

**Bone Turnover in
Alaskan Husky Pups**
ELISA of Bone Collagen
Fragments (BCE) in Urine

B

**Bone Turnover in
Alaskan Husky Pups**
Chemical Assay of
LP Cross-Links
in Urine

Figure 3. Analysis of changes in bone turnover in Alaskan Husky pups, using an ELISA to measure the concentration of bone collagen fragments (BCE), to determine the BCE/CR ratio in urine (A). A chemical assay was used to determine the LP/CR ratio (B). Each value represents the average from analysis of four successive 6 hour urine collections. The percentage change per month of these values is shown in Table 1.

PERCENTAGE CHANGE PER MONTH IN BCE/CR							
Age (Months)	Killer (F)	Pebbles (F)	Smudge (F)	Glacier (M)	Avg	STD	95% CI
4–7	24.1	26.0	22.0	20.0	23.0	2.6	18.9–27.2
7–12	14.3	9.7	10.4	13.5	12.0	2.3	8.4–15.6

PERCENTAGE CHANGE PER MONTH IN LP/CR							
Age (Months)	Killer (F)	Pebbles (F)	Smudge (F)	Glacier (M)	Avg	STD	95% CI
4–7	19.7	18.4	14.3	18.3	17.7	2.3	14.0–21.4
7–12	9.9	12.7	13.4	9.9	11.5	1.8	8.6–14.4

Table 1. Percentage change per month in the ratio of BCE/CR and LP/CR in Alaskan Husky urine, as shown in Figure 3.

Urinary BCE, HP, LP and CR excretion were also measured in older adult (8- to 11-yr-old) Alaskan Huskies. This included one 8-year-old female, two 8-year-old males, and one 11-yr-old male. The BCE/CR values ranged from 39 to 159 pmoles/μmole and the LP/CR values ranged from 1.8 to 4.8 pmoles/μmole. With an assumed 44.2 mg of bone per nmole of LP as described above, bone loss per 24 hours ranged from 0.9 to 2.9 gm in these older dogs and there was no apparent association of any of the values with either age or gender.

Age Related Changes in Bone Turnover in Golden Retrievers

Bone turnover was also measured in four Golden Retriever pups. At 7, 9, and 11 months of age, four successive six hour urine collections were analyzed for BCE, HP, LP, and CR. As shown in **Figure 4**, the slope of the BCE/CR and LP/CR was essentially identical to that found in the 7- to 12-month-old Alaskan Husky pups. During the 4 month period, the change in BCE/CR was 12.9±0.9% per month, while the LP/CR decreased at a rate of 14.1±1.3% per month. The relationship between the results obtained with ELISA and chemical assays of urine of

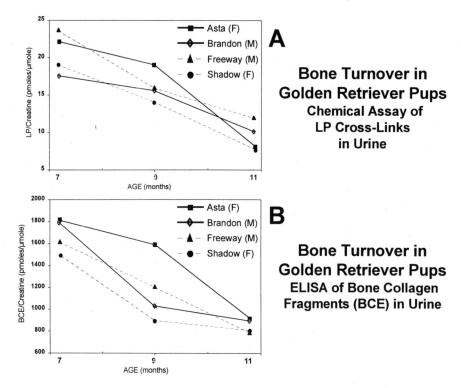

Figure 4. Analysis of changes in bone turnover in Golden Retriever pups, using a chemical assay of the LP/CR ratio (A) and an ELISA of the BCE/CR ratio (B) in urine. Each value represents the average from analysis of four successive 6 hour urine collections.

46

Alaskan Husky and Golden Retriever pups suggests that these are equally good, non-invasive methods of measuring age related changes in canine bone turnover.

Effects of Dietary Protein. An experiment that is nearing completion was designed to determine if differences in bone turnover were induced by differences in the levels of protein, fat, or calcium in the diet of growing dogs. Twenty- four 12-week-old pups were divided into three equal groups that were fed diets containing 32%, 26%, or 20% protein on a dry matter basis, providing 32%, 26%, and 20% of calories as protein, respectively. All three diets supplied energy at 4.7 kcal/g, and carbohydrate was used to replace protein in the lower protein diets. All pups were fed the intermediate protein (basal) diet for one week (week 0), and urine was collected for four successive six hour periods to determine the levels of BCE, HP, LP and CR at the start of the 4 weeks on a formulated diet. The pups were arbitrarily assigned to the three diet groups, each group was fed the same diet for 4 weeks, and urine was collected at weekly intervals for analysis of BCE, HP, LP and CR. At the end of the 4 weeks the pups were fed the basal diet for a 2 week washout. After each week on the basal diet, urine was collected for ELISA and chemical analysis. *Figure 5* illustrates the average weekly change in BCE/CR ratio in the first three dogs fed for 4 weeks with the high, intermediate or low protein diet, followed by 2 weeks on the basal diet. The slope of change in BCE/CR is similar in the high and low protein diet group and none of the slopes changed during the last 2 weeks when all pups

Effects of Diet on Canine Bone Turnover

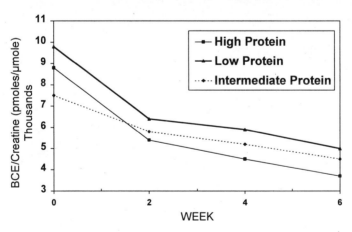

Effects of Dietary Protein on
Bone Turnover in Dogs
ELISA of Bone Collagen Fragments (BCE) in Urine

Figure 5. Analysis of the effects of dietary protein on bone turnover, using assays of the BCE/CR ratio in urine of pups fed from 0 to 4 weeks with high (30%), control (25%), or low (20%) protein diets followed by a washout feeding of all pups for 2 weeks with the control diet. Each value represents the average of the BCE/CR ratio in pooled 24 hour urine samples from 3 dogs in each diet group. Note that there was no change in the slopes of the BCE/CR ratio during the last 2 weeks when pups being fed the high and low protein diets were switched back to the control diet.

were fed the basal diet. This may indicate that the protein level had no effect on bone turnover, although completion of all animals through the study is necessary to verify this conclusion.

Effects of Dietary Fat. The second week on the basal diet was considered as week 0 for the next experimental diet. At the end of this week the diets were changed to examine the effects of dietary fat levels on bone turnover. Each pup was assigned to a different diet group, and the groups were fed diets with 21%, 14%, or 8% fat for 4 weeks. This resulted in 46%, 34%, and 21% of the caloric intake being provided by fat in the high, medium, and low fat diets, respectively. The low fat diet was formulated to the AAFCO Growth and Reproduction recommended minimum for fat. Dogs in the high and medium fat groups were pair fed to the low fat group, resulting in a 20 and 10% greater caloric intake for the high and medium fat groups relative to the low fat group. After 4 weeks in their respective diet groups, the pups were again fed basal diet for a 2 week washout. At weekly intervals, urine was collected for four successive six hour periods for analysis of BCE, HP, LP, and CR concentrations. *Figure 6* illustrates the changes in the average BCE/CR ratio in urine of the first 3 pups fed the high, basal, and low fat diet. Although final conclusions about the significance of the data must await the complete data set, the slopes suggest that bone turnover decreased at approximately the same rate in the pups fed

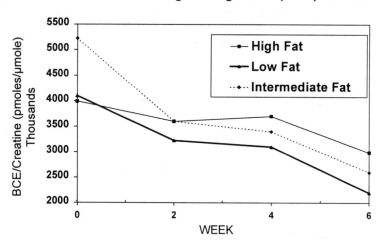

Effects of Dietary Fat on Bone Turnover in Dogs
ELISA of Bone Collagen Fragments (BCE) in Urine

Figure 6. Analysis of the effects of dietary energy on bone turnover, using assays of the BCE/CR ratio in urine of pups fed from 0 to 4 weeks with high (5 kcal/gm), control (4 kcal/gm), or low (3 kcal/gm) energy diets, followed by a washout feeding of all pups for 2 weeks with the control diet. Each value represents the average of the BCE/CR ratio in pooled 24 hour urine samples from 3 dogs in each diet group. Note that in the pups fed the high energy diet, the BCE/CR ratio did not decrease as expected during the 4 weeks on diet, but decreased more rapidly during the last 2 weeks when pups were all switched back to the control diet.

low and medium fat diets, while the expected decrease in bone turnover was absent during the 4 weeks that the pups were fed the high fat diet. Nevertheless, when the diets were returned to basal fat levels during the last 2 weeks, bone turnover again decreased at the expected rate in all three groups of pups. Increased skeletal growth and bone modeling in the pups in the high fat diet could account for these observations.

Effects of Dietary Calcium. The second week of the basal diet was again considered as week 0 for the next diet. At the end of this week the diets were changed to examine the effects of dietary calcium levels in bone turnover. Puppies were assigned to three diet treatment groups (high, intermediate, or low calcium diets) for 4 weeks. The diets were formulated to contain calcium at 0.48%, 0.80%, or 2.7% of dry matter with a constant calcium to phosphorus ratio (1.2:1). All diets supplied 4.7 kcal/g of dry matter, and contained identical concentrations of other nutrients. Analysis of the calcium content of these diets produced values of 0.57%, 0.80%, and 2.68% calcium for each of the diets. Although the number of samples are still too small to permit conclusions, the initial data suggest that throughout the 4 weeks on diet, there was an increase in bone turnover in the pups fed the high calcium diet (**Figure 7**). During the last 2 weeks on the experiment, when all pups were fed the basal diet, the rates of bone turnover decreased more rapidly in the

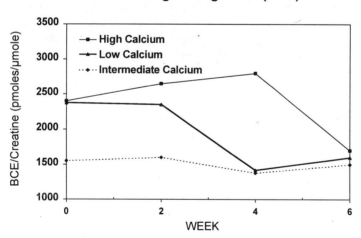

Figure 7. Analysis of the effects of dietary calcium on bone turnover, using assays of the BCE/CR ratio in urine of pups fed from 0 to 4 weeks with high (2.9%), control (1.0%), or low (0.63%) calcium diets, followed by a washout feeding of all pups for 2 weeks with the control diet. Each value represents the average of the BCE/CR ratio in pooled 24 hour urine samples from 3 dogs in each diet group. Note that in the pups fed the high calcium diet, the BCE/CR ratio increased instead of decreasing during the 4 weeks on diet, but decreased very rapidly during the last 2 weeks when pups were all switched back to the control diet.

pups that had been fed the high calcium diet. By the end of week 2 on the basal diet, the rates of excretion of BCE/CR were essentially identical in all of the pups. Thus, the results of assays of both the BCE/CR and LP/CR in all 8 pups in each of these diet groups should be quite interesting.

One might predict that the 0.57% calcium diet would result in stimulation of PTH production and cause increased degradation of bone collagen with increased mobilization of calcium. Instead, the BCE/CR increased during the 4 weeks the pups were fed the high calcium diet and decreased during this period in both the basal and low calcium group (*Figure 7*). If similar differences in bone turnover occur in the remaining pups in each diet group, further studies will be required to determine if increased bone formation and remodeling account for the increased degradation of bone matrix in pups fed the high calcium diet. This is one physiologic mechanism that could account for these observations. However, recent *in vitro* studies demonstrated that high extracellular calcium levels stimulated cultured mouse osteoblast-like bone cells to undergo osteoclast-like cell formation and increased bone resorption.[13] The culture medium of high calcium-stimulated osteoblast-like cells also stimulated osteoclast-like cell formation from hematopoietic stem cells. Nevertheless, our results were surprising because all of the pups were 31-weeks-old at the end of the three experiments, so skeletal growth was nearing completion and the rate of excretion of bone collagen fragments was approaching the levels required for skeletal maintenance.

Conclusions   Analysis of BCE/CR and LP/CR in urine have proven to be two non-invasive methods of analyzing bone turnover in both growing and mature dogs. Even though these assays require only 1 ml of urine, both assays require 24 hour urine collections and analysis of pooled aliquots. With both assays, there is minimal variation in the values obtained with multiple assays of each sample, but there is considerable temporal variation in excretion of creatinine and bone collagen cross-links in canine urine. Recent data indicate that the NTX fragments of bone collagen detected by the Osteomark ELISA result from the degradation of bone by osteoclasts,[14] but there are no data on the degradation products of bone collagen released by osteoblastic or osteocytic osteolysis.

Since the LP in hydrolysates of urine will contain LP released from NTX fragments, as well as free LP that was released by the complete proteolytic degradation of bone collagen into its constituent amino acids,[15] our working hypothesis is that the BCE/CR values may be a more sensitive indicator of rapid changes in bone turnover, while the LP/CR values may permit a more quantitative analysis of the total amount of bone degradation. Completion of the assays of urine of all 8 dogs in each diet group described above should determine the sensitivity and variability that can be expected of each of these methods. The data should also provide important information on the effects of dietary protein, energy and calcium levels on bone turnover in the growing dog. Knowledge of the amounts of variation in the excretion of the bone collagen cross-links in canine urine should help design studies of the effects of different dietary supplements, pharmacological agents and disease on skeletal growth, maintenance and repair in the dog.

The excellent technical assistance of Barbara Hover, Annette Otis, and Joe Wakslag is greatly appreciated. Dr. Fernando de Noronha kindly contributed to the development of the ELISA assays of canine BCE. This research was supported by The Iams Company.

Acknowledge-ments

References

1. Eyre DR, Oguchi H. The hydroxypyridinium cross-links of skeletal collagens: Their measurement, properties and a proposed pathway of formation. *Bioch Biophys Res Commun* 1980; 92:403-410.

2. Eyre D, Koob TJ, Van Ness KP. Quantitation of hydroxypyridinium cross-links in collagen by high-performance liquid chromatography. *Analyt Biochem* 1984; 137:380-388.

3. Eyre D. Collagen cross-linking amino acids. *Methods in Enzymol* 1987; 144:115-139.

4. Beardsworth LJ, Eyre DR, Dickson IR. Changes with age in the urinary excretion of lysyl- and hydroxylysylpyridinoline, two new markers of bone collagen turnover. *J Bone Mineral Res* 1990; 5:671-676.

5. Black D, Duncan A, Robins SP. Quantitative analysis of pyridinoline cross-links of collagen in urine using ion-paired reversed phase high-performance liquid chromatography. *Analyt Biochem* 1988; 169:197-203.

6. Hanson DA, Weis MAE, Bollen A-M, Maslan SL, Singer FR, Eyre DR. A specific immunoassay for monitoring human bone resorption: Quantitation of type I collagen cross-linked N-telopeptides in urine. *J Bone Mineral Res* 1992; 7:1251-1258.

7. Hanson DA, Eyre DR. Molecular site specificity of pyridinoline and pyrole cross-links in type I collagen in human bone. *J Biol Chem* 1996; 271:26508-26516.

8. Gertz BJ, Shao P, Hanson DA, Quan H, Harris ST, Genant HK, Chesnut CH, Eyre DR. Monitoring bone resorption in early postmenopausal women by an immunoassay for cross-linked collagen peptides in urine. *J Bone Mineral Res* 1994; 9:135-141.

9. Naylor KE, MacLean J, Eastell R. Cross-linked N-telopeptides of type I collagen: Response to cyclical etidronate therapy in osteoporosis. *Bone* 1997; 20:101S.

10. Pratt D, Daniloff Y, Duncan A, Robins SP. Automated analysis of pyridinium cross-links of collagen in tissue and urine using solid-phase extraction and reversed-phase high-performance liquid chromatography. *Analyt Biochem* 1992; 207:168-175.

11. Schlemmer A, Hassager C, Jensen SB, Christiansen C. Marked diurnal variation in urinary excretion of pyridinium cross-links in premenopausal women. *J Clin Endocrinol Metab* 1992; 74:476-480.

12. Eastell R, Calvo MS, Burritt MP, Offord KP, Graham R, Russell G, Riggs BL. Abnormalities in circadian patterns of bone resorption and renal calcium conservation of type I osteoporosis. *J Clin Endocrinol Metab* 1992; 74:487-494.

13. Kaji H, SugimotoT, Kanatani M, Chihara K. High calcium stimulates osteoclast-like cell formation and bone-resorbing activity in the presence of osteoblastic cells. *J Bone Mineral Res* 1996; 11:912-919.

14. Apone S, Lee MY, Eyre DR. Osteoclasts generate cross-linked collagen N-telopeptides (NTx) but not free pyridinolines when cultured on human bone. *Bone* 1997; 21:129-136.

15. Colwell A, Eastell R. The renal clearance of free and conjugated pyridinium cross-links of collagen. *J Bone Mineral Res* 1996; 11:1976-1980.

Nutritional Management
of the Large Breed Puppy

Allan J. Lepine, PhD
Research Nutritionist, Research and Development
The Iams Company, Lewisburg, Ohio, USA

Body size and conformation in the canine often reflect the role for which a breed was originally developed. This can range in the extreme from the long, low profile of the Dachshund, or literally "badger dog," to the velocity-inspired aerodynamics of the Greyhound. Frequently, the successful accomplishment of the specific task assigned to the dog necessitated great size and strength as essential breed characteristics. Evidence of this heritage remains for dogs such as the Great Dane, Irish Wolfhound, and Scottish Deerhound, originally used to hunt large game, the Great Pyrenees and Mastiff bred to protect property, and breeds such as the Newfoundland and Saint Bernard working as rescue or pack animals. In large measure, however, breeds such as these are no longer required to perform the functions for which they were originally bred, but are instead maintained as pets and show dogs by individuals who appreciate their unique breed characteristics. A common outcome of this distancing of a breed from its original purpose is a shift in criteria for genetic selection away from function and towards phenotypic considerations which may enhance success in the show ring. One dramatic example of this phenomenon is the increase in mature body size of the Great Dane in recent years. Growth curves published in 1974 (**Figure 1**) indicate that the typical Great Dane of that era grew to approximately 130 lb mature body weight by 12–18 months of age. Today, mature body weights of 180 lb or more during that same 12–18 month growth phase are not uncommon for this breed.

Introduction

An important consideration of the genetic selection process which is often not considered or discounted as insignificant is that selection for a given trait does not occur as an isolated event. Selecting for one trait may often affect other traits, for genes may influence more than one characteristic. Such is clearly evidenced by the Great Dane growth data referenced above. Selection for increased body weight during the past 25 years not only increased mature body size, but likewise increased the potential for growth velocity since the duration of the growth process has not been extended. It must therefore be recognized that selection pressure for a specific desirable trait may result in the unintentional selection of additional desirable or undesirable genetically linked traits and that the effect of these associated traits may not be inconsequential. Many large and giant breed dogs suffer from an increased propensity for the development of specific skeletal abnormalities resulting from the selection for enhanced growth rate and larger mature body size. The predominant

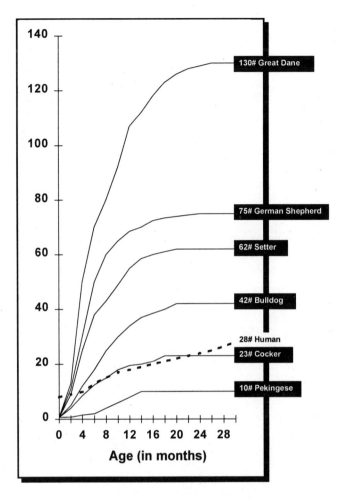

Figure 1. Representative growth curves of a variety of breeds. Adapted from *Current Veterinary Therapy V*, 1974.

skeletal abnormalities include hypertrophic osteodystrophy, osteochondrosis, and hip dysplasia.

Hypertrophic osteodystrophy is a metabolic bone disease that primarily affects young, rapidly growing large and giant breed dogs. Several breeds, including the Great Dane, Irish Wolfhound, Saint Bernard, Borzoi, Boxer, Dalmation, Irish Setter, Weimaraner, German Shorthaired Pointer, Doberman Pinscher, German Shepherd, Labrador Retriever, Collie, and Greyhound have been reported to be affected.[1-4] Hypertrophic osteodystrophy is most commonly observed at 3 to 6 months of age and is characterized by anorexia, pyrexia, lameness, and by swollen, painful and hyperthermic long bone metaphyses. The grossly apparent swellings are the result of a fibrous thickening of the periosteum accompanied by periosteal new bone formation. Commonly affected are the metaphyseal regions of the long bone distal to the elbow and stifle; however, all long bone metaphyses can be affected. Two distinct radiographic patterns have been reported to be associated with hypertrophic osteodystrophy.[5] In one there is a widening of the metaphysis and irregular periosteal new bone formation and soft tissue swelling, while the other shows a radiolucent band parallel to but separated from the physeal cartilage.

Osteochondrosis is a common cause of lameness in growing large and giant breed dogs and is especially prevalent in the Great Dane, Labrador Retriever, Newfoundland, and Rottweiler.[6] Acute pain, swelling, and lameness is observed most commonly in the shoulder, elbow, hock, and stifle.[7] Although the etiology is considered to be mulifactorial, the damaged articular cartilage is reported to result from a biomechanically weak subchondral spongiosa which is unable to provide adequate support for the epiphyseal articular cartilage.[8] Secondary disturbances then occur in the function and metabolism of the chondrocytes in the developing joint surface.

Canine hip dysplasia is a developmental disease of the coxofemoral joint resulting from a genetic predisposition which is generally accepted as polygenic in its mode of inheritance. Hip dysplasia predominantly affects growing large and giant breed dogs although it can occur in any breed. During growth a disparity develops between the strength of the soft tissues supporting the joint and increasing biomechanical forces associated with weight gain resulting in a loss of congruity between the femoral head and the surfaces of the acetabulum. This subluxation produces remodeling of the joint including a shallowing of the acetabulum, a flattening of the femoral head, and eventually, osteoarthritis. Chronically affected dogs may be asymptomatic or may indicate only mild discomfort particularly following periods of relatively intense exercise. In contrast, severe hip dysplasia produces marked lameness, pain, abnormal gait, reluctance to rise, and atrophy of the thigh muscle.

A collective feature of hypertrophic osteodystrophy, osteochondrosis, and canine hip dysplasia is the genetic predisposition for the development of these diseases. This is supported by an increased incidence in certain breeds, particularly growing large and giant breed dogs. Furthermore, nutritional management has been implicated as a factor important in influencing the expression of the genetic potential for skeletal disease. As a result, numerous feeding management recommendations, supported or unsupported by controlled research, are currently advanced as effective in enhancing the skeletal integrity of the large and giant breed dog. *Table 1* provides a representative list of such myths and misconceptions. Two points become immediately obvious from even a cursory inspection of these feeding management recommendations. First, considerable diversity exists across the recommendations, and second, contradictory recommendations are not uncommon. Consequently, the confusion and uncertainty often associated with determining the correct method of feeding the large and giant breed dog during growth is quite understandable. Nevertheless, three nutritional considerations can be summarized as those most consistently presented as areas of primary concern during large and giant breed dog growth. These include 1) dietary protein concentration, 2) energy density of the diet, and 3) calcium supplementation.

Table 1. Common myths and misconceptions about feeding large and giant breed puppies.

- Vitamin and mineral supplements can be given.
- Mineral and vitamin supplementation is OK but should be on the advice of a veterinarian.
- Supplement with calcium carbonate.
- Dolomite can be substituted for calcium carbonate every third day.
- Provide additional calcium (tablets, cottage cheese, yogurt).
- You can supplement with eggs, milk, and cheese if you wish.
- Apple cider vinegar improves calcium absorption and flushes acid crystals out of muscles and joints.
- Feed puppy at least three diluted milk drinks a week with an egg yolk added.
- Provide daily multi-vitamins and vitamin C tablets.
- It is encouraged that you give your puppy a vitamin supplement daily.
- Vitamin C is thought to be helpful for giant breeds.
- High doses of vitamin C may prevent growth disorders such as hip dysplasia.
- Cod liver oil can be added to the diet in periods of bad weather.
- Vitamin E supplementation will lead to a healthier coat.
- High protein can cause skeletal problems.
- Keep puppies on a low protein diet (<24% protein) until at least 1 year of age.
- Very low protein diets (<15% protein) are best for large and giant breed puppies.
- High protein diets (>30% protein) are required to provide for collagen deposition and muscle growth.
- Add 1/8 cup of oatmeal to the diet daily.
- Include vegetables, potatoes, chicken, turkey, eggs, rice, cottage cheese and noodles.
- Give a piece of banana and carrots every morning.
- Cooked vegetables (especially cooked from table scraps) may be added to the diet.
- Kelp granules or powder can help enrich the natural color of the coat.
- A teaspoon of polyunsaturated oil added to the daily meal helps to provide necessary oils and fats.
- Puppy foods are not a good idea for large and giant breeds.

Dietary protein level has been implicated as influencing the incidence and severity of skeletal disease in the growing large and giant breed puppy. It is often stated that diets that are "too hot" (i.e., contain high levels of dietary protein) promote rapid rates of growth and thereby predispose the dog to skeletal disease. Controlled research, however, does not support the hypothesis of an association between high dietary protein intake and skeletal abnormalities. Great Dane puppies consuming isocaloric diets providing a broad range of dietary protein (31.6%, 23.1% or 14.6% protein) from weaning for 18 weeks displayed no evidence of treatment effect on calcium metabolism or skeletal development.[9,10] Histological and radiologic changes consistent with disturbed endochondral ossification were observed, but were equally distributed across treatment groups indicating the causative factor to be something other than dietary protein. Although the high protein diet did not promote any detectable negative effects on skeletal development, the low protein diet was considered only marginally sufficient for the growing Great Dane in these diets providing approximately 3,600 kcal ME/kg of diet. Body weight was significantly reduced for the dogs consuming the 14.6% protein diet relative to the 31.6% protein group at 13 and 15 weeks of age, while plasma albumin concentrations remained lower for the former diet throughout the study. This demonstrates the necessity to be cognizant of the protein to energy ratio when evaluating the dietary protein concentration.

Skeletal disease in the growing large and giant breed dog often attributed to excess dietary protein is more likely the result of an elevated dietary energy density supporting a more rapid rate of growth. Hedhammer et al.[11] investigated the issue of dietary energy intake by providing growing Great Dane puppies either *ad libitum* or 66% of *ad libitum* intake and observed a dramatic increase in the incidence of skeletal pathology in puppies consuming the higher level of intake. It was apparent that the high plane of nutrition effectively supported the genetic potential for rapid growth and predisposed the large breed puppy to the development of skeletal disease. Great Danes consuming either *ad libitum* or restricted (60–70% of *ad libitum*) intake from weaning through 6 months of age provided further support for this growth rate response.[8] Maximal growth (*ad libitum* intake) resulted in subchondral spongiosa which was less dense and weaker per unit area. The resulting osteopenia and biomechanically weak subchondral bone could not adequately support the articular cartilage of the joint. In addition, the increased growth rate of *ad libitum* feeding more rapidly subjected the joint surface to stresses due to increased body mass. Clearly, a high level of energy intake can promote an excessive rate of growth in the large breed puppy and increase the potential for the development of skeletal disease.

In contrast to dietary protein, calcium concentration has been demonstrated to have a significant effect on development, morphology, and pathology of the skeleton in the large breed puppy. Hazewinkel et al.[12] and Goedegebuure and Hazewinkel[13] evaluated the effect of feeding either a typical calcium diet (1.10% Ca/0.90%P) or a high calcium diet (3.30% Ca/0.90% P) to Great Dane puppies from weaning through 6 months of age. The effect of the high calcium diet on endocrine status (less active parathyroid glands, increased activity of thyroid C cells), circulating mineral concentrations (hypercalcemia, hypophosphatemia), skeletal development (increased osteoblasts, decreased osteoclasts, decreased osteoclast activity, more retained cartilage cones, increased bone mineral mass, delayed bone remodeling), and skeletal disease (increased radiographic irregularities, more osteochondritic lesions) clearly demonstrated the negative impact of excess dietary calcium on skeletal health of the large breed puppy. This conclusion was further supported by the finding that the large breed puppy was ineffective in reducing intestinal calcium absorption when provided a high calcium diet and was therefore unable to protect itself from a chronic high dietary calcium intake.[14] In contrast, intestinal calcium absorption was increased to greater than 90% of calcium intake when a low calcium diet was consumed.

Research published to date clearly documents that 1) maximal growth rate supported by elevated energy intake increases the incidence of skeletal disease, 2) dietary protein level has little influence on the incidence of skeletal disease, and 3) high dietary calcium concentration interferes with normal skeletal development and promotes skeletal pathology in the large breed puppy. Nevertheless, data upon which to base specific dietary recommendations for dietary energy and calcium concentrations for the large and giant breed puppy are lacking. A comprehensive research program sponsored by The Iams Company, and conducted in collaboration with several leading universities, is currently underway to establish the scientific foundation necessary to support improved nutritional recommendations for the large and giant breed puppy. The nutritional philosophy subscribed to within these research efforts is that a managed growth rate in the large and giant breed puppy can be more practically achieved with a diet matrix providing a lower concentration of energy relative to that typical of puppy foods. This managed growth has been accomplished by formulation to a minimum 14% dietary fat balanced with a minimum 26% dietary protein concentration. Results from a portion of this research program, designed to determine the optimal dietary calcium and phosphorus concentrations for this dietary matrix, are presented in manuscripts published in these proceedings and elsewhere. Several response criteria, including effects on growth rate, bone structure, bone biomechanics, body conformation, incidence of skeletal disease, and gait analysis, indicate that the diet of the large and giant breed puppy should provide 0.80% Ca/0.66% P (moderate calcium [MC]) when contrasted with higher (high calcium [HC] = 2.70% Ca/2.20% P) or lower (low calcium [LC] = 0.48% Ca/0.40% P) concentrations. These research results will be briefly summarized herein to demonstrate that scientifically supported, practical directives regarding the most appropriate manner in which to feed the large and giant breed puppy includes a modified calcium and phosphorus concentration to complement a reduced dietary energy density.

Lauten et al.[15] reported that the growth rate of Great Dane puppies consuming a diet providing 26% protein and 14% fat was influenced substantially by dietary calcium and phosphorus concentration. Providing 0.80% Ca and 0.66% P (MC) promoted more rapid growth compared to providing either 0.48% Ca/0.40% P (LC) or 2.70% Ca/2.20% P (HC). This response was likewise confirmed during measurement of the length of the humerus, radius, femur, and tibia and circumference of the thigh and radius.[16] It must be recognized, particularly in view of the necessity to manage the growth rate of the large and giant breed dog, that the growth rates of all three treatment groups were less than the genetic potential, due to the reduced energy density of the diet relative to typical puppy foods and feeding management (time restricted feeding). All puppies, however, reached a similar body size at maturity. This effect on growth rate suggests that the 0.80% Ca/0.66% P inclusion rate most effectively provided for the specific nutritional requirements of the growing Great Dane when growth is effectively managed with a 26% protein, 14% fat diet.

Bone mineral content (BMC) as determined by DEXA reflected dietary calcium concentration with differences observable very early in growth (2 months of age).[15] Bone mineral content, as a percentage of body weight, at 2 months of age was 1.07% (LC), 1.42% (MC) and 1.85% (HC), and had increased to 2.91% (LC), 3.45% (MC) and 3.84% (HC) by 6 months of age.[17] Furthermore, bone mineral density (BMD) values were likewise different by 8 weeks of age (0.442 g/cm², 0.456 g/cm² and 0.482g/cm² for LC, MC, and HC, respectively). Treatment group BMD differences continued through 6 months of age after which time the magnitude of the response began to decrease. By 12 months of age, BMD values were 0.976 g/cm² (LC), 1.046 g/cm² (MC) and 1.054 g/cm² (HC). Surprisingly, these same diet matrices did not result in the expected bone turnover rates relative to BMC and BMD as measured by urinary excretion of N-terminal, pyridinoline cross-linked fragments of bone collagen or total urinary lysinopryidinoline in growing Alaskan Husky puppies. Elevated bone turnover was apparent for puppies consuming HC while reduced bone turnover was evident with LC relative to the MC diet.[18] It was anticipated that bone turnover would be lower with a high dietary calcium concentration due to the need to temper elevated circulating Ca concentrations while the opposite would result from the low dietary Ca. Further research will be required to elucidate the physiological rationale behind this response.

Bone mechanical properties likewise demonstrate specific effects in response to dietary calcium concentrations in the diet matrix described above. Total cross sectional area as well as cortical and medulary areas of the femur, humerus, third metacarpal, and third metatarsal was greater for 18-month-old Great Danes fed MC and HC compared to those fed LC.[19] This suggests that there may be no advantage to supplementing a diet containing 26% protein and 14% fat with Ca and P beyond 0.80% and 0.67%, respectively. Although statistical significances were not apparent, MC yield force (see Crenshaw chapter[19]) was similar to LC and numerically greater than HC (1,799 and 1,860 *v* 1,684 kg-mm, respectively). Likewise, maximum force was responsive to diet with MC and HC similar and numerically greater than LC (4,534 and 4,652 *v* 4,042 kg-mm, respectively). These data suggest that the Ca and P concentration provided by the MC diet (0.80% Ca/ 0.67% P) may be most appropriate relative to bone strength as measured by force when incorporated into a 26% protein, 14% fat matrix.

Overall body conformation was evaluated and reported to be consistently poorer for Great Dane puppies fed the HC diet compared to those fed either the MC or LC.[16] This was also reflective of the fact that 86% of all clinical lameness observed were associated with the HC diet.[20] Furthermore, all cases of hypertrophic osteodystrophy were observed in puppies consuming HC.[16] Likewise, repeated kinetic gait analyses conducted throughout growth (4, 6, 8, 12, and 18 months of age) on 4 puppies per treatment group indicated that all of the puppies consuming LC or HC had some evidence of gait asymmetry.[21] In contrast, 3 of the 4 dogs on the MC had satisfactory ground reaction force symmetry at all exams. Conformation and kinetics of the Great Dane, when evaluated throughout growth, are positively influenced by the consumption of 0.80% Ca and 0.67% P in an appropriately reduced energy density matrix.

Summary
The results of ongoing research clearly documents that the unique nutritional demands of the large breed puppy are best provided by a diet matrix containing minimum 26% protein (high quality, animal-based source), minimum 14% fat, 0.80% Ca, and 0.67% P. Support for this recommendation is based on the following research observations:

- A reduced dietary energy density relative to typical puppy foods provides for easier management of growth rate to a level moderately restricted relative to the genetic potential. Mature body size is genetically determined and will simply be attained at a slightly older age with a more gradual growth rate.
- A diet containing 26% protein, 14% fat, 0.80% Ca, and 0.67% P more adequately supplies the nutrient requirements for the large breed puppy during managed growth as evidenced by the inferior performance of puppies consuming diets containing higher or lower Ca and P concentrations.
- Bone mineral content and bone mineral density were lower for the puppies consuming the diet containing 0.48% Ca indicating an inadequate level of supplementation in this diet matrix. Furthermore, BMC and BMD responses occurred very early in the growth phase indicating the need to address the nutritional requirements of the large breed puppy immediately after weaning.
- Bone cross sectional area was increased and bone strength positively influenced by the 0.80% Ca/0.67% P dietary level.
- Orthopedic examination revealed higher incidence of abnormalities in the puppies consuming the diet containing 2.70% Ca, indicative of Ca oversupplementation in this diet matrix containing a reduced energy density.
- Fewer gait abnormalities were observed throughout growth of the giant breed puppy when a 26% protein, 14% fat diet contained 0.80% Ca and 0.67% P than if the dietary concentration of these minerals was increased or decreased.

Conclusion
Long term health and well-being of the large and giant breed dog is dependent on proper nutrition during growth of the puppy. When considered in total, the research cited above strongly supports the conclusion that a a diet matrix containing 26% protein and 14% fat to assist in the management of growth velocity in the large and giant breed puppy should provide 0.80% Ca and 0.67% P to properly support growth and skeletal development.

References
1. Grondalen J. Metaphyseal osteopathy (hypertrophic osteodystrophy) in growing dogs: A clinical study. *J Sm Anim Prac* 1976; 17:721-735.
2. Woodward JC. Canine hypertrophic osteodystrophy, a study of the spontaneous disease in littermates. *Vet Pathol* 1982; 19:337-354.

3. Schulz KS, Payne JT, Aronson E. *Escherichia coli* bacteria associated with hypertrophic osteodystrophy in a dog. JAVMA 1991; 199:1170-1173.

4. Watson ADJ, Blair RC, Farrow BRH, Baird JD, Cooper HL. Hypertrophic osteodystrophy in the dog. *Austr Vet J* 1973; 49:433-439.

5. Schrader SC. Differential diagnosis of nontraumatic causes of lameness in young growing dogs. In: Bonagura JD, ed. *Kirk's Current Veterinary Therapy XII*. Philadelphia: W.B. Saunders Co., 1995; 1171-1180.

6. Slater MR, Scarlett JM, Donoghue S. Diet and exercise as potential risk factors for osteochondritis dissecans in dogs. *Am J Vet Res* 1992; 53:2119-2124.

7. Slater MR, Scarlett JM, Kaderley RE. Breed, gender and age risk factors for canine osteochondritis dissecans. *J Vet Comp Orthop Traum* 1991; 4:100-106.

8. Dammrich K. Relationship between nutrition and bone growth in large and giant dogs. *J Nutr* 1991; 121:S114-S121.

9. Nap RC, Hazewinkel HAW, Voorhout G, Van Den Brom WE, Goedegebuure SA, Van 'T Klooster ATh. Growth and skeletal development in Great Dane pups fed different levels of protein intake. *J Nutr* 1991; 121:S107-S113.

10. Nap RC, Hazewinkel HAW, Voorhout G, Biewenga WJ, Koeman JP, Goedegebuure SA, Van't Klooster ATh. The influence of the dietary protein content on growth in giant breed dogs. *J Vet Comp Ortha Traumatol* 1993; 6:1-8.

11. Hedhammer A, Wu F, Krook L, Schryver HF, Delahunta A, Whalen JP, Kallfez FA, Numez EA, Hintz HF, Sheffy, Ryan GD. Overnutrition and skeletal disease. An experimental study in Great Dane dogs. *Cornell Vet* 1974; 64(Suppl. 1):1-160.

12. Hazewinkel HAW, Goedegebuure SA, Poulos PW, Wolvekamp WThC. Influences of chronic calcium excess on the skeletal development of growing Great Danes. JAAHA 1985; 21:377-391.

13. Goedegebuure SA, Hazewinkel HAW. Morphological findings in young dogs chronically fed a diet containing excess calcium. *Vet Pathol* 1986; 23:594-605.

14. Hazewinkel HAW, Van Den Brom WE, Van 'T Klooster ATh, Voorhout G, Van Wees A. Calcium metabolism in Great Dane dogs fed diets with various calcium and phosphorus levels. *J Nutr* 1991; 121:S99-S106.

15. Lauten SD, Goodman SA, Brawner WR, Cox NR, Hathcock JT, Jungst SB, Kincaid SA, Montgomery RA, Rumph PF, Baker HJ, Reinhart GA, Lepine AJ. Growth and body composition of the large breed puppy as affected by diet. In: Reinhart GA, Carey DP, eds. *Recent Advances in Canine and Feline Nutrition, Vol. II: 1998 Iams Nutrition Symposium Proceedings*. Wilmington: Orange Frazer Press, 1998; 63-70.

16. Goodman SA, Montgomery RD, Fitch RB, Hathcock JT, Lauten SD, Cox NR, Kincaid SA, Rumph PF, Baker HJ, Lepine AJ, Reinhart GA. Serial orthopedic examinations of growing Great Dane puppies fed three diets varying in calcium and phosphorus. In: Reinhart GA, Carey DP, eds. *Recent Advances in Canine and Feline Nutrition, Vol. II: 1998 Iams Nutrition Symposium Proceedings*. Wilmington: Orange Frazer Press, 1998; 3-12.

17. Lauten SD, Brawner Jr WR, Goodman SA, Lepine AJ, Reinhart GA, Baker HJ. Dual energy x-ray absorptiometry measurement if body composition and skeletal development in giant breed dogs fed diets differing in calcium and phosphorus. *FASEB J* 1997; 11:A388.

18. Minor R, Wootton JAM, Reynolds AJ, Erb HN, Lepine AJ, Eyre D. Studies of bone turnover in the dog. In: Reinhart GA, Carey DP, eds. *Recent Advances in Canine and Feline Nutrition, Vol. II: 1998 Iams Nutrition Symposium Proceedings.* Wilmington: Orange Frazer Press, 1998; 41-52.

19. Crenshaw TD, Budde RA, Lauten SD, Lepine AJ. Nutritional effects on bone strength in the growing canine. In: Reinhart GA, Carey DP, eds. *Recent Advances in Canine and Feline Nutrition, Vol. II: 1998 Iams Nutrition Symposium Proceedings.* Wilmington: Orange Frazer Press, 1998; 29-40.

20. Brawner Jr WR. Imaging techniques evaluating skeletal development of the large breed puppy. In: Reinhart GA, Carey DP, eds. *Recent Advances in Canine and Feline Nutrition, Vol. II: 1998 Iams Nutrition Symposium Proceedings.* Wilmington: Orange Frazer Press, 1998; 13-28.

21. Rumph P. Kinetic gait analysis in developing Great Dane dogs. In: Reinhart GA, Carey DP, eds. *Recent Advances in Canine and Feline Nutrition, Vol. II: 1998 Iams Nutrition Symposium Proceedings.* Wilmington: Orange Frazer Press, 1998; 71-80.

Growth and Body Composition of the Large Breed Puppy As Affected By Diet

Susan D. Lauten, MAg, PhD Candidate
Scott-Ritchey Research Center, Auburn University, Alabama, USA

S.A. Goodman, MS, DVM[a];
W.R. Brawner, Jr., DVM, PhD, DACVR[b]; N.R. Cox, DVM, PhD[a];
J.T. Hathcock, DVM, MS, DARS[b]; S.B. Jungst[c]; S.A. Kincaid, DVM, PhD[d];
R.A. Montgomery, DVM, MS, DACVS[e]; P.F. Rumph, DVM[d];
H.J. Baker, DVM[a]; Allan J. Lepine, PhD[f]; Gregory A. Reinhart, PhD[f]
[a]Scott-Ritchey Research Center
[b]Department of Radiology
[c]Department of Animal Dairy Sciences
[d]Department of Anatomy and Histology
[e]Department of Small Animal Medicine and Surgery
College of Veterinary Medicine, Auburn University, Alabama, USA
[f]Research and Development, The Iams Company, Lewisburg, Ohio, USA

Introduction

Large and giant breed dogs experience a disproportionately high incidence of skeletal developmental disease compared to medium and small breeds. These diseases often become clinically apparent during the rapid growth phase which occurs between four to six months of life. The etiologies and pathogeneses of these diseases have not been elucidated, but nutrition is known to play an important role in their development and may exacerbate an inherited predisposition. Exaggerated growth rate and development of large and giant breeds may contribute to these problems.

New absorptiometry technology was used to study the changes that occur in bone mineral content, lean body mass, and fat tissue during the growth and development of Great Dane puppies. The calcium and phosphorus content of diets was altered, while a constant calcium to phosphorus ratio was maintained, to determine potential affects on growth rate, skeletal development, and accretion of lean body tissue and fat tissue. Monthly changes in body composition of growing Great Dane puppies from 2 to 18 months of age were documented. Early analyses of results indicate that dietary intake of calcium and phosphorus has an affect on the rate of growth, bone mineral deposition, and the development of skeletal disease.

A brief review of some factors which influence changes in growth and development of large breed dogs illustrate the need for specific research on the nutritional requirements of these unique animals. First, there has been an increase in the mature size of many breeds of dogs. Breed standards for the American Kennel Club (AKC)[1] show very few size limitations imposed on the large and giant breeds. As a result, most breeds have increased in size in an attempt to provide visual appeal and a positive response from judges in conformation competition. AKC registered breeds that do not specify a maximum allowable height with a disqualification penalty for oversize have, over time, created a larger dog by selection for increased size. In 1971, Kirk reported a growth curve for the Great Dane with a mature weight of 130 pounds.[2] Currently, the mature weight of a male Great Dane in the United States often exceeds 180 pounds.

Secondly, in addition to selecting for larger dogs, there has been an emphasis on rapid achievement of mature height and weight. This trend results from economic concerns because the earlier a dog reaches maturity, the faster the prerequisites for placement into a planned breeding program can be accomplished.

The third area of change relates to the composition of commercial pet diets. High quality, palatable, nutrient dense diets can result in overfeeding if appropriate feeding management is not exercised. These puppies are more likely to grow rapidly because of the increased caloric content and high digestibility of typical diets formulated for growth. These changes have contributed to larger, heavier puppies, which grow at rates that may impact skeletal development and disease. Nutritionists are responding to these issues by studying the rates of growth and development of various tissues, and proposing appropriate changes to current dietary recommendations.

A study using Great Danes as a model of large and giant breeds of dogs was conducted. Because of the availability of Dual Energy X-ray Absorptiometry, this project was designed using non-invasive, continuous, repeated measures to study the growth and development of Great Dane puppies.

Dual Energy X-ray Absorptiometry (DEXA)

The ability to perform non-invasive, repeated measures of growth and body composition, made possible by DEXA, is a major technical advancement for growth and development studies. Prior to the introduction of absorptiometry, accurate measurements of bone mineral content were possible only by terminating the animals and performing an analysis on the bone ash. It is now possible to study animals over time to measure changes in skeletal development, and accretion of lean and fat tissue.

The first instrument in this class was introduced in 1963 as a single photon absorptiometer.[3] In response to demands for improved technology, equipment which uses dual x-ray spectroscopy became available in 1987. Although DEXA utilizes x-rays, a total body scan produces only about one-tenth of the exposure of a thoracic radiograph, making the equipment safe for the patient as well as for the operator. Since its introduction, DEXA has been used extensively in the study of human bone diseases, such as osteoporosis, and has been adapted for use in veterinary research.

In addition to quantifying bone mineral content, DEXA allows the quantification of lean body mass and percentage fat tissue. By utilizing beams of two energy levels (38 keV and 70 keV), the software of the instrument is able to distinguish bone mineral tissue and differentiate between fat and lean soft tissues. This is possible because of the different attenuation properties of these tissues. For example, the high energy beam easily penetrates bone and soft tissue, while the photons from the low energy beam are absorbed by bone. Comparison of the attenuation factors to the data collected allows the computer software to determine the composition of the scanned patient in a pixel-by-pixel format. Although designed for analysis of human body scans, it is possible to utilize the software capabilities to examine other species. Regional data, such as analyses of specific areas of the body (i.e., front legs, rear legs), has been validated in humans, but has not yet been completed in animals. Anatomical differences between human and animals in the shoulder and hip areas will restrict interpretation of regional data until software can be rewritten to accommodate these species differences.

Methods of positioning animals (dogs, cats, and birds) were developed to allow for minimal tissue overlap, a factor that can introduce error into scans (*Figure 1*). Initial precision values, reported as a coefficient of variation, were in excess of 2% (expected range of 1-3%), but were reduced to 0.92% by improved positioning techniques.

With DEXA, the distance between the radiation source and detector is fixed, as is the patient platform. As a result, it is possible to measure the length of specific bones. Specific regions of the spine (i.e., L1-L4) can also be examined and the development of bone size and mineral content studied. The output from anterior-posterior spine scans includes vertebral width, height, area, and bone mineral content in each vertebrae.

DEXA is not without limitations, however, and the accurate measurement of fat tissue under varying circumstances remains a subject of debate. All methods of total body analysis are dependent upon certain assumptions. With DEXA, the water content of soft tissue is assumed to be 0.73 mL/g. The greater the fat content of the patient being scanned, the greater the error factor introduced by this assumption. Long term studies that involve large changes in fat content appear to be subject to error, the extent of which has not been reported in dogs. A validation project is being conducted to measure body composition of dogs with different body conditions and quantify this error in the dog. Recently, scientists studying human patients used DEXA to study weight loss, diabetes, effects of menopause, exercise physiol-

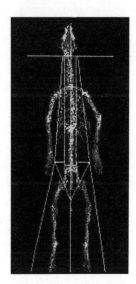

Figure 1. Total body scan image produced by Lunar DPX-L densitometer.

ogy and aging, which demand more accurate body fat calculations. Improved technology for evaluation of body composition will likely be developed in response to this demand.

In summary, DEXA has potential use for research and clinical assessments in many species. It can be used to study the growth and development of bone, lean and fat tissue under various conditions, to evaluate disease, to measure treatment effects, and to help determine optimum nutritional requirements for animals.

Growth Rate and Body Composition in Giant Breed Puppies

As part of a recently completed study of dietary mineral requirements of giant breed puppies, DEXA was used to measure growth rate and body composition of Great Danes from 2 through 18 months of age. The puppies used in this project were born and raised according to the following protocol. Breeding stock was housed in indoor/outdoor facilities and fed identical adult maintenance diets for more than 6 months. As pregnancies were confirmed (>29 days post breeding), the bitches were placed on a growth formula diet which was fed until the pups were weaned. Thirty-two puppies from four litters were fed diets varying only in the levels of calcium and phosphorus. The ratio of calcium to phosphorus (Ca:P) in all diets was 1.2:1. Each test diets was isonitrogenous (26% crude protein) and isocaloric (14% fat). The calcium and phosphorus content of the treatment diets is presented in **Table 1**.

As puppies were being weaned at approximately five weeks of age, they were assigned randomly to the three diet groups. Puppies were then separated into their respective diet groups and fed twice daily for 30 minute intervals. During the weaning transition, the puppies were returned to the bitch after each supplemental feeding. This supplemented bitch care continued until the pups were fully weaned at 7 weeks of age. For the remainder of the study, pups were fed their assigned test diets at two daily 30 minute feedings. Data collection began at 8 weeks and continued through 18 months of age. Animals were housed in indoor/outdoor runs, with unlimited access to water and exercised regularly.

DEXA scanning was performed using a Lunar DPX-L absorptiometer. The pups were fasted and general anesthesia was induced using isofluorane for approximately 40 minutes while procedures were performed. Dogs were recovered from anesthesia and returned to their runs. This DEXA scanning procedure was repeated monthly until the puppies were eight months old, then bimonthly thereafter (10,12,14,16, and 18 months.).[4] Total body scans were performed initially using the DEXA pediatric software (version 1.5g), changing from the small to medium and then to large scan modes as suggested by the manufacturer. Appropriate scan modes were selected based on body weight of the dog to be scanned. It became necessary to change to the adult software (version 1.31) package after the puppies exceeded 35 kg body weight. Although a change from pediatric to adult software imposes some variability, our study involved animals with weights ranging from 5 kg to 58 kg, making this change unavoidable.

Table 1. Calcium content of diets fed to Great Dane puppies.

Dietary Treatment Group	Ca:P Content (w/w%)
Low Diet (LD)	0.48% : 0.40%
Medium Diet (MD)	0.80% : 0.67%
High Diet (HD)	2.70% : 2.20%

Results and Discussion

The Association of American Feed Control Officials (AAFCO)[5] recommendations state that calcium level in a growth ration should be 1.0% with a maximum of 2.5%.[5] The test diets in this study ranged from 0.4% to 2.7% calcium. The Low Diet (LD) contained considerably less calcium than the recommended levels in a ration formulated for growth, and the High Diet (HD) was close to the maximum amount of calcium recommended in a growth diet. Pups fed LD appeared to grow normally, but at a slower rate than the puppies on the other dietary treatments. Pups fed the Medium Diet (MD) grew the fastest and remained clinically healthy throughout the study.[6] The HD puppies experienced the most rapid early growth, which peaked at 5 months, then declined rapidly; they also tended to be leaner at the conclusion of the study.

Analysis of DEXA data (**Table 2**) revealed a significant treatment effect on bone mineral content of puppies beginning as early as 2 months of age. The effect of dietary calcium on bone mineral accretion correlated positively with bone mineral content (BMC). These dietary differences were reflected rapidly in BMC changes of the puppies. BMC was statistically different by 8 weeks of age with the puppies fed LD having the lowest BMC and the pups fed the HD having the greatest bone mineral. These differences were apparent after supplementing suckled bitch milk with test diet for approximately 2 weeks and feeding the test diets exclusively for one week.

Hazewinkel et al.[7] reported that calcium balance in puppies is highly positive. Calcium absorption occurs by the following two mechanisms: active transport involving vitamin D, and simple diffusion. It is suggested that the mechanism utilized by young puppies is predominantly limited to simple diffusion. The results of this study agree with those previously reported, suggesting that the regulatory mechanisms for calcium absorption and excretion may not be fully developed at 8 weeks of age. The bone mineral differences between diet groups continued to increase through 7 months of age. By the time pups were 12 months old, the differences were minimal and at 14, 16, and 18 months, there were no further statistically significant differences. Mechanisms of calcium homeostasis, regulated by parathyroid hormone, calcitonin, and vitamin D do not appear to be fully mature and functional until approximately 7 months of age in the Great Danes

Table 2. Bone mineral content of puppies fed different levels of calcium.

	BONE MINERAL CONTENT (GRAMS OF BMC)		
	LD	MD	HD
2 months	77.55[b]	83.27[b]	110.38[a]
6 months	905.06[b]	1066.63[c]	1201.87[c]
12 months	1768.64[b]	1916.68[a,b]	2072.70[a]
14 months	2031.21	2069.72	2132.20

[a,b,c] Values within a row with different superscripts differ (P<.05)

studied. These puppies seemed unable to adequately regulate absorption and excretion of excesses or deficient levels of calcium until about 7 months, when the data indicated a change in the monthly mineral accretion rates. The data also indicate that the accretion rates remain higher in the pups fed LD, while accretion rates in the MD and HD groups declined after seven months of age.

Soft tissue weight also showed a significant difference among all diet groups between 5 and 12 months of age (*Table 3*). Soft tissue represents both the fat tissue fraction and the lean body mass fraction of body weight. When soft tissue is analyzed by its respective components of fat and lean tissue, no statistical differences exist.

Statistical differences were not observed in the test animals based on gender. Differences in body weights were seen, but these differences appeared to be transient. No statistical differences existed in total body composition data after age 12 months based on gender.

Several of the puppies fed HD developed conformational and skeletal problems by the time they were 6 months old. Conformational changes included an abnormally crouched stance in the hind quarters and thin body condition. Five of the ten pups fed the HD developed hypertrophic osteodystrophy and three of these four also developed a condition resembling craniomandibular osteopathy, a developmental disease involving the bones of the jaw which is not typically seen in the Great Dane. These changes indicate the need to re-evaluate the influence of dietary minerals on bone disease in dogs.

Conclusions   This study indicated that significant changes in dietary recommendations for large and giant breed puppies are justified. Currently, puppies that begin to experience skeletal problems or appear to be growing too rapidly frequently are changed to an adult maintenance diet. The goal of this practice is to reduce growth

Table 3. Soft tissue weights of puppies fed different levels of calcium.

SOFT TISSUE WEIGHTS, KG

	LD	MD	HD
2 months	6.208[b]	6.202[b]	6.175[a]
6 months	29.636[b]	29.475[c]	29.339[a]
12 months	46.180[b]	46.031[a,b]	45.875[a]
14 months	46.104	46.066	46.004

[a,b,c] Values within a row with different superscripts differ (P<.05)

rate and to correct overweight conditions by reducing caloric intake. Secondly, the AAFCO guidelines for calcium in an adult maintenance food is 0.6% compared to 1.0% found in growth rations. Unfortunately, feeding an adult ration may in fact increase calcium intake if the volume of food is increased to adjust for the lower calorie content of the adult ration, or if the adult ration is also high in calcium content.

Results of this study suggest that a calcium level lower than 1.0% is beneficial to large breed puppies. A lower calcium puppy ration should be fed from the time puppies are weaned. Severe skeletal problems were already present in animals by 6 months of age, suggesting that lowering calcium levels at that time probably would be too late. Although data presented here were derived from a study done only in Great Danes, and the results involve nonnutritional factors such as a genetic predisposition, it may be useful to attempt interpretation of these results for application to other rapidly growing, large body size dogs. In making these interpretations, it is important to recognize that the composition of the diet used in this study was intentionally made with lower than normal energy and mineral content. Therefore, diets not similarly composed could have substantially different effects than those reported here. The most dramatic differences between dietary groups were observed up to 6 months of age. Analysis of data from ages greater than 6 months show diminishing differences between dietary groups, particularly skeletal lesions. Taking all of these factors into consideration in an attempt to provide guidance to breeders of large dogs, we speculate that feeding diets with calcium content of 0.80% or less, starting at weaning and extending for periods beyond 6 months and perhaps as long as 12 to 18 months, depending on the maximum body weight achieved by a given breed, may promote optimal growth and development, and may prevent dietarily induced skeletal disease.

1. The American Kennel Club, AKC Breed Standards, on-line www.AKC.org/breeds.htm. 1997.   *References*

2. Kirk RW. *Current Veterinary Therapy VI*. Philadelphia: W.B. Saunders Co., 1971; 1366.

3. Cameron EC, Boyd RM, Luk D, McIntosh HW, Walker V. Cortical thickness measurements and photon absorptiometry for determination of bone quantity. *J Can Med Assoc* 1977; 116:145-147.

4. Lauten SD, Brawner WR, Goodman SA, Lepine AJ, Reinhart GA, Baker HJ. Dual energy x-ray absorptiometry measurement of body composition and skeletal development in Great Dane puppies fed diets differing in calcium and phosphorus. *FASEB Journal* 1997; 11:A388.

5. Association of American Feed Control Officials. *Official Publication*, 1997.

6. Lauten SD, Brawner Jr WR, Goodman SA, Lepine AJ, Reinhart GA, Vaughn DM, Baker HJ. Body composition of growing Great Dane puppies fed diets varying in calcium and phosphorus concentration evaluated by dual energy x-ray absorptiometry. American College of Veterinary Radiologists conference, Chicago, IL, December 1996.

7. Hazewinkel HAW, van den Brom WE, Hackeng WHL, Bosch R. Effects of chronic calcium excess on calciotropic hormones and calcium homeostatis in growing large breed dogs. In: *Influences of Different Calcium Metabolism and Skeletal Development in Young Great Danes*. The Netherlands, 1969; 77-91.

Kinetic Gait Analysis in
Developing Great Dane Dogs

Paul F. Rumph, DVM, MS
Professor of Veterinary Anatomy
Department of Anatomy, Physiology, and Pharmacology
College of Veterinary Medicine, Auburn University, Alabama, USA

During the past century, biomechanical analysis has been used to under-   *Introduction*
stand basic patterns of locomotion, study the performance of athletes, and aid in
diagnosis and treatment of orthopedic diseases in human beings and other animals.
A variety of gait analysis techniques have been devised to measure variables
including angular displacement, velocity and acceleration, internally measured mass
distribution, and externally measured ground reaction forces.

Kinetic and kinematic analyses have become popular additions to traditional subjective evaluations of locomotor performance because they provide
noninvasively collected objective data. The availability and sophistication of
measurement devices, computers, and specialized software to acquire and analyze
large quantities of complex data have reinforced their popularity.

The term kinetics refers to the study of forces or loads that cause or change
motion. A number of tools are available for kinetic analysis of gait. These include
press maps, pedobarographs, force sensitive resistors, accelerometers, and force
platforms. Force platform gait analyses can be conducted over ground or on a
treadmill.

Ground reaction forces have been measured in dogs using platforms
containing force sensitive transducers during normal and abnormal locomotion.
These analyses have been used to characterize the gaits of dogs of various breeds,
describe the sources of variation in ground reaction forces, compare orthopedic
surgical techniques in dogs, evaluate the efficacy of surgical procedures, and monitor
the progress of treatments in clinical cases.

During locomotion the force of the foot strikes the ground at a complex
angle that changes rapidly as the stance phase progresses. The electrical signals from
a force platform during stance are mathematically resolved into the orthogonal
vector components of the ground reaction force. The resulting variables representing these orthogonal components have been described as mediolateral force [Fx],
craniocaudal force [Fy] (also called shear or braking/propulsion), and vertical force
[Fz] (*Figure 1*). The characteristic waveforms and the magnitudes of these compo-

AMTI Biomechanics Force Platform

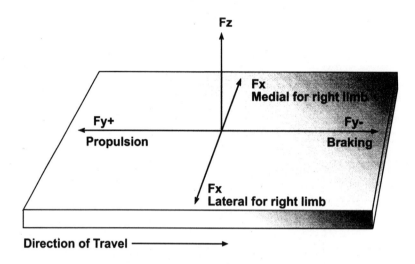

Figure 1. Orthogonal vectors of ground reaction force shown on AMTI Force Platform.

nents reflect species, gait, and limb function. The vertical component [Fz] has the greatest magnitude, lowest variability and has been the most frequently studied. Many other factors have been reported to influence these variables in dogs. The effects of subject velocity, limb velocity, morphometric features, gait, variation among and within subjects, handlers, habituation, and pathological conditions have been documented.

Data acquisition from force platforms can be simultaneous with kinematic data acquisition and software is available to permit concurrent analysis and study of the results. Results of force platform analyses have been reported for normal dogs at the walk, trot, and jumping and they have also been used to study the gaits of horses and cattle. The Greyhound has been the most frequently mentioned breed in the growing body of literature describing biomechanical gait analysis in dogs. Other reports do not specifically mention the breed of dogs studied and there are none that include giant breeds.

The objective of this study was to evaluate the vertical ground reaction force in three groups of growing Great Dane dogs fed different levels of dietary calcium. The expected outcomes were to describe the normal patterns of ground reaction force in a rapidly growing giant breed and gather evidence of musculoskeletal dysfunction.

Materials
and Methods

Great Dane puppies from five separate litters were randomly assigned to three dietary groups. In each group, the litters and sexes were equally represented. Starting at 4–5 weeks, pups were fed one of three isocaloric diets that varied only in levels of calcium and phosphorous with the ratios of these minerals kept constant at 1.2:1.0 Ca:P. The calcium:phosphorous content of the diets was as follows: **Low** = 0.48%:0.40%; **Medium** = 0.80%:0.67%; and **High** = 2.7%:2.2%.

Force platform gait analyses were conducted on four dogs from each dietary group at 4, 6, 8, 12, and 18 months of age. Five or six additional dogs from each dietary group were randomly examined at 4,6,12, or 18 months.

The force platform[a] (46.4 x 50.8 cm) was located in the middle of a 9.4 meter runway. Signals from the platform were amplified and delivered to a computer[b] containing an analog/digital conversion board. The two other important features in the lab were a stop/interrupt timing device and a video camera. For these large dogs at a trot, the comfortable forward velocity range was 1.9–2.4 meters per second.

Each gait analysis session consisted of multiple trials. The dogs were led at a trot (1.9–2.4 m/s) along the runway (**Figure 2**). A valid trial occurred when a dog passed over the force platform with only ipsilateral fore and hind feet landing entirely on the platform surface. This provided data for both limbs. Electronic sampling proceeded at the rate of 200 Hz. for a duration of 1 second. The process was repeated until data from 5–7 valid trials were recorded for both the right and left limbs. Data were saved using the software accompanying the force platform.[c]

Figure 2. Great Dane trotting across floor mounted force platform.

[a] Model OR6-5-1, Advanced Mechanical Technologies Inc, Newton, MA.
[b] IBM Compatable (286 with coprocessor), CPR Systems, Auburn AL.
[c] Bedas-2, Advanced Mechanical Technologies Inc, Newton, MA.

The raw vector data were graphed using a FORçAN[d] software analysis program. The vertical force [Fz] graphs for all trials were subjectively evaluated. On a vertical force versus time graph, the first part of the signal was generated by the forelimb, and the second part by the hind limb (*Figure 3*). The hind limb peak was usually of less magnitude than the forelimb and this reflected the different proportion of mass supported over the limbs.

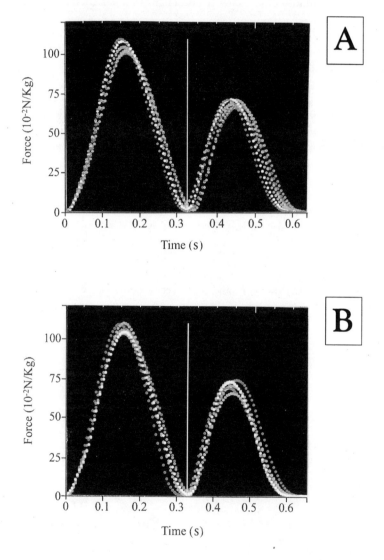

Figure 3. Vertical ground reaction force versus time graphs of right limbs (A- seven repetitions) and left limbs (B- six repetitions) of a Great Dane dog at a trot and showing excellent right/left symmetry. Forelimb data are to the left of the vertical line and hind limb data are to the right of the vertical line.

[d] FORçAN, Lander J, Rumph P, Department of Anatomy and Histology, Auburn University AL.

The raw force data were normalized using a common transformation (force/body weight) to account for weight variation among dogs. Peak vertical force data were then reported as 10^{-2} N/kg. A force/time history, called the impulse, was also calculated. This total force during the stance phase is an expression of the area or integral under the force/time curve and was expressed as 10^{-2} N/kg/s.

A calculation of gait symmetry was used to draw attention to and screen the dogs for evidence of gait abnormality. The symmetry calculation on peak vertical force or impulse of vertical force is:

$$\text{Symmetry Index (SI)} = \frac{\text{right — left}}{[(\text{right} + \text{left})/2]} * 100$$

With this symmetry index, 0 indicates perfect symmetry while 200 represents complete asymmetry and the sign (+, right) or (–, left) indicates the side of the body that had the greater value (and was presumed to indicate the healthier side). Dogs were screened for peak vertical force SI $\leq \pm$ 9 and vertical force impulse SI $\leq \pm$ 15. Experience has shown that 95% of dogs having no evidence of musculoskeletal abnormality will have symmetry indices equal to or less than these values.

Results

Full analysis and evaluation of vertical [Fz] and craniocaudal [Fy] ground reaction force data are in progress and the following preliminary observations are based on the vertical force vector only. The average vertical ground reaction force variables from the Great Dane dogs that had acceptable right/left symmetry are shown in *Table 1*.

Table 1.

AGE	Forelimb Peak Vertical Force*	Hind Limb Peak Vertical Force*	Forelimb Vertical Force Impulse†	Hind Limb Vertical Force Impulse†
4 months	113.35	72.30	15.93	10.01
6 months	111.77	66.99	17.64	10.13
8 months	111.35	69.07	19.05	10.91
12 months	108.66	71.53	19.34	10.99
18 months	110.57	70.74	20.16	10.68

* peak vertical force expressed as 10^{-2} N/kg
† vertical force impulse expressed in 10^{-2} N/kg/s

The four dogs in the low calcium group that were scheduled to have gait analyses at 4,6,8,12, and 18 months all had symmetry indices suggesting a gait abnormality at some time during the study. Likewise, none of the high calcium group had satisfactory symmetry on every exam. Three of the four dogs on medium calcium diet had satisfactory symmetrical ground reaction force at every exam. However, these three dogs were later found to have radiographic evidence of panosteitis at some time during the study, and two had mild degenerative joint disease of the shoulder and one had bilateral hip dysplasia. Five dogs showed ground reaction force evidence of lameness at one of the scheduled sessions, but it did not persist and on subsequent gait analyses, the dogs appeared to be sound again. Two of these dogs were in the low group and three were in the high calcium group.

Results of the exams of the randomly examined dogs did not clearly associate dietary group with incidence of gait abnormality (*Table 2*).

Table 2.

Group	No evidence of gait abnormality on force platform examination	Evidence of gait abnormality on force platform examination
Low	3 dogs (3 exams) at 4, 12, and 18 mo	3 dogs (3 exams) at 4, 6, and 18 mo
Medium	1 dog at 4 mo	5 dogs (6 exams) at 6, 12, and 18 mo
High	3 dogs (4 exams) at 4, 12, and 18 mo	3 dogs (3 exams) at 4 and 18 mo

Discussion   Gait analyses has been conducted in the laboratory on dogs at the extremes of size. The smallest dog to date was a 3.5 kg Maltese terrier and the largest was a Great Dane weighing 61.3 kg. Performing analyses on dogs at these extremes of size presents some special problems while collecting the data and other problems in the analysis phase. As a group, the large physical size of Great Dane dogs created problems that increased as the dogs grew. Often a dog would trot along the runway without touching the force platform or with only one foot landing in a satisfactory position. This necessitated additional repetitions to assemble a sufficient number of valid trials and required special software modifications capable of isolating signals from individual feet. As with other breeds the vertical force component was highly individualized and subjective evaluation of fore/hind proportion of force suggested that it did not change as the dogs grew.

The ground reaction force patterns and normalized magnitudes for vertical peak and impulse were generally comparable to those found in other breeds. By subjective evaluation, there appeared to be substantial increase in the forelimb vertical force impulse (force/time history) as the dogs developed and our preliminary examination of the data suggest that this was due to an increasing stance time which is the duration of time that the foot is in contact with the force plate. Although originally not included in the proposal, the stance time will be examined more closely.

When the project was envisioned, there was concern that there might be only a few incidences of skeletal disease among the relatively small study population of Great Danes. The force platform gait analysis was included to augment the study and help pinpoint the presence of musculoskeletal abnormality. Conformation defects were common among the five litters with carpal and tarsal valgus deformities being the most frequent. These deformities were also accompanied by a relatively high incidence of developmental and inflammatory skeletal disease. Most dogs had some degree of osteochondritis dissecans and many had elbow dysplasia. Hip dysplasia was also common. Many dogs had panosteitis at some time during the 18 months of the study.

Of primary importance was how the results of force platform analyses reflected changes in locomotor function. Generally, it was found that pain resulted in less vertical force and shorter stance times as would be expected if you had a stone in the heel of your shoe. The high incidence of multiple skeletal deformities in the presence of developmental and /or inflammatory skeletal disease made it extremely difficult to associate any force platform pattern with any specific disease. In several dogs the retrospective comparisons of the results of force platform gait analysis with radiographic, orthopedic or necropsy results suggested a relationship between force platform asymmetries and specific diseases. Episodes of panosteitis were especially obvious and the most severe cases of skeletal disease identified by radiography had clear concurrent force plate asymmetries.

The study protocol precluded necropsy examination of the right limbs and, therefore, when the symmetry indices did not point to the presence of a musculo-skeletal disease, the condition may have been subclinical with the dog not responding to the pain of the disease in one limb. It is also possible that roughly equal discomfort was present in contralateral limbs resulting in symmetrical gait alteration. At this time we hesitate to associate the results of force plate analysis, the incidence of musculoskeletal disease, and dietary group.

Dueland R, Bartel DL, Antonson E. Force-plate technique for canine gait analysis of total hip and excision arthroplasty. *J Am Anim Hosp Assoc* 1977; 13:547-552.

Budsberg SC, Verstraete MC, Soutas-Little RW. Force plate analysis of the walking gait in healthy dogs. *Am J Vet Res* 1987; 48:915-918.

Vilensky JA. Locomotor behavior and control in human and non-human primates: comparisons with cats and dogs. *Neurosci Behavior Rev* 1987; 11:263-274.

Budsberg SC, Verstraete MC, Soutas-Little RW, Flo GL, Probst CW. Force plate analyses before and after stabilization of canine stifles for cruciate injury. *Am J Vet Res* 1988; 49:1522-1524.

O'Connor BL, Visco DM, Heck DA, Myers SL, Brandt KD. Gait alterations in dogs after transection of the anterior cruciate ligament. *Arthritis Rheum* 1989; 32:1142-1147.

McLaughlin R, Miller C, Taves C, Hearn TC, Palmer NC, Anderson GI. Force plate analysis of triple pelvic osteotomy for the treatment of canine hip dysplasia. *Vet Surg* 1991; 20:291-297.

Riggs CM, DeCamp CE, Soutas-Little RW, Braden TD, Richter MA. Effects of subject velocity on force plate-measured ground reaction forces in healthy Greyhounds at the trot. *Am J Vet Res* 1993; 54:1523-1526.

Jevins DJ, Hauptman JG, DeCamp CE, Budsberg SC, Soutas-Little RW. Contributions to variance in force-plate analysis of gait in dogs. *Am J Vet Res* 1993; 54:612-615.

Rumph PF, Kincaid SA, Baird DK, Kammermann JR, Visco DM, Goetze LF. Vertical ground reaction force distribution during experimentally induced acute synovitis in dogs. *Am J Vet Res* 1993; 54:365-369.

Budsberg SC, Jevens DJ, Brown J, Foutz TL, DeCamp CE, Reece L. Evaluation of limb symmetry indices, using ground reaction forces in healthy dogs. *Am J Vet Res* 1993; 54:1569-1574.

Griffon DJ, McLaughlin RM, Roush JK. Vertical ground reaction force redistribution during experimentally induced shoulder lameness in dogs. *Vet Comp Ortho Traum* 1994; 7:154-157.

McLaughlin RM, Roush JK. Effects of subject stance time and velocity on ground reaction forces in clinically normal Greyhounds at the trot. *Am J Vet Res* 1994; 55:1666-1671.

Roush JK, McLaughlin RM. Effects of subject stance time and velocity on ground reaction forces in clinically normal Greyhounds at the walk. *Am J Vet Res* 1994; 55:1672-1676.

Rumph PF, Lander JE, Kincaid SA, Baird DK, Kammermann JR, Visco DM. Ground reaction force profiles from force platform gait analyses of clinically normal mesomorphic dogs at the trot. *Am J Vet Res* 1994; 55:756-761.

McLaughlin RM, Roush JK. Effects of increasing velocity on braking and propulsion times during force plate gait analysis in Greyhounds. *Am J Vet Res* 1995; 56:159-161.

Budsberg SC, Verstraete MC, Brown J, Reece L. Vertical loading rates in clinically normal dogs at a trot. *Am J Vet Res* 1995; 56:1275-1280.

Rumph PF, Kincaid SA, Visco DM, Baird DK, Kammermann JR, West MS. Redistribution of vertical ground reaction force in dogs with experimentally induced chronic hindlimb lameness. *Vet Surg* 1995; 24:384-389.

Budsberg SC, Chambers JN, Van Lue SL, Foutz TL, Reece L. Prospective evaluation of ground reaction forces in dogs undergoing unilateral total hip replacement. *Am J Vet Res* 1996; 57:1781-1785.

Jevens DJ, DeCamp CE, Hauptman JG, Braden TD, Richter M, Robinson R. Use of force-plate analysis of gait to compare two surgical techniques for treatment of cranial cruciate ligament rupture in dogs. *Am J Vet Res* 1996; 57:389-393.

Cross AR, Budsberg SC, Keefe TJ. Kinetic gait analysis assessment of meloxicam efficacy in a sodium urate-induced synovitis model in dogs. *Am J Vet Res* 1997; 58:626-631.

Diabetes Management

Pathogenesis of Feline Diabetes

Jacquie S. Rand, BVSc, DVSc
Reader, Division of Companion Animal Clinical Sciences
School of Veterinary Science, The University of Queensland, Queensland, Australia

Diabetic cats can be difficult to treat because of fluctuating blood glucose, variable response to insulin, severe hypoglycemia, and in some cats, spontaneous resolution of the diabetic state. Knowledge of the metabolic abnormalities associated with type II diabetes helps to understand why some of these problems occur. Feline diabetes is characterized by decreased insulin secretion, amyloid deposition in the pancreatic islets, and probably insulin resistance. Profound loss of β-cell function from the effects of glucose toxicity and amyloid deposition are the likely reasons that the majority of diabetic cats require insulin therapy to control hyperglycemia.

Abstract

Introduction

Diabetes in many cats is analogous to human type II diabetes, and is characterized by decreased insulin secretion, amyloid deposition in pancreatic islets, and probably insulin resistance.[1] Diabetic cats can be difficult to treat because blood glucose often fluctuates markedly following insulin administration, and blood glucose concentration may vary considerably from day to day, despite the same dose of insulin. Severe hypoglycemia with seizures or coma may occur if tight glycemic control is attempted, and occurs in some cats as the diabetic state spontaneously resolves. This article discusses the pathogenesis of feline diabetes. Knowledge of the metabolic abnormalities associated with type II diabetes helps to explain some of the problems that occur with management.

Classification of Diabetes

Diabetes mellitus is a heterogenous syndrome with hyperglycemia as its primary manifestation.[2]

Primary Diabetes. Feline diabetes usually occurs as a primary disease, but may occur secondary to other diseases which decrease insulin secretion or cause insulin resistance.[1] Primary diabetes is further subdivided into type I and type II diabetes. In humans, the term insulin dependent diabetes is used interchangeably with type I diabetes, because typically these patients require insulin for survival. Non-insulin dependent diabetes is used to describe type II diabetes, because insulin is not required for sustaining life, although many patients are treated with insulin to control hyperglycemia.[3] Direct translation of this terminology to feline diabetes has led to confusion and inaccurate classification. There is good evidence that both type

I and II diabetes occur in cats, but type II appears to be much more frequent. In contrast to humans, the majority of cats are treated with insulin. In this paper, type I and II are used to imply a specific underlying pathology, and the terms insulin dependence or non-dependence are used only as a description of the clinical characteristics of the disease.

Secondary Diabetes. Secondary diabetes, also called type III diabetes, is the result of another disease process causing decreased insulin secretion or impaired insulin action.[1] In cats, pancreatic neoplasia is a significant cause of diabetes, accounting for as many as 18% of cases. [4,5] Pancreatitis is increasingly being recognized as associated with feline diabetes and in a recent study was present in 51% of necropsied diabetic cats.[5] Whether pancreatitis is usually a cause of diabetes or a result is unclear. Humans with type II diabetes also have lesions consistent with pancreatitis.[6] Evidence that pancreatitis may result from hyperlipidemia associated with diabetes comes from data in humans with hyperlipoproteinemia, where pancreatitis is a major secondary complication.[7,8]

Secondary diabetes also results from chronically elevated levels of hormones which oppose insulin action, causing insulin resistance. In cats, this occurs iatrogenically, most commonly after progesterone use, and spontaneously with growth hormone excess, hyperadrenocorticism, and hyperthyroidism.[9,10,11] Whether diabetes resolves with resolution of the primary disease process, or whether insulin therapy is required, depends on the duration and degree of hyperglycemia.[12,13] This is because progressive loss of beta cells occurs after several weeks of elevated plasma glucose.[13,14,15]

Pathogenesis of Type I Diabetes	Type I diabetes is caused by autoimmune destruction of the pancreatic beta cells by T cells and antibodies.[16] Eventually there is almost total loss of beta cells, and insulin is required for survival.[16] In humans, antibodies to islet cell components are detectable in 85-90% of patients at diagnosis, and are usually present for more than 12 months prior to the onset of clinical signs.[17] Type I diabetes is thought to be a common cause of diabetes in dogs because 50% of diabetic dogs have islet cell antibodies.[18] In contrast, type I diabetes has not been well documented in cats, although lymphocytic insulitis has been reported associated with diabetes, and islet cell antibodies were found in a diabetic kitten.[19,20] The prevalence of islet cell antibodies in feline diabetes has not been reported.

Pathogenesis of Type II Diabetes	In contrast to type I diabetes where the pathogenesis is now largely understood, the cause of type II diabetes is still unknown. Hallmarks of type II diabetes in humans are impaired insulin secretion, insulin resistance and amyloid deposition in the islets, and there is strong evidence that these occur in diabetic cats.[1,21,22] In humans, the major risk factors for type II diabetes are increasing age, obesity, and physical inactivity.[3] These acquired factors interact with genetic factors to cause expression of the disease.[3] These same risk factors are probably also important in cats.

Age. In cats, age is the most significant risk factor for the development of diabetes.[23,24] An Australian study of 45 diabetic cats found that 90% were 7 years or older, and 66% were over 10 years of age.[24] In North America, of 333 diabetic cats, 72% were 7 years or older.[23] Similarly, most humans with type II diabetes are older than 45 years of age.[25] The reason for the effect of age in humans and cats is unknown.[3] However, the age of onset is consistent with the theory that type II diabetes results from β-cell exhaustion, following prolonged excessive demand for insulin secretion.[26]

Obesity. In cats, obesity is a significant risk factor for diabetes.[23] Many cats are obese when clinical signs first develop, although by the time they are examined by a veterinarian, obesity has often resolved. There is good evidence in cats and humans that obesity predisposes to diabetes because it produces insulin resistance.[27,28] Insulin resistance reduces glucose uptake for a given amount of insulin. This occurs because obesity causes abnormalities at the receptor level, such as decreased insulin receptors, and more importantly, at the postreceptor level, affecting metabolic events that occur after insulin binds to its receptor.[29]

In humans, the longer the duration of obesity, the greater the risk of diabetes.[30] The pattern of fat deposition is also important. Deposition of fat in the abdomen (central obesity) increases the risk of diabetes significantly, compared to deposition in the thighs (peripheral obesity).[3] There are no studies in cats of the effect of fat distribution on diabetes prevalence.

Genetics. There are no published studies of the genetics of feline diabetes. No breed susceptibility was identified in a North American study of 333 diabetic cats.[23] However, Burmese cats are predisposed to diabetes in Australia, and comprise approximately 20-25% of diabetic cats, compared to 7% of the cat population.[24]

In humans, specific genes are believed to determine whether a person develops diabetes, but the actual genes involved have not been identified.[3] However, other factors including obesity, age, and physical activity have an important modifying effect on the genotype, as shown in studies of twins.[3] In identical twins, diabetes only develops in 20-40% of the co-twins, if the other twin has diabetes. In non-identical twins, less than 10% of the co-twins develop diabetes.[3,31]

Gender. In both Australia and North America, more diabetic cats are males, with a ratio of approximately 1.5:1, although more Burmese diabetics were female.[23,24] In humans, there is some effect of gender amongst different ethnic groups, although worldwide there is no gender predisposition.[3,32]

Exercise. Exercise increases insulin sensitivity in normal and diabetic humans, and reduces insulin requirements in diabetics.[33,34] Physical inactivity increases the risk of diabetes directly via decreased insulin sensitivity (insulin resistance) and indirectly by contributing to obesity.[3,35] Although there are no studies in cats of the effect of inactivity on the risk of diabetes, most cats are physically less active after domestication when food is provided, than feral cats which hunt to obtain food. In human native populations living traditional life styles, the prevalence of diabetes is very low, compared to urban natives living less active western life styles.[3]

| Features of Type II Diabetes | The hallmarks of type II diabetes in humans are abnormal insulin secretion, insulin resistance, and amyloid deposition, and there is good evidence that all of these occur in feline diabetics.[1] |

Abnormal Insulin Secretion. In cats and humans with milder forms of diabetes and impaired glucose tolerance, insulin secretion that occurs in the first 10 minutes (first phase secretion) after an increase in glucose is very reduced or absent (**Figure 1**).[36,37] Second phase secretion is often delayed, higher than normal, and prolonged because of persisting hyperglycemia. With increasing loss of insulin secretion during the second phase, fasting glucose progressively increases. Once persistent hyperglycemia occurs, insulin secretion is further decreased via a glucose toxic effect on β-cells.[38] With loss of 80-90% of total insulin secretory capacity, fasting glucose concentration exceeds the renal threshold and overt signs of diabetes occur, such as polyuria, polydipsia, and polyphagia with weight loss.[36] Cats usually have greater loss of insulin secretory capacity than humans with type II diabetes, and most require insulin for survival.[1] This is probably associated with greater loss of β-cells from glucose toxicity and amyloid deposition.

Insulin Resistance. Insulin resistance is the second feature of human type II diabetes. With insulin resistance, more insulin is needed to produce the same glucose lowering effect.[36] Insulin resistance occurs primarily after insulin binds to its receptor. It decreases the amount of glucose metabolized for storage as glycogen and fat, but has less effect on oxidation of glucose for energy.[27] There is considerable debate whether decreased insulin secretion or insulin resistance is the initial defect in type II diabetes. Insulin sensitivity has not been measured accurately in diabetic cats. However, there is evidence that insulin resistance is a feature of feline diabetes. Cats with impaired glucose tolerance that still have adequate second phase insulin secretion, have higher insulin concentration relative to glucose concentration than normal cats.[39] Special tests are required to measure insulin resistance in diabetic cats because insulin concentration is very low and no results have yet been reported.

In humans, insulin resistance is largely inherited, but is worsened by obesity.[36] In cats, there is evidence that obesity also causes insulin resistance because insulin concentration is increased relative to glucose concentration.[28] Insulin resistance is also increased by persistent hyperglycemia.[38] Therefore, once persistent hyperglycemia in diabetes occurs, the added insulin resistance compounds the effect of decreased insulin secretion.

Because insulin resistance is so widespread in human native populations and is largely genetically determined, it raises the question whether insulin resis-

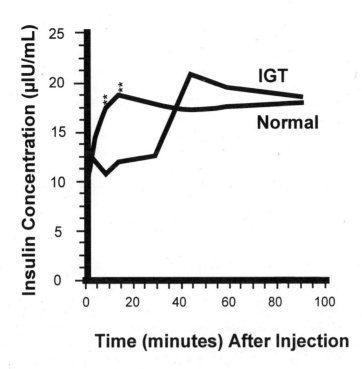

Time (minutes) After Injection

Figure 1. In cats with impaired glucose tolerance, insulin secretion that occurs in the first 10 minutes (first phase secretion) after an increase in glucose is very reduced or absent. Adapted from Lutz and Rand, 1995.[1]

tance is advantageous.[26,40] There have been some interesting theories advanced, and the carnivore connection theory best explains the high incidence of insulin resistance and type II diabetes in urbanized native populations compared to Europeans.[26,40] The essential components of the theory are that our primate ancestors who lived 2 to 4 million years ago, lived in a mild climate and ate a high carbohydrate diet containing lots of fruit and root vegetables. During that time, the brain and reproductive tissues evolved a specific requirement for glucose as a source of fuel.[41] In contrast, in the last 2 million years when humans evolved, the climate was dominated by ice ages and our human ancestors ate a low carbohydrate, high protein diet.[41] They were hunters of large game and their diets during the coldest part of the year contained virtually no carbohydrate, except for minor amounts in the liver or gut contents of animals. To maintain a normal blood glucose on a very low glucose intake required metabolic adaptations. Studies in humans and animals have shown that the adaptive response to a low carbohydrate intake is insulin resistance.[26,42]

Thus, insulin resistance is the mechanism for coping with a shortage of dietary glucose.[26] It allows blood glucose levels to be maintained immediately after eating a low carbohydrate meal, when insulin is secreted in response to other food components, such as amino acids. The ice ages, therefore, potentially selected for individuals with insulin resistance, resulting in a high proportion of people with genetically determined insulin resistance.[2]

Europeans were one of the first to develop agriculture about 10,000 years ago.[43] This resulted in a change to a high carbohydrate diet and relaxation of the selection pressure for insulin resistance.[26] With the advent of the industrial revolution and milling of cereals, the diet changed to highly processed carbohydrate that was quickly digested and absorbed. In humans, the increase in glucose concentration and corresponding increase in insulin is two to three times greater after eating milled cereals, compared to eating coarsely ground grains.[26,44] With the change to this type of highly processed carbohydrate diet came a demand on β-cells to secrete large amounts of insulin throughout life. In this scenario, insulin resistance is a disadvantage because of the added demand on the β-cells to secrete even more insulin.[26]

In contrast, native populations with a high prevalence of insulin resistance and diabetes, such as the Pima Indians and Nauruians, did not adopt agriculture until 2,000 years ago.[26] Therefore, until relatively recently insulin resistance was an advantage.[26] In addition, after the arrival of Europeans, many native populations were decimated by infectious disease and food shortages. Starvation results in similar metabolic changes to a low carbohydrate–high protein diet, that is, increased insulin resistance and gluconeogenesis.[45] Therefore, in native populations in the last 100 years, acute starvation from disease and famine may have resulted in intense selection for insulin resistance.[26] Only in the last few generations have these populations adopted a highly processed carbohydrate diet, in which insulin resistance is a disadvantage, because it puts a huge demand on the beta cells to produce insulin.[26]

The carnivore connection theory and the change in man's diet, therefore, provide an explanation of why insulin resistance and diabetes is so widespread in native populations.[26] The prolonged, excessive demand on β-cells is postulated to eventually lead to β-cell exhaustion and failure of insulin secretion.[26] Although the mechanism of cellular exhaustion is not yet understood, it is a recognized phenomena in other cell types.[46,47]

The carnivore connection theory can also be applied to the development of diabetes in domestic cats. Cats are obligate carnivores and in contrast to dogs, do not need any carbohydrate in their diet to reproduce.[48] Insulin resistance is necessary for cats to maintain glucose supply to the brain and developing fetus, because insulin is secreted in response to a high protein, low carbohydrate meal.[26]

Insulin resistance is not necessarily pathologic or static. Changing insulin sensitivity is a potent mechanism for maintaining glucose homeostasis. A vivid example of this occurs in cats after intravenous injection of arginine, where a 4-fold increase in insulin concentration occurs with only a minute decrease in glucose concentration.[49] For blood glucose to be maintained, rapid and profound insulin resistance is necessary.

There is evidence that cats are genetically insulin resistant, and that they appear to develop type II diabetes when exposed to a high carbohydrate diet.[26] Some commercial brands of cat food contain significant amounts of processed cereal, and are very different in composition from the diet that cats evolved to eat. In addition, most domestic cats are physically less active and have more body fat than feral cats, which hunt to obtain food. In cats, insulin resistance increases with increased body fat, and based on other species, increases with inactivity.[28,34] Inherited insulin resistance is an advantage on a high protein diet and in times of little food. It is probably not advantageous for domestic cats eating a relatively high carbohydrate diet of processed cereal, and with acquired insulin resistance from increased body fat and inactivity. Cats today probably require much higher levels of insulin secretion than what cats evolved to need. It is not surprising that in some cats, β-cells cannot meet the demand, and that type II diabetes ensues.

Amyloid Deposition. The third feature of type II diabetes is excessive amyloid deposition in pancreatic islets.[50] In cats and humans, this is the most consistent histological finding. Islet amyloid is a precipitate of the hormone amylin, which is co-secreted with insulin by β-cells.[51] Amylin is also called islet amyloid polypeptide or IAPP.[51] *Figure 2* is of a normal cat islet with an immunohistochemical label for amylin, and shows intracellular amylin and very small amounts of extracellular amyloid. In normal cats, amyloid does not comprise more than 20% of the islet volume.[52] In contrast, *Figure 3* shows massive amounts of islet amyloid replacing islet cells in a cat with diabetes. Amyloid deposition in diabetic cats is often more extensive than in human diabetics.[52]

Amyloid replaces islet cells, but in many diabetic cats and humans, the reduction in β-cell mass does not appear to be sufficient to lead to diabetes.[4] Recent work has shown that development of diabetes is not dependent on large amyloid deposits, and that amorphous inter- and extracellular aggregates of amylin are associated with β-cell death.[53] In an *in vitro* study, amyloid fibrils resulted in death of the majority of islet cells within 96 hours, demonstrating their potent toxicity to β-cells.[54,55]

For amylin to precipitate as amyloid, it requires a specific amino acid sequence to fold up into pleated sheets. This occurs in cats, dogs and humans, but in few other species.[51] A high local concentration of the hormone also seems necessary for amyloid formation because canine amylin has the same amino acid sequence as feline amylin, but amyloid only forms in insulinomas, which also oversecrete amylin.[56] There is some evidence that cats have higher concentrations of amylin than other species, and that cats with impaired glucose tolerance have higher amylin concentrations than normal or diabetic cats.[37] This higher amylin concentration may contribute to amyloid formation.

Amylin has an important physiologic role because it has been found in all warm blooded species investigated to date, although its function is not fully understood.[57] Amylin is thought to be important in maintaining blood glucose by stimu-

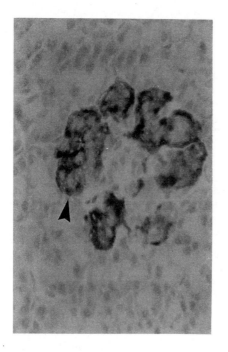

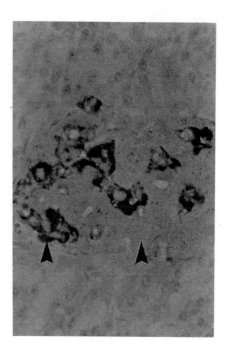

Figure 2. Normal cat islet with an immunohistochemical label for amylin. Intracellular amylin (arrow, darker, clouded areas) is present in β-cells located in the periphery of the islet. Very small amounts of amyloid (lighter area) are present around cells. In normal cats, amyloid does not comprise more than 20% of the islet volume. (Courtesy of Dr. T. Lutz, University of Zürich, Switzerland)

Figure 3. Islet from diabetic cat, showing massive amounts of islet amyloid (arrow, dark area) replacing islet cells. Reduced numbers of amylin containing β-cells are present (arrow, light area). (Courtesy of Dr. T. Lutz, University of Zürich, Switzerland)

lating the breakdown of muscle glycogen (*Figure 4*).[58] This occurs via antagonism of insulin-stimulated glucose uptake into muscle, and direct inhibition of glycogen synthetase.[58] Breakdown of glycogen releases lactate, which is used by the liver for glucose production (gluconeogenesis), which maintains blood glucose between meals. In species getting a significant postprandial glucose surge, gluconeogenesis only functions between meals to maintain glucose at normal levels for brain and reproductive function.[26,58] If there is very little carbohydrate in the diet, gluconeogenesis also occurs postprandially.[26] In cats, gluconeogenesis functions continuously to maintain blood glucose.[48] As amylin appears to be important in maintaining adequate blood glucose, it would be logical that cats have a continuous and greater requirement for amylin secretion compared to humans and would, therefore, be at greater risk of amyloid deposition. Greater amyloid deposition results in loss of more β-cells, and reduces the likelihood of sufficient β-cells remaining for adequate insulin secretion in response to oral hypoglycemic drugs. These drugs largely work by stimulating β-cells to secrete insulin. More extensive amyloid deposition, therefore, is one reason why diabetic cats are more often insulin dependent than humans with type II diabetes.

Amylin's Actions

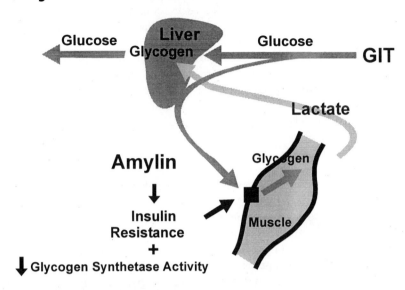

Figure 4. Amylin is thought to be important in stimulating the breakdown of muscle glycogen. This occurs via antagonism of insulin-stimulated glucose uptake into muscle, and direct inhibition of glycogen synthetase. Breakdown of glycogen releases lactate, which is used by the liver for glucose production, which maintains blood glucose between meals. Adapted from Gaeta and Rink, 1994.[58]

Glucose toxicity appears to be an important feature of feline diabetes and its significance needs to be understood when managing diabetic cats. Glucose toxicity is defined as impaired insulin secretion from β-cells as a result of prolonged hyperglycemia.[38] Initially, this glucose-mediated suppression of insulin secretion is functional and reversible.[13,38] Later, structural changes occur in β-cells. With time, these become irreversible, resulting in loss of β-cells.[13,15]

Suppression of insulin secretion by glucose toxicity is postulated to be the reason that measuring insulin concentration in cats prior to initiating therapy is not useful for predicting which cats will respond to oral hypoglycemic drugs, and which require insulin.[28] Generally, insulin concentrations are inappropriately low, even in cats with sufficient β-cell mass to respond to oral hypoglycemic drugs.[28,59]

Studies in cats and dogs demonstrate that persistent hyperglycemia can reduce insulin secretion so profoundly that even animals with previously normal β-cell mass may become permanent diabetics.[14,15] The insulin suppressive effect of glucose toxicity begins within two days of persistent hyperglycemia.[13] The severity of the glucose toxic effect is dependent on the degree of the hyperglycemia, and is more potent if β-cell mass is already reduced.[13,14,15] These findings have important clinical implications. Preservation of β-cell mass in diabetics is important, because studies have shown that glycemic control in humans is significantly better if there

Glucose
Toxicity

are some functioning β-cells.[60] In addition, 20 to 40% of feline diabetics will have remission of their diabetes for months or years, if β-cell mass is not destroyed.[61,62] Therefore, early initiation of therapy aimed at minimizing the long term effects of glucose toxicity is important for achieving good long term glycemic control or remission. Unfortunately, cats with reduced β-cell mass from spontaneous disease such as pancreatitis or islet amyloid deposition, are at greater risk of further loss of β-cells from glucose toxicity.[14,15] At least one to two weeks of insulin therapy and good glycemic control is required before β-cells can recover from moderate glucose toxicity.[13] Severe glucose toxicity may take several months to resolve, but in some cases, it is irreversible because of total destruction of β-cells.[15,28,59]

It is likely that cats have greater loss of β-cells from glucose toxicity compared to humans with type II diabetes, because cats often have marked hyperglycemia and clinical signs for longer than humans before treatment is sought. In addition, once treatment is initiated, cats usually have poorer glycemic control and much higher glucose concentrations than humans. Diabetic cats also often have much more extensive amyloid deposition in pancreatic islets than human diabetics.[52] As amyloid deposition progresses, there is progressive loss of β-cells.[52,63] Therefore, although cats appear to have type II diabetes (also called non-insulin dependent diabetes), more cats require insulin therapy than humans with type II diabetes, probably because of the loss of β-cells from the effects of chronic glucose toxicity and extensive amyloid deposition.

In summary, knowledge of the major abnormalities of type II diabetes of decreased insulin secretion, insulin resistance, and amyloid deposition is important for understanding some of the problems associated with managing feline diabetic patients.

Acknowledgements   Adapted with permission from Rand JS, Understanding feline diabetes. *Aust Vet Practit* 1997; 27:17-26, and from Rand JS, Management of feline diabetes. *Aust Vet Practit* 1997; 27:68-78.

References   1. Lutz TA, Rand JS. Pathogenesis of feline diabetes. In: Peterson M, Greco D, eds. Diabetes Mellitus, *Vet Clin N Am* 1995; 25:527-552.

2. National Diabetes Data Group. Classification and diagnosis of diabetes mellitus and other categories of glucose intolerance. *Diabetes* 1979; 28:1039.

3. Harris MI. Epidemiologic studies on the pathogenesis of non-insulin-dependent diabetes mellitus (NIDDM). *Clin Invest Med* 1995; 18:231-239.

4. O'Brien TD, Hayden DW, Johnson KH, Fletcher TF. Immunohistochemical morphometry of pancreatic endocrine cells in diabetic, normoglycaemic glucose-intolerant and normal cats. *J Comp Path* 1986; 96:357.

5. Goossens J, Nelson R, Feldman E. Response to therapy and survival in diabetic cats. *J Vet Int Med* 1995; 9:181.

6. Clark A, De-Koning EJ, Hattersley AT, Hansen BC, Yajnik CS, Poulton J.

Pancreatic pathology in non-insulin dependent diabetes (NIDDM). *Diabetes Res Clin Pract* 1995; S39:47.

7. Greenberger NJ. Pancreatitis and hyperlipemia. *New Eng J Med* 1973; 289:586-587.

8. Thompson GR. Clinical consequences of hyperlipidaemia. *J Inher Metab Dis* 1988; 11:18-28.

9. Petersen ME, Javenovic L, Petersen CL. Insulin-resistant diabetes mellitus associated with elevated growth hormone concentrations following megestrol acetate treatment in a cat. In: *Proc ACVIM*, 1981; 63.

10. Petersen ME, Taylor RS, Greco DS, Nelson RW, Randolph JF, Foodman MS, Moroff SD, Morrison SA, Lothrop CD. Acromegaly in 14 cats. *J Vet Med* 1990; 4:192.

11. Feldman EC, Nelson RW. Canine Diabetes Mellitus. In: Feldman EC, Nelson RW, eds. *Canine and Feline Endocrinology and Reproduction*. Philadelphia: Saunders. 1995; 256-340.

12. Eigenmann JR. Diabetes mellitus in elderly female dogs: Recent findings on pathogenesis and clinical implications. *J Am Anim Hosp Assoc* 1981; 17:805.

13. Link KRJ, Rand JS. Glucose toxicity in cats. *J Vet Int Med* 1996; 10:185.

14. Dohan FC, Lukens FDW. Experimental diabetes produced by the administration of glucose. *Endocrinology* 1948; 42:244-262.

15. Imamura T, Koffler M, Helderman JF, Prince D, Thirlby R, Inman L, Unger RH. Severe diabetes induces in subtotally depancreatized dogs by sustained hyperglycemia. *Diabetes* 1988; 37:600-609.

16. Boitard C, Avner P. The immunology of diabetes mellitus. *Nature* 1991; 351:519.

17. Schiffrin A, Colle E, Ciampi A, Henricks L, Poussier P. Different rates of conversion to IDDM in siblings of type 1 diabetic children: the Montreal family study. *Diabetes Res Clin Pract* 1993; 21:75-84.

18. Hoenig M. Pathophysiology of canine diabetes. In: Peterson M, Greco D, eds. Diabetes Mellitus, *Vet Clin N Am* 1995; 25:253-256.

19. Nakayama H, Uchida K, Ono K, Goto N. Pathological observation of six cases of feline diabetes mellitus. *Jap J Vet Sci* 1990; 52:819.

20. Woods JP, Panciera DL, Snyder PS, Jackson MW, Smedes SL. Diabetes mellitus in a kitten. *J Am Anim Hosp Assoc* 1994; 30:177.

21. Johnson KH, Hayden DW, O'Brien TD, Westermark P. Spontaneous diabetes mellitus - islet amyloid complex in adult cats. *Am J Path* 1986; 125:416.

22. Sacks DB, McDonald JM. The pathogenesis of Type II diabetes mellitus: A polygenic disease. *Am J Clin Pathol* 1996; 105:149-154.

23. Panciera DL, Thomas CB, Eicker SW, Atkins CE. Epizootiologic patterns of diabetes mellitus in cats: 333 cases (1980-1986). *J Am Vet Med Assoc* 1990; 197:1504.

24. Rand JS, Bobbermein LM, Hendrikz JK. Over-representation of Burmese in cats with diabetes mellitus in Queensland. *Aust Vet J* 1997; in press.

25. Harris MI, Hadden WC, Knowler WC, Bennett PH. Prevalence of diabetes and impaired glucose tolerance and plasma glucose levels in US population aged 20-74 yr. *Diabetes* 1987; 36:523-534.

26. Brand Miller JC, Colagiuri S. The carnivore connection: dietary carbohydrate in the evolution of NIDDM. *Diabetologia* 1994; 37:1280-1286.

27. Bloomgarden ZT. American Diabetes Association Annual Meeting 1996: The etiology of Type II diabetes, obesity, and the treatment of Type II diabetes. *Diabetes Care* 1996; 19:1311-1315.

28. Nelson RW, Himsel CA, Feldman EC, Bottoms GD. Glucose tolerance and insulin response in normal-weight and obese cats. *Am J Vet Res* 1990; 51:1357.

29. Olefsky JM, Ciaraldi TP, Dolterman OG. Mechanisms of insulin resistance in noninsulin-dependent (type II) diabetes. *Am J Med* 1985; 79:12-21.

30. Everhart JE, Pettitt DJ, Bennett PH, Knowler WC. Duration of obesity increases the incidence of NIDDM. *Diabetes* 1992; 41:235-240.

31. Newman B, Selby JV, King MC, Slemenda C, Fabstiz R, Friedman GD. Concordance for type 2 (non-insulin dependent) diabetes mellitus in male twins. *Diabetologia* 1987; 30:763-768.

32. King H, Rrewers M. Global estimates for prevalence of diabetes mellitus and impaired glucose tolerance in adults. *Diabetes Care* 1993; 16:157-177.

33. Arslanian S, Nixon PA, Becker D, Drash AL. Impact of physical fitness and glycaemic control on *in vivo* insulin action in adolescents with IDDM. *Diabetes Care* 1990; 13:9-15.

34. Henriksson J. Influence of exercise on insulin sensitivity. *J Cardiovasc Risk* 1995; 2:303.

35. Regensteiner JG, Mayer EJ, Shetterly SM, Eckel RH, Haskell WL, Marshall JA, Baxter J, Hamman RF. Relationship between habitual physical activity and insulin levels among nondiabetic men and women. San Luis Valley Diabetes Study. *Diabetes Care* 1991; 11:1066-1074.

36. Porte (Jr) D. Beta-cells in type 2 diabetes mellitus. *Diabetes* 1991; 40:166.

37. Lutz TA, Rand JS. Plasma amylin and insulin concentrations in normo- and hyperglycemic cats. *Can Vet J* 1996; 37:27-34.

38. Yki-Jarvinen H. Glucose toxicity. *Endocrine Reviews* 1992; 13:415-430.

39. O'Brien TD, Hayden DW, Johnson EH, Stevens JB. High dose intravenous glucose tolerance test and serum insulin and glucagon levels in diabetic and non-diabetic cats: relationships to insular amyloidosis. *Vet Path* 1985; 22:250.

40. Neel JV. Diabetes mellitus: a 'thrifty' genotype rendered detrimental by 'progress'? *Am J Hum Genet* 1962; 14:353-362.

41. Gaulin SJC, Konner M. On the natural diet of primates, including humans. In: Wurtman RJ, Wurtman JJ, eds. *Nutrition and the Brain*, Vol 1. New York: Raven Press, 1977; 1-86.

42. Rossetti L, Rothman DL, DeFronzo RA, Schulman GI. The effect of dietary protein on *in vivo* insulin action and liver glycogen repletion. *Am J Physiol* 1989; 257:E212-E219.

43. Eaton SB, Konner M. Paleolithic nutrition. A consideration of its nature and current implications. *New Engl J Med* 1985; 312:283-289.

44. Heaton KW, Marcus SN, Emmett PM, Bolton CH. Particle size of wheat, maize, and oat test meals: effects on plasma glucose and insulin responses and on the rate of starch digestion in vitro. *Am J Clin Nutr* 1988; 47:675-682.

45. DeFrozo RA, Soman V, Sherwin RT, Handler R, Felig P. Insulin binding to

monocytes and insulin action in human obesity, starvation and refeeding. *J Clin Invest* 1978; 62:204-213.

46. Chowdhury AR, Gautam AK, Venkatakrisha-Bhatt H. DDT (2,2,bis(p-chlorophenyl) 1,1,1-trichloroethane) induced structural changes in adrenal glands of rats. *Bull Environment Contamination & Toxicol* 1990; 45:193-196.

47. Terasaki PI, Koyama H, Cecka JM, Gjertson DW. The hyperfiltration hypothesis in human renal transplantation. *Transplantation* 1994; 57:1450-1454.

48. MacDonald ML, Rogers QR, Morris JG. Nutrition of the domestic cat, a mammalian carnivore. *Ann Rev Nutr* 1984; 4:521-562.

49. Link KRJ, Rand JS. Arginine and phentolamine response tests in cats. *J Vet Int Med* 1996; 10:185.

50. Johnson KH, O'Brien TD, Betsholtz C, Westermark P. Islet amyloid, islet-amyloid polypeptide and diabetes mellitus. *New Engl J Med* 1989; 321:513.

51. Johnson KH, O'Brien TD, Betsholtz C, Westermark P. Biology of disease: Islet amyloid polypeptide: Mechanisms of amyloidogenesis in the pancreatic islets and potential roles in diabetes mellitus. *Lab Invest* 1992; 66:522.

52. Lutz TA, Ainscow J, Rand JS. Frequency of pancreatic amyloid deposition in cats from south-eastern Queensland. *Aust Vet J* 1994; 71:254-255.

53. Janson J, Soeller WC, Roche PC, Nelson RT, Torchia AJ, Kreutter DK, Butler PC. Spontaneous diabetes mellitus in transgenic mice expressing human islet amyloid polypeptide. *Proc Natl Acad Sci USA* 1996; 93:7283-8.

54. Lorenzo A, Razzaboni B, Weir GC, Yanker BA. Pancreatic islet cell toxicity of amylin associated with Type 2 diabetes mellitus. *Nature* 1994; 368:756.

55. O'Brien TD, Butler PC, Dreutter DK, Kane LA, Eberhardt NL. A model of intracellular amyloidogenesis. *Am J Pathol* 1995; 147:609-16.

56. Jordan K, Murtaugh MP, O'Brien TD, Betsholtz C, Johnson KH. Canine IAPP cDNA sequence provides important clues regarding diabetogenesis and amyloidogenesis in type 2 diabetes. *Biochem Biophys Res Commun* 1990; 169:502.

57. O'Brien TD, Butler PC, Westermark P, Johnson KH. Islet amyloid polypeptide: a review of its biology and potential roles in the pathogenesis of diabetes mellitus. *Vet Pathol* 1993; 30:317.

58. Gaeta LSL, Rink TJ. Amylin: A new hormone as a therapeutic target in diabetes mellitus and other metabolic diseases. *Med Chem Res* 1994; 3:483.

59. Kirk CA, Feldman FC, Nelson RW. Diagnosis of naturally acquired type-I and type-II diabetes mellitus in cats. *Am J Vet Res* 1993; 54:463.

60. Service FJ, Nelson RL. Characteristics of glycemic stability. *Diabetes Care* 1980; 3:58.

61. Nelson RW, Feldman EC, Ford SL, Kirk C. Transient diabetes mellitus in the cat. *Proceed ACVIM*, San Diego, 1992; 794.

62. Martin GJW, Rand JS. Lack of correlation between food ingestion and blood glucose in diabetic cats. *Proceedings of 15th American College of Veterinary Internal Medicine Forum*. 1997.

63. Lutz TA, Rand JS. Detection of amyloid deposition in various regions of the feline pancreas by different staining techniques. *J Comp Path* 1997; 116:157.

Effect of Carboxymethylcellulose on Postprandial Glycemic Response in Healthy Dogs

Richard W. Nelson, DVM, DACVIM
Professor, Department of Medicine and Epidemiology
School of Veterinary Medicine, University of California, Davis, California, USA

Gregory D. Sunvold, PhD
Research and Development, The Iams Company, Lewisburg, Ohio, USA

Introduction

The most common disorder of the endocrine pancreas in dogs and cats is diabetes mellitus, with a reported incidence of 1 in 100 to 1 in 500 patients presenting to small animal veterinary hospitals.[1] Diabetes mellitus results from a relative or absolute deficiency of insulin secretion by the beta cells. Insulin deficiency, in turn, causes decreased tissue utilization of glucose, amino acids, and fatty acids. Glucose obtained from the diet or from hepatic gluconeogenesis accumulates in the circulation, causing hyperglycemia and eventually glycosuria and an osmotic diuresis. The resultant obligatory polyuria and compensatory polydipsia constitute two of the classic clinical signs of diabetes mellitus.

Regardless of the underlying etiology, the primary goal of therapy for diabetes mellitus is the elimination of owner-observed clinical signs that occur secondary to hyperglycemia and glycosuria. Persistence of clinical signs (i.e., polyuria, polydipsia, polyphagia, weight loss) and the development of chronic complications (e.g., cataracts, peripheral neuropathy) is directly correlated with the severity and duration of hyperglycemia. Limiting fluctuations in the blood glucose concentration and maintaining near normal glycemia helps minimize clinical signs and prevents the complications associated with poorly-controlled diabetes. This goal is accomplished through appropriate insulin therapy, modifications of diet and exercise, administration of oral hypoglycemic medications, and the avoidance or control of concurrent inflammatory, infectious, neoplastic, and hormonal disorders.

Role of Dietary Fiber for Treating Diabetes

Dietary therapy plays an integral role in the successful management of the diabetic patient and should be initiated in all diabetic dogs and cats, regardless of the type of diabetes present (i.e., insulin-dependent or noninsulin-dependent diabetes mellitus). Dietary therapy should be directed at correcting obesity, maintaining consistency in the timing and caloric content of the meals, and furnishing a diet that minimizes postprandial fluctuations in blood glucose concentration.[2] Fluctuations in the postprandial blood glucose concentration can be controlled to some degree by feeding a canned or dry kibble food which contains a predominance of complex carbohydrates.[3] Increasing the fiber content of the diet is also beneficial in reducing postprandial fluctuations in the blood glucose concentration and improving control of glycemia in diabetic patients. Several studies have documented improved control of glycemia in diabetic human beings after increasing daily fiber consumption.[4-6] Preliminary studies in dogs suggest a similar benefit of dietary fiber. Fiber consumption decreased postprandial hyperglycemia in healthy dogs,[7] reduced the fluctuation in postprandial glycemia after an afternoon meal in dogs with naturally developing diabetes mellitus,[8] and improved control of glycemia in dogs with alloxan-induced and naturally developing diabetes mellitus.[9,10]

Proposed beneficial effects of fiber consumption include a delay in gastric emptying, slowing of carbohydrate absorption from the intestinal tract, augmented insulin sensitivity in the liver and other tissues, and alterations in secretion of gastrointestinal tract hormones that control nutrient metabolism.[6,11,12] The ability of dietary fiber to form a viscous gel and thus impair convective transfer of glucose and water to the absorptive surface of the intestine appears to be of greatest importance.[6] The more viscous soluble fibers slow glucose diffusion to a greater degree than do the less viscous insoluble fibers and, as such, are believed to be of greater benefit in improving control of glycemia in diabetic human beings.[4-6] Others have found both fiber types to be beneficial in diabetic human beings[13,14] and dogs with alloxan-induced diabetes.[9] Differences between studies evaluating the efficacy of soluble and insoluble fiber in improving control of glycemia may be attributable, in part, to differences in type and quantity of fiber and other dietary ingredients, insulin treatment regimen utilized, existence and severity of diabetic complications, study duration, and client/patient compliance.[13,15,16]

Several forms of cellulose are available with the common characteristic of being poorly fermentable. One form of cellulose fiber, α-cellulose (Solka Floc®) is relatively insoluble in water and nonviscous.[17] In contrast, semisynthetic cellulose polymers are water-soluble and viscous fiber sources. These fibers include methylcellulose (MC), carboxymethylcellulose (CMC), and hydroxypropylmethylcellulose (HPMC). Methylcellulose is a methyl ester of cellulose; CMC is a cellulose polymer with carboxymethyl group side chains; and HPMC is the propylene glycol ether of MC in which both hydroxypropyl and methyl groups are attached to cellulose.[18] Studies in healthy dogs have identified a linear relationship between the viscosity of HPMC added to an orally-administered sodium chloride-polyethylene glycol solution, the viscosity of gastrointestinal intraluminal contents and the subsequent decrease in the rate of transit of intestinal contents,[19] and a relationship between the viscosity of an orally-administered HPMC-containing glucose solution and its effectiveness in delaying glucose absorption from the gastrointestinal tract.[20] High-viscosity HPMC also reduced postprandial blood glucose concentrations in humans with noninsulin-dependent diabetes mellitus fed a carbohydrate-rich meal,[21] and the postprandial glucose response was reduced in healthy rats fed an MC-supplemented high carbohydrate meal, compared with an insoluble fiber-supplemented high carbohydrate meal.[22]

Research addressing the effect of consuming these semisynthetic cellulose polymers on minimizing the postprandial glycemic response to a conventional meal in dogs have apparently not been reported. The effect of consuming dog food containing different quantities and viscosities of CMC on postprandial serum glucose and insulin concentrations in 5 healthy adult hound-type dogs was recently evaluated. Five experimental diets were evaluated in this study; all diets were in dry form. The same protein (chicken, fish meal, egg), fat, and carbohydrate (corn) sources were used to make the 5 diets. Additional ingredients, including vitamins and minerals, were added in identical amounts to make the diets nutritionally complete and balanced for adult dogs. One percent or 2.9% CMC of low (<15 centipoise) or high (>5000 centipoise) viscosity (Metsä-Serla, Aänekoski, Finland) was added to four of the experimental diets; CMC did not replace any ingredient in the diets. The resultant diets contained 1% CMC and had low viscosity, 1% CMC and high viscosity, 2.9% CMC and low viscosity, and 2.9% CMC and high viscosity. One experimental diet was not supplemented with CMC.

Each dog went through five 2 week feeding trials with a 2 week control period between each 2 week feeding trial. A Latin square design was used to randomize the sequence of experimental diets fed. Dogs were fed Eukanuba® Adult Maintenance Formula (The Iams Company, Lewisburg, Ohio) during the 2 week control periods. The effect of each experimental diet on postprandial serum glucose and insulin concentrations was evaluated on day 14 of each 2 week feeding trial. On day 14 of each feeding trial, blood was obtained for measurement of serum glucose and insulin concentrations 15 minutes prior to and immediately prior to eating the meal, and 30, 60, 90, and 120 minutes, and then hourly for an additional six hours after consumption of the meal. The normal fluctuation in serum glucose and insulin concentrations in the nonfed state (i.e., fasting) was determined 2 weeks after the last evaluation of the experimental diets. Dogs were not fed for 24 hours prior to the eight hour blood sampling interval; blood was obtained for measurement of serum glucose and insulin concentrations at the times previously described.

Two dogs developed soft, semi-formed feces and one dog developed watery diarrhea when fed the 2.9% CMC-high viscosity diet and one dog developed soft, semi-formed feces when fed the 2.9% CMC-low viscosity diet. Soft feces and diarrhea resolved within 72 hours after the dogs began eating the commercial dog food during the control period. None of these dogs developed problems when fed the 1% CMC diets. Presumably, 2.9% CMC induced a secretory diarrhea in these dogs.

The serum glucose concentration consistently decreased below the normal fasting range for serum glucose concentration 30 minutes postprandial for the CMC-containing diets but not for the no CMC diet; findings which suggest the CMC was intact and active in delaying gastric emptying and initially slowing nutrient absorption in the dogs.[20] A statistically significant difference in postprandial glycemic response was not identified for any of the CMC-containing diets, suggesting the amount and viscosity of CMC evaluated in this study had no effect on postprandial glycemic response in healthy dogs. However, large standard deviations were the result of one dog which consistently had higher serum glucose and insulin results, compared with the other dogs. When results of the study were evaluated independent of statistical analysis, dogs had the lowest postprandial increase in serum glucose and insulin concentrations when fed the 1% CMC-high viscosity diet, while the 2.9% CMC diets had the highest postprandial increase in serum glucose and insulin concentrations. The higher values for the 2.9% CMC diets are difficult to explain, although these results suggest that the 2.9% CMC in the diet may have actually enhanced glucose absorption, resulting in higher total postprandial glucose absorption and insulin secretion, compared with the 1% CMC diets. The idea that increased dietary viscosity could improve nutrient absorption is supported by findings in rats indicating that amino acid digestibility in the small intestine is enhanced with relatively high dietary viscosity.[23] The time for the postprandial blood glucose concentration to return to the normal fasting range was prolonged for the 1% CMC-high viscosity diet, compared with the other diets; findings which also suggest a delay in gastrointestinal transit time and glucose absorption for this diet. Results for the 1% CMC-low viscosity and no CMC diets were similar, suggesting that there was not enough viscosity in the 1% CMC-low viscosity diet to see an effect on postprandial serum glucose and insulin concentrations.

Implications and Future Research

Slowing digestion and absorption of dietary carbohydrates dampens the increase in postprandial blood glucose concentration and the increase in pancreatic insulin secretion required to re-establish euglycemia. In a healthy dog, slowing digestion and absorption of dietary carbohydrates is not critical, since the healthy pancreas can secrete adequate amounts of insulin in response to an increase in portal blood glucose to prevent or minimize the increase in postprandial blood glucose concentration. Unfortunately, diabetic dogs are unable to increase pancreatic insulin secretion in response to an increase in portal blood glucose. As a result, an increase in blood glucose concentration typically occurs in the general circulation shortly after the dog consumes a meal. Depending on the composition of the meal consumed, the postprandial increase in blood glucose concentration may exceed 200 mg/dl.

Diets which cause the lowest increase in postprandial blood glucose concentration should be recommended for the treatment of diabetes mellitus in dogs. Although the present study was conducted in healthy dogs, results would suggest that the 1% CMC-high viscosity diet is the preferred diet of those evaluated for future studies in diabetic dogs. Dogs had the lowest postprandial glycemic response when fed the 1% CMC-high viscosity diet and had no identifiable adverse effects as a result of consuming the diet. Additional studies will be needed to determine what effect, if any, the 1% CMC-high viscosity diet has on improving control of glycemia in diabetic dogs and, if improvement is documented, how this diet compares to other commercially-available fiber diets currently recommended for the treatment of diabetes mellitus in dogs.

1. Panciera DL, Thomas CB, Eicker SW, Atkins CE. Epizootiologic patterns of diabetes mellitus in cats: 333 cases (1980-1986). *J Am Vet Med Assoc* 1990; 197:1504-1508.

2. Nelson RW, Lewis LD. Nutritional management of diabetes mellitus. *Seminars Vet Med Surg* 1990; 5:178-186.

3. Holste LC, Nelson RW, Feldman EC, Bottoms GD. Effect of dry, soft moist, and canned dog foods on postprandial blood glucose and insulin concentrations in healthy dogs. *Am J Vet Med* 1989; 50:984-989.

4. Weinstock RS, Levine RA. The role of dietary fiber in the management of diabetes mellitus. *Nutrition* 1988; 4:187-193.

5. Anderson JW, Akanji AO. Dietary fiber-An overview. *Diabetes Care* 1991; 14:1126-1131.

6. Nuttall FQ. Dietary fiber in the management of diabetes. *Diabetes* 1993; 42:503-508.

7. Blaxter AC, Cripps PJ, Gruffydd-Jones TJ. Dietary fibre and post prandial hyperglycaemia in normal and diabetic dogs. *J Sm Anim Pract* 1990; 31:229-233.

8. Graham PA, Maskell IE, Nash AS. Canned high fiber diet and postprandial glycemia in dogs with naturally occurring diabetes mellitus. *J Nutr* 1994; 124:2712S-2715S.

9. Nelson RW, Ihle SL, Lewis LD, Salisbury SK, Miller T, Bergdall V, Bottoms GD. Effects of dietary fiber supplementation on glycemic control in dogs with alloxan-induced diabetes mellitus. *Am J Vet Res* 1991; 52:2060-2066.

10. Nelson RW, Duesberg CA, Ford SL, Feldman EC, Davenport DJ, Kiernan C, Neal L. Effect of dietary insoluble fiber on control of glycemia in dogs with naturally developing diabetes mellitus. *J Am Vet Med Assoc* 1997 (in press).

11. Meyer JH, Gu YG, Jehn D, Taylor TL. Intragastric versus intraintestinal viscous polymers and glucose tolerance after liquid meals of glucose. *Am J Clin Nutr* 1988; 48:260-266.

12. Anderson JW, Ziegler JA, Deakins DA, Floore TL, Dillon DW, Wood CL, Oeltgen PR, Whitley RJ. Metabolic effects of high carbohydrate, high fiber diets for insulin dependent diabetic individuals. *Am J Clin Nutr* 1991; 54:936-943.

13. Villaume C, Beck B, Gariot P, Desalme A, Debry G. Long-term evolution of the effect of bran ingestion on meal-induced glucose and insulin responses in healthy men. *Am J Clin Nutr* 1984; 40:1023-1026.

14. Vaaler S. Diabetic control is improved by guar gum and wheat bran supplementation. *Diabetic Med* 1986; 3:230-233.

15. Vinik AI, Jenkins DJA. Dietary fiber in management of diabetes. *Diabetes Care* 1988; 11:160-173.

16. Riccardi G, Rivellese AA. Effects of dietary fiber and carbohydrate on glucose and lipoprotein metabolism in diabetic patients. *Diabetes Care* 1991; 14:1115-1125.

17. Ang JF. Water retention capacity and viscosity effects of powdered cellulose. *J Food Sci* 1991; 56:1682.

18. Johnson IT, Southgate DAT. *Dietary Fiber and Related Substances*. London: Chapman and Hall, 1994; 14-38.

References

19. Reppas C, Meyer JH, Sirois J, Dressman JB. Effect of hydroxypropylmethyl-cellulose on gastrointestinal transit and luminal viscosity in dogs. *Gastroenterology* 1991; 100:1217-1223.

20. Reppas C, Dressman JB. Viscosity modulates blood glucose response to nutrient solutions in dogs. *Diabetes Res Clin Pract* 1992; 17:81-88.

21. Reppas C, Adair CH, Barnett JL, Berardi RR, DuRoss D, Swidan SZ, Thill PF, Tobey SW, Dressman JB. High viscosity hydroxypropylmethylcellulose reduces postprandial blood glucose concentrations in NIDDM patients. *Diabetes Res Clin Pract* 1993; 22:61-69.

22. Cameron-Smith D, Collier GR, O'Dea K. Effect of soluble dietary fiber on the viscosity of gastrointestinal contents and the acute glycaemic response in the rat. *Brit J Nutr* 1994; 71:563-571.

23. Larsen FM, Wilson MN, Moughan PJ. Dietary fiber viscosity and amino acid digestibility, proteolytic digestive enzyme activity and digestive organ weights in growing rats. *J Nutr* 1994; 124:833-841.

Influence of Chromium on Glucose Metabolism and Insulin Sensitivity

Jerry W. Spears, PhD
Professor, Department of Animal Science
North Carolina State University, Raleigh, North Carolina, USA

Talmage T. Brown, Jr., DVM, PhD[a];
Gregory D. Sunvold, PhD[b]; Michael G. Hayek, PhD[b]
[a]Department of Veterinary Microbiology, Pathology and Parasitology
North Carolina State University, Raleigh, North Carolina, USA;
[b]Research and Development, The Iams Company, Lewisburg, Ohio, USA

Schwartz and Mertz[1] reported in 1959 that chromium (Cr) was an essential component of a glucose tolerance factor that corrected impaired glucose metabolism in rats fed certain diets. Severe Cr deficiency, associated with abnormal glucose utilization and insulin resistance, was later observed in humans receiving long-term total parenteral nutrition.[2-4] Low dietary intake of Cr or impaired metabolism of Cr may be a factor associated with the development of diabetes in humans. Chromium supplementation has improved glucose tolerance in diabetic human subjects.[5]

Chromium has received little attention in canine nutrition. Recent studies in cattle[6] and swine[7] have indicated that Cr addition to practical diets can increase glucose uptake by tissues following glucose or insulin administration. Supplementation of Cr to canine diets may also increase insulin sensitivity and result in improved animal health. Various types of diabetes occur in dogs.[8] Inadequate intake of Cr by dogs may increase their risk of developing diabetes. Furthermore, based on previous human studies, some diabetic dogs may benefit from Cr supplementation.

This paper will discuss the role of Cr in insulin function and describe our recent Cr studies with dogs.

Introduction

Chromium functions as a potentiator of insulin action.[9] The active form of Cr involved in facilitating insulin function has traditionally been referred to as the glucose tolerance factor. Glucose tolerance factor was initially isolated from brewer's yeast and shown to contain trivalent Cr, two molecules of nicotinic acid, glutamic acid, glycine and cysteine.[10] However, the chemical identity of the biologically active form of Cr that facilitates insulin activity in the body is not known.[9]

Chromium and Insulin Activity

A number of studies have indicated improved glucose tolerance and/or reduced circulating insulin concentrations following Cr supplementation. Rats fed diets low in Cr and raised in a controlled environment, designed to minimize Cr contamination, had severely impaired glucose clearance rates.[11] Striffler et al.[12] recently reported not only impaired glucose tolerance but also hypersecretion of insulin in rats fed diets low in Cr.

The most convincing evidence of Cr essentiality has been derived from three case reports of severe Cr deficiency in humans receiving total parenteral nutrition.[2-4] All three individuals developed severe glucose intolerance and insulin resistance and two of the subjects experienced sudden weight loss. Addition of 150 to 250 µg of Cr/day to the infusate corrected the impaired glucose tolerance and eliminated or at least alleviated the need for exogenous insulin.

Glucose clearance rate decreases with age in humans due to tissues becoming less responsive to insulin. Depending on the severity of the decline, adult or maturity-onset diabetes may develop. Early studies indicated that some individuals with impaired glucose tolerance responded positively to inorganic Cr supplementation. Three of 6 humans with mild diabetes showed improved glucose tolerance following oral supplementation with Cr chloride.[13] In elderly subjects with abnormal glucose tolerance, Cr chloride supplementation improved glucose tolerance curves to normal in 4 of 10 subjects.[14] Supplementation of Cr tripicolinate reduced fasting blood glucose concentrations in humans with adult-onset diabetes.[15]

Chromium requirements may be higher in humans with insulin-dependent diabetes because of increased urinary losses of Cr.[5] In research trials, humans have generally been supplemented with 200 µg Cr/day. Supplementing diabetic patients, that were receiving exogenous insulin or hypoglycemic agents, with 600µg Cr (as Cr chloride)/day decreased fasting blood glucose concentrations from 254 to 119 mg/dl.[16] It has been postulated that some insulin-dependent diabetics may lose their ability to convert inorganic Cr to the biologically active form.[5] Injection of a glucose tolerance factor purified from yeast decreased blood glucose within 2 hours in diabetic rats.[17] The amount of glucose tolerance factor injected in the streptozotocin diabetic rats in this study supplied only 12.5 ng of Cr.

Responses to Cr supplementation have been variable and some investigators have reported no effect of Cr supplementation on glucose tolerance.[9] A response to Cr supplementation would not be expected unless an animal or individual was deficient in Cr. At the present time there is no reliable indicator of Cr status. Anderson[18] suggested that the only reliable measurement of Cr status was to monitor glucose and lipid metabolism before and after Cr supplementation.

The mechanism whereby Cr enhances insulin activity has not been elucidated. Several hypotheses have been suggested including direct interaction of Cr with insulin,[19] an effect on the production of insulin receptors[20] or a post receptor action.[15] Insulin binding and insulin receptor numbers on red blood cells of hypoglycemic patients were increased by Cr supplementation.[20] *In vitro* addition of glucose and insulin to striated muscle and adipose tissue increased ^{51}Cr binding in these tissues.[21]

Studies in rats and humans have clearly indicated that Cr is poorly absorbed. Chromium absorption in humans consuming self-selected diets ranged from 0.5 to 2.0%.[22] Rats consuming ^{51}Cr incorporated into kale, wheat, and eggs absorbed and retained from 1.1 to 2.3% of the dose after 9 days.[23]

Although the active form of Cr in the body has not been identified, it is apparent from studies with humans that inorganic Cr can be converted into a physiologically active form in most individuals. For example, in humans on total parenteral nutrition and showing signs of severe Cr deficiency, parenteral administration of inorganic Cr chloride rapidly corrected abnormalities.[2-4]

Excretion of absorbed Cr from the body occurs primarily via the urine.[9] Certain types of stress have been shown to increase urinary losses of Cr and may increase the likelihood of Cr deficiency. Stresses reported to increase urinary Cr losses include strenuous exercise, physical trauma, lactation, and consumption of high sugar diets.[24]

Chromium metabolism is altered in humans with insulin dependent diabetes. Absorption of Cr is higher but urinary excretion of Cr is greatly elevated in diabetic subjects.[25] Lower tissue and hair Cr concentrations have been observed in diabetics.[25]

A number of supplemental Cr sources have been evaluated including inorganic Cr chloride, high Cr yeast preparations, and complexes of Cr picolinate and Cr nicotinate. Forms of supplemental Cr may vary in regard to their ability to enhance insulin activity in mammals. Differences in either absorption or post absorptive utilization of different Cr sources could account for variation in physiological responses observed in animals or humans. Considerable research has been conducted evaluating the ability of different forms of Cr to potentiate insulin activity *in vitro* using tissues or isolated cells grown in culture. Results of such studies are difficult to interpret because Cr compounds may not be absorbed and delivered to tissues in the same form in which they are ingested. Since the biologically active form of Cr in the body has not been identified, it is unclear what modifications occur from the time a Cr source is ingested until it is utilized for a biochemical function.

In earlier studies with Cr, a brewer's yeast extract (glucose tolerance factor) containing Cr was found to be a potent facilitator of insulin activity. Using an *in vitro* fat cell assay, the yeast extract increased glucose oxidation to carbon dioxide in the presence of a fixed concentration of insulin.[26] The addition of inorganic Cr chloride to fat cells did not potentiate insulin activity. However, synthetic Cr complexes containing nicotinic acid and glycine or glutathione did increase insulin activity. Glucose tolerance was improved and fasting glucose decreased in elderly humans given supplemental Cr chloride and nicotinic acid.[27] However, neither Cr or nicotinic acid alone affected glucose metabolism. This supports the hypothesis that nicotinic acid functions together with Cr in potentiating insulin activity.

Evans and Pouchnik[28] compared the effects of Cr chloride, Cr tripicolinate and Cr dinicotinate on insulin activity *in vitro*. Insulin activity (measured as glucose oxidation) in isolated adipose tissue was enhanced by Cr dinicotinate but not by the other forms of Cr. However, in skeletal muscle cultures only Cr tripicolinate increased insulin activity.

The absorption and retention of ^{51}Cr, given orally as Cr chloride, Cr nicotinate and Cr picolinate, was recently studied in rats.[29] Rats were killed at 1, 3, 6, and 12 hours after being dosed with ^{51}Cr and tissues were removed and assayed for ^{51}Cr. Rats given radioactive Cr in the form of Cr nicotinate had higher retention of ^{51}Cr in a number of tissues than rats dosed with Cr chloride or Cr picolinate. In contrast, Polansky et al.[30] dosed rats with a single oral dose of ^{51}Cr from various forms including chloride, trinicotinate and tripicolinate and a dinicotinic acid-amino acids (diglycine-cysteine-glutamic acid) complex, and found no significant differences between sources in Cr absorption and retention. In another study, Cr concentrations in tissues were measured after rats were fed different forms of Cr for 3 weeks.[31] Kidney Cr concentrations were highest in animals fed the Cr dinicotinic acid-amino acid complex followed by Cr tripicolinate, Cr trinicotinate and Cr chloride. However, Cr concentrations in the liver and lung were highest in rats fed Cr tripicolinate.

Current
Research

Until recently, Cr had not been evaluated as an essential trace mineral for dogs, and in the most recent NRC nutrient requirement publication for dogs, no requirement was given for Cr.[32] Therefore, two experiments were recently conducted to determine the effect of dietary Cr on glucose clearance rate and circulating insulin concentrations in dogs.

Experiment 1. Twenty-four female Beagle dogs, 2 to 4 years of age, were randomly assigned to diets containing 0, 0.3 or 0.6 ppm of supplemental Cr.[33] Chromium was supplemented in the form of Cr tripicolinate. A glucose tolerance test was conducted after dogs had received the experimental diets for 35 days. Dogs were fasted for 18 hours, then infused via jugular catheter with a 50% glucose solution to provide 0.5 grams of glucose/kg of body weight. Blood samples were collected at 0, 5, 10, 15, 30, 45, 60, and 90 minutes post infusion for plasma glucose and serum insulin concentrations. On day 36 an insulin challenge was conducted by infusing dogs with 0.1 IU of porcine insulin/kg of body weight. Blood was obtained for plasma glucose and serum insulin at 0, 5, 10, 15, 30, 45, 60, and 120 minutes after insulin administration.

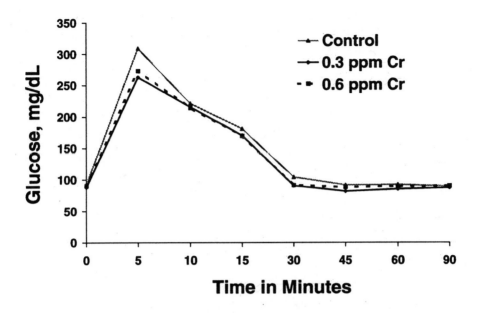

Figure 1. Effect of dietary chromium on plasma glucose concentrations after glucose challenge (Experiment 1). Pooled standard errors of the mean for 0, 5, 10, 15, 30, 45, 60, and 90 minutes were 1.7, 21.8, 7.3 7.3, 7.3, 4.5, 2.2, and 1.5, respectively.

Dogs supplemented with Cr tended to have lower plasma glucose concentrations for 30 minutes following intravenous glucose administration than controls (*Figure 1*). By 30 minutes after glucose infusion, plasma glucose concentrations had generally returned to baseline values. Glucose clearance rate was calculated between 10 and 30 minutes post-infusion. Although not significantly affected by treatment, glucose clearance rate tended to be slightly higher in Cr-supplemented dogs (*Table 1*). Glucose concentrations and glucose clearance rates were similar in dogs supplemented with 0.3 and 0.6 ppm of Cr.

Table 1. Effect of dietary chromium on glucose clearance rate following a glucose tolerance test.

Glucose Clearance Rate*	Dietary Chromium (ppm)				
	Control	0.15	0.30	0.60	SEM
Experiment 1	4.01		4.32	4.29	0.27
Experiment 2	6.08	6.53	6.80		0.40
Combined analysis†	5.05		5.56		0.25

*Expressed as %/minute. Clearance rate was calculated from 10 to 30 minutes post infusion.
†Pooled statistical analysis of data from both experiments. Treatment means differ (P<0.08).

Serum insulin concentrations increased greatly then returned to baseline concentrations by 30 minutes following glucose challenge (**Figure 2**). Dietary Cr did not affect insulin release in response to glucose.

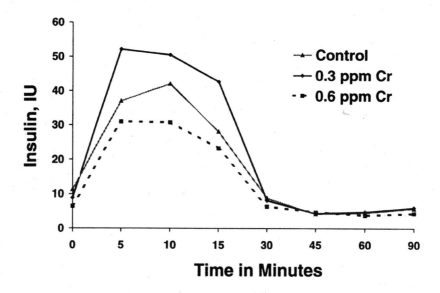

Figure 2. Effect of dietary chromium on serum insulin concentrations after glucose challenge (Experiment 1). Pooled standard errors of the mean for 0, 5, 10, 15, 30, 45, 60, and 90 minutes were 2.1, 8.0, 8.9, 6.4, 1.9, 0.8, 0.6, and 1.0, respectively.

Following insulin infusion, plasma glucose concentrations decreased throughout the 15 minute sampling and then returned to baseline values by 120 minutes post-infusion (**Figure 3**). Plasma glucose concentrations were affected by Cr (P<0.01) and sampling time (P<0.01) but not a Cr X sampling time interaction. Dogs given supplemental Cr had lower plasma glucose concentrations. The lower fasting (time 0) blood glucose concentrations observed in Cr-supplemented dogs is consistent with previous human studies where Cr has reduced fasting blood glucose levels.[5] Plasma glucose also appeared to return to pre-challenge concentrations more rapidly in control dogs. This would suggest that tissues from Cr-supplemented dogs may have been more sensitive to insulin or the administered insulin had a longer lasting effect in these animals.

Experiment 2. Twenty-four female Beagle dogs, 2 to 3 years of age, were used in this study. All dogs were fed the control diet for 10 days. A blood sample was then obtained from each dog, following an 18-hour fast, for plasma glucose determination. Dogs were randomly assigned to treatments based on fasting glucose concentrations. Treatments consisted of 0, 0.15 or 0.30 ppm of supplemental Cr in the form of Cr tripicolinate. Dogs were catheterized in the jugular vein after being fed the experimental diets for 81 days. A glucose tolerance test was then conducted as described for experiment 1.

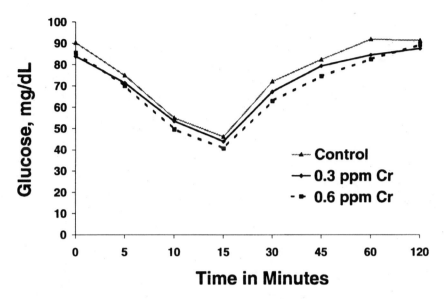

Figure 3. Effect of dietary chromium on plasma glucose concentrations after insulin challenge (Experiment 1). Pooled standard errors of the mean for 0, 5, 10, 15, 30, 45, 60, and 120 minutes were 1.7, 1.9, 2.4, 2.5, 3.3, 2.3, 2.5, and 1.9, respectively.

Results obtained after glucose infusion were similar to those observed in experiment 1. Plasma glucose levels were not significantly affected by treatment but tended to be lower in Cr-supplemented dogs for 30 minutes after glucose dosing (*Figure 4*). Glucose clearance rate also tended to be higher in dogs supplemented with Cr (*Table 1*). Serum insulin concentrations in response to glucose challenge was not affected by Cr (*Figure 5*).

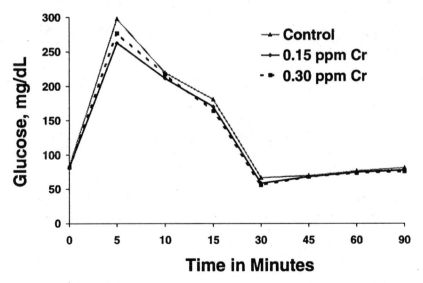

Figure 4. Effect of dietary chromium on plasma glucose concentrations after glucose challenge (Experiment 2). Pooled standard errors of the mean for 0, 5, 10, 15, 30, 45, 60, and 90 minutes were 2.6, 18.6, 11.2, 6.4, 5.2, 2.5, 1.5, and 1.4, respectively.

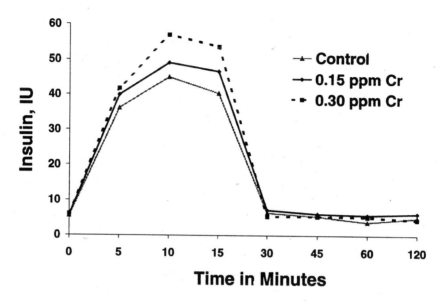

Figure 5. Effect of dietary chromium on serum insulin concentrations after glucose challenge (Experiment 2). Pooled standard errors of the mean for 0, 5, 10, 15, 30, 45, 60, and 90 minutes were 1.1, 7.2, 9.9, 8.8, 0.7, 0.9, 0.7, and 0.8, respectively.

Pooled Analysis. Since similar trends were observed in both experiments, data from the two studies were combined and analyzed statistically for dogs fed the control and 0.3 ppm Cr treatments. Data from dogs fed 0.15 and 0.60 ppm of Cr were not used in the analysis because these treatments were not represented in both experiments. The statistical model included experiment, treatment, and treatment X experiment interaction. When data from the two studies were pooled, plasma glucose concentrations after glucose administration were significantly ($P<0.05$) lower in Cr-supplemented dogs (data not shown). Glucose clearance rate was higher ($P<0.08$) for dogs supplemented with 0.3 ppm of Cr.

Summary and Perspectives

The present studies suggests that Cr supplementation in the form of Cr picolinate to practical dog diets can affect glucose metabolism. When data from two experiments were pooled, dogs fed 0.3 ppm of supplemental Cr had lower plasma glucose concentrations than control dogs following an intravenous glucose tolerance test. Glucose clearance rate between 10 and 30 minutes following glucose administration also tended to be higher for Cr-supplemented dogs. The improved glucose tolerance observed in our studies is consistent with recent studies where Cr picolinate supplementation increased glucose clearance rates in swine[7] and cattle.[6] Serum insulin concentrations were not affected by Cr supplementation. Therefore, the higher glucose clearance noted in Cr-supplemented dogs occurred in the absence of a detectable change in circulating insulin concentrations.

The responses observed in glucose clearance rate with Cr supplementation were relatively small (~10%). However, this change could affect long term health in dogs. Improvement in glucose tolerance in young animals could help prevent diabetes and other disorders associated with impaired glucose tolerance that occur with aging. Responses in glucose and/or insulin to Cr supplementation may also be greater in diabetic dogs or older dogs with impaired glucose tolerance. Further studies are warranted to test these hypotheses.

References

1. Schwarz K, Mertz W. Chromium (III) and the glucose tolerance factor. *Arch Biochem Biophys* 1959; 85:292-295.

2. Jeejeebhoy KN, Chu RC, Marliss EB, Greenberg GR, Bruce-Robertson A. Chromium deficiency, glucose intolerance, and neuropathy reversed by chromium supplementation, in a patient receiving long-term total parenteral nutrition. *Am J Clin Nutr* 1977; 30:531-538.

3. Freund H, Atamian S, Fischer JE. Chromium deficiency during total parenteral nutrition. *J Am Med Assoc* 1979; 241:496-498.

4. Brown RO, Forloines-Lynn S, Cross RE, Heizer WD. Chromium deficiency after long-term total parenteral nutrition. *Dig Dis Sci* 1986; 31:661-664.

5. Anderson RA. Chromium, glucose tolerance, and diabetes. *Biol Trace Element Res* 1992; 32:19-24.

6. Bunting LD, Fernandez JM, Thompson DL, Southern LL. Influence of chromium picolinate on glucose usage and metabolic criteria in growing Holstein calves. *J Anim Sci* 1994; 72:1591-1599.

7. Amoikon EK, Fernandez JM, Southern LL, Thompson DL, Ward TL, Olcott BM. Effect of chromium tripicolinate on growth, glucose tolerance, insulin sensitivity, plasma metabolites and growth hormone in pigs. *J Anim Sci* 1995; 73:1123-1130.

8. Stogdale L. Definition of diabetes mellitus. *Cornell Vet* 1986; 76:156-174.

9. Offenbacher EG, Pi-Sunyer FX, Stoecker BJ. Chromium. In: O'Dell BL, Sunde RA, eds. *Handbook of Nutritionally Essential Mineral Elements*. New York: Marcel Dekker Inc, 1997; 389-412.

10. Mertz W. Chromium history and nutritional importance. *Biol Trace Element Res* 1992; 32:3-9.

11. Mertz W. Roginski EE, Schroeder HA. Some aspects of glucose metabolism of chromium-deficient rats raised in a strictly controlled environment. *J Nutr* 1965; 86:107-112.

12. Striffler JS, Law JS, Polansky MM, Bhathena SJ, Anderson RA. Chromium improves insulin response to glucose in rats. *Metabolism* 1995; 44:1314-1320.

13. Glinsmann WH, Mertz W. Effect of trivalent chromium on glucose tolerance. *Metabolism* 1966; 15:510-520.

14. Levine RA, Streeten DHP, Doisy RJ. Effects of oral chromium supplementation on the glucose tolerance of elderly human subjects. *Metabolism* 1968; 17:114-125.

15. Evans GW. The effect of chromium picolinate on insulin controlled parameters in humans. *Intl J Biosoc Med Res* 1989; 11:163-180.

16. Mossop RT. Effects of chromium (III) on fasting glucose, cholesterol, and cholesterol HDL levels in diabetics. *Cent Afr J Med* 1983; 29:80-82.

17. Mirsky N. Glucose tolerance factor reduces blood glucose and free fatty acid levels in diabetic rats. *J Inorg Biochem* 1993; 49:123-128.

18. Anderson RA. Chromium and parenteral nutrition. *Nutr* 1995; 11:83-86.

19. Mertz W. Chromium occurrence and function in biological systems. *Physiol Rev* 1969; 49:163-238.

20. Anderson RA, Polansky MM, Bryden NA, Bhathena SJ, Canary JJ. Effects of supplemental chromium on patients with symptoms of reactive hypoglycemia. *Metabolism* 1987; 36:351-355.

21. Morris BW, Gray TA, MacNeil S. Glucose-dependent uptake of chromium in human and rat insulin-sensitive tissues. *Clin Sci* 1993; 84:477-452.

22. Anderson RA, Kozlovsky AS. Chromium intake, absorption and excretion of subjects consuming self-selected diets. *Am J Clin Nutr* 1985; 41:1177-1183.

23. Johnson CD, Weaver CM. Chromium in kale, wheat, and eggs:intrinsic labeling and bioavailability to rats. *J Agr Food Chem* 1986; 34:436-440.

24. Anderson RA. Stress effects on chromium nutrition of humans and farm animals. In: *Biotechnology in the Feed Industry; Proceedings of the Alltech 10th Annual Symposium*. Nottingham, England: University Press, 1994; 267-274.

25. Doisy RJ, Streeten DHP, Freiberg JM, Schneider AJ. Chromium metabolism in man and biochemical effects. In: Prasad AS, Oberleas D, eds. *Trace Elements in Human Health and Disease. Vol. 2 Essential and Toxic Elements*. New York: Academic Press Inc., 1976; 79-104.

26. Anderson RA, Brantner JH, Polansky MM. An improved assay for biological active chromium. *J Agric Food Chem* 1978; 26:1219-1221.

27. Urberg M, Zemel MB. Evidence for synergism between chromium and nicotinic acid in the control of glucose tolerance in elderly humans. *Metabolism* 1987; 36:896-899.

28. Evans GW, Pouchnik DJ. Composition and biological activity of chromium-pyridine carboxylate complexes. *J Inorg Biochem* 1993; 49:177-187.

29. Olin KL, Stearns DM, Armstrong WH, Keen CL. Comparative retention/absorption of [51]chromium (^{51}Cr) from ^{51}Cr chloride, ^{51}Cr nicotinate and ^{51}Cr picolinate in a rat model. *Trace Elements Electrolytes* 1994; 11:182-186.

30. Polansky MM, Bryden NA, Anderson RA. Effects of form of chromium on chromium absorption. *FASEB J* 1993; 7:A77.

31. Anderson RA, Bryden MM, Polansky MM. Form of chromium effects tissue chromium concentrations. *FASEB J* 1993; 7:A204.

32. NRC. *Nutrient Requirements of Dogs*. Washington DC: National Academy Press, 1985.

33. Keeling KL. Effect of chromium picolinate on glucose metabolism and immune response in dogs. MS Thesis. North Carolina State University, Raleigh, 1997.

Modulation of Intestinal Function and Glucose Homeostasis in Dogs by the Ingestion of Fermentable Dietary Fibers

Michael I. McBurney, PhD, FACN
Professor of Nutrition, Dept. of Agricultural, Food, and Nutritional Science
University of Alberta, Edmonton, Alberta, Canada

Stefan P. Massimino, MSc[a]; Catherine J. Field, PhD, RD[a];
Gregory D. Sunvold, PhD[b]; Michael G. Hayek, PhD[b]
[a]Department of Agricultural, Food and Nutritional Science,
University of Alberta, Edmonton, Alberta, Canada;
[b]Research and Development, The Iams Company, Lewisburg, Ohio, USA

Introduction

The nutrient requirements of animals are met by the digestion and absorption of foods from the gastrointestinal tract. Humoral changes associated with physiological state (pregnancy, lactation) and disease (diabetes mellitus) influence small intestinal mass and its digestive and absorptive capacity, independent of food intake. Although numerous intestinal hormones have been proposed to regulate intestinal adaptation (gastrin, cholecystokinin, epidermal growth factor, secretin), there is evidence to suggest that proglucagon-derived peptides are the most important. Intestinal hormones also account for >50% of the insulin response to a meal, an effect known as the 'incretin' response. Of the incretin hormones, proglucagon-derived peptides seem to be the most important. Thus, intestinal proglucagon-derived peptides are reported to modulate the capacity of the intestine to absorb glucose and stimulate insulin secretion to facilitate glucose disposal into tissues. The purpose of this paper will be to summarize recent insights into dietary fiber-proglucagon gene interactions within the intestinal tract which appear to be important in the management of glucose metabolism.

Proglucagon-derived Peptides

Proglucagon is a 160 amino acid polypeptide encoded by the glucagon gene[1] of L cells found along the gastrointestinal tract and in greatest concentration in the distal ileum and large intestine.[2] Several highly conserved proglucagon-derived peptides, related in structure to glucagon and processed from the proglucagon prohormone[3,4] have been identified including: glicentin, a C-terminal extended form of glucagon called oxyntomodulin; glucagon-like peptide (GLP)-1; intervening peptide-2; and GLP-2. Prohormone convertases [(PC1, also known as PC3) and PC2], or calcium-dependent serine proteases, are found throughout the body and cleave at lysine-arginine or arginine-arginine sequences to generate peptides which have the C-terminal end removed by the exopeptidase, carboxypeptidase E.[5] It appears from transformed cell line experiments that PC1 produces glicentin, oxyntomodulin, GLP-1, and GLP-2 in equal proportions.[6-8]

The sequence of GLP-1 is completely conserved in all mammalian species investigated,[9] suggesting its importance in glucose metabolism. GLP-1 stimulates the release of insulin by interacting with specific receptors on pancreatic β-cells in the presence of elevated, but not normal, blood glucose concentrations.[2,10] GLP-1 also stimulates proinsulin expression and proinsulin biosynthesis.[11] Recent studies suggest that GLP-1 action may occur via inhibition of gastric emptying and delayed glucose absorption.[12-13] Pancreatic responsiveness to GLP-1, but not GIP, is preserved in noninsulin-dependent diabetes mellitus (NIDDM) subjects and exogenous GLP-1 administration is being proposed in the management of NIDDM subjects.[10,14,15,16]

Many studies have established a strong relationship between cell proliferation and elevated plasma levels of proglucagon-derived peptides.[17-20] GLP-2 seems particularly relevant since preinjection with anti-glucagon-like peptide antibodies blocks the expected increase in basolateral glucose transporter (GLUT2) abundance seen with luminal perfusion of glucose in rats.[21] Moreover, nude mice bearing subcutaneous proglucagon-producing tumours exhibit marked proliferation of the small intestinal epithelium and GLP-2 is the peptide responsible for the enhanced epithelium proliferation.[22] Reimer and McBurney[23] reported that the ingestion of fermentable fiber stimulates proglucagon gene expression and postprandial release of glucagon-like peptides. Feeding fiber supplemented diets to Sprague-Dawley rats for 14 days resulted in dose-dependent increases in intestinal proglucagon mRNA expression.[24] Gee et al.[20] reported that plasma concentrations of proglucagon-derived peptides were increased with the ingestion of fermentable fibers and decreased with the removal of fermentable fiber from the diet. Proglucagon mRNA abundance is greater in rats fed equal amounts of fermentable versus less fermentable fibers.[25] Göke et al.[26] reported that GLP-1 secretion was 80% greater than that of controls after seven days of administration of an α-glucosidase inhibitor which would increase carbohydrate delivery to the large intestine. These observations are consistent with an effect of short chain fatty acids (SCFA), end products of microbial fermentation of dietary fiber, on small bowel hypertrophy. Indeed, the addition of SCFA to total parenteral nutrition formulations significantly increased intestinal proglucagon expression and GLUT2 mRNA, mucosal mass, and ileal uptakes of D-glucose were greater at three and seven days in rats following 80% small bowel resection.[27] Moreover, intestinal proglucagon and glucose transporter mRNA and transporter protein abundances and plasma GLP-2 concentrations increase within six hours of intravenous SCFA infusion in rats receiving parenteral nutrition.[28]

Hypothesis   The consumption of fermentable fiber diets will increase proglucagon mRNA abundance which will be associated with increased postprandial GLP-1 and insulin secretion and a net improvement in glucose homeostasis despite a greater small intestinal capacity to transport glucose.

A crossover experimental design was conducted whereby dogs (n=16) were randomly assigned for 14 day periods to one of two diets which were formulated to be isoenergetic and isonitrogenous. The diets provided 19.5 MJ/kg diet with approximately 30% of the energy from protein, 50% from fat, and the remainder from carbohydrate. The diets differed in the fermentability of the fiber being consumed. The low fermentable fiber (LFF) diet contained wood cellulose with an *in vitro* fermentability of 9 mmol SCFA/kg of fiber organic matter, whereas the high fermentable fiber (HFF) diet contained a mixture of plant fibers and had an *in vitro* fermentability of 229 mmol SCFA/kg of fiber organic matter. The total dietary fiber content of the diets, determined by AOAC methods were 8.3g/100g LFF diet and 7.3g/100g HFF diet. The HFF diet contained 1.5 g fructooligosaccharide powder/ 100g diet and the AOAC method does not recover oligosaccharides; therefore, the actual fiber content of the HFF diet was calculated to be 8.7 g/100g HFF diet assuming that 95% of the fructooligosaccharide powder was dietary fiber.

Eight dogs were fed the HFF diet for 14 days followed by the LFF diet, whereas the other 8 dogs were fed the diets in the opposite order. Because all 16 dogs could not be accommodated at one time, dogs were paired throughout the cross-over design. All dogs were individually fed to meet energy requirements and water was provided *ad libitum*. After an overnight fast, an oral glucose tolerance test was conducted on days 14 and 28. Peripheral blood samples were obtained for glucose, insulin and GLP-1 analyses. On day 28, the dogs were anesthetized and intestinal samples were taken for northern and western blot analyses, histology, and nutrient uptake assays. All procedures received ethical approval from the Health Sciences Animal Welfare Committee of the University of Alberta and are consistent with the guidelines of the Canadian Council on Animal Care.

Animal weights did not differ by experimental diet or by period. Consumption of HFF *v* LFF resulted in significantly greater proglucagon mRNA abundance in the ileum and the colon ($P \leq 0.05$). The incremental areas under the curve were significantly greater for GLP-1 and insulin whereas glucose were lower in dogs fed the HFF diet *v* LFF diet (**Table 1**).

Consumption of the HFF diet resulted in significantly greater maximal D-glucose uptakes in the jejunum (182 ± 15 *v* 133 ± 13, $P \leq 0.05$) but not in the ileum. The Michaelis affinity constant (Km) for glucose was not affected by diet ($P > 0.05$). Estimates of paracellular D-glucose uptake, determined by L-glucose uptake at 16 mM, were not significantly affected by diet ($P > 0.05$).

Diet did not affect gene expression of brush border sodium-dependent glucose transporters (SGLT-1 mRNA abundance) in any of the intestinal segments measured ($P > 0.05$) but the consumption of HFF *v* LFF was associated with greater abundance of the SGLT-1 transporter protein in the jejunum (22.2 ± 3.7 *v* 6.6 ± 3.7 densitometer units, $P \leq 0.01$) and a tendency to be higher in the ileum (13.4 ± 0.7 *v* 0.4 ± 0.7 densitometer units, $P = 0.09$). The ingestion of HFF diets was associated with greater abundance of basolateral glucose transporter protein (GLUT2) in both the jejunum and ileum.

Table 1. Incremental areas under the curve for plasma GLP-1, glucose, and insulin following an oral glucose tolerance test (2 g glucose/kg live body weight) in dogs fed a high (HFF) or low (LFF) fermentable diet for 14 days.

	HFF n=16	LFF n=16	Pooled SEM
GLP-1 (pmol / L·h)	988[a]	648	92
Insulin (pmol / L·hr)	15781[a]	11209	1371
Glucose (mmol / L·hr)	219[a]	291	22

[a] Indicates means within a row are significantly different at $P<0.05$

Discussion

The addition of dietary fibers to meals are known to reduce postprandial hyperglycemia and decrease exogenous insulin requirements.[29-32] Although the ingestion of fiber supplements with a meal also improves glucose tolerance to a subsequent meal[30-33] and long term consumption of fiber increases plasma insulin concentrations and improves glucose homeostasis to oral glucose tolerance tests,[34-40] the mechanisms of action remain unclear.

Reimer and McBurney[23] proposed that the ingestion of high fiber diets increases proglucagon gene expression and subsequently reported that proglucagon mRNA abundances reflect the fermentability of the fiber being consumed.[25] The current study demonstrates that the ingestion of HFF diets for 14 days results in significantly greater abundances of intestinal proglucagon mRNA, greater incremental GLP-1 and insulin secretion, and improved glucose tolerances (decreased glucose area under curve) in dogs. It was not determined whether L-cell number increased or if proglucagon expression and GLP-1 production per L-cell changed. However, Hoyt et al.[41] used in situ hybridization techniques and reported that proglucagon mRNA abundance increased per cell with refeeding. GLP-1 has been proposed to be an antidiabetogenic agent because of its biological functions as an inhibitor of gastric acid secretion and emptying,[12,33,42,43] glucagon secretion,[42,44,45] and as a potent insulin secretagogue.[2,3,42,45-47]

The mechanism whereby diet modulates intestinal proglucagon expression and GLP-1 synthesis and secretion remains unknown. L-cells have a pyramid shape with the apical process being located in the microvilli of the intestinal lumen and the base, rich in endocrine granules, is adjacent to the basal lamina, suggesting that L-cells respond to luminal events with a basal discharge of granular contents.[41] However, it is unknown if L-cells respond directly to nutrients, the transport of nutrients or if some other signals are involved. Colonic infusions of various fibers and SCFA do not affect GLP-1 release in fasted rats,[48] but SCFA administration in rats receiving parenteral nutriton does affect plasma proglucagon-derived peptide concentrations.[28]

The GLP-1 antibody used in the radioimmunoassay in this study was specific for c-terminal-amidated GLP-1 isomers and does not distinguish between intestinal GLP-1(7-36)NH_2, the DP-IV-truncated GLP-1(9-36)NH_2 or pancreatic GLP-1(1-36)NH_2. However, the latter two moities do not stimulate insulin secretion.[49] Therefore, we conclude that the greater insulin secretion observed in dogs fed the HFF diets is a function of enhanced intestinal GLP-1(7-36)NH_2 secretion.

Long term consumption of fiber-supplemented diets is associated with changes in intestinal motility, mass and length,[50-53] the rate of intestinal cell turnover, enterocyte migration along the crypt-villus axis, enterocyte life span, and villus appearance.[53-55] Dogs which consumed the HFF had significantly longer jejunal villi and greater D-glucose transport capacity. Karasov and Diamond[56] reported that protein mediated transport is predominantly altered by changes in Vmax. The mechanistic basis for an alteration in the absorption rate of a single nutrient is usually the result of a change in the number of transport sites per enterocyte arising from an altered rate of synthesis or degradation of that transport site.[57] Consumption of the HFF diet was significantly associated with upregulated jejunal SGLT-1 and jejunal and ileal GLUT2 glucose transporter levels. It was proposed that SCFA, endproducts of dietary fiber fermentation, modulate proglucagon mRNA abundance and GLP-2 secretion. SCFA have been reported to significantly increase functional adaptation by increasing total, mucosal and submucosal weight, and increasing ileal DNA, RNA, and protein concentrations.[27,58] Intravenous supplementation of SCFA was associated with significantly increased ileal D-glucose uptake in rats.[28] GLP-2 is co-secreted with GLP-1.[4-8] GLP-2 stimulates small intestinal epithelial proliferation[22] and modulates basolateral GLUT2 abundance in rats.[21]

A significant increase in proglucagon gene abundance and intestinal and plasma GLP-1 concentrations was observed in dogs fed HFF diets. Thus, it is proposed that the increase in transporter abundance observed in dogs in this study may reflect increased secretion of GLP-2. The observed improvements in glucose homeostasis suggests, however, that either enhanced insulin secretion or tissue sensitivity must occur to compensate for the greater glucose transport capacity seen in dogs fed the HFF diet. There is evidence that GLP-1 increases insulin-dependent glucose disposal.[59] GLP-1 is also known to inhibit gastric emptying,[12-13] an effect which could slow glucose delivery to glucose transporters located within the small intestine that carry glucose to the systemic circulation. In this study, gastric emptying rates were not determined. Thus the relative importance of GLP-1-mediated actions on gastric emptying versus measured changes in small intestinal glucose transport and the secretion and action of insulin on glucose homeostasis cannot be elucidated. The net effect, however, despite increased intestinal glucose transport capacity, is a measurable improvement in glucose homeostasis of healthy dogs ingesting fermentable fiber diets. Consequently, we propose a new model (*Figure 1*) to characterize dietary fiber-proglucagon gene interactions which may lead to the development of novel nutritional strategies that improve glucose homeostasis and reduce health complications associated with hyperglycemia.

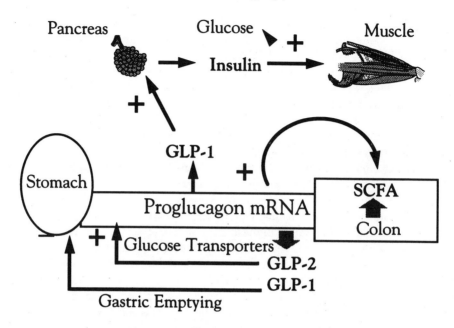

Figure 1. Model portraying the relationship among large bowel fermentation, proglucagon gene expression, gastric emptying, small intestinal glucose transport, pancreatic insulin secretion and insulin-facilitated glucose uptake into muscle.

Take Home Message

The ingestion of fermentable fiber diets by dogs is associated with increased synthesis and secretion of proglucagon-derived peptides. These peptides modulate intestinal nutrient transport capacity and stimulate insulin secretion to facilitate glucose disposal. These results suggest that canine diets can be formulated which will reduce the risk of health complications associated with pathological conditions such as diabetes mellitus.

References

1. Bell GI, Sanchez-Pescador R, Laybourn PJ, Najarian RC. Exon duplication and divergence in the human preproglucagon gene. *Nature* 1983; 304:368-371.

2. Holst JJ. Glucagonlike peptide 1: a newly discovered gastrointestinal hormone. *Gastroenterol* 1994; 107:1848-1855.

3. Mojsov S, Weir GC, Habener JF. Insulinotropin: glucagon-like peptide 1-(7-37) co-encoded in the glucagon gene is a potent stimulator of insulin release in the perfused rat pancreas. *J Clin Invest* 1987; 79:616-619.

4. Ørskov C, Holst JJ, Knuhtsen S, Baldissera FG, Poulsen SS, Nielsen OV. Glucagon-like peptides GLP-1 and GLP-2, predicted products of the glucagon gene, are secreted separately from pig small intestine but not pancreas. *Endocrinol* 1986; 119:1467-1475.

5. Steiner DF, Rouille Y, Gong Q, Martin S, Carroll R, Chan SJ. The role of prohormone convertases in insulin biosynthesis: evidence for inherited defects in their action in man and experimental animals. *Diabetes & Metab* 1996; 22:94-104.

6. Rouillé Y, Martin S, Steiner DF. Differential processing of proglucagon by the subtilisin-like prohormone convertases PC2 and PC3 to generate either glucagon or glucagon-like peptide. *J Biol Chem* 1995; 270:26488-26496.

7. Dhanvantari S, Seidah NG, Brubaker PL. Role of prohormone convertases in the tissue-specific processing of proglucagon. *Molec Endocrinol* 1996; 10:342-355.

8. Rothenberg ME, Eilertson CD, Klein K, Mackin RB, Noe BD. Evidence for redundancy in propeptide/prohormone convertase activities in processing proglucagon: an antisense study. *Molec Endocrinol* 1996; 10:331-341.

9. Adelhorst K, Hedegaard BB, Knudsen LB, Kirk O. Structure-activity studies of glucagon-like peptide-1. *J Biol Chem* 1994; 269:6275-6278.

10. Gutniak M, Ørskov C, Holst JJ, Ahrén B, Efendic S. Antidiabetogenic effect of glucagon-like peptide-1 (7-36) amide in normal subjects and patients with diabetes mellitus. *N Engl J Med* 1992; 326:1312-1322.

11. Drucker DJ, Philippe J, Mojsov S, Chick WL, Habener JF. Glucagon-like peptide I stimulates insulin gene expression and increases cyclic AMP levels in a rat islet cell line. *Proc Natl Soc Acad Sci USA* 1987; 93:7911-7916.

12. Schirra J, Katschinski M, Weidmann C, Schafer T, Wank U, Arnold R, Goke B. Gastric emptying and release of incretin hormones after glucose ingestion in humans. *J Clin Invest* 1996; 97:92-103.

13. Willms B, Werner J, Holst JJ, Ørskov C, Creutzfeldt W, Nauck MA. Gastric emptying, glucose responses, and insulin secretion after a liquid test meal: effects of exogenous glucagon-like peptide-1 (GLP-1)-(7-36) amide in type 2 (noninsulin-dependent) diabetic patients. *J Clin Endocrinol* 1996; 81:327-332.

14. Nauck MA, Heimesaat AM, Ørskov C, Holst J, Ebert R, Creutzfeldt W. Preserved incretin activity of glucagon-like peptide I but not of synthetic human gastric inhibitory polypeptide in patients with type-2 diabetes mellitus. *J Clin Invest* 1993; 91:301-307.

15. Deacon CF, Nauck MA, Toft-Nielsen, M, Pridal L, Willms B, Holts JJ. Both subcutaneously and intravenously administered glucagon-like peptide 1 are rapidly degraded from the NH_2-terminus in Type II diabetic patients and in healthy subjects. *Diabetes* 1995; 44:1126-1131.

16. Nauck MA, Wollschlager D, Werner J, Holst JJ, Ørskov C, Creutzfeldt W, Willms B. Effects of subcutaneous glucagon-like peptide 1 (GLP-1 [7-36 amide]) in patients with NIDDM. *Diabetologia* 1996; 39:1546-1553.

17. Sagor GR, Al-Mukhtar MYT, Ghatel MA, Wright NA, Bloom SR. The effect of altered luminal nutrition on cellular proliferation and plasma concentrations of enteroglucagon and gastrin after small bowel resection in the rat. *Br J Surg* 1982; 69:14-18.

18. Sagor GR, Ghatel MA, Al-Mukhtar MYT, Wright NA, Bloom SR. Evidence for a humoral mechanism after small intestinal resection: exclusion of gastrin but not enteroglucagon. *Gastroenterol* 1983; 84:902-906.

19. Gornacz GE, Al-Mukhtar, MYT, Ghatei MA, Sagor GR, Wright NA, Bloom SR. Pattern of cell proliferation and enteroglucagon reponse following small bowel resection in the rat. *Digestion* 1984; 29:65-72.

20. Gee JM, Lee-Finglas W, Wortley GW, Johnson IT. Fermentable carbohydrates elevate plasma enteroglucagon but high viscosity is also necessary to stimulate small bowel mucosal proliferation in rats. *J Nutr* 1996; 126:373-379.

21. Cheeseman CI, Tsang R. The effect of gastric inhibitory polypeptide and glucagon-like peptides on intestinal hexose transport. *Am J Physiol* 1996; 261:G477-482.

22. Drucker DJ, Erlich P, Asa SL, Brubaker PL. Induction of intestinal epithelial proliferation by glucagon-like peptide 2. *Proc Nat Acad Sci USA* 1996; 93:7911-7916.

23. Reimer RA, McBurney MI. Dietary fiber modulates intestinal proglucagon mRNA and postprandial secretion of GLP-1 and insulin in rats. *Endocrinol* 1996; 137:3948-3956.

24. McBurney MI, Reimer RA, Tappenden KA. Short chain fatty acids, intestinal adaptation and nutrient utilization. *Proc 5th Vahouny Conf Dietary Fiber*, Washington DC, March 1996, Plenum Press Inc; in press.

25. Reimer RA, Thomson ABR, Rajotte R, Basu TK, Oorakuil B, McBurney MI. A physiological level of rhubarb fiber affects proglucagon gene expression and intestinal glucose uptake in rats. *J Nutr*; in press.

26. Göke B, Fuder H, Wieckhorst G, Theiss U, Stridde E, Littke T, Kleist P, Arnold R, Lücker PW. Vogliose (AO-128) is an efficient a-glucosidase inhibitor and mobilizes the endogenous GLP-1 reserve. *Digestion* 1995; 56:493-501.

27. Tappenden KA, Thomson ABRT, Wild GE, McBurney MI. Short chain fatty acids increase proglucagon and ornithine decarboxylase messenger RNAs following intestinal resection in rats. *JPEN* 1996; 20:357-362.

28. Tappenden KA, Drozdowski LA, McBurney MI. Short chain fatty acid supplemented total parenteral nutrition leads to rapid increases in proglucagon mRNA and plasma GLP-2 concentrations. *ASPEN*, San Francisco, CA, Jan 26-29, 1997.

29. Anderson JW, O'Neal DS, Riddell-Mason S, Floore TL, Dillon DW, Oeltgen PR. Postprandial serum glucose, insulin and lipoprotein responses to high- and low-fiber diets. *Metab: Clin & Expt* 1995; 44:848-854.

30. Jenkins DJA, Wolever TM, Nineham R, Sarson DL, Bloom SR, Ahern J, Alberti KG, Hockaday TD. Improved glucose tolerance four hours after taking guar with glucose. *Diabetologia* 1980; 19:21-24.

31. Jenkins DJA, Wolever TM, Taylor RH, Barker HM, Fielden H, Jenkins AL. Effect of guar crispbread with cereal products and leguminous seeds on blood glucose concentrations of diabetics. *Br Med J* 1980; 281:1248-1250.

32. Wolever TM, Jenkins DJ, Nineham R, Alberti KG. Guar gum and reduction of post-prandial glycaemia: effect of incorporation into solid food, liquid food, and both. *Br J Nutr* 1979; 41:505-510.

33. Trinick TR, Laker MF, Johnston DG, Keir M, Buchanan KD, Alberti KG. Effect of guar gum on second-meal glucose tolerance in normal man. *Clin Sci* 1986; 71:49-55.

34. Aro A, Uusitupa M, Voutilainen E, Hersio K, Korhonen T, Siitonen O. Improved diabetic control and hypocholesterolaemic effect induced by long-term dietary supplementation with guar gum in type 2 (insulin-independent) diabetes. *Diabetologia* 1981; 21:29-33.

35. Hagander B, Schersten B, Asp NG, Sartor G, Agardh CD, Schrezenner J, Kasper H, Ahren B, Lundquist I. Effect of dietary fibre on blood glucose, plasma immunoreactive insulin, C-peptide and GIP responses in non-insulin dependent (type 2) diabetes and controls. *Acta Medica Scand* 1984; 215:205-213.

36. Lovejoy J, DiGirolamo M. Habitual dietary intake and insulin sensitivity in lean and obese adults. *Am J Clin Nutr* 1992; 55:1174-1179.

37. Groop PH, Aro A, Stenman S, Goop L. Long-term effects of guar gum in subjects with non-insulin-dependent diabetes mellitus. *Am J Clin Nutr* 1993; 58:513-518.

38. Miranda PM, Horowitz DL. High-fiber diets in the treatment of diabetes mellitus. *Ann Internal Med* 1978; 88:482-486.

39. O'Dea K, Traianedes K, Ireland P, Niall M, Sadler J, Hopper J, De Luis M. The effects of diets differing in fat, carbohydrate, and fiber on carbohydrate and lipid metabolism in type II diabetes. *J Am Dietet Assoc* 1989; 89:1076-1086.

40. Pastors JG, Blaisdell PW, Balm TK, Asplin CM, Pohl SL. Psyllium gum reduces rise in postprandial glucose and insulin concentrations in patients with non-insulin-dependent diabetes. *Am J Clin Nutr* 1991; 53:1431-1435.

41. Hoyt EC, Lund PK, Winesett DE, Fuller CR, Ghatei MA, Bloom SR, Ulshen MH. Effects of fasting, refeeding and intraluminal triglyceride on proglucagon expression in jejunum and ileum. *Diabetes* 1996; 45:434-439.

42. Wettergren A, Schjoldager B, Mortensen PE, Myhre J, Christiansen J, Holst JJ. Truncated GLP-1 (proglucagon 78-107 amide) inhibits gastric and pancreatic functions in man. *Digest Dis Sci* 1993; 38:665-673.

43. Layer P, Holst JJ, Grandt D, Goebell H. Ileal release of glucagon-like peptide-1 (GLP-1). Association with inhibition of gastric acid secretion in humans. *Dig Dis Sci* 1995; 40:1074-1082.

44. Hvidberg A, Nielsen MT, Hilstead J, Ørskov C, Holst JJ. Effect of glucagon-like peptide-1 (proglucagon 78-107 amide) on hepatic glucose production in healthy man. *Metab: Clin & Expt* 1994; 43:104-108.

45. Ørskov C, Wettergren A, Holst JJ. Biological effects and metabolic rates of glucagon-like peptide-1 7-36 amide and glucagon-like peptide-1 7-37 in healthy subjects are indistinguishable. *Diabetes* 1993; 42:658-661.

46. Ahren B, Larsson H, Holst JJ. Effects of glucagon-like peptide-1 on islet function and insulin sensitivity in noninsulin-dependent diabetes mellitus. *J Clin Endocr & Metab* 1997; 82:473-478.

47. Qualmann C, Nauck MA, Holst JJ, Ørskov C, Creutzfeldt W. Insulin-otropic actions of intravenous glucagon-like peptide-1 (GLP-1) [7-36 amide] in the fasting state in healthy subjects. *Acta Diabetologica* 1995; 32:13-16.

48. Plaisancie P, Dumoulin V, Chayvialle JA, Cuber JC. Luminal glucagon-like peptide-1(7-36) amide-releasing factors in the isolated vascularly perfused rat colon. *J Endocrinol* 1995; 145:521-526.

49. Suzuki S, Kawai K, Ohashi S, Mukai H, Yamashita K. Comparison of the effects of various C-terminal and N-terminal fragment peptides of glucagon-like peptide-1 on insulin and glucagon release from the isolated perfused rat pancreas. *Endocrinol* 1989; 125:3109-3114.

50. Bornet FR. Undigestible sugars in food products. *Am J Clin Nutr* 1994; 59:763S-769S.

51. Jacobs LR. Effects of dietary fiber on mucosal growth and cell proliferation in the small intestine of the rat: a comparison of oat bran, pectin, and guar gum with total fiber deprivation. *Am J Clin Nutr* 1983; 37:954-960.

52. Jacobs LR, Lupton JR. Effect of dietary fibers on rat large bowel mucosal growth and cell proliferation. *Am J Phyisol* 1984; 246:G378-385.

53. Johnson IT, Gee JM, Mahoney RR. Effect of dietary supplements of guar gum and cellulose on intestinal proliferation, enzyme levels and sugar transport in the rat. *Br J Nutr* 1984; 52:477-487.

54. Brown RC, Kelleher RS, Losowsky MS. The effect of pectin on the structure and function of the rat small intestine. *Br J Nutr* 1979; 42:357-365.

55. Chiou PW, Yu B, Lin C. Effect of different components of dietary fiber on the intestinal morphology of domestic rabbits. *Comp Biochem Biophysiol* 1994; 108:629-638.

56. Karasov W, Diamond J. A simple method for measuring intestinal solute uptake in vitro. *J Comp Physiol* 1983; 152:105-116.

57. Ferraris RP, Diamond J. Regulation of intestinal sugar transport. *Am J Physiol* 1997; 262:G1069-1073.

58. Koruda MMJ, Rolandelli RH, Bliss DZ, Hastings J, Rombeau JL, Settle RG. Parenteral nutrition supplemented with short-chain fatty acids: effect on the small-bowel mucosa in normal rats. *Am J Clin Nutr* 1990; 51:685-689.

59. D'Alessio DA, Kahn SE, Leusner C, Ensinck J. Glucagon-like peptide 1 (7-36 NH$_2$) enhances glucose tolerance both by stimulation of insulin release and by increasing insulin independent glucose disposal. *J Clin Invest* 1994; 93:2263-2266.

The Glycemic Response to Dietary Starch

Gregory D. Sunvold, PhD
Research Nutritionist, Research and Development
The Iams Company, Lewisburg, Ohio, USA

Guy F. Bouchard, DMV, MS, DACT
Sinclair Research Center, Columbia, Missouri, USA

Glycemic Response

The ingestion of food results in a postprandial increase in blood glucose followed by an increase in blood insulin levels. Because the diabetic has difficulty in storing blood glucose, glucose levels remain higher for longer periods of time than in normal individuals. Therefore, to re-establish a state of normalcy more quickly in these individuals, diets which minimize the postprandial glucose response are of benefit to diabetics.

The primary dietary component likely responsible for the rise in blood glucose immediately following a meal is starch.[1] One way to minimize the starch composition of diets is to replace it with high amounts of nonfermentable dietary fiber. However, high fiber diets can be associated with several side effects.[2] Modest amounts of selected dietary fibers can have beneficial effects on the glycemic response; this information is discussed elsewhere in this proceedings by McBurney and coworkers,[3] and Nelson and Sunvold.[4] In order for an animal to maintain its weight, caloric needs must be derived from protein, carbohydrates, or fat. If the carbohydrate fraction of food is reduced, the other two primary macronutrients, protein and fat, must increase. Replacing starch entirely with protein is difficult to do on a practical basis since many commercially available protein sources contain a significant amount of fat. Replacing the starch with fat results in a food that is extremely calorically dense and thereby poses the health risk of creating (or sustaining) obesity. Additionally, increased dietary fat has been reported to decrease insulin sensitivity.[5,6] Keeping starch as a component of the diet is important for maintaining nutritional balance; extreme dietary formulations should be avoided.

Glycemic Index

For nearly two decades, human nutritionists have been aware of the differing glycemic responses of various carbohydrate-containing foods.[7] The term "glycemic index" was defined as a way to comparatively rank foods based on their glycemic response[8] (**Figure 1**). The human glycemic index initially utilized glucose as the standard and all other foods were ranked accordingly. Later, the standard for comparison was changed to white bread due to concerns about excessive sweetness and the osmotic effect of glucose on gastric emptying.[9] Glycemic index and dietary level of carbohydrate has been used to explain approximately 90% of the reason for differences in glucose and insulin responses to a meal.[10] Therefore, starch source is an important consideration when determining what diet may be optimal for diabetics.

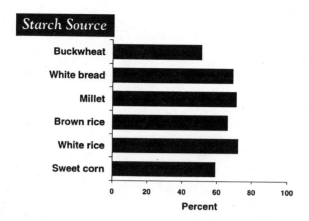

Figure 1. The glycemic index of several high carbohydrate human foods expressed as a percentage of glucose. Adapted from Jenkins et al., 1981.[8]

Starch Sources for Human Diabetics

One common recommendation for human diabetics is that whole grain sources of starch should be consumed rather than highly refined starch sources. This concept is substantiated by results from Järvi et al.[11] These researchers compared a minimally processed meal containing parboiled rice, red kidney beans, and bread made from whole-wheat grains to a highly processed meal containing sticky rice, ground red kidney beans, and bread made from ground wheat. Results indicated that a lower postprandial blood glucose and insulin response occurred when human subjects consumed the minimally processed meal. Thus, consumption of whole grains appears to improve glycemic control of humans.

The source of starch has also been implicated in affecting the glycemic response to a meal. For example, Bantle et al.[12] found that a greater blood glucose and insulin response results when wheat starch is consumed compared to potato starch. In a review of several studies evaluating starch sources, Wolever and Miller[13] concluded that classifying carbohydrates as simple (e.g., sucrose) or complex (e.g., starch) does not predict the blood glucose and insulin response. Therefore, *in vivo* analysis of a starch's influence on blood glucose and insulin is important to determine its influence on glucose response.

Other evaluations of the impact of starch sources on glycemic response have suggested a benefit of barley. Human subjects that ingested barley had a lower glycemic response than with potato, white bread, and spaghetti.[14] Liljeberg et al.[15] indicated that not all barleys may have the same influence on the glycemic response to a meal. Therefore, certain barley sources appear to be important in controlling the glycemic response to a meal.

Glucose metabolism of the dog has been studied extensively using various experimental techniques.[16,17,18] In spite of this, the amount of information regarding the influence of starch on glycemic response in dogs is extremely limited while other components such as fiber have received much more attention.[18,19,20] Presumably, the greatest influence of starch source on glucose metabolism would occur during the postprandial glycemic response. Thus, techniques which emphasize this time frame would be useful in understanding the role of starch.

A publication by Holste et al.[21] reported the comparison of dry, semi-moist, and canned foods fed to healthy dogs. Results indicated that the semi-moist food resulted in a greater rise in postprandial glucose and insulin than the other two diets. Area under the insulin curve was also greatest in the semi-moist fed dogs. Reasons for these differences may include the source of carbohydrates and the amount of carbohydrates. The semi-moist food was the only diet that contained corn syrup. Additionally, Holste et al.[21] reported that the semi-moist food contained the greatest amount of carbohydrates per unit of energy. Regardless of specific reasons for these differences, these results introduce the possibility of dietary carbohydrate influencing the postprandial glycemic response in dogs.

Present
Evaluation
of Starch
and Glycemic
Response

Approximately 25 to 60% of a dog's daily caloric intake is derived from carbohydrates. Based on this fact and previous research with other species, the potential ability of dietary carbohydrate to influence postprandial response in the dog was of interest. To study this, diets needed to be equivalent in starch content so that glycemic response was not influenced by differences in carbohydrate intake. Evaluation of carbohydrate sources in a complete diet matrix was also of interest. To do this, protein was allowed to vary primarily along with minor variations in fat level. The protein, fat, and starch concentration across all diets was 31.6 ± 4.5; 10.6 ± 0.5; and 29.9 ± 1.4, respectively. Supplementation of micronutrients was held constant among diets since certain vitamins[22,23] and minerals[24,25] have been shown to alter signs of glycemic status.

Methods

Animals. Thirty adult ovariohysterectomized female Beagles were used in this experiment. The average body weight of the dogs was 9.62 kg ± 0.78 at the initiation of the study. Fresh water was provided *ad libitum* during the entire period of study.

Experimental Design. Following a stabilization period of 7 weeks, the dogs were randomized into 1 of 5 dietary treatment groups of 6 dogs each. The dogs were re-randomized and assigned to a different experimental diet for the second replicate. Replicates I and II lasted a minimum of 2 weeks each.

Glycemic Response Tests. Glycemic response tests were performed at the end of each replicate. The dogs were fasted for 24 hours prior to the initiation of the glycemic test. Two baseline samples were collected approximately five minutes apart.

Immediately after the last baseline samples were collected, the dogs were fed their diets (amount equal to 1% of body weight) and allowed a maximum of 15 minutes to eat the experimental diets. Dogs not consuming the experimental diet within 15 minutes were excluded from the glycemic test for that day and retested the next day. Additional blood samples were collected at 10, 20, 30, 45, 60, 120, 180, and 240 minutes after the food was consumed.

Experimental Diets. During the stabilization period, dogs were fed an extruded maintenance diet (Eukanuba® Adult Maintenance, The Iams Company, Lewisburg, Ohio, USA) for 7 weeks. During the study period, 5 experimental diets were evaluated. All diets were formulated to contain a similar starch content (30%) from different cereal sources (corn, wheat, barley, rice, and sorghum).

Statistical Analysis. Glucose and insulin levels were analyzed according to split plot analysis for repeated measurements over time.[26] The results of glucose and insulin assays from the two baseline samples were averaged as one baseline value. Area under the curve (AUC) for the glucose and insulin responses was calculated. Statistical significance was considered at $P<0.05$. The data was analyzed with the SAS statistical software package.[27]

Results. The rice diet resulted in the greatest ($P<0.05$) average glucose (**Figure 2**) and glucose AUC (**Figure 3**). In contrast, the sorghum diet resulted in the lowest average glucose (**Figure 2**) and glucose AUC (**Figure 3**). The rice diet resulted in a higher ($P<0.05$) average insulin (**Figure 4**) and insulin AUC (**Figure 5**) compared to other diets. Conversely, the barley diet resulted in the lowest average insulin (**Figure 4**) and insulin AUC (**Figure 5**). The wheat diet generally was intermediate for most response criteria. The corn diet resulted in a relatively low average glucose and glucose AUC but resulted in intermediate insulin responses.

Discussion. Results from this experiment indicate that starch source can influence the postprandial glycemic response in normal dogs. Rice clearly exacer-

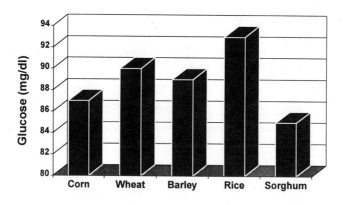

Figure 2. Average postprandial glucose response to selected starch-containing diets (Average = average of baseline, 10, 20, 30, 45, 60, 120, 180, and 240 minute samples).

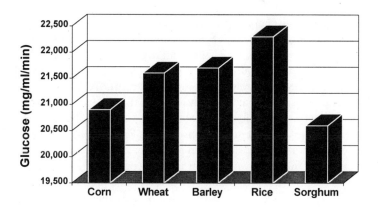

Figure 3. Area under curve (AUC) of postprandial glucose response to selected starch-containing diets.

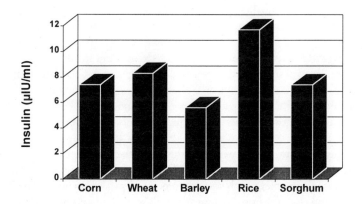

Figure 4. Average postprandial insulin response to selected starch-containing diets (Average = average of baseline, 10, 20, 30, 45, 60, 120, 180, and 240 minute samples).

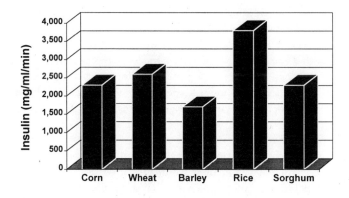

Figure 5. Area under curve (AUC) of postprandial insulin response to selected starch-containing diets.

bated the postprandial glycemic response. Previous studies with humans have indicated that the postprandial rate of glucose absorption was also affected by the characteristics of dietary starch.[28-32] Results from an experiment performed in humans where individuals consumed equivalent amounts of starch (50 g) indicated a greater postprandial glucose response from boiled rice than bread.[33] This is in contrast, however, with other research that generally indicates that wheat is among the highest glycemic response (i.e., glycemic index) foods.[11,14,15,34] This may be explained by the apparent variability in the glycemic response to rice. For example, the glycemic index of two different rice sources has been reported to vary by 26 percentage units.[11] One explanation for this is the variation in amylose content of rice sources. For instance, a diet made of rice with normal-amylose content produced higher overall average glucose and peak glucose level than that of a rice diet containing high-amylose with low fiber content in human subjects.[29,32] Thus, it is plausible that the amylose content was greatest in the rice diet.

The relatively low glycemic response to barley is consistent with the general indication for its use in the diet of human diabetics. Barley is reported to have the lowest glycemic index compared to other starch sources such as corn, wheat, and rice.[35] The glucose and insulin response of human subjects to boiled barley was generally lower than bread.[14] Presumably the extremely low insulin response to barley is due to attenuated absorption of dietarily-derived glucose. The fiber composition and β-glucan content may contribute to alterations in the postprandial rate of glucose absorption and the subsequent insulin response.[15,36] Indeed, the barley diet contained the greatest concentration of fiber and β-glucans of all starch sources.

Limited information is available regarding the influence of sorghum on glycemic response. However, the relatively low blood glucose response by dogs to the sorghum diet is in agreement with research reported by Lakshmi and Vimala.[37] These researchers found that non-insulin dependent diabetic humans had a lower postprandial glucose response when fed sorghum compared to wheat as their carbohydrate source.

Rice-based diets result in significantly higher postprandial glucose and insulin responses. Sorghum generally resulted in the lowest postprandial glucose response while barley resulted in the lowest postprandial insulin response. These findings suggest that the source of starch influences the postprandial glucose and insulin response in dogs. Dietary recommendations for improving glucose control in dogs should include barley and sorghum. Rice as a starch source is contraindicated for those animals with poor glucose control (e.g., diabetes, obesity).

Applications of Starch Technology

Diabetes, obesity, gestation, and aging are all life stages/conditions where proper glucose control may be impaired. Results reported herewith indicate that starch sources can differ in glycemic response. Thus, the potential exists to improve animal health in individuals with compromised glucose tolerance and/or insulin resistance by altering starch source. While further study of the influence of starch source on animals with compromised health is needed, it would be imprudent to ignore the potential health risk associated with rice starch. Reciprocally, the potential health benefit associated with barley and sorghum starches should also not be ignored.

Eukanuba is a registered trademark of The Iams Company.

1. Milla C, Doherty L, Raatz S, Schwarzenberg SJ, Regelmann W, Moran A. Glycemic response to dietary supplements in cystic fibrosis is dependent on the carbohydrate content of the formula. *J Parent Enter Nutr* 1996; 20:182-186.

2. Sunvold GD. Dietary fiber for dogs and cats: An historical perspective. In: Carey DP, Norton SA, Bolser SM, eds. *Recent Advances in Canine and Feline Nutritional Research: Proceedings of the 1996 Iams International Nutrition Symposium.* Wilmington: Orange Frazer Press, 1996; 3-14.

3. McBurney MI, Massimino SP, Field CJ, Sunvold GD, Hayek MG. Modulation of intestinal function and glucose homeostasis in dogs by the ingestion of fermentable dietary fibers. In: Reinhart GA, Carey DP, eds. *Recent Advances in Canine and Feline Nutrition, Vol. II: 1998 Iams Nutrition Symposium Proceedings.* Wilmington: Orange Frazer Press, 1998; 113-122.

4. Nelson RW, Sunvold GD. Effect of carboxymethylcellulose on postprandial glycemic response in healthy dogs. In: Reinhart GA, Carey DP, eds. *Recent Advances in Canine and Feline Nutrition, Vol. II: 1998 Iams Nutrition Symposium Proceedings.* Wilmington: Orange Frazer Press, 1998; 97-102.

5. Rocchini AP, Marker P, Cervenka T. Time course of insulin resistance associated with feeding dogs a high-fat diet. *Am J Physiol* 1997; 272:E147-E154.

6. Swinburn BA, Boyce VL, Bergman RN, Howard BV, Bogardus C. Deterioration in carbohydrate metabolism and lipoprotein changes induced by modern, high fat diet in Pima Indians and Caucasians. *J Clin Endocrin Metab* 1991; 73:156-165.

7. Otto H, Niklas L. Different glycemic responses to carbohydrate-containing food-implications for the dietary treatment of diabetes mellitus. *Hyg (Geneve)* 1980; 38:3424-3429 (in French).

8. Jenkins DJA, Wolever TMS, Taylor RH, Barker H, Fielden H, Baldwin JM, Bowling AC, Newman HC, Jenkins AL, Goff DV. Glycemic index of foods: A physiological basis for carbohydrate exchange. *Am J Clin Nutr* 1981; 34:362-366.

9. Jenkins DJA, Wolever TMS, Jenkins AL, Thorne MJ, Lee R, Kalmosky J, Reichert R, Wong GS. The glycaemic index of foods tested in diabetic patients: A new basis for carbohydrate exchange favouring the use of legumes. *Diabetologia* 1983; 24:257-264.

10. Wolever TMS, Bolognesi C. Prediction of glucose and insulin responses of normal subjects after consuming mixed meals varying in energy, protein, fat, carbohydrate and glycemic index. *J Nutr* 1996; 126:2807-2812.

11. Järvi AE, Karlström YE, Granfeldt YE, Björck IME, Vessby BOH, Asp N-GL. The influence of food structure on postprandial metabolism in patients with non-insulin-dependent diabetes mellitus. *Am J Clin Nutr* 1995; 61:837-842.

12. Bantle JP, Laine DC, Castle GW, Thomas JW, Hoogwerf BJ, Goetz FC. Postprandial glucose and insulin responses to meals containing different carbohydrates in normal and diabetic subjects. *N Engl J Med* 1983; 309:7-12.

References

13. Wolever TMS, Miller JB. Sugars and blood glucose control. *Am J Clin Nutr* 1995; 62:212S-227S.

14. Wolever TMS, Bolognesi C. Source and amount of carbohydrate affect postprandial glucose and insulin in normal subjects. *J Nutr* 1996; 126:2798-2806.

15. Liljeberg HGM, Granfeldt YE, Björck IME. Products based on a high fiber barley genotype, but not on common barley or oats, lower postprandial glucose and insulin responses in healthy humans. *J Nutr* 1996; 126:458-466.

16. Bergman RN, Ider YZ, Bowden CR, Cobelli C. Quantitative estimation of insulin sensitivity. *Am J Physiol* 1979; 236:E667-E677.

17. Rottiers R, Mattheeuws D, Kaneko JJ, Vermeulen A. Glucose uptake and insulin secretory responses to intravenous glucose loads in the dog. *Am J Vet Res* 1981; 42:155-158.

18. Nelson RW, Ihle SL, Lewis LD, Salisbury SK, Miller T, Bergdall V, Bottoms GD. Effects of dietary fiber supplementation on glycemic control in dogs with alloxan-induced diabetes mellitus. *Am J Vet Res* 1991; 52:2060-2066.

19. Maskell IE, Winner LM, Markwell PJ, Boehler S. Does the canning process alter the physiological effects of dietary fiber in the dog? *J Nutr* 1994; 124:2704S-2706S.

20. Blaxter AC, Cripps PJ, Gruffydd-Jones TJ. Dietary fibre and post prandial hyperglycaemia in normal and diabetic dogs. *J Sm Anim Pract* 1990; 31:229-233.

21. Holste LC, Nelson RW, Feldman EC, Bottoms GD. Effects of dry, soft moist, and canned dog foods on postprandial blood glucose and insulin concentrations in healthy dog. *Am J Vet Res* 1989; 50:984-989.

22. Ceriello A, Giugliano D, Quatraro A, Donzella C, Dipalo G, Lefebvre PJ. Vitamin E reduction of protein glycosylation in diabetics: New prospect for prevention of diabetic complications. *Diabetes Care* 1991; 14:68-72.

23. Jain SK, McVie R, Jaramillo JJ, Palmer M, Smith T. Effect of modest vitamin E supplementation on blood glycated hemoglobin and triglyceride levels and red cell indices in type 1 diabetic patients. *J Amer Coll Nutr* 1996; 15:458-461.

24. Brun J-F, Guintrand-Hugret R, Fons C, Carvajal J, Fedou C, Fussellier M, Bardet L, Orsetti A. Effects of oral zinc gluconate on glucose effectiveness and insulin sensitivity in humans. *Biol Trace Element Res* 1995; 47:385-391.

25. Thompson KH, Godin DV. Micronutrients and antioxidants in the progression of diabetes. *Nutr Res* 1995; 15:1377-1410.

26. Gill JL, Half HD. Analysis of repeated measurements of animals. *J Anim Sci* 1971; 30:331-336.

27. SAS *User's Guide: Statistics*. Cary: SAS Institute, Inc., 1989.

28. Behall KM, Schofield DJ, Yuhaniak I, Canary J. Diets containing high amylose vs amylopectin starch: Effect on metabolic variables in human subjects. *Am J Clin Nutr* 1989; 49:337-344.

29. Goddard MS, Young G, Marcus R. The effect of amylose content on insulin and glucose responses to ingested rice. *Am J Clin Nutr* 1984; 39:388-392.

30. Devi K. Comparitive observations on blood sugar level in normal adults following common cereal and millet diets. M.S. Thesis, A.P. Agril. University, Hyderabad, India, 1972.

31. Behall KM, Howe JC. Effect of long-term consumption of amylose vs. amylopectin starch on metabolic variables in human subjects. *Am J Clin Nutr* 1995; 61:334-340.

32. Coulston AM, Hollenbeck CB, Liu GC, Williams RA, Starich GH, Mazzaferri EL, Reaven GM. Effect of dietary carbohydrate on plasma glucose, insulin, and gastric inhibitory polypeptide responses to test meals in subjects with noninsulin-dependent diabetes mellitus. *Am J Clin Nutr* 1984; 40:965-970.

33. Goni I, Garcia-Alonso A, Saura-Calixto F. A starch hydrolysis procedure to estimate glycemic index. *Nutr Res* 1997; 17:427-437.

34. Wolever TMS, Jenkins DJA, Jenkins AL, Josse RG. The glycemic index: Methodology and clinical implications. *Am J Clin Nutr* 1991; 54:846-854.

35. Powell K, Miller JB. International tables of glycemic index. *Am J Clin Nutr* 1995; 62:871S.

36. Halfrisch J, Scholfield DJ, Behall KM. Diets containing soluble oat extracts improve glucose and insulin responses of moderately hypercholesterolemic men and women. *Am J Clin Nutr* 1995; 61:379-384.

37. Lakshmi KB, Vimala V. Hypoglycemic effect of selected sorghum recipes. *Nutr Res* 1996; 16:1651-1658.

Obesity

Assessment of Obesity and Associated Metabolic Disorders

Gregory D. Sunvold, PhD
Research Nutritionist, Research and Development
The Iams Company, Lewisburg, Ohio, USA

Guy F. Bouchard, DMV, MS, DACT
Sinclair Research Center, Columbia, Missouri, USA

Gastrointestinal, renal, and dermatological conditions are physiological disorders that are readily accepted as diseases. As a result, clinical interest in treatment of these diseases is obvious and seldom questioned. The recognition of obesity as a disease, however, has yet to come to full acceptance. In the human, overweight individuals are often assumed to be gluttonous and without self-control. As a consequence, obesity is not thought of as a disease but rather a psychologically-induced phenomena. Since these same phenomena are unlikely to occur in dogs and cats, the presence of overweightness in dogs and cats is a physiological example of why obesity must be treated as a disease.

Introduction

The prevalence of overweightness in dogs and cats has been reported to occur in up to 40% of dogs and cats seen by veterinarians.[1-6] Therefore, the clinical relevance of this disease is astounding. Since obesity is fundamentally related to the diet, information on how to improve dietary formulations to prevent or treat obesity is useful in improving the health and well-being of the dog and the cat.

For purposes of this discussion, overweightness will be defined as being greater than 5% over the normal or ideal body weight of an individual. Being greater than 20% over the ideal body weight will be defined as being obese. Overweightness can be caused by 1) overeating, 2) endocrine disorders, 3) loss in normal body thermogenesis, 4) lack of physical activity, or 5) any combination of the previous factors. Some of these factors are psychologically influenced within the animal, others are likely to be genetically determined, still others may be induced by dietary factors. Determination of the causative factors of overweightness is the key to the treatment of obesity. Treatments employed without proper assessment of the precipitating cause(s) have a good chance of failure.

Causes

Overweightness is a chronic condition that usually takes months and sometimes years to occur. Overweightness can be detrimental to optimal health

Detrimental Effects

from several perspectives: increased blood pressure,[7-10] increased blood triglycerides,[11] impaired locomotor functions, skeletal stress,[5,12] increased dystocia,[13] and difficulty in self-regulation of body temperature. In addition to the detrimental effects of carrying too much weight, secondary physiological problems are often associated with overweightness. These problems include cardiac disease,[5,14] diabetes mellitus,[15,16] and thyroid dysfunction.[17]

Traditional
Treatment

Common treatment modalities often include the use of high fiber-containing diets.[18,19] This type of treatment is not always effective (see chapter by Center[20]) and can add additional problems to compromised animals. Problems include the following: 1) constipation, 2) excessive stool output/frequency, 3) poor skin and hair coat, 4) decreased nutrient digestibility, and 5) decreased mineral absorption.[21]

Determination
of
Overweightness

Accurate assessment of overweightness is important for achieving optimal treatment and for well-controlled research. A basic form of assessing overweightness is to compare body weight to what is considered normal. To do this, a normal or "ideal" body weight must be defined by the examiner. Therefore, a subjective assessment of the animal is made. Another form of assessing overweightness is accomplished by assessing the body condition score (BCS) of the animal. An advantage of this system is that it is relatively simple. In a clinical setting, comparison of an owner's pet to a predefined chart (**Figures 1** and **2**) can improve the ability of the owner to honestly assess the body weight condition of an animal. Use of these charts can also aid in providing motivation to get their animal to lose weight. The disadvantage of BCS assessment is that the technique has relatively low sensitivity compared to more rigorous body composition determination techniques. Therefore, when challenged with the need to precisely and accurately determine body composition of an individual, other techniques must be considered.

Several techniques to determine body composition have been utilized. The definitive technique used to determine body composition has been the dissection method. Because this technique can only be used one time on an individual it has limited usefulness. Other techniques have been developed that can be used multiple times on an individual and, therefore, be useful in longitudinal studies. The challenge in using these techniques is knowing how well they relate to the actual body composition.

Techniques for
Assessing Body
Composition

Three major components are of interest when assessing whole body composition: muscle or lean body mass (LBM), fat mass (FM), and bone mineral content (BMC). These three compartments make up the total body pool. The LBM is the largest pool (**Tables 1** and **2**) except in extreme cases of obesity. As weight loss occurs, loss of FM with minimal loss of LBM and BMC is most desirable.

Figure 1. Body condition score assessment of dogs.

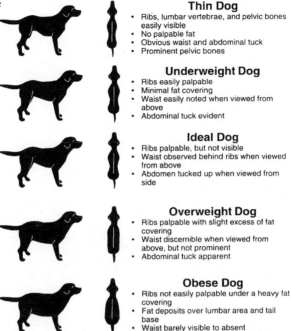

Thin Dog
- Ribs, lumbar vertebrae, and pelvic bones easily visible
- No palpable fat
- Obvious waist and abdominal tuck
- Prominent pelvic bones

Underweight Dog
- Ribs easily palpable
- Minimal fat covering
- Waist easily noted when viewed from above
- Abdominal tuck evident

Ideal Dog
- Ribs palpable, but not visible
- Waist observed behind ribs when viewed from above
- Abdomen tucked up when viewed from side

Overweight Dog
- Ribs palpable with slight excess of fat covering
- Waist discernible when viewed from above, but not prominent
- Abdominal tuck apparent

Obese Dog
- Ribs not easily palpable under a heavy fat covering
- Fat deposits over lumbar area and tail base
- Waist barely visible to absent
- No abdominal tuck; may exhibit obvious abdominal distention

Figure 2. Body condition score assessment of cats.

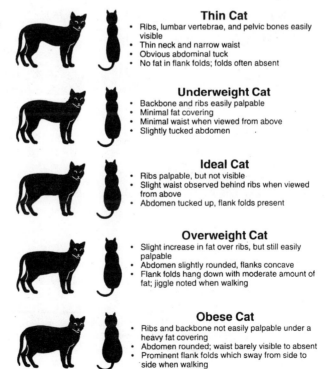

Thin Cat
- Ribs, lumbar vertebrae, and pelvic bones easily visible
- Thin neck and narrow waist
- Obvious abdominal tuck
- No fat in flank folds; folds often absent

Underweight Cat
- Backbone and ribs easily palpable
- Minimal fat covering
- Minimal waist when viewed from above
- Slightly tucked abdomen

Ideal Cat
- Ribs palpable, but not visible
- Slight waist observed behind ribs when viewed from above
- Abdomen tucked up, flank folds present

Overweight Cat
- Slight increase in fat over ribs, but still easily palpable
- Abdomen slightly rounded, flanks concave
- Flank folds hang down with moderate amount of fat; jiggle noted when walking

Obese Cat
- Ribs and backbone not easily palpable under a heavy fat covering
- Abdomen rounded; waist barely visible to absent
- Prominent flank folds which sway from side to side when walking

Table 1. Actual body composition of dogs.

Age	LBM,[a] %	Body Fat, %	BMC,[b] %	Reference
Newborn	88.6	6.0	5.4	Sheng and Huggins, 1971[4]
10-days-old	88.2	6.7	5.1	Sheng and Huggins, 1971[4]
46-days-old	73.4	19.1	7.2	Sheng and Huggins, 1971[4]
< 3-months-old	88.4	8.2	3.3	Wedekind et al., 1992[32]
177–185-days-old	69.6	21.5	8.9	Sheng and Huggins, 1971[4]
Adult	79.4	11.5	9.1	Sheng and Huggins, 1971[4]
Adult	ND/NR[c]	20.1	ND/NR	Harrison et al., 1936[48]
Adult	ND/NR	15.4	ND/NR	Behnke, 1941-42[49]

[a]LBM = lean body mass; calculated as % water + % protein
[b]BMC = bone mineral content; assumed to be equivalent to % ash
[c]ND/NR = not determined/not reported

Table 2. Actual body composition of cats.

Age	LBM,[a] %	Body Fat, %	BMC,[b] %	Reference
Newborn	95.6	1.8	ND/NR[c]	Widdowson, 1950[50]
Newborn	93.0	3.6	ND/NR	Kienzle et al. (1991)[51]
1-day-old	94.5	1.7	2.6%	Thomas (1915) as reported by Munday (1994)[52]
9-days-old	92.7	4.0	2.2	Thomas (1915) as reported by Munday (1994)[52]
14-days-old	88.8	7.1	2.5	Thomas (1915) as reported by Munday (1994)[52]
103-days-old	86.8	7.9	3.2	Thomas (1915) as reported by Munday (1994)[52]
4–12-weeks-old	81.0	12.0	ND/NR	Kienzle et al. (1991)[51]
12–14-weeks-old	83.6	10.9	ND/NR	Jansen et al. (1975)[53]
Adult	83.3	13.0	ND/NR	Spray and Widdowson (1950)[54]
Adult	86.8	7.9	ND/NR	Hatai (1917) as reported by Pace and Rathbun (1945)[55]
Adult	ND/NR	12.0	ND/NR	Kienzle et al. (1991)[51]
Adult	79.6	16.8	3.6	Wedekind et al. (1992)[32]

[a]LBM = lean body mass; calculated as % water + % protein
[b]BMC = bone mineral content; assumed to be equivalent to % ash
[c]ND/NR = not determined/not reported

Several research techniques often used in humans only distinguish between fat and non-fat tissue (muscle plus bone). These two compartments are referred to as the fat and fat-free mass of the individual.

Current techniques for assessing body composition include 1) anthropometry, 2) densitometry, 3) hydrometry (total body water), 4) body potassium, 5) total body electroconductivity (TOBEC), 6) bioelectrical impedance, 7) regional imaging analysis, and 8) absorptiometry techniques. A brief description of each technique follows.

Anthropometry. This technique involves the measurement of skin and subcutaneous fat thickness to estimate percent-body fat. It is currently used in humans to provide a rapid, inexpensive assessment of percent-body fat. An experienced technician uses a skinfold caliper to measure adipose tissue thickness in predefined sites. Use of skinfold measurements requires extensive validation and technician expertise to insure accurate and reliable results. A lack of technical expertise and technique standardization makes this method marginally useful for dogs and cats.

Densitometry. Densitometry is a technique which allows indirect estimation of the fat and fat-free components of the body. The weight of an individual in water is used to calculate body density. This density value will range between the density of pure fat (0.9007 g/cc) and pure bone (approximately 3.000 g/cc[22]). Consequently, this density value is used to estimate the percent-body fat and fat-free mass of the individual. Advantages of this technique include its high reliability. An obvious disadvantage for dogs and cats is the great difficulty in applying the technique.

Total Body Water. Assessment of total body water is a technique that is based on the assumption that fat is anhydrous and that water occupies a relatively fixed fraction of the fat-free body.[23] Doubly labeled water (^2H_2O, $H_2^{18}O$) or radioactive water (^3H_2O) is consumed by the subject. The dilution of this water by the water present in the breath, blood, or urine is then used to calculate the total body pool of water. Lean body mass is then estimated from the total body pool of water. This technique has been used to assess the lean body mass of athletic dogs.[24]

Body Potassium. Another method of assessing body composition involves the detection of nuclear energy emitted from an isotope of potassium (i.e., potassium 40: ^{40}K).[25] In this procedure, the body is surrounded by a liquid that can convert nuclear energy emitted from gamma-rays of ^{40}K to light energy. The light energy is then counted in pulses by a whole body liquid scintillation counter. From this, the amount of potassium in the body can be determined since it is known that ^{40}K represents 0.0118% of naturally occurring potassium. Since the human body has been determined to contain a defined amount of K per unit of fat-free mass (2.50 g/Kg for females, 2.66 g/Kg for males), the fat-free mass can be calculated once the quantity of ^{40}K has been determined.[25] While this technique has been used successfully on humans[26] and animals,[27] its application is limited to those who have access to the relatively sophisticated equipment required. Additionally, the technique does not directly assess each one of the three body components, LBM, FM, and BMC.

Total Body Electroconductivity. In this technique an individual is passed through an electrical field. The conductance of electricity in this field is related to the body water content of the individual. Therefore, the LBM can be estimated from the electrical conductivity of the individual. An advantage of TOBEC is its high level of precision. The following four major limitations exist for the application of TOBEC to dogs and cats: 1) results from this technique are greatly dependent on the subject population used to develop the predictive equations, 2) TOBEC instruments are relatively expensive and inaccessible, 3) only LBM is measured with this technique, and 4) special animal handling techniques would need to be developed for animals analyzed with TOBEC.

Bioelectrical Impedance. This technique operates on the principle that electrical resistivity in fat is much greater than resistivity in the fat-free body. Electrodes attached to the body measure electrical resistivity through an individual's body. This value is then used in a predetermined regression equation to predict the LBM of an individual. This technique offers portability and relative ease of use.[28] However, regression equations would need to be developed before the technique could be applied to dogs and cats. Additionally, bioelectrical impedance only provides a measurement of LBM.

Regional Imaging Analysis. Ultrasound, computer assisted axial tomography (CAT), and magnetic resonance imaging (MRI) are techniques that are often used to determine regional body composition. Ultrasound is used extensively to evaluate body fat deposits and areas of selected muscles.[29] Ultrasound gives poor image quality but is relatively cheap, portable technology. Further development of this technology would be necessary before routine use of it would be feasible with dogs and cats.

CAT requires the use of several x-rays to make transectional images of the body. These images discriminate well between bone, muscle, and adipose tissue,[29] but resultant high exposure to x-rays limits the use of CAT. MRI uses a magnetic field to assess the presence of hydrogen nuclei and the environment in which they exist. The magnetic "signature" of the hydrogen nucleus changes with association of free water or as a component of triglycerides.[29] The resulting image is similar to CAT, but since x-rays are not used, it is highly preferable. The drawbacks of MRI include extreme equipment expense and accessibility. Long term, MRI is an exciting technique for obtaining high precision imaging.

Absorptiometry Techniques. Dual photon absorptiometry (DPA) has been used to assess spine and femur bone mineral content.[30] This has been adapted to evaluate osteoporosis.[28] Its predecessor, single photon absorptiometry (SPA), was limited to bone mineral assessment of bones in the forearm.[30] Dual Energy X-ray Absorptiometry (DEXA) represented yet another advancement in that it is capable of whole body as well as regional body analysis of the three major body tissues, BMC, body fat, and LBM.

Of these techniques, DEXA has much appeal as it is relatively quick, determines the three major components of body composition, LBM, FM, and BMC, and is highly repeatable. However, little validation of this method with dogs and cats has been performed.

Present Knowledge Regarding Body Composition

Several groups have reported the body chemical composition of both developing and adult dogs and cats (**Tables 1** and **2**). In general, LBM declines and body fat increases as the animal develops into an adult. Interestingly, LBM is generally greater in cats than dogs. This difference may be related to several factors including: 1) the highly carnivorous nature of the cat, 2) the higher protein content of feline versus canine diets, and 3) differences in metabolism between cats and dogs.[31]

As previously indicated, little information is available regarding validation of body composition methods for dogs and cats. The DEXA method holds great promise for assessing body composition since it is highly reliable, minimally dependent on technician expertise, repeatable without side effects, and extremely rapid. The validation of this method has only been attempted once with one dog and two cats.[32] Thus, validation of this method is greatly needed to understand its potential strengths and weaknesses. The following experiments were designed to assess the value of DXA in determining dog and cat body composition.

DEXA Validation

Animals. Fifteen young adult female, mongrel dogs (18.2±1.6 kg) and 15 young adult female and male cats (2.9±1.4 kg) were used.

Chemical Analyses. Chemical composition of whole body homogenate samples was determined using standard AOAC methods for protein, moisture, fat, and calcium.[33] Chemically determined values for protein and moisture were added together as an indication of lean body mass (LBM). Chemical analysis for fat was used as an indicator of body fat. The chemically determined calcium concentration was divided by 0.4 to estimate the hydroxyapatite concentration. Similar to Wedekind et al.,[32] hydroxapatite concentration was assumed to be equivalent to bone mineral content (BMC). Body composition values derived from this procedure were considered actual values.

Body Composition Assessment

A Hologic QDR 2000 Plus DEXA unit was used to perform whole body scans of each animal. Scans of dogs were performed using two modes, single beam, and array. Scans of cats were performed using human infant and human adult software. Body composition values derived from this procedure were considered predicted values.

Statistical Analysis

The least significant difference test of the General Linear Models procedure in SAS[34] was used to compare means between DEXA predicted values and actual (chemical) measurements. The Regression procedure in SAS[34] was used to determine the correlation between DEXA predicted values and actual measurements.

Dogs. For LBM and body fat, actual and DEXA values were similar (**Figures 3** and **4**) and were highly correlated ($R^2 > 0.85$). The single beam scanning mode of DEXA resulted in values numerically closer to the actual values than did the array scanning mode.

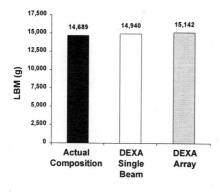

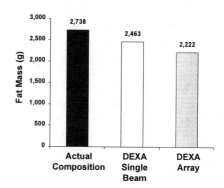

Figure 3. Predicted (DEXA) compared to actual lean body mass (LBM) values for dogs.

Figure 4. Predicted (DEXA) compared to actual fat mass values for dogs.

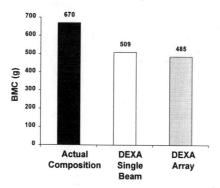

Figure 5. Predicted (DEXA) compared to actual bone mineral content (BMC) values for dogs.

DEXA predicted values for BMC were substantially (>20%) lower than actual composition values (**Figure 5**). BMC as predicted by DEXA resulted in a relatively low correlation ($R^2 < 0.30$) with actual BMC. Results for BMC are somewhat surprising. The inaccurate prediction and low correlation of BMC may be due to a difference in bone mineral density of human reference values for which the software was developed.

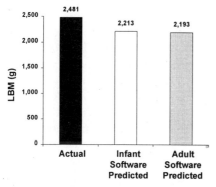

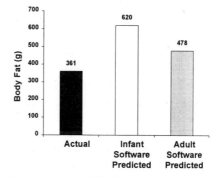

Figure 6. Predicted (DEXA) compared to actual lean body mass (LBM) values for cats.

Figure 7. Predicted (DEXA) compared to actual fat mass values for cats.

In sum, LBM and body fat is estimated quite well in dogs by DEXA, especially when the single beam scanning mode is used. Results from this experiment did not indicate a highly accurate or precise prediction of BMC in dogs.

Cats. Body fat and LBM as predicted by DEXA using either software source (i.e., human or infant) were similar to actual values (*Figures* **6** and **7**). DEXA predicted values for body fat and LBM were highly correlated ($R^2>0.85$) with actual values regardless of the software that was used. DEXA values for LBM were within 12% of the actual values. While the DEXA software source used to determine LBM did not seem to influence prediction accuracy, the software source used to determine body fat, at least numerically, appeared to influence prediction accuracy. DEXA infant software resulted in body fat predicted values being nearly twice the actual body fat values, while DEXA adult software resulted in predicted values within 35% of the actual values. Therefore, to assess changes in body fat of cats, the adult software would be preferable.

DEXA predicted values for BMC were highly correlated ($R^2>0.85$) with actual values regardless of the software that was used. The predicted values for BMC were substantially lower from the adult software, but not from the infant software, than the actual values (*Figure* **8**). These results indicate that infant software for DEXA would be preferred when assessing BMC.

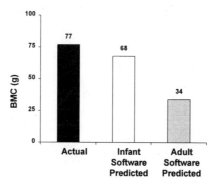

Figure 8. Predicted (DEXA) compared to actual bone mineral content (BMC) values for cats.

Obesity is associated with several metabolic disorders. Each of these disorders constitutes a health risk to the animal. Maintaining optimal body composition during weight loss presents a better visual appearance of the animal. However, greater loss of fat mass compared to LBM may also help minimize obesity associated metabolic disorders. Use of body composition techniques such as DEXA will allow the study of nutritional strategies to alleviate obesity and thus reverse metabolic disorders associated with obesity. The remaining discussion outlines three metabolic disorders that occur with excessive fat accumulation and concludes with dietary recommendations for weight loss.

Glucose Tolerance. Disturbances in normal glucose metabolism through hyperinsulinemia and insulin resistance is relatively common in obese humans.[35] Additionally, research with humans indicates that individuals whose postprandial insulin response is increased have a greater propensity to control their energy balance.[36] Empirically, it is difficult to separate diabetic effects of insulin resistance from obesity. It has been demonstrated in both obese dogs and cats that glucose tolerance is impaired.[15,16,37] Biourge et al.[38] demonstrated that insulin resistance can be decreased when obese cats are returned to normal body weight. This study was done using healthy, ideal body weight cats fattened to obesity. However, obesity may act as a causitive factor in precipitating non-insulin dependent diabetes mellitus in humans.[35] In this case, the impaired glucose metabolism would be irreversible. Therefore, nutritional strategies to improve glucose tolerance in some obese individuals would be useful both during and after weight loss.

Hepatic Lipidosis. Obesity predisposes cats to a greater risk of hepatic lipidosis. Biourge et al.[39] clearly demonstrated that a substantial reduction in food intake by obese cats resulted in excessive fat infiltration of the liver. Biourge et al.[40,41] went on to report that dietary components may play a role in influencing fatty acid accumulation. Further discussions of dietary factors that may be important in controlling feline hepatic lipidosis are covered elsewhere in this proceeding by Bruckner and coworkers.[42] Since hepatic lipidosis is a concern during feline weight loss, proper adherence to feeding guidelines and careful clinical monitoring is essential to safe weight loss (see chapter by Center[20]). A commercial weight loss product for felines has been evaluated for its ability to limit induction of hepatic lipidosis.[43,44]

Hypertriglyceridemia. Closely associated with hepatic lipidosis are disturbances in fatty acid metabolism. These disturbances are clinically manifested by hypertriglyceridemia. Indeed, Pazak et al.[45] reported that cats with idiopathic hepatic lipidosis also had increased blood triglyceride levels. A dietary solution to hypertriglyceridemia is to simply reduce fat intake. Another potential solution is to increase consumption of omega-3 fatty acids and fish oil. Berry[46] reviewed the effects of supplementing n-3 fatty acids and fish oil in diabetic patients and found that of 22 reported studies, 19 resulted in decreased triglycerides while only three studies did not report an effect. Therefore, in order to achieve optimal blood triglyceride reduction, one should consider simultaneously reducing total dietary fat as well as the ratio of n-6:n-3 fatty acids.

Goals During Weight Loss

A new approach regarding weight loss is suggested (**Figure 9**). This approach includes rapid weight loss done in a safe manner. This will help achieve owner compliance and assure animal well-being. Additionally, this approach includes feeding a diet that avoids the traditional side effects associated with high fiber.

To achieve this new approach to weight loss, dietary therapies should include: 1) normal fiber levels, 2) documentation of diet's effectiveness, and 3) documentation of diet's safety (e.g., normal blood chemistries and no incidence of hepatic lipidosis). Loss of body fat with minimal loss of LBM should occur during weight loss. A technique that has been substantiated to reliably assess body composition is DEXA. Its current use is oriented toward research studies to determine diet efficacy. As costs of this technology decrease and accessibility increases, its use in clinical settings will occur.

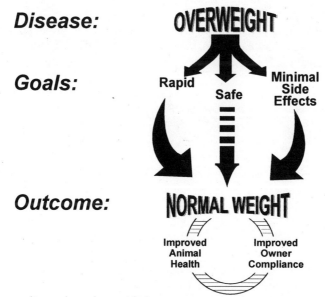

Figure 9. A new paradigm to dog and cat weight loss.

Conclusions

Proper assessment of body composition is important for researchers and clinicians. Dietary strategies that promote excellent body composition while weight loss occurs should be the primary objective in the development of weight loss diets for dogs and cats and the application of those diets by clinicians. Additionally, dietary strategies proven to minimize the risk of hepatic lipidosis should be utilized to maintain optimal animal well-being. Dietary strategies such as high fiber diets should be avoided as they are associated with detrimental side effects.

References

1. Sloth C. Practical management of obesity in dogs and cats. *J Sm An Pract* 1992; 33:178-182.

2. Glickman LT, Sonnenschein EG, Glickman NW, Donoghue S, Goldschmidt MH. Pattern of diet and obesity in female adult pet dogs. *Vet Clin Nutr* 1995; 2:6-13.

3. Mason E. Obesity in pet dogs. *Vet Rec* 1970; 86:612-616.

4. MacEwen EG. Physiologic and metabolic aspects of obesity. *Proc 6th Ann ACVIM* 1988; 663.

5. Edney ATB, Smith PM. Study of obesity in dogs visiting veterinary practices in the United Kingdom. *Vet Rec* 1986; 118:391-396.

6. Brown RG. Dealing with canine obesity. *Can Vet J* 1989; 30:973-975.

7. Brands MW, Hall JE. Insulin resistance, hyperinsulinemia, and obesity-associated hypertension. *J Am Soc Neph* 1992; 3:1064-1077.

8. Hall JE, Brands MW, Hildebrandt DA, Mizelle HL. Obesity-associated hypertension. *Hypertension* 1992; 19:I45-I55.

9. Rocchini AP. Insulin resistance, obesity and hypertension. *J Nutr* 1995; 125:1718S-1724S.

10. West DB, Wehberg KE, Kieswetter K, Granger JP. Blunted natriuretic response to an acute sodium load in obese hypertensive dogs. *Hypertension* 1992; 19:I96-I100.

11. Chikamune T, Katamoto H, Ohashi F, Shimada Y. Serum lipid and lipoprotein concentrations in obese dogs. *J Vet Med Sci* 1995; 57:595-598.

12. Joshua JO. The obese dog and some clinical repercussions. *J Sm An Pract* 1970; 11:601-606.

13. Clutton RE. The medical implications of canine obesity and their relevance to anesthesia. *Brit Vet J* 1988; 144:21-28. ,

14. Rocchini AP, Moorehead C, Wentz E, Deremer S. Obesity-induced hypertension in the dog. *Hypertension* 1987; 9:64-68.

15. Mattheeuws D, Rottiers R, Baeyens D, Vermeulen A. Glucose tolerance and insulin response in obese dogs. *J Am Anim Hosp Assoc* 1984a; 20:287-293.

16. Mattheeuws D, Rottiers R, Kaneko JJ, Vermeulen A. Diabetes mellitus in dogs: Relationship of obesity to glucose tolerance and insulin response. *Am J Vet Res* 1984; 45:98-103.

17. Ferguson DC. Nonthyroidal illness and drug effects on thyroid function tests: Should we pay attention? *Proc 14th ACVIM* 1996; 89-92(Abstract).

18. Borne AT, Wolfsheimer KJ, Truett AA, Kiene J, Wojciechowski T, Davenport DJ, Ford RB, West DB. Differential metabolic effects of energy restriction in dogs using diets varying in fat and fiber content. *Obes Res* 1996; 4:337-345.

19. Ballèvre O, Barrie J, Piguet-Welsch C, Nash AS, Anantharaman-Barr G. Body composition during a weight reduction programme in obese dogs. *BSAVA Congress Proc* 1994; 148.

20. Center SA. Safe weight loss in cats. In: Reinhart GA, Carey DP. *Recent Advances in Canine and Feline Nutrition, Vol. II: 1998 Iams Nutrition Symposium Proceedings.* Wilmington: Orange Frazer Press, 1998; 165-182.

21. Sunvold GD. Dietary fiber for dogs and cats: An historical perspective. In: Carey DP, Norton SA, Bolser SM, eds. *Recent Advances in Canine and Feline Nutritional Research: Proceedings of the 1996 Iams International Nutrition Symposium.* Wilmington: Orange Frazer Press, 1996; 3-14.

22. Brozek J, Grande J, Anderson JP, Keys A. Densitometric analysis of body composition: Revision of some quantitative assumptions. *Ann New York Acad Sci* 1963; 110:113.

23. Lukaski HC. Methods for the assessment of human body composition: Traditional and new. *Am J Clin Nutr* 1987; 46:537-556.

24. Hinchcliffe KW, Reinhart GA, Burr JR, Schreier CJ, Swenson RA. Metabolizable energy intake and sustained energy expenditure in Alaskan sled dogs during heavy exertion in the cold. *Am J Vet Res* 1997; 58:(in press).

25. Forbes GB. *Human Body Composition: Growth, Aging, Nutrition and Activity.* New York: Springer-Verlag, Inc., 1987.

26. Flynn MA, Nolph GB, Krause G. Comparison of body composition measured by total body potassium and infrared interactance. *J Amer Coll Nutr* 1995; 14:652-655.

27. DiCostanzo A, Lipsey RJ, Siemens MG, Meiske JC, Hedrick HB. Prediction of carcass and empty body composition of steers by ^{40}K emisson detection. *J Anim Sci* 1995; 73:2882-2887.

28. Jensen MD. Research techniques for body composition assessment. *J Am Dietetic Assoc* 1992; 92:454-460.

29. Fuller MF, Fowler PA, McNeil G, Foster MA. Imaging techniques for the assessment of body composition. *J Nutr* 1994; 124:1546S-1550S.

30. Lohman TG. *Advances in Body Composition Assessment.* Monograph No. 3. Champaign: Human Kinetics Publishers, 1992; 25-36.

31. Morris JG, Rogers QR. Why is the nutrition of cats different from that of dogs? *Tijdschrift Voor Diergeneeskunde* 1991; 116:64S-67S.

32. Wedekind K, Toll P, Richardson D, Burkholder W. Validation of dual energy x-ray absorptiometry as a quantitative measure of body composition in small subjects. *J Bone Min Res* 1992; 7:5253(Abstr.).

33. Association of Official Analytical Chemists. *Official Methods of Analysis,* Arlington, VA, 1994.

34. *SAS User's Guide: Statistics.* Cary: SAS Institute Inc, 1990.

35. Plaisted CS, Istfan NW. Metabolic abnormalities of obesity. In: Blackburn GL, Kanders BS, eds. *Obesity: Pathophysiology, Psychology, and Treatment.* New York: Chapman and Hall, 1994; 80-97.

36. Tremblay A, Nadeau A, Deprés JP, Bouchard C. Hyperinsulinemia and regulation of energy balance. *Am J Clin Nutr* 1995; 61:827-830.

37. Nelson RW, Himsel CA, Feldman EC, Bottoms GD. Glucose tolerance and insulin response in normal-weight and obese cats. *Am J Vet Res* 1990; 51:1357-1362.

38. Biourge V, Nelson RW, Feldman EC, Willits NH, Morris JG, Rogers QR. Effect of weight gain and subsequent weight loss on glucose tolerance and insulin response in cats. *J Vet Intern Med* 1997; 11:86-91.

39. Biourge VC, Groff JM, Munn RJ, Kirk CA, Nyland TG, Madeiros VA, Morris JG, Rogers QR. Experimental induction of hepatic lipidosis in cats. *Am J Vet Res* 1994; 55:1291-1302.

40. Biourge VC, Massat B, Groff JM, Morris JG, Rogers QR. Effects of protein, lipid, or carbohydrate supplementation on hepatic lipid accumulation during rapid weight loss in obese cats. *Am J Vet Res* 1994b; 55:1406-1415.

41. Biourge V, Groff JM, Fisher C, Bee D, Morris JG, Rogers QR. Nitrogen balance, plasma free amino acid concentrations and urinary orotic acid excretion during long-term fasting in cats. *J Nutr* 1994; 124:1094-1103.

42. Bruckner GG, Szabo J, Sunvold GD. Implications of nutrition on feline hepatic fatty acid metabolism. In: Reinhart GA, Carey DP, eds. *Recent Advances in Canine and Feline Nutrition, Vol. II: 1998 Iams Nutrition Symposium Proceedings.* Wilmington: Orange Frazer Press, 1998; 149-164.

43. Sunvold GD, Bouchard G. Effectiveness and safety of a low fiber, low calorie diet for feline weight loss. *Proc 15th ACVIM* 1997; 696.

44. Bouchard GF, Sunvold GD, Daristotle L. Dietary modification of feline obesity with a low fat, low fiber diet. In: Reinhart GA, Carey DP, eds. *Recent Advances in Canine and Feline Nutrition, Vol. II: 1998 Iams Nutrition Symposium Proceedings.* Wilmington: Orange Frazer Press, 1998; 183-192.

45. Pazak HE, Bartges JW, Scott MA, Cornelius LC, Huber TL, Gross K. Characterization of serum lipoprotein profiles of healthy adult cats and idopathic feline hepatic lipidosis patients. *Waltham Intl Symp* 1997; 72.

46. Berry EM. Dietary fatty acids in the management of diabetes mellitus. *Am J Clin Nutr* 1997; 66:991S-997S.

47. Sheng H-P, Huggins RA. Growth of the beagle: Changes in chemical composition. *Growth* 1971; 25:369-376.

48. Harrison HE, Darrow DC, Yannet H. The total electrolyte content of animals and its probable relation to the distribution of body water. *J Biol Chem* 1936; 113:515-529.

49. Behnke Jr AR. Physiologic studies pertaining to deep sea diving and aviation, especially in relation to the fat content and composition of the body. *Harvey Lectures* 1942; 37:198-226.

50. Widdowson EM. Chemical composition of newly born mammals. *Nature* 1950; 6:626-628.

51. Kienzle E, Stratmann B, Meyer H. Body composition of cats as a basis for factorial calculations of energy and nutrient requirements for growth. *J Nutr* 1991; 121:S122-S123.

52. Munday HS. Assessment of body-composition in cats and dogs. *Int J Obes* 1994; 18:S14-S21.

53. Jansen GR, Deuth MA, Ward GM, Johnson DE. Protein quality studies in growing kittens. *Nutr Rep Int* 1975; 11:525-536.

54. Spray CM, Widdowson EM. The effect of growth and development on the composition of mammals. *Brit J Nutr* 1950; 4:332.

55. Pace N, Rathbun EN. Studies on body composition. 3. The body water and chemically combined nitrogen content in relation to fat content. *J Biol Chem* 1945; 158:685-690.

Implications of Nutrition on Feline Hepatic Fatty Acid Metabolism

Geza G. Bruckner, PhD
Professor, Department of Clinical Sciences/Division of Clinical Nutrition
University of Kentucky, Lexington, Kentucky, USA

Joseph Szabo, DVM, PhD[a]; Gregory D. Sunvold, PhD[b]
[a]Department of Animal Nutrition, University of Veterinary Medicine,
Budapest, Hungary
[b]Research and Development, The Iams Company, Lewisburg, Ohio, USA

Summary

Feline hepatic lipidosis (FHL) is a well-recognized hepatopathy which is characterized by extensive lipid accumulation in liver parenchymal cells. Although diabetes mellitus and acute pancreatitis appear to contribute to the pathogenesis of FHL, the majority of cases are believed to result from the nutritional and biochemical peculiarities of the cat[1,2] which to date are not understood. A large number of the nutritional idiosyncrasies exhibited by the cat can be regarded as evolutionary adaptations to a carnivorous diet and may in particular influence liver fatty acid metabolism and the feline's requirements for essential fatty acids. Cats, unlike most other pets, may develop hepatic lipidosis during a fast. The three most likely mechanisms involved are 1) increased triglyceride synthesis, 2) decreased fatty acid oxidation, and/or 3) decreased very low density lipoprotein (VLDL) transport from the hepatocyte.

The special dietary requirements of the cat appear to make it more susceptible to hepatic lipidosis than other species. The cat has minimal $\Delta 6$ desaturase enzyme activity[3,4] and, therefore, common vegetable oil sources, such as corn oil, appear to be inadequate for meeting its essential fatty acid requirement. Essential fatty acid deficiency is known to induce fatty livers in cats[5] and other animal models.[6,7] Essential fatty acid deficiency (EFAD) is also known to effect lipoprotein lipase, lipoprotein transport from the liver, lecithin cholesterol acyltransferase, and fatty acid synthetase activities;[8] alterations of any one of these parameters may contribute to the development of FHL. Based on these previously reported observations, it is plausible that the feline is more susceptible to EFAD and the associated changes in liver lipid metabolism. Diets which have recently been used to induce and study FHL are deficient in essential fatty acids (e.g., arachidonic acid, docosahexaenoic acid), most likely even when supplemented with corn oil.[9,10]

Dietary protein is also important in the management of FHL and it has been shown that feeding 25% of the calculated energy requirement (CE) as high quality protein will attenuate the hepatic lipidosis but does not ameliorate the condition (reduced liver lipid content by approximately 50% compared to corn oil supplemented animals).[9] It is assumed that these changes are associated with increased lipoprotein transport from the liver as VLDL; however these studies are flawed in design because other nutrient deficiencies (vitamin/mineral) not controlled for may be present. There are no studies which address the potential protein-lipid interactions on the development of FHL.

The objective of this chapter is therefore to review the literature related to 1) essential fatty acid metabolism in the feline, 2) lipid and lipoprotein metabolism in the feline, 3) how dietary protein quality impacts on the etiology of FHL, 4) the interaction between protein and polyunsaturated fatty acids (PUFAs), and 5) other nutritional factors which may alter hepatic lipogenesis.

Background

Essential Fatty Acid Metabolism. In all mammalian species so far studied there exists a dietary requirement for all cis-18 carbon polyunsaturated fatty acids. Polyunsaturated fatty acids (PUFAs) are defined as fatty acids that contain two or more unsaturated double bonds. In mammalian systems, PUFAs can be classified into two broad categories termed "essential" and "nonessential" fatty acids (*Figure 1*). Essential PUFAs (E-PUFAs) are considered by most to include fatty acids of both the n-6 and n-3 fatty acid families, for example, all-cis-18:2n6 and all-cis-18:3n3. These essential fatty acids must be provided in the diet because they cannot be synthesized from simple carbon precursors in a mammalian cellular system. However, nonessential PUFAs (NE-PUFAs) can be synthesized from simple acetate units. The condensation of these acetate units via fatty acid synthetase yields primarily 16- and 18-carbon saturated fatty acids, which can be further desaturated and elongated to yield NE-PUFAs, for example, all-cis-20:3n9, all-cis-20:4n7. If E-PUFAs are provided in the diet, the synthesis of the NE-PUFA is minimal, and only trace amounts can be detected in cellular storage lipids and membrane phospholipids. However, if a dietary deficiency of essential fatty acids occurs or is induced, the synthesis of NE-PUFAs is increased, and both physiological and biochemical homeostasis is perturbed.[11]

Classical essential fatty acid deficiency symptoms are growth retardation, fatty liver, increased membrane permeability, sterility, capillary fragility, elevated NE-PUFA (20:3n9), decreased E-PUFA (20:4n6), increased insensible water loss, altered QRS complex, decreased eicosanoid synthesis, and altered platelet aggregation.[11,12] It is apparent from both the biochemical and gross observations that in mammalian systems the increased synthesis of NE-PUFA cannot substitute for the biological functions that are associated with n-6 and n-3 fatty acids.[13]

Linoleic acid is required in the diets of most animal species in the range of 0.5–2.0 energy percent of the diet depending on the sex and species; however, the cat may have an even lower requirement provided that the n-6 fatty acid is provided as 20:4n6. The minimum requirements for n-3 fatty acids have not yet been established. When animals are fed fat-free or completely saturated fat diets, tissue lipids

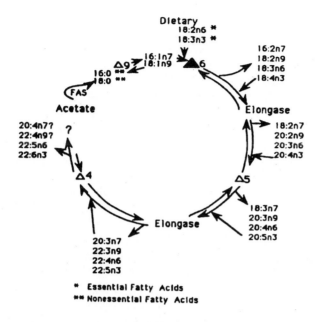

Figure 1. Essential and nonessential fatty acid desaturation and elongation pathways. $\Delta 6$, $\Delta 5$, $\Delta 4$ represent respective desaturase steps. FAS, fatty acid synthetase.

have only small amounts of n-3 or n-6 PUFAs and accumulate PUFAs of the n-9 and n-7 series. As one includes n-3 and n-6 fatty acids in the diets of these essential fatty acid-deficient animals, the endogenous PUFAs of the n-7 and n-9 series are rapidly replaced by n-6 and n-3 fatty acids at the sn-2 position of phospholipids; there is a preference for n-6 fatty acids to be incorporated into phosphatidylcholine and for n-3 fatty acids to be acylated to phosphatidylethanolamine. As reported by Lands et al.,[14] there exists a quantitative relationship among fatty acids for a limited number of esterification sites, and, although dietary fat can influence the levels of membrane fatty acids, there is an overall similarity in tissue composition between rats and humans and most likely other animal species. As the regulation of membrane fatty acid composition appears to be tightly controlled, one might assume that cellular function is closely associated with membrane form. Therefore, as slight changes in phospholipid fatty acid composition are induced, membrane function might be altered in either a positive or negative sense. Membrane fluidity has been shown to influence insulin receptor sensitivity, phenylalanine transport, succinate oxidase activity, transport of hexose sugars, and Ca ATPase activity.[15-19] Not only the enzyme activities but also membrane receptor affinities may be altered by dietary fatty acids.

Dietary linoleic and α-linolenic acids are metabolized by desaturation and chain elongation to yield longer, more unsaturated derivatives. Since fatty acid chain desaturation and elongation in mammals occurs between the fatty acid carboxyl group and the nearest double bond, the number of carbons from the methyl end to the first double bond remains fixed. There is no inter-conversion between the n-6, n-3, n-9, or n-7 fatty acid families. The first desaturase enzyme, Δ6 desaturase, is the rate-limiting enzyme for n-3 and n-6 fatty acids[20] (**Figure 1**). This enzyme is regulated by feedback inhibition and is sensitive to competitive inhibition by other PUFAs. In the key regulatory role, Δ6 desaturase can influence the highly unsaturated fatty acid (HUFA) composition of membranes and the bioactive lipid end products formed. By feeding HUFAs (20:4n6, 20:5n3, and 22:6n3), the conversion of 18:2n6 and 18:3n3 to more unsaturated fatty acids by this enzyme can be inhibited. It has repeatedly been demonstrated that high dietary levels of 20:5n3 and/or 22:6n3 will decrease phospholipid and neutral lipid arachidonic acid concentration. This occurs through inhibition of the Δ6 desaturase as well as competition for the phospholipid acylation sites. The feeding of other fatty acids that are past the rate-limiting Δ6 desaturase step, for example γ-linolenic acid (18:3n6), may also inhibit this enzyme and alter the amount of bioactive lipids produced. The balance or optimal dietary levels of n-3 and n-6 fatty acids have not been determined.

Essential Fatty Acids in Cats. Rivers et al.[4] reported that cats fed purified diets containing vegetable oils which provided EFA only as linoleate or as a mixture of linoleate (18:2n6) and α-linolenate (18:3n3) developed clinical signs compatible with EFA deficiency. Analysis of plasma phospholipids in these cats showed they all had very low levels of HUFAs in plasma phospholipids. Animals which were fed linoleate and linoleate plus α-linolenate, accumulated high levels of these fatty acids in tissue phospholipids. These authors and others[10] have therefore concluded that cats fed 18:2n6 and or 18:3n3 became EFA deficient because they lacked the ability to convert dietary EFA into long chain HUFAs. It has been postulated that this was due to a lack of Δ6 and Δ8 desaturases. Later it was also suggested that the cat lacked a Δ5 desaturase.[20,21,22] Therefore, it has been implied that the feline requires preformed arachidonic, eicosapentaenoic and docosahexaenoic fatty acids in its diet. McLean[10] and others[3] have not successfully duplicated these earlier experiments. Cats maintained up to 8 years on diets, which contained safflower seed oil (linoleate) as the sole source of dietary lipid, appeared normal but could not reproduce more than two viable litters and exhibited hepatic lipidosis. Differences between other dietary constituents may account for the differences noted between these studies, such as taurine levels in the diet and/or the presence or absence of hydrogenated coconut oil.

One study with cats fed purified γ-linolenate (18:3n6) noted changes in the fatty acid composition of erythrocyte phospholipids which suggested that Δ5 desaturase activity was present,[23] but an earlier study suggested the absence of this enzyme.[21] More recently Pawloski et al.[3] have shown that both Δ5 desaturase and Δ6 desaturase activity are present in the feline but the level of activity does not appear to be adequate for maintaining the tissue stores of long chain HUFAs. Both linoleate and α-linolenate were desaturated and elongated to HUFAs in low concentrations. Cats fed linoleate-rich diets for 10 months showed a marked decrease in arachidonate and an elevation of 18:2n6 and 20:2n6, together with a 6-fold increase in 5,11,14-20:3.[10] Most likely this fatty acid was produced from the elongation of linoleic acid and a subsequent Δ5 desaturase. In other tissues of cats fed an EFA deficient diet there appeared an unknown fatty acid which was isolated and characterized as 5,8,11-20:3 (20:3n9), which is the classic indicator of EFA deficiency.[7] Most likely in the absence of Δ6 desaturase this is produced by the action of the Δ8 and Δ5 desaturases. Therefore, the potentially limiting step in linoleic acid and α-linolenic acid metabolism in the cat remains the Δ6 desaturase enzyme. The levels of 20:3n9 or the ratio of 20:3n9 to 20:4n6 are not reliable indicators of the EFA status of the cat and, therefore, it is necessary to use features such as the absolute amount of EFA and their HUFA metabolites to identify deficiencies in this species.

EFA Requirements in the Feline. It has been stated previously that linoleic acid alone is not capable of maintaining reproduction in cats.[10] The addition of γ-linolenic acid to linoleic acid in the diet improved wound healing and estrus, but did not normalize litter viability.[24] However, MacDonald et al. [24] fed supplements of 20:4n6 to cats at .04% of the dietary energy and demonstrated complete reproductive capacity in felines. If tuna oil was added to the diets of the cats fed 20:4n6 the earlier noted reproductive benefits were attenuated, suggesting that n-3 fatty acids were competing for the membrane phospholipid acylation sites and possibly for subsequent eicosanoid production. It is clear from these studies that the exact EFA requirements of normal cats and the EFA requirements of cats under metabolic stress conditions are not known.

Lipoproteins. Lipoproteins are the key transport vehicles for cholesterol, cholesterol esters, and triglycerides. These lipoproteins are in a constant state of flux as lipids are absorbed, packaged, and transported throughout the body. In the intestine, absorbed lipids are packaged into chylomicrons (CM) containing apolipoproteins B48 A-1 and A-V. These chylomicrons are transported through the thoracic lymph duct into the systemic circulation, where they acquire apo E and apo C from the circulating high-density lipoproteins (HDL). As the chylomicron comes into contact with the capillary endothelium, the enzyme lipoprotein lipase (LPL) hydrolyzes the triglycerides (TG) from the chylomicron. Thus the TG core of the chylomicron is decreased until only a cholesterol-enriched CM remnant remains. These CM remnants are catabolized by the liver (**Figure 2**).

Hepatic Lipid and Lipoprotein Metabolism

If there is an excess in caloric intake from carbohydrates, fats, and/or proteins, there is an increase in acetate units available for fat or cholesterol biosynthesis. In the liver the synthesized fatty acids and cholesterol are processed into VLDL containing apolipoproteins B-100, C, and E and secreted into the circulation. Once again LPL removes the trigylcerides from these VLDL micelles. As the TG content is decreased and the relative cholesterol portion increased, the micelle particle is designated as intermediate density lipoprotein (IDL) and ultimately as low-density lipoprotein (LDL). Constant exchange occurs between the various lipoprotein fractions and HDLs as they are transported to and from the liver. The LDL is a cholesterol-rich particle and can be removed from the circulation by the liver, endothelial cells, and/or the macrophage scavenger pathway.

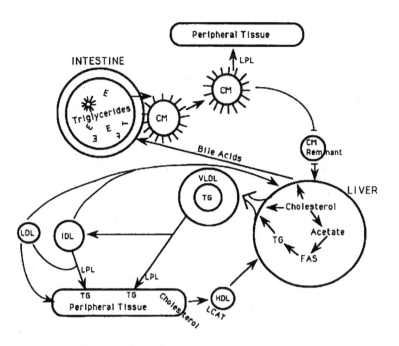

Figure 2. Triglyceride (TG) absorption transport and metabolism. Fat is absorbed and packaged as chylomicrons (CM) and lipoprotein lipase (LPL) releases TG to yield the CM remnant. Very low density lipoprotein (VLDL), synthesized by the liver, is broken down by LPL to yield intermediate density lipoprotein (IDL) and ultimately, low density lipoprotein (LDL). High density lipoprotein clears cholesterol from the cell through lecithin-cholesterol acyltransferase (LCAT).

Fish oils (rich in n-3 fatty acids) have been found to effectively lower plasma VLDL levels in a number of animal species as well as in humans.[25] The average reduction in VLDL is greater in hypertriglyceridemic subjects than in normal individuals. Decreased serum TGs (VLDL) are not due to changes in lipoprotein lipase or hepatic triglyceride lipase activities, which indicates that the n-3 fatty acid effects are most likely due to altered synthesis rates. As shown by Nestel et al.,[26] the net synthesis of liver triglyceride as VLDL is greatly reduced. The reduced output of liver VLDL is dose-dependent and appears to be due to 1) increased mitochondrial and peroxisomal β-oxidation of fatty acids, 2) decreased fatty acid synthesis, 3) increased phospholipid versus TG synthesis, and 4) decreased activity of the esterifying enzymes. It is speculated that lipogenesis is reduced owing to feedback inhibition of the acetyl CoA carboxylase, the rate-limiting enzyme. Apoprotein B-l00, which is an integral part of VLDL synthesis, is also suppressed by the n-3 fatty acids. Harris[27] summarized the lipoprotein changes that result from n-3 fatty acid dietary supplementation. The effects of n-3 fatty acids on hepatic lipogenesis in felines have not been studied.

Feline Lipoprotein Metabolism. Triglyceride accumulation in the liver occurs when the rate of removal from the liver is less than the rate of synthesis. The majority of lipids from the liver are removed as triglyceride packaged into VLDL or oxidized through peroxisomal or mitochondrial β-oxidation. In the feline, VLDL levels are low compared to HDL and LDL.[42,43] Significant differences in lipoprotein concentrations were not noted between obese and lean cats,[42] nor were differences noted following 28 days of a rapid weight reduction. Fatty acids which are incorporated into triglycerides in the liver are derived from primarily three sources which include CM remnants from dietary fat, *de novo* synthesis of fatty acids from acetate and malonyl CoA, and fatty acids released from adipose stores and transported via albumin to the liver. Only in a few species (including cats, rhesus monkeys, and humans) does liver dysfunction occur with hepatic lipidosis. Obesity has been associated with increased hepatic triglyceride content in humans and because obese cats are most often afflicted with FHL, it has been suggested that obesity also plays a role in FHL. However, two studies[28,29] found no differences between hepatic vacuolar changes in obese versus nonobese cats; thus obesity is not directly correlated with FHL.

It has been shown that cats with FHL have 30 times more triglyceride and 20 times more cholesterol ester stores in hepatocytes than normal controls.[30] These authors note significant changes in tissue fatty acid compositon between control and FHL cats. In particular the liver lipids reflect the adipose tissue stores suggesting that the mobilization of adipose stores may serve as the primary source for liver triglyceride synthesis and accumulation in FHL. It should be noted that the changes in liver fatty acid composition between EFAD and FHL cats differ. Cats fed an EFAD diet show drastically reduced levels of 18:2n6 versus cats with FHL; this is most likely due to increased mobilization of lipid stores in FHL (fasting) compared to EFAD (fed, lacking EFAs). Interestingly, the triglyceride hepatic fatty acid composition of cats with FHL showed patterns which are indicative of HUFA EFAD. In both the liver and adipose tissue, arachidonic and docosahexaenoic acid levels were drastically reduced in the FHL cats versus control cats. As speculated by other investigators,[6,10] the essential fatty acid status of the feline may be compromised due to the limiting nature of the Δ6 desaturase. Since the majority of lipids stored in adipose tissue of healthy felines are saturated and monounsaturated fatty acids and the predominant PUFA is linoleic acid, it may be that during an anorectic period the longer chain PUFAs (20:4n6 and 22:6n3) are not adequately synthesized from precursor fatty acids for meeting the animals' needs and this lack of E-HUFA contributes to the pathogenesis of FHL. It is hypothesized that EFAD, which may develop during starvation in the feline, contributes to the pathogenesis of FHL as follows:

1) EFAs (20:4n6, 22:6n3) are needed for specific phospholipid synthesis to form components of VLDL. With diminished VLDL synthesis, triglyceride transport from the liver would be decreased and hepatic triglyceride accumulation may occur. It has been shown that in EFAD rats the VLDL fraction is decreased and is markedly different than in EFA sufficient animals.[31]

2) EFAs (20:4n6, 22:6n3), which are required as components of specific phospholipids, would be absent for functional intracellular organelle membrane formation. This may result in altered mitochondrial and/or peroxisomal function and thus decrease fatty acid β-oxidation in both peroxisomes and mitochondria.

One would predict increased accumulation of long chain saturated and monounsaturated fatty acids in FHL due to a peroxisomal defect. Peroxisomes can be damaged during starvation by as yet unknown mechanisms. It has been shown that both in cats with FHL and in malnourished humans peroxisome numbers are greatly reduced.[33,34]

Other Factors Related to FHL

Carnitine. Fatty acid oxidation may also be altered by the availability of carnitine for transport into the mitochondria for β-oxidation — carnitine is not required for peroxisomal oxidation *(Figure 3)*. The hypothesis that a relative carnitine deficiency may be involved in FHL is supported by a study in which cats were fed 25% of their maintenance energy requirements with normal or extra carnitine supplementation.[35] In the cats receiving the additional carnitine supplementation there was minimal lipid accumulation compared to the control group, suggesting that there may be limiting carnitine during times of increased lipid mobilization. However, cats with FHL have increased serum concentrations of β-hydroxybutyrate, a byproduct of fatty acid oxidation, suggesting that carnitine may not be limiting for transport of fatty acids into the mitochondria for β-oxidation; one cannot rule out that additional carnitine might not further enhance β-oxidation.

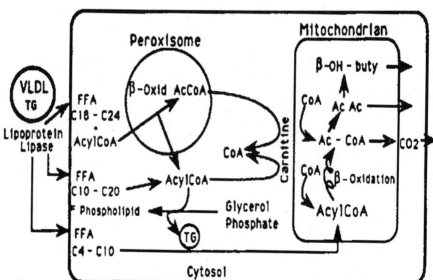

Figure 3. β-oxidation pathways of fatty acids with differing chain lengths; VLDL (very low density lipoprotein), TG (triglyceride), and FFA (free fatty acid). Short chain fatty acids (C_4– C_{10}) can be directly oxidized via mitochondria β-oxidation, and carnitine is not required. Longer chain fatty acids can be oxidized via mitochondrial β-oxidation directly or, after chain shortening, through peroxisomal oxidation.

Protein and Amino Acids. The synthesis of VLDL is also dependent on the availabilty of amino acids for apoprotein formation. Prolonged starvation reduces the synthesis of all proteins and thus decreases the amount of VLDL; the reduced synthesis of VLDL may cause increased hepatic triglycerides. Anorectic cats have low levels of arginine, alanine, methionine, taurine, citrulline, and tryptophan. Arginine insufficiency, which is an essential amino acid for felines[36] and is needed for the urea cycle, may stimulate the synthesis of orotic acid as a result of urea cycle inhibition.[37] Also, orotic acid has been suggested to contribute to hepatic lipidosis in the rat. However, orotic acid even at high concentrations did not alter the histopathology in normal and FHL cats, suggesting that orotic acid most likely does not contribute to FHL.[38,39] It is apparent that the amount of dietary protein plays a role in the pathogenesis of hepatic lipidosis as shown by Biourge et al.[9] in the feline and in humans with Kwashiorkor.[40] Cats provided with 25% of the CE as a mixed protein had less lipid accumulation than cats fed the same caloric equivalents as corn oil or dextrin. Others have shown that obese cats fed 25% of CE requirements developed hepatic lipidosis but cats fed 50 or 60% of ME did not develop FHL. It is evident that long term nutrient deprivation is required for inducing hepatic lipidosis in the cat as shown by Biourge et al.[41]

Conclusion. The etiology of feline FHL is mutifactorial with an interplay between factors regulating the compositon and deposition of fatty acids into membrane and storage lipids, mobilization of fatty acids from lipid stores, peroxisomal and mitochondrial oxidation of fatty acids, reesterification of fatty acids into liver triglycerides and the transport of these from the liver via VLDL. In order to understand these mechanisms, studies need to be conducted using diets carefully formulated to address only single variables of the mechanisms involved. To date the studies which have induced FHL used primarily starvation diets. Other studies have fed only single nutrients (protein, carbohydrate or fat) resulting in possibly multi-nutrient deficiencies (minerals, vitamins, etc.). Therefore, our current ongoing study is designed to study lipid/protein interactions as they might influence the pathogenesis of feline HL.

Current Ongoing Study

Objective. Using a modification of the obese/low calorie weight reduction feline model (female retired breeder, purpose bred, spayed cats) and a 2x2 factorial design, effects of low and high biological value proteins and their interaction with EFAD and EFA sufficient diets fed at 25% of lean bodyweight maintenance energy requirement (MaE) were tested.

Factorial Experimental Design

Corn gluten plus corn oil	Corn gluten plus blend of poultry fat, borage oil, and fish oil
Casein plus corn oil	Casein plus blend of poultry fat, borage oil, and fish oil

Animals for Dietary Studies. Twenty-four female cats, retired breeders (Harlan Sprague Dawley, IN – purpose bred) were procured, anesthetized (ketamine and isoflurane), and spayed; blood samples (10ml) were taken two days prior to surgery and a wedge liver biopsy taken during surgery (all surgical procedures and protocol were carried out according to the *Guide for the Care and Use of Laboratory Animals* and were IACUC approved). Following surgery, cats were fed a high quality, energy dense diet (Eukanuba Veterinary Diets® Nutritional Recovery Formula® [NRF] and Iams® Ocean Fish Formula Cat Food) *ad libitum* until they gained a minimum of 30% over their arrival weight. Once the animals attained the 30 plus % obesity, they were assigned randomly to the four treatment groups (6 animals/trt) in staggered intervals (4 animals/wk; 1/each trt/wk); blood samples (10ml) were taken again two days prior to surgery for a wedge liver biopsy. The cats are currently being maintained on the weight reduction diets for 7–8 weeks or until they reach body weights similar to but not less than -10% of the body weight established for healthy cats of the same body type and length. Other limitations to the fast include bilirubin levels >0.4 mg/dl.

Diets. All of the experimental diets were formulated and provided by The Iams Company, Dayton, Ohio, USA. The composition of the diets fed during the weight reduction is shown in **Table 1**. Diets were fed at 25% of MaE as described by others [(lean Bwt x 30) + 70] x 1.4/4 = 25% MaE.[28,37] Vitamins, choline, taurine, and minerals were supplemented at 4x the NRC so that animals consuming 25% MaE would be supplied with the normally required NRC amounts. Water was provided to all cats *ad libitum* and a 12 hour dark/light cycle maintained.

Table 1. Composition of diets fed to obese cats at 25% of maintenance energy for weight reduction.

	Gluten-corn oil	Gluten-oil blend	Casein-corn oil	Casein-oil blend
Ingredients				
Corn gluten meal	68.30	68.30		
Casein			52.00	52.00
Corn oil	13.00		18.70	3.90
Poultry fat		11.70		13.50
Corn starch	5.00	5.00	19.60	19.60
Calcium carbonate	3.70	3.70	0.02	
Dried beet pulp	3.00	3.00	3.00	3.00
Monosodium phosphate	2.40	2.40	0.49	0.49
Choline chloride	1.50	1.50	1.80	1.80
Minerals	1.20	1.20	1.20	1.20
Vitamins	1.20	1.20	1.20	1.20
Sodium chloride			1.00	1.00
DL-methionine			0.32	0.32
Fish oil		0.90		0.90
Borage oil		0.15		0.15
Ground flax		0.15		0.15
Taurine	0.15	0.15	0.15	0.15
Potassium chloride	0.49	0.49	0.54	0.61
Nutrients				
Protein, % (4kcal/g)	45.09	44.37	42.97	41.94
Moisture, %	5.81	7.62	10.28	10.85
Ash, %	7.87	7.98	7.36	7.06
Fat, % (9 kcal/g)	17.18	17.29	17.10	18.51
Crude fiber, %	2.22	2.34	2.28	1.59
N-free extracts, % (4 kcal/g)	21.84	20.40	19.79	19.97
Calculated energy (kcal/kg)	4223.4	4146.9	4049.4	4142.3

Measurements and Collections.

Body weights were recorded weekly and the results are presented in
Figure 4.

Blood samples (10 ml/collection period) were taken at baseline, following
weight gain and after 21 days on the weight loss diets from the jugular vein of
anesthetized cats. Samples were drawn into EDTA or glass tubes for plasma and
serum.

Liver biopsies were performed on the anesthetized cats as a wedge biopsy at
the beginning of the protocol (during the spaying procedure), after the cats attained
a minimum of 30% weight gain, and following the loss of at least 30% of the weight
gained. Liver samples were fixed in 10% formalin or 3% glutaraldehyde for assessment of histopathology or extracted into hexane-isopropanol for lipid analysis.

Biochemical assessment was done on serum samples at baseline, following
maximum weight gain, and 21 days after starting the weight reduction feeding
protocol (*Table 2*); values for the end of the weight reduction period are not
complete at this time but will be reported at the 1998 Iams Nutrition Symposium.

Lipoproteins (VLDL, LDL, and HDL) will be measured using a modification of the procedures reported by Dimski et al.[37]

Isotopomer spectral analysis, following administration of deuterium
labeled water and ^{13}C glycerol, will be utilized to determine the rate of 1) triglyceride synthesis and turnover, 2) cholesterol synthesis, and 3) VLDL synthesis *in vivo*,
modified on the basis of work described by Kelleher et al.[41] and Paul Lee et al.[45]

Statistical Analysis. Data are analyzed by one way analysis of variance
(ANOVA) followed by least square means analysis (LSM) to measure significant
differences between treatment groups.

Body Weight Changes. The body weight gains of the cats increased consistently following spaying until about 75 days post surgery after which the weights
plateaued (**Figure 4**). Weight loss on the 25% MaE diets showed no significant
differences between the groups during the 21 days of weight loss, suggesting that
neither low or high quality protein and/or EFA status alter weight loss during the
first 21 days. The rate of weight loss on our 25% MaE diets was similar to that
reported by others during a complete fast.[9,41] The cats lost about 8 to 11% of their
bodyweight during the first week, 5 to 6% during the second week and 4 to 5% in
the third week.

Cholesterol and Triglycerides(TG). Obese cats had significantly higher serum
cholesterol concentrations compared to their baseline values (193±45 *v* 107±23 mg/
dL respectively). Following 21 days of weight loss, the cholesterol values decreased

Preliminary
Results/
Discussion

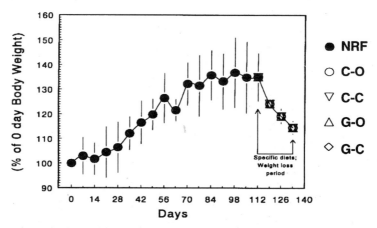

Figure 4. Body weight changes of cats following spaying. Cats were fed a high energy dense diet (NRF=Eukanuba Veterinary Diets Nutritional Recovery Formula; 0-112 days) and then placed on the following diets fed at 25% maintenance energy requirement of lean bodyweight: C-O=Casein-oil blend; C-C= Casein-corn oil; G-O=Gluten-oil blend; G-C=Gluten-corn oil.

but did not return to baseline values; there were no significant differences between treatment groups (**Table 2**). Triglyceride concentrations were elevated (not significantly) in the obese cats versus their baseline values. The weight reduction lowered serum TG in all dietary groups, but no significant differences were noted at 21 days of weight loss. These results differ from that reported by Dimski et al.[29] since they reported no significant differences in cholesterol or TGs between obese and control animals prior to weight reduction; following 28 days of weight loss, the control animals had a higher concentration of serum cholesterol than the obese animals. Differences between this study and that reported by Dimski et al.[29] may be due to the amount of MaE provided; their protocol provided ~ 50% of their previous diet intake while the diets used in this study were fed at 25% MaE (based on lean bodyweight).

Biochemistries. Other significant changes were not noted for the chemistries listed in **Table 2**, suggesting that indicators of FHL pathogenesis are not evident at 21 days of weight loss on the 25% MaE diets. One of the cats in the study broke a tooth and did not consume any diet for 7 weeks. This cat developed classical signs associated with FHL in that total bilirubin, ALT, and LDH were elevated and the liver had massive lipid infiltration. These observations are identical to those reported by others in obese cats undergoing a total fast.[9,41]

Fatty Acids. Preliminary data from 2 cats, one fed the casein–oil blend and the other the casein–corn oil, shows that in the liver phospholipid fraction, the amount of long chain fatty acids accumulates; although as yet unidentified, these fatty acids appear beyond 20:0. Additionally, the levels of 20:4n6 and 22:6n3 are also reduced, suggesting a trend similar to that reported by Hall et al.[30] Cats on the other diets have not yet been analyzed.

Table 2. Biochemistry of cats prior to weight gain (Baseline) at a minimum of 30% weight gain above lean body weight (Obese) and following a 3 week weight loss on diets providing 25% of maintenance energy requirements.

	Baseline	Obese	Casein-oil blend	Casein-corn oil	Gluten-oil blend	Gluten-corn oil
Cholesterol (mg/dL)	107.52± 23.78	193.39± 45.18	121.67± 26.39	109.8± 19.42	125.33± 31.14	110.50± 10.62
Triglyceride (mg/dL)	48.61± 37.2	60.65± 38.2	40.50± 13.52	42.8± 6.61	38.5± 4.04	48.33± 23.8
Total Bilirubin (mg/dL)	0.17± 0.19	0.10± 0.06	0.08± 0.04	0.06± 0.05	0.08± 0.04	0.05± 0.05
Glucose (mg/dL)	139.39± 54.73	201.61± 73.46	190.5± 56.06	148.6± 41.79	136.5± 50.72	142.17± 44.03
Insulin (mU/L)	2.65± 2.49	2.55± 1.87	2.1± 1.51	2.84± 2.7	1.86± 0.95	2.55± 2.34
ALT (IU/L) Alanine aminotransferase	78.61± 40.61	73.13± 33.59	61.50± 20.21	59.60± 21.82	78± 54.55	51.67± 16.9
AST (IU/L) Aspartate aminotransferase	32.87± 9.72	31.74± 15.68	22.33± 3.93	24.4± 4.51	48.50± 58.44	23.50± 11.50
LDH (IU/L) Lactate dehydrogenase	131.41± 52.29	116.30± 49.69	91.67± 33.25	85.60± 22.61	120.67± 74.53	88.00± 27.22
ALP (IU/L) Alkaline phosphatase	22.09± 10.00	32.41± 11.01	28.83± 4.45	29.40± 10.57	25.00± 6.69	31.67± 14.00
CK (IU/L) Creatine kinase	437.61± 281.60	145.17± 131.02	88.67± 40.46	82.40± 22.66	72± 19.49	79.83± 38.66
Creatinine (mg/dL)	1.47± 0.20	2.00± 0.22	1.87± 0.15	2.04± 0.09	2.07± 0.22	1.9± 0.27
BUN (mg/dL) Blood urea nitrogen	20.48± 3.64	26.17± 4.00	19.33± 3.93	20.40± 2.07	19.83± 0.75	22.83± 1.72
TP (g/dL) Total protein	6.27± 0.49	6.55± 0.48	5.88± 0.27	6.30± 0.58	6.28± 0.56	5.96± 0.22
ALB (g/dL) Albumin	3.15± 0.40	3.46± 0.32	3.28± 0.20	3.52± 0.22	3.50± 0.25	3.40± 0.18
GLOB (g/dL) Globulin	3.12± 0.37	3.09± 0.53	2.60± 0.32	2.78± 0.49	2.78± 0.50	2.55± 0.32
Ca (mg/dL)	9.53± 0.89	9.81± 0.57	9.65± 0.52	10.00± 0.26	9.98± 0.26	9.83± 0.24
P (mg/dL)	4.55± 0.99	5.24± 0.67	4.87± 0.33	5.00± 0.44	4.98± 0.89	4.90± 0.28
Mg (meq/L)	2.13± 0.16	2.17± 0.25	2.10± 0.13	2.14± 0.35	2.18± 0.34	2.02± 0.13
Na (mmol/L)	154.48± 2.64	155.48± 5.74	154.17± 3.37	158.8± 10.47	156.5± 2.26	155.83± 3.31
K (mmol/L)	3.94± 0.36	4.26± 0.46	4.02± 0.30	3.90± 0.53	3.40± 0.85	3.58± 0.60
Cl (mEq/L)	121.26± 2.47	121.22± 6.25	122.00± 2.37	128.40± 12.30	120.33± 1.21	120.67± 1.86

The results of prolonged weight loss on lipid and lipoprotein metabolism in cats fed diets with low and high protein quality and/or diets containing only 18:2n6 or 18:2n6 and HUFA will be presented at the 1998 Iams Nutrition Symposium.

Acknowledgements   A special thank you to Wissam Ibrahim, Daria Cloyd, Ken Dickey, and Janet Rodgers for their valuable assistance with the animal surgeries. Research supported by a grant from The Iams Company.

Eukanuba Veterinary Diets, Nutritional Recovery Formula, and Iams are registered trademarks of The Iams Company.

References   1. Zawie DA, Garvey MS. Feline hepatic disease. *Vet Clin North Am Small Anim Prac* 1984; 14:1201-1230.

2. Dimski DS, Taboada J. Feline idiopathic hepatic lipidosis. *Vet Clin North Am Small Anim Prac* 1995; 25:357-373.

3. Pawlosky R, Barnes A, Salem N. Essential fatty acid metabolism in the feline: relationship between liver and brain production of long-chain polyunsaturated fatty acids. *J Lipid Res* 1994; 35:2032-2040.

4. Rivers JPW, Sinclair AJ, Crawford MA. Inability of the cat to desaturate essential fatty acids. *Nature* 1975; 258:171-173.

5. MacDonald ML, Rogers QR, Morrison, JG. Role of linoleate as an essential fatty acid for the cat, independent arachidonate synthesis. *J Nutr* 1983; 113:1422-1433.

6. Sinclair AJ, Collins FD. Fatty livers in rats deficient in essential fatty acids. *Biochim Biophys Acta* 1968; 152:498-510.

7. Holman RT. Essential fatty acid deficiency. *Prog Chem Fats and Other Lipids* 1971; 9:275-284.

8. Sano M, Privett OS. Effects of an essential fatty acid deficiency on serum lipoproteins in the rat. *Lipids* 1980; 15:337-344.

9. Biourge VC, Massat B, Groff JM, Morris JG, Rogers QR. Effects of protein, lipid, carbohydrate supplementation on hepatic lipid accumulation during rapid weight loss in obese cats. *Am J Vet Res* 1994; 55:1406-1415.

10. McLean JG, Monger EA. Factors determining the essential fatty acid requirements of the cat. In: Burger IH, Rivers JPW, eds. *Nutrition of the Cat and Dog*. Cambridge: Cambridge University, 1989; 329-341.

11. Holman RT. Biological activities of and requirements for polyunsaturated fatty acids. In: Holman RT, ed. *Progress in the Chemistry of Fats and Other Lipids*. Oxford: Pergamon, 1970; 61-86.

12. Vergroesen AJ. Early signs of polyunsaturated fatty acid deficiency. *Biblthca Nutr Dieta* 1976; 23:19-24.

13. Vergroesen AJ. In: Vergroesen AJ, Crawford M, eds. *The Role of Fats in Human Nutrition*. San Diego: Academic Press, 1988; 1.

14. Lands WEM, Letellier P, Rowe LH, Vanderhock J. Inhibition of prostaglandin biosynthesis. *Adv Biosci* 1973; 9:15-20.

15. Spector AA, Yorek MA. Membrane lipid composition and cellular function *J Lipid Res* 1985; 26:1015-1023.

16. Ginsberg BH, Jabour J, Spector AA. Effect of alterations of membrane lipid unsaturation on the properties of the insulin receptor of Ehrlich ascites cells. *Biochimi Biophys Acta* 1982; 690:157-162.

17. Im WB, Deutchler JT, Spector AA. Effects of membrane fatty acid composition on sodium independent phenylalanine transport in Ehrlich cells. *Lipids* 1979; 14:1003-1007.

18. McMurchie EJ, Raison JK. Membrane lipid fluidity and its effect on the activation energy of membrane associated enzymes. *Biochimi Biophys Acta* 1979; 554:364-371.

19. Innis SM, Clandinin MT. Dynamic modulation of mitochondrial membrane physical properties and ATPase activity by diet lipid. *Biochem J* 1981; 198:167-172.

20. Hassam AG, Rivers JPW, Crawford MA. The failure of the cat to desaturate linoleic acid: Its nutritional implications. *Nutr Met* 1977; 21:321-328.

21. Frankel TL, Rivers JPW. The nutritional and metabolic impact of γ-linolenic acid (18:3n6) on cats deprived of animal lipid. *Brit J Nutr* 1978; 39:227-231.

22. Rivers JPW, Frankel TL. Fat in the diet of cats and dogs. In: Anderson RS, ed. *Nutriton of the Dog and Cat.* Oxford: Pergamon Press, 1980; 67-99.

23. Sinclair AJ, McLean JG, Monger EA. Metabolism of linoleic acid in the cat. *Lipids* 1979; 14:932-936.

24. MacDonald ML, Anderson BC, Rogers QR, Buffington CA, Morris JG. Essential fatty acid requirements of cats: Pathology of essential fatty acid deficiency. *Am J Vet Res* 1984; 45:1310-1317.

25. Connor WE, DeFrancesco CA, Connor SL. n-3 fatty acids from fish oil: effects on plasma lipoproteins and hypertriglyceridemic patients. *Ann NY Acad Sci* 1993; 683:16-34.

26. Nestel PJ, Connor WE, Reardon MR, Connor S, Wong S, Boston R. Suppression by diets rich in fish oil of very low density lipoprotein production in man. *J Clin Invest* 1993; 683:16-34.

28. Armstrong P. Feline hepatic lipidosis. In: *Proc ACVIM,* San Diego, CA 1989; 335-337.

29. Dimski DS, Buffington CA, Johnson SE, Sherding RG, Rosol TJ. Serum lipoprotein concentrations and hepatic lesions in obese cats undergoing weight loss. *Am J Vet Res* 1992; 53:1259-1262.

30. Hall JA, Barstad LA, Connor WE. Lipid composition of hepatic and adipose tissue from normal cats and from cats with idiopathic hepatic lipidosis. *J Vet Int Med* 1997; 11:238-242.

31. De Pury CG, Collins FD. Very low density lipoproteins and lipoprotein lipase in serum of rats deficient in essential fatty acids. *Lipids* 1972; 7:268-275.

32. Sano M, Privett OS. Effects of essential fatty acid deficiency on serum lipoproteins in the rat. *Lipids* 1980; 15:337-344.

33. Center SA, Guida L, Zanciii MJ, Dougherty E, Cummings J, King J. Ultrastructural hepatocellular features associated with severe hepatic lipidosis in cats. *Am J Vet Res* 1993; 54:724-731.

34. Doherty JF, Golden MH, Brooks SEH. Peroxisomes and the fatty liver in malnutrition: an hypothesis. *Am J Clin Nutr* 1991; 54:674-677.

35. Armstrong P, Hardie E, Cullen J, Keene B, Hand M, Babineau C. L-carnitine reduces hepatic fat accumulation during rapid weight reduction in cats. In: *Proc ACVIM*, San Diego, CA 1992; 810.

36. Burrows C, Chiapclla A, Jezyk P. Idiopathic feline hepatic lipidosis: The syndrome and speculations on its pathogenesis. *Florida Vet J* 1981; 10:18-20.

37. Dimski DS. Feline hepatic lipidosis. *Sem Vet Med Surg* 1997; 12:28-33.

38. Dimski D. Idiopathic hepatic lipidosis: a research update. *Proc ACVIM*. Washington, DC, 1993; 198-201.

39. Dimski DS, Taylor HW, Taboada J, Van Steenhouse JL, Sweenson DH, Marx BD. Toxic and vascular nephropathy associated with orotic acid administration on laboratory cats. *Nephron* 1994; 68:275-276.

40. Lewis B, Hansen JDL, Wittman W, Krut LH, Stewart F. Plasma free fatty acids in kwashiorkor and the pathogenesis of the fatty liver. *Am J Clin Nutr* 1964; 15:161-168.

41. Biourge VC, Groff JM, Munn RJ, Kirk CA, Nyland TG, Madeiros VA, Morris JG, Rogers QR. Experimental induction of hepatic lipidosis in cats. *Am J Vet Res* 1994; 55:1291-1302.

42. Dimski DS, Buffington CA, Johnson SE, Sherding RG, Rosol TJ. Serum lipoprotein concentrations and hepatic lesions in cats undergoing weight loss. *Am J Vet Res* 1992; 53:1259-1262.

43. Watson TDG, Butterwick RF, McConnell M, Markwell PJ. Development of methods for anylyzing plasma lipoprotein concentrations and associated enzyme activities and their use to measure the effects of preganancy and lactation in cats. *Am J Vet Res* 1995; 56:289-296.

44. Kelleher JK, Kharroubi AT, Tayseer A, Shambat IB, Kennedy KA, Holleran AL, Masterson TM. Isotopomer spectral analysis of cholesterol synthesis: application in human hepatoma cells. *Am J Physiol* 1994; 29:E384-395.

45. Paul Lee WN, Bassilian S, Ajie HO, Schoeller DA, Edmond J, Bergner EA, Byerley LO. *In vivo* measurement of fatty acid and cholesterol synthesis using D_2O and mass isotopomer analysis. *Am J Physiol* 1994; 266:E699-E708.

Safe Weight Loss in Cats

Sharon A. Center, DVM, DACVIM
Professor, Internal Medicine, College of Veterinary Medicine
Cornell University, Ithaca, New York, USA

Obesity, defined as body condition exceeding ideal weight by 15%, is considered the most common nutritional disorder in man and small companion animals. Clinical estimation of obesity in the cat is obfuscated by differences in skeletal frame size among individuals and their tendency to deposit adipose in inguinal and abdominal sites. Although the average cat weighs between 3.5 and 4.5 kg, some cats have remarkably large skeletal frames which easily accommodate lean body weights ranging up to 8 or 9 kg. Although recently developed methods for quantitative assessment of body condition (absorptiometry and subcutaneous ultrasonography) have improved identification and classification of the degree of obesity in research animals, clinical recognition of obesity relies heavily on subjective assessments. Use of body condition scores has reduced the subjectivity of these appraisals. Most applicable in feline practice are comparisons of patient conformation to feline silhouettes depicting different degrees of overweight body condition (**Figure 1**).

Introduction

In man, obesity is considered to have a multifactorial etiology.[1,2] Some patients have acquired metabolic derangements leading to a lower than normal metabolic rate and energy requirement. Additional abnormalities involve variations in biofeedback mechanisms related to satiety and appetite, quantitative increases in adipocyte numbers, impaired ability or desire to exercise, or psychologic factors that lead to excessive food consumption. The common unifying factor in all circumstances is a greater intake of calories than required for energy expenditure. Subsequently, excessive energy is transformed into triglyceride in adipose stores. The development of obesity involves an initial dynamic phase followed by a static or maintenance phase.[1] During the dynamic phase, energy intake exceeds requirements and adipose stores accumulate triglyceride. During the static phase, body weight stabilizes and appetite is controlled by normal feedback mechanisms. Food intake during the static phase may be as normally expected or reduced.

A four year prospective study of body condition in 1,400 pet cats in 27 veterinary hospitals in North America has confirmed that approximately 20% of cats receiving veterinary examination are overweight.[3] Up to 5% of cats were overtly obese. Findings of this study suggest that body condition has significant effects on feline health. Overweight cats had an increased risk for certain diseases and an increased risk for dying when middle aged.[4] Previous studies have docu-

Weight Loss Protocol Sheet

Case Number: _____ Sex: M MC F FS   Breed: _____

Client Name: _____ Current Body Weight: _____ kg

Patient Name: _____ Estimated Ideal Body Weight: _____ kg
(Circle the best fit body condition   Current Wt. (Current Body Weight x % Overweight)
silhouette in the Estimation of Body
Condition chart below)   **MER for Ideal Body Weight:**
     60 kcal/kg x Ideal Body Weight

Caloric Intake per Day: _____kcal/day
Diet Selected: _____
Caloric Density of Diet: _____kcal/can or kcal/oz fed
Amount of Diet to Feed: _____

Estimation of Body Condition

Normal   **Overweight Profiles**

         15%   **20%**   **30%**   **40%**

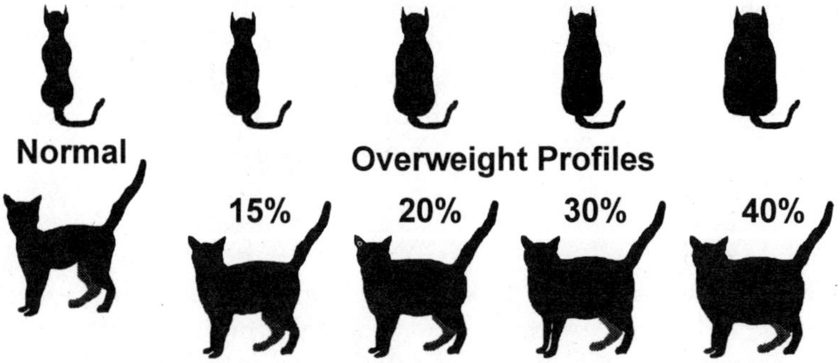

<u>*Specific Reducing Protocol Considerations*</u>
Meal Frequency – Divide total food quantity into 2 or 3 meals per day.
Body Weight Determinations – Single calibrated pediatric scale; record weights to 1 decimal point in Kilograms. (2.2 pounds = 1 kg)
Abdominal Girth Determinations – Made at the widest point of the abdomen, use indelible pen to mark site of tape measure positioning. Consistent determinations require single operator and consistently used tape measure. Girths reflect weight loss *through week 8*, only if patient losing 1.5% of body weight per week.
If body weight stabilizes and goal weight not attained – Restrict calorie intake by 15%
If weight loss >2.5% per week – Increase caloric intake by 15% .
Re-evaluate physical condition +/– biochemistry and urinalysis (check for bilirubinuria)

Figure 1. Clinical weight loss protocol sheet showing feline obesity scoring silhouettes, energy intake calculations, and general instructions.

mented feline obesity at frequencies ranging between 9 and 40%.[5,6] Collectively, surveys have disclosed increased risk for obesity in cats that have a sedentary lifestyle, that are neutered, that are restricted as indoor-only pets, that are fed certain prescription or specialty cat foods or dry cat food *ad libitum*, and that do not hunt.[5-7] Prescription or specialty diets associated with obesity had higher fat contents than "grocery" distributed canned cat foods or other specialty type cat foods.[7] Interestingly, there was no association between body condition and consumption of table foods. Neutered cats were 3.4 times more likely to be overweight as compared to intact animals.[4] This comes as no surprise as ovariohysterectomy and castration have been shown to lead to reduced metabolic rate and activity.[8-10] Estrogens specifically have been shown to impart appetite suppression. Simply being obese also is thought to augment the tendency for a lowered metabolic rate favoring a continued imbalance between energy intake and utilization.[11] This may also be true in cats as shown in a study of energy requirements for cats varing in size and activity levels.[12]

The medical consequences of obesity for human beings has received considerable attention in both the lay and scientific literature. Consequently, it is well acknowledged that obesity is "unhealthful". Specific risks seemingly associated with obesity in the cat include the following: a propensity for hepatic lipidosis, diabetes mellitus, feline urologic syndrome, constipation, osteoarthritis and ligament injuries, perineal dermatitis, and decompensated cardiac function in cats with cardiomyopathy. Obesity may also complicate routine physical diagnostic evaluations, radiographic imaging, and render normally routine surgical procedures difficult to hazardous.

Clinical Approach to the Obese Cat

Successful completion of a weight reduction protocol and subsequent long term weight control in pet cats requires a number of essential considerations. First and most importantly, the owner must be committed to the enterprise and maintain good compliance with a reasonable regimen. Secondly, the weight reduction protocol must be individualized for the patient, the owners ability for compliance, and the management complexities introduced by other household pets. The regimen must be convenient, affordable, and produce visible results within 4 to 6 weeks to encourage owner cooperation. The reducing regimen must satisfy all essential nutrients, be adequate in vitamins, micronutrients and protein, being deficient only in energy. Finally, the diet must be well accepted by the patient, inducing neither anorexia nor a negative nitrogen balance. Several prescription reducing diets are now available for use in cats that satisfy these requirements.

Initial Patient Appraisal

Management of feline obesity first requires that the owner recognize that the pet is overweight. This realization can sometimes prove awkward if the owner also is markedly overweight. Discussions of pet obesity are assisted by use of body condition silhouettes and owner identification of the "best fit" for the pet's physique (**Figure 1**). Description of pertinent health risks of obesity for the cat can provide pivotal persuasion. It is essential that the owner be committed to weight control/normalization for the pet as a 20–25% safe weight reduction protocol requires a minimum of 16 to 18 weeks. Owner participation and vigilance are essential during the entire program. Personalization of the weight loss protocol includes selection of the most palatable diet for the individual cat, a determination of feeding frequency (multiple feedings are better than a single large feeding), and careful titration of energy intake versus observed weight change. The progress of the weight loss regimen is best represented to the client and in the medical record by use of a single data sheet on which all dates and body weights are recorded and graphic representation of the percentage change of initial body weight over time (*Figure 2*).

During the initial visit, the health status of the cat is determined, reasonable weight loss goals established, an appropriate ration selected, and the level of dietary intake estimated. A reasonable maximal goal of 20 to 25% body weight reduction over 18 weeks is possible without complications. The cat is weighed to establish baseline body weight. Weights should be consistently determined using a single calibrated pediatric scale to optimize accuracy of sequential weight determinations. Owner participation in weight determinations will cultivate their involvement in the weight loss protocol. During the first 8 weeks of weight reduction, changes in animal girth also can reflect declining adiposity. Meaningful girth measurements require use of a single tape measure, consistent positioning around the largest dimension of the abdomen, and a single operator using reproducible techniques. Placing an indelible ink mark on the abdominal skin will ensure that girths are measured from the same area. Emphasis on the desirability for a slim waist in humans makes this assessment particularly appealing to some pet owners.

Before implementation of the weight reduction protocol, optimal patient assessment should include a rigorous review of the medical history, a complete physical examination, and routine baseline screening tests (complete blood cell count, serum chemistry profile, and complete urinalysis). Review of the medical history will disclose whether the cat has a propensity for lower urinary tract or gastrointestinal (vomiting, diarrhea) signs following dietary alterations. It is of particular importance, biochemically, to ascertain the status of liver enzymes which reflect pre-existent hepatic disease. The serendipitous discovery of increased liver enzyme activity during weight loss may erroneously suggest iatrogenically induced hepatic lipidosis. The hepatic lipidosis syndrome is most common in obese, neutered female cats undergoing short term energy deprivation (2 to 7 days of partial or complete anorexia).[13] Abrupt onset of jaundice associated with marked increases in liver enzyme activities (alkaline phosphatase [ALP] fold increase exceeding γ-glutamyl transferase [γGT] fold increase), hepatomegaly, and hyperechoic hepatic parenchyma on ultrasonographic evaluation of liver tissue, are most common. Blood glucose evaluations will exclude the possibility of pre-existent diabetes mellitus. Urinalysis will disclose whether hematuria or crystalluria precede diet change.

Date	Week of Protocol	Body Wt (kg)	% Wt Loss Ideal Wt = ____ kg	Abdominal Girth (cm)	Owner estimated food ingestion per day (quantity = kcal)
	0				
	2				
	4				
	6				
	8				
	10				
	12				
	14				
	16				
	18				

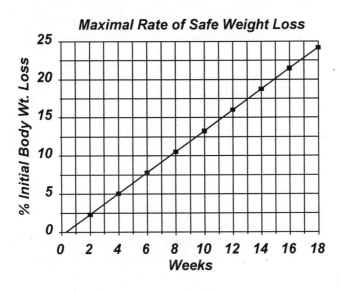

Figure 2. Data recording forms for sequential weight and girth determinations, and % change from initial body weight. A graph designed for plotting rate of weight loss over 18 weeks is provided with reference rate representing the maximal rate of safe weight loss.

Diets formulated for feline weight reduction must be highly palatable and balanced in essential nutrients, micronutrients, and vitamins. No matter what diet is selected, it is important that acclimization gradually occur over a 7 day interval to assure that the diet is well accepted. If a cat refuses a particular reducing ration, alternative diets should be offered until a preferred one is identified.

There are several general nutritional approaches to weight reduction. One approach is to simply reduce the quantity of a maintenance diet being fed and to restrict other feeding opportunities. This usually is unrewarding as changes in body weight develop very slowly (over months) and the cat's perserverence in obtaining extra food often vanquishes the clients dedication to the weight loss venture. Furthermore, important nutritional deficiencies may develop if the cat is underfed essential nutrients/micronutrients/or protein as can occur when some maintenance rations are simply restricted.

A second approach to weight reduction in cats is to restrict feeding opportunities to well defined "meal-times" for glutinous cats accustomed to free choice feeding. Since cats are generally "nibblers", this restriction is thought by some to result in a reduced daily caloric intake. Sadly, this technique also is fraught with failure. Many cats will adapt to the designated feeding interval by rapidly consuming their ration, demanding more food at each sitting, and otherwise preoccupy their time obnoxiously seeking other food sources.

The third approach to weight reduction and the most successful, involves the use of specially formulated feline weight reduction or control diets. These are calorie restricted diets which encompass a variety of nutritional approaches including modification in fat and fiber provision, and formula supplementation with essential micronutrients and protein. Each approach has been shown to be successful, although fat restriction has not been shown to be essential and fiber supplementation has not been received well by all cats.

The caloric balance or the proportion of total energy intake supplied by protein, fat, or carbohydrate, has important implications in the cat. As obligate carnivores, cats are unable to conserve nitrogen because of nonadaptive hepatic enzymes involved in the catabolism of amino acids.[14,15] These enzymes are set to handle a high protein diet and therefore lead to large losses of amino acid nitrogen when a protein deficient diet is fed.[15] Sequential measurements of serum albumin concentrations, physical assessments, as well as evaluation of body composition by absorptiometry of cats undergoing rapid weight reduction, have estimated safe protein intake in moderately to markedly obese cats (20 to 40% overweight cats). At a rate of weight loss of 1.5 to 3.0% initial body weight per week, protein intake ranging between 3.0 and 4.0 g/kg body weight per day was sufficient to maintain >85% of the original lean tissue mass while not inducing hepatic lipidosis.[16-18] Sufficient protein intake for cats undergoing more rapid weight reduction has not been as closely examined.

The level of fat in weight reduction diets remains a controversial issue. Although diet composition can play a role in obesity treatment in man, its greatest potential effect occurs not during weight reduction but during maintenance of a reduced body weight.[19] During weight reduction, the extent of negative energy balance is the greatest determinant of the amount and rate of weight loss, and any effects of diet composition are thought to be very small. Conversely, during the maintenance period after weight reduction, maintenance energy requirements are reduced and the rate of fat oxidation may be slow in enhancing the weight gaining effects of fat intake.[19] Low dietary fat is desirable simply because, on a weight basis, fat provides more than twice the calories as soluble carbohydrate or protein. Fat restricted diets also are argued to induce a greater meal associated thermic effect which reflects initial energy expended for food utilization as well as a sustained postprandial influence. It is assumed that obese animals, like obese people, undergo greater meal-induced heat production and thus energy utilization following carbohydrate and protein ingestion than following fat ingestion.[20] As much as 50% of excess energy intake can be disseminated as heat from meal-induced thermogenesis.[20] A further argument for preferential derivation of energy from carbohydrate and protein calorie sources over fat relates to their influence as insulin secretagogues—increased insulin promotes increased metabolic rate and energy utilization.[21] Since fat is least potent as an insulin secretagogue, it does not render this benefit.

Although fiber supplementation is widely recommended in the popular press as a method of weight reduction in human beings, little scientific information substantiates its effectiveness. There is some evidence that fiber ingestion reduces voluntary food and energy intake in overweight cats.[10,22] This purportedly occurs through induction of satiety or gastric "fullness".[23] There also is contradictive evidence that dietary fiber has limited effect on food intake or the perception of hunger.[24] This is not surprising as satiety is a complex phenomenon influenced by numerous endogenous and exogenous factors. Protein derived energy has value in weight reduction diets in respect to its satiating effect on appetite.[5] Dietary protein and carbohydrates each may play important roles in satiety through their influence on brain delivery of serotonin precursors.[25] This is important, as serotonin is instrumental in regulation of food consumption and satiation. Studies also suggest that fat may independently modulate food intake through changes in the rate of hepatic fatty acid oxidation; increased fatty acid oxidation appears to reduce food intake.[26]

Alternatively, some nutritionists argue that reduced palatability plays a role in the efficacy of high fiber reducing rations. The effectiveness of a high fiber, low fat reducing diet was studied in obese cats fed free choice or food-restricted to 60% of their MER for estimated ideal body weight.[22] Estimates of required calories for ideal body weight MER were approximated at 60 kcal/kg ideal body weight per day. When this diet was fed free choice, cats consumed approximately 70% of their estimated ideal body weight MER (equivalent to a calorie intake of 35 to 40 kcal/kg ideal body weight). Both groups of cats lost weight rapidly such that by 14 weeks they had attained weight losses spanning 6.7 to 21.0% (food restricted feeding) and

2.4 to 17.1% (free-choice feeding) of initial body weight. This rate of weight loss approximates 0.2 to 1.5% of initial body weight per week and is quite safe. Although this diet has been clinically successful in many cats, some patients either do not prefer high fiber rations and will not accept it, or do not consume adequate quantities. Without strict veterinary supervision, a small subset of cats can lose weight too rapidly when fed high fiber diets, which can have serious metabolic complications (*Figure 3*).[27]

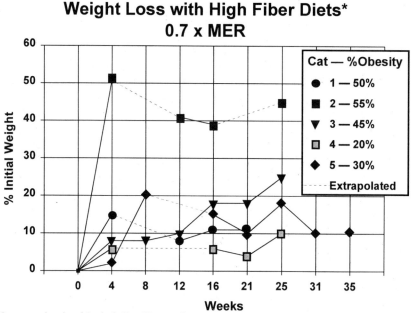

*Commercial, reduced fat, high fiber feline product.
Gentry, 1993.[27]

Figure 3. Results of a clinical weight loss protocol using high fiber, restricted fat diets in 5 obese pet cats.[22] Cats were restricted to 70% of calculated MER (60 kcal/kg/day). Cat number 2 lost weight at a dangerously rapid weight over the first month of diet introduction. No cat attained its targeted body weight at a slow, steady safe rate. Individualization of the weight loss protocol was seemingly not done.

It is also well acknowledged that dietary fiber supplementation may have risks associated with decreased nutrient digestibility and metabolizable energy.[28] These concerns have particular importance in profoundly obese cats undergoing weight reduction which are seemingly predisposed to development of the hepatic lipidosis syndrome. Of particular concern is that protein digestibility has been shown to be significantly impaired in cats receiving a variety of low-digestible dietary components.[29] While small amounts of fiber are important in regulating gut peristalsis in cats, other potentially objectionable clinical effects of increased dietary fiber include excessive defecation or constipation.

What MER Calculation Works for Weight Loss Targeting in the Cat?

Maintenance energy requirements (MER in kcal/kg per day) for cats are indicated by the commonly used formulas for MER as 60 to 90W (W=body weight in kg) for active cats, 60 to 70W /day for inactive cats, $138W^{0.404}$ for cats of all body size and activity, or calculation of MER using body surface area (shown in ***Figure 4***).[12,30] The range of estimated MER values is quite broad. For example, MER for a 4 kg cat would range between 240 to 360 kcal/day. Recent information suggests that some overweight cats have MER considerably lower than normal weight healthy cats, as low as approximately 40 kcal/kg/day; in a 4 kg obese cat this would correspond with 160 kcal per day.[12]

Calculation of MER Using
Body Surface Area (BSA) for Cats
500 x $BSA^{0.5}$ (square root of BSA = √BSA)

Body Weight (kg)	BSA	√BSA	MER for Cats 500 x √BSA
2.0	0.15	0.40	200
3.0	0.20	0.45	225
4.0	0.25	0.50	250
5.0	0.29	0.54	270
6.0	0.33	0.57	285
7.0	0.36	0.60	300
8.0	0.40	0.63	315
9.0	0.43	0.66	330
10.0	0.46	0.68	340
11.0	0.49	0.70	350

Figure 4. Method of MER determination using body surface area.[19]

Variables that may influence the level of required energy for metabolic needs are numerous and complex. One important variable causing differences between metabolic rates in overweight human beings is their differing body compositions (fat versus fat-free mass).[31] Such differences in body composition can elicit surprising differences in metabolic rates among overweight individuals when compared to lean individuals of similar age, sex, and skeletal frame. These differences in metabolic rate significantly influence the success of weight reduction programs and predictions of the rate of weight loss on standardized protocols.[11] Unfortunately, the range of metabolic rates in obese pet cats has not been rigorously investigated in clinical patients due to lack of practical and convenient methods of assessment. Subsequently, a trial and error approach is necessitated in calculating energy intake with initial measures of energy restriction erring on the conservative side.

In developing a safe and effective reducing regimen, a target or goal weight is first identified. This is best determined on combined assessments derived from veterinary examination and owner estimation of body condition from a historical perspective and feline body condition/silhouette scoring. Based on experimental and clinical work in obese cats estimated to be between 20 and 40% overweight, no greater than 60 kcal/kg should be used for initial target weight MER calculations using a low fiber, moderate or low fat diet. Ordinarily, initial energy intake is estimated at 60% of calculated MER as more conservative restrictions result in objectionably slow rates of weight loss (**Figure 5**).[16-18,22,32] With this level of energy intake, caloric ingestion ranges between 21 and 27 kcal/kg initial body weight per day while providing an intake of 36 kcal/kg of ideal weight. Obviously, weight loss will be faster during the first two months of the protocol unless caloric intakes are readjusted to maintain a steady rate of weight loss. Some cats require several energy intake adjustments during an 18 week protocol to maintain weight loss approximating 1.0 to 1.5% initial body weight per week. In 24 cats with degrees of obesity ranging between 20 to 40% (median = 25%), 13 cats attained 90% of targeted weight loss within 18 weeks when fed a low fiber, moderate fat reducing diet (fed at a level of 60% ideal body weight MER [60 kcal/kg]) (**Figure 6**).[17] Six of 7 cats estimated as 30% or greater overweight, required longer than 18 weeks to achieve their target weights. Overall, median weight loss in these cats was 20% over 18 weeks. Energy intake in this study was not adjusted during the reducing interval unless cats had attained their target weights as all lost weight at a relatively steady rate. Based on this study and experience with clinical patients, if a 30% or greater weight loss is estimated, a reducing interval longer than 18 weeks will be necessary. As cats lose weight on a well balanced ration, they become more active and playful and maintain a healthy appearance. Their apparent well being encourages further client effort in adhering to a protracted reducing regimen.

It is less clear how many calories to feed cats when a high fiber weight loss diet is offered. Clinical experience suggests that some cats voluntarily limit intake of fiber supplemented reducing diets resulting in energy restrictions more severe than anticipated (**Figure 3**). In addition, the lower digestibility and/or assimilation of nutrients may reduce derived energy.[29] With these diets as well as all other reducing diets, it is very important that food intake be closely monitored and that ration allowances be individually adjusted to attain a slow steady loss of weight over 16 to 18 weeks.

If there is unequivocally no weight loss after 4 weeks on a reducing regimen, the level of caloric restriction is increased to 45% of the MER for the targeted body weight. Before this is done there should be careful scrutiny for poor client compliance in permitting alternative eating opportunities or hunting behavior allowing prey consumption. If after another 4 weeks the cat fails to achieve a 1.5% per week rate of weight loss, the caloric intake is further reduced by 10 to 15% of calculated ideal weight MER.

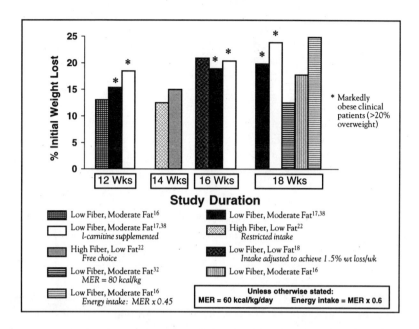

Figure 5. Comparison of results derived from different weight loss protocols and nutritional formulas in research and pet cats. References are given for each study. Unless otherwise stated, MER was derived on the basis of 60kcal/kg/day "ideal" body weight (subjectively determined). Energy intake was calculated as 60% MER, unless otherwise defined. Results suggest that similar rates of weight loss are derived using a low fiber, moderate fat or a low fiber, low fat diet. Cats receiving carnitine supplementation (white bar) and their complementary placebo group (black bar) are shown at weeks 12, 16, and 18. Cats receiving carnitine lost weight at a rate similar to cats with more severe energy restriction (45% lean body weight MER [horizontally striped bar]) receiving the same ration. See text and reference citations for particulars of each study. This data confirm that successful weight loss can be safely achieved using a variety of nutritional approaches and protocols in cats.

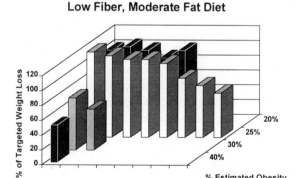

Figure 6. Success achieved over 18 weeks in obese cats (expressed as percentage of targeted weight loss) using a simple protocol (ideal body weight MER [60 kcal/kg/day] x 0.6 for daily energy intake). Cats were fed a low fiber, moderate fat diet.[17] Estimated percentage obesity was subjectively determined. Data indicates that cats approximately 20 to 25% overweight can successfully achieve 90% of targeted weight loss over 18 weeks whereas cats estimated as >25% obese require a longer weight reduction interval.

An alternative feeding option for weight loss is to restrict energy intake on an as needed basis. By having the owner match the animal to its stage of body condition (*Figure 1*), the owner can visually identify the cat's overweightness. The animal is then placed on a "phased" weight loss program. The cat's initial weight is recorded and put on a restricted energy intake with a commercial weight loss product. The owner is asked to periodically bring the animal back to the clinic for weight rechecks. If the cat loses too much or too little weight, the animal's food intake is adjusted to achieve the appropriate weight loss. As stated previously, the cat should not lose greater than 1.5% of its body weight per week. This concept has previously been applied with cats to lose >20% of their body weight.[18]

Rate of Weight Loss and Influence on Body Condition

The effect of weight reduction on lean tissue mass and body adipose tissue is thought to be influenced by several factors. These include the starting body composition, the degree of diet-induced energy restriction, the level of protein intake, individual metabolic adaptations, and the degree of regular exercise. Generally, the greater the body adipose composition the greater the reduction in adiposity during a weight reduction protocol. In humans undergoing weight reduction, lean tissue mass is preserved better with a higher protein content of a low calorie diet formulation.[33] However, estimates made in human beings suggest that 1 gram of lean body mass is lost for every 3 grams of fat and that with more severe energy restriction, greater loss of lean body mass occurs. In two studies using different diets formulated for weight reduction, each fed at a level attaining minimal weight loss of 1 to 1.5% initial body weight per week, weight loss was predominantly due to reduction in body fat as determined by absorptiometry estimation of body composition.[16,18] Cats losing weight more rapidly (caloric restriction to 45% target weight MER) had a trend for greater loss of lean tissue as compared to cats losing weight more slowly (on average 19.1% v 8.2%, respectively) and a lower loss of body fat (79.6% v 90.5, respectively) as a proportion of total body weight loss.[16] It is important to recognize that these diets provided protein at a level of 3.0 to 4.0 gm/kg/day which seemingly maintained nitrogen balance.

Recommendations regarding the safe rate of weight loss in veterinary patients are variable, with some nutritionists suggesting a loss of up to 3% of initial body weight per week. On the basis of the previously cited body condition studies, this rate of weight loss may be too fast for optimal maintenance of lean tissue. When cats lose more than 12% of their body weight during the first 4 weeks of weight reduction, concern should be warranted regarding inappropriate caloric restriction, reduced diet consumption, and/or illness. Biochemical testing should be done to detect early changes consistent with hepatic lipidosis. Therefore, a more safe approach to weight loss is obtained at 1 to 1.5% body weight loss per week.

Clinical Monitoring During Weight Reduction

After acclimization to a reducing diet the owner must remain vigilant to verify that the cat is consuming adequate quantities to optimize the safety of weight loss. Monitoring weight loss requires that baseline body weights and abdominal girths be determined one week before and at the time of diet initiation. Acquiring two baseline measurements for each parameter will help clarify changes solely due to operator error in girth determination and in weight attributable to retained urinary and alimentary contents. Variations in the quantity of urine and ingesta can importantly confuse interpretation of sequential weight determinations because of the small feline body mass. An effort should be made to record body weights at the same time of day using a single calibrated pediatric scale, at 2 week intervals during the first 8 weeks. Standardization as to time of day may help reduce weight and girth fluctuations due to daily eating and elimination patterns. Patient re-evaluation should include a quick physical examination and substantiation of the observed diet consumption. Recheck visits should be kept as short as possible to reduce client inconvenience and patient stress. Data is plotted in graphic form for both client illustration and to facilitate adjustment of energy intake (*Figure 2*). A simple computer generated graphic can be made using one of several popular spread sheets (Quatro Pro[a], Excel[b]). Weight loss ranging between 1.5 and 2.5% initial body weight per week is safe and provides encouraging evidence that the owners efforts have been successful. Graphic depiction of the rate of weight loss over 6 weeks also can be used to predict when the weight reduction program will achieve the targeted ideal body weight.

Signs of illness at any time during the weight reduction protocol should be investigated by complete physical examination and evaluation of liver enzyme activities, total bilirubin concentration, and complete urinalysis. Urine should be tested for bilirubin using an Ictotest7[c] tablet which is the most sensitive method for detection of bilirubinuria. Finding bilirubin in the urine of a cat is always abnormal and should initiate patient evaluation for its cause. Cats with hepatic lipidosis develop increased transaminase (ALT formerly SGPT, AST formerly SGOT), and ALP activities, and bilirubinuria as the earliest routine clinicopathologic indications of the syndrome. If these abnormalities are found, weight reduction is immediately suspended and the cat provided nutritional support as suggested for hepatic lipidosis.[34] In the author's hospital, these cats are given l-carnitine 250 mg per day, supplementary taurine (250 to 500 mg/day), B-complex vitamins with additional thiamine (50 to 100 mg per day), vitamin K1 (0.5–1.5 mg/kg SQ or IM one to three doses at 12 to 24 hour intervals) and supplementary zinc (7–8 mg/kg/day), mixed with a non-protein restricted feline diet.

Metabolic Manipulation of Fat Utilization

There are a variety of different "nutriceuticals" that have been suggested to have an ergonomic effect and to facilitate optimization of lean tissue mass and weight reduction in human beings.[35] These include l-carnitine, DHEA (dehydroepiandrosterone), chromium, and coenzyme Q_{10}. The only substance that has been clinically investigated in cats is l-carnitine.

Carnitine is an essential cofactor of fatty acid metabolism facilitating entrance of activated fatty acids into the mitochondrial matrix and, in a non-obligatory way, the transfer of long chain fatty acids from peroxisomes to mitochondria.[36,37] Carnitine is either acquired preformed from the diet or synthesized from

[a] Quatro-Pro: Novell, Inc.
[b] Microsoft Excel for Windows 95, Microsoft Corp., Roselle, Illinois, USA.
[c] Ictotest: Bayer Corp, Elkhart, Indiana, USA.

precursors in body cells. Precursors include methionine, lysine, iron, niacin, ascorbate, and vitamin B_6. A preliminary study of the influence of l-carnitine on rapid weight reduction (18 weeks) in markedly obese pet was investigated because of its perceived therapeutic benefit in cats afflicted with the hepatic lipidosis syndrome.[38] Results from that study suggest that supplemental l-carnitine accelerates weight loss and increases the rate of fatty acid β-oxidation. This was a double blinded placebo controlled trial in which markedly obese cats (weights exceeding estimated ideal body weights by ≥20%) were divided into 2 groups (l-carnitine treated (n=14) and placebo treated (n=10)). A low fiber moderate fat reducing diet was fed at a level providing 22 to 29 kcal/kg of initial starting body weight (food intake was not adjusted to attain a specific rate of weight loss). Cats receiving l-carnitine had significantly faster weight loss compared to the placebo control group (**Figure 7**). Although l-carnitine treated cats initially were significantly heavier than the control group, at all subsequent weekly intervals, there was no difference in body weight between groups. Determinations of acetylcarnitine, free carnitine, and total carnitine moieties demonstrated increased concentrations compared to baseline values in each group. All animals undergoing weight loss appropriately should have an increased synthesis and mobilization of carnitine. However, cats treated with l-carnitine, had significantly greater quantities of acetylcarnitine as well as a fractional distribution of total carnitine as the acetyl-ester. This highly suggests a facilitory influence on the rate of fatty acid oxidation. Diets contained measurable quantities of carnitine exceeding levels in other commercial canned diets (unpublished observations). Although these results are intriguing, it is premature to suggest that weight reduction in cats be augmented by supplemental l-carnitine as this effect requires further investigation.

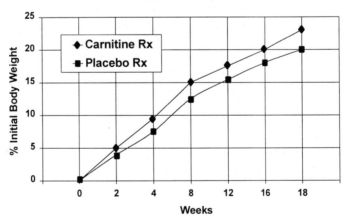

Weight Loss: % Baseline Weight
Low Fiber, Moderate Fat Diet

Figure 7. Weight loss achieved in cats fed a low fiber, moderate fat diet using a simple protocol (ideal body weight MER [60 kcal/kg/day] x 0.6 for daily energy intake). Fourteen cats received supplemental l-carnitine (250 mg per day) and 10 cats an identical appearing placebo. Although considered a preliminary observation, cats treated with supplemental l-carnitine lost weight at a significantly faster rate.[17,38]

For sustained management of normal body weight, changes in cat behavior, feeding opportunities, and modification of a sedentary lifestyle are recommended long term goals. Unfortunately, these are difficult to accomplish in the obese cat. Modification of the sedentary lifestyle may be possible through introduction of toys, interactive play, or acquisition of a companion pet. Selection of diets such as "lite foods" with caloric density ≤ 4.0 kcal/gm, not high in fat, and avoidance of free choice maintenance dry foods are suggested.[7] One of the most common obstacles to tight control of "glutinous" cats feeding opportunities is the presence of non-obese companion cats that prefer to have free choice feeding or that are fed calorically dense rations. Long term weight control in previously obese pet cats is undertaken with maintenance diets specifically designed for calorie restriction. Long term success of these diets for weight control in previously obese pet cats has not been rigorously evaluated in the home environment.

Aftermath of Weight Reduction: Weight Control

References

1. Weinsier RL, Wadden TA, Ritenbaugh C, Harrison GG, Johnson FS, Wilmore JH. Recommended therapeutic guidelines for professional weight control programs. *Am J Clin Nutr* 1984; 40:865-872.

2. Bray GA. Pathyophysiology of obesity. *Am J Clin Nutr* 1992; 55:S488-S494.

3. Scarlett JM, Donoghue S, Saidla J, Wills J. Overweight cats: prevalence and risk factors. *International J Obes* 1994; 18(Suppl 1):S22-S28.

4. Scarlett JM, Donoghue S. Health effects of obesity in cats. *Proc Waltham Intl Symp* 1997; 90.

5. Anderson RS. Obesity in the dog and cat. *Vet Ann* 1973; 13:182-186.

6. Sloth C. Practical management of obesity in dogs and cats. *J Small Anim Pract* 1992; 33:178-182.

7. Donoghue S, Scarlett JM. Diet and feline obesity. *Proc Waltham Intl Symp* 1997; 106.

8. Czaja JA, Gay RW. Ovarian hormones and food intake in female guinea pigs and rhesus monkeys. *Horm Behav* 1975; 6:329-349.

9. Tarttelin MR, Gorski RA. Variations in food and water intake in normal and acyclic female rats. *Physiol Behav* 1971; 8:847-852.

10. Lewis LD, Morris ML, Hand MS. Obesity. In: *Small Animal Clinical Nutrition III.* Topeka: Mark Morris Associates 1987; 6-1–6-39.

11. Pavlou KN, Hoefer MA, Blackburn GL. Resting energy expenditure in moderate obesity. Predicting velocity of weight loss. *Ann Surg* 1986; 203:2136-2141.

12. Earle KE, Smith PM. Digestible energy requirments of adult cats at maintenance. *J Nutr* 1991; 121:S45-S46.

13. Center SA, Crawford MA, Guida L, Erb HN, King J. A retrospective study of cats (n=77) with severe hepatic lipidosis: (1975-1990). *J Vet Int Med* 1993; 7:349-359.

14. Rogers QR, Morris JG, Freedland RA. Lack of hepatic enzymatic adaptation to low and high levels of dietary protein in the adult cat. *Enzyme* 1977; 22:348-356.

15. Hendriks WH, Moughan PJ, Tarttelin MF. Dietary excretion of endogenous nitrogen metabolites in adult domestic cats using a protein-free diet and the regression technique. *J Nutr* 1997; 127:623-629.

16. Butterwick RF, Watson TDG, Markwell PJ. The effect of different levels of energy restriction on body weight and composition in obese cats. *Proc 13th ACVIM Forum* 1995; 1029.

17. Center SA, Reynolds AP, Harte J, Watson T, Markwell PJ, Erb HN, Millington DS, Wood P, Yeager AE, Watrous D. Clinical effects of rapid weight loss in obese pet cats with and without supplemental L-carnitine. *J Vet Int Med* 1997; 11:118. (abstract)

18. Sunvold GD, Bouchard G. Use of a low fiber, low calorie diet for feline weight loss. *J Vet Int Med* 1997; 11:149. (abstract)

19. Hill JO, Drougas H, Peters JC. Obesity treatment: can diet composition play a role? *Ann Intern Med* 1993; 119:694-697.

20. Swaminathan R, King RF, Holmfield J, Siwek RA, Baker M, Wales JK. Thermic effect of feeding carbohydrate, fat, protein and mixed meal in lean and obese subjects. *Am J Clin Nutr* 1985; 42:177-181.

21. Danforth Jr E. The role of thyroid hormones and insulin in the regulation of energy metabolism. *Am J Clin Nutr* 1983; 38:1006-1017.

22. Hand MS. Effects of low fat / high fiber in the dietary management of obesity. *Proc 6th ACVIM Forum* 1988; 702-703.

23. Deutsch JA. The role of the stomach in eating. *Am J Clin Nutr* 1985; 42(5 Suppl):1040-1043.

24. Butterwick RF, Markwell PJ. Effect of level and source of dietary fibre on food intake in the dog. *Waltham Symp Nutr Comp Anim* 1993.

25. Blundell JE. Serotonin and biology of feeding. *Am J Clin Nutr* 1992; 55:S155-S159.

26. Bray GA. Treatment for obesity: A nutrient balance/nutrient partition approach. *Nutr Rev* 1991; 49:33-45.

27. Gentry SJ. Results of the clinical use of a standardized weight-loss program in dogs and cat. *J Am Anim Hosp Assoc* 1993; 29:371-376.

28. Baer DJ, Rumpler WV, Miles CW, Fahey GC. Dietary fiber decreases the metabolizable energy content and nutrient digestibility of mixed diets fed to humans. *J Nutr* 1997; 127:579-586.

29. Kienzle E, Meyer H, Schneider R. Investigations on palatability, digestibility and tolerance of low digestible food components in cats. *J Nutr* 1991;121:S56-57.

30. Hill RC. A rapid method of estimating maintenance energy requirement from body surface area in inactive adult dogs and in cats. *J Am Vet Med Assoc* 1993; 202:1814-1816.

31. Donoghue S, Kronfeld DS. A comparative medical approach to obesity. *Proc 6th ACVIM Forum* 1988; 705-707.

32. Butterwick RF, Wills SM, Sloth C, Markwell PJ. A study of obese cats on a calorie-controlled weight reduction programme. *Vet Rec* 1994; 134:372-377.

33. Prentice AM, Goldberg GR, Jebb SA, Black AE, Murgatroyd PR, Diaz EO. Physiological responses to slimming. *Proc Nutr Soc* 1991; 50:441-458.

34. Center SA. Hepatic lipidosis, glucocorticoid hepatopathy, vacuolar heptopathy, storage disorders, amyloidosis, and iron toxicity. In: Guilford WG, Center SA, Strombeck DR, Williams DA, Meyer DJ, eds. *Strombeck's Small Animal Gastroenterology*, 3rd Edition. Philadelphia: W.B. Saunders Co., 1996; 766-801.

35. Bucci LR. Nutritional ergogenic aids. In: Wolinsky I, Hickson JF, eds. *Nutrition in Exercise and Sport,* 2nd Edition. Ann Arbor: CRC Press, 1993; 295-346.

36. Goa KL, Brogden RN. l-carnitine: A preliminary review of its pharmacokinetics, and its therapeutic use in ischaemic cardiac disease and primay and secondary carnitine deficiencies in realtionship to its role in fatty acid metabolism. *Drugs* 1987; 34:1-24.

37. Brehmer J. Carnitine-metabolism and functions. *Physiological Rev* 1983; 68:1420-1480.

38. Center SA, Reynolds AP, Harte J, Watson T, Markwell PJ, Erb HN, Millington DS, Wood P, Yeager AE, Watrous D. Metabolic influence of oral l-carnitine during a rapid 18 week weight loss program in obese cats. *J Vet Int Med* 1997; 11:118.

Dietary Modification of Feline Obesity with a Low Fat, Low Fiber Diet

Guy F. Bouchard, DMV, MS, DACT
Director, Sinclair Research Center, Columbia, Missouri, USA

Gregory D. Sunvold, PhD; Leighann Daristotle, DVM, PhD
Research and Development, The Iams Company, Lewisburg, Ohio, USA

Abstract

The prevalence of obesity varies in cats but has been reported to range between 35 and 40%. Obesity constitutes the most common nutritional problem in cats. Current weight loss therapies often include the use of diets containing high amounts of fiber. This type of therapy frequently results in excessive defecation or constipation. Uncontrolled weight loss in cats can also induce hepatic lipidosis. In an effort to develop an efficient but safe anti-obesity diet for cats, an experimental diet formulation that contained low fiber levels (<3% crude fiber) and minimal calories from fat (23%) was formulated. This diet contained 33.5% protein, 9.2% fat, and 8.0% moisture.

The objective of this study was to evaluate this low fiber and low fat diet in a weight loss regimen. After a fattening period, ten overweight ovariohysterectomized cats were fed the experimental low fiber, low calorie diet for 16 weeks. Weekly body weight (BW) values were recorded and intakes were adjusted to achieve 1.5% BW loss per week. Body condition score (BCS) and body composition were measured at 0, 3, 5, 9, 13, and 16 weeks during feeding of the experimental diet. Liver biopsies were obtained at 0, 3, 5, 13, and 16 weeks during feeding of the experimental diet.

During the 16 week period, the average BW loss of the cats was 21.0%, and BCS declined 34.3%. Body composition changed from 71.0% lean body mass (LBM), 28.0% fat mass (FM), and 1.0% bone mineral content (BMC) at the initiation of the weight loss period to 80.0% LBM, 18.8% FM, and 1.2% BMC at 16 weeks after consuming the experimental diet. Nearly 50% of the animals' body fat was lost during the 16 week period. Liver histology was assessed on a six-point scale (0 = **normal** to 5 = **severe**) that indicated the degree of lipid infiltration. A score of 3 or greater indicates a clinical diagnosis of hepatic lipidosis. At no point during the 16 weeks of feeding the experimental diet was a liver histological score greater than 1 observed in any of the cats. These results indicate that a low fiber, low calorie diet for cats can effectively and safely result in weight loss.

Obesity is the most common nutritional problem in cats.[1,2] Recent estimates of the prevalence of obesity have ranged from 35% to 40% .[1,3] Obesity can be easily overlooked in cats, partly because obesity is often less visually apparent in cats than in dogs. The excess of adipose tissue is often located intra-abdominally and cranial to the inguinal area, forming an "apron".[4,5] In addition, excessive weight gain is usually an insidious process in cats. Consumption of only one extra kibble of commercial cat food per day for one year can lead to a 1% gain in body weight as fat, and may result in an animal that is 20% overweight by middle age.

Obesity can be simply defined as an excessive accumulation of fat in the adipose tissues of the body. It is generally the result of excessive caloric intake in relation to the individual's requirement.[1] Risk factors that can lead to obesity in pets include neutering, confined lifestyle, inactivity, middle age, male gender, and pet owner lifestyle.[1-4,6] Consumption of commercial dry pet foods is also considered a risk factor for obesity, possibly due to the high palatability of these diets.[3,4] A body weight that is above 15 to 20% of the "ideal" body weight is indicative of obesity.[1,6] The "ideal" body weight is a somewhat subjective determination. In most cases, the body weight of cats during their first year of age is a good reflection of their "ideal" weight. A body condition scoring system introduced by Edney and Smith[7] is an important clinical tool to assess the obesity status of an animal.

Obesity is known to be associated with significant health risks in humans, including diabetes mellitus, hypertension, neoplasia, bacterial and viral infections, and dermatoses.[4] Although there is a paucity of information to show that cats experience the same health complications, it is assumed that obesity may play a role in some of these problems. Obesity in cats has been reported to be associated with the development of hepatic lipidosis,[1,4,6] feline urological syndrome,[8,9] diabetes mellitus,[10,11,12] impaired glucose tolerance and altered insulin response to glucose infusion,[13] and skin problems from difficulties in self-grooming.[1,14] Undocumented clinical associations have been made with constipation, dystocia, and articular/locomotor problems. Obese cats have a higher risk of complications during anesthesia and intra-abdominal surgery and are more likely to have postsurgical wound dehiscence.[1,4] Furthermore, obesity interferes with veterinary examination and diagnostic procedures, such as auscultation, abdominal palpation, radiography, and ultrasound. Because of these health risks and associated problems, protocols and commercial diets for weight loss are becoming an increasingly important consideration in feline veterinary practice.

Most commercial feline diets formulated to promote clinically significant weight loss contain at least 25% fiber. Such high fiber diets may be associated with excessive fecal output, constipation, poor skin and haircoat, and decreased palatability and nutrient digestibility in cats.[15-18] The objective of the study reported here was to determine whether a low fat and low fiber diet can effectively and safely promote weight loss in cats.

*Materials
and Methods*

Animals. Ten ovariectomized purpose-bred female domestic shorthair cats participated in this study. They were observed to be free of internal and external parasites, and were current on their vaccination schedule. All cats were housed individually in cages or runs. They had access to a resting board, toys, and clay litter. Fresh water was provided *ad libitum*.

Study Design. The study consisted of two phases: a weight-gain and a weight-loss period. During the 9 week weight-gain phase, the cats were fed a high-energy diet (Eukanuba Veterinary Diets' Nutritional Recovery Formula®) and expected to gain approximately 20% of their baseline body weight (**Figure 1**). During this phase, fresh food was provided *ad libitum* daily.

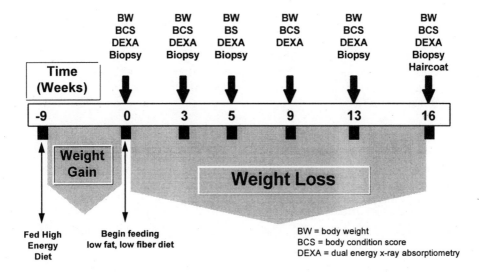

Figure 1. Experimental timeline.

The 16 week weight-loss phase was initiated immediately following a five day diet transition period. During the weight-loss phase, the cats were fed a pre-scribed amount of a dry test diet once daily (**Table 1**). The amount of diet fed was calculated weekly for each cat, based on the historical feed consumption and body weight patterns. Feeding amounts were adjusted to achieve approximately 1.5% loss in body weight per week. If animals lost more than 2% or less than 1% of their body weight in a one week period, the amount of diet offered was adjusted accordingly.

The test diet (Eukanuba Veterinary Diets Restricted-Calorie® Formula/ Feline) contained 9.2% fat, 33.5% protein, and 1.9% fiber on a dry matter basis (**Table 2**), and only 23% of the calories provided were from fat. The dietary protein quality was extremely high, with a protein efficiency ratio of 96% when compared with that of egg.

Table 1. Ingredients in the low fat, low fiber diet.

Chicken By-Product Meal	Choline Chloride	Thiamine Mononitrate
Rice Flour	Salt	Pyridoxine Hydrochloride
Ground Corn Grits	Vitamin E Supplement	(Vitamin B_6)
Dried Beet Pulp	Zinc Oxide	Vitamin B_{12} Supplement
Fish Meal	Manganese Sulfate	Riboflavin Supplement
Poultry Digest	Ethoxyquin (a preservative)	Inositol
Dried Egg Product	Niacin	Vitamin D_3 Supplement
Chicken Fat (preserved w/BHA)	Ascorbic Acid	Folic Acid
Potassium Chloride	Vitamin A Acetate	Potassium Iodide
Calcium Carbonate	Biotin Supplement	Sodium Selenite
Brewers Dried Yeast	Copper Sulfate	Cobalt Carbonate
DL-Methionine	Calcium Pantothenate	

Data Collection. Food consumption and body weights were measured daily and weekly, respectively, during both phases of the study. Body weights were measured using a weighing cage and scale in the dynamic mode, and were reported to the nearest 0.0001 kg.

Body composition was estimated by subjective scoring or use of a Dual Energy X-ray Absorptiometer (DEXA; QDR-2000 Plus, Hologic) at the initiation of each phase and every 2 to 4 weeks during the weight-loss phase (**Figure 1**). Subjective body composition score (BCS) was also evaluated by two observers, using a scale from 1 to 5, as proposed by Edney and Smith in 1986.[7] For DEXA measurements, cats were initially anesthetized with a combination of atropine, acepromazine, and ketamine and maintained under anesthesia with isoflurane. The cats were placed in dorsal recumbency with the limbs stretched caudally to avoid overlapping the body. The animals were scanned using enhanced-array whole-body software. Bone mineral content (BMC), lean mass, fat mass, estimated body weight, and percent fat were determined.

Table 2. Nutrient profile of the low fat, low fiber diet.

Nutrient	%, Dry Matter Basis
Protein	33.5
Moisture	8.0
Fat	9.2
Crude Fiber	1.9
Ash	5.8
Calcium	0.88
Phosphorus	0.85
Magnesium	0.09
n-6:n-3 fatty acid ratio	5.7:1

Because idiopathic hepatic lipidosis can be experimentally induced in overweight cats by restriction of nutrient intake,[19] ultrasound-guided liver biopsies were performed in fasted, isoflurane-anesthetized cats after blood and urine sample collection. Liver biopsies were collected on weeks 0, 3, 5, 13, and 16 during the weight-loss phase (*Figure 1*). An ultrasound (Pie Medical Scanner 200, Classic Medical Supply, Inc.) equipped with a 7.5-MHZ mechanical sectorial probe was used. Histologic results were scored by degree of lipid infiltration on a scale of 0 to 5 as proposed by Biourge and others in 1994a.[19]

At the end of the study, hair coat parameters were assessed. Haircoat shine, scale, and ease of epilation also were graded from 0 to 5, according to a scale proposed by Campbell and Roudebush in 1995[20] (*Table 3*). The cats were also monitored daily for clinical conditions.

Table 3. Scoring system for skin and haircoat evaluation.

	SCORE		
Score	**Shine**	**Scale**	**Ease of Epilation**
0	dull	none	none
1	poorly reflective	fine over back	slight
2	slightly reflective	fine over body	moderate
3	medium reflective	medium over body	marked
4	glistens	medium	severe
5	greasy	severe	spontaneous

From reference 20.

Statistical Analysis. Data were evaluated at the following three time points: initiation of weight-gain phase, end of weight-gain phase or initiation of weight-loss phase, and end of weight-loss phase. Descriptive statistics and Student t-tests were performed on body weights, body condition scores, and body composition parameters measured by DEXA. Descriptive statistics were calculated for hair coat parameters and liver biopsies.

Weight-gain Phase. The cats gained 25.7% of their initial body weight during the weight-gain phase. The gain in body weight was statistically significant ($P<0.01$). The BCS increased 0.9 units during the weight-gain phase. The gain in BCS was also statistically significant ($P<0.01$).

Results

Body composition measurements as determined by DEXA revealed that the weight gain was distributed over BMC, lean mass, and fat mass. *Table 4* summarizes the DEXA results for the initiation of weight-gain and weight-loss phases, and end of the weight-loss phase. The animals gained 9.4, 12.1, and 48.8% of their initial

BMC, lean mass, and fat mass, respectively (data not shown). The gain in lean and fat masses were statistically significant (P<0.05).

Weight-loss Phase. Over the 16 week period of consuming the test diet, cats lost 21.0% of their body weight. The loss in body weight was statistically significant (P<0.05). The body weight at the end of the weight-loss phase was not different than that at the initiation of the weight-gain phase. On average, cats lost 1.5% of their body weight per week. The BCS decreased during the weight-loss phase by 34.3%. The decrease in BCS was statistically significant (P<0.05). The BCS at the end of the weight loss phase was not different than that at the initiation of the weight-gain period.

Table 4. Body composition (in percent) as measured by DEXA.

Time	BMC, %	FM, %	LBM, %
Initiation of Weight Gain	1.1	22.0	76.9
Initiation of Weight Loss	1.0	28.0	71.0
End of Weight Gain	1.2	18.8	80.0

The diet-induced weight loss was 2.8, 14.2, and 48.7% for BMC, lean mass, and fat mass, respectively, when body composition was determined by DEXA (**Table 4**). **Figure 2** illustrates the body composition (in percent) of cats before and after feeding the low fiber, low fat diet for 16 weeks. The reductions in lean and fat mass were statistically significant (P<0.05). There were no statistical differences between the BMC, lean mass, and fat mass at the end of the weight-loss phase versus at the initiation of the weight-gain phase.

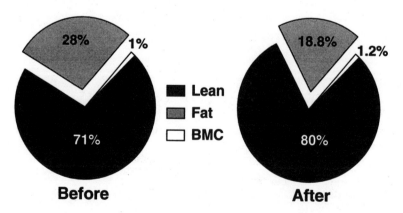

Figure 2. Body composition of cats before and after feeding the low fat, low fiber diet for 16 weeks.

Liver biopsy results were similar before and during the weight-loss phase (data not shown). Scores were not greater than 1, and did not increase with weight loss. The weight-reduction diet did not affect the shine of the hair coat, nor did it produce scale or increase hair epilation. No clinical conditions were observed during the course of the study.

Discussion

The present study introduces a unique animal model of obesity to evaluate weight-loss diets. The cat obesity model was designed with the risk factors for feline obesity in mind. It consists of older, ovariectomized, ex-breeder queens (1.5- to 3-years-old) maintained in a confined environment to promote an inactive lifestyle and fed a highly palatable, high energy diet. Queens were used instead of toms because of availability. However, the queens gained 25.7% of their body weight over 9 weeks, which exceeded expectations. This obesity model provides a reliable, easily standardized, and efficient method of producing obese cats. It also provides a good level of control over the final percentage of fat.

In the present study, the weight-loss rate was 1.5% per week over a 16 week period. In previous experimental weight-loss programs, the rates were 0.8 and 1.0%.[5,21] Achieving 2 to 3% weight loss per week is generally recommended as safe for canine weight-loss programs.[4,6] However, the potential for development of hepatic lipidosis is a major concern when obese cats undergo caloric restriction. In this study, 1.5% weight loss per week over 16 weeks was found safe and efficient for cats. All of the cats were clinically normal and no significant hepatic lipid accumulation was observed in any of the cats.

A low rate of weight loss in this study, in addition to a high protein intake, was likely responsible for the lack of hepatic lipidosis in these cats. Although the pathogenesis of hepatic lipidosis has not been completely elucidated, affected cats commonly have a history of obesity followed by significant weight loss.[22,23,24] Hepatic lipidosis has been observed in two reports in which cats fasted for 5 to 7 weeks. The rate of weight loss was between 7 and 15% for the first week, and 3 to 6% for the subsequent weeks.[25] Clinical signs, histologic lesions, and changes in blood parameters consistent with hepatic lipidosis were observed within 5 to 7 weeks. Protein supplementation has been shown to reduce hepatic lipid accumulation in fasted cats,[25,26] with methionine and arginine implicated as the limiting amino acids for preventing hepatic lipidosis.[27]

The Dual Energy X-ray Absorptiometer has been found to be specific and highly sensitive in measuring body composition in cats.[28] The DEXA is particularly suitable to determine body composition fluctuations over time. During the weight-loss phase, the cats' weight losses were chiefly attributable to changes in fat mass with a minor lean mass component. Although the cats lost 14.2 and 48.7% of lean and fat masses, respectively, during the weight-loss phase, the lean mass absolute value was not statistically different from the lean mass prior to the weight-gain phase. However, the relative lean mass at the end of the weight-loss phase (82%)

was significantly higher (P<0.05) than that at the initiation of the weight-gain phase (76.9%), indicating that the lean mass:body weight ratio had been protected despite body weight loss.

A loss in lean mass is to be expected during a weight-loss program. Forbes[29] describes it as "the companionship of lean and fat tissue". The composition of weight loss in humans is such that the obese patient on low calorie intake will lose nitrogen (estimate of lean mass) at a slower relative rate than the non-obese patient. In other words, the fat content at the beginning of a weight-loss program will determine the change in the ratio of lean mass:total body weight. Obese patients lost less lean mass than non-obese patients and obese patients being severely restricted lost more lean mass than those being moderately restricted.[29,30,31] This pattern may also be evident in cats. In a recent feline weight-reduction study, the initial percent of fat was 35.8%, compared with 27.0% for this study, and their weight loss composition was 90.5 and 8.2% for fat and lean masses, respectively.[21] Their weight loss rate was approximately 1% versus 1.5% for this study. At the end of their weight-loss regimen, 5 of the 13 cats were still obese (>25% fat). In this study, only one cat had more than 25% fat. Thus, the higher percentage of lean mass lost in this study might be attributable to a lower initial percentage of fat, a faster rate of weight loss, and/or a more profound weight loss. Butterwick and Markwell[21] also found that the body weight loss from fat correlated significantly with the highest initial fat content in cats.

Clinical experience suggests that deterioration of skin and coat quality may be a problem with some feline weight-loss diets. Such was not the case for the test diet in this study, however. Cats consuming this diet had glossy coats with little scale and slight to moderate ease of epilation at the end of the feeding period. One potential explanation for the preservation of hair and skin condition in these cats is the 5.7:1 balance of omega-6:omega-3 (n-6:n-3) fatty acids in the diet. Feeding dogs a diet containing a 5:1 to 10:1 ratio of n-6 to n-3 fatty acids resulted in less inflammatory changes in the skin at the cellular level.[32] Although similar results are not available for cats, n-3 fatty acid supplementation (i.e., lower n-6:n-3 ratio) has been shown to have beneficial effects in cats with dermatologic disease.[33]

Overweight cats are common in veterinary practice and clinical experience suggests that obese cats may be more likely to develop complications from anesthesia and surgery. Recent data suggest that obese cats are more likely to develop a number of clinical conditions including diabetes mellitus, skin problems, and lameness.[34] Results from this study demonstrated that the diet used in this study induced safe and effective weight loss and suggests that such a diet should be clinically useful in the treatment of obesity and the prevention of obesity-associated pathology.

The results of this study demonstrated that feeding the test diet to obese cats could induce safe and effective weight loss. On average, cats consuming this diet lost 1.5% of their body weight per week over a 16 week period, without evidence of hepatic lipidosis or deterioration of skin and coat condition.

The authors thank Dr. Larry Thornburg, Columbia, Missouri, USA for *Acknowledgements* histologic evaluation of the liver biopsy specimens.

References

1. Sloth D. Practical management of obesity in dogs and cats. *J Small Anim Pract* 1992; 33:178-182.
2. Crane SW. Occurrence and management of obesity in companion animals. *J Small Anim Pract* 1991; 32:275-282.
3. Scarlett JM, Donoghue S, Saidla J, Wills J. Overweight cats: Prevalence and risk factors. *Int J Obesity* 1994; 18(Suppl 1):S22-S28.
4. Hand MS, Armstrong PJ, Allen TA. Obesity: Occurrence, treatment, and prevention. *Vet Clin of North Am* 1989; 9:447-474.
5. Butterwick RF, Wills JM, Sloth C, Markwell PJ. A study of obese cats on a calorie-controlled weight reduction programme. *Vet Rec* 1994; 134:372-377.
6. Buffington CAT. Management of obesity: the clinical nutritionist's experience. *Int J Obesity* 1994; 18(Suppl 1):S29-S34.
7. Edney ATB, Smith PM. Study of obesity in dogs visiting veterinary practices in the United Kingdom. *Vet Rec* 1986; 118:391.
8. Walker AD, Weaver AD, Anderson RS, Crighton GW, Fennell C, Gaskell CJ, Wilkinson GT. An epidemiological survey of the feline urological syndrome. *J Small Anim Pract* 1977; 18:283-301.
9. Willeberg P, Priester WA. Feline urological syndrome: Associations with some time, space, and individual patient factors. *Am J Vet Res* 1976; 37:975-978.
10. Crenshaw KL, Peterson ME. Pretreatment clinical and laboratory evaluation of cats with diabetes mellitus: 104 cases (1992-1994). JAVMA 1996; 209:943-949.
11. Moise NS, Reimers TJ. Insulin therapy in cats with diabetes mellitus. JAVMA 1983; 182:158-164.
12. Panciera DL, Thomas CB, Eiker SW, Atkins CE. Epizootiologic patterns of diabetes mellitus in cats: 333 cases (1980-1986). JAVMA 1990; 197:1504-1508.
13. Nelson RW, Himsel CA, Feldman EC, Bottoms GD. Glucose tolerance and insulin response in normal-weight and obese cats. *Am J Vet Res* 1990; 5:1357-1362.
14. Rodriguez JM, Perez M. Cutaneous myiasis in three obese cats. *Vet Quart* 1996; 18:102-103.
15. Dimski DS, Buffington CA. Dietary fiber in small animal therapeutics. JAVMA 1991; 199:1142-1146.
16. Burrows CF, Kronfeld DS, Banta CA, Merritt AM. Effects of fiber on digestibility and transit time in dogs. *J Nutr* 1982; 112:1726.
17. Fahey Jr GC, Merchen NR, Corbin JE, Hamilton AK, Bauer LL, Titgemeyer EC, Hirakawa DA. Dietary fiber for dogs: III. Effects of beet pulp and oat fiber additions to dog diets on nutrient intake, digestibility, metabolizable energy, and digesta mean retention time. *J Anim Sci* 1992; 70:1169.

18. Sunvold GD, Fahey Jr GC, Merchen NR, Bourquin LD, Titgemeyer EC, Bauer LL, Reinhart GA. Dietary fiber for cats: *In vitro* fermentation of selected fiber sources by cat fecal inoculum and *in vivo* utilization of diets containing selected fiber sources and their blends. *J Anim Sci* 1995; 73:2329.

19. Biourge VC, Groff JM, Munn RJ, Kirk CA, Nyland TG, Madeiros VA, Morris JG, Rogers QR. Experimental induction of hepatic lipidosis in cats. *Am J Vet Res* 1994a; 55:1291-1302.

20. Campbell KL, Roudebush P. Effects of four diets on serum and cutaneous fatty acids, transepidermal water losses, skin surface lipids, hydration and condition of the skin and haircoat of dogs. *Proc 11th AAVD/ACVD* 1995; 80.

21. Butterwick RF, Markwell PJ. Changes in the body composition of cats during weight reduction by controlled dietary energy restriction. *Vet Rec* 1996; 138:354-357.

22. Barsanti JA, Jones BD, Spano JS, Taylor HW. Prolonged anorexia associated with hepatic lipidosis in three cats. *Fel Pract* 1977; 52:57.

23. Center SA, Crawford MA, Guida L, Erb HN, King J. A retrospective study of 77 cats with severe hepatic lipidosis: 1975-1990. *J Vet Int Med* 1993; 7:349-359.

24. Jacobs G, Cornelius L, Allen S, Greene C. Treatment of idiopathic hepatic lipidosis in cats: 11 cases (1986-1987). *JAVMA* 1989; 195:635-638.

25. Biourge VC, Pion P, Lewis J, Morris JG, Rogers QR. Spontaneous occurrence of hepatic lipidosis in a group of laboratory cats. *J Vet Int Med* 1993; 7:194-197.

26. Dimski DS. Feline hepatic lipidosis. *Seminar in Vet Med & Surg (Small Animal)* 1997; 12:28-33.

27. Biourge VC, Massat B, Groff JM, Morris JG, Rogers QR. Effects of protein, lipid, or carbohydrate supplementation on hepatic lipid accumulation during rapid weight loss in obese cats. *Am J Vet Res* 1994b; 55:1406-1415.

28. Sunvold GD, Bouchard G. Dual energy x-ray absorptiometry validation for cats. *FASEB J* 1996; 10:A209 (Abstr.)

29. Forbes GB. Lean body mass-body fat interrelationships in humans. *Nutr Rev* 1987; 45:225-231.

30. Forbes GB, Drenick EJ. Loss of body nitrogen on fasting. *Am J Clin Nutr* 1979; 32:1570-1574.

31. Prentice AM, Goldberg GR, Jebb SA, Black AE, Murgatroyd PR. Physiological responses to slimming. *Proc Nutr Soc* 1991; 50:441-458.

32. Vaughn DM, Reinhart GA, Swaim SF, Lauten SD, Garner CA, Boudreaux MK, Spano JS, Hoffman CE, Conner B. Evaluation of effects of dietary n-6 to n-3 fatty acid ratios on leukotriene B synthesis in dog skin and neutrophils. *Vet Derm* 1994; 5:163.

33. Miller WH, Scott DW, Wellington JR. Efficacy of DVM Derm Caps Liquid™ in the management of allergic and inflammatory dermatoses of the cat. *J Am Anim Hosp Assoc* 1993; 29:38-40.

34. Scarlett JM, Donoghue S. Obesity in cats: Prevalence and prognosis. *Vet Clin Nutr* 1996; 3:128.

Neonatal Health

Development of the Canine and Feline Gastrointestinal Tract

Randal K. Buddington, PhD
Professor, Department of Biological Sciences
Mississippi State University, Mississippi State, Mississippi, USA

Daniel B. Paulsen, DVM, PhD, DACVP
College of Veterinary Medicine
Mississippi State University, Mississippi State, Mississippi, USA

The highest level of mortality for cats and dogs occurs during the first weeks after birth, with up to 30% of puppy mortality within the first two weeks.[1] Although the causes are numerous, and often hard to identify, many have been attributed to problems associated with nutrition and/or dysfunctions and limitations of the developing gastrointestinal tract (GIT). Because of this, our ability to care for and feed orphaned kittens and puppies and those suffering from diseases will be improved by gaining a better understanding of the developing GIT and the interactions with nutrition.

Changes in the GIT actually occur over three time scales. The first is during the evolution of a species and involves setting genetic determinants of the GIT to maximize digestive efficiency for the natural diet. For example, pancreatic secretions of carnivores are characterized by low amylase, but high protease activities compared to omnivores. They also lack or have reduced regions of the GIT that are specialized for bacterial fermentation. The digestive and metabolic specializations of domestic cats to a carnivorous diet are exemplary.[2] The second time scale is during the life of individuals and involves the age-related changes in the GIT which are timed to coincide with expected shifts in diet composition,[3] such as those at weaning. The third time scale includes the rapid and reversible changes in GIT structure and functions that allow individuals to respond to daily and seasonal fluctuations in the amounts and composition of dietary inputs. It is important to consider all three time scales of adaptation when designing diets for individual species (maybe breeds) and different ages.

The present contribution focuses on what is known about the developing GIT of cats and dogs. It should be considered as a supplement to a previous description of cat and dog GIT development[4] and will include results and insights obtained during the short interval. Where appropriate, some overlap is included to prevent confusion and to enhance understanding. First, some of the age-related changes in dietary inputs that are relevant to this discussion of GIT development are described(see chapter by Lepine[5]). Information about structural and functional development of the GIT is then presented. Age-related changes in exocrine pancreatic secretions are discussed in the chapter by Elnif and Buddington.[6] A final section is devoted to the GIT microbiota in light of its importance in health and disease (see chapter by Buddington and Sunvold[7]). It must be remembered that despite the focus on digestion, the GIT has at least three other critical functions, all of which are known to undergo age-related changes. These include immunity (see chapter by Nelson[8]), osmoregulation, and endocrine control of digestion and metabolism.

| *Diets of Developing Dogs and Cats* | The functional demands placed on the GIT of cats and dogs change dramatically during development. Prior to birth, fetuses swallow amniotic fluid, which contains nutrients (albeit at low concentrations) and a diversity of biologically active molecules. It has been established that swallowing amniotic fluid is critical for normal development of the GIT during gestation.[9] |

Colostrum, the first milk produced after birth is higher in protein and lower in fat and carbohdyrate compared to later, or mature, milk.[10] However, the higher protein content is largely because of the high concentrations of antibodies, many of which are transferred by the fetal enterocytes to the blood of kittens and puppies, thereby providing passive immunity. As a consequence, the 'digestible' protein content of colostrum may be similar to that of mature milk. In the dog, colostrum also stimulates rapid hypertrophy and hyperplasia of the intestinal mucosa and causes changes in the activities of some enzymes.[11,12,13] The effects are not caused solely by nutrients since milk replacer does not elicit the same degree of growth and maturation. Although similar responses to colostrum are seen in pigs and other species,[3] they are not universal as evident from the virtual lack of increase in the intestinal mass during the first days to week after kittens are born.[4,14]

The composition of mature milk varies widely among mammals,[15] and even between females.[16] The reduced growth and failure to thrive of kittens and puppies fed cow's milk or other 'homemade' replacers can be partly attributed to a composition that does not adequately match that of queen's and bitch's milk.[17] It is also possible that because of the limited digestive functions of the suckling GIT, some alternative sources of nutrients may not be adequately digested.

Weaning is a complex phenomenon and represents another critical time for cats and dogs.[18] In natural settings, internal (genetic) and external (diet) signals determine when animals wean. These include 1) when the volume of milk available is not sufficient to provide adequate energy and nutrients, 2) when alternative foods are available, and 3) when the developing GIT can process the alternative foods. Data for dogs indicate milk intake is relatively constant from postnatal weeks 2 to 7, but declines as a percentage of body weight (from 11% to 0.26%). During this period consumption of solid food gradually increases from 1.4% of body weight at week 3 to 4.4% at week 7. As the proportions of milk and solid food change, there are corresponding changes in the functional demands placed on the developing GIT.

Domestic cats and dogs are sometimes weaned abruptly, based on the subjective evaluation of the breeder/owner, and not by the capabilities of the growing animal to tolerate solid food. When and how to wean remain important questions in companion animal nutrition, but clearly GIT development is an important consideration.

Intestinal Dimensions. Corresponding with other carnivores, the intestines of adult dogs and cats are relatively short compared to those of omnivores and herbivores.[19] Throughout most of development, the relative length of the small intestine (cm/kg body weight) is greater for cats than dogs (**Figure 1A**), but in adults the intestines are similar in length when normalized to body weight. Cats also tend to have more absorptive surface area relative to body weight than dogs (**Figure 1B**). The exceptions are at birth and again at 3 weeks of age when the cats studied had a sharp drop in surface area for as yet unexplained reasons. However, by weaning, values had recovered and were higher than at any other stage of development.

The small intestine averages about 2.5–7% of body weight throughout development of cats and dogs, with a peak at weaning (**Figure 1C**). The values are within the range for other mammals. Why cats, dogs, and other carnivores tend to have shorter, thicker intestines whereas omnivores have longer and thinner intestines is not adequately understood. A consistent feature among mammals, regardless of feeding type and intestinal length, is that the amount of mucosa declines from the duodenum to the ileum.[20] This has profound implications in the regional distribution of hydrolytic and absorptive processes.

In dogs, the relative mass of stomach (g/kg body weight) increases after birth, particularly during suckling, with maximum values at the time of weaning (**Figure 2**). After weaning there is a slight decline with the stomachs of 25 week old beagles being about 1.7% of total body weight.[21] Values are not available for adult dogs and developing cats.

The peak at weaning for the relative weight of small intestine and stomach contrasts with other organs, which represent a higher percentage of body weight at birth and decline thereafter.[21] However, the pattern of GIT development coincide with the high metabolic rates and weight specific food intake of developing cats and dogs. Specifically, rates of body mass gain and food consumption for Beagles are greatest between weaning and puberty (2–5 months of age), and the large amount of intestinal tissue would be needed to process the dietary inputs. The subsequent decline in intestinal mass relative to body weight corresponds with reduced growth, and lower weight-specific metabolic rates and dietary inputs.

Although at present there is very little known about interbreed variation, a survey of the literature and a review of research results reveal that intestinal dimensions do vary between, and maybe even within, breeds. A portion of the

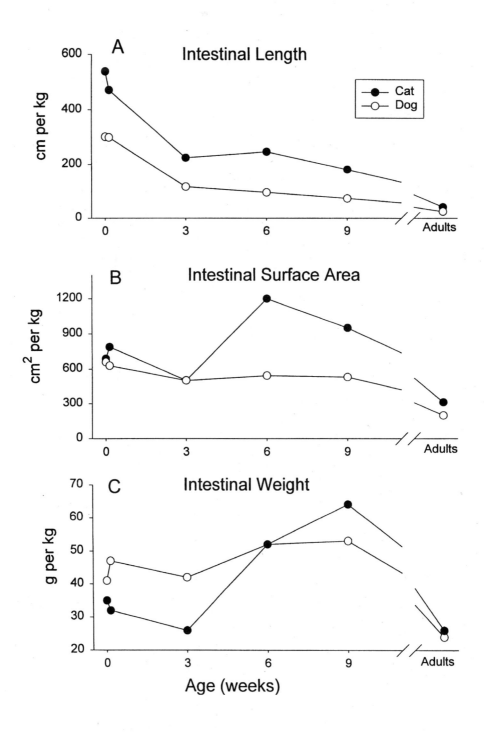

Figure 1. Intestinal length (A), surface area (B), and wet weight (C) normalized to total body weight for cats and dogs from birth to adulthood.

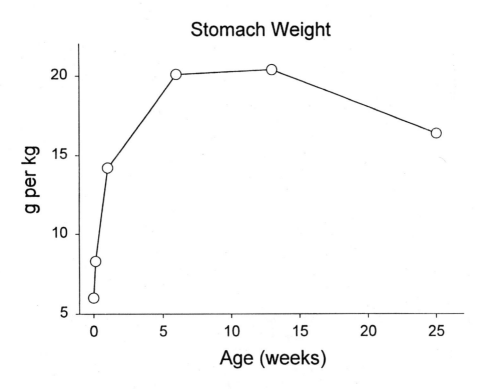

Figure 2. Stomach weight of beagles. Adapted from Deavers et al., 1972.[21]

variation can be explained by investigators using different protocols. However, even when the same procedures are used, differences have been detected between stocks of cats, pigs, and mink that would have been thought to be genetically similar. Factors that are known to be important determinants of growth and final body weight for cats and dogs include sex and birth weight, maternal weight, parity, nutritional state, and litter size, and genetic background.[22] It would not be surprising to find these same factors also influence GIT development.

Intestinal Histology. Mucosal histology can be used as an indicator of functional characteristics in healthy dogs[23] and those suffering from intestinal dysfunctions.[24] This section, therefore, briefly presents an account of basic intestinal histology that supplements a previous account[4] before describing changes that occur during normal postnatal development of cats and dogs.

The villi of the cat and dog small intestine are roughly cylindrical with a conical to club-shaped top. The epithelial layer of the villi consists of the abundant, tall, columnar enterocytes and scattered mucus secreting goblet cells. The luminal surface of the enterocyte is formed in numerous tiny projections known as microvilli. These, in conjunction with the villi, amplify the absorptive surface area of the intestine several hundred times over that of a smooth bore cylinder.

Under the epithelial layer is a loose connective tissue core called the lamina propria, which contains a blind-ended lymphatic vessel (lacteal), capillaries, strands of smooth muscle, and in adults, variable numbers of lymphocytes and plasma cells. Numerous solitary lymphoid nodules and clusters of lymphoid nodules, known as Peyer's patches, are present within the lamina propria, with a greater abundance in the ileum.

Opening between the villi and extending down through the lamina propria to the muscularis mucosa, are simple tubular glands called the crypts of Lieberkuhn (crypts). The epithelium of the crypts is continuous with the epithelium of the villi. Stem cells within the crypts produce the cells that migrate up the villus and differentiate into the enterocytes and goblet cells, as well as those that migrate down deeper into the crypts and become enterochromaffin cells and other cell types with secretory functions.

The muscularis mucosa separates the lamina propria from the submucosa, which is a loosely arranged connective tissue stroma containing blood and lymphatic vessels and nerve ganglia. It is surrounded by a tunica muscularis composed of inner circular and outer longitudinal layers of smooth muscle. Finally, the tunica muscularis is covered with a thin serosal membrane.

Small intestinal histology of cats and dogs is similar, and it is not surprising that the microscopic changes that occur during postnatal development of the intestine are also similar. At birth, the villi of cats and dogs are relatively long and slender, and the crypts are short (*Figures 3 and 4*). The tendencies for the villi and the crypts to be longer in the proximal portions of the intestine, and a constant villus:crypt ratio along the length of intestine are retained into adulthood. At birth, before the start of suckling, the enterocytes covering the villi are of moderate height and have a well-developed brush border. The cytoplasm is brightly eosinophilic with a mild granularity. Enterocyte nuclei are haphazardly located in the cat, whereas they tend to be centrally to apically located in the dog. The lacteals are collapsed and rarely visible. Only a few goblet cells are seen in the proximal and middle segments, but they are moderate in number in the distal segment. Lymphocytes are few and scattered in the lamina propria. The crypts are lined by a low columnar epithelium with basilar nuclei. The mitotic rate is moderate, with usually 0–2 mitotic figures visible per crypt. The muscularis mucosa is poorly developed at birth, and the submucosa is highly cellular with little extracellular matrix. The tunica muscularis of newborns is relatively cellular compared with that of adults. The inner circular layer thickness is from 4–5 times that of the outer longitudinal layer, compared with about 1.5:1 in the adult.

Perhaps the most striking microscopic change during development of the intestine occurs in the villus mucosa of the dog during the first 24 hours after birth coinciding with the ingestion of colostrum (*Figure 5*). In the middle and distal segments, and to a lesser extent in the proximal segment, there is a dramatic expansion of the villi. This is primarily caused by two factors, a marked enlargement

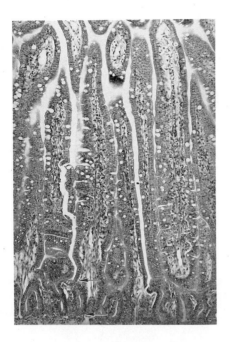

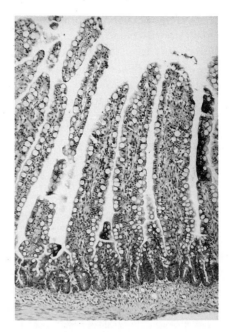

Figure 3. Canine small intestine, middle jejunum, at birth. Notice the long slender villi relative to the shallow crypts (between arrows). The distinct, round, clear cells in the villous epithelium are goblet cells. Original magnification, 100X.

Figure 4. Feline small intestine, middle jejunum, at birth. Note the slightly smaller dimensions than in the dog (Figure 3) but similar long villi compared with relatively short crypts. Goblet cells are more abundant than in the dog. The increased villus spacing compared with Figure 3 is an artifact caused by different extent of muscular contraction at the time of fixation. Original magnification, 100X.

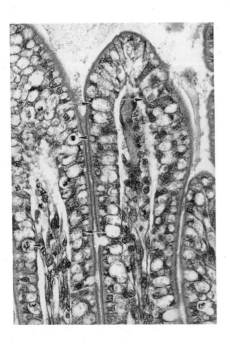

Figure 5. Canine small intestinal villi, middle jejunum, at 24 hours after birth in a nursing puppy. Notice that essentially all enterocytes contain one or more vacuoles filled with flocculent to globular, proteinaceous material (arrows) acquired from the uptake of colostrum. A few neutrophils are seen in transmucosal exocytosis (arrowheads). Goblet cells are not apparent. Original magnification, 400X.

of the enterocytes and a dilation of the lacteals. Both are associated with the intense uptake of colostral proteins that occurs in the first hours of suckling. The enterocyte cytoplasm is distended by large protein globules and large vacuoles containing flocculent proteinaceous material, with greater densities toward the basilar cytoplasm. Likewise, the lacteals contain globular to granular proteinaceous material. Enterocytes along the entire length of the villus are involved, but particularly those on the upper half of the villi. A mild inflammatory reaction accompanies these changes and is evident from a limited neutrophil infiltration with transmucosal exocytosis. Tissues below the level of the villi are little changed during this period of time.

Quite surprisingly, the changes seen in the cat during the first 24 hours after birth are far less dramatic (*Figure 6*). Only a few scattered enterocytes on the villus tips contain proteinaceous cytoplasmic globules; one cat did have cellular characteristics that were similar to those described for dogs but only in the distal segment. There is a slight vacuolation of the enterocyte cytoplasm, primarily on the apical side of the nucleus, which is similar to that seen in the enterocytes of more mature animals and is presumed to be an effect of nutrient absorption. Only occasional lacteals contain proteinaceous material. The cat, like the dog, has a mild, neutrophilic, inflammatory response.

The two most plausible explanations for the differences between the 24-hour-old cats and dogs have clinical implications. First, the neonatal cat may have lower abilities to absorb colostral proteins and antibodies compared with dogs. Second, 24-hour-old cats may have already absorbed the colostral proteins and cleared them systemically, indicating absorption of colostral antibodies occurs

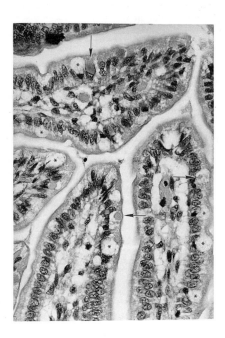

Figure 6. Feline small intestinal villi, middle jejunum, at 24 hours after birth in a nursing kitten. Notice the paucity of vacuoles containing flocculent to globular, colostral protein (arrows) compared with the dog intestine in Figure 4. Do not confuse these goblet cells (asterisks), which are more abundant than in the dog. Original magnification, 400X.

during a much shorter window of time. The first possibility seems more likely since 24 hour increases in circulating immunoglobulins were less in cats than dogs.

Surprisingly, villus length varies little from birth to the adult. This is consistent throughout the length of small intestine in both the cat and dog. Villus diameter does increase with age as a result of several factors. Adult enterocytes are taller with a pseudostratified appearance, and there is an increase in the smooth muscle and extracellular matrix of the lamina propria, which is accompanied by increased densities of lymphocytes and plasma cells.

In contrast with the villi, crypt depth increases 3–5-fold from birth to adulthood. As a result, villus:crypt ratios decrease from about 5.5–7.5:1 at birth to 1.1–1.5:1 in adult cats and dogs. The crypt mitotic activity remains moderate throughout development, but as a result of the increasing crypt depths, more mitotic figures can be seen per crypt in older animals.

With increasing age the lamina propia contains more lymphocytes and plasma cells at the base of the crypts and the connective tissues separating the crypts increases slightly more in the distal segments, from 1 to 1–3 layers. During the first 9 weeks after birth the muscularis mucosa develops further and the submucosa becomes progressively more collagenized. With increasing age the tunica muscularis gets thicker and cellular density decreases.

Coinciding with different dietary inputs, the enterocytes of fetal, suckling, and weaned cats and dogs have distinct functional characteristics.

Functional Development

Brush Border Membrane Hydrolases. Although development of the cat and dog GIT prior to birth has not been described in detail, it is likely to be similar to that of other mammals. If so, after the appearance of enterocytes along the villi, the activities of the various brush-border (BB) enzymes will increase up until the time of birth. What differs among mammals is when enterocytes and digestive functions first appear during gestation.[25] The greatest increases in BB hydrolase activities occur during the period just prior to birth, preparing newborns for the first swallows of milk. As a consequence of the late maturation, the GIT of kittens, puppies, and other mammals born premature has underdeveloped abilities to hydrolyze dietary inputs, increasing the risks for problems of digestion and nutrition.

Similar to other mammals, lactase activity is highest at birth in cats and dogs, with a declining proximal-to-distal gradient of activity.[26,27] The postnatal decline in lactase activity and concurrent increases in activities of α-glycosidases (maltase, sucrase, trehalase) coincides with the gradual replacement of fetal enterocytes by cells that are similar to those of adults. Although all mammals undergo the same basic pattern of changes, there are differences.[28] This is evident from the wide species variation in postnatal changes for the activities of the α-glycosidases maltase and sucrase (**Figure 7**), as well as the absence of trehalase in cats and other felids.[29]The postnatal patterns for cats and dogs are more similar to that of pigs than those for rats and humans. It is uncertain if the differences between species are related to the length of gestation (long for humans, short for mice and rats, and intermediate for dogs, cats, and pigs).

α-Glucosidase Activity at Birth

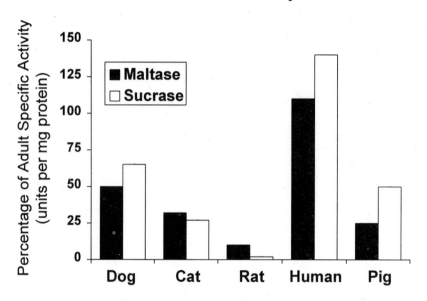

Figure 7. The increase in maltase and sucrase specific activities between birth and maturity for dogs, cats, rats, humans, and pigs. Adapted from Galand, 1989.[28]

The patterns of BB enzyme development have important clinical implications in that they are related to a species ability to utilize alternative foods. The presence of high α-glycosidase activities in newborn human infants allows them to digest and do well on formulas that have lactose completely replaced by sucrose or maltodextrins. In contrast, suckling rats have severe diarrhea when disaccharides other than lactose are fed. Kittens, puppies, and pigs should be able to tolerate limited amounts of other disaccharides. However, because of the decline in lactase activity and low sucrase activity, adult cats are unable to tolerate substantial dietary levels of lactose and sucrose.[26,30]

Nutrient Absorption. Rates of carrier-mediated uptake for glucose are highest at birth then decline in both cats and dogs (*Figure 8A*). A steeper decline for galactose coincides with its loss from the diet at weaning and also suggests there is more than one form of aldohexose transporter present in the intestine, as previously reported for the cat.[31] However, a second transporter, in addition to the well understood sodium-dependent glucose transporter (SGLT-1), has yet to be isolated and described from the intestine of any mammal.

Despite the decline in rates of glucose transport per mg of tissue, because of intestinal growth the capacities of the entire intestine to transport glucose (mmol/day) actually increase several-fold between birth and adulthood for both cats and dogs (**Figure 8B**). However, the magnitude of increases is lower when compared to those measured of omnivores, such as pigs.[32]

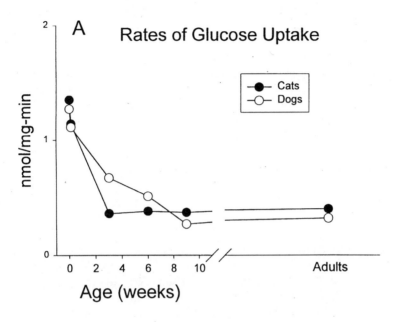

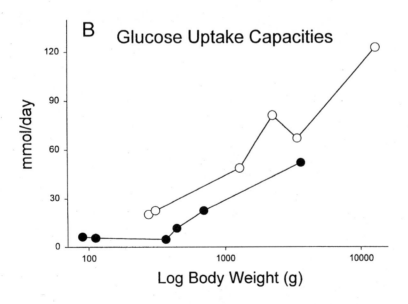

Figure 8. Rates of glucose uptake (A) and total capacities of the entire length of small intestine to transport (B) during postnatal development of cats and dogs.

Several different transporters are known to transport the different classes of amino acids (i.e., acidic, basic, neutral, imino) and include both sodium dependent and independent forms.[33] Our studies of amino acid absorption by the intestines of developing dogs and cats have revealed several fascinating characteristics. The postnatal decline for amino acid absorption per mg of tissue is not as dramatic as that for glucose and appears to be more related to changes in the amount of absorptive surface than lower densities of transporters per unit intestine.

The carrier-mediated components of amino acid absorption in both cats and dogs have been estimated by measuring rates of uptake over a broad range of concentrations and then analyzing the data using model equations that include one or more saturable carrier-mediated pathway(s) of absorption and a linear component that represents the passive, carrier-independent influx. When this was done, it was discovered that for some amino acids there was little, if any, evidence for a saturable component, indicating a low abundance of transporters. This is confirmed by calculating ratios for the uptake of tracer levels of radiolabeled amino acid in high and low concentrations of unlabeled amino acid. These ratios for glucose exceed 1.0 at all ages and are highest at birth in both cats and dogs when the densities of SGLT-1 are also highest.

Ratios for amino acid uptake by the cat showed that transporters were present at birth for the different classes of amino acids. The highest values were for the basic amino acid arginine, corresponding with the cat's hyperessential requirements. Values for all amino acids declined during suckling with some ratios not significantly exceeding 1.0. This suggests the transporters had either been lost or only a very few remained. The declining ratios for taurine coincide with a previously speculated loss of transporters.[34] Although the same amino acids were not studied in the cat and dog, there were some obvious similarities based on amino acid accumulation ratios. First, in both species the transporters for some amino acids are not in great abundance at any age (e.g., transporters for the acid amino acid aspartate). Second, in both species transporters' densities declined with increasing age (e.g., proline). Third, transporters for leucine are evident in both species, but more so in the dog. Dogs also differ from cats in having few, if any, transporters for basic amino acids (e.g., lysine and arginine).

The possibility that for several amino acids, cats and dogs, and also mink (unpublished data) have few available transporters presents a paradox. This is particularly true since cats, dogs, and mink are able to digest proteins very efficiently and some feeding studies suggest that amino acids are more available when presented in free form than as components of intact proteins.[35] Furthermore, transporters for the different classes of amino acids are known to be present in the intestines of mice, which are omnivores and eat natural and laboratory diets that are lower in protein than those fed to cats and dogs. These findings led us to expect the intestines of cats and dogs would have high densities of carriers for all amino acids.

The above suggests that cats, dogs, and mink may not need to fully hydrolyze dietary proteins before absorption. The most likely alternative is that proteins are hydrolyzed to di- and tripeptides. These could then be absorbed by peptide transporters, which would provide the advantages of more rapid and efficient absorption.[33] The presence of peptide transporters also explains why defects in amino acid transporters are rarely manifested as deficiencies since the affected amino acids would be absorbed as constituents of di- and tripeptides. If an amino acid deficiency is diagnosed, it can usually be attributed to either dysfunctions causing inadequate protein hydrolysis (e.g., exocrine pancreatic insufficiency[36]) or to the lack of a functional amino acid transporter in the kidney.[37] There is an obvious need to better understand the relative roles of peptide and amino acid transporters as they relate to metabolism and protein digestion by cats and dogs. Furthermore, such information may enhance therapeutic strategies since some antibiotics, such as β-lactams, are absorbed by peptide transporters.[33]

Finally, some of the early studies on nutrient transport provided evidence that carriers for sugars and amino acids were present in the large intestines of dogs.[38] The functional significance is uncertain, but this regional distribution differs from that of most other mammals. It is unknown if the colon of adult cats has carriers for sugars and amino acids.

Macromolecular Absorption. The intestine has the capacity to absorb intact a wide diversity of macromolecules, particularly during early development.[39] The pattern of development for the ability to absorb maternal antibodies and transfer them to the neonate's circulation varies widely among mammals. This ability can be detected in human fetuses but ceases (commonly called 'closure') before term. In rats, the capacity for antibody transfer appears just prior to birth and persists until weaning. Pigs are intermediate in that the ability to acquire maternal antibodies appears before birth with closure occurring only a few hours after onset of suckling. Although cats and dogs are thought to be like pigs in that they must receive colostrum during the first 24–48 hours,[1] definitive studies have yet to be performed. There is circumstantial evidence that indicates there are differences between these two species. Specifically, between birth and 24 hours of suckling, both species show an increase in serum antibody levels. However, the magnitude of increase is markedly higher for dogs compared to cats. Corroborating this is the lower ability of the intestines of kittens to absorb polyvinyl pyrrolidone (PVP) compared to pigs.[40] The ability varied widely between litters of kittens, and even siblings, as we also saw based on histological observations of 24-hour-old cats. The capacity of macromolecular absorption is related to the presence of intracellular vacuoles, which were less prevalent in the newborn cats studied compared to those seen in the dogs (see Histology section of this contribution).

Even though the ability to transfer immunoglobulins to the circulation may be short-lived after exposure to colostrum (6–12 hours), internalization of other macromolecules may continue for several days after birth. For example, the mucosa of pigs, rats, and even cats continues to internalize PVP for 10–14 days after birth.[40]

The persistence of macromolecular absorption may compensate for underdeveloped exocrine pancreatic functions during suckling by using intracellular enzymes to digest macromolecules. However, the possible implications in providing energy and nutrients have not been quantified for any mammal.

<p>

<table>
<tr><td>Adaptation and
Regulation of
GIT Digestive
Processes</td><td>

The ability of cats and dogs to adapt digestive processes is of obvious relevance when formulating diets. Although there are surprisingly few data available for adult cats and dogs, there are still obvious differences between these two species that are related to their respective natural diets. The strict carnivorous diet of cats coincides with an inability to regulate pancreatic secretion of amylase,[41] production of BB disaccharidases,[26,30] rates of transport for sugars and amino acids,[14] and alters metabolic patterns to match changes in dietary levels of sugars.[2] Despite these limitations, cats do have the ability to regulate secretion of chymotrypsin.[41]

</td></tr>
</table>

Results from several different studies suggest the GIT of the more omnivorous dog is more responsive to diet composition. Macronutrient composition of the diet is known to influence exocrine pancreatic secretion, activities of the BB disaccharidases,[42] cell populations in the proximal small intestine,[43] and the presence of unabsorbed nutrients in the distal intestine of dogs influences digestive functions in the proximal bowel.[44] This 'ileal brake' involves signalling pathways[45] that act to enhance hydrolysis and absorption in the jejunum such that nutrient concentrations in the distal bowel are reduced. The addition of fermentable fiber (fructooligosaccharides and beet pulp) to the diet elicits an increase in intestinal dimensions and induces the expression of sugar and amino acid transporters, causing a significant increase in the ability to absorb nutrients.[46] The latter study is insightful for two reasons. First, even though proline transporters were not evident in the intestines of control dogs fed a diet lacking fermentable fiber, they were apparently induced in dogs fed a diet with fermentable fiber. Second, the increased densities of both glucose and proline transporters indicate signals other than the substrates for the transporters are responsible for causing the upregulation.

It is not known if any studies of the adaptive capacities of the GIT of suckling kittens and puppies have been reported. The first question to consider is whether sucklings of either species have the capacity to adaptively modulate the GIT during the first weeks after birth. Throughout evolution, sucklings consume a diet relatively stable in composition. Only when the diet would normally change should these abilities develop, and only in species with adult diets that are variable in composition (i.e., dogs but not cats). Secondly, it is of interest to know when the GIT normally undergoes the changes that surround weaning.

The specific signals that influence adaptation and development of the GIT are not completely understood for any species with much less known for cats and dogs. The signals can originate from three different sources. First, exogenous signals can be present in the diet. Colostrum and milk both contain numerous and high concentrations of biologically active molecules that have the potential to influence GIT development.[47] Even some of the proteins present in milk release biologically active peptides during hydrolysis. Although there has been intense interest in identifying regulatory molecules that could be added to formulas and milk replacers, none have been shown to have a profound effect on the developing GIT. It is likely that several different molecules act synergistically and that studies using just one or a few may not be able to match the combined influences of colostrum. Second, the signals can come from the intestine itself. The influences of gastrin, CCK, GLP-1 and -2, and other peptides are well established.[48] Third, there can be other endogenous sources distant from the GIT, such as the adrenal cortex, which produces glucocorticoids that are known to be important mediators of GIT development.

The GIT can be considered as a complex ecosystem which includes several distinct 'habitats' (e.g., stomach, small intestine, colon) that have different physical, chemical, and biological characteristics (see chapter by Buddington and Sunvold[7]). The populations of bacteria present in the various regions of the GIT differ widely between animals. This reflects a combination of several factors.[49] Those considered most important are 1) the variation in GIT structure and functions, 2) host age, 3) the surrounding environment, and 4) the amounts and types of substrates available to the bacteria. The influence of diet is evident from the differences between breast fed and formula fed infants.[50] Feeding fermentable fiber also changes the fecal bacteria of cats[51] and humans.[52]

Development of the GIT Ecosystem

The bacterial populations present in the mammalian GIT change dramatically during development. The GIT of fetuses is sterile, but during passage through the birth canal, fecal and vaginal microbiota are introduced with extrauterine fluids that are swallowed by newborns. Additional bacteria enter the GIT as neonates begin to suckle. The first invading bacteria rapidly transit the GIT, effectively colonizing all regions, and within three hours after birth can be detected in the distal colon.[53] Over the next several months there are gradual changes in the microbiota present in the different regions, eventually culminating in the adult 'ecosystem'.

Within 24 hours after birth, densities of bacteria in fecal samples from kittens and puppies have reached levels comparable to those of adults (unpublished data). However, from 24 hours after birth to adulthood there are changes in the relative proportion of the total bacterial population represented by the different groups (**Figure 9**). For example, aerotolerant groups dominate the fecal flora of 24-hour-old puppies and are a significant component of fecal bacteria of cats with enterics representing more than half of the aerotolerant forms. This corresponds with the faster proliferation rates of aerobic relative to anaerobic bacteria. With time, the relative densities of enterics decline as other groups increase in abundance. The shifts in populations can be partly attributed to a combination of interactions between bacteria and different dietary inputs. Although not as well understood, it is likely that age related changes in pancreatic secretions, bile acid secretion and absorption, and structural and functional characteristics of the intestine are also important factors.

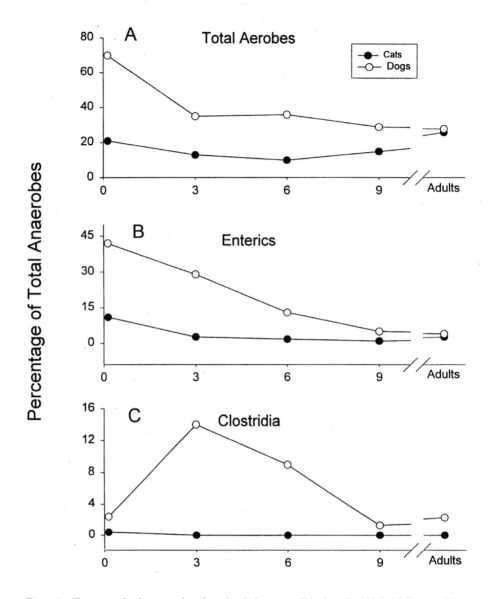

Figure 9. Changes in the densities of total aerobes (A), enterics (B), clostridia (C), bifidobacteria (D), lactobacilli (E), and bacteroides (F) in fecal samples of cats and dogs from birth to maturity. Values are expressed as percentages of total anaerobe counts.

The bacterial populations present in the GIT differ between cats and dogs. Bifidobacteria were detected at all ages in the cats but were not recovered in the stools of the dogs, even during suckling. In contrast, aerotolerant forms as well as lactobacilli, clostridia and bacteroides were more abundant in dogs than cats. Only a small number of the bacterial groups known to be present in the GIT of cats and dogs were studied and identifications were not taken to level of species. It is likely that future studies will reveal other differences.

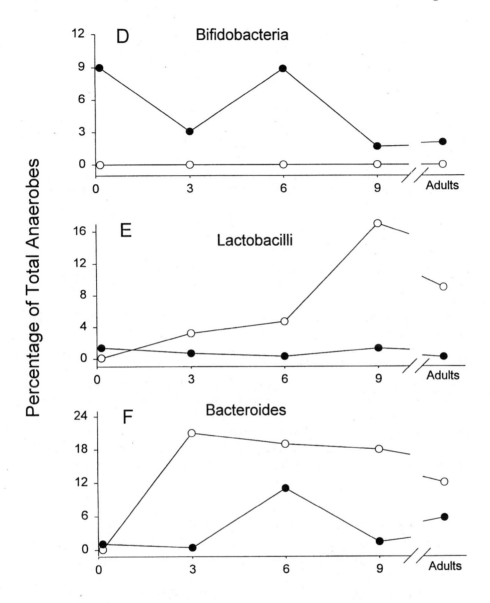

The clinical implications of the differences between species and ages and the effects of dietary inputs and antibiotics on the developing microbiota have yet to be elucidated. Also to be considered is the relationship between the GIT bacteria and host diet, nutrition, and metabolism. In adult cats, the majority of starch digestion in the GIT is by the colonic bacteria, not the actions of carbohydrases secreted by the pancreas and intestine.[54] This not only complicates measurements of digestibility, it also raises questions about the metabolism of dietary carbohydrate.

Conclusions and Perspectives

Although diets for companion animals have been commercially available for over 130 years, studies of the GIT functions of cats and dogs did not become evident in the literature until the 1960's. A large fraction of the published research since then has emphasized either pathological conditions of the adult cat and dog GIT or the use of the dog as a model for biomedical studies. As a consequence, the relations between digestion, nutrition, and GIT development are not well understood for these two species. Although data for these relations are more available for omnivorous species, such as mice, rats, and pigs, they are only partly applicable to cats and dogs because of the digestive and metabolic specializations to evolutionary diets. Additional studies of cats and dogs are needed for a better understanding of the relations between nutrition and the GIT during development. And although not enough is known yet about development from birth to maturity, even less is known about the changes that occur during senescence.

Finally, there is a pressing need to develop chronic experimental approaches that will allow investigators to study the GIT during the life history of individuals and the responses to diet. This will provide much needed insights that are not available from acute studies that are limited to obtaining data from individuals at only one time.

Acknowledgements

Results reported in this contribution were made possible by the efforts of numerous participants. These include Mr. Mike Bassett, Dr. Karyl Buddington, Mr. Jason Peters, and other animal care personnel; Mr. J.C. Cuadra and Ms. Katie Brand for recording and analyzing GIT morphometrics; Mr. Rick Sands for assisting in histologic procedures; Ms. Jillian Buckingham for participating in the measurements of nutrient transport, and Mr. Ken Jackson for bacteriologic analysis of cat and dog intestinal contents.

References

1. Poffenbarger EM, Olson PN, Ralston SL, Chandler ML. Canine neonatology. Part II. Disorders of the neonate. *Comp Cont Edu Pract Vet* 1991; 13:25-37.

2. Legrand-Defretin V. Differences between cats and dogs: a nutritional view. *Proc Nutr Soc* 1994; 53:15-24.

3. Widdowson EM. Development of the digestive system: comparative animal studies. *Am J Clin Nutr* 1985; 41:384-390.

4. Buddington RK. Structure and functions of the dog and cat intestine. In: Carey DP, Norton SA, Bolser SM, eds. *Recent Advances in Canine and Feline Nutritional Research: Proceedings of the 1996 Iams International Nutrition Symposium.* Wilmington: Orange Frazer Press, 1996; 61-77.

5. Lepine AJ. Nutrition of the neonatal canine and feline. In: Reinhart GA, Carey DP, eds. *Recent Advances in Canine and Feline Nutrition, Vol. II: 1998 Iams Nutrition Symposium Proceedings.* Wilmington: Orange Frazer Press, 1998; 249-256.

6. Elnif J, Buddington RK. Adaptation and development of the exocrine pancreas in cats and dogs. In: Reinhart GA, Carey DP, eds. *Recent Advances in Canine and Feline Nutrition, Vol. II: 1998 Iams Nutrition Symposium Proceedings.*

Wilmington: Orange Frazer Press, 1998; 217-230.

7. Buddington RK, Sunvold GD. Fermentable fiber and the gastrointestinal tract ecosystem. In: Reinhart GA, Carey DP, eds. *Recent Advances in Canine and Feline Nutrition, Vol. II: 1998 Iams Nutrition Symposium Proceedings*. Wilmington: Orange Frazer Press, 1998; 449-462.

8. Nelson PD, Kern MR, Kelly-Quaglianna K, Qu X-L, Boyle C, Buddington RK. Influence of age on the immune system. In: Reinhart GA, Carey DP, eds. *Recent Advances in Canine and Feline Nutrition, Vol. II: 1998 Iams Nutrition Symposium Proceedings*. Wilmington: Orange Frazer Press, 1998; 231-248.

9. Trahair JF, Sangild PT. Systemic and luminal influences on the perinatal development of the gut. *Equine Vet J* 1998; in press.

10. Lonnerdal B. Lactation in the dog and cat. In: Carey DP, Norton SA, Bolser SM, eds. *Recent Advances in Canine and Feline Nutritional Research: Proceedings of the 1996 Iams International Nutrition Symposium*. Wilmington: Orange Frazer Press, 1996; 79-87.

11. Heird WC, Schwarz SM, Hansen IH. Colostrum-induced enteric mucosal growth in beagle puppies. *Ped Res* 1984; 18:512-515.

12. Yamashiro Y, Mitsuyoshi S, Shimizu T, Oguchi S, Maruyama K, Kitamura S. Possible biological growth factors in breast milk and postnatal development of the gastrointestinal tract. *Acta Paediatr Jpn* 1989; 31:417-423.

13. Schwarz SM, Heird WC. Effects of feeding on the small intestinal mucosa of beagle pups during the first 5 d of life. *Am J Clin Nutr* 1994; 60:879-886.

14. Buddington RK, Diamond JM. Ontogenetic development of nutrient transporters in cat intestine. *Am J Physiol* 1992; 263:G605-G616.

15. Jenness R, Sloan RE. The composition of milk from various species-a review. *Dairy Sci Abstr* 1970; 32:599-614.

16. Oftedal OT. Lactation in the dog: Milk composition and intake by puppies. *J Nutr* 1984; 114:803-812.

17. Chandler ML, Miller E, Olson PN, Ralston SL. Serum chemistry and lipid profiles in neonatal beagle puppies fed homemade milk replacer formulas. *Cornell Vet* 1993; 83:107-116.

18. Malm K, Jensen P. Weaning in dogs: within- and between-litter variation in milk and solid food intake. *Appl Anim Behav Sci* 1996; 49:223-235.

19. Stevens CE, Hume ID. *Comparative Physiology of the Vertebrate Digestive System* 2nd ed. Cambridge Univ Press, 1995; 400.

20. Laganiere S, Berteloot A, Maestracci D. Digestive and absorptive functions along dog small intestine: Comparative distributions in relation to biochemical and morphological parameters. *Comp Biochem Physiol* 1984; 79A:463-472.

21. Deavers S, Huggins RA, Smith EL. Absolute and relative organ weights of the growing beagle. *Growth* 1972; 36:195-208.

22. Loveridge GG. Some factors affecting kitten growth. *Anim Famil* 1987; 2:9-16.

23. Hart IR, Kidder DE. The quantitative assessment of normal canine small intestinal mucosa. *Res Vet Sci* 1978; 25:157-162.

24. Hart IR, Kidder DE. The quantitative assessment of mucosa in canine small intestinal malabsorption. *Res Vet Sci* 1978; 25:163-167.

25. Buddington RK. Nutrition and ontogenetic development of the intestine. *Can J Physiol Pharmacol* 1980; 72:251-259.

26. Kienzle E. Carbohydrate metabolism of the cat. 4. Activity of maltase, isomaltase, sucrase, and lactase in the gastrointestinal tract in relation to age and diet. *J Anim Physiol A Anim Nutr* 1993; 70:89-96.

27. Welsh JD, Walker A. Intestinal disaccharidase and alkaline phosphatase activity in the dog. *Proc Soc Exp Biol Med* 1965; 120:525-527.

28. Galand G. Brush border membrane sucrase-isomaltase, maltase-glucoamylase and trehalase in mammals. Comparative development, effects of glucocorticoids, molecular mechanisms, and phylogenetic implications. *Comp Biochem Physiol* 1989; 94B:1-11.

29. Hore P, Messer M. Studies on disaccharidase activities of the small intestine of the domestic cat and other carnivorous mammals. *Comp Biochem Physiol* 1968; 24:717-725.

30. Morris JG, Trudell J, Pencovic T. Carbohydrate digestion by the domestic cat (Felis catus). *Br J Nutr* 1977; 37:365-373.

31. Wolffram S, Eggenberger E, Scharrer E. Kinetics of D-glucose transport across the intestinal brush-border membrane of the cat. *Comp Biochem Physiol* 1989; 94A:111-115.

32. Puchal AA, Buddington RK. Postnatal development of monosaccharide transport in pig intestine. *Am J Physiol* 1992; 262:G895-G902.

33. Ganapathy V, Brandsch M, Leibach FH. Intestinal transport of amino acids and peptides. In: Johnson LR, ed. *Physiology of the Gastrointestinal Tract*, 3rd Ed. New York: Raven Press, 1994; 1773-1794.

34. Wolffram S, Hagemann C, Scharrer E. Regression of high-affinity carrier-mediated intestinal transport of taurine in the adult cats. *Am J Physiol* 1991; 261:R1089-R1095.

35. Hirakawa DA, Baker DH. Comparative performance as well as nitrogen and energy metabolism of young puppies fed three distinctly different experimental dog foods and one commercial product. *Comp Anim Prac* 1988; 2:25-32.

36. Batt RM. Diagnosis and management of malabsorption in dogs. *J Sm Anim Pract* 1992; 33:161-166.

37. Tsan M-F, Jones TC, Wilson TH. Canine cystinuria: Intestinal and renal amino acid transport. *Am J Vet Res* 1972; 33:2463-2468.

38. Robinson JWL, Luisier A-L, Mirkovitch V. Transport of amino-acids and sugars by the dog colonic mucosa. *Pflugers Arch* 1973; 345:317-326.

39. Gardner MLG. Absorption of intact proteins and peptides. In: Johnson LR, ed. *Physiology of the Gastrointestinal Tract* 3rd ed. New York: Raven Press, 1994; 1795-1820.

40. Clarke RM, Hardy RN. Structural changes in the small intestine associated with the uptake of polyvinyl pyrrolidone by the young ferret, rabbit, guinea-pig, cat and chicken. *J Physiol* 1970; 209:669-687.

41. Kienzle E. Carbohydrate metabolism of the cat. 1. Activity of amylase in the gastrointestinal tract of the cat. *J Anim Physiol A Anim Nutr* 1993; 69:92-101.

42. Kienzle E. Enzymaktivitat in pancreas, darmwand und chymus des hundes in abhangigkeit von alter und futterart. *J Anim Physiol Anim Nutr* 1988; 60:276-288.

43. Edwards JF, Fossum TW, Willard MD, Cohen ND, Patterson WB IV, Carey DP. Changes in the intestinal mucosal cell populations of German Shepherd dogs fed diets containing different protein sources. *Am J Vet Res* 1995; 56:340-348.

44. Macarone-Palmieri R, Mirkovitch V, Blanc D, Robinson JWL, Saegesser F. Structural and functional differences in response to small intestinal resection or by-pass in the dog. *Helv Chir Acta* 1979; 46:195-204.

45. Bastidas JA, Orandle MS, Zinner MJ, Yeo CJ. Small-bowel origin of the signal for meal-induced jejunal absorption. *Surgery* 1990; 108:376-383.

46. Buddington RK, Buddington KK, Sunvold GD. The influence of ferment-able fiber on the small intestine of the dog: Intestinal dimensions and transport of glucose and proline. *Am J Vet Res* submitted.

47. Kelly D. Colostrum, growth factors and intestinal development in pigs. In: Souffrant W-B, Hagemeister H, eds. *Proceedings of the VI International Symposium on Digestive Physiology in Pigs*. 1994; 151-166.

48. Walsh JH. Gastrointestinal hormones. In: Johnson LR (ed). *Physiology of the Gastrointestinal Tract* 3rd ed. New York: Raven Press, 1994; 1-128.

49. Collins MD, Gibson GR. Nutritional modulation of microbial ecology. *Am J Clin Nutr* 1998; (in press).

50. Gothefors L. Effects of diet on intestinal flora. *Acta Paediatr Scand.* 1989; 351:118-121.

51. Sparkes, AH, Papasouliotis K, Sunvold G, Werrett G, Gruffydd-Jones EA, Egan K, Gruffydd-Jones TJ, Reinhart G. The effect of dietary supplementation with fructo-oligosaccharides on the faecal flora of healthy cats. *Am J Vet Res* 1998; (in press).

52. Buddington RK, Williams CH, Chen S, Witherly SW. A dietary supple-ment of neosugar alters the fecal flora and decreases the activities of some reductive enzymes in human subjects. *Am J Clin Nutr* 1996; 63:709-716.

53. Swords WE, Wu CC, Champlin FR, Buddington RK. Postnatal changes in selected bacterial groups of the pig colonic microflora. *Biol Neonate* 1993; 63:191-200.

54. Kienzle E. Carbohydrate metabolism of the cat. 2. Digestion of starch. *J Anim Physiol A Anim Nutr* 1993; 69:102-114.

Adaptation and Development of the Exocrine Pancreas in Cats and Dogs

Jan Elnif, MSc
Associate Professor, Department of Animal Science and Animal Health
The Royal Veterinary and Agricultural University, Copenhagen, Denmark

Randal K. Buddington, PhD
Professor, Department of Biological Sciences
Mississippi State University, Mississippi State, Mississippi USA

The exocrine pancreas is composed of greater than 80% acinar cells. These are the principal source of the digestive enzymes that are responsible for hydrolyzing the macronutrient components of food (proteins, fats, carbohydrates, nucleic acids). The exocrine pancreas also produces antibacterial factors which are included in the pancreatic juice. The remainder of the pancreas is mainly ductal tissue that secretes water with ions and high concentrations of bicarbonate. The anatomical arrangement of the cat and dog pancreas has been reviewed by Williams.[1]

Introduction

Over 20 proteins are secreted in the pancreatic juice at a concentration of 4 mg/ml. When the high concentrations of protein and large volumes of juice (about 100 ml/kg body weight each day in pigs[2]) are considered together, the rate of protein synthesis and secretion per gram of pancreas exceeds that of any other tissue in the body.[3] The rates of synthesis and secretion may be of even greater magnitude in carnivorous mammals, such as the dog, fox, cat, and mink, which have relatively short intestines (only 4 to 5 times longer than body length[4]) and very short passage times for digesta (only 4 hours in mink). These characteristics place a large burden on the exocrine pancreas for efficient digestion of the nutrient dense foods of carnivores. In mink, the apparent digestibility of nitrogen was as low as -120%[5] when based on measurements in the chyme from the first part of the intestine 1.5 hours after a meal. These findings are indicative of a very high rate of exocrine pancreatic secretion.

A large portion of what is known about pancreatic functions of cats and dogs is based on pathological conditions (see reviews by Williams[1] and Williams and Guilford[6]). Although there is a growing base of information about adaptation of dog pancreatic secretions to diet, much less is known for the cat and even less is available about age-related changes in exocrine pancreatic secretions of both species.

Several recent reviews describe the composition and regulation of pancreatic secretions in mammals.[7-11] In addition to the large volume of water added to the intestine, pancreatic juice includes three functional groups of solutes: hydrolytic enzymes, antibacterial factors, and bicarbonate and electrolytes.

Hydrolytic Enzymes. Readers are referred to reviews for detailed descriptions of the various enzymes,[7] the structure-function relations of the pancreatic acinar cells and enzyme synthesis,[3,8] and the signals and signal transduction pathways regulating secretion.[9-11] Briefly, proteases secreted by the acinar cells of the pancreas include endopeptidases and exopeptidases that function to reduce proteins into small peptides with the release of some free amino acids. The major endopeptidase of the cat and dog is trypsin, with lower activities of chymotrypsin and elastase. The different types of endoproteases cleave proteins at different sites, releasing a diversity of oligopeptides. Exopeptidases, of which carboxypeptidases A and B dominate, remove specific amino acid residues from the carboxyl and amino terminal ends of proteins and peptides. To prevent autodigestion prior to secretion, the proteases are secreted as proenzymes (zymogens) which are normally activated only after entering the intestine. Enterokinase produced by the intestinal mucosa activates trypsin which then can activate additional trypsin as well as chymotrypsin and other proteases. Autodigestion in the pancreas prior to secretion is also prevented by the presence of protease inhibitors, enzymes which specifically degrade trypsin, and an inherent resistance to the various pancreatic hydrolases.

Other enzymes present in pancreatic juice include: phospholipases that hydrolyze phosphoglycerides; lipase and its necessary cofactor, colipase, for degrading long chain triglycerides; amylase for digestion of complex carbohydrates and ribonucleases; and deoxybribonucleases for degradation of nucleic acids.

Antibacterial Factors. The pancreatic juice of dogs has been shown to possess antibacterial properties.[12] Similar antibacterial activity has been reported in the pancreatic juice of other mammals, but is absent in the secretions of rats.[13] The active component is a protein with a molecular weight of about 4,000 D and an alkaline pH optimum. It retains activity until pancreatic juice is diluted at least 10-fold. The protein is relatively heat stable since it retains and even has increased activity when exposed to 65° C for 15 minutes, but it is inactivated at 100°.[14] It is resistant to degradation by pancreatic proteases.

The antibacterial factor present in dog pancreatic secretions has a broad spectrum of activity.[12] It has bactericidal activity against *E. coli*, *Shigella*, *Salmonella*, and *Kebsiella*, and is bacteriostatic for coagulase positive and negative staphylococci and *Pseudomonas*. It also inhibits growth of *Candida albicans*. It does not affect certain bacterial groups, many of which are considered to be symbiotic (*Bacteroides* and *Streptococcus faecalis*). It is unknown if it affects groups considered to be beneficial, such as lactobacilli, bifidobacteria, and eubacteria. If the antibacterial factors are selective, this may help to establish and maintain gastrointestinal bacterial populations that enhance the health of the host.

The amount of dietary inputs appears to affect the secretion of the antibacterial factor in cattle,[14] suggesting it is secreted concurrent with other exocrine secretions. However, the composition of the diet did not influence the antibacterial qualities of the pancreatic juice.

Studies of age-related changes in the antibacterial activities of pancreatic juice in cats and dogs are unknown, however, the activity is lower in pigs during suckling with a dramatic increase at the time of weaning.[14] The speculation is that at the time of weaning there is a need to have enhanced antibacterial activity to compensate for the loss of antibacterial factors present in milk and to protect against the increased numbers of food-borne bacteria, many of which are potential pathogens.

The presence of antibacterial activity in pancreatic juice partly explains why exocrine pancreatic insufficiency (EPI) is often accompanied with bacterial overgrowth in the upper small intestine. Although dietary interventions, particularly the use of diets lower in fat, may reduce the incidence of diarrhea and improve the condition of many dogs,[15,16] this remains controversial.[17] Low fat diets do not address the problem of bacterial overgrowth which typically requires treatment with broad spectrum antibiotics. Supplementing diets with some preparations of pancreatic secretions or tissues may increase digestibility and improve weight recovery and condition, but this too does not adequately address the bacterial overgrowth.[18] Although the antibacterial properties of feline pancreatic secretions are unknown, it is of interest that the upper small intestine of many cats normally harbors densities of bacteria that are characteristic of overgrowth in dogs.[19]

Pancreatitis is a common problem for dogs, but the pathogenesis and epidemiology remain uncertain.[20] To date, the majority of studies have focused on the possible influence of diet, hypersecretion, and a variety of other risk factors. Whether reduced production or dysfunctional antibacterial factors plays a role in some cases has yet to be investigated.

Bicarbonate and Electrolytes. Whereas the concentrations of Na^+ and K^+ are relatively stable in pancreatic juice and coincide with plasma levels, values for bicarbonate (HCO_3^-) and Cl^- are reciprocally related and vary considerably.[21] Much of the information about fluid and electrolyte secretion by the ductal tissue is from studies of cat pancreas. These studies have shown that HCO_3^- concentrations are directly related to the rate of fluid production. This makes functional sense as the needs for fluid and HCO_3^- would occur in parallel and be co-dependent on the amount of digesta entering the intestine from the stomach.

The responses of fluid and HCO_3^- secretion to hormonal stimulation are better developed in cats and dogs as compared to rats. This may be related to the relatively large but sporadic meals consumed by dogs and cats that would require larger volumes of fluid and high concentrations of HCO_3^-. In contrast, omnivores that tend to eat smaller, more frequent meals would need a more constant secretion of fluid and HCO_3^- and apparently reduced secretory responses to stimulation.

*Clinical and
Research
Assessments of
Exocrine
Pancreatic
Secretion*
Clinicians are generally dependent on indirect measures of exocrine pancreatic secretion. The most commonly used approaches involve assaying for the activities of enzymes in peripheral blood or in fecal samples. A variety of methods have been developed to assist clinicians in making such measurements (reviewed by Williams and Guilford[6]). Fecal samples, though easy to collect, probably do not accurately reflect secretory activities due to auto and bacterial degradation of secreted enzymes. The contribution of enzymes with similar activities by the bacteria present in the alimentary canal can be accounted for by using species-specific radioimmunoassays and substrates that are enzyme-specific. Measurement of trypsin activity in blood samples tends to be preferred by many clinicians and has proven to be dependable for diagnosing EPI. An *in vivo* approach sometimes used involves feeding N-benzoyl-L-tyrosyl-p-aminobenzoic acid (Bentiromide). Plasma or urine concentrations of p-aminobenzoic acid that are absorbed after hydrolysis of Bentiromide are used to assess if there is adequate secretion of pancreatic enzymes. Although the indirect measures are of great diagnostic use for clinicians, as of now they have only limited applications for establishing the patterns of secretion during development and in response to changes in diet composition.

Direct measures of pancreatic secretions include the use of acute samples, usually obtained at necropsy, and chronic studies involving repeated collection of pancreatic secretions from a single individual. By collecting the entire pancreas and assaying for activity, investigators are able to determine the total secretory capacity of an animal. However, the data are restricted to a single point in time and it is difficult to account for diurnal rhythms, meal induced patterns of synthesis and secretion, and changes over time. Surgical methods have been developed to permit chronic collection of pancreatic secretions. These involve either sampling the contents of the duodenum just distal to the entrance of the pancreatic duct, or by surgical placement of catheters into the pancreatic duct for direct collection of the exocrine secretions. The second approach has proven to be very informative as it is possible to measure the volume and composition of the secretions over prolonged periods of time. By use of reentrant catheters into the duodenum, aliquots can be removed and the remainder of the secretions can be introduced into the intestine, thereby not disturbing normal digestive functions. To date, chronic investigations of pancreatic juice have been restricted to the dog. Similar studies with cats are not known.

Although chronic methods have proven to be very useful to investigators studying adaptation and regulation of exocrine pancreatic secretion, they are not practical for clinicians trying to diagnose animals with digestive disorders who are seeking only positive or negative answers. The validity and application of serum enzyme activities to actual pancreatic synthesis and secretion of enyzmes needs to be better evaluated. This could be addressed by developing correlative relationships based on chronic and simultaneous measurements of activities in blood samples and pancreatic juice.

Ever since the experiments with dogs from Pavlov's laboratory more than 100 years ago, it has been known that both rates of secretion and composition of the pancreatic juice are responsive to changes in diet composition. The omnivorous rat has been the principal model used for studying dietary modulation of pancreatic enzyme secretion. These studies have shown the magnitude of adaptation is greater for proteases and carbohydrases than for lipase which is only slightly responsive to amounts of fat in the diet.[22,23]

There are reports of a correlation between composition of diet and secretion of pancreatic enzymes by carnivores, but the patterns of adaptation are not as well understood. This may be related to the different methods that have been used to obtain secretions and measure enzyme activities. Direct analysis of pancreatic juice collected from cannulated dogs fed diets either high in protein or fat has shown there is substrate adaptation in dogs.[24] The dietary influences are not as obvious when pancreatic enzyme activity is measured indirectly using feces or serum samples. Although there are increases in fecal protease activity when dogs are fed a diet high in protein, the differences between individual dogs are great and may obscure diet effects.[25,26] Individual variation is also a problem when measuring serum trypsin-like immunoreactivity (TLI). Values for some dogs are unchanged, even after a 6-fold increase in dietary protein,[27] which would have resulted in higher values in pancreatic juice.

Although pancreatic secretions are modulated to match the quantitative distribution of protein, fat and carbohydrate in the diet, the qualitative aspects of the nutrients are also important. Dogs adapted for 8 months on either of two isocaloric diets differing only in fat source (sunflower oil or olive oil) had different secretory patterns. Dogs fed the polyunsaturated sunflower oil had higher amylase and lipase activity but lower activity of chymotrypsin compared to those fed olive oil.[28]

The degree of carnivorousness appears to be an indicator of the ability to modulate secretion of pancreatic enzymes. A comprehensive series of studies on the digestion and metabolism of carbohydrate by cats showed that, compared to dogs, pancreatic amylase activity and other indicators of carbohydrate digestion and utilization were lower and not responsive to dietary loads of starch.[29-32] This was attributed to a more carnivorous natural diet that would expose cats to consistently lower levels of dietary carbohydrate. The mink, which is another strict carnivore, has no capacity to adapt secretion of proteases and amylase to changes in dietary levels of protein or carbohydrate.[32] However, lipase activity did increase slightly when the fat content was doubled.

There are also differences between species in how they respond to enzyme inhibitors present in feedstuffs. This is particularly true for the trypsin inhibitors present in leguminous plants, such as peas and soybeans, which are often considered as lower cost sources of protein. Feeding adult dogs diets containing up to 15% raw soybean does not affect pancreatic growth or secretion of digestive enzymes.[34,35] This contrasts sharply with the pronounced pancreatic hypertrophy reported in young rats and chickens fed similar diets. There are also differences between species for the sensitivity of proteases to the inhibitors. We have found that mink trypsin is up to 3,000 times more sensitive to inhibitors extracted from peas than trypsin from pigs and rats.[36]

Development
of Pancreatic
Enzymes

The functions of the gastrointestinal tract during early development are of vital importance for growth and survival of offspring. They are also of interest when formulating diets for young mammals and deciding when to wean. Despite this, there is very little information available about the development of pancreatic functions in cats and dogs. The following presents the first data about development of the exocrine pancreas in the cat and dog. These data are compared with reports for other carnivores, as well as omnivorous species, taking into account differences between species and methodologies.

Postnatal development of trypsin, chymotrypsin, and lipase activity was studied in the intestinal contents (chyme) collected from cats and dogs ranging in age from 1 day to adulthood (Elnif et al., unpublished data). In both species and for all enzymes, the lowest activities were measured at 1 day of age (**Figure 1**).

Trypsin activity peaked at 3 weeks in dogs and remained relatively stable, despite a slight decline at 6 weeks. Chymotrypsin was lower (<2% of trypsin for all ages), and only doubled from 1 day to 3 weeks, with maximum values at 9 weeks. Similar findings have been reported by Kienzle for growing dogs.[37]

Trypsin and chymotrypsin activity were not detected in 1-day-old kittens; the exception was one kitten that had very low values. Maximum activities were not attained until after adolescence with activities in adults 2.5 to 3 times higher than those measured in 9-week-old cats. Interestingly, adult protease values for the cats were almost three times higher than those for the adult dogs.

Lipase activity increased 4-fold between 1 day and 3 weeks in dogs with peak activity recorded in 9-week-old animals. Values for adult dogs showed a decline and were similar to those at 3 weeks of age. Lipase activity was only occasionally detected in 1-day-old cats. Similar to the proteases activity increased after 1 day and was relatively constant from 3 weeks to 9 weeks of age, with highest activities measured in adults.

In addition to a pancreatic source, lipase activity detected in the intestines of the cats and dogs could have originated from lingual or gastric secretions and from lipases present in milk.[38] To assess the possible contribution from other sources, lipase activity was also measured in the contents of the stomach of cats and dogs (**Figure 2**). In both species, the highest activities in the stomach were detected in 1-day-old animals. These findings indicate that lipases originating from other

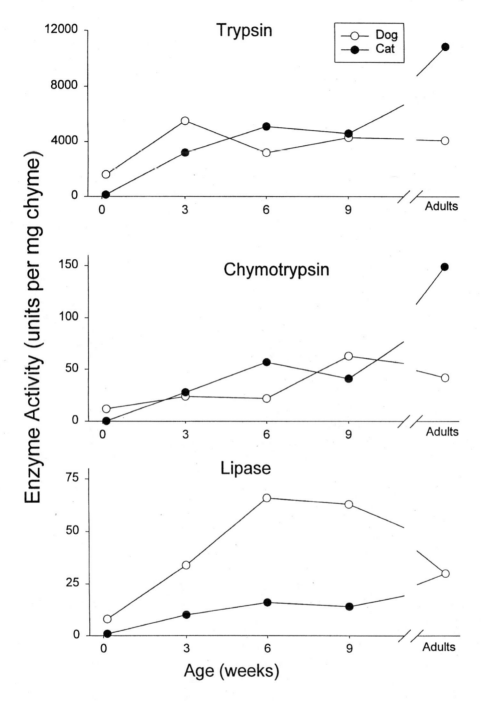

Figure 1. The activity of trypsin, chymotrypsin, and lipase in freshly collected chyme from the proximal third of the small intestine from dogs and cats at the ages of 1 day, 3, 6, and 9 weeks, and in adults.

sources may partly compensate for the low pancreatic secretion during the neonatal period and may be of particular importance for neonatal cats.

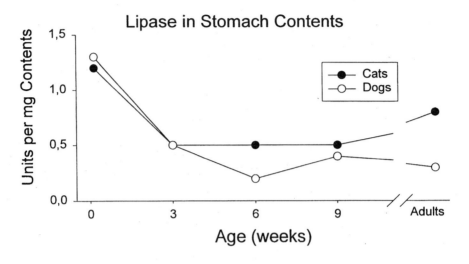

Figure 2. The activity of lipase in freshly collected chyme from the stomach of dogs or cats at the ages of 1 day, 3, 6, and 9 weeks, and in adults.

The above patterns for age-related changes in pancreatic secretion of proteases and lipase by cats and dogs are comparable to those of mink which has been studied in greater depth based on assays of intact pancreas.[39] Mink kits are born at an earlier stage of development. As a consequence, secretion of pancreatic proteases and lipase is not fully developed until mink kits are more than 3 months old (**Figure 3**). Mink are more similar to cats in that the highest activities for the proteases and lipase are measured in adults, not in younger animals as in dogs.

Pancreatic amylase activity is surprisingly high in mink kits for the first 4 weeks after birth (**Figure 3**). This is followed by a gradual decrease to the low values characteristic of adults. The low activities of adults are more similar to those of cats. Although amylase data for cats and dogs are not presented, in dogs there is a 10-fold increase in activity between 4 and 8 weeks of age.[37] A possible explanation for the high amylase activities during the first 4 weeks after mink are born is that this reflects the retention of an evolutionary trait from the ancestors of the marten family (*Mustelidae*) which includes omnivorous representatives (e.g., the badger and the skunk) and the mink. In contrast, all members of the cat family (*Felidae*) are strict carnivores and have a limited tolerance for dietary carbohydrate.[40] It is also possible that during suckling, mink synthesize but do not secrete amylase, causing high concentrations to accumulate within the acinar cells. After weaning, rates of synthesis may decline in conjunction with increased secretion resulting in lower activities in intact pancreas.

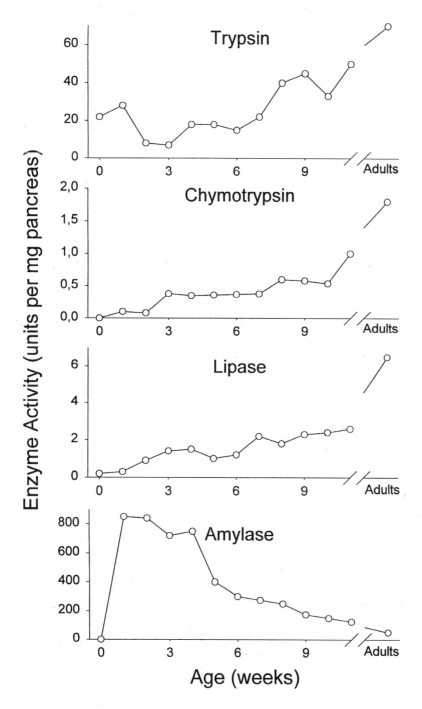

Figure 3. The activity of trypsin, chymotrypsin, lipase, and amylase in pancreatic tissue collected from mink kits from birth to 11-weeks-old and from adults.

Comparisons of enzyme activities in pancreatic secretions from pigs[41] reveal similarities with cats, dogs, and mink, as well as differences. Similar to cats and dogs, the activities of amylase, lipase, and the various proteases are low in pancreatic secretions collected from the pancreatic duct of suckling pigs (0–4 weeks of age). At the time pigs are weaned, there are marked increases in the activities of the pancreatic enzymes, as well as a heightened response to hormonal stimulation. A key difference between pigs and carnivores is the relative proportion of the pancreatic output represented by the various enzymes. For example, in weaned pigs the ratio for the specific activity of amylase is nearly 200 times higher than that for trypsin. Values for adult mink are less than 1.0. Values from the literature and actual measurements indicate ratios for cats and dogs are also much lower compared to pigs. This corresponds with the composition of the evolutionary diets of the three species.

| Conclusions and Perspectives | The differences between carnivores and omnivores in the relative activities of the enzymes secreted by the pancreas are apparently matched by genetic determinants to the natural diet. These genetic determinants are set during a species' evolution and match enzyme secretions with expected changes in diet (milk to the adult diet). They also appear to set limitations to how much an animal can adapt to changes in diet composition. Similar digestive adaptations and specializations are known for the enzymes and transporters associated with the enterocytes that line the small intestine (see chapter by Buddington and Paulsen).[42] |

The inability of cats, mink, and possibly dogs to fully adapt pancreatic enzyme secretion to match changes in diet composition, in addition to the late development of pancreatic secretion and regulation, are important considerations when formulating diets. The differences in pancreatic functions and regulatory capacities among carnivores, much less between animals with different feeding habits, restrict direct application of results from one species to others. This highlights the need to obtain additional information about adaptation and development of pancreatic functions in cats and dogs.

Acknowledgements   The authors would like to thank Mr. Mike Bassett, Dr. Karyl Buddington, Mr. Jason Peters, and other animal care personnel who assisted in the project, and Mr. Michael Bishop, Ms. Jillian Buckingham, and Ms. Katie Brand for providing technical support in the enzyme assays.

References   1. Williams DA. The Pancreas. In: Guilford WG, Center SA, Strombeck DR, Williams DA, Mejer DJ, eds. *Strombeck's Small Animal Gastroenterology* 3rd. edition. Philadelphia: W.B. Saunders Company, 1996; 381-410.

2. Zebrowska T, Low AG. The influence of diets based on whole wheat, wheat flour and wheat bran on exocrine pancreatic secretion in pigs. *J Nutr* 1987; 117:1212-16.

3. Rinderknecht H. Pancreatic secretory enzymes. In: Vay Liang W. Go, et al., ed. *The Pancreas: Biology Pathology, and Disease*. 2nd edition. New York: Raven Press Ltd., 1993; 219-251.

4. Stevens CE, Hume IA. *Comparative Physiology of the Vertebrate Digestive System*. 2nd edition. New York: Cambridge University Press, 1995; 400.

5. Scymeczko R, Skrede A. Protein digestion in mink. *Acta Agric. Scand* 1990; 40:189-200.

6. Williams DA, Guilford WG. Procedures for the evaluation of pancreatic and gastrointestinal tract diseases. In: Guilford WG, Center SA, Strombeck DR, Williams DA, Mejer DJ, eds. *Strombeck´s Small Animal Gastroenterology* 3rd edition. Philadelphia: W.B. Saunders Company, 1996; 77-114.

7. Lowe ME. The structure and function of pancreatic enzymes. In: Johnson, LR et al., eds. *Physiology of the Gastrointestinal Tract* 3rd edition. Raven Press, New York, 1993; 1531-1543.

8. Gorelick FS, Jamieson JD. The pancreatic acinarcell: Structure-function relationships. In: Johnson LR, et al., eds. *Physiology of the Gastrointestinal Tract* 3rd edition. New York: Raven Press, 1994; 1353-1376.

9. Jensen RT. Receptors on pancreatic acinar cells. In: Johnson LR, et al. (eds.). *Physiology of the Gastrointestinal Tract* 3rd edition. New York: Raven Press, 1994; 1377-1346.

10. Yule DI, Williams JA. Stimulus-secretion coupling in the pancreatic acinus. In: Johnson LR, et al., eds. *Physiology of the gastrointestinal tract*. 3rd. edition. New York: Raven Press, 1994; 1447-1472.

11. Solomon TE. Control of exocrine pancreas secretion.In: Johnson LR, et al., eds. *Physiology of the Gastrointestinal Tract* 3rd edition. New York: Raven Press, 1994; 1499-1531.

12. Rubenstein E, Mark Z, Haspel J, Ben-Ari G, Dreznik Z, Mirelman D, Tadmor A. Antibacterial activity of the pancreatic fluid. *Gastroenterology* 1985; 88:927-32.

13. Pierzynowski SG, Sharma P, Sobczyk J, Garwacki S, Barej W, Weström B. Comparative study of antibacterial activity of pancreatic juice in six mammalian species. *Pancreas* 1993; 8:546-550.

14. Pierzynowski SG, Sharma P, Sobczyk J, Garwacki S, Barej W. Influence of feeding regimen and postnatal developmental stages on antibacterial activity of pancreatic juice. *Intl J Pancrea* 1992; 12:121-125.

15. Simpson JW, Maskell IE, Quigg J, Markwell PJ. Long term management of canine exocrine pancreatic insufficiency. *J Sm Anim Prac* 1994; 35:133-138.

16. Pidgeon G. Effect of diet on exocrine pancreatic insuffiency in dogs. *JAVMA* 1982; 181:232-235.

17. Westermarck E, Junttila JT, Wiberg ME. Role of low dietary fat in the treatment of dogs with exocrine pancreatic insufficiency. *Am J Vet Res*.1995; 56:600-605.

18. Westermarck E, Myllys V, Aho M. Effect of treatment on jejunal and colonic bacterial flora of dogs with exocrine pancreatic insufficiency. *Pancreas* 1993; 8:559-562.

19. Johnston K, Batt RM. Relationship between the intestinal flora and disaccharidase activities in healthy cats. *Vet Rec* 1993; 132:362-363.

20. Cook AK, Breitschwerdt EB, Levine JF, Bunch SE, Linn LO. Risk factors associated with acute pancreatitis in dog: 101 cases (1985-1990). *JAVMA* 1993; 203:673-679.

21. Argent BE, Case RM. Pancreatic ducts: Cellular mechanism and control of bicarbonate secretion. In: Johnson LR, et al., eds. *Physiology of the Gastrointestinal Tract* 3rd edition. New York: Raven Press, 1994; 1473-1498.

22. Grossman MI, Greengard H, Ivy AC. The effect of dietary composition on pancreatic enzymes. *Am J Phys* 1942; 138:676-682.

23. Desnuelle P, Reboud JP, Ben Abdeljill A. Influence of the composition of the diet on the enzyme content of rat pancreas. In: Reuck AVS, Cameron MP, eds. *The Exocrine Pancreas Normal and Abnormal Functions*. London: Ciba Foundation, 1962; 90-114.

24. Behrman HR, Kare MR. Adaptation of pancreatic enzymes to diet composition. *J Physiol* 1969; 205: 667-676

25. Merrit AM, Burrows CF, Cowgill L, Streett W. Fecal fat and trypsin in dogs fed a meat-base or cereal-base diet. *JAVMA* 1979; 174:51-61.

26. Canfield PJ, Fairburm AJ. Effect of various diets on faecal analysis in normal dogs. *Res Vet Sci* 1983; 34:24-27.

27. Carro T, Williams DA. Relationship between dietary protein concentration and serum trypsin-like immunoreativity in dogs. *Am J Vet Res* 1989; 50:2105-2107.

28. Ballesta MC, Mañas M, Mataix FJ, Martínez-Victoria E, Seiquer I. Long-term adaptation of pancreatic response by dogs to dietary fats of different degrees of saturation: olive and sunflower oil. *Brit J Nutr* 1990; 64:487-496.

29. Kienzle E. Carbohydrate metabolism of the cat. 1. Activity of amylase in the gastrointestinal tract of the cat. *J Anim Physiol a Anim Nutr* 1993; 69:92-101.

30. Kienzle E. Carbohydrate metabolism of the cat. 2. Digestion of starch. *J Anim Physiol a Anim Nutr* 1993; 69:102-114.

31. Kienzle E. Carbohydrate metabolism of the cat. 3. Digestion of sugars. *J Anim Physiol a Anim Nutr* 1993; 69:203-210.

32. Kienzle E. Carbohydrate metabolism of the cat. 4. Activity of maltase, isomaltase, sucrase and lactase in the gastrointestinal tract in relation to age and diet. *J Anim Physiol a Anim Nutr* 1993; 70:89-96.

33. Simoes-Nunes C, Charlet-Léry G, Rougeot J. Adaptation of the exocrine pancreas secretion to diet composition in mink. *Proc III Congr Anim Fur Prod* 1984; 16/1-16/6.

34. Patten JR, Richards EA, Wheeler J. The effect of dietary soybean trypsin-inhibitor on the histology of the dog pancreas. *Life Science* 1971; 10:145-150.

35. Patten JR, Richards EA. The effect of raw soybean on the pancreas of adult dogs. *Proc Soc Exp Biol Med* 1971; 137:59-63.

36. Elnif J, Hansen NE, Mortensen K, Sørensen H. Properties of mink trypsinogen/trypsin and chymotrypsinogen/chymotrypsin compared with corresponding properties of these enzymes from other animals. *Proc IV Int Congr Fur Anim Prod* 1988; 308-320.

37. Kienzle E. Enzymaktivität in Pancreas, Darmwand und Chymus des Hundes in Abhängigkeit von Alter und Futterart. *J Anim Physiol a Anim Nutr* 1988; 60:276-288.

38. DeNigris SJ, Hamosh M, Kasbekar DK, Lee TC, Hamosh P. Lingual and gastric lipases: species differences in the origin of prepancreatic digestive lipases and in the localization of gastric lipase. *Biochem Biophys Acta* 1988; 959:38-45.

39. Elnif J, Hansen NE, Mortensen K, Sørensen K. Production of digestive enzymes in mink kits. *Proc IV Int Congr Fur Anim Prod* 1988; 320-329.

40. Legrand-Defretin V. Keynote Lecture 2. Differences between cats and dogs: a nutritional veiw. *Proc Nutr Soc* 1994; 53:15-24.

41. Pierzynowski SG, Weström BR, Svendsen J, Svendsen L, Karlsson BW. State-of-the-Art: Development and regulation of porcine pancreatic function. *Int J Pancreatology* 1995; 18:81-94.

42. Buddington RK, Paulsen DB. Development of the canine and feline gastrointestinal tract. In: Reinhart GA, Carey DP, eds. *Recent Advances in Canine and Feline Nutrition, Vol. II: 1998 Iams Nutrition Symposium Proceedings.* Wilmington: Orange Frazer Press, 1998; 195-216.

The Influence of Age on the Immune System

Phillip D. Nelson, DVM, PhD
Associate Dean, College of Veterinary Medicine
Mississippi State University, Mississippi State, Mississippi, USA

Margaret R. Kern, DVM, DACVIM; Kindra Kelly-Quaglianna, BS;
Xian-Lu Qu, MD; Carolyn Boyle, MS, PhD; Randal K. Buddington, PhD
College of Veterinary Medicine, Mississippi State University,
Mississippi State, Mississippi, USA

Introduction

Our understanding of the immune system has advanced dramatically over the past decade, thanks to significant advances in biotechnology and the impetus provided by the threat of human AIDS. These advances have provided us the ability to describe in molecular detail the effects of immaturity and advanced age on the immune response. In almost every immunological study, the effect of age must be considered, particularly in geriatric and pediatric subjects. Cellular and humoral immune responses of the juvenile mammal are known to become more effective over time as maturity approaches,[1-5] while a decline in immune function has been documented in several species.[6-13]

The effect of advanced age on the immune system (immunosenescence) is generally characterized by depressed helper T cell activity and changes in signal transduction.[5,13-16] Several investigators have published results that indicate this change may be due to both functional changes of immune cells as well as a shift in phenotype subsets.[12,16,17] Functional changes include reports of changes in patterns of cytokine gene expression,[17] a decline in cytotoxic activity,[8] and decreased proliferative responses to mitogen stimulation.[15] Age-related T cell dysfunction in particular is associated with increased autoimmunity and tumor incidence.[5] Age-related subset changes in various species include clonal expansion of CD4+ cell clones, and conflicting reports concerning the decrease or increase of CD4+, CD8+, γδ +, and/or B cells.[5,6,11,18] The reported characteristics of immunosenescence also differ according to gender, species, breed or race.[11] These confounding parameters make it impossible to make broad sweeping assumptions from human or mouse studies and apply them to the dog and cat.

A decline in cytotoxic T lymphocyte (CTL) activity has also been observed, and been found to be at least partially due to the loss of lytic T cell activity with advanced age.[8] This age related decline in T cell activity has been correlated with a reduction in serine esterase production in the process of generating CTL.[8]

Still, the culmination of knowledge describing the immune systems of the canine and feline species, using recently developed molecular techniques, is incomplete and largely derived from investigations involving animal models of human diseases. Our knowledge concerning lymphocyte distribution and CD4 or CD8 receptor expression in the major lymphoid organs during the development of the immune system in the dog and cat is incomplete. The importance of acquiring such knowledge would provide investigators valuable information on the age effects of immaturity on the anticipated responses to *in vivo* and *in vitro* analysis of the immune system. For example, it has been shown that murine CD8$^+$4$^+$ double positive (DP) cells can have different progenitor potentials in different fetal organs,[19] and that lymphocyte responses to mitogen stimulation vary between lymphocytes from different organ sources.[20] The same may be true in the dog and the cat, exerting significant age effects on results obtained from newly applied biotechniques. Further, primary and secondary lymphatic organs may have differing lymphocyte subset populations that are affected by both age and species. The following is a brief review of the present literature concerning lymphocyte subpopulations in lymphoid organs of selected species.

Lymphocyte
Development

Some knowledge of normal lymphocyte development is a prerequisite for any investigation concerning the normal proportions and/or distributions of lymphocyte phenotypes. It is important to understand that particularly in pediatric patients, the expression of certain markers may be age and tissue dependant.

Present knowledge of lymphocyte development suggests that most T cell development and instruction occurs in the thymus.[21-27] At least in the human fetus, thymic precursors initially reside in the fetal liver and migrate via the blood to seed the thymus during the first 8 weeks of gestation.[19] During the sixteenth week of gestation, the fetal liver colonizes the bone marrow and, approximately 6 weeks later, thymic precursors are derived from the bone marrow. These bone marrow derived, thymic precursors are generally assumed to have the capability to develop into either T cells, natural killer cells, or dendritic cells. These cells can also develop into B cells in the mouse.[19]

A small number of B cells have been reported to exist in the thymus of normal mice and humans cells.[28,29] Though these cells are generally progenitor cells, it has been reported that they can mature in the thymus, and do not migrate peripherally.[29] The developmental pathways resulting in a mature B cell in the thymic environment is unknown. It is speculated that they play some role in antigen presentation to T cells and may be involved in negative selection.[28,29,30]

With respect to the CD4 and CD8 receptors, the CD4$^-$CD8$^-$ precursors differentiate and mature to a CD8$^+$4^{low} or CD4$^+$8^{low} cell. The cell then becomes CD8$^+$4$^+$ double positive (DP). Most DP thymocytes express a T cell receptor (TCR) that cannot recognize self major histocompatibility complex (MHC) and are sentenced to a programmed cell death within 3–4 days. Those DP thymocytes that are self-MHC restricted are positively selected to develop into functionally mature CD4+ or CD8+ single positive (SP) cells (**Figure 1**).[31,32]

Thymocyte Maturation

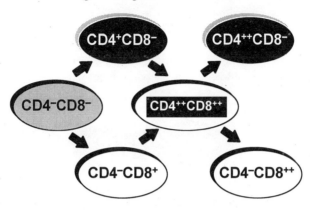

Figure 1. Phenotypic changes during normal maturation of the thymocyte as they are described for the CD4 and CD8 molecules in the mouse and human.

Several models have been proposed to explain CD4/CD8 receptor expression and functional differentiation during positive selection of the T-lymphocyte.[31,32] The stochastic/selection models emphasize the importance of the MHC molecule in lymphocyte development and differentiation. This model proposes that a first interaction of the T cell receptor (TCR) and co-receptor with either MHC class I or class II molecules results in a partial down-regulation of either CD4 or CD8 receptors. The TCR and co-receptor of these cells (CD8+4^{low} or CD4+8^{low}) must then interact with MHC class I or class II, respectively, to become mature single positive (CD8+ or CD4+) T cells. A proposed variant of the above model suggests that all T cell precursors are destined to become CD4+ cells unless there is a sustained TCR/MHC class I interaction, resulting in a transient down-regulation of CD8 before CD4 receptor expression becomes permanently down regulated. Alternatively, the instructional model proposes CD4 or CD8 receptor commitment is determined by the co-engagement of TCR/CD4 or TCR/CD8 on DP thymocytes, resulting in a down regulation of the remaining co-receptor (reviewed by Groves et al.[31]). A recent report suggests that TCR signaling may be important for the induction of early maturational events *in vivo*, but may not be sufficient or even critical for late maturational events to occur in the DP thymocyte.[32]

The progressive expression of the CD4 and CD8 co-receptors in the maturing lymphocyte represent a factor that must be considered when ascertaining subpopulations of the thymus and, possibly, other lymphoid organs in the immature mammal. Further, since extra-thymic maturation of T cells is also possible,[19] maturational effects should also be considered in investigations of other lympoid organs.

Several immunohistological studies of the immune system have been devoted to the description of lymphocyte subset distribution in the intestines of various species.[33-40] Results have been generally reported by phenotype (CD4[+], CD8[+], IgA, etc.) and their structural location (villi *v* crypts, lamina propria *v* epithelium, follicle *v* inter-follicular area, small intestines *v* large intestines). The recognition of normal distribution patterns should provide clues to functional mechanisms of defense and abnormal distribution in disease should shed some light on immunopathologic mechanisms. Tissues associated with the mucosal immunology of the gastrointestinal tract are presented in **Figure 2**.

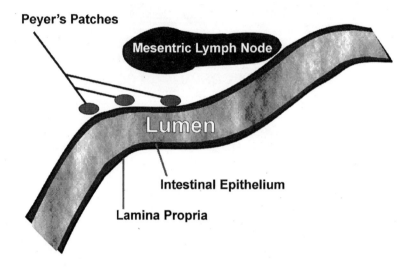

Figure 2. Lymphoid organs and tissues associated with the gastrointestinal tract.

Intestinal lymphocytes supposedly have the dichotomous responsibility of defending against gut pathogens without reacting with ubiquitous gut luminal contents.[20] The ability of intestinal lymphocytes to tolerate ubiquitous gut antigens has been shown to be the result of down regulation by intestinal mucosal cells, which are primarily CD4[+].[20] This is consistent with the accepted theory that MHC Class II cells respond to exogenous antigen and relegates MHC Class I cells (primarily located in the epithelium) to a cytotoxic role in the epithelium.[20] Experimental evidence suggests that when down-regulation is absent, or when intestinal lymphocytes become activated despite down-regulation, chronic inflammatory mucosal disease can occur.[39,41] This is supported by the observations that in some immune-mediated, allergic, and parasitic intestinal diseases, an increase in intraepithelial lymphocytes (IELs) and/or lamina proprial lymphocytes is seen,[39,40] whereas a decrease in mucosal lymphocytes has been described in viral diseases.[38]

Co-receptor expression within the epithelium and gut-associated lymphoid tissues differ between species with respect to population and distribution. The age of the subject also affects the relative proportions of lymphocyte sub-populations. Lymphocyte populations of the GI tract for selected species are described in *Table 1*.

Table 1. Lymphocyte populations of the gastrointestinal tract of various species.

Species	Intestinal Epithelium	Lamina Propria	Peyer's Patches
Human	Predominantly CD8⁺	60% CD4⁺ 40% CD8⁺	
Murine	Predominantly CD8⁺		
Ovine	CD8⁺ in epithelia basement membrane	CD4⁺ in central villus	95% B cells
Bovine		Predominantly CD4⁺	ileal: predominantly B cells jejunal: predominantly CD4⁺
Porcine			ileal: 10:1 T/B ratio jejunal: 50:50 T/B ratio
Canine	42% B cells 22% CD4⁺ 3% CD8⁺		jejunal: predominantly CD4⁺

Humans. In humans, T cells comprise up to 15% of cells in the intestinal epithelium and over 40% in the lamina propria.[20,39] IELs are predominantly CD4⁻CD8⁺ whereas, at least in the human, T cells in the lamina propria express CD4⁺ (60%) or CD8⁺ (40%) molecules similar to that in peripheral blood.[40]

Murine. In the mouse, gut IELs display a cytotoxic activity in *in vitro* assays despite CD4/8 lineage or the presence of α/β or γ/δ chains.[42] Gastrointestinal IELs have been reported to have dual origins (reviewed by Guy et al.[42]). Approximately 45% are thymodependent destined to proliferate in Peyer's patches under antigenic stimulation then migrate through the thoracic duct lymph and the blood to seed the gut mucosa.[43] These cells are TCR-α/β and are primarily CD8⁺, though some CD4⁺ cells are present. The remaining 55% of gut IELs are thymoindependent that arise from bone marrow, migrate directly to gut, and bear TCR-α/β or γ/δ. Unlike the thymodependant IELs, thymoindependant IELs bear CD8 molecules made of homodimeric α chains (CD8-α/α).[42] It has been speculated that IELs may be involved in the defense of the epithelia by rapidly eliminating altered enterocytes in pathological conditions.[42]

Ovine. In sheep, lymphocytes appear to be non-randomly distributed throughout the lamina propria with the greatest density occurring in the villus rather than the crypt areas. As in humans, CD8[+] cells are located around the epithelial basement membrane, while CD4[+] cells are localized towards the central villus area of the lamina propria.[34] Many of the CD8[+] cells are γ/δ cells, which have been reported to be a prominent lymphocyte subset in ruminants except for goats.[33,34] In sheep, these cells are widely distributed in both lamina propria and epithelium.[34]

Ruminant Peyer's patches (PP) differ dramatically in structure and lymphocyte composition (reviewed by Landsverk et al.[44]). Detailed discussion of ruminant PP is beyond the scope of this article. Briefly, the ileal PP is comprised of 95% B cells and <1% T cells, eliciting the suspicion that this structure may be a bursal analogue in lambs.[45,46] The ileal PP begins to involute at 12 weeks of age until it becomes a few small follicles at about 18 months of age.[45] In contrast, the jejunal and large intestine PP remain throughout life and are 16–25% T cells, most of which are CD4[+].[46,47] The B cell populations of the jejunal and large intestine PP are approximately 60% and 70% of the total lymphocyte populations in the lamb, respectively.[46]

Bovine. When comparing lymphocyte subset distributions between the cow and the calf, Parsons et al.[48] described different lymphocyte profiles for the various structural areas of the gut. Compared to the calf, the cow has fewer B cells in the ileum and greater numbers of T cells throughout the gut. The T cell sub-populations (CD4[+] and CD8[+]) were higher in the cow in the mucosa of the jejunum, ileum, and cecum. The colonic mucosa of the cow and calf were similar except for an increased number of CD8[+] cells in the cow.[48] Bovine CD4[+] cells are primarily located in the lamina propria of small and large intestines (as described in humans and sheep above) with the greatest number being in the small intestines.[38,49] These cells are evenly distributed in the crypt regions and focally distributed in some villi. In contrast to sheep, bovine CD8[+] and γδ cells were infrequently observed in the lamina propria. These cells were found instead in the epithelium of villi and crypts of the small intestine and crypts of the large intestine.[38,49] Bovine PP are numerous and heterogeneous in lymphocyte as well as epithelial composition.[44] Briefly, the bovine ileal PP is principally made up of B cells, whereas jejunal PP are primarily CD4[+] T cells.

Porcine. The relative numbers of T cells and B cells, as well as their distribution, also vary between the types of porcine PP (reviewed by Stokes et al.[50]). Unlike bovine PP, porcine jejunal PP have equal numbers of T and B cells, whereas ileal PP contain a 10:1 T cell to B cell ratio. A unique characteristic of porcine adult PP is that they also contain a significant population of functional CD2[+] CD4[+] CD8[+] double positive cells.[50]

At birth, T cells are rare in the porcine lamina propria (LP) and are negative for CD4 and CD8 molecules. There is a dramatic increase in the lamina proprial CD4[+] T cell population during the first week after birth. CD8[+] T cells increase moderately 5–6 weeks later. Rothkotter et al.[51] also reported the identification of a CD2+CD4-CD8- population (88%) during the first 12 days of life. This null population gradually decreased in proportion, and was not found after day 12. In 6-week-old pigs, LP T cells are either CD4+ or CD8+, and these cells have increased by 150- and 20-fold, respectively, since birth. B cells are extremely rare in the porcine neonatal LP until day 12, when IgA+ cells can be detected. IgA+ cells are higher in number in the crypts than in the villi. As in other species, CD4+ cells concentrate in the core of the villus lamina propria in the adult pig while T cells located below the epithelial cells and adjacent to the basement membrane express CD8 molecules.[51]

Canine. Canine studies of the gut using immunohistochemical staining have been reported in dogs aged from 2 months to 13 years.[35,36,37,52] Follicles of the gastric mucosa were reported to have an organized distribution of lymphocytes with a predominantly B cell area containing some CD4+ and CD8+ cells. Follicles in the fundus and body regions possessed similar percentages of lymphocytes averaging 42% (B cells), 22% (CD4+), and 3% (CD8+). The predominance of CD4+ T cells is similar to that reported for jejunal PP in the lamb.[47] Age related changes in lymphocyte distribution were not found.[36]

In another investigation (Hogenesch et al.[52]), regional differences in morphology and lymphocyte distribution within canine Peyer's patches (PP) were reported. The distinct types of canine PP is similar to that known to exist in lambs, calves, and pigs. Duodenal and jejunal PP contain more T cells than the ileal PP. The analysis performed examined the distribution of immunoglobulin isotypes within the domes of PP. The plasma cells in the canine lamina propria of the distinct PP were IgA+, while the plasma cells in the domes of the PP were principally IgG+.[52] Lymphocytes in the paracortical and interfollicular areas of PP are predominantly T cells that express the CD4 molecule (70–80%), whereas a minority of the T cells express the CD8 molecule (20–30%).[35]

The lymphocyte blastogenesis assay measures the degree of cell replication (DNA synthesis) after mitogen stimulation. The ability of the lymphocyte population to replicate in response to mitogen stimulation is used as an indirect measure of the intrinsic ability of the lymphocyte to respond to antigen. Mitogens used in lymphocyte blastogenesis assays deliver a signal that is transmitted across the membrane via the release of two messenger molecules, diacylglycerol and inositol 1,4,5-tris-phosphate (IP_3), which are involved in the activation of protein kinase C (PK-C) and the increase in cytosolic free Ca^{2+}.[16]

Lympho-proliferative Responses to Mitogens

Studies in humans and rodents have documented a decline in mitogen responses with age.[12,13,14] The investigators offer the following reasons for the observed decline: 1) a decline in calcium mobilization and PK-C activity, resulting in decreased IL-2 production and IL-2 receptor expression;[14,15] 2) transition with age from a predominance of naive cells to memory cells;[16] and 3) changes in the patterns of cytokine secretion.[17] It has been reported that, at least in the mouse, basal levels of both free cytoplasmic Ca^{2+} concentration and inositol phosphates are consistently higher in lymphocytes derived from old mice resulting in a net decrease in concentration changes of second messengers.[15] The sum of the data suggests that depressed mitogen activation of aged T cells is due to problems at the levels of Ca^{2+} mobilization, phosphatidylinositol phosphate hydrolysis, and/or PK-C activation (reviewed by Thoman et al.[16]).

In vitro response to mitogen stimulation appears to be affected by the tissue source. Human lymphocytes collected from intestinal mucosa have shown a depressed response to mitogen stimulation (reviewed by Khoo et al.[20]). However, discounting possible species differences, age may have a more profound effect on mitogen response capability in that IELs from 4-week-old calves are capable of blastogenic responses and interferon-γ production at levels similar to peripheral blood lymphocytes.[53] This is inconsistent with the expectation of depressed mitogen response noted in IELs of mature humans.[20]

Lymphoproliferative responses to mitogens have been found to be significantly depressed in older dogs when compared to young or middle aged dogs. The mean CPM responses of older dogs to concanavalin A (Con A), staphyloccal enterotoxin B, phytohemagglutinin (PHA), and pokeweed mitogen (PWM) were found to be significantly depressed when compared to that of younger dogs.[11] This data is consistent with age-related data noted in other species.[12,13,14]

Feline lymphocytes respond to Con A, PHA, PWM, and marginally respond to lipopolysaccharide.[54,55] Feline lymphocytes have been found to be sensitive to the induction of apoptosis when cultured overnight in medium.[56] Holznagel et al.[56] suggests this sensitivity to apoptotic induction may be based on the high constitutive expression of MHC II (indicating activation) on a B cell subpopulation. The loss of such cells may explain the limited response of feline lymphocytes to lipopolysaccharide stimulation. To the authors' knowledge, there is no reported data on the age effects on mitogen response of feline lymphocytes.

Lymphocyte Subset Distribution

Peripheral Blood.

Human. Numerous studies of lymphocyte subsets in peripheral blood have been conducted using flourescent activated cell sorting (FACS) analysis of various species.[11,12,18,56-60] Diverse age-related changes in the human have been cited, making it difficult to provide a concise description of subset changes.[12,16,18] At least one investigator suggests that there is a gradual increase in the percentage of T cells and $CD8^+$ cells with a simultaneous decrease in B cells in the elderly human.[18] However, the majority of the literature supports a decrease in the proportion of T lymphocytes with a decrease in both $CD4^+$ and $CD8^+$ cells (reviewed by Thoman et al.[16]). It is proposed that the increase in percentage of T cells is due to a lower rate of decline in absolute numbers. The functional implications of these changes has yet to be determined.[11] In humans, the percentage of T lymphocytes is reportedly significantly lower in very old patients than in young adults. The decrease is generally attributed to a decrease in $CD8^+$ cells.[12]

Canine. In puppies 1–9 weeks of age, T cell percentages gradually increase so that by 9 weeks of age T cells comprise nearly 80% of the lymphocyte population whereas B cells comprise approximately 10–15%.[59,61] This pattern is similar to that seen in the aged human in peripheral blood lymphocytes.[61] As the dog ages from 2 to 6 years there is an increase in T cells accompanied by an increase in the percentage of CD8+ lymphocytes, while B cells decreased during the same period.[11]

Feline. Cytometric analysis of T-lymphocyte subsets in adult SPF and random source cats reveal that T-lymphocytes, CD4+8− cells, CD8+4− cells, and Ig+ (or B) cells comprise 21–64%, 6–33.9%, 19–23%, and 23–45% of the peripheral lymphocyte population, respectively.[54,58,62] There were no significant differences between the two sources of cats (SPF *v* random source) in the study by Dean et al.[62] Reported ranges for CD4+ and CD8+ population numbers in adult random source and SPF cats are approximately 900–2600 and 700–1000 cells/μL, respectively.[60,63]

Normal SPF kittens have quite different blood lymphocyte profiles. In kittens (0–8 weeks of age) lymphocyte subset populations (T-lymphocytes, CD4+8− cells, CD8+4− cells, and Ig+ (or B cells) are reported to change over time from 17 to 50%, 25 to 35%, 6 to 10%, and 31 to 45%, respectively.[64] As in the dog, feline lymphocytes with pan T cell markers increase in number and proportion during the first 8 weeks of life. In contrast to canine reports, feline T cell subset populations increase in total numbers over the first 8 weeks of age, while Ig+ cells also increase in number and proportion from birth to 4 weeks of age.[64] These T cell changes are similar to changes in the aged human and the early post-natal canine. However, B cell dynamics in the kitten appear to differ from that exhibited by the puppy.

Thymus.
Canine. Canine values (FACS) of lymphocyte subset distributions in the thymus of dogs 4–8 weeks of age have been reported as follows: T cells, 95%; CD4+8− cells, 10%; CD8+4− cells, <3%; CD4+8+ cells, 75%; and CD4−8− cells, 10%.[59] Using immunohistochemical techniques on adult dogs, Rabanal et al.[35] reported that 90% of thymic lymphocytes were T cells, whereas an anti-B cell monoclonal antibody recognized 5% of lymph cells near trabeculae. CD4+ and CD8+ cells were described in the cortex and in the medulla at a proportion of 3:2, respectively. It should be noted that the anti-CD4 antibody also reacted with cells thought to be thymic epithelial cells.[35]

Feline. Feline lymphocytes with T cell properties (rosettes) and/or markers make up 35–45% of thymic lymphocytes, while 2.9% are B cells. CD4+8− and CD8+4− cells have been found to comprise 52% and 63–76% of thymic lymphocytes, respectively (reviewed by Lin).[54] The finding of B cells in the canine and feline thymus is consistent with reports that small numbers of B cell progenitors (sIg−, B220med, and CD43+) have been found in the thymus of mouse and humans.[29]

Reported values of lymphocyte distribution in other lymphoid organs in the canine and feline species are not as complete, and will not be addressed in this review.[54,59,65]

| Experimental | Much of the present knowledge concerning the canine and feline immune |

Experimental
Design
and Methods

Much of the present knowledge concerning the canine and feline immune system has long been inferred from human and murine studies undertaken in the murine and human systems. Until recently, the lack of species specific molecular agents and the resultant void of species specific index data have greatly curtailed our ability to determine the effects of nutrition and/or disease on the immune response in the dog and cat. This study focused on the characterization of the lymphocytic functional and phenotypical development during the early post-natal (first 9 weeks) period. Although final data are not available at the time of this writing, the specific objectives of this study are as follows: 1) to describe CD4$^+$, CD8$^+$, CD4$^+$CD8$^+$ (DP), and Ig$^+$ lymphocyte population distribution in the spleen, thymus, mesenteric lymph node, popliteal lymph node, bone marrow, and peripheral blood in the kitten; 2) to assess lymphocyte responses of the same lymphatic tissues to mitogen stimulation in the kitten; 3) to describe CD4$^+$, CD8$^+$, CD4$^+$CD8$^+$ (DP), and Ig$^+$ lymphocyte population distribution in the spleen, thymus, mesenteric lymph node, popliteal lymph node, bone marrow, and peripheral blood in the puppy; and 4) to describe the distribution of the CD4$^+$ and the CD8$^+$ lymphocyte in the canine small intestines. At the 1998 Iams Nutrition Symposium, the percentages of CD4$^+$ and CD8$^+$ receptor single- (SP) and co-expression (DP) will be described, as well as Ig$^+$ cell percentages in various lymphatic organs. A correlation to data derived from lymphocyte blast transformation assays performed on the same lymphocyte populations in the feline and immunohistochemical analysis of the canine small intestines during the same time period will be attempted.

Animals. Samples were obtained from random source normal dogs (86) and cats (65) free of overt disease. Each animal was destined to be used in a a subsequent study. Samples were obtained immediately prior to any other procedure being performed. The animals ranged in age from 0–9 weeks of age and 1–3 years of age.

Lymphocyte Collection. Blood samples were collected via venopuncture. Tissue samples were collected from the thymus, spleen, bone marrow from the femur, mesenteric and popliteal lymph nodes. Tissue samples from each organ source were forced through a fine wire mesh screen and suspended in RPMI with 10% calf serum. Each cell suspension (including peripheral blood buffy coat in PBS) was then layered over a differential gradient of Percol (1.083 for cat, 1.068 for dog), and the lymphocyte rich layer was collected, resuspended in RPMI +10% FBS, run through a 20mM Nylon mesh to obtain a single cell suspention, and hand counted on a hemocytometer using a phase contrast microscope.

Antibodies. Tissues were collected as described above for FACS analysis of lymphocyte subpopulations using a panel of monoclonal antibodies developed at North Carolina State University.[66] *Canine antibodies include:* fluorescein conjugated goat anti-mouse Igs (Cappel # 55499); biotin conjugated goat anti-mouse Igs (Cappel #55590); fluorescein conjugated goat anti-dog IgG (Cappel #55330); Streptavidin RPE (Dako #R0438); biotin conjugated mouse anti-dog CD8, biotin conjugated mouse anti-dog T, and FITC conjugated mouse anti-dog CD4 (courtesy of North Carolina State University). *Feline antibodies include:* fluorescein conjugated goat anti mouse Igs (Cappel # 55499); Rhodamine conjugated goat anti-mouse Igs (Cappel # 55532); fluorescein conjugated rabbit anti-goat IgG (EY Labs #FAF-013-2); fluorescein conjugated goat anti-feline IgG (Cappel #55291); PE conjugated mouse anti-feline T- (572); PE conjugated mouse anti-feline CD4- (30A), and fluorescein conjugated mouse anti feline CD8- (357) (courtesy of North Carolina State University).

FACS Analysis. The suspended lymphocytes from each tissue were then phenotyped using two-color flow cytometric analysis. Cells were purified and prepared for flow analysis as previously described.[63] Briefly, 1 x 10[6] cells were aliquoted into tubes, placed on ice, and washed with PBS and incubated with direct FITC conjugated and direct biotin conjugated mAbs for 30 minutes. Cells were then washed with PBS, and Strep PE applied for five minutes. Finally cells were washed with PBS, resuspended in 0.2% NaCl for 20 seconds, then fixed with an additional 3 ml of 4% Formalin in PBS. Cells were again pelleted, and the pellet resuspended in 1 ml PBS. The percentage of fluorescently stained lymphocytes was determined by dual color flow cytometric analysis using a Becton Dickinson FACScan.

Lymphocyte Blast Transformation. Feline tissue lymphocytes (spleen, thymus, mesenteric lymph node, popliteal lymph node, femur) were collected as described above. Slides for each tissue were streaked, air dried, and H&E stained to verify cell types.

Blastogenesis samples were suspended in media at a concentration of 1 x 10[5] cells per well (175µl) and alloquoted into 96 well plates according to an established template. The mitogens used were as follows: pokeweed pure (PWM) [EY Laboratories, San Mateo, CA, #L-1901-5]; lipopolysaccharide rough strain from E. *coli* (LPS) [List Biological Labs, Campbell, CA, #302]; phytohemagglutinin (PHA-P) [Sigma, St. Louis, MO, #L-9132]; and concanavalin A (ConA) [Sigma, #C-5275]. Mitogens were then applied (25µl) and mixed gently. Final mitogen concentrations were as follows: LPS; 10µg/mL, 5µg/mL, 2.5µg/mL, ConA; 10µg/mL, 7.5µg/mL, 5µg/mL, PHA; 5µg/mL, 2.5µg/mL, 1.25µg/mL, PWM; 4µg/mL, 1µg/mL, 0.25µg/mL. All samples were stimulated in triplicate. Plates were then placed in an incubator at 5% CO_2, 90% humidity, 37° C. At 54 hours, 0.5µCi [^{3}H]-thymidine was added (10 µL) to each well and gently mixed. Plates were then replaced in the incubator for 18 hours. At 72 total hours, cells were harvested onto filter disks and radioactive emissions were measured in a scintillation counter. Data was adjusted to a stimulation index (SI) by using counts per minute (cpm) in the test sample divided by cpm of the unstimulated control.

Immunohistochemistry. Sections from the duodenal, ileal, and jejunal portions of the small intestines were collected from each canine subject, placed in OCT media, and quick frozen in liquid nitrogen. Samples were then held in a -70° C freezer until processed. The tissues were cut and stained using the indirect ABC method as previously described.[67] The expression of CD4 and CD8 receptors was demonstrated using rat anti-canine CD8 and rat anti-canine CD4 (MCA1039 and MCA1038, Serotec, 22 Bankside England, Station Approach, Kidlington, Oxford OX5 1JE, England) and Vectastain Elite Rat IgG ABC Kit (PK 6104, Vector Labs, 30 Ingold Road, Burlingame, CA 94010, USA).

Discussion

The results of the study described above have been submitted for statistical analysis at the time of this writing. Preliminary evaluations suggest the following conclusions: 1) juvenile canine and feline lymphoid organs have markedly different lymphocyte subset populations when compared to the adult; 2) the response of juvenile feline lymphocytes to *in vitro* mitogen stimulation is affected by the tissue source and may be affected by age; and 3) the distribution of CD4+ and CD8+ lymphocytes in the puppy differs from that of the adult dog.

The data cited in this article suggest that the development and age-related change of lymphocyte subset populations in various lymphatic organs may reflect species specific patterns. However, at least one investigator has concluded that age effects are undetectable in adult cats ranging in age from 1–15 years of age, with a median age of 3 years.[58] Considering the fact that the study by Walker et al.[57] was on adult cats only, the possibility remains that age influence is only important in the developmental (pediatric) and the geriatric periods of life. This has been documented in humans where the greatest age influence on lymphocyte subset populations have been found to be in the pediatric and elderly subjects.[12-14,16,18,19,68] The influence of age, gender, species, breed, and organ of interest present a complex problem in describing the immune system. The problem is further complicated by the use of various agents, techniques, and cell lines when different investigators seek to characterize a particular immunologic response. These factors provide ample justification for delineation of various immune parameters and processes specific for the dog and cat. Animal models of human diseases that affect the immune system are often based on similar phenotypic expression in the immune response. However, immunophenotypic differences may simply reflect operational differences between two species. Utilizing newly developed agents and biotechniques, it is now possible to more definitively describe the canine and feline immune systems, and potentially provide insight that may result in the identification of new animal disease models.

The need for characterizing the canine and feline immune systems is important if appropriate immunological models of human diseases are to be identified, or for pathogenic investigations of the effect of disease on the immune system, or if immunologic evaluations of novel therapies are to be studied.[59,61,69-71] The complex effects of species, age, and gender on various immunologic measured responses further strengthens this need. The results to be presented at the 1998 Iams Nutrition Symposium will provide information on the developing immune system in the early post-natal period in the canine and feline species.

Acknowledgements

The authors wish to thank Doug Gebhard, and Drs. Mary and Wayne Tompkins for providing mAbs for this study.

1. Gazzolo L, Moscovici M, Moscovici C. Susceptibility and resistance of chicken macrophages to avian RNA tumor viruses. *Virology* 1975; 67:553-565.

2. Levy M, Wheelock E. Impaired macrophage function in Friend virus leukemia: Restoration by statolon. *J Immunol* 1975; 114:962-964.

3. Marcelletti J, Furmanski P. Spontaneous regression of Friend virus-induced erythroleukemia. *J Immunol* 1978; 120:1-8.

4. Mogensen S. Role of macrophages in natural resistance to virus infections. *Microbiol Rev* 1979; 43:1-26.

5. Makinodan T, Kay M. Age influence on the immune system. *Adv Immunol* 1980; 29:287-330.

6. Schwab R, Szabo P, Manavalan JS, Weksler ME, Posnett DN, Pannetier C, Kourilsky P, Even J. Expanded CD4+ and CD8+ T cell clones in elderly humans. *J Immunol* 1997; 158:4493-4499.

7. Beckman I, Dimopoulos K, Xu X, Ahern M, Bradley J. Age-related changes in the activation requirements of human CD4+ T-cell subsets. *Cell Immunol* 1991; 132:17-25.

8. Bloom E, Umehara H, Bleackley R, Okumura K, Mostowski H, Babbitt JT. Age-related decrement in cytotoxic T lymphocyte (CTL) activity is associated with decreased levels of mRNA encoded by two CTL-associated serine esterase genes and the perforin gene in mice. *Eur J Immunol* 1990; 20:2309-2316.

9. De Paoli P, Battistin S, Santini G. Age-related changes in human lymphocyte subsets: progressive reduction of the CD4 CD45R (suppressor inducer) population. *Clin Immunol Immunopathol* 1988; 48:290-296.

10. Erkeller-Yuksel F, Deneys V, Yuksel B, Hannet I, Hulstaert F, Hamilton C, Mackinnon H, Stokes LT, Munhyeshuli V, Vanlangendonck F, et al. Age-related changes in human blood lymphocyte subpopulations. *J Pediatr* 1992; 120:216-222.

11. Greeley EH, Kealy RD, Ballam JM, Lawler DF, Segre M. The influence of age on the canine immune system. *Vet Immunol Immunopathol* 1996; 55:1-10.

12. Lehtonen L, Eskola J, Vainio O, Lehtonen A. Changes in lymphocyte subsets and immune competence in very advanced age. *J Gerontol* 1990; 45:M108-M112.

13. Muràsko DM, Weiner P, Kaye D. Decline in mitogen induced proliferation of lymphocytes with increasing age. *Clin Exp Immunol* 1987; 70:440-448.

14. Gillis S, Kozak R, Durante M, Weksler MEl. Immunological studies of aging. *J Clin Invest* 1981; 67:937-942.

15. Proust JJ, Filburn CR, Harrison SA, Buchholz MA, Nordin AA. Age-related defect in signal transduction during lectin activation of murine T lymphocytes. *J Immunol* 1987; 139:1472-1478.

16. Thoman M, Weigle W. The cellular and subcellular bases of immunosenescence. *Adv Immunol* 1989; 46:221-261.

17. Hobbs MV, Weigle WO, Noonan DJ, Torbett BE, McEvilly RJ, Koch RJ, Cardenas GJ, Ernst DN. Patterns of cytokine gene expression by CD4+ T cells from young and old mice. *J Immunol* 1993; 150:3602-3614.

18. Hulstaert F, Hannet I, Deneys V, Munhyeshuli V, Reichert T, De Bruyere M, Strauss K. Age-related changes in human blood lymphocyte subpopulations. II. Varying kinetics of percentage and absolute count measurements. *Clin Immunol Immunopathol* 1994; 70:152-158.

19. Blom B, Res P, Noteboom E, Weijer K, Spits H. Prethymic CD34+ progenitors capable of developing into T cells are not committed to the T cell lineage. *J Immunol* 1997; 158:3571-3577.

20. Khoo UY, Proctor IE, Macpherson AJ. CD4+ T cell down-regulation in human intestinal mucosa: evidence for intestinal tolerance to luminal bacterial antigens. *J Immunol* 1997; 158:3626-634.

21. Barcena A, Galy A, Punnonen J, Muench MO, Schols D, Roncarolo MG, de Vries JE, Spits H. Lymphoid and myeloid differentiation of fetal liver CD34+lineage- cells in human thymic organ culture. *J Exp Med* 1994; 180:123-132.

22. Anderson S, Perlmutter R. A signaling pathway governing early thymocyte maturation. *Immunol Today* 1995; 16:99-105.

23. Chan S, Cosgrove D, Waltzinger C, Benoist C, Mathis D. Another view of the selective model of thymocyte selection. *Cell* 1993; 73:225-236.

24. Chan S, Waltzinger C, Baron A, Benoist C, Mathis D. Role of coreceptors in positive selection and lineage commitment. *EMBO J* 1994; 13:4482-4489.

25. Crump AL, Grusby MJ, Glimcher LH, Cantor H. Thymocyte development in major histocompatibility complex-deficient mice: evidence for stochastic commitment to the CD4 and CD8 lineages. *Proc Natl Acad Sci USA* 1993; 90:10739-10743.

26. Davis M, Bjorkman P. T-cell antigen receptor genes and T-cell recognition. *Nature* 1988; 334:395-402.

27. Davis C, Killeen N, Crooks M, Raulet D, Littman DR. Evidence for a stochastic mechanism in the differentiation of mature subsets of T lymphocytes. *Cell* 1993; 73:237-247.

28. Miyama-Inaba M, Kuma S, Inaba K, Ogata H, Iwai H, Yasumizu R, Muramatsu S, Steinman RM, Ikehara S. Unusual phenotype of B cells in the thymus of normal mice. *J Exp Med* 1988; 168:811-816.

29. Mori S, Inaba M, Sugihara A, Taketani S, Doi H, Fukuba Y, Yamamoto Y, Adachi Y, Inaba K, Fukuhara S, Ikehara S. Presence of B cell progenitors in the thymus. *J Immunol* 1997; 158:4193-9.

30. Spencer J, Choy M, Hussell T, Papadaki L, Kington JP, Isaacson PGl. Properties of human thymic B cells. *Immunology* 1992; 75:596-600.

31. Groves T, Parsons M, Miyamoto NG, Guidos CJ. TCR engagement of CD4+CD8+ thymocytes *in vitro* induces early aspects of positive selection, but not apoptosis. *J Immunol* 1997; 158:65-75.

32. Vanhecke D, Verhasselt B, De Smedt M, De Paepe B, Leclercq G, Plum J, Vandekerckhove B. MHC class II molecules are required for initiation of positive selection but not during terminal differentiation of human CD4 single positive thymocytes. *J Immunol* 1997; 158:3730-737.

33. Navarro JA, Seva J, Caro MR, Sanchez J, Gomez MA, Bernabe A. Postnatal development of lymphocyte subpopulations in the intestinal mucosa in goat. *Vet Immunol Immunopathol* 1997; 55:303-311.

34. Little D, Alzuherri HM, Clarke CJ. Phenotypic characterisation of intestinal lymphocytes in ovine paratuberculosis by immunohistochemistry. *Vet Immunol Immunopathol* 1996; 55:175-187.

35. Rabanal R, Ferrer L, Else R. Immunohistochemical detection of canine leucocyte antigens byspecific monoclonal antibodies in canine normal tissues. *Vet Immunol Immunopathol* 1995; 46:95-100.

36. Kolbjornsen O, Press C, Moore P, Landsverk T. Lymphoid follicles in the gastric mucosa of dogs. Distribution and lymphocyte phenotypes. *Vet Immunol Immunopathol* 1994; 40:299-312.

37. HogenEsch H, Felsburg P. Immunohistology of Peyer's patches in the dog. *Vet Immunol Immunopathol* 1992; 31:1-10.

38. Liebler EM, Kusters C, Pohlenz JF. Experimental mucosal disease in cattle: changes in the number of lymphocytes and plasma cells in the mucosa of the small and large intestine. *Vet Immunol Immunopathol* 1996; 55:93-105.

39. Corazza GR, Frazzoni M, Gasbarrini G. Jejunal intraepithelial lymphocytes in coeliac disease: are they increased or decreased? *Gut* 1984; 25:158-62.

40. Russell GJ, Parker CM, Sood A, Mizoguchi E, Ebert EC, Bhan AK, Brenner MB. p126 (CDw101), a costimulatory molecule preferentially expressed on mucosal T lymphocytes. *J Immunol* 1996; 157:3366-3374.

41. Schreiber S, MacDermott R, Raedler A, Pinnau R, Bertovich MJ, Nash GS. Increased activation of isolated intestinal lamina propria mononuclear cells in inflammatory bowel disease. *Gastroenterology* 1991; 101:1020-1030.

42. Guy-Grand D, Malassis-Seris M, Briottet C, Vassalli P. Cytotoxic differentiation of mouse gut thymodependent and independent intraepithelial T lymphocytes is induced locally. Correlation between functional assays, presence of perforin and granzyme transcripts, and cytoplasmic granules. *J Exp Med* 1991; 173:1549-52.

43. Husband A, Gowans J. The origin and antigen-dependent distribution of IgA-containing cells in the intestine. *J Exp Med* 1978; 148:1146-1160.

44. Landsverk T, Halleraker M, Aleksandersen M, McClure S, Hein W, Nicander L. The intestinal habitat for organized lymphoid tissues in ruminants; comparative aspects of structure, function and development. *Vet Immunol Immunopathol* 1991; 28:1-16.

45. Reynolds J, Morris B. The evolution and involution of Peyer's patches in fetal and postnatal sheep. *Eur J Immunol* 1983; 13:627-635.

46. Aleksandersen M, Hein W, Landsverk T, McClure S. Distribution of lymphocyte subsets in the large intestinal lymphoid follicles of lambs. *Immunology* 1990; 70:391-397.

47. Hein W, Dudler L, Mackay C. Surface expression of differentiation antigens on lymphocytes in the ileal and jejunal Peyer's patches of lambs. *Immunology* 1989; 68:365-370.

48. Parsons KR, Howard CJ, Jones BV, Sopp P. Investigation of bovine gut associated lymphoid tissue (GALT) using monoclonal antibodies against bovine lymphocytes. *Vet Pathol* 1989; 26:396-408.

49. Parsons KR, Hall GA, Bridger JC, Cook RS. Number and distribution of T lymphocytes in the small intestinal mucosa of calves inoculated with rotavirus. *Vet Immunol Immunopathol* 1993; 39:355-64.

50. Stokes C, Haverson K, Bailey M. Antigen presenting cells in the porcine gut. *Vet Immunol Immunopathol* 1996; 54:171-177.

51. Rothkotter HJ, Ulbrich H, Pabst R. The postnatal development of gut lamina propria lymphocytes: number, proliferation, and T and B cell subsets in conventional and germ-free pigs. *Pediatr Res* 1991; 29:237-242.

52. HogenEsch H, Felsburg PJ. Isolation and phenotypic and functional characterization of cells from Peyer's patches in the dog. *Vet Immunol Immunopathol* 1992; 31:1-10.

53. Corbeil L. Workshop summary: local/mucosal immunity. *Vet Immunol Immunopathol* 1996; 54:187-189.

54. Lin D. Feline immune system. *Comp Immunol Microbiol Infect Dis* 1992; 15:1-11.

55. Lin D, Bowman D, Jacobson R, Barr MC, Fevereiro M, Williams JR, Noronha FM, Scott FW, Avery RJ. Suppression of lymphocyte blastogenesis to mitogens in cats experimentally infected with feline immunodeficiency virus. *Vet Immunol Immunopathol* 1990; 26:183-189.

56. Holznagel E, Hofmann-Lehmann R, Allenspach K, Huttner S, Willett B, Groscurth P, Niederer E, Lutz H. Flow cytometric detection of activation-induced cell death (apoptosis) in peripheral blood lymphocyte subpopulations from healthy cats. *Vet Immunol Immunopathol* 1996; 52:1-14.

57. Walker C, Malik R, Canfield P. Analysis of leucocytes and lymphocyte subsets in cats with naturally-occurring cryptococcosis but differing feline immuno-deficiency virus status. *Aust Vet J* 1995; 72:93-97.

58. Walker C, Canfield P, Love D. Analysis of leucocytes and lymphocyte subsets for different clinical stages of naturally acquired feline immunodeficiency virus infection. *Vet Immunol Immunopathol* 1994; 44:1-12.

59. Somberg RL, Robinson JP, Felsburg PJ. T lymphocyte development and function in dogs with X-linked severe combined immunodeficiency. *J Immunol* 1994; 153:4006-4015.

60. English R, Nelson P, Johnson C, Nasisse M, Tompkins WA, Tompkins MB. Development of clinical disease in cats experimentally infected with feline immuno-deficiency virus. *J Infect Dis* 1994; 170:543-552.

61. Somberg RL, Tipold A, Hartnett BJ, Moore PF, Henthorn PS, Felsburg PJl. Postnatal development of T cells in dogs with X-linked severe combined immuno-deficiency. *J Immunol* 1996; 156:1431-1435.

62. Dean G, Quackenbush S, Ackley C, Cooper MD, Hoover EA. Flow cytometric analysis of T-lymphocyte subsets in cats. *Vet Immunol Immunopathol* 1991; 28:327-335.

63. Tompkins M, Nelson P, English R, Novotney C. Early events in the immunopathogenesis of feline retrovirus infections. *J Am Vet Med Assoc* 1991; 199:1311-1315.

64. Sellon R, Levy J, Jordan H, Gebhard DH, Tompkins MB, Tompkins WA. Changes in lymphocyte subsets with age in perinatal cats: late gestation through eight weeks. *Vet Immunol Immunopathol* 1996; 53:105-113.

65. Parodi A, Femenia F, Moraillon A, Crespeau F, Fontaine JJ. Histopathologi-cal changes in lymph nodes of cats experimentally infected with the feline immuno-deficiency virus (FIV). *J Comp Pathol* 1994; 111:165-174.

66. Tompkins M, Gebhard D, Bingham H, Hamilton MJ, Davis WC, Tompkins WA. Characterization of monoclonal antibodies to feline T lymphocytes and their use in the analysis of lymphocyte tissue distribution in the cat. *Vet Immunol Immunopathol* 1990; 26:305-317.

67. Day M. Immunophenotypic characterization of cutaneous lymphoid neoplasia in the dog and cat. *J Comp Pathol* 1995; 112:79-96.

68. Offner F, Van-Beneden K, Debacker V, Vanhecke D, Vandekerckhove B, Plum J, Leclercq G. Phenotypic and functional maturation of TCR gamma delta cells in the human thymus. *J Immunol* 1997; 158:4634-4641.

69. Martinez MA, Martinez CM, Blanco A, Hernandez-Rodriguez S. Immunological and histological study of T- and B-lymphocyte activity in canine visceral leishmaniosis. *Vet Parasitol* 1993; 51:49-59.

70. Martinez MA, Moreno T, Martinez MFJ, Acosta I, Hernandez S. Humoral and cell-mediated immunity in natural and experimental canine leishmaniasis. 1995; 48:209-220.

71. Iwatsuki K, Okita M, Ochikubo F, Gemma T, Shin YS, Miyashita N, Mikami T, Kai C. Immunohistochemical analysis of the lymphoid organs of dogs naturally infected with canine distemper virus. *J Comp Pathol* 1995; 113:185-190.

Nutrition of the Neonatal Canine and Feline

Allan J. Lepine, PhD
Research Nutritionist, Research and Development
The Iams Company, Lewisburg Ohio USA

The neonatal period, broadly defined for use in the following discussion as the interval from birth through the weaning transition, is a span of time comprising a number of inherent challenges which require the puppy or kitten to demonstrate appropriate developmental adaptations if survival is to be assured. Following an abrupt expulsion from the protection and support of the uterine milieu into a comparatively hostile external environment, the neonatal canine or feline becomes responsible for the acquisition of nutrition and initial defense against disease through the active process of nursing. Failure to rapidly and effectively make the transition to meet these new environmental demands is a major contributor to the high mortality rates observed during the neonatal period. Further complicating this situation is the constantly changing nutritional matrix presented to the neonate, not only during the nursing phase, but throughout the entirety of the neonatal period. The objective herein is to briefly review nutritional support of the canine and feline during the neonatal period with special emphasis on supplemental nutrition provided by milk replacers.

Introduction

The essentiality of ensuring milk intake by the canine and feline neonate was expounded upon during the 1996 Iams International Nutrition Symposium.[1] Briefly, mammary secretions provide for the following needs of the neonate: 1) maintenance of hydration, 2) passive immunity, 3) nutrition, and 4) non-nutritional factors. Failure of maternal provision of an adequate quantity of mammary secretions or an inadequate acquisition by the neonate demands a surrogate source of nutrition for the neonate, most often in the form of a milk replacer.

Mammary Secretions and Passive Immunity

A primary concern regarding the provision of milk replacer is the lack of passive immunity acquisition should the failure of mammary secretion intake begin immediately postpartum. The endothelialchorial placenta of the canine and feline limits the *in utero* passage of maternal antibodies, thereby increasing the importance of colostral antibodies to provide immune protection to the neonatal canine and feline. Very little information currently exists in the scientific literature regarding the development of active immunity in the neonatal canine and feline. Such data would be extremely beneficial in evaluating potential mechanisms by which the development of the neonatal immune system could be potentiated, thus reducing the risk potential to the orphaned canine and feline neonate. A review of the present knowledge in neonatal canine and feline immunology and summary of current research to expand this essential area is presented by Nelson[2] in these proceedings.

Formulation of a milk replacer is a daunting task since mammary secretions are extremely complex and constantly change throughout the course of lactation. It is also not appropriate to consider the compositional analysis of milk from another species as a model for the nutrient profile of a canine or feline milk replacer since the composition of mammary secretions differs markedly across species.[3,5,6,7] It is therefore essential that the compositional uniquenesses of canine and feline milk be appreciated to allow a critical evaluation of the key nutritional characteristics of milk replacers for the puppy and kitten.

Milk Protein   The protein content of feline milk has been reported to decrease from days 1 to 3 of lactation and then increase throughout the remainder of lactation.[3,4] Protein content on a dry matter basis was reported to range from a low of approximately 30% to a high of 43% in these studies. A similar pattern of feline milk protein was observed in an earlier study although lower overall concentrations (20 to 35%) levels were reported.[5] Canine milk protein content was demonstrated to increase in a manner similar to that observed for the feline with protein concentrations ranging from 21.5% on a dry matter basis in early lactation to 30% in late lactation.[6] Oftedal[7] reported a similar lactational pattern with somewhat higher protein values of 30% and 34% in early and late lactation, respectively. Based on the reported protein values for canine and feline milk, a milk replacer containing 35 to 40% protein on a dry matter basis should be appropriate.

It is important to recognize, however, that the total protein content of a milk replacer provides little information regarding the profile of amino acids being provided to the neonate. This, rather, is determined by the specific milk proteins comprising the protein component of the replacer. In general, milk proteins can be classified into two categories, casein proteins, and whey proteins, with the relative proportion of casein proteins to whey proteins being species specific. Approximately 60 to 80% of the protein in human milk is present as whey proteins[8] while, conversely, approximately 80% of the protein in bovine milk are caseins.[9] This is of considerable importance since the ratio of casein proteins to whey proteins determines the amino acid profile provided to the neonate.

A graphic demonstration of the amino acid profiles resulting from changes in the relative proportion of bovine casein and whey proteins in a protein blend is evidenced in *Figure 1*. It is readily apparent that the content of several amino acids increase (isoleucine, cystine, tryptophan) while others decrease (arginine, leucine, lysine, methionine, phenylalanine, tyrosine) as the proportion of whey proteins increase and casein proteins decrease. This becomes particularly relevant when it is realized that the ratio of casein proteins to whey proteins are substantially different in canine and feline milks. In feline milk, the ratio of casein proteins to whey proteins slowly increases from 40:60 in colostrum to 56:44 in milk by the end of lactation with an overall ratio of 50:50 most apparent.[4] The major whey proteins in feline milk have been determined as lysozyme, β-lactoglobulin A and B, and transferrin while the casein proteins are primarily phosphorylated forms of β-casein.[3,10,11] In contrast, ongoing research is demonstrating canine milk to be more similar to the proportion of casein proteins to whey proteins of bovine milk, in other words, predominantly casein proteins (Lepine, unpublished data).

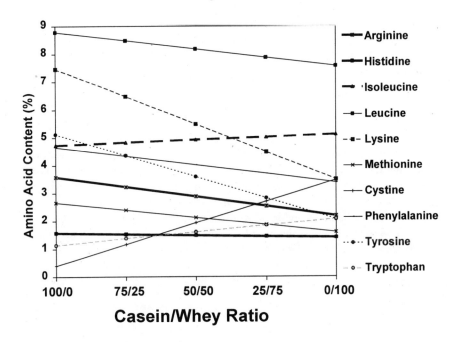

Figure 1. Relative changes in the amino acid profile of a protein containing various ratios of casein proteins to whey proteins.

Although it is not possible to determine the actual ratio of casein proteins to whey proteins in a milk replacer by a review of the ingredient panel, the relative predominance of the protein classes can be assessed. The typical protein sources used in canine and feline milk replacers are dried skimmed milk and Na- or Ca-caseinate. Since both of these ingredients are of bovine origin, any resulting protein blend comprised of these sources must be casein predominant. This is obviously inappropriate for the kitten since the ratio of casein proteins to whey proteins in the milk produced by this species is at unity.[3] An appropriate amino acid profile is more closely provided by the use of casein and whey protein sources, each providing 50% of the milk protein component.

The energy requirement of the nursing puppy or kitten is substantial and reflects the rapid growth rate occurring during this period. The bulk of this energy

Milk Fat

requirement is provided by the relatively high fat content of the mammary secretions. Feline milk fat was determined to increase during the lactation period from
approximately 17% (dry matter basis) in early lactation to 30% in later lactation.[5]
More recent compositional analysis has yielded higher fat concentrations for feline
milk with post-colostral fat concentrations increasing from about 25% to 40% by
the 28th day of lactation.[3,4] Variation in milk fat concentration has also been
observed in the canine. The fat concentration of canine milk has been reported to
be as high as 42%[7] (dry matter basis), but also to range from 12% in early lactation
to 30% in late lactation.[3,4] The variability in values may reflect lactation diet,
analytical technique or collection method. Lonnerdal[12] speculated that the higher
values may be indicative of a more complete expression of the mammary gland
during milk collection and may not be entirely reflective of the ability of the puppy
or kitten to empty the gland during a normal bout of nursing. It is suggested that
feline and canine milk replacers containing approximately 35% and 30% fat on a
dry matter basis, respectively, are adequate.

Of perhaps greater significance is the need for the milk replacer fat source
to provide an appropriate fatty acid profile. Analysis of canine and feline milk fatty
acid profiles has shown oleic, palmitic, linoleic, and stearic acids as the predominant
fatty acids (Lepine, unpublished data). Most milk replacers are based on soybean oil
or vegetable oil as the predominant fat source with the occasional use of butter fat
or corn oil. The use of a vegetable oil will likely provide marginal levels of oleic,
palmitic, and stearic acids while providing excessive quantities of linoleic acid. The
addition of an animal-based fat such as butter oil will increase the level of stearic
and palmitic acids but will not substantially improve the oleic acid concentration.
Inclusion of a high oleic acid source such as canola oil is necessary to elevate oleic
acid concentrations in the milk replacer.

Several studies have suggested the need for dietary preformed sources of
docosahexaenoic acid during the neonatal period when elongation and desaturation
of the precursor α-linolenic acid is not sufficient to meet the needs of rapid development. Altered neurological and visual function has been observed in the growing
monkey[13] and rat[14,15] coincident with a decreased docosahexaenoic acid concentration in the brain and retina following feeding with omega-3 (n-3) deficient diets.
Furthermore, feeding of conventional infant diets resulted in a lower
docosahexaenoic acid concentration in erythrocyte phospholipids as compared with
breast fed infants.[16,17] Breast fed infants also had a higher level of docosahexaenoic
acid in their cerebral cortex than did formula fed infants.[18]

Supplementation of preterm formulas with docosahexaenoic acid in the
form of marine oil resulted in increased docosahexaenoic acid incorporation into
erythrocyte phospholipids and resulted in improved visual function when compared
to infants not receiving n-3 supplementation.[19-21] Infant growth, however, was
poorer for infants receiving docosahexaenoic acid supplementation which was
correlated with a compromised arachidonic acid status. Work in the neonatal pig
demonstrated that supplementation of infant formulas with docosahexaenoic acid

not only increases the content of this fatty acid in membrane phospholipids, but also decreases the arachidonic acid content of the cell membrane.[22] It was suggested that altered eicosanoid production resulting from docosahexaenoic acid supplementation in the absence of arachidonic acid supplementation may contribute to the resulting reduced infant growth rate. These data therefore support the addition of both docosahexaenoic acid and arachidonic acid to infant formulas to ensure adequate membrane concentrations of these fatty acids.

Data to that discussed above is not yet available in the canine and feline. Nevertheless, compositional data has demonstrated the presence of significant quantities of both docosahexaenoic acid and arachidonic acid in the milk of both of these species (Lepine, unpublished data). The inclusion of these fatty acids into the milk implies a biological significance to their presence, one which is likely similar to that demonstrated in other species. It is, therefore, prudent to supplement milk replacers for puppies and kittens with docosahexaenoic acid and arachidonic acid to levels similar to that found in the natural milk. This is not current practice for the majority of milk replacers currently available.

As mentioned previously, the neonatal canine and feline are exposed to changing nutrient profiles not only during the course of the nursing period but also during and following the transition to the intake of solid food. **Figures 2** and **3** graphically depict the typical changes in dietary protein, carbohydrate and fat concentrations as presented to the canine and feline at various life stages. The progressive decrease in the level of dietary fat and increase in dietary carbohydrate load is readily apparent. The most dramatic dietary shift appears during the weaning transition. This transition is arguably the most dramatic shift in nutrient profile that the canine or feline will undergo during the entire life process. Perhaps less obvious, but of equal or greater importance, is the fact that accompanying this absolute change in nutrient load is a qualitative change in the source of the dietary proteins, fats, and carbohydrates. During weaning, the neonatal canine or feline begins consuming meat proteins (or vegetable proteins in lower quality foods) in place of milk proteins (casein and whey proteins), animal fats and oils in place of milk fat, and plant carbohydrates (starches) in place of milk sugar (lactose). This demands substantial adaptations of the digestive and absorptive processes in the neonatal canine and feline if these new sources of nutritional support are to be effectively used. These adaptations are multifactorial and include changes in intestinal morphology and histology, functional characteristics of intestinal brush border membrane enzymes, exocrine pancreatic hydrolase activities, and the kinetics of intestinal nutrient transport systems. These functional adaptations in the neonatal canine and feline will be presented in detail elsewhere in these proceedings.[23,24] The enhanced understanding of intestinal ontogeny resulting from this research will further the ability to provide nutritional matrices for the neonatal canine and feline which more closely matches the physiological stage of development and, thereby, enhance animal well-being.

Typical Changes in Dietary Protein, Carbohydrate, and Fat Concentrations

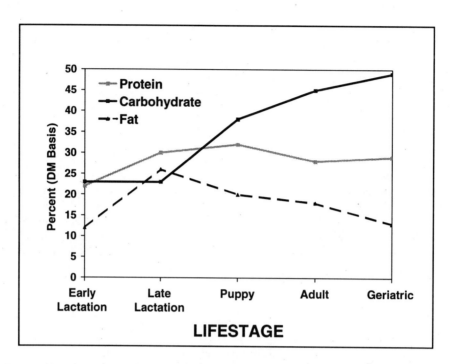

Figure 2. Typical percentage of protein, carbohydrate and fat in the diet of the canine as influenced by lifestage.

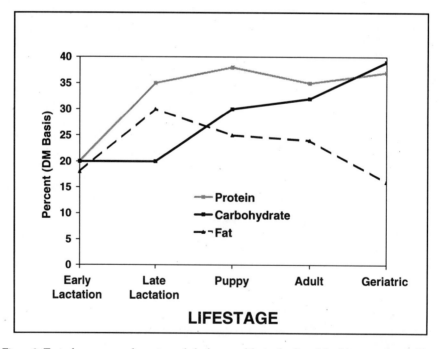

Figure 3. Typical percentage of protein, carbohydrate, and fat in the diet of the feline as influenced by lifestage.

The nutrient source presented to the canine and feline throughout the neonatal period is an extremely complex and constantly changing nutrient matrix. The nutrient profile of milk is not static but is substantially affected by the stage of lactation. Recent research reported herein provides a more complete definition of canine and feline milk composition and, thereby, contributes much needed information regarding the appropriate characteristics as applied to milk replacers for these species. These include not only suitable percentages of protein and fat, but also milk protein profiles, amino acid profiles, and fatty acid profiles more closely approximating those typical in natural milk. Futhermore, a substantial transition in nutrient source and composition occurs during the weaning transition. An increased understanding of the normal ontogenic processes which occur in the canine and feline is imperative if the nutritional needs of this transitional period are to be most optimally provided.

Summary

1. Lepine, AJ. Canine and feline reproduction and neonatal health: A nutritional perspective. In: Carey DP, Norton SA, Bolser SM, eds. *Recent Advances in Canine and Feline Nutritional Research: Proceedings of the 1996 Iams International Nutrition Symposium.* Wilmington: Orange Frazer Press, 1996; 53-60.

2. Nelson, PD. Age correlation and characterization of lymphocyte populations in lymphoid organs in the dog and cat. In: Reinhart GA, Carey DP, eds. *Recent Advances in Canine and Feline Nutrition, Vol. II: 1998 Iams Nutrition Symposium Proceedings.* Wilmington: Orange Frazer Press, 1998; 231-248.

3. Adkins Y, Zicker SC, Lepine A, Lonnerdal B. Changes in milk nutrient and protein composition of cat milk during lactation. *Am J Vet Res* 1997; 58:370-375.

4. Adkins Y, Zicker SC, Lepine AJ, Lonnerdal B. Protein and nutrient composition of cat milk throughout lactation. *FASEB J* 1995; 9:A1019.

5. Keen CL, Lonnerdal B, Clegg MS, Hurley LS, Morris JG, Rogers QR, Rucker RB. Developmental changes in composition of cats' milk: trace elements, minerals, protein, carbohydrate and fat. *J Nutr* 1982; 112:1763-1769.

6. Lonnerdal B, Keen CL, Hurley LS, Fisher GL. Developmental changes in the composition of Beagle dog milk. *Am J Vet Res* 1981; 42:662-666.

7. Oftedal OT. Lactation in the dog: milk composition and intake by puppies. *J Nutr* 1984; 114:803-812.

8. Kuntz C, Lonnerdal B. Re-evaluation of the whey protein/casein ratio of human milk. *Acta Paediatr* 1992; 81:107-112.

9. Ruegg R, Blanc B. Structure and properties of the particulate constituents of human milk. A review. *Food Microstructure* 1982; 3:25-47.

10. Adkins Y, Lonnerdal B, Lepine AJ. Isolation and characterization of cat milk proteins. *FASEB J* 1996; 10:A751.

11. Adkins Y, Lonnerdal B, Lepine AJ. Analysis and characterization of cat milk casein by column chromatography and gel electrophoresis. *FASEB J* 1997; 11:A414.

References

12. Lonnerdal B. Lactation in the dog and cat. In: Carey DP, Norton SA, Bolsen SM, eds. *Recent Advances in Canine and Feline Nutritional Research: Proceedings of the 1996 Iams International Nutrition Symposium.* Wilmington: Orange Frazer Press, 1996; 79-87.

13. Neuringer M, Connor WE, Lin DS, Barstad L, Luck S. Biochemical and functional effects of prenatal and postnatal ω-3 fatty acid deficiency on retina and brain in rhesus monkeys. *Proc Natl Acad Sci USA* 1986; 53:4021-4025.

14. Anderson GJ, Connor WE. Uptake of fatty acids by the developing rat brain. *Lipids* 1988; 23:286-290.

15. Yamamoto N, Saitoh M, Moriuchi A, Nomura M, Okuyama H. Effect of dietary α-linolenate/linoleate balance in brain lipid compositions and learning behavior of rats. *J Lipid Res* 1987; 28:144-151.

16. Carlson SE, Rhodes PG, Furguson MG. Docosahexaenoic acid status of preterm infants at birth and following feeding with human milk or formula. *Am J Clin Nutr* 1986; 44:798-804.

17. Putnam JC, Carlson SE, Devoe PW, Barness LA. The effect of variations in dietary fatty acids on the fatty acid composition of erythrocyte phosphatidylcholine and phosphatidylethanolamine in human infants. *Am J Clin Nutr* 1982; 36:106-114.

18. Farqharson J, Cockburn F, Patrick WA, Jamieson WC, Logan RW. Infant cerebral cortex phospholipid fatty-acid composition and diet. *The Lancet* 1992; 340:810-813.

19. Carlson SE, Cooke RJ, Rhodes PG, Peeples JM, Werkman SH, Tolley EA. Long-term feeding of formulas high in linolenic acid and marine oil to very low birth weight infants: Phospholipid fatty acids. *Pediatric Res* 1991; 30:404-412.

20. Carlson SE, Cooke RJ, Rhodes PG, Peeples JM, Werkman SH. Effect of vegetable and marine oils in preterm infant formula on blood arachidonic and docosahexaenoic acids. *J Pediatr* 1992; 120:S159-S167.

21. Carlson SE, Werkman SH, Rhodes PG, Tolley EA. Visual-acuity development in healthy preterm infants: effect of marine-oil supplementation. *Am J Clin Nutr* 1993; 58:35-42.

22. Huang MC, Craig-Schmidt MC. Arachidonate and docosahexaenoate added to infant formula influence fatty acid composition and subsequent eicasanoid production in neonatal pigs. *J Nutr* 1996; 126:2199-2208.

23. Buddington RK, Paulsen D. Development of the canine and feline gastrointestinal tract. In: Reinhart GA, Carey DP, eds. *Recent Advances in Canine and Feline Nutrition, Vol. II: 1998 Iams Nutrition Symposium Proceedings.* Wilmington: Orange Frazer Press, 1998; 195-216.

24. Elnif J, Buddington RK. Adaptation and development of the exocrine pancreas in cats and dogs. In: Reinhart GA, Carey DP, eds. *Recent Advances in Canine and Feline Nutrition, Vol. II: 1998 Iams Nutrition Symposium Proceedings.* Wilmington: Orange Frazer Press, 1998; 217-230.

Physical Stress Nutrition

Hydration Strategies for Exercising Dogs

Arleigh J. Reynolds, DVM, PhD, DACVN
Assistant Professor of Clinical Nutrition, College of Veterinary Medicine
Cornell University, Ithaca, New York, USA

Kim Sneddon, BS[a]; Gregory A. Reinhart, PhD[b];
Kenneth W. Hinchcliff, BVSc, MS, PhD, DACVIM[c]; Richard A. Swenson[d]
[a]College of Veterinary Medicine, Cornell University, Ithaca, New York, USA;
[b]Research and Development, The Iams Company, Lewisburg, Ohio, USA;
[c]Department of Veterinary Clinical Sciences, College of Veterinary Medicine,
The Ohio State University, Columbus, Ohio, USA;
[d]Lightning Bolt Express Kennels, Two Rivers, Alaska, USA

Introduction

The late Dr. Rolland Lombard is often credited with being the first competitive musher to realize the importance of watering his dogs during the racing season. During his day, most mushers believed that their dogs got all the water they needed by just eating snow. The dependence of performance upon good hydration is just one of the legacies left behind by the innovative and dominant force that was Rolland Lombard. Over the past 25 years, racing and research have demonstrated the benefits of providing working dogs with sufficient amounts of protein, fat, vitamins, and minerals. Still, a working dog may tolerate a dietary deficiency in one of these nutrients for several days or even weeks before any adverse effects on its performance or health are observed. In contrast, dehydration may lead to diminished performance and, in severe cases, even to death within hours of onset.

To understand why dehydration leads to such rapid and severe performance problems, one must first understand the many vital roles this important nutrient plays in the maintenance of nearly all body functions. A typical healthy dog has a total body water content of about 70% of its body weight. This water is divided into four compartments as shown in **Table 1**. Most (65%) of the total body water (TBW) resides within the individual cells of the dog's body.[1] This water is the solvent in which all reactions of the cell take place. It thus facilitates the generation of energy, the synthesis of new cell materials, the storage of products, and the detoxification of wastes. Intracellular water is also the medium of transport for all materials within the cells.

The extracellular water is divided up between three spaces.[1] The interstitial space (20% TBW) is the second largest compartment; it represents the water which lies immediately outside of the cells and bathes them. The main role of the interstitial water is as a transport medium for nutrients and other materials into, and wastes and other products out of, the cells. The plasma space (10% TBW) is the water

Table 1. Division of total body water (TBW) content of a typical healthy dog.

Compartment	% Body Weight	% Total Body Water
Total Body Water	70	100
Intracellular	45	65
Extracellular	25	35
Interstitial	14	20
Plasma	7	10
Transcellular	4	5

found in the liquid or non-cellular part of blood. This water transports materials between all locations of the body. The transcellular compartment (5% TBW) is a conglomerate of all other extracellular spaces and is made up of the water found in the aqueous humor, the synovial fluid, the cerebral-spinal fluid (CSF), and the secretions of the gastrointestinal tract. This water acts as a medium for the passage of light and as a source of lubrication and shock absorption in the joints and CSF. In the GI tract it is a solvent for digestion and a transport medium to facilitate absorption of digested nutrients.

Under normal circumstances, water is free to shift between these compartments. The direction of that shift will depend on the conditions to which the body is exposed. During exercise for example, the metabolic changes occurring within the muscle cell increases the concentration of solutes or dissolvable particles within these cells. This increase in solute concentration causes water to move into the cell from the interstitial fluid.[2] This loss of interstitial fluid volume is then replaced by the movement of water from the plasma compartment into the interstitial space.[2] The result of exercise is thus an expansion of the intracellular compartment and a contraction of the plasma compartment. This fluid shift is in part responsible for the increased size of a weight lifter's muscles after a work out.[2]

The small loss of plasma volume that normally occurs during short bouts of exercise does not usually adversely affect performance. If exercise is prolonged, or if a dog is losing significant amounts of water through other means, the loss of water from the plasma may lead to a potentially dangerous contraction of plasma volume. As plasma volume diminishes, the heart has to work harder to circulate the blood because there is less fluid travelling through the vessels, and that fluid is more viscous.[3] The result of these changes is a decreased delivery of oxygen and nutrients to, and a slower rate of waste removal from, muscle cells. In this situation working muscle cells have less fuel available and accumulate wastes more rapidly, a combination which restricts the sustainable intensity and duration of exercise. In severe cases plasma volume contraction can lead to major organ failure and even death.[3]

Dehydration is almost always easier to prevent than it is to treat. Still, early recognition of the problem gives the dog the greatest chance for a rapid and complete recovery. As dehydration progresses from the mild to the moderate and severe states, the animal's ability to correct the problem on its own diminishes. Dogs suffering from advanced dehydration usually refuse to eat or drink. Such animals need veterinary attention immediately since loss of only 15% of TBW may result in death.[4] Correction of moderate and severe dehydration usually requires intravenous administration of fluids. Mildly dehydrated animals may be able to restore their water deficit by drinking but will often recover more rapidly if at least some of the fluid is replaced parenterally.

To prevent dehydration, one must try to balance the dog's daily water loss with its daily water intake and production. To achieve this goal one must first understand how water is added to and lost from a dog's body, and how each of these components of water balance change with changes in the dog's workload, environment, and health status. A dog may add to its total body water through its diet, by drinking water, and by burning fuels for energy in its muscles. When a dog is fed a meat diet or a dry dog food soaked in water, 70–80% of what that animal eats is actually water. Water that is taken in as part of food is called "preformed water." Many sled dogs get half or more of their daily water intake from preformed water. Most of the rest of their daily water intake comes from drinking water and eating snow. A small amount of water is also generated when fats, carbohydrates, and proteins are converted to energy in the muscle. For each 100 kcal of energy burned about 13 ml of water is generated and for each gram of muscle glycogen used, 3–4 ml of water are produced.[5] Water produced in the body by these processes is referred to as "metabolic water." Metabolic water may contribute as much as 10% of the total water gained by a dog each day.

Usually, the amount of water gained each day by a dog is exactly balanced by the amount lost. Each day a dog loses water through its urine, feces, saliva, breath, and sweat. Unlike humans and horses, dogs do not lose much water due to sweating. In fact, the only place a dog sweats is through its foot pads. The dog's inability to sweat from the rest of its skin probably stems from its large surface area to volume ratio. Water loss from such a large surface area would put the animal at constant risk of dehydration if it perspired from its entire skin surface. In larger animals like humans and horses, a relatively small surface area and large volume inhibits heat dissipation. Dehydration due to sweating is less of a risk than heat accumulation in these larger animals.

Most of the water a dog loses each day leaves its body through urine, feces, respiratory vapor, and saliva. The contributions of each of these factors depend greatly upon the dog's health, environment, workload, and diet. For example, consider the same 20 kg (44 lb) sled dog as a sedentary house dog, a sprint racing dog, and a distance racing dog. Each day the house dog, living in a climate controlled environment, loses about 1000 ml of water through urine, about 100 ml of water through its feces, and about 300 ml of water through evaporation of respiratory water and saliva. If that dog is moved outside and he becomes an open class sprint racing dog, he will lose about 1500 ml of water through his urine and 150 ml of water through his feces. Assuming an ambient temperature of at least 0° F, this dog will also lose about 300 ml of water from evaporation during a one hour run and about 800 ml of water from evaporation during the remaining 23 hours of the day. If this dog now becomes a distance racing dog his water loss to urine and feces will increase to about 2250 ml/day and 250 ml/day, respectively. Assuming he works 12 hours at about a 40% of VO_2 maximum workload and rests 12 hours in an ambient temperature of -20° C or below, he will lose between 2000 and 2500 ml of water during exercise and about 400 ml of water during rest to evaporation from his mouth and respiratory tract. A summary of the water balance for these three dogs is shown in *Figure 1*.

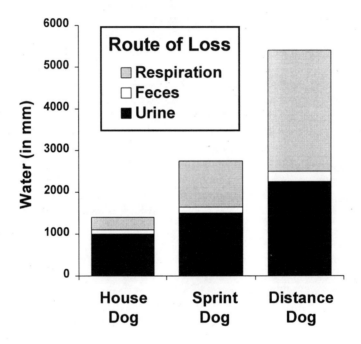

Figure 1. Amount and sources of daily water loss associated with exercise and environment.

The combination of exercise and living in a cold environment dramatically increases the dog's daily water requirement. The increase in this requirement is about 2-fold for the sprint dog and about 4-fold for the distance dog as compared to the house dog. The greater losses of urine and fecal water seen in working dogs are mostly due to their increased food intake. A greater food intake leads to an increased production of feces which are usually 80–90% water. More food also means the generation of more metabolic wastes which must be filtered by and excreted from the kidneys. The excretion of these additional wastes results in an increased urine volume and consequently a greater urinary water loss.

The most remarkable increase in water loss observed in working dogs is due to the increase in evaporation from the mouth and respiratory tract. Depending on the dog's exercise intensity, and the environmental temperature and humidity, evaporative water losses may increase 10- to 20-fold during exercise.[6] At cold temperatures, the air a dog breathes in has very little moisture in it. When this cold air reaches the lungs it is saturated with water so that about 6% of every exhaled breath is water. In warm climates the inhaled air is more nearly saturated with water and so the dog loses less water from its lungs with each breath. However, since dogs pant to cool themselves off, water loss through the evaporation of saliva often leads to evaporative losses in warm conditions equal to or in excess of those seen in cold environments.[7]

The numbers given above are estimates for specific cases, but they give an idea of the influence that exercise and environment have on a dog's daily water requirement. Health problems may also greatly influence daily water loss. Urinary water losses increase dramatically in renal disease, systemic infections, diabetes, and other hormonal abnormalities. Most of these dogs are sick enough that they would not be able to perform as sled dogs and would require veterinary attention. Increased water loss from the gastrointestinal tract is more common and often less serious. Nearly all kennels experience stress diarrhea and the "flu" during the course of a season. Often, dogs will continue to perform well with these conditions as long as their hydration can be maintained. However, the rate of dehydration resulting from severe diarrhea, as in the case of parvovirus infection, can be a life threatening situation. The severity of the situation can usually be assessed by the frequency and volume of fluid eliminated. In any case the fluid lost through the feces must be replaced or the dog's health will deteriorate rapidly.

The factors which contribute to water loss in the dog are complex and constantly changing. If one had to exactly calculate a dog's daily water requirement in order to hydrate it properly, it would be nearly an impossible task. Fortunately nature has designed a complex system to regulate water intake and output, thus allowing the dog to maintain hydration across a wide range of environmental conditions. As a dog's plasma begins to lose water, the increase in concentration of salts is detected centrally, triggering thirst.[8] Since it takes some time for water to be absorbed into the plasma, the quenching of thirst does not immediately rely on the return of salt concentrations to normal. Instead, stretching in the stomach and a drop in throat temperature are the signals that lead to thirst satiation.[8] This system is so well tuned that a healthy dog will adapt to changes in water loss just as quickly as these changes occur. Theoretically, the dog will drink as much as it needs as long as water is available when it is thirsty.

Therein lies the problem of keeping sled dogs well hydrated. They are not always thirsty when water is available, and water is not always available when they are thirsty. For this reason strategies were explored that would promote hydration in these specialized athletes. For years mushers have tried to encourage relatively large amounts of water consumption during the relatively short periods of time that water could be made available by flavoring the water with palatable additives. This technique, known as "baiting the water", has proven to be successful under all but the most severe environmental and racing conditions.

Recently there has been much attention focused on the use of glycerol containing solutions to hyperhydrate human endurance athletes performing in hot, humid environs.[9,10,11] Glycerol acts as a hydrating agent because it is osmotically active, rapidly absorbed, and freely crosses all cell membranes.[12] Compared to subjects ingesting an equal volume of water alone, cyclists consuming dilute glycerol solutions prior to exercise in hot and humid conditions have exhibited an increased sweat rate, decreased rectal temperature, and decreased urine output.[11] Time to exhaustion was also significantly greater in the glycerol treated cyclists.[11]

The ingestion of glycerol containing solutions has been shown to result in a state of hyperhydration.[13,14] "Water loading", as this practice is often referred to as, has been achieved in both human and rat models. The effect of a single loading dose may increase total body water up to 5% for as long as 48 hours.[14] The mechanism by which this hyperhydrated state is achieved has yet to be determined. One recent study has found that glycerol containing solutions increase anti-diuretic hormone secretion and increase renal medullary concentration gradient.[15] The hyperhydrated state may thus be mediated through a decrease in urinary water loss.[15]

Critics of glycerol induced hyperhydration note the risk of gastrointestinal upset and the potentially serious risk of excessive cellular swelling that may result from the practice.[16] Indeed, fatal rhabdomyolysis and acute renal failure have been induced in rats given massive oral doses of glycerol.[16] The solutions used in the studies noted above were moderate doses and ranged from 1 to 5%; they were not associated with any significant side effects.[9,10,11]

Recently three studies were undertaken to evaluate the effect of glycerol supplementation on the hydration status of working sled dogs. In the first study, the effects of a single loading dose of a glycerol solution(1 liter of 1% glycerol) versus an equal volume of water on total body water (TBW) in 8 sedentary dogs was examined. Using a deuterium oxide dilution technique, it was found that glycerol ingestion significantly increased TBW (**Figure 2**) without increasing creatine kinase concentration (**Figure 3**) or altering any measured parameter on a serum biochemistry panel or a complete blood cell count analysis.

Once it was established that glycerol solutions could induce a hyperhydrated state, the safety and efficacy of such a treatment for dogs exercising in cold and dry or warm and humid environs was investigated. In the cold weather study two age, ability, and sex matched groups of 12 dogs each were given either 1 L of a 1% glycerol solution or 1 L of water two hours prior to a 30 mile run. This procedure was repeated for three days. Immediately after and six hours after each run all dogs were given access to 1 L of baited water. Blood samples for TBW, hematocrit, and serum chemistry analysis were drawn immediately before the first administration of fluid on day 1 and after the last bout of exercise on day 3. The

Total Body Water (TBW)

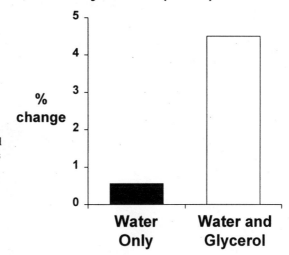

Figure 2. Percentage change in total body water (TBW) in sedentary dogs three hours after ingestion of 1 L of water or 1 g/kg body weight glycerol in 1 L water.

Serum Creatine Kinase (CK)

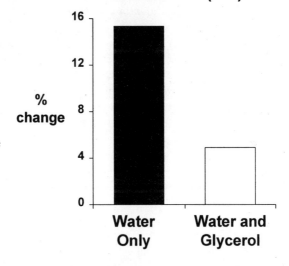

Figure 3. Percentage change (pre to post fluid ingestion) in serum creatine kinase (CK) values measured in sedentary dogs three hours after ingesting 1 L of water or 1 L of water with 1 g glycerol/kg body weight.

ambient temperature during the experiment averaged -35° C. The dogs receiving the glycerol solution maintained their hydration at pre-exercise levels while those receiving just water became approximately 3% dehydrated (*Figure 4*). There was no difference in creatine kinase concentrations between the two treatment groups at any time in the study.

In the warm weather study, 2 groups of 8 dogs each were treated and measured as described above for the cold weather study, except that they were exercised on a hot walking wheel in a warm (25° C), humid (85% relative humidity) environment until their rectal temperature reached 41° C. Data from the warm

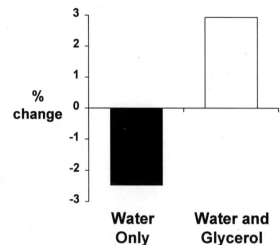

Total Body Water (TBW)

Figure 4. Percentage change in total body water (TBW) after a three day exercise period in which dogs were given water only or water with 1 g/kg body weight glycerol.

weather study is still being collected and analyzed at this writing. The results of this study will be available at the time of the 1998 Iams Nutrition Symposium.

The results of the first two studies have indicated that ingestion of a dilute glycerol solution is a safe and effective way to induce a mild state of hyperhydration in the dog. The degree of hyperhydration achieved did not have any observable adverse effect on gastrointestinal, renal or muscle function and may instead help these animals maintain hydration while exercising under extreme environmental conditions. These findings may also have clinical applications in the formulation of oral rehydrating solutions. Due to the long lasting effect of glycerol on hydration, glycerol solutions may promote a greater and longer lasting state of rehydration than is presently achievable from standard glucose electrolyte solutions. Further research will undoubtedly clarify the role of glycerol supplementation in the clinically dehydrated patient.

References

1. Swenson MJ. Physiological properties and chemical constituents of blood. In: Swenson MJ, ed. *Duke's Physiology of Domestic Animals*, Tenth Edition, Vol. One. Ithaca: Cornell University Press, 1984; 15-40.

2. Pivornik JM. *Water and Electrolytes During Exercise*. Boca Raton: CRC Press, 1989.

3. Harrison MH, Edwards RJ, Leitch DR. Effect of exercise and thermal stress on plasma volume. *J Appl Physiol* 1975; 39:925-931.

4. Lewis LD, Morriss ML, Hand MS. *Clinical Nutrition III*. Topeka: Mark Morriss Associates, 1989; 5-17.

5. Houpt TR. Water balance and excretion. In: Swenson MJ, ed. *Duke's Physiology of Domestic Animals*, Tenth Edition, Vol. One. Ithaca: Cornell University Press, 1984; 15-40.

6. Ferrus L, Commenges D, Gire G, Varene P. Respiratory water loss as function of ventilatory or environmental factors. *Resp Physiol* 1984; 56:11-20.

7. Young DR, Mosher R, Erve P, et al. Temperature and heat exchange during treadmill running in dogs. *J Appl Physiol* 1959; 14:839-843.

8. Houpt TR. Water, electrolytes, and acid base balance. In: *Duke's Physiology of Domestic Animals*, Tenth Edition, Vol. One. Ithaca: Cornell University Press, 1984; 15-40.

9. Montner P, Stark D, Riedesel, Murata G, Robergs R, Timms M, Chick T. Pre-exercise glycerol hydration combined with standard intra-exercise oral replacement solution improves endurance performance. *J Am Coll Sports Med* 1992; Abstract 14:S3.

10. Lyons TP, Riedesel ML, Meuli LE, Chick TW. Effects of glycerol induced hyperhydration prior to exercise in the heat on sweating and core temperature. *Med Sci Sports Med* 1990; 22:477-483.

11. Sawka MN, Freund GJ, Roberts DE, O'Brien C, Dennis RC, Baleri CR. Total body water, extracellular fluid, and plasma responses to hyperhydration with aqueous glycerol. *Med Sci Sports Med* 1995; 25:S35.

12. Lin ECC. Glycerol utilization and its regulation in mammals. *Annu Rev Biochem* 1977; 46:765-795.

13. Maw GJ, Mackenzie IL, Comer DAM, Taylor NAS. Whole body hyperhydration in endurance trained males determined using radionuclide dilution. *Med Sci Sports Exerc* 1996; 24:934-940.

14. Koenigsberg PS, Martin KK, Hlava HR, Riedesel ML. Sustained hyperhydration with glycerol ingestion. *Life Sciences* 1995; 57:6645-653.

15. Freund BJ, Montain SJ, McKay JM, Laird JE, Young AJ. Renal responses to hyperhydration using aqueous glycerol vs. water alone provides insight to the mechanism of glycerol's effectiveness. *J Am Coll Sports Med* 1993; 25:S35.

16. Zurovsky Y. Models of glycerol induced acute renal failure in rats. *J Basic Clin Physiol Pharmacol* 1993; 4:213-228.

Exercise and Oxidant Stress

Kenneth W. Hinchcliff, BVSc, MS, PhD, DACVIM
Associate Professor, Department of Veterinary Clinical Sciences
College of Veterinary Medicine, The Ohio State University, Columbus, Ohio, USA

Gregory A. Reinhart, PhD[a]; Arleigh J. Reynolds, DVM, PhD, DACVN[b];
Richard A. Swenson[c]
[a]Research and Development, The Iams Company, Lewisburg, Ohio, USA
[b]Department of Clinical Sciences, College of Veterinary Medicine,
Cornell University, Ithaca, New York, USA
[c]Lightning Bolt Express Kennels, Two Rivers, Alaska, USA

Introduction

Aerobic metabolism is inevitably and inextricably associated with the production of free radicals of oxygen. While production of free radicals may be beneficial to the body, such as in the oxidative burst of a neutrophil in response to phagocytosis of a bacterium, recent studies have implicated reactive oxygen species (ROS) in the pathogenesis of many diseases, including ischemia/reperfusion injury, spinal cord and brain trauma, and some chronic degenerative diseases. The role of ROS in exercise-associated conditions, such as delayed muscle soreness and rhabdomyolysis, has attracted attention in part because of the pervasive public health recommendations that sedentary humans exercise, and in part because of the recognition that the increase in oxygen consumption that accompanies exercise likely results in an increase in ROS production.

Overview of Oxidant Stress

A radical is a molecule or molecular fragment containing an unpaired electron. In the context of this discussion, the radicals of oxygen, or their reactive metabolites, are: $O_2^{\bullet -}$, the superoxide radical; H_2O_2, hydrogen peroxide; $OH^{\bullet}$, hydroxy radical; $ROOH^{\bullet}$, peroxyl radical. These substances are often referred to as reactive oxygen species (ROS), and have a strong tendency to attract electrons from others sites in order to become more chemically stable. Depending on the source of the attracted electron, ROS may cause damage to cell structures such as the cell membranes and nuclear material. Note that not all ROS are oxygen free radicals, but include non-radicals (H_2O_2) that are capable of inciting or propagating oxidant damage.[1]

Reactive oxygen species are produced as an inevitable consequence of aerobic metabolism. Approximately 3–5% of the oxygen consumed is univalently reduced to the ROS at various locations within the cell; the remainder of the oxygen is converted to water and carbon dioxide in the electron transport chain. Because all aerobic organisms must deal with the continual production of ROS, numerous antioxidant systems have evolved to render the ROS less harmful to the cell or organism. Under normal, resting conditions the antioxidant resources are adequate to render the continually produced ROS harmless. However, under situations in which the production of ROS is dramatically increased, such as is believed to be the case during exercise, or when antioxidant mechanisms are reduced, such as in vitamin E or selenium deficiency, cell damage or death may occur.

The site of production of ROS during exercise is unclear, although several theories have been propounded. Because the majority of oxygen consumed by mammals cells is reduced in the mitochondria by the electron transport chain, it has been assumed that the mitochondria are therefore a site of increased production of ROS during exercise. However, although there is no direct evidence of increased ROS production by mitochondria during exercise, there is indirect evidence of increased ROS production in mitochondria during and after exercise of which the most persuasive is that the extent of oxidative damage is proportional to the workload.

Another potential site of ROS production during exercise is tissues containing xanthine dehydrogenase/oxidase. It is well documented that xanthine oxidase catalyzed reactions in the ischemic and reperfused heart are one of the major sources of ROS. In order for this reaction to proceed, there must be adequate quantities of xanthine and hypoxanthine, oxygen, and the xanthine oxidase. These conditions may be met in very high intensity exercise, as hypoxanthine accumulates under these conditions, and xanthine oxidase is presumed to be active, based on the increase in uric acid production observed during intense exercise. Interestingly, inhibition of xanthine oxidase by allopurinol leads to a decrease in the formation of reactive oxygen species during and after intense exercise by horses.[2] However, the evidence to support this mechanism of ROS production during exercise is not conclusive at this time.

Neutrophils produce ROS in response to various stimuli including cytokines. It has been suggested that inflammation of muscle that occurs after intense exercise may be mediated by neutrophils and ROS. However, the time required for neutrophil infiltration into tissues and subsequent degranulation and production of ROS means that this mechanism is likely not an important source of ROS during short-term, intense exercise. It may, however, be important in the recovery phase and during endurance exercise.[3]

Antioxidants   Antioxidants are substances that prevent or slow the oxidation of oxidizable substrates such as proteins, lipids, carbohydrates, and DNA when present in small amounts.[1] Antioxidants may prevent oxidant damage by 1) preventing ROS production, 2) scavenging of reactive intermediates produced by ROS, 3) preventing the conversion of less reactive ROS to more reactive ROS (O_2^- to $OH^•$), 4) facilitating repair of damage caused by ROS, and 5) providing an environment favorable for activity of other antioxidants.[1] The mammalian body contains a number of antioxidant systems, most of which are interrelated, and can be thought of as being enzymatic and non-enzymatic (*Table 1*).

Table 1. Potential antioxidants.

Non-enzymatic	Comment
Vitamin E	Major lipid soluble antioxidant
Vitamin C	Water soluble antioxidant
Glutathione	Major intracellular antioxidant, regenerates vitamins E and C
Ubiquinone (Q10)	Potential antioxidant *in vivo*
Uric acid	End product of purine metabolism, *in vivo* antioxidant role not defined
α-lipoic acid	Active form may be dihydrolipoic acid
β-carotene	Powerful quencher of singlet oxygen; provitamin A
Flavinoids	Phenolic antioxidants derived from plants
Ceruloplasmin	Catalyzes Fe(II) to Fe(III) without release of oxygen radical intermediates
Enzymatic	**Comment**
Superoxide dismutase	Catalyzes reaction: $O_2 + 2e^- + 2H^+ \rightarrow H_2O_2 + O_2$
Catalase	Catalyzes reaction: $2H_2O_2 \rightarrow H_2O + O_2$
Glutathione peroxidase	Catalyzes reaction: $2GSH + H_2O_2 \rightarrow 2H_2O + GSSG$
Glutathione reductase	Catalyzes reaction: $2NADPH + GSSG \rightarrow 2NADP + 2GSH$

Non-enzymatic Antioxidants. **Vitamin E** is the most important fat soluble antioxidant. It functions as a chain breaking antioxidant in that it donates hydrogen molecules that block lipid peroxides from further reaction.[4] During the course of this reaction, vitamin E is oxidized to a weakly reactive radical that is then reduced by ascorbate to the active form. Vitamin E is a fat-soluble molecule that is concentrated in the lipid membranes of the cell. In these sites vitamin E both quenches singlet oxygen species and reacts with lipid peroxy and alkoxy radicals, the latter action breaking the chain reaction of peroxidation by scavenging chain-propagating radicals.[5]

Vitamin E is an essential vitamin for mammals with deficiency causing a wide range of diseases including retinal degeneration, myopathy, cardiomyopathy, neurologic disease, and red cell fragility, among others. Vitamin E deficiency is associated with an increase in the concentration of markers of lipid peroxidation in the dog and other species.[6] The requirement for vitamin E in the diet is increased by diets rich in unsaturated fats. However, short term absence of vitamin E from the diet may not be deleterious because of the large body stores of the vitamin.

Vitamin C (ascorbate) is an effective antioxidant both by directly quenching radicals and, perhaps more importantly, by regenerating reduced vitamin E, although this mechanism is unproved.[7] Vitamin C is a water soluble antioxidant that is present in greatest concentration in the cytosol and extracellular fluid where it scavenges free radicals formed in the aqueous phase, thereby preventing damage to erythrocyte membranes. At relatively high concentrations, such as those achieved *in vivo* after the administration of large doses, vitamin C acts as a pro-oxidant.[3] Because most species synthesize vitamin C, deficiencies of this vitamin are difficult to produce experimentally.

β-carotene is a lipid-soluble antioxidant that quenches superoxide and other free radicals. β-carotene has a potent inhibitory effect on lipid peroxidation initiated by oxygen generated free radicals.[3]

Antioxidant Enzymes. **Superoxide dimutase (SOD)** activity constitutes the primary intracellular defense against $O_2^{•-}$ by dismutase to hydrogen peroxide.[3] Superoxide dismutases are found in cellular cytosol and in mitochondria, and may contain either copper and zinc or manganese at their active site. Highest activity of SOD is found in liver, kidney, brain, adrenal gland, heart and skeletal muscle (in decreasing order of activity).

Catalase (CAT) catalyses the conversion of hydrogen peroxide to water and oxygen. Within the cell the highest activity of CAT is found in peroxisomes, with lesser activity in mitochondria. As with SOD, skeletal muscle has a relatively low activity of CAT, compared with that in liver.

Glutathione peroxidase (GPX) catalyzes the reaction of H_2O_2 or other hydroperoxides including long chain fatty acid hydroperoxides, and glutathione (GSH) to water and oxidized glutathione (glutathione disulfide, GSSG). Glutathione peroxidase (GPX) is a selenium containing enzyme. The enzyme is located in the cytosol and mitochondrial matrix, with most of the enzyme being located in the cytosol. Relative to red blood cells, the activity of GPX is low in skeletal muscle. Oxidative fibers have a higher activity of GPX than do glycolytic fibers. Selenium deficiency dramatically reduces the activity of GPX in all tissues.

Glutathione reductase is required for the regeneration of GSH from GSSG, and thus is essential for the continued function of the glutathione antioxidant system.

Exercise has been associated with an increase in the concentration or production of various putative markers of oxidative stress or lipid peroxidation, such as an increase in urinary excretion of malondialdehyde or thiobarbituric acid reactive substances, in a number of species.[1] Electron paramagnetic resonance studies have demonstrated increases of 70% in the concentration of free radicals in active intact muscle, compared with resting muscle.[8] The production of ROS during exercise appears to be proportional to the intensity of the exercise, presumably because intense exercise has a greater oxygen requirement.[9,10,11] While others have not demonstrated evidence of free radical injury during or after exercise or training,[12] the consensus appears to be that strenuous exercise in many species results in evidence of lipid peroxidation.

Exercise. An acute bout of exercise increases SOD and CAT activities in many tissues including heart and skeletal muscle, although the increases in CAT were dependent upon the muscle type.[13] There has not been a consistent effect of exercise on GPX activity reported. However, concentrations of GSSG increase in skeletal muscle, liver, and plasma after a bout of intense exercise[14] and this change is associated with a reduction in GSH concentration. Reductions in tissue and serum vitamin E concentration occur as a consequence of acute exercise in a number of species, and are probably caused by consumption of vitamin E in ROS neutralizing reactions. However, others have reported an increase in vitamin E concentration during acute exercise. The effect of exercise on vitamin E concentration probably depends on the effect of exercise on the amount of vitamin E in the plasma (the vitamin E content of the vascular space) and exercise-induced changes in plasma volume.

Training. Habitual physical activity (training) increases endogenous antioxidant activity, probably because of the chronic and intermittent exposure of the active tissues to ROS.[1] The increases in antioxidant activity are attributable to increases in activity of the major antioxidant enzymes, SOD, CAT and GPX, with the greatest increases occurring in skeletal muscle.[13] Within skeletal muscle, the greatest increases in SOD activity are in type 1 fibers, with the amount of the increase being determined by the duration of the exercise, rather than its intensity, during training. A similar pattern was found in the GPX response to training with the exception that the largest increases in activity were in type 2a fibers.[15]

Vitamin E deficiency has been consistently shown to decrease exercise performance in a number of species.[7] In animals that are deficient, vitamin E supplementation clearly has a beneficial effect on exercise capacity and markers of lipid peroxidation. However, even in non-deficient animals and humans, vitamin E supplementation attenuates the exercise-induced increase in markers of lipid peroxidation in both blood and tissues.

The situation is not as clear regarding either the requirement for vitamin C or the effect of vitamin C supplementation on exercise capacity and markers of exercise-induced lipid peroxidation. Vitamin C supplementation does not improve run time of rats, but it does decrease the production of thiobarbituric reactive substances in young men running for 30 minutes at 80% VO_2max.[4] Consumption of an antioxidant cocktail (592 IU vitamin E, 1000 mg vitamin C, and 30 mg β-carotene) by healthy males attenuated the exercise-induced increases in pentane and malondialdehyde production.[10]

Oxidant Stress in Dogs

Sedentary Dogs. Experimental vitamin E deficiency (combined with selenium deficiency) and vitamin E-responsive syndromes have been reported in dogs, although the latter are in general poorly characterized.[16-20] Combined vitamin E and selenium deficiency in dogs is characterized by increases in plasma creatine kinase activity and anorexia, muscular weakness, depression and subcutaneous edema. In 2 beagles fed a vitamin E deficient diet for 109 weeks, depletion of nerve (tibial), plasma and fat vitamin E occurred before histologic and functional changes were observed in peripheral nerves.[19]

Vitamin E deficiency appears to increase red cell hemolysis in response to an osmotic or detergent challenge.[20] Vitamin E deficient diets or diets very high in omega-3 fatty acids,[21] decrease the concentration of vitamin E in many canine tissues, including nervous tissue,[19] and increase the concentration of markers of lipid peroxidation in various tissues of dogs is unknown.[6] The effect of vitamin E deficiency on indicators of oxidative stress or damage of exercising dogs is unknown.

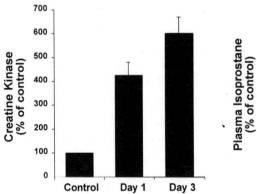

Figure 1. Increases in serum creatine kinase activity in 16 Alaskan sled dogs running 36 miles on each of three consecutive days.

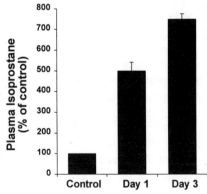

Figure 2. Increases in plasma isoprostane concentration in 16 Alaskan sled dogs running 36 miles on each of three consecutive days.

Exercise. Recently it was demonstrated that three days of strenuous exercise by Alaskan sled dogs increases plasma isoprostane concentration and serum creatine kinase activity. Isoprostane is a sensitive and specific marker of lipid peroxidation,[22] and creatine kinase is a specific marker of skeletal muscle damage. The increases in isoprostane and creatine kinase activity (**Figures 1** and **2**) were highly correlated ($R^2=0.75$), suggesting a causal relationship between lipid peroxidation and skeletal muscle damage in these dogs. Concurrent with the increase in isoprostane concentration was a decrease in serum vitamin E concentration

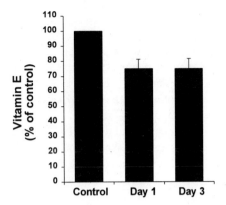

Figure 3. Decreases in serum vitamin E concentration in 16 Alaskan sled dogs running 36 miles on each of three consecutive days.

(**Figure 3**). This suggests that three days of exercise reduced the antioxidant capacity of the dogs, and that this reduction in antioxidant capacity was temporally associated with an increase in lipid peroxidation and skeletal muscle cell damage. However, this hypothesis needs to be tested using studies of appropriate design.

Review Papers

Sen CK. Oxidants and antioxidants in exercise. *J Appl Physiol* 1995; 79: 675-686.

Ji LL, Leichtweis S. Exercise and oxidative stress: sources of free radicals and their impact on antioxidant systems. *Age* 1997; 20:91-106.

Goldfarb A, Sen CK. Antioxidant supplementation and the control of oxygen toxicity during exercise. In: Sen CK, Packer L, Hanninen O, eds. *Exercise and Oxygen Toxicity.* Amsterdam: Elsevier Science, 1994; 163-189.

Jenkins RR. Exercise, oxidative stress and antioxidants: a review. *Inter J Sport Nutr* 1993; 3:356-375.

Sen CK. Hanninen O. Physiological antioxidants. In: Sen CK, Packer L, Hanninen O, eds. *Exercise and Oxygen Toxicity.* Amsterdam: Elsevier Science, 1994; 89-126.

References

1. Sen CK. Oxidants and antioxidants in exercise. *J Appl Physiol* 1995; 79:675-686.

2. Mills PC, Smith NC, Harris RC, Harris P. Effect of allopurinol on the formation of reactive oxygen species during intense exercise in the horse. *Res Vet Sci* 1997; 62:11-16.

3. Ji LL, Leichtweis S. Exercise and oxidative stress: sources of free radicals and their impact on antioxidant systems. *Age* 1997; 20:91-106.

4. Goldfarb A, Sen CK. Antioxidant supplementation and the control of oxygen toxicity during exercise. In: Sen CK, Packer L, Hanninen O, eds. *Exercise and Oxygen Toxicity.* Amsterdam: Elsevier Science, 1994; 163-189.

5. Halliwell B, Gutteridge JMC. In: Halliwell B, Gutteridge JMC, eds. *Free Radicals in Biology and Medicine*, 2nd ed. Oxford: Clarendon Press, 1989; 234-276.

6. Dratz EA, Farnsworth CC, Loew EC, Stephens RJ, Thomas DW, Van Kuijk FJ. Products of *in vivo* peroxidation are present in tissues of vitamin E-deficient rats and dogs. *Ann N Y Acad Sci* 1989; 570:46-60.

7. Jenkins RR. Exercise, oxidative stress and antioxidants: a review. *Inter J Sport Nutr* 1993; 3:356-375.

8. Jackson MJ, Edwards RHT, Symons MCR. Electron spin resonance studies of intact mammalian skeletal muscle. *Biochem Biophys Acta* 1985; 847:185-190.

9. Alessio HM, Goldfarb AH. MDA content increases in fast- and slow twitch skeletal muscle with the intensity of exercise in rats. *Am J Physiol* 1988; 255:C874-877.

10. Kanter MM, Nolte LA, Holloszy JO. Effect of an antioxidant mixture on lipid peroxidation at rest and postexercise. *J Appl Physiol* 1993; 74:965-969.

11. Ji LL, Fu RG, Mitchell E. Glutathione and antioxidant enzymes in skeletal muscle: effect of fiber type and exercise intensity. *J Appl Physiol* 1992; 73:1854-1859.

12. Dernbach AR, Sherman WM, Simonsen JC, Flowers KM, Lamb DR. No evidence of oxidant stress during high-intensity rowing training. *J Appl Physiol* 1993; 74:2140-2145.

13. Ji LL. Exercise and oxidative stress: role of cellular antioxidant systems. *Exercise and Sport Science Reviews* 1995; 23:135-166.

14. Lew H, Pyke S, Quintanilha A. Changes in the glutathione status of plasma, liver and muscle following exhaustive exercise in rats. *FEBS Lett* 1985; 185:262-266.

15. Powers SK, Criswell D, Lawler J. Influence of exercise intensity and fiber type on antioxidant enzyme activity in skeletal muscle. *Am J Physiol* 1994; 266:R375-R380.

16. Green PD, Lemckert JW. Vitamin E and selenium responsive myocardial degeneration in dogs. *Can Vet J* 1977; 18:290-291.

17. van Rensburg IB, Venning WJ. Nutritional myopathy in a dog. *J S Afr Vet Assoc* 1979; 50:119-121.

18. Van Vleet JF. Experimentally induced vitamin E-selenium deficiency in the growing dog. *J Am Vet Med Assoc* 1975; 166:769-774.

19. Pillai SR, Traber MG, Steiss JE, Kayden HJ. Depletion of adipose tissue and peripheral nerve α-tocopherol in adult dogs. *Lipids* 1993; 28:1095-1099.

20. Pillai SR, Steiss JE, Traber MG, Kayden HJ, Wright JC. Comparison of four erythrocyte fragility tests as indicators of vitamin E status in adult dogs. *J Comp Pathol* 1992; 107:399-410.

21. Wander RC, Hall JA, Gradin JL, Du SH, Jewell DE. The ratio of dietary (n-6) to (n-3) fatty acids influences immune system function, eicosanoid metabolism, lipid peroxidation and vitamin E status in aged dogs. *J Nutr* 1997; 127:1198-1205.

22. Morrow JD, Roberts LJ. The isoprostanes: current knowledge and directions for future research. *Biochem Pharmacol* 1996; 51:1-9.

The Role of Fat in the Formulation of Performance Rations: Focus on Fat Sources

Arleigh J. Reynolds, DVM, PhD, DACVN
Assistant Professor of Clinical Nutrition, College of Veterinary Medicine
Cornell University, Ithaca, New York, USA

Gregory A. Reinhart, PhD
Research and Development, The Iams Company, Lewisburg, Ohio, USA

Introduction

Several studies have demonstrated the benefits of feeding high fat diets to working dogs.[1-4] Recently significant attention has been focused on the types of fats used in working dog rations. The sources of fats used in these diets may influence not only the rate of digestion and utilization, but also alter inflammatory processes, blood coagulation, and even oxygen consumption. Much attention has been focused on how altering dietary fat sources effects many of these parameters. Initial studies examined the effects of omega-3 fatty acid supplementation on platelet aggregation, clotting time, and maximal oxygen uptake. More recently, the effects of medium chain triglyceride supplementation on the maximal rate of fat oxidation have been examined.

Omega-3
Fatty Acid
Supplementation

Due to their potential influence on various inflammatory processes, dietary supplementation with omega-3 (n-3) fatty acids has generated considerable interest from the research and medical communities over the past three decades. Enhanced n-3 fatty acid intake has been associated with a reduction in the incidence and severity of coronary artery disease,[5] hypertension,[6] and hyperlipidemia[7] in humans, as well as immune mediated joint,[8] renal,[9] gastrointestinal,[10] respiratory,[11] and skin disease[12,13] in humans and other species. In addition to their role in disease prevention and treatment, this class of fatty acids has also been implicated as an ergogenic aid to athletic performance. A recent study of well conditioned human subjects found that those fed n-3 enriched diets experienced a small increase in VO$_2$ max when compared to non-supplemented controls.[14]

Although the benefits of n-3 supplementation may be significant, they do not appear to be universal. Parallel studies on the same organ system have often resulted in conflicting conclusions. Such conflicting results may be due to differences in relative proportions of other unsaturated fatty acids in the diet (n-6:n-3 ratio), dosages or duration of treatment. Skeptics of the practice of n-3 supplementation have noted that prolonged intakes at high doses have led to impaired hemostasis in humans.[15]

In light of the potential enhancement in VO$_2$ max and the potential risk of hemorrhage, the effects of n-3 fatty acid supplementation on prothrombin time (PT), activated partial thromboplastin time (APTT), platelet function, and VO$_2$ max in a group of sled dogs during a strenuous training program were examined.

Three age, sex, and ability matched groups of 24 sled dogs (8 dogs per group) were fed one of three experimental diets for the 12 week duration of the study. All diets were equal in nutrient content except for adjustments in their omega-6:omega-3 ratio and the sources of these fatty acids. Diet S was supplemented with safflower oil to reach a 50:1 ratio, diet X was supplemented with flax oil to reach a 5:1 ratio, and diet F was supplemented with fish oil to reach a 5:1 ratio. The dogs were trained to peak fitness before the onset of the study and maintained at this level of training for the entire study period. Platelet aggregation, PT, APTT, and VO$_2$ max were measured before and 6 and 12 weeks after introduction of the experimental diets.

There were no effects of diet on any of the parameters measured in this study. The data for VO$_2$ max, platelet aggregation, PT, and APTT are presented in **Tables 1–4**. Based on previous reports of Inuit Populations[5,15] an increase in clotting time and a decrease in platelet aggregation parameters might have been expected in the F and X groups of this study. The n-3 intake and n-3:n-6 ratios of the F and X diets fed were lower than those reported for the traditional Inuit diet.[15,16,17] In studies on humans where n-3 intake was similar to that of the F and X fed dogs, no changes were seen in coagulation profiles.[18] Previous work in sedentary dogs supplemented with nearly as high an n-3 intake as was fed here also failed to show an increase in clotting time or a change in platelet number.[19]

The only changes observed in clotting profiles or platelet aggregation parameters in the present study were associated with time. Whether these effects were associated with the duration of the diets fed or the duration of training cannot be differentiated. Previous studies have demonstrated an exercise associated decrease in bleeding times in humans[20] and so an interaction between diet and training cannot be ruled out in the present study.

Unlike a previous report on human subjects, there was not an increase, or any effect, of n-3 supplementation on VO$_2$ max. The values measured in these sled dogs are 2–3 times those reported in a study of human subjects where n-3 supplementation was associated with a small increase in VO$_2$ max.[14] These findings suggest that species specific differences may exist in the effects of n-3 supplementation on VO$_2$ max. Further studies defining the mechanisms limiting VO$_2$ max and the role n-3 fatty acids play in these mechanisms would be necessary to validate this hypothesis.

Several commercial rations contain concentrations of n-3 fatty acids similar to those fed in the present study. At this level of intake, n-3 fatty acids supplementation had no effect on VO$_2$ max in well trained sled dogs. This degree of n-3 fatty acids intake also had little effect on APTT, PT, or platelet number and function. The magnitude of n-3 fatty acids intake studied here thus appears to be safe for dogs undergoing strenuous training.

Arleigh J. Reynolds

Table 1. Change in VO$_2$ max after 12 weeks of dietary fatty acid supplementation. Values presented are percentage change from pre-supplemented values.

	% Change VO$_2$ max
Fish oil	26.8 ± -21.9
Flax oil	36.5 ± -28.2
Safflower oil	-5.1 ± -13.4

Table 2. Primary response platelet aggregation induced by 5 mcg collagen at 6 and 12 weeks post supplementation. Values given as percentage change from pre-supplemented measurements.

	6 weeks	12 weeks
Fish oil	6.7 ± -26.9	8.2 ± -25.6
Flax oil	25.0 ± -25.9	-9.3 ± -22.2
Safflower oil	20.9 ± -39.5	1.4 ± -26.0

Table 3. Prothrombin time at 6 and 12 weeks post supplementation. Values given as percentage change from pre-supplemented measurements.

	6 weeks	12 weeks
Fish oil	0.9 ± -6.9	2.4 ± -5.3
Flax oil	6.1 ± -6.9	5.3 ± -8.1
Safflower oil	8.1 ± -8.1	6.8 ± -6.6

Table 4. Activated partial thromboplastin time at 6 and 12 weeks post supplementation. Values given as percentage change from pre-supplemented measurements.

	6 weeks	12 weeks
Fish oil	5.7 ± -7.7	8.9 ± -6.7
Flax oil	5.9 ± -7.4	12.6 ± -6.7
Safflower oil	10.0 ± -9.1	11.9 ± -6.5

Unique Properties with Unique Benefits. Medium chain triglycerides (MCTs) are composed of fatty acids between 6 and 12 carbons in length.[21] The relatively short length of these fatty acids permits them a more rapid rate of digestion and absorption than is possible for longer chain moieties.[22] Fatty acids derived from MCTs are more water soluble and can enter the blood stream directly after digestion.[23] MCTs do not require pancreatic lipase or bile for digestion and absorption.[23] Early studies in rats showed that significant amounts of MCTs can be absorbed as intact triglycerides.[24]

Alternatively, long chain triglyceride (LCT) digestion and absorption requires pancreatic lipase and bile.[25] LCT derived fatty acids must be first incorporated into chylomicron triglycerides and travel through the lymphatic system before entering the general circulation.[25] Once in circulation LCT fatty acids are not available for peripheral cells until they are first removed from triglycerides by lipoprotein lipase.[26] Unlike MCT, LCT fatty acids require carnitine for transport across the inner mitochondrial membrane before oxidation for energy can occur.[22] Thus MCT fatty acids are more rapidly and readily available for energy after a meal than LCT fatty acids.

From a clinical point of view MCT supplementation may help increase caloric intake in cases where the normal avenues of fat digestion and absorption are unavailable or contraindicated. Such clinical conditions include pancreatic exocrine insufficiency, pancreatitis, cholestasis, short bowel syndrome, and lymphangiectasia.[21]

Like any dietary supplement there are limits to the benefits of MCT supplementation. There is little or no storage of MCT in the animal body.[27] Thus if MCT is fed at a rate greater than it can be oxidized, the excess must be elongated in the liver, esterified into triglycerides, and secreted as VLDL.[27] In some species such overfeeding of MCT's has been associated with the development of hepatic lipidosis. Presently there is no recommended allowance of MCT's for cats because of this risk.[28] Some authors have recommended that 25% of calories is the upper safe limit for dogs.[29] MCT can also present a challenge in clinical application as many forms are unpalatable.

Sled Dogs and MCTs. The effects of MCT oil supplementation on the maximal rate of fat oxidation in a group of highly trained sled dogs was investigated. The dogs were split into 2 groups of 8 dogs matched for age, sex, and ability. The control group (LCT) was fed a commercially available performance ration supplemented to 25% of the calories with corn oil, and the experimental group (MCT) was fed the same ration supplemented to 25% of the calories with MCT oil. After 4 weeks of diet adaptation, 12 hour post prandial maximal rates of fat oxidation were calculated from VO_2 and VCO_2 measurements made on an open flow gas exchange system. These measurements were also made one hour post ingestion of 400 kcal of either LCT or MCT. The data from this experiment was still being collected and analyzed at the time of this writing. The final results will be presented at the 1998 Iams Nutrition Symposium.

1. Kronfeld DS. Diet and performance in racing sled dogs. *J Am Vet Med Assoc* 1973; 162:470-474.

2. Downey RL, Kronfeld DS, Banta CA. Diet of beagles affects stamina. *J Am Anim Hosp Assoc* 1980; 273-277.

3. Reynolds AJ, Fuhrer L, Dunlap HL, Kallfelz FA. The effect of diet and training on muscle glycogen storage and utilization in trained and untrained sled dogs. *J Appl Phys* 1995; 79:1601-1607.

4. Reynolds AJ, Fuhrer L, Dunlap HL, Kallfelz FA. Lipid metabolite responses to diet and training in sled dogs. *J Nutr* 1994; 124:2754S-2759S.

5. Dyerberg J. n-3 Fatty acids: the beginnings. In: Frolich JC, von Schacky C, eds. *Fish, Fish Oil and Human Health*. New York: W. Zuckschwerdt Verlag, 1992; 1-13.

6. Knapp HR. Dietary omega-3 fatty acids and blood pressure control. In: Drevon CA, Baksaas I, Krokan HE, eds. *Omega-3 Fatty Acids: Metabolism and Biological Effects*. Basel/Switzerland: Birkhauser Verlag, 1993; 241-249.

7. Delany JP, Vivian VM, Snook JT, Anderson PA. Effects of fish oil on serum lipids in men during a controlled feeding trial. *Am J Clin Nutr* 1990; 52:477-485.

8. Kremer JM. Omega-3 fatty acid dietary supplementation in patients with rheumatoid arthritis. In: Frolich JC, von Schacky C, eds. *Fish, Fish Oil and Human Health*. New York: W. Zuckschwerdt Verlag, 1992; 135-143.

9. Plotnick AN. The role of omega-3 fatty acids in renal disorders. *J Am Vet Med Assoc* 1996; 209:906-910.

10. Allen PC, Danforth HD, Levander OA. Diets high in n-3 fatty acids reduce cecal lesion scores in chickens infected with *Eimeria tenella*. *Poult Sci* 1996; 75:179-185.

11. Thien FCK, Lee TH. n-3 Fatty acids in asthma. In: Frolich JC, von Schacky C, eds. *Fish, Fish Oil and Human Health*. New York: W. Zuckschwerdt Verlag, 1992; 155-166.

12. Ziboh A. n-3 Fatty acids in dermatology. In: Frolich JC, von Schacky C, eds. *Fish, Fish Oil and Human Health*. New York: W. Zuckschwerdt Verlag, 1992; 144-154.

13. Vaughn DM, Reinhart GA, Swaim SF, Lauten SD, Garner CA, Boudreaux MK, Spano JS, Hoffman CE, Conner B. Evaluation of effects of dietary n-6 to -3 fatty acid ratios on leukotriene B synthesis in dog skin and neutrophils. *Vet Derm* 1994; 5:163-173.

14. Brilla LR, Landerholm TE. Effects of fish oil supplementation and exercise on serum lipids and aerobic fitness. *J Sports Med Phys Fitness* 1990; 30:173-180.

15. Dyerberg J, Bang HO. Haemostatic function and platelet polyunsaturated fatty acids in Eskimos. *Lancet* 1979; ii:433-435.

16. Bang HO, Dyerberg J, Sinclair HM. The composition of the Eskimo food in north western Greenland. *Am J Clin Nutr* 1990; 33:2657-2661.

17. Innis SM. Sources of ω3 fatty acids in artic diets and their effects on red cell and breast milk fatty acids in Canadian Inuits. In: Galli C, Simopouolos A, eds. *Dietary ω3 and ω6 Fatty Acids: Biological Effects and Nutritional Essentiality*. New York: Plenum Press, 1988; 135-146.

18. Lox CD. The effects of dietary marine fish oils on coagulation profiles in men. *Gen Pharm* 1990; 12:241-246.

19. Cahill PD, Sarris GE, Cooper AD, Wood PD, Kosek JC, Mitchell RS, Miller DC. Inhibition of vein graft intimal thickening by eicosapentaenoic acid: reduced thromboxane production without change in lipoprotein levels or low-density lipoprotein receptor density. *J Vasc Surg* 1988; 7:108-118.

20. Hansen JB, Nordoy A. The effect of fish oil and lovastatin on lipoproteins and blood-vessel wall reactivity in familial hypercholesterolemia. In: Drevon CA, Baksaas I, Krokan HE, eds. *Omega-3 Fatty Acids: Metabolism and Biological Effects*. Basel: Birkhauser Verlag, 1993; 231-240.

21. Rombeau JL, Rolandelli RH. *Clinical Nutrition: Enteral and Tube Feeding*. Philadelphia: W.B. Saunders Co., 1997; 129.

22. Bach AC, Babayan BK. Medium chain triglycerides: an update. *Am J Clin Nutr* 1982; 36:950-962.

23. Gottschlich MM. Selection of optimal lipid sources in enteral and parenteral nutrition. *Nutr Clin Pract* 1992; 7:152-165.

24. Playoust MR, Isselbacher KJ. Studies on the intestinal absorption and intramucosal hydrolysis of a medium chain triglyceride. *J Clin Invest* 1964: 43; 878-875.

25. Isselbach KJ. Mechanisms of absorption of long and medium chain triglycerides. In: Senior JR, ed. *Medium Chain Triglycerides*. Philadelphia: University of Pennsylvania Press, 1968; 21-33.

26. Beitz DC, Allen RS. Lipid metabolism. In: Swenson MJ, ed. *Dukes Physiology of Domestic Animals, 110th Edition*. Ithaca: Cornell University Press, 1984; 386-396.

27. Shieg R. Hepatic metabolism of medium chain triglycerides. In: Senior JR, ed. *Medium Chain Triglycerides*. Philadelphia: University of Pennsylvania Press, 1968; 39-47.

28. MacDonald ML, Anderson BG, Rogers QR, Buffington CA, Morriss JG. Essential fatty acid requirements of cats: pathology of essential fatty acid deficiency. *Am J Vet Res* 1984; 45:1310-1317.

29. Lewis LD, Morriss ML, Hand MS. *Clinical Nutrition III*. Topeka: Mark Morris Associates, 1989; 7-45.

Effect of Racing on Water Metabolism, Serum Sodium and Potassium Concentrations, Renal Hormones, and Urine Composition of Alaskan Sled Dogs

Kenneth W. Hinchcliff, BVSc, MS, PhD, DACVIM
Associate Professor, Department of Veterinary Clinical Sciences
College of Veterinary Medicine; The Ohio State University, Columbus, Ohio, USA

Gregory A. Reinhart, PhD[a]; John R. Burr, DVM[a];
Curtis J. Schreier[a]; Richard A. Swenson[b]
[a]Research and Development, The Iams Company, Lewisburg, Ohio, USA
[b]Lightning Bolt Express Kennels, Two Rivers, Alaska, USA

Introduction

Human, equine, and canine athletes all perform some sort of endurance exercise. Humans compete in marathon and ultra-marathon races, horses compete in single and multiple day endurance rides, and sled dogs run 100 miles per day for 10 to 14 consecutive days. The physiological implications of such prolonged exercise are profound. Sustained exertion requires maintenance of an elevated metabolic rate for hours at a time, often with minimal rest periods to permit recovery. Sustained high metabolic rates require the provision of adequate energy substrates, either derived from body stores or by ingestion of food, and maintenance of adequate hydration. Of the athletic species, Alaskan sled dogs clearly are the superior endurance athletes. Consequently, the stresses imposed on these animals by competition in long distance sled races must be the greatest of any of the athletic species. However, performance failure is relatively uncommon in Alaskan sled dogs[1] indicating the capacity of these dogs to cope with the physiological strain of sustained exertion in frigid conditions. Optimal care and management of athletic Alaskan sled dogs requires an understanding of the physiology of sustained exertion. The results of studies of the physiology of fluid and electrolyte balance in these dogs follow.

Energy Intake and Water Turnover

It has been previously reported that the energy expenditure and intake of Alaskan sled dogs while racing is extraordinarily high for large mammals.[1,2] Energy expenditure of racing Alaskan sled dogs can exceed 10,000 kcal per day for several consecutive days. This large energy expenditure is met almost entirely by ingestion of energy in the form of a high fat diet. The typical diet of racing Alaskan sled dogs, and of the dogs in this study, consists of 60% of calories from fat, 25% of calories from protein, and the balance from carbohydrate and fiber. The ingestion of 2500 kcal per day as protein has some important implications to water balance in these dogs.

Ingested material is excreted from the body in the feces, urine, and breath. Undigested nutrients are excreted in the feces, whereas carbon from fat and carbohydrate is excreted mainly as carbon dioxide in the breath. The main route of excretion of nitrogen, produced from the metabolism of endogenous and ingested protein, is in the urine as urea. Similarly, electrolytes including sodium and potassium are excreted in the urine — fecal losses of these substances are minimal in normal dogs.[3,4] The amount or quantity of substances ingested that must be excreted in the urine is referred to as the renal solute load (RSL).[5] The potential renal solute load of the diet can be estimated:

$$RSL = urea + 2(Na + K)$$
$$or$$
$$RSL = N/28 + 2(Na + K)$$

where urea, Na, and K are expressed in mmols and N (nitrogen) is expressed in mg (N/28 = mmol of urea, as there is 28 mg of N per mmol of urea).[5]

The ingestion of large quantities of protein, therefore, results in the excretion of large amounts of urea in urine. Because the amount of urine produced is related to the amount of urea that needs to be excreted per day and the concentration of the urine, ingestion of an increasing amount of protein will likely mandate an increase in urine volume. In other words, urine volume is related to urine osmolality and the renal solute load of the diet; for a given urine osmolality, urine volume increases as intake of solutes that are excreted in the urine increases.[5] Urine production can, therefore, be estimated from the renal solute load in the diet and urine osmolality. Racing Alaskan sled dogs consume over 45,000 kJ·d^{-1} of which approximately 900 g is protein.[2] An intake of 900 g·d^{-1} of protein, equivalent to approximately 5.1 mol·d^{-1} of urea, would necessitate the excretion of 4.6 liters of urine with a urea concentration of 1100 mosmol·kg^{-1}.

It is apparent that the high energy intake of racing Alaskan sled dogs will result in the production of large quantities of urine, even if that urine is relatively concentrated, and will cause these dogs to have a high water turnover. In fact, when water turnover in racing Alaskan sled dogs was measured (as a corollary to measurement of energy expenditure using the doubly labelled water technique) the dogs had water turnover of slightly more than 6 liters per day (about 250 ml/kg body weight).[2]

Effect of Racing on Electrolyte Status

Prolonged exertion by horses and human beings often results in a reduction in serum sodium concentration and variable changes in serum potassium concentration.[6-9] Large losses of sodium and potassium occur in sweat during prolonged exercise by these species; concurrent urinary and gastrointestinal losses are small relative to the sweat losses and likely contribute only minimally to exercise-associated cation loss.[6,7,9-13] The large losses of sodium and potassium in sweat during exercise, if not offset by ingestion of these electrolytes, results in a reduction in the total body content of these cations.[8,9,11,14] The estimated reduction in total body cation content may or may not be apparent as a reduction in serum sodium concentration depending on changes in total body water.[15,16,17]

Theoretically, serum sodium concentration can be considered to be determined in mammals, including dogs,[6] by the relationship:[15,17]

Serum sodium conc. = ([Na$_e$] + [K$_e$])/TBW

where [Na$_e$] and [K$_e$] are the body contents of exchangeable sodium and potassium, respectively, and TBW is total body water. Thus, a decrease in serum sodium concentration can be considered to be attributable to a depletion of exchangeable sodium, exchangeable potassium, or both, with maintained body water volume.

Exertion-associated hyponatremia and/or cation depletion is reported in species that thermoregulate by sweating, but to our knowledge an exertion-associated reduction in serum sodium concentration had not been reported in dogs until very recently.[18] The exertion-associated hyponatremia in dogs, a species that thermoregulates by evaporation of water from the respiratory tract, was surprising given that cation depletion in human beings and horses is caused by cation loss in sweat. Therefore, to determine if the exertion-associated reduction in serum sodium concentration of sled dogs is associated with a decrease in estimated total exchangeable cation depletion, serum electrolyte concentrations, body weight, and total body water of trained Alaskan sled dogs were measured before, during, and after a 300 mile sled dog race, in conjunction with the measurement of energy expenditure described above.[19]

Total body exchangeable cation content (TECC) was estimated:[15,20]

TECC = [Na$^+$] x 0.66 x BW

where [Na$^+$] is serum sodium concentration, 0.66 is the proportion of body weight that was water, and BW is body weight (kg). Body water volume was measured in 9 of the dogs by deuterium dilution and, expressed as a proportion of body weight, did not change significantly over the course of the race.[2] Serum sodium and potassium concentrations decreased significantly ($P<0.01$) during the race (*Table 1*), as did serum calcium, total protein, albumin and globulin concentrations, and packed cell volume ($P<0.01$). Serum chloride concentration increased during the race ($P<0.01$) (*Table 1*).

Body weight and estimated total exchangeable cation content of the dogs decreased significantly ($P<0.001$) during the race (23.5 ± 0.8, 23.6 ± 0.8 and 22.9 ± 0.7 kg, and 2307 ± 79, 2262 ± 75, and 2182 ± 80 mEq, at the start, mid-point, and finish of the race, respectively). When expressed as a function of body weight, estimated exchangeable cation content declined significantly ($P<0.001$) during the race (98.1 ± 1, 95.9 ± 1, and 95.7 ± 1 mEq/kg, respectively).

Table 1. Packed cell volume (PCV) and concentrations of venous plasma constituents of 14 Alaskan sled dogs before (Pre-race), during (Mid-race), and after (Post-race) a 300 mile sled dog race. From Hinchcliff et al. 1997.[19]

Variable	SITE		
	Pre-race*	Mid-race*	Post-race*
PCV (%)	60.3 ± 2.6	52.3 ± 4.6†	45.6 ± 6.1†
Sodium (mEq/L)	148.5 ± 0.3	145.3 ± 0.4†	145.1 ± 0.5†
Potassium (mEq/L)	4.8 ± 0.1	4.6 ± 0.1†	3.8 ± 0.1†
Chloride (mEq/L)	116 ± 1	116 ± 1	119 ± 1†
Calcium (mg/dL)	10.0 ± 0.1	8.9 ± 0.1†	8.6 ± 0.1†
Total protein (g/dL)	6.2 ± 0.1	5.7 ± 0.1†	5.0 ± 0.1†
Albumin (g/dL)	3.4 ± 0.5	3.3 ± 0.1	2.9 ± 0.1†
Globulin (g/dL)	2.8 ± 0.1	2.5 ± 0.1†	2.1 ± 0.1†

* Mean ± SE
† P<0.01 vs Pre-race value

This study demonstrated that prolonged submaximal exercise by Alaskan sled dogs is associated with decreases in serum sodium, potassium, calcium, and protein concentrations, changes not observed after exercise of shorter duration.[21,22] Measurement of serum sodium concentration and body weight of dogs before, during, and immediately after the race allowed changes in total body cation content to be estimated, demonstrating that the decrease in serum sodium concentration could be explained by a decrease in estimated total body cation content with no significant change in total body water.

Urinary and Renal Hormone Responses to Racing

Total body water of the dogs in the study described above was not different before and after the race, thereby implicating a reduction in total exchangeable cation content as the cause of the decrease in serum sodium concentration. Alternatively, there may have been a selective increase in extracellular fluid volume due to the presence of an unmeasured ion whose distribution was confined to the extracellular space. Selective expansion of the extracellular space may have decreased serum sodium concentration without a decrease in total body cation content. Evidence to support a selective expansion of the extracellular space includes the reduction in hematocrit and serum protein and calcium concentrations. Conversely, there is no evidence of an increase in the anion gap that would be suggestive of the presence of unmeasured anions.

The route of cation loss, if any, in the dogs in the above study is unknown, although several mechanisms, including increased losses in feces and/or urine, are plausible. Unlike humans and horses, dogs do not sweat to an appreciable extent and thermoregulation in dogs is achieved principally by panting (evaporative cooling from the respiratory tract) and by conductive and radiative heat loss.[23,24] Therefore, physiologically important loss of cations in sweat of the dogs is considered unlikely, and other routes for sodium and potassium loss must be considered. Sodium and potassium can be lost from the body in urine and feces. Assessment of fecal sodium loss in free ranging dogs is problematic because of problems in ensuring complete collection of feces, but the amount of sodium lost is likely small.[3,4] However, excretion of sodium in urine may be substantial.[3,4]

Regardless of the exact mechanism, exercise-associated hyponatremia in humans and horses is associated with substantial losses of sodium in sweat and a reduction in urine osmolality (compared to values before exercise).[8,12,13] The occurrence of hyponatremia has been observed in 33 of 283 Alaskan sled dogs sampled during the 1995 Iditarod Trail Sled Dog Race (Hinchcliff et al., unpublished observation), and total body cation depletion of dogs during a shorter race.[19] It is speculated that exercise-associated hyponatremia in these dogs is attributable to solute diuresis and urine sodium loss mandated by the large metabolizable energy intake of racing Alaskan sled dogs. Therefore, a study measuring water turnover, serum electrolyte concentration and osmolality, urine osmolality, plasma concentrations of vasopressin, aldosterone and atrial natriuretic peptide and renin activity in dogs during a 300 mile race was conducted.[25] Similar variables were measured at the same time in a group of similarly trained dogs that did not race.

Average temperature during the 3 days of the race was -36, -34, and -27 °C and the dogs completed the 300 mile race in 65 hours. Water turnover was significantly higher in the dogs that ran ($P<0.001$, 5.0 ± 1.8 L·d^{-1} [190 ± 19 ml·kg^{-1}·d^{-1}]) than in those that did not (1.13 ± 0.3 L·d^{-1}, 51 ± 13 ml·kg^{-1}·d^{-1}). Serum sodium, potassium, calcium, and total protein concentrations and osmolality of racing dogs decreased during the race (**Table 2**), but there was no change in these values in the dogs that did not run. Serum urea nitrogen concentrations increased in the dogs that ran, but not in the sedentary dogs.

Plasma concentrations of vasopressin concentrations decreased significantly ($P<0.001$) from 2.3 ± 0.5 ng/L before the race to 1.2 ± 0.3 ng/L after the race in dogs that ran. In contrast, plasma aldosterone and plasma renin activity increased from 28 ± 26 to 82 ± 46 ng/L and 2.1 ± 1.5 to 6.8 ± 5.2 μ/L/h, respectively, over the course of the race.

Urine osmolality was unchanged during the race (1500 ± 390 and 1410 ± 450 mosmol/kg before and after the race, respectively) whereas urine sodium (96 ± 38 and 26 ± 19 mEq/L) and potassium (157 ± 56 and 66 ± 35 mEq/L) decreased. Urine urea nitrogen concentration increased ($P=0.06$, 940 ± 247 to 1150 ± 403 mmol/L) over the course of the race.

The decrease in serum sodium concentration in exercising dogs, but not in the sedentary dogs, in the present study was associated with large water turnover,

Table 2. Concentrations of serum constituents of 12 Alaskan sled dogs before (Pre-race), during (Mid-race), and after (Post-race) a 490 km sled dog race. Modified from Hinchcliff et al. 1997.[25]

Variable	SITE		
	Pre-race*	Mid-race*	Post-race‡
Sodium (mmol·L⁻¹)	148.6 ± 2.8	144.9 ± 2.7†	139.7 ± 1.9†
Potassium (mmol·L⁻¹)	4.8 ± 0.2	4.7 ± 0.2	4.0 ± 0.4†
Chloride (mmol·L⁻¹)	115.7 ± 2.2	114.7 ± 3.2	117.3 ± 2.5
Calcium (mmol·L⁻¹)	2.4 ± 0	2.2 ± 0.1†	2.2 ± 0.1†
Total protein (g·L⁻¹)	63 ± 3	58 ± 4†	54 ± 6†
Urea nitrogen (mmol·L⁻¹)	8.7 ± 3.0	11.6 ± 3.1†	11.3 ± 2.7†
Creatinine (μmol·L⁻¹)	61.9 ± 17.7	61.9 ± 17.7	53.0 ± 8.8
Osmolality (mOsmol·kg⁻¹)	306.2 ± 9.3	303.4 ± 9.5	295.6 ± 5.7†

* Mean ± SD
† P<0.05 vs Pre-race value

renal sodium conservation in the absence of signs of dehydration, and maintained high urine osmolality. Urine osmolality was maintained, in spite of a marked reduction in urine sodium and potassium concentration, largely by an increase in urine urea concentration. The increase in urine urea concentration likely reflected the increased renal solute load mandated by the dogs' diet. Therefore, it is speculated that the large water turnover of Alaskan sled dogs during a race is attributable in large part to the high renal solute load in the diet, and that the reduction in serum sodium concentration is a consequence of solute diuresis and inadequate sodium intake in these dogs. These findings suggest the novel explanation that exercise-induced hyponatremia in Alaskan sled dogs is secondary to a solute diuresis induced by the solute load mandated by the dogs' high energy expenditure and diet.

Respiratory water losses, estimated assuming a total daily carbon dioxide production of 90 moles,[2] 5% CO_2 in expired air, V_E of 27 L·min⁻¹, inspired air temperature of 0° C, inspired humidity of 0 Torr, and a respiratory rate of 60 breaths per min, was 800 ml·d⁻¹.[26] Together, fecal and respiratory losses were likely less than 1 L·d⁻¹, indicating that water loss in the urine must have been substantial (4.5 L·d⁻¹).

The large urine volume mandated by the dogs' diet imposes an obligatory urinary sodium loss. The excretion of 4.6 L·d⁻¹ of urine with a sodium concentration of 50 mmol·L⁻¹ results in the excretion of 230 mmol of sodium per day of the race. This quantity of sodium is equivalent to 25% of a 25 kg dog's exchangeable sodium content, assuming an extracellular fluid volume of 250 ml·kg⁻¹.[27] Sodium intakes of 8.2 grams (360 mmol) of sodium were measured during the race, although this value may underestimate actual intake because of problems ensuring complete collection of a representative diet. Therefore, the obligatory excretion of urea by racing Alaskan sled dogs apparently mandates excretion of a physiologically significant quantity of sodium even in the face of homeostatic mechanisms that act to reduce urinary sodium concentration. The large losses of sodium in the urine are apparently not met by similar increases in sodium intake and result in the development of total body sodium depletion and hyponatremia.

Together, these studies demonstrate the consequences of the high energy expenditure mandated by the sustained exercise performed by Alaskan sled dogs. Because of the sustained and prolonged exertion, the dogs ingest large quantities of protein which is excreted as urea in the urine. Excretion of the large quantity of urea necessitates production of a large quantity of concentrated urine. In spite of a hormonal milieu that favors conservation of sodium in the kidney, the large volume of urine produced in response to the urea load causes the excretion of substantial amounts of sodium. The loss of sodium in urine, if not compensated for by ingestion of sodium in the diet, may result in the development of hyponatremia.

Conclusions

1. Hinchcliff KW, Reinhart GA, Burr JR, Schreier CJ, Swenson RA. Energy metabolism and water turnover in Alaskan sled dogs during running. In: Carey DP, Norton SA, Bolser SM eds. *Recent Advances in Canine and Feline Nutritional Research: Proceedings of the 1996 Iams International Nutrition Symposium*, Wilmington: Orange Frazer Press, 1996; 199-206.

2. Hinchcliff KW, Reinhart GA, Burr JR, Schreier CJ, Swenson RA. Metabolizable energy intake and sustained energy expenditure of Alaskan sled dogs during heavy exertion in the cold. *Am J Vet Res* 1997; 58:1457-1462.

3. Needle MA, Kaloyanides GJ, Schwartz WB. The effects of selective depletion of hydrochloric acid on acid-base and electrolyte equilibrium. *J Clin Invest* 1964; 43:1836-1846.

4. Schwartz WB, Brackett NC, Cohen JJ. The response of extracellular hydrogen ion concentration to graded degrees of chronic hypercapnia: the physiologic limits of defense of pH. *J Clin Invest* 1965; 44:291-301.

5. Kohn CW, DiBartola SP. Composition and distribution of body fluids in dogs and cats. In: DiBartola SP, ed. *Small Animal Fluid Therapy*. Philadelphia: W.B. Saunders Co., 1993; 1-33.

6. Andrews FM, Ralston SL, Sommardahl CS, Maykuth PL, Green EM, White SL, Williamson LH, Holmes CA, Geiser DR. Weight, water, and cation losses in horses competing in a three-day event. *J Am Vet Med Assoc* 1994; 205:721-724.

7. Hinchcliff KW, Kohn CW, Geor R, McCutcheon LJ, Foreman J, Andrews FM, Allen AK, White SL, Williamson LH, Maykuth PL. Acid:base and serum biochemistry changes in horses competing at a modified 1 Star 3-day-event. *Equine Vet J Suppl* 1995; 20:105-110.

References

8. Irving RA, Noakes TD, Buck R, van Zyl Smit R, Raine E, Godlonton J, Norman RJ. Evaluation of renal function and fluid homeostasis during recovery from exercise-induced hyponatremia. *J Appl Physiol* 1991; 70:342-348.

9. Hiller WDB. Dehydration and hyponatremia during triathlons. *Med Science Sports Exerc* 1989; 21:S219-S221.

10. Frizzell RT, Lang GH, Lowance DC, Lathan SR. Hyponatremia and ultramarathon running. *J Am Med Assoc* 1986; 255:772-774.

11. McCutcheon LJ, Geor RJ, Hare MH, Ecker GL, Lindinger MI. Sweating rate and sweat compostion during exercise and recovery in ambient heat and humidity. *Equine Vet J* 1996; Suppl. 20:153-157.

12. Snow DH, Kerr MG, Nimmo MA, Abbott EM. Alterations in blood, sweat, urine, and muscle composition during prolonged exercise in the horse. *Vet Rec* 1982; 110:377-384.

13. Galun E, Tur-Kaspa I, Assia E, Burstein R, Strauss N, Epstein Y, Popovtzer MM. Hyponatremia induced by exercise: a 24-hour endurance march study. *Miner Electrolyte Metab* 1991; 17:315-320.

14. Surgenor S, Uphold RE. Acute hyponatremia in ultra-endurance athletes. *Am J Emerg Med* 1994; 12:441-444.

15. Edelman IS, Leibman J, O'Meara MP, et al. Interrelations between serum sodium concentration, serum osmolality and total exchangeable sodium, total exchangeable potassium, and total body water. *J Clin Invest* 1958; 37:1236-1256.

16. Leaf A. The clinical and physiologic significance of the serum sodium concentration. *New Eng J Med* 1962; 267:77-83.

17. Saxton CR, Seldin DW. Clinical interpretation of laboratory values. In: Kokko JP, Tannen RL, eds. *Fluids and Electrolytes*. Philadelphia: W.B.Saunders, 1986; 3-62.

18. Burr JR, Reinhart GA, Swenson RA, Swaim SF, Vaughn DM, Bradley DM. Comparison of biological changes before and after racing, and between dogs competing in long distance sled dog races. In: Carey DP, Norton SA, Bolser SM eds. *Recent Advances in Canine and Feline Nutritional Research: Proceedings of the 1996 Iams International Nutrition Symposium*. Wilmington: Orange Frazer Press, 1996; 207-218.

19. Hinchcliff KW, Reinhart GA, Burr JR, Schreier CJ, Swenson RA. Effect of racing on serum sodium and potassium concentrations and acid-base status of Alaskan sled dogs. *J Am Vet Med Assoc* 1997; 210:1615-1618.

20. Carlson GP. Hematology and body fluids in the equine athlete. In: Gillespie JR, Robinson NE, eds. *Equine Exercise Physiology 2*. Davis: ICEEP Publications, 1987; 102-111.

21. Hammel EP, Kronfeld DS, Ganjam VK, Dunlap Jr HL. Metabolic responses to exhaustive exercise in racing sled dogs fed diets containing medium, low, or zero carbohydrate. *Am J Clin Nut* 1977; 30:409-418.

22. Querengaesser A, Iben C, Leibetseder J. Blood changes during training and racing in sled dogs. *J Nutr* 1994; 124:2760S-2764S.

23. Phillips CJ, Coppinger RP, Schimel DS. Hyperthermia in running sled dogs. *J Appl Physiol* 1981; 51:135-142.

24. Baker MA, Turlejska E. Thermal panting in dehydrated dogs: effects of plasma volume expansion and drinking. *Pflugers Arch* 1989; 413:511-515.

25. Hinchcliff KW, Reinhart GA, Burr JR, Swenson RA. Exercise-associated hyponatremia in Alaskan sled dogs: urinary and hormonal responses. *J Appl Physiol* 1997; 83:824-829.

26. Ferrus L, Commenges D, Gire J, Swenson RA. Respiratory water loss as a function of ventilatory or environmental factors. *Respiration Physiol* 1984; 56:11-20.

27. Cardozo RH, Edelman IS. The volume of distribution of sodium thiosulfate as a measure of the extracellular fluid space. *J Clin Invest* 1952; 31:280-290.

Geriatric Nutrition

Vitamin E and Immune Response in Aged Dogs

Simin Nikbin Meydani, DVM, PhD
Professor of Nutrition and Immunology, Tufts University
Chief of the Nutritional Immunology Laboratory at the
Jean Mayer USDA Human Nutrition Research Center on Aging
at Tufts University, Boston, Massachusetts, USA

Michael G. Hayek, PhD[a]; Dayong Wu, MD[b]; Mohsen Meydani, DVM, PhD[b]
[a]Research and Development, The Iams Company, Lewisburg, Ohio, USA
[b]Tufts University, Boston, Massachusetts, USA

Aging is associated with altered regulation of the immune system[1] which contributes to increased incidence of infectious diseases and tumors. Of the four major cell types (stem cells, macrophages, B cells, and T cells) of the immune system, the major alterations occur in the T cells.[1,2] A very important aspect to the decline in T cell function is increased susceptibility to viral and intracellular pathogens as well as neoplastic diseases. Altered T cell-mediated immunity is reflected *in vivo* in the inability of the aged to mount a delayed-type hypersensitivity (DTH) skin response as well as a decrease in antibody production. The decrease in specific antibody production has been observed for both primary and secondary antibody responses. Among *in vitro* indices of T cell-mediated function, the ability of T cells to proliferate in response to antigens or the polyclonal T cell mitogens concanavalin A (Con A) or phytohemagglutinin (PHA), and their production of interleukin (IL)-2 have been shown to consistently decrease with age.[1] An age-associated increase in prostaglandin (PG) E_2, and its contribution to reduced antibody production, DTH, IL-2 production, and lymphocyte proliferation has been reported.[3-5]

Many factors contribute to the age-associated decline in T cell function. Since the aged are at higher risk for low consumption of several micro-nutrients needed for the proper function of the immune system, it has been suggested that the nutritional status of the aged is an important determinant of their immune response. It has long been accepted that deficiencies of many macro- and micronutrients impair the ability of a host to mount an immune response and defend against an invading pathogen. More recent research has suggested that supplementation above accepted requirements of certain nutrients may improve the immune response and thus increase resistance to immune related diseases.

Researchers have been interested in studying the role of nutrients, in particular that of antioxidant nutrients, in maintaining an optimal immune response in the aged. Vitamin E is the most powerful biological lipid soluble antioxidant; its main function is to protect cellular lipids against oxidation. Studies in recent years, however, have shown that some of vitamin E's biological effects (e.g., regulation of signal transduction) is independent of its antioxidant effect.[6]

The oxidant/antioxidant balance is an important determinant of immune cell function, not only for maintaining the integrity and functionality of membrane lipids, cellular proteins, and nucleic acids, but also for control of signal transduction and gene expression in immune cells. The cells of the immune system are particularly sensitive to changes in the oxidant/antioxidant balance because of the relatively high percentage of polyunsaturated fatty acids in their plasma membrane. They are also frequently exposed to changes in this balance because high levels of reactive oxygen intermediates are produced as byproducts of their normal function. When exposed to a pathogen (e.g., influenza virus) the cellular level of antioxidant nutrients such as vitamin E declines.[7] It is, therefore, not surprising that the cells of the immune system have higher concentrations of vitamin E compared to other cells[8, 9] and that severe or marginal deficiency of vitamin E adversely affects the immune response in animal models and humans.[10] Furthermore, many studies have indicated that supplementation with higher than the recommended dietary allowance levels of vitamin E enhances cell-mediated and humoral immune responses, as well as resistance to infections in a variety of species.[11]

Vitamin E and the Aging Immune Response

An optimal level of vitamin E is needed for maintenance of the immune response across all age groups. This need, however, appears to be more critical in the aged. A consistently reported biological phenomena in the aged is an increase in free radical formation and lipid peroxidation. Enzymatic and non-enzymatic products of lipid peroxidation have been shown to decrease T cell mediated function.[3,5,12] Given that enzymatic antioxidant defenses are reduced in aging and that the level of some antioxidant nutrients is reduced in the elderly, the aged immune response might particularly benefit from increased intake of vitamin E.

To test this hypothesis, the effect of vitamin E supplementation on the immune responsiveness of aged mice was evaluated.[13] Old mice were fed diets containing 30 ppm or 500 ppm dl-α-tocopheryl acetate for 6 weeks, and their immune response was compared to that of young mice fed 30 ppm tocopherol. Splenocytes from old mice fed 500 ppm dietary vitamin E had a significantly higher proliferative response to ConA and LPS, but not to PHA, than control animals fed 30 ppm of vitamin E. In addition, vitamin E supplementation significantly increased DTH to 2,4-dinitro-7-fluorobenzene. This immunostimulatory effect of vitamin E was associated with increased production of IL-2 and a decreased production of PGE$_2$ (*Table 1*).

Vitamin E supplementation to humans in a double-blind, placebo-controlled study demonstrated that certain *in vivo* and *in vitro* indices of the immune response could be improved with vitamin E supplementation.[14] In this study, 34

Table 1. Effects of vitamin E on immune response of 24-month-old mice. Data adapted from Meydani et al.[13]

PARAMETERS	30 ppm†	500 ppm†
Serum α-tocopherol	71	194*
Delayed hypersensitivity	36*	75
T cell lymphocyte proliferation	5*	38
B cell lymphocyte proliferation	24*	85
Ex vivo splenic PGE₂ synthesis	123*	89
Interleukin-2	44*	85

† All values expressed as a percentage of 3-month-old control group (fed 30 ppm vitamin E).
* Significantly different from control and other experimental group, $P \leq 0.05$.

healthy men and women (>60 years) were supplemented with either a placebo containing soybean oil or 800 mg dl-α-tocopherol (400 mg capsules twice daily) for 30 days. The study evaluated the subjects' DTH and mitogenic response as well as IL-1, IL-2, and PGE₂ formation. Vitamin E supplementation was associated with increases in plasma vitamin E, DTH score, and mitogenic response to ConA and IL-2 production (**Figure 1**). Vitamin E supplementation was also associated with decreases in PHA-stimulated PGE₂ production by peripheral blood mononuclear cells (PBMC), as well as plasma lipid peroxide levels.[14] No effects on mitogenic response of PBMC to PHA or in IL-1 production were observed.

To determine the optimal level of vitamin E, a long term, double-blind, placebo-controlled study was undertaken. Healthy elderly subjects were randomly assigned to one of the four following groups: placebo, 60, 200 or 800 IU/day of vitamin E.[15] In addition to DTH, the ability of subjects to produce antibodies in response to primary T cell-dependent (hepatitis B), secondary T cell-dependent (tetanus/diphtheria), and T cell-independent (pneumococcal) vaccines was determined. There was no significant increase in DTH of the placebo group. However, a significant increase in DTH was observed in all 3 vitamin E-supplemented groups. As shown in **Figure 2**, the group supplemented with 200 IU/day had the highest percent increase in DTH. Furthermore, the change in DTH of the 200 mg/day group was significantly different from that of the placebo group, while no significant difference in percent changes of the 60 and 800 IU/day group with that of the placebo group was observed. There was no significant increase in antibody titer against hepatitis B in the placebo or 60 IU/day group. However, both the 200 and 800 IU/day groups showed a significant increase in the antibody titer against hepatitis B (**Table 2**). The 200 mg/day group had the highest percent change in the antibody titer. There was no significant change in response to pneumococcal or diphtheria vaccine due to vitamin E supplementation. A significant increase in antibody titer to tetanus toxoid, however, was observed in the group supplemented with 200 IU/day. The results of this study confirmed previous findings and indicated that of the 3 doses tested, the 200 IU/day was the optimal level for enhancement of the immune response in the elderly.

To date no information related to the effect of vitamin E supplementation on the immune response of geriatric companion animals is available. Recently, a study was undertaken to determine if supplementation with vitamin E will enhance the immune response of young and old dogs. Twenty young (mean age 2 years) and 20 old (mean age 9.2 years) Beagles were fed a standard commercial chicken/corn-based diet formulated to contain 27 IU/kg diet of vitamin E (NRC recommendation) (control diet) for 1 month prior to the commencement of the experiment in order to stabilize the dogs' vitamin E levels. Young and old dogs were then randomly

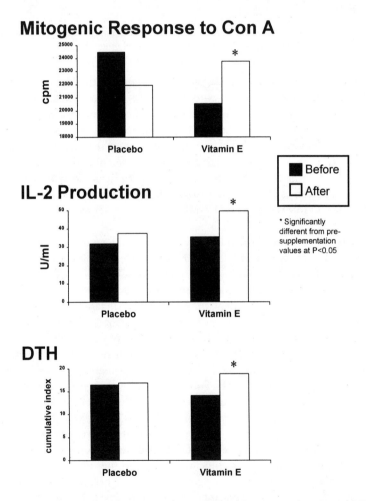

Figure 1. Effect of vitamin E supplementation on mitogen response, IL-2 production, and DTH in elderly humans. Thirty-four elderly men and women were supplemented with either placebo or 800 IU α-tocopherol for 30 days. Data adapted from Meydani et al., 1990.[14]

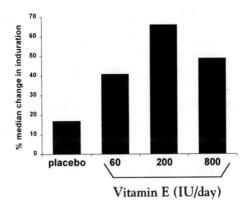

Figure 2. Effect of vitamin E supplementation on DTH of healthy elderly. Subjects were supplemented with placebo or 60, 200, 800 IU/day of vitamin E for 4.5 months. DTH was assessed before and after supplementation using Multi-test CMI. Data represent sum of induration of all positive responses. Data adapted from Meydani et al., 1997.[15]

assigned to the diets containing 27 IU/kg diet of vitamin E or 280 IU/Kg diet of vitamin E for 8 weeks. Blood was collected before and after 8 weeks of dietary treatments for measurement of plasma vitamin E levels and assessment of lymphocyte mitogenic response to ConA and PHA. Prior to dietary treatment and similar to other species, old dogs had significantly lower mitogenic response to PHA and ConA than young dogs. Surprisingly, there was a significant decrease in plasma vitamin E level of young and old dogs fed 27 IU/kg diet of vitamin E with the young dogs exhibiting a higher percentage decrease (35% in old v 50% in young, P=0.12). Examination of the vitamin E content of the commercial chow fed to the study dogs before their arrival at the facility indicated that on average, the commercial chow contained 60 IU/kg diet of vitamin E. Thus, decline in plasma vitamin E levels can be attributed to the lower levels of vitamin E in the control diet compared to that of commercial dog chow. Both young and old dogs supplemented with vitamin E showed a significant increase in plasma vitamin E levels, with the young dogs exhibiting a significantly higher percent increase than old dogs (20% in old v 50% increase in young dogs, P=0.02). The young dogs fed the 27 IU/kg diet of vitamin E also had a significant decrease in ConA and PHA-stimulated proliferation during the 8 week feeding period. No such decrease was observed in dogs supplemented with 280 IU/kg diet of vitamin E. The old dogs fed 27 or 280 IU/kg diet of vitamin E did not show a significant change in mitogen-stimulated lymphocyte proliferation.

The results of this study indicate that 1) old dogs have lower proliferative response to ConA and PHA than young dogs, and 2) young and old dogs respond differently to changes in dietary vitamin E levels. Young dogs are more sensitive to short term decreases in dietary vitamin E levels than old dogs, which is most likely due to their lower storage level of vitamin E. On the other hand, young dogs achieve significantly higher plasma vitamin E levels than old dogs following supplementation with levels of vitamin E above current recommendations. This

Table 2. Effect of vitamin E supplementation on antibody titer to hepatitis B in elderly subjects. Adapted from Meydani et al., 1997.[15]

GROUP	GEOMETRIC MEAN, IU/ML		% WITH DETECTABLE HEP B TITER†
	PRE-SUPPLEMENTATION	POST-SUPPLEMENTATION*	
Placebo (n=16)	4.0	7.3	19
60 mg E (n=18)	4.0	10.4	28
200 mg E (n=18)	4.0	23.9‡	41
800 mg E (n=18)	4.0	9.2‡	42

A standard dose of hepatitis B was administered on day 156 of the study. Two additional hepatitis B booster doses were administered on days 186 and 216 of the study. Blood for serum antibody level measurement was collected before vaccination and after each hepatitis B booster administration. Sera with undetectable levels were assigned 4 units/ml for the purpose of calculating geometric means.

* refers to antibody titer after the third booster

† ≥ 8 IU/ml as detected by RIA after third hepatitis B (Hep B) booster

‡ post-supplementation compared with baseline using Wilcoxon signed rank test followed by Bonferroni correction for multiple comparisons

difference can be due to either lower absorption or higher utilization of vitamin E in old dogs compared to young dogs and might imply a different vitamin E requirement for young and old dogs. This is supported by the observation of a higher level of H_2O_2 production by mononuclear cells of old dogs compared to young dogs. Further studies are needed to determine the mechanism of observed differences in vitamin E levels between young and old dogs and the appropriate level of vitamin E needed to enhance the immune response in aged dogs.

Vitamin E and Resistance to Infection

The immunostimulatory effect of vitamin E is associated with increased resistance to infection.[11] Tengerdy et al.[16] showed that supplementation with 150–300 mg/kg of vitamin E significantly reduced *E. coli*-induced mortality in chickens (from 50 to 5%). Similarly, the mortality of mice infected with *streptococcus* pneumonia Type I decreased from 80 to 20% after vitamin E supplementation.[17] The protective effect of vitamin E has been associated with higher antibody titer and an increase in the number of plaque-forming cells. Vitamin E was also shown to be protective against *E. coli*-induced mortality in turkeys[18] and pigs.[19]

The incidence of and mortality from respiratory infections increases with age. These diseases are among the leading causes of death in the elderly. To determine the clinical significance of the immunostimulatory effect of vitamin E for the aged, the effect of vitamin E supplementation on resistance to influenza in young and old C57BL/NIA mice was investigated. As expected, the old mice fed diets containing 30 ppm vitamin E had significantly higher lung influenza viral titers compared to the young mice fed 30 ppm vitamin E. Old mice fed 500 ppm vitamin E, however, had significantly lower lung viral titers than old mice fed 30 ppm vitamin E. Vitamin E had a more dramatic effect in old mice so that there was no difference in lung viral titers of young mice fed 30 or 500 ppm vitamin E and those of old mice fed 500 ppm vitamin E.[20] Others have reported protective effects against viral infection as well.[21-23] Epidemiological studies also indicate a lower incidence of infections in the elderly with higher plasma levels of tocopherol.[24] Preliminary results in humans[16] showed that elderly supplemented with vitamin E tended (P=0.098) to have a 30% lower incidence of self-reported infections compared to those supplemented with placebo. These findings, while encouraging, need to be confirmed in a larger number of subjects using more rigorous method of infection documentation. Currently, a large clinical trial is evaluating the effect of one year supplementation with 200 IU/day of vitamin E on the incidence of respiratory infections in elderly residents of long term care facilities.

Conclusions

Studies in different species of animals indicate a consistent age-related change in T cell-mediated function. This is believed to be an important contributing factor to the higher incidence of infectious and neoplastic diseases with aging. Studies in mice and humans indicate that supplementation with vitamin E enhances the immune response of the aged and that this could be of clinical significance to them. Few studies have evaluated age-related changes in companion animals[25,26] and currently there are no reports regarding the effect of micro-nutrients on the immune response of old dogs and cats. The preliminary studies reported here indicate that similar to other species, lymphocytes from older dogs respond less vigorously to mitogenic stimulation than those of young dogs. Furthermore, they respond differently to changes in dietary vitamin E levels than young dogs. Further studies are needed to determine the appropriate level of vitamin E needed to enhance the immune response of the older dogs, as well as to determine the mechanism of differences in plasma vitamin E level following dietary manipulation.

Acknowledge-ments

The author's work has been funded at least in part with Federal funds from the U.S. Department of Agriculture, Agricultural Research Service under contract number 53-K06-01, as well as NIA Grant #1R01 AG091, USDA Grant #94-055-77, and grants from The Iams Company and Hoffman LaRoche, Inc. The authors would like to thank Timothy S. McElreavy, MA, for preparation of this manuscript.

References

1. Miller RA. The cell biology of aging: Immunological models. *J Gerontol* 1989; 44:B4-B8.
2. Makinodan T. Cellular basis of immunological aging. In: *Biological Mechanisms in Aging*: USDA, NIH, 1981; 488-500.

3. Goodwin JS, Ceuppens J. Regulations of the immune response by prostaglandins. *J Exp Med* 1982; 155:943-948.

4. Hayek MG, Meydani SN, Meydani M, Blumberg JB. Age differences in eicosanoid production of mouse splenocytes: Effects on mitogen-induced T-cell proliferation. *J Gerontol* 1994; 49:B197-B207.

5. Beharka AA, Wu D, Han S-N, Meydani SN. Macrophage prostaglandin production contributes to the age-associated decrease in T-cell function which is reversed by the dietary antioxidant vitamin E. *Mech Age Dev* 1997; 94:157-165.

6. Azzi A, Boscobonik D, Hensley C. The protein kinase C family. *Euro J Biochem* 1992; 208:547-557.

7. Hennet T, Peterhans E, Stocker R. Alterations in antioxidant defenses in lung and liver of mice infected with influenza A virus. *J Gen Virol* 1992; 73:39-46.

8. Coquette A, Vray B, Vanderpas J. Role of vitamin E in the protection of the resident macrophage membrane against oxidative damage. *Arch Int Physiol Biochem* 1986; 94:529-534.

9. Hartman LJ, Kayden HJ. A high-performance liquid chromatographic method for the determination of tocopherol in plasma and cellular elements of the blood. *J Lipid Res* 1979; 20:639-645.

10. Meydani SN, Wu D, Santos MS, Hayek MG. Antioxidants and immune response in the aged: Overview of the present evidence. *Am J Clin Nutr* 1995; 62:1462S-1476S.

11. Meydani SN, Hayek MG. Vitamin E and immune response. In: Chandra RK, ed. *Proceedings of the International Congress on Nutrition and Immunity.* St Johns, Newfoundland, Canada: ARTS Biomedical Publishers and Distributors, 1992; 105-128.

12. Franklin RA, Arkins S, Li YM, Kelley KY. Macrophages suppress lectin-induced proliferation of lymphocytes from aged rats. *Mech Ageing Dev* 1993; 67:33-46.

13. Meydani SN, Meydani M, Verdon CP, Shapiro AC, Blumberg JB, Hayes KC. Vitamin E supplementation suppresses prostaglandin E$_2$ synthesis and enhances the immune response of aged mice. *Mech Ageing Dev* 1986; 34:191-201.

14. Meydani SN, Barklund PM, Lui S, Meydani M, Miller RA, Cannon JG, Morrow FD, Rocklin R, Blumberg JB. Effect of vitamin E supplementation on immune responsiveness of healthy elderly subjects. *Am J Clin Nutr* 1990; 52:557-563.

15. Meydani SN, Meydani M, Blumberg JB, Leka LS, Siber G, Loszewski R, Thompson C, Pedrosa MC, Diamond RD, Stollar BD. Vitamin E supplementation enhances *in vivo* immune response in healthy elderly subjects: A randomized controlled trial. *JAMA* 1997; 277:1380-1386.

16. Tengerdy RP, Heinzerling RH, Mathias MM. Effect of vitamin E on disease resistance and immune response. In: de Dune C, Hayaishi O, eds. *Tocopherol, Oxygen and Biomembranes.* Amsterdam: Elsevier Scientific Pub. Co., 1978; 191-200.

17. Heinzerling RH, Tengerdy RP, Wick LL, Leuker DC. Vitamin E protects mice against Diplococcus pneumonia type I infection. *Infect Immun* 1974; 10:1292-1295.

18. Julseth DR. *Evaluation of Vitamin E and Disease Stress on Turkey Performance.* Fort Collins CO. Colorado State University, 1984.

19. Ellis RP, Vorhies MW. Effect of supplemental dietary vitamin E on the serologic response of swine to an *Escherichia coli* bacteria. *J Am Vet Med Assn* 1986; 168:231-232.

20. Hayek MG, Taylor SF, Bender BS, Han SN, Meydani M, Smith D, Eghtesada S, Meydani SN. Vitamin E supplementation decreases lung viral titer in mice infected with influenza. *J Infect Dis* 1997; 176:273-276.

21. Wang Y, Hwang DS, Licing B, Watson RR. Nutritional status and immune responses in mice with murine AIDS are normalized by vitamin E supplementation. *J Nutr* 1994; 124:2024-2032.

22. Reddy PG, Morill JL, Minocha HC, Morill MB, Dayton AB, Frey RA. Effects of supplemental vitamin E on the immune system of calves. *J Dairy Sci* 1985; 69:164-171.

23. Teige J, Tollersrud S, Lund A, Larson HJ. Swine dysentery: the influence of dietary vitamin E and selenium on the clinical and pathological effect of *Treponema hydyseteriae* infections in pigs. *Res Vet Sci* 1982; 32:95-160.

24. Booth T, Phillips D, Barritt A, Berry S, Martin DN, Melotle C. Patterns of mortality in homes for the elderly. *Age Aging* 1983; 12:240-244.

25. Sheffy BE, Williams AJ, Zimmer JF, Ryan GD. Nutrition and metabolism of the geriatric dog. *Cornell Vet* 1985; 75:324-347.

26. Greeley EH, Kealy RD, Ballam JM, Lawler DF, Segre M. The influence of age on the canine immune system. *Vet Immunol & Immunopath* 1996; 55:1-10.

Effect of Omega-6:Omega-3 Fatty Acid Ratios on Cytokine Production in Adult and Geriatric Dogs

John J. Turek, PhD
Associate Professor, Department of Basic Medical Sciences
School of Veterinary Medicine, Purdue University, West Lafayette, Indiana, USA

Michael G. Hayek, PhD
Research and Development, The Iams Company, Lewisburg, Ohio, USA

Aging is associated with a decline in the immune response of several species. Since omega-3 fatty acids have been shown to interact with the immune system, this study was undertaken to determine the effect of omega-3 fatty acids on cytokine production for peripheral blood cells and peritoneal macrophages in young and old Fox Terriers and Labrador Retrievers. Young and old dogs were acclimated to a diet containing an omega-6:omega-3 (n-6:n-3) ratio of 25:1 for 60 days. Blood and peritoneal cells were collected, cells were isolated, stimulated with lipopolysacharide, and cultured for cytokine production. Half of the dogs were then switched to a diet with a 5:1 n-6:n-3 ratio and all were maintained on their respective diets for an additional 60 days before collection of blood and peritoneal cells. Interleukin-1, Interleukin-6, and Tumor Necrosis Factor-α production from peripheral blood mononuclearcytes or peritoneal macrophages were not affected by age or diet. Significant age x breed interactions (P<0.01) were noted for arachidonic acid and eicosapentaenoic acid. Arachidonic acid levels were increased in the serum of old Labrador Retrievers and decreased in old Fox Terriers, while eicosapentaenoic acid decreased in old Labrador Retrievers and increased in old Fox Terriers. Significant diet x breed interactions (P<0.01) were noted with α-linolenic acid, arachidonic acid, eicosapentanoic acid, docosapentaenoic acid, total n-6, n-3, and n-6:n-3 ratio. Fox Terriers had higher serum levels of omega-3 fatty acid metabolites than Labrador Retrievers. It appears that dietary fatty acid utilization is differentially regulated by breed and age in the dog. These breed associated differences in fatty acid metabolism may explain why not all atopic dogs respond to fatty acid therapy. Consideration of specific dietary fatty acid profiles may be warranted for different breeds and stages of life.

Summary

The process of aging and nutritional factors such as dietary lipids can both influence the immune system. For the aging immune system, the nutritional components may possess additional significance as modulating agents since the aging immune system takes on attributes that have been characterized as a "dysregulation" of normal function. This dysregulation is manifested in decreased

Introduction

antibody response to foreign antigens and increased autoantibody production along with increased incidence of infectious disease and cancer.[1,2] At the cellular level, aging results in fundamental changes to lymphocyte cell populations and signal transduction mechanisms, as well as alterations in cytokine production by inflammatory cells. Because dietary lipids may directly or indirectly modulate the immune system via regulation of cytokines,[3-5] eicosanoids,[6-8] enzymes of cell activation such as protein kinase C,[9] and changes in membrane receptor expression,[10-12] these dietary components may provide a "natural" means to modify some of the detrimental effects of aging on the immune system. Studies in rodents and humans have shown that dietary lipids are capable of attenuating or reducing the incidence of geriatric conditions such as arthritis and cancer. As research in this area progresses, it will hopefully result in dietary methods to enhance long term health and well-being of companion animals.

Although there has been extensive research on the effects of aging and/or dietary lipids in humans and rodents, there is currently little data on how these factors affect the canine immune system. The present study was designed to determine the effect of different ratios of omega-6:omega-3 fatty acids on canine peripheral blood mononuclear cell (PBMC) and peritoneal macrophage cytokine production in adult and geriatric dogs.

Effects of Aging on the Immune System

With aging, there is a decline in the number of T cells able to respond to activators such as Concanavalin A (ConA),[13,14] and a decrease in the proportion of cells able to produce a calcium signal in response to receptor dependent and independent agents.[15-17] These responses are due, in part, to a shift in T cell populations from naive T cells to memory T cells. Memory T cells are more resistant than naive T cells in their responsiveness to Con A stimulation of intracellular calcium increases in both young and old animals.[16,18,19] Concurrent with these T cell changes there is a modification in IL-2 production capacity. The evidence from a variety of rodent models[20-24] and human studies[18,25,26] is that aging results in reduced interleukin (IL)-2 production, and in some cases increased interferon (IFN)-γ[20,21,24] and IL-4.[24,27] In addition, aging may result in defects in transcriptional factors such as AP-1 and nuclear factor of activated T cells (NF-AT) which are important for IL-2 production.[28] In elderly individuals with decreased IL-2 there was impairment in the activation of these transcriptional factors, but in elderly with normal levels of IL-2 production they had normal activation of AP-1 and NF-AT. This same study also looked at the level of nuclear transcription factor NF-κB, and although it was lower in the elderly it did not correlate with altered IL-2 production.[28] However, NF-κB is important in the regulation of other cytokines such as IL-6.[29] Cells exposed to a NF-κB inducer such as lipopolysaccharide (LPS) rapidly phosphorylate and degrade the inhibitor protein IκB which allows NF-κB to translocate to the nucleus and activate gene expression.[30] Reductions in the level of NF-κB as reported for T cells[31] could be responsible for some of the other observed changes in cytokine production with aging.

In a study using human peripheral blood mononuclear cells, unstimulated and LPS-stimulated production of IL-1 was significantly higher in subjects older than 55 years than in the group aged less than 55 years. No difference was observed in tumor necrosis factor (TNF) or prostaglandin (PG)E$_2$ production from PBMC.[32] Another study in elderly humans observed that TNF-α, IL-4, and IL-6 were unchanged in mitogen stimulated mononuclear cell cultures, but IFN-γ and IL-2 production were decreased. This same study also examined aged mice and observed decreased IFN-γ, IL-2, and TNF-β, and increased IL-4 and IL-5.[33] Other experiments have resulted in the observation that IL-1 and TNF-α secretion by PBMC increased in the elderly, with no change in IFN-γ levels.[34] A study of elderly patients with pneumonia observed lower levels of IL-1β, TNF-α, and IL-8 in the sera compared to young patients with pneumonia. These researchers also observed lower levels of these cytokines from LPS-stimulated PBMC of healthy elderly compared to young normal individuals.[35] Peritoneal macrophages from aged rats fed a standard diet produced less IL-1 and TNF, than young and middle-aged rats.[36]

Interleukin-6 is one cytokine which is systemically elevated in aging animals and humans.[37] It appears that with aging this cytokine is produced constitutively, which results in a continual influence on the immune system.[38] Interestingly, the increase in IL-6 levels can be reduced via calorie restriction[37,39,40] or supplementation with dehydroepiandrosterone (DHEA), an adrenal steroid that decreases with aging.[38] In mice, the age associated increase in IL-6 in serum appears to have a genetic basis. It was found that in the MRL/lpr strain, IL-6 increased with age but did not increase in aged Balb/C or C3H/HeN strains.[41] Interleukin-6 also plays a major role in the acute phase response[42] and affects the hypothalamic-pituitary-adrenal axis (HPA-axis).[43] The chronic elevation of this cytokine in the aged may explain why acute phase proteins such as C-reactive protein are also elevated in the elderly.[44] It is unknown if constitutive production of IL-6 has a role in the age related decline in DHEA levels from the adrenal gland.

There is also some evidence that the anti-inflammatory cytokine, IL-10, is elevated with aging. Splenic CD4$^+$ cells from aged C57Bl/6NNIA mice that were stimulated *in vitro* with immobilized anti-CD3 ϵ mAB produced 10-fold more IL-10 than young adult mice.[45] Similar findings of elevated IL-10 production from peritoneal cells and splenocytes were also observed by others, and as with IL-6, the levels of IL-10 could be reduced by DHEA.[46] Higher levels of IL-10 and INF-γ were also observed in aged mice in response to intraperitoneal LPS injection.[47] There is also an increase in CD5$^+$ B cells in the elderly.[48] These cells are a major source of B cell derived IL-10 and may contribute to increased levels of this cytokine in the elderly.[46]

Since natural killer (NK) cells are in part regulated by Th$_1$ cytokines such as IL-2, it is important to mention that aging appears to cause functional changes in this cell as well. There are reports of increased, decreased, and unchanged NK activity with aging. In a study using geriatric dogs, it was found that NK cell activity was not significantly affected by age.[49] One study reported that the maximum cytotoxic potential of the NK cells from elderly humans was four times higher than that of young adults.[50] Later studies by this research group demonstrated that NK cells accumulated during human immunosenescence. It was found that the mean NK cell subset ratio ($\%CD56^+CD57^+$ / $\%CD56^+CD57^-$) increased from a level of 0.7 in the young adult to over 4.6 in the elderly. This was due primarily to increased numbers of $\%CD56^+CD57^+$ cells coupled with a modest decrease in the $\%CD56^+CD57^-$ cells.[51] It has also been reported that basal and induced NK activity decline with age.[52] NK cells were stimulated with Con A, polyinosinic acid-polyctidylic acid (poly I:C stimulant for cytokine production) and LPS, and a reduced NK cell response to poly (I:C) and LPS was correlated with decreased expression of the IFN-γ gene. However, the reduced NK cell response in aged animals to Con A was independent of the expression of IL-2 or IFN-γ genes.[52]

Dietary Lipid Modulation of the Immune System

Sources of Omega-3 and Omega-6 Polyunsaturated Fatty Acids (PUFA). The parent fatty acid for PUFA of the omega-3 (or n-3) family is α-linolenic acid (ALA, 18:3n-3). It is found primarily in green leafy vegetables and some vegetable oils such as canola and linseed.[53] The longer chain (n-3) PUFA such as eicosapentaenoic (EPA, 20:5n-3) and docosahexaenoic acid (DHA, 22:6n-3) are formed to varying degrees in mammals via elongation and desaturation of ALA, but cold water marine fish are the primary source.[54] Eicosapentaenoic acid gives rise to prostanoids of the 3-series and leukotrienes of the 5-series. The parent compound for omega-6 (or n-6) PUFA is linoleic acid (LA, 18:2n-6). Linoleic acid is desaturated and elongated to form dihomo-γ-linolenic acid (DGLA, 20:3n-6) and arachidonic acid (AA, 20:4n-6), which give rise to the 1- and 2-series prostanoids and 3- and 4-series leukotrienes, respectively.[55] The n-6 PUFA LA is highly enriched in many vegetable oils (corn, safflower, sunflower) and AA is a major component of mammalian cell membranes.

Effects of Dietary PUFA. One focal area of research is on the effects of dietary lipids on eicosanoid metabolism.[56-63] The n-3 PUFA EPA competes with AA for available cyclooxygenase and lipoxygenase enzymes.[64] This decreases eicosanoid formation from arachidonic acid and increases the levels from EPA.[65,66] The physiological response to n-3 derived eicosanoids is more moderate, since the n-3 derived eicosanoids are less pro-inflammatory.[55] An important consideration in the formulation of diets is that the regulation of eicosanoid synthesis by dietary lipids is dependent upon the ratio of n-6:n-3 fatty acids and not on the total amount of n-3 fatty acids.[67] Dietary lipid modulation of eicosanoids is important because PGE_2 derived from AA acts primarily as a negative feedback modulator of the immune response. Prostaglandin E_2 suppresses T lymphocyte proliferation and cytotoxic activities of natural killer cells.[68,69] It also induces suppresser T cells,[70,71] down- modulates Ia antigen expression[72] and interleukin-2 production by T cells,[73] down-regulates macrophage TNF-α to basal levels,[74,75] and inhibits IL-12 production.[76] Also, there is evidence that at equamolar concentrations, PGE_3 and LTB_5 derived enzymatically from EPA are just as potent as PGE_2 and LTB_4 in inhibiting lymphocyte proliferation.[77] However, in biological systems, concentrations of LTB_5 and PGE_3 are lower than their LTB_4 and PGE_2 counterparts (Hayek et al., unpublished data).

Effects of PUFA on inflammatory mediators have been reported in recent years.[3-5,78-82] Fish oil diets decreased TNF-α and IL-1β production,[3] as well as IL-2 production and phytohemagglutinin (PHA)-induced proliferation of human peripheral blood mononuclear cells.[83] In a study comparing young and older women, n-3 fatty acid supplementation reduced total IL-1β, TNF, and IL-6 in both groups, and also PHA-induced T cell mitogenesis in older women. The effects of n-3 fatty acid supplementation were more dramatic in the older women.[4]

The reduction in mononuclear cell mediators and proliferative activity has been hypothesized to account for some anti-inflammatory properties of n-3 fatty acids. However, in rodents, diets containing n-3 PUFA have anti-inflammatory properties,[84] but also enhance TNF,[85] IL-1 production,[80] and cell mediated cytotoxicity.[7] The increased production of TNF from diets enriched in n-3 PUFA is also evident *in vivo* in mice challenged with LPS.[81] However, a paradoxical phenomenon in rodents, compared to other species, is that although diets enriched in n-3 PUFA lead to increased production of inflammatory cytokines, there is less morbidity and mortality associated with LPS challenge. In research where rats were fed diets enriched in LA 18:2n-6 or ALA (18:3n-3), the ALA fed rats had no mortality and low morbidity to a 25 mg/Kg intraperitoneal LPS challenge, but the rats fed the n-6 enriched diet experienced 30% mortality and increased morbidity.[86] This paradox may be explained in part by the fact that macrophages from rats fed an n-3 enriched diet had a different activation range compared to rats fed an n-6 enriched diet. It was determined by leucine aminopeptidase levels that an n-3 enriched diet leads to a higher activation state in a non-stimulated peritoneal macrophage. However, if an inflammatory response is elicited via an adjuvant, the macrophages from rats fed an n-6 enriched diet activate to a greater extent compared to macrophages from n-3 fed animals.[5] This controlled response to activation may explain why n-3 enriched diets appear to enhance some immune functions, but may also prevent an over activation that results in a pathological inflammatory response.

Interactions of Aging and Fatty Acids with the Immune System. From the above background it is evident that there are many areas where dietary lipids and aging impact on the same cell type or metabolic pathway, as illustrated in **Figure 1**. The items enclosed by single bounding boxes are affected by aging and dietary lipids. There is currently only evidence for an effect of aging on items surrounded by a double bounding box. These interactions illustrate both the challenge and the promise of using dietary components for optimal health over an entire life span.

Diet. The formulation of the diet is in **Table 1**. The n-6:n-3 fatty acid ratio of the diets was 25:1 for the control diet and 5:1 for the test diet. The choice of the 5:1 n-6:n-3 ratio was influenced by the fact that this ratio was demonstrated to decrease LTB_4 synthesis while increasing LTB_5 synthesis by neutrophils and skin of dogs.[78]

Materials and Methods

Figure 1. Cytokine production/induction and inhibition pathways influenced by aging and/or dietary lipids. Items surrounded by a single bounding box are affected by aging and dietary lipids. There is currently only evidence for an effect of aging on items surrounded by a double bounding box. HPA = hypothalamic-pituitary-adrenal; PMN = polymorphonuclear leukocyte; NK = natural killer; IL = interleukin; Th = T helper; TNF = Tumor necrosis factor.

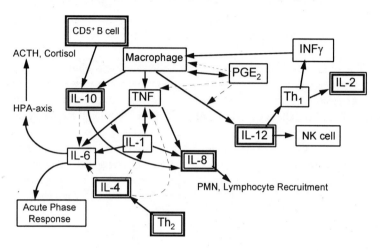

Cytokine Production / Induction (——▶) and Inhibition (- -▶)

Pathways Influenced By Aging and/or Dietary Lipids

Table 1. Composition of diets.

| | n-6:n-3 fatty acid ratio | |
| | 25:1 | 5:1 |
Ingredient	%	%
Corn	27.00	27.00
Rice	26.00	26.00
Chicken Protein	26.00	26.00
Chicken Fat	8.21	6.50
Beet Pulp	4.00	4.00
Egg	2.50	2.50
Chicken Digest	2.00	2.00
Fish oil	—	1.65
Yeast	1.00	1.00
Mineral Mix	2.91	2.91
Vitamin Mix	0.27	0.27
Ground Flax Seed	—	0.24
Methionine	0.15	0.15

Dogs. Eighteen geriatric (9 Labrador Retriever, mean age of 9.6 years; and 9 Fox Terrier, mean age of 11.5 years) and 18 adult (9 Labrador Retriever, mean age of 1.5 years; and 9 Fox Terrier, mean age of 1.8 years) dogs were used in this study. During phase I, all dogs were fed a diet containing an n-6:n-3 ratio of 25:1 for 60 days; peritoneal fluid and 2 blood samples were collected on day 60. The second blood sample was collected 14 days after the first sample. During phase II, 9 old and 9 young dogs were then placed on a diet with an n-6:n-3 ratio of 5:1 for an additional 60 days and the remaining dogs stayed on the n-6:n-3 diet with the 25:1 ratio. After 60 days, blood and peritoneal fluid were collected as in phase I.

Peripheral Blood Mononuclear Cells. Peripheral blood mononuclear cells were isolated by centrifugation on a Ficoll-Hypaque gradient. Cells were cultured in RPMI-1640 medium in the presence of 10 µg/mL of LPS for 24 hours. The culture supernatant fluids were collected and any nonadherent cells pelleted by centrifugation. The cell-free supernatant was frozen at -80° C until analysis and the nonadherent cells and adherent cells digested with 1N ammonium hydroxide and 0.2% Triton X-100 for total cellular DNA quantitation.[87]

Peritoneal Macrophages. The peritoneal cells were cultured in RPMI-1640 medium containing 5 mg/mL bovine serum albumin (BSA), 100 U/mL penicillin, 100 µg/mL streptomycin, and 1% L-glutamine for 2 hours. The nonadherent cells were washed off with medium, and the remaining adherent macrophages cultured for 24 hours in medium containing 10 µg/mL of LPS. Culture supernatant fluids were collected and stored and the cells digested for total DNA as described above.

Fatty Acid Analysis. A baseline fatty acid analysis was performed by gas-liquid chromatography on plasma after 45 days on the control diet (phase I) and again after an additional 60 days on the control diet or the test diet (phase II).

TNF Bioassay. Assay for TNF-like activity was performed on L929 murine fibroblasts. L929 cells were grown in RPMI 1640 medium with 1×10^5 U/L penicillin, 6.9×10^{-5} mol/L streptomycin, 2×10^{-3} mol/L L-glutamine and 10% calf serum. Dilutions of peritoneal macrophage or PBMC culture supernatant fluid (1:50 or 1:100) were added in octuplicate to 96 well culture plates containing L929 murine fibroblasts. Medium supplemented with actinomycin-D (3.98×10^{-6} mol/L) was added to the wells and after incubation for 20 hours at 37° C, the fluid in the wells was discarded, and 75 µL of 7.24×10^{-7} mol/L tetrazolium salt reduction (MTT) in Hank's balanced salt solution added to each well. After three hours, 100 µL of a solution of 6.9×10^{-1} mol/L SDS in 6.45 mol/L N,N dimethylformamide, pH 4.7 was added to each well and incubated at 37° C overnight.[88] The absorbency at 600 nm was then determined using microplate reader. To determine the amount of TNF-like activity, a standard curve was produced for each assay using human recombinant TNF-α (Genzyme, Boston, MA).

IL-6 Bioassay. Interleukin-6 bioassay was performed using B9 cells.[89] The cells were grown in Iscove's Modified Dulbecco's medium supplemented with 10%

fetal calf serum (FCS), 4pg/100mL of mouse recombinant IL-6, and 50 mM 2-mercaptoethanol (2-ME). Dilutions of PBMC or peritoneal macrophage culture supernatant fluid (1:100 or 1:200) were added in octuplicate to 96 well culture plates containing B9 cells. After 72 hours of incubation, 20 mL of 5mg/mL MTT in HBSS was added to each well and then six hours later 100 mL of SDS-dimethylformamide. The absorbancy at 550 nm was recorded after an overnight incubation at 37° C. A standard curve was generated for each assay using mouse recombinant IL-6.

IL-1 Bioassay. A mouse plasmacytoma cell line (T1165.17) which proliferates in response to IL-1 was used to assay for IL-1 activity.[90] The IL-1 receptor on the T1165.17 cell line was blocked using a monoclonal antibody (LA 15.6) to the IL-1 receptor. The cell line and antibody were generously supplied by Dr. Andrew Glasebrook, Eli Lilly and Co., Indianapolis, Indiana, USA. The cells were seeded in 96 well plates (5 x 10^5/mL), and samples are assayed in quadruplicate. Four wells were blocked with antibody (1μg/mL) 30 minutes before addition of samples and 4 wells were unblocked. Samples diluted 1:100 to 1:200 were added and incubated for 18 hours, and then MTT added as described for the IL-6 bioassay. Six hours later SDS-dimethylformamide was added and the plates incubated and absorbancy measured as described for the IL-6 assay. The difference in absorbancy between blocked and unblocked wells, corrected for control levels, determined the amount of IL-1 activity in the PBMC culture medium. A standard curve was generated for each assay using mouse recombinant IL-1β.

Statistical Analysis. Data from the fatty acid analysis and cytokine bioassays were analyzed using SAS for individual treatment effects and interactions based upon age, breed, and diet. ANOVA P values less than 0.05 were considered statistically significant.

Results
　　　　　　　Fatty Acid Analysis of Plasma. Results of the fatty acid analysis of phase I and II plasma samples are presented in **Figures 2** and **3**, respectively. During phase I, all of the dogs were fed the control diet with an n-6:n-3 ratio of 25:1. However, there were differences in plasma fatty acid levels based upon both breed and age of dog. Gamma-linolenic acid levels were significantly higher in Fox Terriers. There was also a significant interaction of age x breed for AA and EPA levels. Arachidonic acid levels were higher in old Labrador Retrievers (OLR) compared to old Fox Terriers (OFT) and were lower in young Labrador Retrievers (YLR) compared to young Fox Terriers (YFT). EPA was significantly higher in OFT compared to OLR. The overall level of n-6 PUFA in the plasma was also significantly higher in the Labrador Retrievers compared to the Fox Terriers during phase I.

　　　　　　　During phase II, control (C) dogs were fed the 25:1 and test (T) dogs the 5:1 n-6:n-3 ratio diets. The levels of GLA were significantly higher (P=0.001) in the control dogs. There were significant diet x breed (P=0.004) and age x diet effects on ALA levels. Old Fox Terriers fed either control or test diets and YFT fed the test

Fatty Acid Analysis of Plasma: Phase I

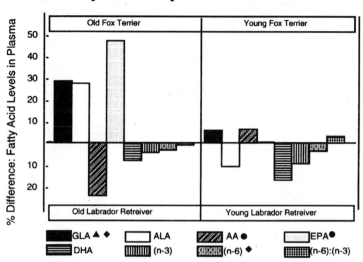

Figure 2. Comparison of fatty acid levels in plasma during phase I. The percentage difference compares old Fox Terriers *v* old Labrador Retrievers, and young Fox Terriers *v* young Labrador Retrievers. GLA = γ-linolenic acid; ALA = α-linolenic acid; AA = arachidonic acid; EPA = eicosapentaenoic acid; DHA = docosahexaenoic acid. Statistically significant effects at $P<0.05$; ▲ = diet effect; ◆ = breed effect; ● = age x breed effect.

Fatty Acid Analysis of Plasma: Phase II

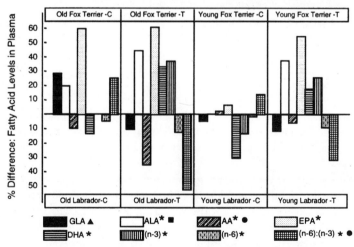

Figure 3. Comparison of fatty acid levels in plasma during phase II. The percentage difference compares the old and young dogs of each breed based upon control (C) or test (T) diets. GLA = γ-linolenic acid; ALA = α-linolenic acid; AA = arachidonic acid; EPA = eicosapentaenoic acid; DHA = docosahexaenoic acid; O = Old; Y = Young; FT = Fox Terrier; LR = Labrador Retriever. Statistically significant effects at $P<0.05$; ▲ = diet effect; ◆ = breed effect; ● = age x breed effect; * = diet x breed effect; ■ = age x diet effect.

diet had higher levels of ALA. For AA, there were significant differences in the concentration based upon diet x breed (P=0.009) and age x breed (P=0.004). The levels of AA were higher in OLR fed control or test diets and YLR fed the test diet. As expected, the levels of EPA were significantly higher in the test animals. However, there were significant breed (P=0.001) and diet x breed (P=0.001) effects. The levels of this fatty acid were higher in FT fed either control or test diets. There were also significant breed (P=0.008) and diet x breed effects (P=0.0001) on DHA levels. The levels of this fatty acid were higher in OTFT and YTFT compared to OTLR and YTLR. However, the levels of DHA were higher in OCLR and YCLR compared to OCFT and OTFT. These differences in the levels of the individual fatty acids resulted in significant differences based upon diet x breed for the total levels of n-3 and n-6 fatty acids, and the n-6:n-3 fatty acid ratio in the plasma. For the test diet, the total levels of n-3 fatty acids in the plasma were higher in the FT and the total levels of n-6 fatty acids were higher in the LR. The n-6:n-3 ratio was significantly lower in FT fed the test diet compared to LR, but this ratio was significantly higher in FT fed the control diet.

   Cytokine Production. There were no significant differences in TNF, IL-6, or IL-1 bioactivity based upon diet, breed, or age of dog. The results of the TNF bioassay of supernatants from PBMC and peritoneal macrophages are in *Figures 4* and *5*. Comparison of cytokine levels between phases is conducted to determine the effect of diet on individual dogs.

   The results of the IL-6 assay of supernatants from PBMC and peritoneal macrophages are in *Figures 6* and *7*. As was observed for TNF, the phase II levels of IL-6 from PBMC were higher compared to phase I for all groups. The phase II IL-6 production by peritoneal macrophages tended to be lower in old test and young control dogs and higher in young test and old control dogs compared to phase I levels, but not significantly.

   The results of the IL-1 assay of supernatants from PBMC and peritoneal macrophages are in *Figures 8* and *9*. The mean levels of phase II IL-1 production were lower in all old dogs and in young control dogs compared to phase I levels, but not significantly. The mean levels of IL-1 production from the peritoneal macrophages during phase II were higher compared to phase I for all groups of dogs.

Discussion   The results of the fatty acid analysis from the phase I period indicate that there may be breed differences in how the fatty acids are utilized with aging. The parent n-3 and n-6 fatty acids ALA and LA compete for available Δ6-desaturase enzyme. The fact that GLA is higher in OFT coupled with lower AA levels and increased EPA may indicate that in OFT there may be a preference or more efficient use of the n-3 fatty acids as a substrate. Since the levels of ALA are not significantly different in both breeds, differences in metabolism of n-3 fatty acids likely occur after the initial desaturation of ALA and probably involves the elongase and Δ5-desaturase enzymes that are needed to form EPA. Further analysis of these samples

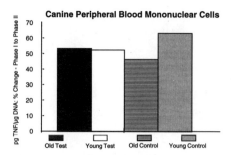

Figure 4. Percent change in tumor necrosis factor (TNF) bioactivity from phase I to phase II for old and young dogs. TNF-like bioactivity measured in lipopolysaccharide (LPS) stimulated canine peripheral blood mononuclear cells after culturing for 24 hours.

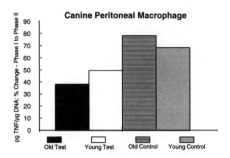

Figure 5. Percent change in tumor necrosis factor (TNF) bioactivity from phase I to phase II for old and young dogs. TNF-like bioactivity measured in lipopolysaccharide (LPS) stimulated canine peritoneal macrophages after culturing for 24 hours.

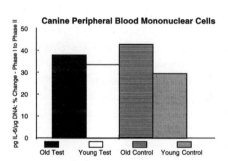

Figure 6. Percent change in interleukin-6 (IL-6) bioactivity from phase I to phase II for old and young dogs. IL-6 bioactivity measured in lipopolysaccharide (LPS) stimulated canine peripheral blood mononuclear cells after culturing for 24 hours.

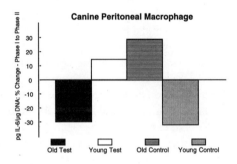

Figure 7. Percent change in interleukin-6 (IL-6) bioactivity from phase I to phase II for old and young dogs. IL-6 bioactivity measured in lipopolysaccharide (LPS) stimulated canine peritoneal macrophages after culturing for 24 hours.

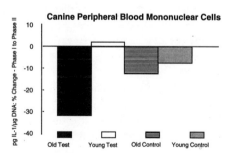

Figure 8. Percent change in interleukin-1 (IL-1) bioactivity from phase I to phase II for old and young dogs. IL-1 bioactivity measured in lipopolysaccharide (LPS) stimulated canine peripheral blood mononuclear cells after culturing for 24 hours.

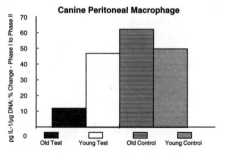

Figure 9. Percent change in interleukin-1 (IL-1) bioactivity from phase I to phase II for old and young dogs. IL-1 bioactivity measured in lipopolysaccharide (LPS) stimulated canine peritoneal macrophages after culturing for 24 hours.

for stearidonic acid (18:4n-3), eicosatetraenoic acid (20:4n-3), and dihomo-γ-linolenic acid (20:3n-6) which are intermediates in the desaturation and elongation pathways from the parent compounds would provide additional evidence for this metabolic difference with aging between the two breeds.

During phase II the levels of EPA in plasma were higher in the test animals compared to controls, but the EPA levels were higher in the FT breed for both young and old animals. This may indicate that in addition to the preference for n-3 PUFA as substrates that was observed in OFT fed the control diet, that in the young FT there may be an induction or enhancement of enzymatic pathways leading to increased EPA formation. The DHA levels were significantly higher in the FT breed for animals fed the test diet. The greatest difference was again evident in the older dogs. DHA is present in the test diet due to the use of fish oil, a natural source of this fatty acid. However, DHA can also be formed via desaturation and elongation of the parent n-3 fatty acid, ALA. There are two proposed mechanisms for this to occur. The first is via an elongation of EPA, followed by a desaturation by Δ4-desaturase, and the second is by an elongation of EPA to 24:5n-3 followed by a Δ6-desaturation and a β-oxidation in peroxisomes.[91] It is possible that in addition to the preference or increased efficiency in the use of n-3 fatty acids as substrates, that in Fox Terriers there may be increased formation of DHA via this β-oxidation pathway. There has been a recognition in recent years that peroxisomes and peroxisome proliferator-activated receptors are closely involved in regulating the metabolism of n-3 fatty acids.[92] The influence of the peroxisomal metabolic pathway on n-3 fatty acids could explain why the n-6:n-3 ratio was significantly lower in Fox Terriers fed the test diet compared to Labrador Retrievers, and why this relationship was not present in the dogs fed the control diet.

This study did not reveal any significant differences in cytokine production by either PBMC or peritoneal macrophages based upon age, breed, or diet. It is known that a dietary n-6:n-3 ratio of 5:1 in dogs will result in reduced LTB$_4$ and increased LTB$_5$ production from neutrophils and skin,[78] and are effective in reducing atopic pruritis in some dogs.[93] However, the latter study observed that not all dogs responded to the decreased ratio of n-6:n-3 fatty acids, due to presumed differences in fatty acid metabolism. The current study provides additional evidence of possible differences in fatty acid metabolism between different dog breeds. If that is true, it could influence the incidence of atopic diseases among certain breeds.

The recent studies in human and rodent models indicate that there is definitely a genetic component to altered cytokine production with aging, [28,41] which could account for some of the contradictory data in this research area. It is unknown if such a condition exists in the canine population, but it would not be an unexpected finding. This unknown factor, coupled with apparent differences in fatty acid metabolism, could contribute sufficient biological variability to our data to obscure possible effects of age or diet. An alternative explanation is that changes in cytokine production with aging are not present in canines. Similarly, the dietary ratio of 5:1 may not be low enough to alter cytokine production in the dog to any appreciable degree. Many of the animal studies on the effects of dietary PUFA on cytokine metabolism have used lower ratios of n-6:n-3 to achieve the alteration in cytokine production.[5,80,94] However, one should keep in mind that high dietary n-3 fatty acids have been shown to suppress T cell responses in humans and dogs.[4,95] A balance needs to be maintained between n-3 effects on cytokine production and T cell function. Additional research in this area is clearly needed to elucidate differences in fatty acid metabolism and to determine if there is a theshhold fatty acid ratio at which cytokine production is modified.

References

1. Haddy RI. Aging, infections, and the immune system. *J Fam Pract* 1988; 27:409-413.

2. Sauder DN, Ponnappan U, Cinader B. Effect of age on cutaneous interleukin 1 expression. *Immunol Lett* 1989; 20:111-114.

3. Endres S, Ghorbani R, Kelley VE, Georgilis K, Lonnemann G, van der Meer JWM, Cannon JG, Rogers TS, Klempner MS, Weber PC, Schaefer EJ, Wolff SM, Dinarello CA. The effect of dietary supplementation with n-3 polyunsaturated fatty acids on the synthesis of interleukin-1 and tumor necrosis factor by mononuclear cells. *N Engl J Med* 1989; 320:265-271.

4. Meydani SN, Endres S, Woods MM, Goldin BR, Soo C, Morrill-Labrode A, Dinarello CA, Gorbach SL. Oral (n-3) fatty acid supplementation suppresses cytokine production and lymphocyte proliferation: Comparison between young and older women. *J Nutr* 1991; 121:547-555.

5. Turek JJ, Schoenlein IA, Bottoms GD. The effect of dietary n-3 and n-6 fatty acids on tumor necrosis factor-α production and leucine aminopeptidase levels in rat peritoneal macrophages. *Prostaglandins Leukot Essent Fatty Acids* 1991; 43:141-149.

6. Lokesh BR, Black JM, Kinsella JE. The suppression of eicosanoid synthesis by peritoneal macrophages is influenced by the ratio of dietary docosahexaenoic acid to linoleic acid. *Lipids* 1989; 24:589-593.

7. Fritsche KL, Johnston PV. Modulation of eicosanoid production and cell-mediated cytotoxicity by dietary α-linolenic acid in BALB/c mice. *Lipids* 1989; 24:305-311.

8. Kinsella JE, Broughton KS, Whelan JW. Dietary unsaturated fatty acids: Interactions and possible needs in relation to eicosanoid synthesis. *J Nutr Biochem* 1990; 1:123-141.

9. May CL, Southworth AJ, Calder PC. Inhibition of lymphocyte protein kinase C by unsaturated fatty acids. *Biochem Biophys Res Commun* 1993; 195:823-828.

10. Opmeer FA, Adolfs MJP, Bonta IL. Regulation of prostaglandin E_2 receptors *in vivo* by dietary fatty acids in peritoneal macrophages from rats. *J Lipid Res* 1984; 25:262-268.

11. Pietsch A, Weber C, Goretzki M, Weber PC, Lorenz RL. N-3 but not n-6 fatty acids reduce the expression of the combined adhesion and scavenger receptor CD36 in human monocytic cells. *Cell Biochem Funct* 1995; 13:211-216.

12. Awazu M, Yared A, Swift LL, Hoover RL, Ichikawa I. Dietary fatty acid modulates glomerular atrial natriuretic peptide receptor. *Kidney Int* 1992; 42:265-271.

13. Fulop T Jr, Utsuyama M, Hirokawa K. Determination of interleukin 2 receptor number of Con A stimulated human lymphocytes with aging. *J Clin Lab Immunol* 1991; 34:31-36.

14. Wikby A, Johansson B, Ferguson F, Olsson J. Age-related changes in immune parameters in a very old population of Swedish people: a longitudinal study. *Exp Gerontol* 1994; 29:531-541.

15. Miller RA. Defective calcium signal generation in a T cell subset that accumulates in old mice. *Ann N Y Acad Sci* 1989; 568:271-276.

16. Miller RA. Accumulation of hyporesponsive, calcium extruding memory T cells as a key feature of age-dependent immune dysfunction. *Clin Immunol Immunopathol* 1991; 58:305-317.

17. Saini A, Sei Y. Age-related impairment of early and late events of signal transduction in mouse immune cells. *Life Sciences* 1993; 52:1759-1765.

18. Linton PJ, Haynes L, Klinman NR, Swain SL. Antigen-independent changes in naive CD4 T cells with aging. *J Exp Med* 1996; 184:1891-1900.

19. Miller RA. Aging and immune function: Cellular and biochemical analysis. *Exp Gerontol* 1994; 29:21-35.

20. Engwerda CR, Fox BS, Handwerger BS. Cytokine production by T lymphocytes from young and aged mice. *J Immunol* 1996; 156:3621-3630.

21. Pahlavani MA, Harris MD. Effect of dehydroepiandrosterone on mitogen-induced lymphocyte proliferation and cytokine production in young and old F344 rats. *Immunol Lett* 1995; 47:9-14.

22. Frasca D, Pucci S, Goso C, Barattini P, Barile S, Pioli C, Doria G. Regulation of cytokine production in aging: Use of recombinant cytokines to upregulate mitogen-stimulated spleen cells. *Mech Ageing Dev* 1997; 93:157-169.

23. Aoki K, Asano K, Okamoto K, Yoshida T, Kuroiwa Y. Age-related changes in ConA-induced cytokine production by splenocytes from senescence accelerated mice SAMP8. *Immunol Lett* 995; 46:169-175.

24. Nagelkerken L, Hertogh-Huijbregts A, Dobber R, Drager A. Age-related changes in lymphokine production related to a decreased number of CD45RBhi CD4+ T cells. *Eur J Immunol.* 1991; 21:273-281.

25. Antonaci S, Jirillo E, Munno I, Colizzi M, Polignano A, Bonomo L. Monocyte- and cytokine-mediated effects on T immunoregulatory activity in the elderly. *Cytobios* 1989; 58:155-164.

26. Chopra RK, Nagel JE, Chrest FJ, Adler WH. Impaired phorbol ester and calcium ionophore induced proliferation of T cells from old humans. *Clin Exp Immunol* 1987; 70:456-462.

27. Kubo M, Cinader B. Polymorphism of age-related changes in interleukin (IL) production: differential changes of T helper subpopulations, synthesizing IL 2, IL 3 and IL 4. *Eur J Immunol* 1990; 20:1289-1296.

28. Whisler RL, Beiqing L, Chen M. Age-related decreases in IL-2 production by human T cells are associated with impaired activation of nuclear transcriptional factors AP-1 and NF-AT. *Cell Immunol* 1996; 169:185-195.

29. Dokter WHA, Koopmans SB, Vellenga E. Effects of IL-10 and IL-4 on LPS-induced transcription factors (AP-1, NF-IL6 and NF-kappaB) which are involved in IL-6 regulation. *Leukemia* 1996; 10:1308-1316.

30. Cordle SR, Donald R, Read MA, Hawiger J. Lipopolysaccharide induces phophorylation of MAD3 and activation of c-Rel and related NF-κB proteins in human monocytic THP-1 cells. *J Biol Chem* 1993; 268:11803-11810.

31. Trebilcock GU, Ponnappan U. Evidence for lowered induction of nuclear factor kappa B in activated human T lymphocytes during aging. *Gerontology* 1996; 42:137-146.

32. Riancho JA, Zarrabeitia MT, Amado JA, Olmos JM, Gonzalez-Macias J. Age-related differences in cytokine secretion. *Gerontology* 1994; 40:8-12.

33. Caruso C, Candore G, Cigna D, DiLorenzo G, Sireci G, Dieli F, Salerno A. Cytokine production pathway in the elderly. *Immunol Res* 1996; 15:84-90.

34. Molteni M, Della BS, Mascagni B, Coppola C, De MV, Zulian, Birindelli S, Vanoli M, Scorza R. Secretion of cytokines upon allogeneic stimulation: effect of aging. *J Biol Regul Homeost Agents* 1994; 8:41-47.

35. Gon Y, Hashimoto S, Hayashi S, Koura T, Matsumoto K, Horie T. Lower serum concentrations of cytokines in elderly patients with pneumonia and the impaired production of cytokines by peripheral blood monocytes in the elderly. *Clin Exp Immunol* 1996; 106:120-126.

36. Bradley SF, Vibhagool A, Kunkel SL, Kauffman CA. Monokine secretion in aging and protein malnutrition. *J Leuk Biol* 1989; 45:510-514.

37. Ershler WB, Sun WH, Binkley N, Gravenstein S, Volk MJ, Kamoske G, Klopp RG, Roecker EB, Daynes RA, Weindruch R. Interleukin-6 and aging: blood levels and mononuclear cell production increase with advancing age and *in vitro* production is modifiable by dietary restriction. *Lymphokine Cytokine Res* 1993; 12:225-230.

38. Daynes RA, Araneo BA, Ershler WB, Maloney C, Li G-Z, Ryu S-Y. Altered regulation of IL-6 production with normal aging: Possible linkage to the age-associated decline in dehyroepiandrosterone and its sulfated derivative. *J Immunol* 1993; 150:5219-5230.

39. Spaulding CC, Walford RL, Effros RB. Calorie restriction inhibits the age-related dysregulation of the cytokines TNF-α and IL-6 in C3B10RF1 mice. *Mech Ageing Dev* 1997; 93:87-94.

40. Volk MJ, Pugh TD, Kim M, Frith CH, Daynes RA, Ershler WB, Weindruch. Dietary restriction from middle age attenuates age-associated lymphoma development and interleukin 6 dysregulation in C57BL/6 mice. *Can Res* 1994; 54:3054-3061.

41. Tang B, Matsuda T, Akira S, Nagata N, Ikehara S, Hirano T, Kishimoto T. Age-associated increase in interleukin 6 in MRL/lpr mice. *Int Immunol* 1991; 3:273-278.

42. Van Snick J. Interleukin-6: An overview. *Annu Rev Immunol* 1990; 8:253-278.

43. Zhou DH, Shanks N, Riechman SE, Liang RM, Kusnecov AW, Rabin BS. Interleukin 6 modulates interleukin-1- and stress-induced activation of the hypothalamic-pituitary-adrenal axis in male rats. *Neuroendocrinology* 1996; 63:227-236.

44. Ballou SP, Lozanski FB, Hodder S, Rzewnicki DL, Mion LC, Sipe JD, Ford AB, Kushner I. Quantitative and qualitative alterations of acute-phase proteins in healthy elderly persons. *Age Ageing* 1996; 25:224-230.

45. Hobbs MV, Weigle WO, Ernst DN. Interleukin-10 production by splenic CD4⁺ cells and cell subsets from young and old mice. *Cell Immunol* 1994; 154:264-272.

46. Spencer NF, Norton SD, Harrison LL, Li G-Z, Daynes RA. Dysregulation of IL-10 production with aging: Possible linkage to the age-associated decline in DHEA and its sulfated derivative. *Exp Gerontology* 1996; 31:393-408.

47. Tateda K, Matsumoto T, Miyazaki S, Yamaguchi K. Lipopolysaccharide-induced lethality and cytokine production in aged mice. *Infect Immun* 1996; 64:769-774.

48. Brohee D, Van Haeuerbeek M, Kennes B, Neve P. Changing patterns of CD5⁺CD20⁺ double positive lymphocytes with ageing and cytotoxix chemotherapy. *Mec Ageing Dev* 1991; 58:127-138.

49. Greeley EH, Kealy RD, Ballam JM, Lawler DF, Segre M. The influence of age on the canine immune system. *Vet Immunol Immunopathol* 1996; 55:1-10.

50. Krishnaraj R, Blandford G. Age-associated alterations in human natural killer cells. 1. Increased activity as per conventional and kinetic analysis. *Clin Immunol Immunopathol* 1987; 45:268-285.

51. Krishnaraj R, Svanborg A. Preferential accumulation of mature NK cells during human immunosenescence. *J Cell Biochem* 1992; 50:386-391.

52. Hsueh CM, Chen SF, Ghanta VK, Hiramoto RN. Involvement of cytokine gene expression in the age-dependent decline of NK cell response. *Cell Immunol* 1996; 173:221-229.

53. Hunter JE. N-3 fatty acids from vegetable oils. *Am J Clin Nutr* 1990; 51:809-814.

54. Raper NR, Cronin FJ, Exler J. Omega-3 fatty acid content of the US food supply. *J Am Coll Nutr* 1992; 11:304-308.

55. Lands WEM. Biochemistry and physiology of n-3 fatty acids. *FASEB J* 1992; 6:2530-2536.

56. Brouard C, Pascaud M. Effects of moderate dietary supplementations with n-3 fatty acids on macrophage and lymphocyte phospholipids and macrophage eicosanoid synthesis in the rat. *Biochim Biophys Acta Lipids Lipid Metab* 1990; 1047:19-28.

57. Guimaràes ARP, Costa Rosa LFBP, Sitnik RH, Curi R. Effect of polyunsaturated (PUFA n-6) and saturated fatty acids-rich diets on macrophage metabolism and function. *Biochem Int* 1991; 23:533-543.

58. Careaga-Houck M, Sprecher H. Effects of fish oil diet on the metabolism of endogenous n-6 and n-3 fatty acids in rat neutrophils. *Biochimica et Biophysica Acta* 1990; 1047:29-34.

59. Somers SD, Chapkin RS, Erickson KL. Alteration of *in vitro* murine peritoneal macrophage function by dietary enrichment with eicosapentaenoic and docosahexaenoic acids in menhaden fish oil. *Cell Immunol* 1989; 123:201-211.

60. Abeywardena MY, McLennan PL, Charnock JS. Differences between *in vivo* and *in vitro* production of eicosanoids following long-term dietary fish oil supplementation in the rat. *Prostaglandins Leukot Essent Fatty Acids* 1991; 42:159-165.

61. Hwang DH, Boudreau M, Chanmugam P. Dietary linolenic acid and longer-chain fatty acids: comparison of effects on arachidonic acid metabolism in rats. *J Nutr* 1988; 118:427-437.

62. Lokesh BR, Kinsella JE. Modulation of prostaglandin synthesis in mouse peritoneal macrophages by enrichment of lipids with either eicosapentaenoic or docosahexaenoic acids *in vitro*. *Immunobiology* 1987; 175:406-419.

63. Lokesh BR, Black JM, German JB, Kinsella JE. Docosahexaenoic acid and other dietary polyunsaturated fatty acids suppress leukotriene synthesis by mouse peritoneal macrophages. *Lipids* 1988; 23:968-972.

64. Mohrhauer H, Holman RT. The effect of dose level of essential fatty acids upon fatty acid composition of the rat liver. *J Lip Res* 1963; 4:151-159.

65. Whelan J, Broughton KS, Kinsella JE. The comparative effects of dietary alpha-linolenic acid and fish oil on 4- and 5-series leukotriene formation *in vivo*. *Lipids* 1991; 26:119-126.

66. Whelan J, Broughton KS, Lokesh B, Kinsella JE. *In vivo* formation of leukotriene E_5 by murine peritoneal cells. *Prostaglandins* 1991; 41:29-42.

67. Boudreau MD, Chanmugam PS, Hart SB, Lee SH, Hwang DH. Lack of dose response by dietary n-3 fatty acids at a constant ratio of n-3 to n-6 fatty acids in suppressing eicosanoid biosynthesis from arachidonic acid. *Am J Clin Nutr* 1991; 54:111-117.

68. Imir T, Sibbitt W, Bankhurst A. The relative resistance of lymphokine activated killer cells to suppression by prostaglandins and glucocorticoids. *Prost Leukotrienes and Med* 1987; 28:111-118.

69. Young MR, Wheeler E, Newby M. Macrophage-mediated suppression of natural killer cell activity in mice bearing Lewis lung carcinoma. *J Natl Can Inst* 1986; 76:745-750.

70. Fisher A, Durandy A, Gricelli C. Role of prostaglandin E_2 in the induction of nonspecific T-lymphocyte suppressor activity. *J Immunol* 1981; 126:1452-1455.

71. Chouiab S, Chatenoud L, Klatzman D, Fradelizi D. The mechanisms of inhibition of human IL-2 production. II. PGE_2 induction of suppressor T lymphocytes. *J Immunol* 1984; 132:1851-1857.

72. Snyder DS, Beller DI, Unanue ER. Prostaglandins modulate macrophage Ia expression. *Nature* 1982; 299:163-165.

73. Chouiab S, Welte K, Mertelsmann R, Dupont B. Prostaglandin E_2 acts at two distinct pathways of T lymphocyte activation: Inhibition of interleukin 2 production and down-regulation of transferrin receptor expression. *J Immunol* 1985; 135:1172-1179.

74. Scales WE, Chensue SW, Otterness I, Kunkel SL. Regulation of monokine gene expression:Prostaglandin E_2 suppresses tumor necrosis factor but not interleukin-1-alpha or beta-mRNA and cell-associated bioactivity. *J Leuk Biol* 1989; 45:416-421.

75. Kunkel SL, Remick DG, Strieter RM, Larrick JW. Mechanisms that regulate the production and effects of tumor necrosis factor-α. *CRC Crit Rev Immunol* 1989; 9:93-117.

76. Van der Pouw Kraan TCTM, Boeije LCM, Smeenk RJT, Wijdenes J, Aarden LA. Prostaglandin-E_2 is a potent inhibitor of human interleukin 12 production. *J Exp Med* 1995; 181:775-779.

77. Shapiro AC, Wu D, Meydani SN. Eicosanoids derived from arachidonic and eicosapentaenoic acids inhibit T cell proliferative response. *Prostaglandins* 1993; 45:229-240.

78. Vaughn DM, Reinhart GA, Swaim SF, Lauten SD, Garner CA. Evaluation of dietary n-6 to n-3 fatty acid ratios on leukotriene B synthesis in dog skin and neutrophils. *Vet Derm* 1994; 5:163-173.

79. Watanabe S, Hayashi H, Onozaki K, Okuyama H. Effect of dietary α-linolenate/linoleate balance on lipopolysaccharide-induced tumor necrosis factor production in mouse macrophages. *Life Sci* 1991; 48:2013-2020.

80. Lokesh BR, Sayers TJ, Kinsella JE. Interleukin-1 and tumor necrosis factor synthesis by mouse peritoneal macrophages is enhanced by dietary n-3 polyunsaturated fatty acids. *Immunol Lett* 1990; 23:281-286.

81. Chang HR, Arsenijevic D, Pechère JC, Piguet PF, Mensi N, Girardier L, Dulloo AG. Dietary supplementation with fish oil enhances *in vivo* synthesis of tumor necrosis factor. *Immunol Lett* 1992; 34:13-18.

82. Somers SD, Erickson KL. Alteration of tumor necrosis factor-α production by macrophages from mice fed diets high in eicosapentaenoic and docosahexaenoic fatty acids. *Cell Immunol* 1994; 153:287-297.

83. Endres S, Meydani SN, Ghorbani R, Schindler R, Dinarello CA. Dietary supplementation with n-3 fatty acids suppresses interleukin-2 production and mononuclear cell proliferation. *J Leuk Biol* 1993; 54:599-603.

84. Leslie CA, Gonnerman WA, Ullman MD, Hayes KC, Franzblau C, Cathcart ES. Dietary fish oil modulates macrophage fatty acids and decreases arthritis susceptibility in mice. *J Exp Med* 1985; 162:1336-1349.

85. Hardard'ottir I, Whelan J, Kinsella JE. Kinetics of tumour necrosis factor and prostaglandin production by murine resident peritoneal macrophages as affected by dietary n-3 polyunsaturated fatty acids. *Immunology* 1992; 76:572-577.

86. Turek JJ, Schoenlein IA. Indomethacin-induced gastrointestinal ulcers in rats: Effects of dietary fatty acids and endotoxin. *Prostaglandins Leukot Essent Fatty Acids* 1993; 48:229-232.

87. Downs TR, Wilfinger WW. Fluorometric quantitation of DNA in cells and tissues. *Anal Biochem* 1983; 131:538-547.

88. Hansen MB, Nielsen SE, Berg K. Re-examination and further development of a precise and rapid dye method for measuring cell growth/cell kill. *J Immunol Methods* 1989; 119:203-210.

89. Aarden LA, De Groot ER, Schaap OL, Lansdorp PM. Production of hybridoma growth factor by monocytes. *Eur J Immunol* 1987; 17:1411-1416.

90. Karavodin LM, Glasebrook AL, Phelps JL. Decline in growth and antibody production of established hybridomas and transfectomas with addition of interleukin 6. *Eur J Immunol* 1989; 19:1351-1354.

91. Sprecher HJ. A reevaluation of the pathway for the biosynthesis of 4,7,10,13,16,19-docosapentaenoic acid. *Omega 3 News* 1992; 7:1-5.

92. Masters C. Omega-3 fatty acids and the peroxisome. *Mol Cell Biochem* 1996; 165:83-93.

93. Scott DW, Miller WHJ, Reinhart GA, Mohammed HO, Bagladi MS. Effect of an omega-3/omega-6 fatty acid-containing commercial lamb and rice diet on pruritus in atopic dogs: results of a single-blinded study. *Can J Vet Res* 1997; 61:145-153.

94. Hardardottir I, Kinsella JE. Tumor necrosis factor production by murine resident peritoneal macrophages is enhanced by dietary n-3 polyunsaturated fatty acids. *Biochim Biophys Acta Mol Cell Res* 1991; 1095:187-195.

95. Wander RC, Hall JA, Gradin JL, Du SH, Jewell DE. The ratio of dietary n-6 to n-3 fatty acids influences immune system function, eicosanoid metabolism, lipid peroxidation and vitamin E status in aged dogs. *J Nutr* 1997; 127:1198-1205.

The Influence of Dietary Omega-6:Omega-3 Ratio on Lameness in Dogs with Osteoarthrosis of the Elbow Joint

Herman A.W. Hazewinkel, DVM, PhD, DECVS
Head, Section of Orthopedics and Neurosurgery
Department of Clinical Sciences of Companion Animals
Utrecht University, The Netherlands

Lars F.H. Theyse, DVM, DRNVA[a]; Walter E. van den Brom, PhD[a];
Pim A.Th. Wolvekamp, DVM, PhD, DECVDI[b];
Gregory A. Reinhart, PhD[c]; Richard C. Nap, DVM, PhD[d]

[a]Department of Clinical Sciences of Companion Animals
[b]Veterinary Radiology, Faculty of Veterinary Medicine
Utrecht University, The Netherlands
[c]Research and Development, The Iams Company, Lewisburg, Ohio, USA
[d]Iams Pet Food International (Europe), Eindhoven, The Netherlands

Introduction

A variety of orthopedic and non-orthopedic diseases eventually lead to osteoarthritis (OA). The number of orthopedic patients with OA exceeds all other categories of causes of lameness.[1] In a variety of breeds, the major factor contributing to OA that involves front leg lameness is elbow dysplasia. This includes fragmented coronoid processes (FCP), osteochondritis dissecans (OCD), and ununited anconeal processes (UCP).[2] Osteoarthritis will continue to influence the clinical signs of lameness and thus the quality of life for the animal and its owner even if the underlying cause of OA can be treated surgically. This is due to the fact that in the course of OA, synovitis will develop, and inflamed synovial cells release a variety of factors that induce chondrocytes to degenerate the cartilaginous matrix. These factors include inflammatory mediators, such as leukotrienes. Leukotrienes (LTs) are a group of compounds (LTA, LTB, LTC, LTD, and LTE) that arise from the metabolism of the fatty acids arachidonic acid (AA; 20:4n-6) and eicosapentaenoic acid (EPA; 20:5n-3) through the 5-lipoxygenase pathway (**Figure 1**). The type of LT that is synthesized by injured cells depends on the proportion of AA and EPA fatty acids which originate from dietary omega-6 (n-6) fatty acids (e.g., linoleic acid) and omega-3 (n-3) fatty acids (e.g., α-linolenic acid; ALA), since there is no conversion in the animal from n-3 to n-6 fatty acid, or vice versa. In addition, docosahexaenoic acid (DHA; 22:6n-3) can serve as a precursor for EPA[3,4] and be metabolized into leukotriene. Arachidonic acid and EPA are the precursors of the leukotrienes LT_4 and LT_5, respectively. LTA is unstable and rapidly converted to LTB or LTC. LTC is subsequently transformed to LTD and LTE.[5,6]

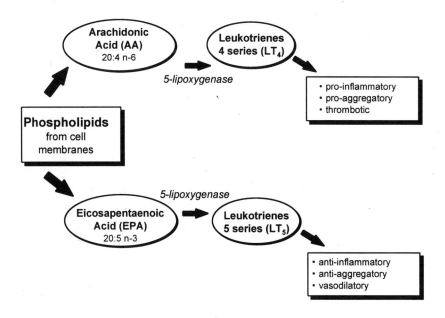

Figure 1. The type of LT that is synthesized by injured cells depends on the fatty acid (AA or EPA) released from the cell membranes.

Increased dietary intake of EPA during 8 weeks by normal human subjects and patients with asthma revealed increased LTB_5 and decreased LTB_4 production by leucocytes, with significantly suppressed chemotactic responses of these cells.[3] Numerous biochemical, physiological, and human clinical studies demonstrated the vasodilatory and anti-platelet aggregatory effects of EPA.[4] In dogs, dietary supplementation with omega-3 fatty acids also shifted the leukotriene biosynthesis from LTB_4 to LTB_5.[7] In the human,[8] the dog,[9] and the cat,[10] skin condition improved when the composition of fatty acids in the diet was changed. It is hypothesized that dietary supplementation of omega-3 fatty acids (EPA, DHA, ALA) might represent a new approach to thromboembolism and anti-inflammatory therapy, including osteoarthrosis in man and companion animals.[3,4]

Normally, dogs receive far more dietary n-6 fatty acids than n-3 fatty acids since most pet food ingredients of mammalian origin have n-6:n-3 fatty acid ratios greater than 10:1. Fish oils, containing large amounts of n-3 fatty acids, are considered to be anti-inflammatory as well as vasodilatory and anti-aggregatory. Vaughn et al.[7] fed 5 diets with different dietary n-6:n-3 ratios (5, 10, 25, 50, and 100:1) to 5 different treatment groups of 6 dogs each. Dogs fed diets with n-6:n-3 ratios of 5:1 and 10:1 had decreased concentrations of LTB_4 and increased concentrations of LTB_5 in LPS-stimulated skin at 12 weeks and in calcium ionophore-challenged neutrophils at 6 and 12 weeks.

It was hypothesized that an intake of predominantly n-3 fatty acids would decrease the clinical signs of OA in dogs. The results of this double blind, prospective study investigated the effects of dietary fatty acid content on locomotion in two groups of dogs suffering from OA of the elbow joints due to elbow dysplasia. One of two diets, differing only in the n-6:n-3 fatty acid ratio, was fed to dogs for 12 weeks after a uniform wash out diet was fed for 6 weeks. In addition to clinical and biochemical measurements, locomotion was objectively evaluated by force-plate analysis.

Dogs. All dogs in this research project were patients of the Utrecht University's Department of Clinical Sciences of Companion Animals and diagnosed as affected by osteoarthritis (OA) secondary to elbow dysplasia without other orthopedic problems. The study included a total of 36 dogs with a breed distribution of 17 Labrador Retrievers, 7 Bernese Mountain Dogs, 4 Rottweilers, 2 Boxers, 3 German Shepherd Dogs, 2 Bouviers, and one Bullmastiff. There were 18 intact males, 10 intact females, and 8 ovariohysterectomized female dogs. The diagnosis elbow dysplasia was based on clinical and radiological examination and made at least 8 months before the start of this study.

Dogs, Materials, and Methods

Materials.

Diets. The formulas used in this investigation (diets A, B, and C) were manufactured specifically for this study with the nutrient compositions as listed in **Table 1**. All diets were formulated to be isonitrogenous and isoenergetic. Ingredient sources and levels were kept constant across all diets, with the exception of fat source. Chicken fat, menhaden fish oil, flax, and safflower oil were used in various combinations to achieve a targeted dietary n-6:n-3 ratio (**Table 2**). Total fat level did not vary across diet. Diet A was used as a wash-out diet while diets B and C were the test formulas. The nutrient profile of Diet A met the NRC '74 requirements with a dietary n-6:n-3 ratio of approximately 25:1. During the test period, a similar nutrient matrix was fed. The test diets differed only in the fatty acid composition with an n-6:n-3 ratio of 5:1 (diet B) or 50:1 (diet C).

Table 1. Nutrient composition of experimental diets.

Item	Diet*		
	A	**B**	**C**
Crude Protein, %	27.77	28.96	27.53
Crude Fat, %	17.69	17.62	17.54
Nitrogen Free Extract, %	47.10	45.42	46.92
Ash, %	5.80	6.20	5.88
Crude Fiber, %	1.64	1.80	2.13
Gross Energy, cal/g	5348	5355	5377
Omega-3 fatty acids, % of total fatty acids	0.9	4.0	0.8
Omega-6 fatty acids, % of total fatty acids	21.8	19.6	38.5
Omega-6:omega-3 fatty acid ratio	23.1:1	4.9:1	50.4:1

*Data expressed on a dry matter basis.

Table 2. Dietary ingredients of experimental diets.

Ingredient	Diet		
	A	**B**	**C**
Chicken protein*	29.0	29.0	29.0
Ground corn	27.0	27.0	27.0
Brewers rice	26.5	26.5	26.5
Chicken fat	6.3	4.3	2.7
Fish oil	—	1.7	—
Flax	—	0.3	—
Safflower oil	—	—	3.6
Beet pulp	4.0	4.0	4.0
Dried whole egg	2.5	2.5	2.5
Liver digest	2.0	2.0	2.0
Brewers yeast	1.0	1.0	1.0
DL-methionine	0.1	0.1	0.1
Vitamins/minerals	1.6	1.6	1.6

*Combination of fresh chicken and chicken by-product meal.

Force Plate Equipment. A quartz crystal piezoelectric force plate was used and mounted flush with the surface in the center of an 11 meter long runway. The central 5 meters of the runway were bordered by a 50 centimeter high fence to direct the dogs over the force plate. The width of the fenced part of the runway and the force plate itself were 60 centimeters. The force plate was 40 centimeters long. Forward velocity was measured, using photoelectric switches and a millisecond timer spaced 3 meters apart and centered on the force plate. The force plate recordings were automatically started and stopped by these photoelectric switches. The signals from three force transducers, corresponding with the ground reaction forces in the transverse direction Fx, the longitudinal direction Fy, and the vertical direction Fz, were amplified and fed into the three channels of an analog-digital converter interfaced with a personal computer. The sampling rate was 100 Hz. Recordings for force plate analysis (FPA) were saved on disk for further processing.

Laboratory Investigations. Blood samples were drawn from the jugular vein with the dog in a sitting position. Urine samples were collected by catheterization. Radiographs were performed without anesthesia, using table-top technique according to Voorhout et al.[11]

Methods.
Protocol. Thirty-six dogs were recruited for this investigation according to the following selection criteria: large breed (>25 kg body weight); sex (equally divided); adult age; body composition (not more than 15% overweight); lame

(noticeably lame due to elbow dysplasia, without other clinical abnormalities); leash trained; owner able and willing to travel and to participate, and willing to feed only the test diet without adding other nutrients or medication. All dogs were healthy in all respects other than the elbow dysplasia.

The physical investigation included a history taking (focused on daily exercise pattern and daily food intake), and a general and orthopedic investigation.[12] The elbow dysplasia diagnosis was made by radiological investigation of all dogs at their referral, at least 8 months before the start of this study, and in some cases, via elbow surgery. Of all clinically affected elbow joints the following radiographic views were made according to the technique published earlier: mediolateral extended, mediolateral flexed, anterior-posterior, anterior-posterior medial oblique, and in some cases the mediolateral 15 degrees exorotated view was also added.[13] When joint surgery was performed, the approach was as reported earlier.[14] In essence, a medial arthrotomy was performed without desmotomy of the medial collateral and/or annular ligament or osteotomy, removal of loose bodies, and thorough flushing before closure. Surgery was performed at least 8 months prior to the start of the study.

Radiological investigation included OA scoring at the start of this study. The criteria of the International Elbow Working Group (IEWG) was utilized on mediolateral views of both elbow joints in a 60 degrees flexed position.[2,11] Body weight was measured and body score[15] registered. Blood analysis included WBC (total and differential), total proteins, protein spectrum, antinuclear antibodies, urea, creatinine, and bile acids. Routine urine screening was performed to confirm general health status and included specific gravity, pH, protein and glucose concentrations.

The owners of healthy dogs with elbow dysplasia were invited to participate in the following program: feeding the test diet to maintain a constant body weight, keeping a daily log, and returning to the university clinic for screening at 6 weeks intervals. The group of 36 dogs was divided randomly into two groups of 18 dogs each which are referred to as diet group B and C.

The following examinations were performed in all dogs at 6 week intervals: history taking, clinical examination, blood analysis, and force plate analysis. Analysis for the presence of non-steroid anti-inflammatory drugs (NSAIDs, including: naproxen, diclofenac, ibuprofen, indomethacin, salicylic acid, diflunisal, sulindac, ketoprofen and piroxicam) and determination of leukotriene B_4 (LTB_4) concentration in plasma was performed at 6, 12, and 18 weeks. At 18 weeks LTB_4 analysis was also conducted in urine.

Feeding Regimen. At the start of the study all dogs were preconditioned on diet A. This food was used as a wash-out diet and fed exclusively for 6 weeks. The owner was then provided with test diet coded B or C; the dietary composition of food B and C was not known to either the owner or the investigators. The code was broken when all findings were reported. After 6 weeks the dogs were fed either food B or C for the next 12 weeks. The owners were thoroughly informed only to feed the test diet and to leave out any treats, bones, table scraps, etc. At each followup visit, the owner was interviewed about the acceptance of the diet during the past 6 week period.

Force Plate Analysis. Force plate analysis (FPA) was performed at the start of the study, after 6 weeks on diet A, and after 6 and 12 weeks on either diet B or C. The dogs were guided over the force plate in an ambling gait by one single handler at a controlled speed. A minimum of 8 recordings per front and hind leg were obtained. The following parameters were used for further analysis: maximum breaking force (Fy_{max}), maximum propulsive force (Fy_{min}), and the maximum vertical force (Fz_{max}) of the front legs. All forces were normalized for body weight.

Statistics. For statistical analysis the front legs were categorized as "most affected limb" and "less affected limb" based on the force plate recordings. Data were evaluated using ANOVA for repeated measures. Differences were considered significant for values of $P<0.05$.

The investigation was approved by the ethical committee of the Department Clinical Sciences of Companion Animal Studies and The Iams Company. The owner was fully informed and approved to cooperate before the start of the study.

Results

One dog was rejected from the study (German Shepherd, 18 months of age, with surgically diagnosed FCP plus UAP in one elbow joint) since NSAID-medication was prescribed for an episode of severe skeletal pain of previously diagnosed panosteitis eosinophylica (enostosis).

Breed, gender, age, weight, and body score for each dietary group is given in **Tables 3** and **4**. Based on the findings of the radiographs made at their first visit, and in some elbows undergoing surgery following this visit, the diagnosis was FCP in one or both elbow joints in 35 dogs. In 3 of these cases, FCP was accompanied with OCD. None of the dogs had incongruity in the elbow joints or other causes of lameness in the front or rear legs. Surgery of the elbow joint was performed in all animals, with 11 of the animals having bilateral surgery. **Tables 3** and **4** indicate if the elbow was treated surgically or non-surgically and the OA score, according to the IEWG, is given for each elbow joint.

Acceptance of the experimental diets was good, except in one case (a 46 kg Bernese Mountain Dog) on food C, but the body weight of this dog did not change during the period of investigation. No dogs were rejected from the study based on major changes in food intake or changes in body weight.

Cytological and biochemical results of blood and urine analysis did not reveal any values outside the range of reference values of our laboratory. None of the

Table 3. Characteristics of dogs and their elbow joints of diet group B.

Breed	Gender	Age (yr–mo)	Body Wt (kg)	Body Score	FCP/– Surgery (+/–) Left Elbow	FCP/– Surgery (+/–) Right Elbow	OA Score Left Elbow	OA Score Right Elbow
lab	F	2–1	26	3	FCP (+)	FCP (–)	3	2
lab	F*	6–1	35	3	– (–)	FCP (+)	0	2
lab	M	2–9	36	2	FCP (+)	FCP (–)	3	3
lab	M	7–9	31	4	FCP (+)	FCP (+)	2	2
lab	M	2–6	40	4	FCP (–)	FCP (+)	2	0
lab	M	1–9	31.5	3	FCP (+)	– (–)	1	0
lab	M	1–11	27	3	FCP (+)	– (–)	3	0
lab	F*	3–0	29	3	FCP and OCD (+)	– (–)	2	0
lab	F*	5–9	29	4	FCP (+)	FCP (+)	3	2
bmd	F	1–8	37	4	FCP (+)	FCP (+)	1	1
bmd	M	1–8	42	3	FCP (+)	FCP (+)	3	3
bmd	M	2–8	43	4	FCP (–)	FCP (+)	3	2
rotw	F*	8–10	35	4	FCP (+)	FCP (–)	2	1
rotw	F	5–1	45	3	FCP (+)	FCP (+)	2	2
bouv	M	2–6	42	4	FCP and OCD (–)	FCP and OCD (–)	3	3
boxer	M	3–9	32	3	FCP (+)	– (–)	1	1
bullma	M	4–1	62	4	– (–)	FCP (+)	0	1

* Ovariohysterectomized; FCP/– = fragmented coronoid process present/not present; OCD = osteochondritis dissecans present; surgery (+/–) = surgery performed/not performed

Table 4. Characteristics of dogs and their elbow joints of diet group C.

Breed	Gender	Age (yr–mo)	Body Wt (kg)	Body Score	FCP/– Surgery (+/–) Left Elbow	FCP/– Surgery (+/–) Right Elbow	OA Score Left Elbow	OA Score Right Elbow
lab	F	5–9	34	4	FCP (+)	FCP (+)	3	3
lab	M	1–8	27	3	FCP (+)	FCP (–)	1	3
lab	M	1–7	35.5	4	FCP and OCD (+)	FCP and OCD (–)	2	2
lab	F*	2–3	30	3	FCP	– (–)	1	0
lab	M	2–11	30	3	FCP (–)	FCP (+)	1	0
lab	M	1–9	34	3	FCP (–)	FCP (+)	3	1
lab	F*	4–8	34.5	4	FCP (–)	FCP (+)	3	3
lab	F*	7–1	37	4	FCP (+)	FCP (–)	3	3
bmd	M	2–9	46	4	FCP (+)	FCP (+)	3	2
bmd	M	6–2	43	3	FCP (+)	FCP (+)	3	3
bmd	F	2–10	33	4	FCP (+)	FCP (+)	2	1
bmd	F	2–8	38	4	FCP (+)	FCP (+)	3	3
rotw	M	1–8	47	4	FCP (+)	FCP (–)	2	2
rotw	F	3–5	38	4	FCP (–)	FCP (+)	3	3
gsh	F	2–4	36	4	FCP (+)	– (–)	3	1
gsh	M	6–0	35	3	FCP (+)	FCP (+)	3	3
bouv	F	2–11	37.5	2	– (–)	FCP (+)	0	3
boxer	M	2–9	34.5	3	FCP (–)	FCP (+)	0	1

* Ovariohysterectomized; FCP/– = fragmented coronoid process present/not present; OCD = osteochondritis dissecans present; surgery (+/–) = surgery performed/not performed owners of the 35 dogs in the study reported medication with NSAIDs, cortico-steroids or any other drugs. The laboratory analysis of the NSAIDs tested did not reveal any plasma concentrations above the detection limit (i.e., 0.2 mg/L plasma) except salicylic acid (0.5–0.7 mg/L) being detected in 3 dogs from both groups. Results on LTB_4 were not available at the time of the report of this study.

The force plate analysis showed no differences between the treatment groups at the start of the study, the treatment groups at week 6 (after the wash-out diet A), and the treatment groups at week 12 and 18 (after diet B or C). The means (and SEM) of Fy_{max}, Fy_{min}, and Fz_{max} for both groups at the start of the study (day 0), at the end of the period of diet A (week 6), after 6 weeks on diet B or C (week 12), and after 12 weeks on diet B or C (week 18), for the most and less affected limb, respectively, are represented in **Figures 2-4**.

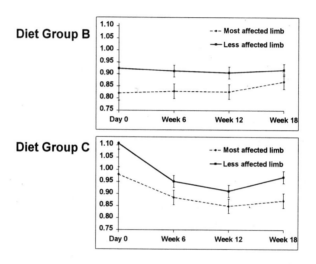

Figure 2. Force plate results Fy_{max} of diet groups B and C.

Discussion

Osteoarthritis due to FCP is frequently seen in large breed dogs with a high incidence in certain breeds (e.g., 18% in Labradors and 72% in Bernese Mountain Dogs of young age in the Netherlands).[16] Despite the removal of the FCP, OA continues to develop in a majority of cases. A variety of measures for conservative treatment of OA or treatment after surgery have been suggested, including limited exercise, decreased body weight, and NSAIDs.[17] Leukotriene B_4 is significantly increased in synovial fluid of humans with rheumatoid arthritis[3] and dogs with infectious and experimental arthritis[18,19] due to its increased production by synoviocytes as well as an increased infiltration of the joint with LT producing macrophages and PMN leukocytes. In the design of this study, a non-invasive evaluation of the OA was chosen in order to not disturb joint integrity by arthrocenthesis. In human patients with rheumatoid arthritis, clinical improvement was reached with the consumption of fish oil, possibly by the decreased production

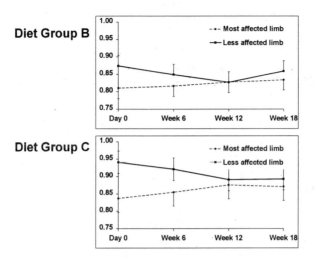

Figure 3. Force plate results Fy_{min} of diet groups B and C.

of LTB_4 and the increased production of LTB_5.[20] The related symptoms of hyperalgesia or tenderness, aching, and stiffness in OA are attributed to the effects of mediators including LTB_4 on the nociceptive pathway of the peripheral nervous system.[3] The n-6 fatty acids are substrates for LT_4 and the n-3 fatty acids for LT_5 production. Leukotriene B_5 is 30–100 times less active in stimulating the LTB receptor than LTB_4.[21]

Based on these reports and the findings that dogs with a lowered dietary n-6:n-3 fatty acid ratio resulted in decreased LTB_4 and increased LTB_5 production,[7]

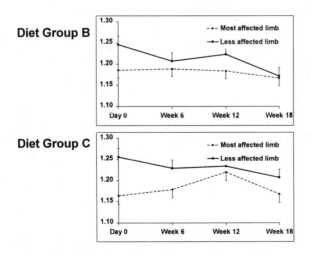

Figure 4. Force plate results Fz_{max} of diet groups B and C.

it was decided to investigate the clinical effects of diets with a constant dietary content that differed in n-6:n-3 fatty acid ratios.

Supplementation of the regular diet of the dogs with n-3 fatty acid containing capsules was not considered since the absolute amount of n-3 fatty acids is not as important as the relative amounts of n-6 and n-3 fatty acids. This is due to the fact that both fatty acids compete for the same enzyme systems (**Figure 1**).[6] Because n-3 fatty acids are unstable, adequate antioxidant protection and increased levels of vitamin E in the diets were necessary. From studies in dogs, dietary n-6:n-3 fatty acid ratios of 5:1 and 10:1 fed for 12 weeks resulted in significant differences in LTB_4 and LTB_5 content in plasma and skin[7] without side effects of lethargy, pruritis, vomiting, diarrhea, or urticaria.[9,22] Similarly, in this study, all dogs were fed a common washout diet for 6 weeks, followed by dietary treatments for an additional 12 weeks.

In reports on the effects of fish oil supplementation in humans, the most mentioned side effect is the fish taste in the mouth, especially after belching.[23] Except for one dog in group C, decreased appetite was not reported. No negative side effects of the food were reported. The salicylic acid concentrations found in three dogs is far under the therapeutic dose as is reported for dogs (i.e., 50–324 mg salicylate per L of plasma).[24] Each owner assured the investigators the salicylic acid did not originate from medication. The vegetable origin of salicylic acid seems to be the most likely explanation.

Ground reaction forces are considered to give an objective reflection of normal[25,26] and disturbed locomotion.[27] In case of a decreased weight bearing of one front leg, Fz forces are decreased on the affected side with a noticeable effect on symmetry. In the case of painful processes in the front leg, maximum breaking and propulsive forces will be decreased. In the case of bilaterally affected animals, evaluation of the most affected limb, based on the first measurements, is an accepted method of investigation of locomotion.[28] Some dogs improved while others deteriorated based on the ground reaction forces after 6 weeks on diet A, or after 6 or 12 weeks on diet B or C. Neither ground reaction forces nor reports of the owners revealed any consistency within dietary treatment groups.

A study in dogs revealed that variations in the dietary n-6:n-3 fatty acid ratio altered LTB_4 generation in the neutrophils after 6 weeks and in the skin after 12 weeks.[7] Although plasma levels of LTB_4 are not available yet for this study, the difference in dietary n-6:n-3 fatty acid ratio did not lead to consistent and significant differences in locomotion in this 12 week period of investigation. It is concluded that the dietary n-6:n-3 fatty acid ratios evaluated in this study were not effective in the treatment of OA of the elbow joint.

Acknowledgements   The following persons are acknowledged: Mr. H. de Groot for technical assistance in force plate measurements, Dr. Th. Wensing, (biochemist Dept. Large Animal Medicine, Utrecht University) for arranging NSAID measurements,

Dr. C.H.P. Pellicaan, (pharmacist Veterinary Faculty, Utrecht University), for randomization.

1. Johnson JA, Austin C, Breur GJ. Incidence of canine appendicular musculoskeletal disorders in 16 veterinary teaching hospitals from 1980-1989. *J Vet Comp Ortho & Trauma* 1994; 7:56-69.

2. Flückiger M. Radiographic diagnosis of elbow dysplasia in the dog: requirements for the internationally standardized screening procedure. *Proceedings International Elbow Working Group*, Birmingham (UK), 1997; 3-4.

3. Goetzl EJ, Goldstein IM. Arachidonic acid metabolism. In: McCarty DJ, ed. *Arthritis and Allied Conditions*. Philadelphia: Lea & Febiger, 1989; 409-425.

4. McIntosh Bright J. Effects of n-3 fatty acid supplementation on feline platelet function. *Proc 11th ACVIM Forum*, Washington DC, 1993; 513-515.

5. Padrid P, Snook S, Mitchell R, Finucane T, Spaethe S, Shiue P, Cozzi P, Ndukwu M, Leff A. Data derived from an expermental model of feline asthma. *Proc 11th ACVIM Forum*, Washington DC, 1993; 142-145.

6. Reinhart GA. Review of omega-3 fatty acids and dietary influences on tissue concentrations. In: Carey DP, Norton SA, Bolser SM, eds. *Recent Advances in Canine and Feline Nutritional Research: Proceedings of the 1996 Iams International Nutrition Symposium*. Wilmington: Orange Frazer Press, 1996; 235-242.

7. Vaughn DM, Reinhart GA, Swaim SF, Lauten SD, Boudreaux MK, Spano JS, Hoffman SD. Evaluation of dietary n-6 to n-3 fatty acid ratios on leukotriene B synthesis in dog skin and neutrophils. *Vet Derm* 1994; 5:163-173.

8. Kunz B, Ring J, Braun-Falco O. Eicosapentaenoic acid (EPA) treatment in atopic eczema (AE): a prospective double-blind trial. *J Allergy Clin Immunol* 1989; 83:196-174.

9. Scott DW, Buerger RG. Non-steroidal anti-inflammatory agents in the management of canine pruritis. *J Am Anim Hosp Assoc* 1988; 24:425-428.

10. Harvey RG. Effect of varying proportions of evening primrose oil and fish oil in cats with crusting dermatosis. *Vet Record* 1993; 133:208-211.

11. Voorhout G, Hazewinkel HAW. Radiological evaluation of the canine elbow joint with special reference to the medial humeral condyle and the medial coronoid process. *Vet Rad* 1987; 28:158-165.

12. Hazewinkel HAW, Meutstege FJ. Locomotor system. In: *Medical History and Physical Examination in Companion Animals*. Norwell: Kluwer Academic Publishers, 1995; 175-201.

13. Hazewinkel HAW, Meij BP, Theyse LFH. Surgical treatment of elbow dysplasia. In: *Canine Skeletal Development & Soundness, Proc TNAVC* 1998; 29-35.

14. Hazewinkel HAW, Kantor A, Meij BP, Voorhout G. Fragmented coronoid process and osteochondritis dissecans of the medial humeral condyle. *Tijdschr Diergeneesk* 1988; 113:41-46.

15. Case LP, Carey DP, Hirakawa DA. Development and treatment of obesity. In: *Canine and Feline Nutrition, A Resource for Companion Animal Professionals*. Boston: Mosby, 1995; 271-292.

References

16. Ubbink GJ, van de Broek, Hazewinkel HAW, Rothuizen J. Risk-estimates for fragmented coronoid process in Dutch purebred dog populations. *Proceedings International Elbow Working Group*, Birmingham (UK), 1997; 13-15.

17. Bennett DB. Joints and joint diseases. In: Whittick WG, ed. *Canine Orthopedics 2nd edition*. Philadelphia: Lea & Febiger, 1990; 761-853.

18. Herlin T, Fogh K, Ewald H, Hansen ES, Kudsen V, Holm I, Kragballe K, Bunger C. Changes in lipoxygenase products from synovial fluid in carragheenan induced arthritis in dogs. *Acta Pathol Micro Immunol Scand 96 (Section C)* 1988; 601-604.

19. Herlin T, Fogh K, Hansen ES, Andreasen A, Knudsen V, Hendriksen TB, Bunger C, Kragballe K. 15-HETE inhibits leukotriene B_4 formation and synovial cell proliferation in experimental arthritis. *Agents and Actions* 1990; 29:52-53.

20. Kremer JM, Jubiz W, Michalek A, Rynes RI, Bartholomew LE, Bigaouette J, Timchalk M, Beeler D, Lininger L. Fish oil fatty acid supplementation in active rheumatoid arthritis. *Ann Intern Med* 1987; 106:497-503.

21. Lee TH, Sethi T, Crea AE, Peters W, Arm JP, Horton CE, Walport MJ, Spur BWI. Characterization of leukotriene B_3: comparison of its biological activities with leukotriene B_4 and leukotriene B_5 in complement receptor enhancement, lysozyme release and chemotaxis of human neutrophils. *Clin Sci* 1988; 74:467-475.

22. Landhmore EW, Cameron CA, Sheridan BL. Reduction of intimal hyperplasia in canine autologous vein grafts with cod liver oil and dipryidamole. *Can J Surg* 1986; 29:357-358.

23. Korstanje MHJ, Bilo HJG, Peltenburg HG, Stoof TJ. Visolie, van voeding tot medicijn? *Ned Tijdschr Geneesk* 1991; 135:828-833.

24. Nap RC, Peters IOM, Willemsen A, de Bruyne JJ. Aspirin medication in dogs, the influence of tablet type and feeding regimen on plasma salicylate concentrations. *Vet Comp Ortho & Trauma* 1991; 4:95-99.

25. Budsberg SC, Verstraete MC, Soutas-Little RW. Force plate analysis of the walking gait in healthy dogs. *Am J Vet Res* 1987; 48:915-918.

26. Budsberg SC, Jevens DJ, Brown J, Foutz TL, DeCamp CE, Reece L. Evaluation of limb symmetry indices using ground reaction forces in healthy dogs. *Am J Vet Res* 1993; 54:1569-1674.

27. Maarschalkerweerd RJ, Hazewinkel HAW, Meij BP, Theyse LTF, Van den Brom WE. Carpal arthrodesis in dogs, a retrospective study with force plate analysis. In: van Sluijs FJ, Auer JA, eds. *Proceedings 5th Annual Meeting of the European College of Veterinary Surgeons*. Addix bv, Wijk bij Duurstede, The Netherlands, 1996; 49.

28. Bouck GR, Miller CW, Taves CL. A comparison of surgical and medical treatment of fragmented coronoid process and osteochondritis dissecans of the canine elbow. *Vet Comp Ortho & Trauma* 1995; 8:177-183.

Microbial Changes in Aged Dogs

Robert J. Kearns, PhD
Associate Professor, Department of Biology
University of Dayton, Dayton, Ohio, USA

Michael G. Hayek, PhD; Gregory D. Sunvold, PhD
Research and Development, The Iams Company, Lewisburg, Ohio, USA

The gastrointestinal tract of man and companion animals represents a *Introduction* complex ecosystem, harboring over 400 different species of microorganisms.[1,2] In addition, this unique ecosystem consists of open, integrated, and interactive units each possessing a microbial community of one or more species indigenous to that specific region.[3] Therefore, it is not difficult to understand that the dynamic relationship that exists between diet and intestinal microflora not only contributes significantly to the health of the host, but has also been instrumental in the development of strategies efficacious in the enhancement and maintenance of bacteria with health promoting properties. The target of these strategies in humans is manipulation of the intestinal tract microflora resulting in an increase in either *Bifidobacterium* or *Lactobacillus*. Modifying the composition of colonic microflora can be achieved by supplementing the diet with probiotics or prebiotics.[4,5,6] Probiotics are defined as "live microbial feed supplements which beneficially affect the host animal by improving its intestinal microbial balance".[4] The major drawback to using probiotics is that although they are effective in promoting the growth of beneficial bacteria, their effects are transient. In an effort to overcome the limitations associated with probiotics, prebiotics have been introduced as a dietary supplement. Prebiotics are defined as "a nondigestible food ingredient that beneficially affects the host by selectively stimulating the growth and/or activity of one or a limited number of bacteria in the colon, and thus improves host health".[5] At present the most effective prebiotics are naturally occurring oligosaccharides of plant origin.[7] A well characterized prebiotic commonly used in promoting health is fructooligosaccharides (FOS), which are a mixture of oligosaccharides consisting of glucose linked to fructose units.[8] There are different mixtures of FOS, all of which are capable of promoting the growth of beneficial bacteria such as *Bifidobacterium* and *Lactobacillus*.[9]

A natural consequence of improving health is increasing life expectancy, both for humans and companion animals. An issue that is currently unresolved is the impact of age and diet on intestinal microflora, specifically regarding increased numbers of health promoting bacteria. In humans, for example, it has been suggested that the intestinal flora remains relatively stable over the lifespan of that individual.[10] At birth, the intestinal tract is colonized by predominately Gram positive bacteria, including bifidobacteria, lactobacilli and clostridia. With age, the composition of intestinal flora gradually changes, although never completely, to Gram negative bacteria such as bacteriodes. It is not until old age that clostridia once again predominate (*Figure 1*). Efforts to enhance human health commensurate with the prevention of geriatric disease by modifying diet have resulted in diminished levels of putrefactive substances, increased numbers of bifidobacteria, and decreased numbers of clostridia, specifically *Clostridium perfringens*.[11] In humans, there appears to be a strong correlation between the predominance of harmful bacteria in the intestinal tract contributing to aging and geriatric diseases. In animals the correlation is not as convincing perhaps due to differences that exist between man and animal relative to the flora of the large intestine, as well as to the anatomical and physiological variances present within the digestive tract.

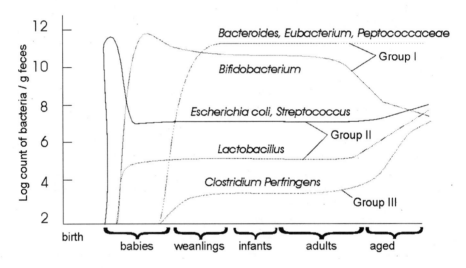

Figure 1. Changes in fecal flora with aging. Figure reprinted with permission. All rights reserved. *Nutrition Reviews*, Vol. 50, No. 12, p. 439. ©1992 by the International Life Sciences Institute, Washington, DC 20036-4810, USA.

Microbial Ecology of the Gastrointestinal Tract

The principal components of the gastrointestinal tract of non-ruminants include the esophagus, stomach, small intestine, cecum, and the large intestine.[3,12,13] Bacterial populations have been isolated from stomach contents; the numbers are variable (~10^3 bacteria/ml) and are influenced by both diet and the environment. Interestingly, the microbes represent transient communities rather than a population of microbes indigenous to this locale. The origin of these microbes is resident in nature, either from ingested material or regions proximal to the stomach. The microbial types most often found are Gram positive and aerobic, representing members of the lactic acid bacteria, including *Bifidobacterium*, *Lactobacillus*, and *Streptococcus*.

The small intestine, which is divided into the duodenum, jejunum, and ileum, has a rather simple microbial population (**Table 1**). The bacterial numbers rarely exceed 10^4 bacteria per ml, except for the distal ileum where counts are estimated to be approximately 10^6 per ml. Streptococci, lactobacilli, and veillonellae are found predominately in the duodenum and jejunum. In the ileum, the predominant microbes are represented primarily by *Escherichia coli* and anaerobic bacteria. The relatively low number of microbes is due primarily to the influence of gastric acidity and bile originating from the stomach, as well as intestinal motility (peristalsis) which allows non-adherent bacteria to simply pass through. An important function of the microflora of the small intestine is preventing the colonization of pathogenic microorganisms. They accomplish this by competing for available nutrients, controlling oxygen levels, as well as producing antibacterial substances.[14] The colonization of puppy small intestine follows exposure to the dam and litter mates, or from the environment. This occurs usually within 2 to 3 weeks of birth. Microorganisms that colonize do so for the life of the animal, but can be influenced by diet.

Table 1. Bacterial flora of various sites of the gastrointestinal tract. Adapted from Mitsuoka, 1982.[12]

	MOUTH	STOMACH	DUODENUM	JEJUNUM	ILEUM	CECUM	RECTUM
	Log number of bacteria per g feces						
Bacteriodes	6.8	0	0	2.1	2.6	10.8	11.0
Eubacteria	0	0	0	0	4.8	10.5	10.7
Peptococcaecea	0	0	0	0	0	10.2	10.4
Bifidobacteria	0	0	0	0	7.0	10.0	10.2
Streptococci	6.0	5.0	3.0	4.0	6.5	8.0	7.8
E. coli	0	0	2.3	2.5	3.0	7.0	6.8
Lactobacilli	7.8	4.0	2.3	3.4	6.8	7.0	6.5
Veillonella	6.7	2.6	2.5	3.2	3.5	3.6	3.5
C. perfringens	0	0	0	0	2.5	3.0	3.2

In contrast to the small intestine, the large intestine (cecum and colon) is heavily colonized by both non-resident and resident microbes, achieving numbers in excess of 10^{11} bacteria for each gram of intestinal contents (**Table 1**).[2,3] Microbes associated with the large intestine are predominately gram negative aerobes, as well as spore- and nonsporeforming anaerobes. Anaerobic bacteria typically account for greater than 90% of the colonic microflora, and consist of *Eubacterium*, *Clostridium*, *Lactobacillus*, *Bifidobacterium*, and *Bacteriodes*. The aerobic organisms that predominate include streptococci and members of the *Enterobacteriaceae*. The large intestine is a complex microbial ecosystem, containing at any one time up to 50 different genera of bacteria representing more than 200 different species.[5] Biologically significant functions of the large intestine include the dehydration of its fecal contents, as well as the absorption and secretion of electrolytes and water.[15,16]

Although diet and the environment significantly influence the composition of this complex ecosystem, numerous endogenous and exogenous factors, such as species of the animal, age, sex, specific physiological parameters including adrenal function, peristalsis, secretion of digestive enzymes, bile, and mucous each contribute to the diversity of gastrointestinal microflora.[17]

Potential Beneficial and Detrimental Impact of Intestinal Microflora on the Host
The gastrointestinal tract of man and animal is characterized by an enormously complex microflora consisting of aerobic and anaerobic indigenous bacteria which are derived almost exclusively from the environment. These bacteria colonize the alimentary canal at birth, and achieve a stable expression that is characteristic for a given host within 3–4 weeks of birth. At present, there exists a wealth of incontrovertible evidence that the gut microbiota plays a major role in providing protection against resident invading bacteria associated with specific infectious diseases. For example, it has been shown that gnotobiotic animals are more susceptible to disease caused by either *Salmonella enteritidis* or *Clostridium botulinum* than their conventional littermates who maintain an intact, stable gut microflora.[18,19] Additionally, animals treated with antibiotics develop a predisposition to infections caused by bacteria such as *Salmonella typhimurium*, *Vibrio cholerae*, *Shigella* sp. and *Clostridium botulinum* (**Table 2**).[20-22] It has also been reported that isolates from the intestinal tract, including either bifidobacteria, lactobacilli, propionibacteria or enterococci inhibited species of pathogenic bacteria including *Clostridium*, *Salmonella*, *Listeria*, *Campylobacter*, and *Shigella*.[23,24] The inhibition of growth mediated by these non-resident colonic bacteria was attributed either to fermentation-derived acids (acetate, lactate), or inhibitory substances, i.e., bacteriocins, unrelated to acid production.[24]

Table 2. Evidence for health protection by indigenous gastrointestinal microbial populations.

Experimental Condition	Outcome
Gnotobiotic Environment	Increased susceptibility to *Salmonella enteritidis*.[18]
Gnotobiotic Environment	Increased susceptibility to *Clostridium botulinum*.[19]
Antibiotic Treatment	Increased susceptibility to *Salmonella typhimurium*.[20]
Antibiotic Treatment	Increased susceptibility to *Vibrio cholerae* and *Shigella* sp.[21]
Antibiotic Treatment	Increased susceptibility to *Clostridium botulinum*.[22]
Inhibition studies	*Clostridium* growth inhibited by lactobacilli, propionibacteria, and enterococci.[23]
Inhibition studies	*E. coli*, *Clostridium perfringens*, *Salmonella*, *Listeria*, *Campylobacter*, *Shigella*, and *Vibrio* growth inhibited by *Bifidobacterium*.[24]

Commensurate with the protective effects associated with gut flora, the colonic microflora of man and animal contributes to host health through the production of vitamins including riboflavin, B_{12}, thiamine, folic, and pantothenic acid, each of which can be absorbed and utilized by the host.[25] Another bacterial metabolite important in maintaining the health of the host are short chain fatty acids (SCFA) which are major end-products of dietary fiber fermentation.[2,17,26] Dietary fiber (non-starch polysaccharides) is a chemically heterogenous substance, the composition of which consists of cellulose, hemicellulose, pectin, gums, mucilages, and lignin. Fermentation of dietary fiber is accomplished by anaerobic bacteria found in the small and large intestine. The principal SCFA are acetate, propionate, and butyrate.[26,27] SCFA produced during carbohydrate fermentation are rapidly absorbed by the colonic mucosa where they stimulate absorption of water, sodium, potassium, and magnesium ions as well as secretion of bicarbonate and chloride ions, reducing the potential risk of diarrhea. Short chain fatty acids, especially butyrate, are used by colonic mucosa as a preferential energy source.[17] It has also been proposed that SCFA may serve as substrates for lipogeneis, gluconeogeneis, and ketogeneis.

The beneficial effects of intestinal bacteria not withstanding, many of these same organisms may form a variety of metabolites that are potentially harmful to the host. These include cadaverine, ammonia, N-nitrosoamines, phenols, and indole, as well as certain vasoconstricting amines such as histamine. Each of these metabolites have been associated with disease in man and animals.[12] In recent years, significant attention has been focussed on various metabolic enzymes of colonic microbes because they have been implicated in the generation of toxins, mutagens, carcinogens, and tumor promoters.[28] Bacterial enzymes mentioned include β-glucuronidase, β-glucosidase, β-galactosidase, nitroreductase, azoreductase, 7-α-steroid dehydrogenase, and 7-α-hydroxy-steroid dehydroxylase. The change in enzyme activity is believed to be influenced by diet; i.e., a diet high in fat/calories and low in dietary fiber provides fermentable substrates for colonic bacteria resulting in the induction of enzymes capable of converting procarcinogens to carcinogens.

The intestinal epithelium forms a barrier separating the internal environment of the host from a myriad of non-resident and resident microorganisms, many of which are potential pathogens. Consequently, the gastrointestinal tract represents a possible portal of entry for many of these colonic microbes, even in the absence of discernable lesions in the colonic mucosa. The passage of viable bacteria from the gastrointestinal tract to otherwise sterile tissues such as mesenteric lymph nodes, liver, spleen, kidney, peritoneal cavity, and bloodstream is referred to as gut translocation.[29-32] Although recognized for years, the clinical significance of gut translocation has remained largely ill-defined. Initially, it was proposed to occur randomly with no untoward ill consequences. More recently, however, evidence suggests that gut translocation by indigenous microflora may be involved in the pathogenesis of numerous diseases in both man and animal. Of particular interest is the strong correlation that exists amongst animals suffering either from inflammatory bowel disease (IBD) or intestinal bacteria overgrowth (IBO) and the development of arthritic lesions.[30,33]

Animal models studies suggest three different mechanisms as plausible explanations for gut translocation.[29,32] These include 1) disruption of the normal symbiotic relationship of intestinal flora subsequent to antibiotic therapy or intestinal obstruction, 2) mucosal atrophy resulting from luminal nutrient deprivation, and 3) host immunosuppression.

In a host whose immune defenses are compromised, or those suffering bacterial overgrowth, the transport of intestinal flora across the epithelial barrier is believed to occur through the mucosal lamina propria. In contrast, alterations in the overall integrity of the mucosal barrier results in enhanced bacterial translocation in the complete absence of bacterial overgrowth or host defenses being compromised. The efficiency of translocation amongst indigenous bacteria varies. Enterobacteria, pseudomonads, and certain Gram positive cocci translocate with greater efficiency than do most other indigenous bacteria, especially obligate anaerobes. Increased sensitivity to oxygen present in mesenteric tissue may in part explain reduced translocation by colonic anaerobes.

Changes in Intestinal Microflora Composition Through Utilization of Probiotics and/or Prebiotics

Amelioration of the harmful or pathogenic influences of colonic microflora, including diarrhea, liver damage, cancer, production of carcinogens, and intestinal putrefaction can be achieved by inducing colonization of beneficial colonic bacteria such as *Lactobacillus* and *Bifidobacterium*. In the past, the most effective strategy towards accomplishing this goal was through dietary modulation involving the utilization of probiotics.[4,34,35] Both *Lactobacillus* and *Bifidobacterium* have been used as probiotics.

At present, it is uncertain as to exactly how probiotics work, but it is likely that one or more of the following attributes may contribute to the efficacy of these preparations.[34] First, a particular probiotic strain is capable of producing antimicrobial substances. For example, it has been demonstrated that bifidobacteria, a major group of saccharolytic bacteria found in the intestinal tract, are potent producers of strong acids (acetate, lactate) which are antibacterial. In addition, a metabolite of bifidobacteria is inhibitory for certain Gram positive and Gram negative bacteria.[24] Secondly, probiotic strains may compete with intestinal pathogens for receptors involved in adhering to intestinal epithelium. Pigs administered a non-pathogenic adhering strain of *E. coli* resisted a challenge dose of a pathogenic strain of the same serotype, supporting the hypothesis that both strains had an affinity for the same receptor.[36] Next, the probiotic strain may compete with pathogenic organisms for the same nutrients. Although the large intestine represents a milieu rich in nutrients, such an effect could result if one nutrient essential for the growth of a specific pathogen was limiting. Lastly, certain probiotic strains may act as immunomodulators. This could be manifested either as an increase in antibody titer, macrophage activation, natural killer cell activity or cytokine production.[37] For example, germ free mice have reduced phagocytic activity and immunoglobulin levels when compared with conventional litter mates.[38] Moreover, *per os* adminstration of *Lactobacillus casei* resulted in augmenting non-specific resistance mechanisms, including macrophage activation and natural killer cell activity.[39]

Although the potential benefit of probiotics is apparent, in order to be effective, probiotics must remain viable and stable over long periods of storage. In addition, each probiotic strain must be able to survive the harsh physical and chemical properties of the gastrointestinal tract and have the capacity to become established within the colon.

It is apparent that the use of probiotics is effective in altering the composition of the gut flora. Unfortunately, the beneficial effects associated with these implanted exogenous bacteria as dietary supplements is transient and therefore limited relative to their reported health promoting properties. An alternative to probiotics in modifying the colonic bacterial balance is the use of prebiotics.

To be classified as a prebiotic, a food ingredient must meet the following criteria: 1) neither be hydrolyzed nor absorbed in the upper part of the gastrointestinal tract; 2) be a selective substrate for one or a limited number of beneficial bacteria commensal to the colon, which are stimulated to grow and/or are metabolically activated; 3) consequently, be able to alter the colonic flora in favor of a healthier composition; and 4) induce luminal or systemic effects that are beneficial to the host health.[5]

Nondigestible carbohydrates, specifically fructooligosaccharides (FOS) have been most effective as prebiotics in modifying the composition and metabolic activity of bacteria in the gastrointestinal tract.[40] Fructooligosaccharides are naturally occurring carbohydrates found in a variety of foods, including bananas, garlic, onions, and tomatoes, as well as common fruits, vegetables, and grains. Fructooligosaccharides consist of several fructosyl residues linked to a terminal glucose residue.[5] Host mammalian digestive enzymes are incapable of hydrolyzing FOS, whereas indigenous intestinal bacteria like *Bifidobacterium* and *Lactobacillus* can metabolize them. The benefits of dietary FOS supplementation include higher densities of beneficial bacteria commensurate with increased production of SCFA, reduced activity of enzymes implicated in carcinogeneis, diminished serum cholesterol levels, suppression of putrefactive substances, and a lowered pH in the large intestine.[41-46] Studies with companion animals have also suggested that diet supplementation with FOS influences the composition of colonic microflora in favor of beneficial microbes, as well as reducing the production of certain putrefactive substances.[47,48,49]

At present, a paucity of information exists regarding the influence of age and diet on colonic microflora, although it is well documented that specific functions of the gastrointestinal tract (i.e., intestinal secretion and motility) are significantly reduced in aged individuals.[15] In humans, for example, there was virtually no difference in the total number of anaerobes or facultative anaerobes in individuals fed random diets versus those maintained on a standard diet.[50] Likewise, only minor differences were noted in intestinal microflora composition in individuals consuming a vegetarian diet versus a meat diet. Others have reported that the numbers of bifidobacteria decreased with advanced age, whereas those of clostridia, lactobacilli,

Current Research

and enterobacteria increased. In a study with Beagle dogs, significantly lower numbers of bacteriodes, eubacteria, bifidobacteria, lactobacilli, and staphylococci were observed in the large bowel of aged dogs (>11 years) when compared with younger (<12 months) animals.[51] Interestingly, the numbers of *Clostridrium perfringens* were significantly higher in aged animals. In studies in aged mice and rats, lower numbers of bifidobacteria and enterobacteria were reported, while lactobacilli remained relatively stable.[52,53]

In recent years, encouraging results have been obtained with human diets supplemented with non-digestible carbohydrates (prebiotics), specifically regarding changes in the number of beneficial bacteria present in the large intestine. For example, the effects of long term administration of different non-digestible carbohydrates (i.e., lactosucrose, neosugar [FOS], oligofructose, and inulin) on the fecal flora of healthy volunteers resulted in a significant increase in bifidobacteria and lactobacilli with a concomitant decrease in the number of enterics, bacteriodes, and clostridia.[41-46,54] In parallel animal model studies, similar results have been obtained.[47-49,55,56] In a study with companion animals in which the diet was supplemented with neosugar, Beagle dogs aged 0–5 years exhibited a significant increase in lactobacilli per gram of feces. In a study in which cats were maintained on a diet supplemented with lactosucrose, there was an increase in lactobacilli in stool samples, and a corresponding decrease in numbers of clostridia and enterobacteria.[49] Finally, in a separate study with dogs experiencing small intestinal bacterial overgrowth (SIBO), it was reported that supplementation of the diet with FOS resulted in significantly fewer aerobic bacteria in the proximal small intestine, although no differences in specific genera were reported.[57]

The purpose of the present study reported here was to assess what effect age and diet have on the composition of fecal microflora, as an indirect measure of ongoing changes within the large intestine. Animals were divided into two groups as follows: 16 young animals less than 12 months of age (10.8 ± 0.54 months) weighing 9.82 ± 1.87 kg, and 16 geriatric animals more than 11 years of age (11.4 ± 2.27 years) weighing 15.52 ± 3.66 kg. Animals were placed on one of the following two diets: a basal diet containing 25.5% protein, 12.2% fat, 1.9% crude fiber, 5.6% ash, and 8.1% moisture; and the basal diet supplemented with 0.8% fructooligosaccharide. This study was designed as a 2 x 2 factorial switchback in order to generate sample size sufficient to allow for statistical analysis. Fecal samples were collected within ten minutes of defecation and stored frozen at -70° C. Samples were analyzed for total aerobic and anaerobic bacterial counts, as well as specific genera of bacteria including enterobacteria, lactobacilli, eubacteria, clostridia, and bacteroides. Briefly, each fecal sample was thawed and 1 gram homogenized in sterile phosphate buffered saline using a Stomacher homogenizer. An aliquot of this homogenized sample was serially diluted to give dilutions between 10^{-2} and 10^{-7} or as judged necessary to reliably obtain plates with a countable number of colonies. One hundred microliters of each dilution was plated in duplicate onto plates of blood agar and EMB agar for aerobic cultures. For anaerobic cultures, sample dilutions were plated onto CDC blood anaerobe agar, LBS agar, BBE agar and rifampicin agar. Aerobic cultures were incubated at 37° C and were examed daily for 72 hours. Plates to be cultured anaerobically were incubated at 37° C for five days in anaerobe jars containing an atmosphere of 80% N_2, 10% CO_2 and 10% H_2.

Data presented in **Table 3** illustrate that there was an increase in both the aerobic and anaerobic population in fecal samples obtained from aged Beagle dogs when compared to numbers of bacteria found in young Beagle dogs. Interestingly, the numbers of enterobacteria were decreased in aged animals. In evaluating the composition of anaerobic microorganisms isolated from stool samples of aged dogs, there was an increase in numbers of bacteriodes, clostridia, eubacteria, and lactobacilli, with the largest increase occurring in the number of clostridia and lactobacilli isolated.

Table 3. Effect of age on the distribution of bacteria in fecal samples obtained from 11-year-old Beagle dogs. Dogs were maintained on a basal diet for 8 weeks and compared with 1-year-old Beagle dogs.

Bacteria	Change
Total Anaerobes	+ 41%
Total Aerobes	+ 24%
Enterobacteria	− 18%
Bacteriodes	+ 31%
Clostridia	+ 344%
Eubacteria	+ 44%
Lactobacilli	+ 118%

The effect of supplementing the basal diet with 0.8% fructooligo-saccharides (FOS) on the distribution of microorganisms in fecal samples of Beagle dogs is presented in **Table 4**. In this study, dogs were maintained either on the basal diet, or the FOS-supplemented diet for a period of 8 weeks at which time stool samples were cultured and the number of fecal microbes determined. Evaluation of the data indicates that a change occurred in the total number of aerobes isolated from fecal samples of dogs maintained on the FOS-supplemented diet. There was no difference, however, in the number of total anaerobes, bacteriodes or clostridia between the two groups. The most dramatic effect of the FOS-supplemented diet was an increase in the number of eubacteria cultured.

Discussion

Results from this study illustrate that age had a signficant impact on the composition of intestinal microflora of Beagle dogs. Fecal samples obtained from 11-year-old Beagle dogs were characterized by a change in both aerobic and anaerobic populations, as indicated by a 24% and 41% increase, respectively, when compared to fecal samples of 1-year-old dogs (**Table 3**). An increase in total numbers of

Table 4. Effect of FOS supplementation on distribution of bacteria in fecal samples. Dogs were maintained on a basal diet supplemented with 0.8% fructooligosaccharides for 8 weeks and compared with dogs fed a basal diet for the same time period.

Bacteria	Change
Total Anaerobes	None
Total Aerobes	+ 55%
Enterobacteria	+ 98%
Bacteriodes	– 1.6%
Clostridia	+ 1.4%
Eubacteria	+ 246%
Lactobacilli	– 64%

anaerobes and aerobes in stool samples may reflect changes affecting anatomically distinct regions of the gastrointestinal tract; i.e., the small intestine. Such a condition may predispose these dogs to canine intestinal bacterial overgrowth (IBO), an important cause of clinical illness, the development of which may be triggered without any clinical signs of disease.[58,59] Levels of bacteriodes, clostridia, eubacteria, and lactobacilli were higher than those in younger animals, whereas the numbers of enterobacteria in aged animals were lower. In a previous paper addressing the impact of age on the intestinal microflora of Beagle dogs, it was observed that elderly dogs had fewer numbers of bacteriodes, eubacteria, and lactobacilli in all regions of the large bowel. In contrast, these same aged dogs expressed an increase in species of clostridia.[51]

Recognizing that the intestinal tract contains a large number of species, a scheme has been developed in an effort to classify these microbes as beneficial, negative or neutral.[60] Beneficial bacteria include bifidobacteria, lactobacilli, and other lactic acid bacteria; negative for general health are bacteria consisting of enterobacteria and clostridia, all other bacteria are considered neutral. Although the data differ somewhat with those of Benno et al,[51] this apparent contradiction may be attributed to the different composition of diets employed, or to differences in the specimen evaluated (fecal versus large bowel). Of particular interest was the dramatic increase in clostridia (↑341%) found in this study in the fecal samples of aged Beagle dogs. An immediate concern raised by this observation is the strong correlation that exists between certain species of bacteria inhabiting the intestinal tract and the genesis of disease in man and animal.[61-63] For example, species of clostridia have been implicated as a major cause of acute and chronic large bowel diarrhea in dogs.[61,62] In addition, species of bacteriodes have also been implicated as a cause of severe disease in animals.[64] What this data and that of others suggest is that aged animals are at risk for developing certain diseases attributable to species of intestinal microflora, and that strategies designed to develop a diet consistent with increasing beneficial bacteria are warranted.

In dogs fed an FOS supplemented diet, there was little or no change in the total number of anaerobes, bacteroides or clostridia when compared with dogs maintained on a basal diet (*Table 3*). There was, however, an increase in total aerobes, enterobacteria, and eubacteria in dogs fed the FOS supplemented diet.

This study represents the first report in which dogs maintained on a diet supplemented with FOS exhibit a dramatic increase in the numbers of eubacteria (↑246%) present in fecal specimens. Moreover, changes in the aerobic population observed in these same dogs may in part be explained by an increase in enterobacteria (↑98%). The impact of these observations relative to the effect of diet on the composition of intestinal microflora is to change existing conventional ideologies regarding which strains of bacteria promote the health of companion animals. For example, *in vitro* studies in humans and companion animals have indicated that fermentation of FOS is mediated almost exclusively by colonic microflora, specifically those possessing "bifidogenic" properties.[27,45,46] Historically speaking, members of the enterobacteria are considered to be representative of bacteria classified as negative for general health when found in the intestinal tract.[60] Recently, however, it has been reported that certain strains of enterobacteria are capable of degrading and fermenting commericial preparations of FOS *in vitro*.[65] These data support previous observations that saprophytic strains of *Escherichia coli* may increase in the presence of FOS, thereby establishing an environment in the intestinal tract that inhibits the survival of pathogenic strains of *E. coli*.[66] It is therefore possible that the increase in eubacteria and enterobacteria observed in this study represents strains of intestinal microflora capable of fermenting FOS, and that these same organisms are involved in preventing the adhesion and survival of potential pathogenic microorganisms, thereby contributing to the overall health status of the animal.

This study contributes to the growth of information regarding the influence of age and diet on the composition of intestinal microflora in man and companion animals. There is clearly an interesting interrelationship that exists among intestinal flora, diet, and aging. Intestinal flora are metabolically diverse, each capable of converting substrates into substances that may be beneficial or detrimental to the host. A nutrient poor diet may provide an environment that selects for intestinal flora capable of producing these harmful substances. An alternative approach is to develop strategies that will enhance the growth of beneficial bacteria, thereby contributing to host health. In the future, one such strategy worth pursuing is maintaining aged animals on a diet supplemented with prebiotics such as fructooligosaccharides.

---

1. Carman RJ, Van Tassell RL, Wilkins TD. The normal intestinal microflora: ecology, variability and stability. *Vet Human Toxicol* 1993; 35(Suppl)1:11-14.

2. Simon LG, Gorbach SL. Intestinal flora in health and disease. *Gastroenterology* 1984; 86:174-193.

3. Savage DC. Microbial ecology of the gastrointestinal tract. *Ann Rev Microbiol* 1977; 31:107-133.

References

4. Fuller R. Probiotics in man and animals. *J Appl Bacteriol* 1989; 66:365-378.

5. Gibson GR, Roberfroid MB. Dietary modulation of the human colonic microbiota: Introducing the concept of prebiotics. *J Nutr* 1995; 125:1401-1442.

6. Fuller R, Gibson GR. Modification of the intestinal microflora using probiotics and prebiotics. *Scand J Gastroenterol* 1997; 32(Suppl)222:28-31.

7. Delzenne NM, Roberfroid MB. Physiological effects of non-digestible oligosaccharides. *Lebensm Wiss Technol* 1994; 27:1-6.

8. Hidaka H, Hirayama M. Useful characteristics and commercial applications of fructo-oligosaccharides. *Biochem Soc Transac* 1991; 19:561-565.

9. Mitsuoka T. Bifidobacteria and their role in human health. *J Ind Microbiol* 1990; 6:263-268.

10. Gorbach SL. Perturbation of intestinal microflora. *Vet Human Toxicol* 1993; 35:15-23.

11. Mitsuoka T. Intestinal flora and aging. *Nutri Rev* 1992; 40:438-446.

12. Mitsuoka T. Recent trends in research on intestinal flora. *Bifidobacteria Microflora* 1982; 1:3-24.

13. Tancrede C. Role of human microflora in health and disease. *Eur J Clin Microbiol Infect Dis* 1992; 11:1012-1015.

14. Greene CE. *Infectious Diseases of the Dog and Cat.* Philadelphia: WB Saunders Company, 1990.

15. Drasar BS, Hill MJ. *Human Intestinal Flora.* London: Academic Press, 1974.

16. Eastwood ML. Colon structure. In: Buston-Ferandes L, ed. *The Colon: Structure and Function.* London: Plenum Medical Book Company, 1982; 1-15.

17. Gorbach SL, Goldin BR. Nutrition and the gastrointestinal microflora. *Nutri Rev* 1992; 50:378-381.

18. Collins FM, Carter PB. Growth of salmonellae in orally infected germfree mice. *Infect Immun* 1978; 21:41-47.

19. Moberg LJ, Sugiyama H. Microbial ecological basis of infant botulism as studied with germfree mice. *Infect Immun* 1979; 25:653-657.

20. Bohnhoff M, Drake BL, Miller CP. Effect of streptomycin on susceptibility of intestinal tract to experimental salmonella infection. *Proc Soc Exp Bio Med* 1954; 86:132.

21. Freter R. Experimental enteric *shigella* and *vibrio* infection in mice and guinea pigs. *J Exp Med* 1956; 104:411.

22. Burr DH, Sugiyama H, Harvis G. Susceptibility to enteric botulinum colonisation of antibiotic-treated adult mice. *Infect Immun* 1982; 36:103-106.

23. Sullivan NM, Mills DC, Riemann HP, Arnon SS. Inhibition of growth of *Clostridium botulinum* by intestinal microflora isolated from healthy infants. *Microbiol Ecol Health Dis* 1988; 1:179.

24. Gibson GR, Wang X. Regulatory effects of bifidobacteria on the growth of other colonic bacteria. *J Appl Bacteriol* 1994; 77:412-420.

25. Deguchi Y, Morishita T, Mutai M. Comparative studies on synthesis of water-soluble vitamins among human species of bifidobacteria. *Agri Biol Chem* 1985; 49:13-20.

26. Kerley MS, Sunvold GD. Physiological response to short chain fatty acid production in the intestine. In: Carey DP, Norton SA, Bolser SM, eds. *Recent*

Advances in Canine and Feline Nutritional Research: Proceeding of the 1996 Iams International Nutrition Symposium. Wilmington: Orange Frazer Press, 1996; 33-40.

27. Sunvold GD, Fahey GC, Merchen NR, Reinhart GA. *In vitro* fermentation of selected fibrous substrates by dog and cat faecal inoculum: influence of diet composition on substrate organic matter disappearance and short chain fatty acid production. *J Anim Sci* 1995; 73:1110-1122.

28. Gorbach SL, Goldin BR. The intestinal microflora and the colon cancer connection. *Rev Inf Dis* 1990; 12:S252-S261.

29. Berg RD. Translocation of enteric bacteria in health and disease. *Curr Stud Hematol Blood Trans* 1992; 59:44-65.

30. Wells CL, Maddaus MA, Simmons RL. Proposed mechanisms for the translocation of intestinal bacteria. *Rev Inf Dis* 1988; 10:958-979.

31. Lichtman SN. Translocation of bacteria from gut lumen to mesenteric lymph nodes–and beyond? *Jour Pediat Gastroenterol Nutr* 1991; 13:433-434.

32. Sedman PC, Macfie J, Sagar P, Mitchell CJ, May J, Mancey-Jones B, Johnstone D. The prevalence of gut translocation in humans. *Gastroenterology* 1994; 107:643-649.

33. Hazenburg MP. Intestinal flora bacteria and arthritis: Why the joint? *Scand J Rheumatol* 1995; 24(Suppl):207-211.

34. Fuller R, Probiotics in human medicine. *Gut* 1991; 32:439-442.

35. Fuller R, ed. *Probiotics: The Scientific Basis*. London: Chapman and Hall, 1992.

36. Davidson JN, Hirsch DC. Bacterial competition as a means of preventing diarrhea in pigs. *Infect Immun* 1976; 13:1773-1774.

37. Perdigon G, Alvarez S. Probiotics and the immune state. In: Fuller R, ed. *Probiotics: The Scientific Basis*. London: Chapman & Hall, 1992; 145.

38. Bealmear PM, Holtermann OA, Mirand EA. Influence of the microflora on the immune response. I. General characteristics of the germ-free animal. In: Coates ME, Gustafsson, BE, eds. *The Germ Free Animal in Biomedical Research*. London: Academic Press, 1984; 335.

39. Perdigon G, DeMacias MEN, Alvarez S, Oliver G, deRuiz Holgado AAP. Effect of perorally administered lactobacilli on macrophage activation in mice. *Infect Immun* 1986; 53:404-410.

40. Fishbein L, Kaplan M, Gough M. Fructooligosaccharide:a review. *Vet Hum Toxicol* 1988; 30:104.

41. Hikada H, Eida T, Takizawa T, Tokunga T, Tashiro Y. Effects of fructooligosaccharides on intestinal flora and human health. *Bifidobact Microflora* 1986; 5:37.

42. Bouhnik Y, Flourie B, Riottot M, Bisett N, Gailing MF, Guibert A, Bornet F, Rambaud JC. Effects of fructo-oligosaccharides ingestion on fecal bifidobacteria and selected metabolic indexes of colon carcinogenesis in healthy humans. *Nutr Cancer* 1996; 26:21-29.

43. Buddington RK, Williams CH, Chen SS, Witherly SA. Dietary supplement of neosugar alters the fecal flora and decreases activities of some reductive enzymes in human subjects. *Am J Clin Nutr* 1996; 63:709-716.

44. Gibson GR, Beatty ER, Wang X, Cummings JH. Selective stimulation of bifidobacteria in the human colon by oligofructose and inulin. *Gastroenterology* 1995; 108:975-982.

45. Williams CH, Witherly SA, Buddington RK. Influence of dietary neosugar on selected bacterial groups of the human faecal microbiota. *Micro Ecol Health Dis* 1994; 7:91-97.

46. Wang X, Gibson GR. Effects of the *in vitro* fermentation of oligofructose and inulin by bacteria growing in the human large intestine. *J Appl Bacteriol* 1993; 75:373-380.

47. Ogata, M. Use of neosugar in pets. *Proc 3rd Neosugar Conference* 1986; 116.

48. Sparkes AH, Papasouliotis K, Sunvold G, Werrett G, Gruffydd-Jones EA, Egan K, Gruffydd-Jones TJ, Reinhart G. The effect of dietary supplementation with fructo-oligosaccharides on the fecal flora of healthy cats. *Am J Vet Sci* 1998; in press.

49. Terada A, Hara H, Kato S, Kimura T, Fujimori I, Hara K, Maruyama T, Mitsuoka T. Effect of lactosucrose (4^G-b-D-Galactosylsucrose) on fecal flora and fecal putrefactive products of cats. *J Vet Med Sci* 1993; 55:291-295.

50. Gorbach SL, Nahas L, Lerner PL, Weinstein L. Studies of intestinal microflora. I. Effects of diet, age, and periodic sampling on numbers of fecal microorganisms in man. *Gastroenterology* 1967; 53:845-855.

51. Benno Y, Nakao H, Uchida K, Mitsuoka T. Impact of the advances in age on the gastrointestinal microflora of beagle dogs. *J Vet Med Sci* 1992; 703-706.

52. Pesti L, Gordon HA. Effects of age and isolation on the intestinal flora in mice. *Gerontologia* 1973; 19:153-161.

53. Morishita Y, Miyaki K. Effects of age and starvation on the gastrointestinal microflora and the heat resistance of fecal bacteria in rats. *Microbiol Immunol* 1979; 23:455-470.

54. Ohkusa T, Ozaki Y, Sato C, Mikuni K, Ikeda H. Long-term ingestion of lactosucrose increases *Bifidobacterium* sp in human faecal flora. *Digestion* 1995; 56:415-420.

55. Terada A, Hara H, Oishi T, Matsui S, Mitsuoka T, Nakajyo S, Fujimori I, Hara K. Effect of dietary lactosucrose on faecal flora and faecal metabolites of dogs. *Micro Ecol Health Dis* 1992; 5:87-92.

56. Howard MD, Gordon DT, Garlep KA, Kerley MS. Dietary fructooligosaccharide, xylooligosaccharide and gum arabic have variable effects on cecal and colonic microbiota and epithelial cell proliferation in mice and rats. *J Nutri* 1995; 125:2604-2609.

57. Willard MD, Simpson RB, Delles EK, Cohen ND, Fossum TW, Kolp D, Reinhart G. Effects of dietary supplementation of fructo-oligosaccharides on small intestinal bacterial overgrowth in dogs. *Am J Vet Res* 1994; 55:654-669.

58. Rutger CH, Batt RM, Elwood CM, Lamport A. Small intestinal bacterial overgrowth in dogs with chronic intestinal disease. *J Am Vet Med Assoc* 1995; 206:187-193.

59. Batt RM, Hall EJ, McLean L, Simpson KW. Small intestinal bacterial overgrowth and enhanced intestinal permeability in healthy beagles. *Am J Vet Res* 1992; 53:1935-1940.

60. Mitsuoka T. Bifidobacteria and their role. *J Indust Micro* 1990; 6:263.

61. Twedt DC. *Clostridium perfringens* associated diarrhea in dogs. *Proc Am Coll Vet Int Med* 1993; 11:121.

62. Berry AP, Levett PN. Chronic diarrhea in dogs associated with *Clostridium difficile* infection. *Vet Rec* 1986; 118:102-103.

63. Jackson SG, Yip-Chuck DA, Clark JB, Brodsky MH. Diagnostic importance of *Clostridium perfringens* enterotoxin analysis recurring enteritis among elderly, chronic care psychiatric patients. J Clin Microbiol 1986; 23:748-751.

64. Myers LL, Shoop DS. Association of enterotoxigenic *Bacteriodes fragilis* with diarrheal disease in young pigs. *Am J Vet Res* 1987; 48:774-775.

65. Hartemink R, Van Laere KMJ, Rombouts FM. Growth of enterobacteria on fructo-oligosaccarides. *J Appl Microbiol* 1997; 83:367-374.

66. Morisse JP, Maurice R, Boilletot E, Cotte JP. Assessment of the activity of a fructo-oligosaccharide on different caecal parameters in rabbits experimental infected with *E. coli* O103. *Ann Zootech* 42:81-87.

Age-related Changes in Physiological Function in the Dog and Cat: Nutritional Implications

Michael G. Hayek, PhD
Research Nutritionist, Research and Development
The Iams Company, Lewisburg, Ohio, USA

Interest in the field of gerontology has been increasing in recent times. Gerontology has been defined as "the scientific study of aging and the aged through the integration of disciplines involving both biological and behavioral sciences."[1] It is important to note that the aging process is a series of stages that begins with conception, continues with maturation, adulthood and senescence (geriatric), and ends with death.[2] Therefore, the study of gerontology is a study of life processes that influence the final stage (i.e., geriatric stage) of the lifespan of the animal.

Increasing attention is being focused on the geriatric portion of our companion animals. Similar to the global human population, the segment of older dogs and cats is substantial as demonstrated by recent demographic surveys conducted in the United States (**Table 1**) and the United Kingdom (**Figure 1**).[3,4] The determination of a chronological age to classify a dog or cat as geriatric has been difficult. This is especially true in the dog in which body size correlates to anticipated life expectancy for that breed. Based on surveys to veterinary clinics, which asked at what age their patients showed geriatric diseases, Goldston[5] proposed the breakdown presented in **Table 2**.

In the past, dietary recommendations for geriatric dogs and cats have been based on generalized changes with age. For instance, it has long been recognized that as dogs and cats age, they become less active. This decrease in physical activity results in a decreased energy requirement for maintenance. Most recommendations suggest an 18-20% decrease in calorie intake. However, as data accumulate it is being recognized that certain physiological changes occur with age that can separate young and geriatric companion animals. Age-associated differences in laboratory values have previously been reported in the dog.[6] A similar trend has been observed in a colony of young and old Fox Terriers and Labrador Retrievers (**Table 3**). While several laboratory parameters were similar between the different age groups, other parameters were either higher or lower in the old dogs. The same observation was noted with young and old cats (**Table 4**). Other physiological systems have been demonstrated to possess age-related changes in other species and are now being

Table 1. Demographics of geriatric dog and cat populations in the United States. Adapted from Wise, 1991.[3]

Total Population	Over 6 years old	Over 11 years old
52.5 million dogs	22 million (41.7%)	7.3 million (13.9%)
57 million cats	19 million (33.4%)	6 million (11%)

Figure 1. Chart A represents a UK survey of 20,786 dogs presented to the Small Animal Practice Teaching Unit (SAPT) at Edinburgh University (1991). Chart B represents a UK survey of 6,417 cats presented to the Small Animal Teaching Unit (SAPT) at Edinburgh University (1991). Adapted from Davies, 1996.[4]

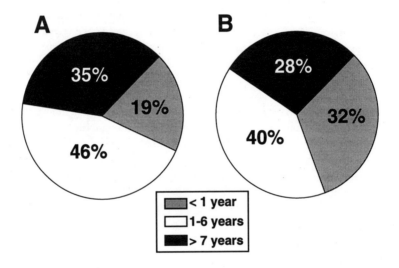

Table 2. Ages dogs and cats start showing diseases associated with aging. Adapted from Goldston, 1995.[4]

Classification	Weight (lb)	Age (yr)
Small Dogs	0 – 20	11.48 ± 1.85
Medium Dogs	21 – 50	10.90 ± 1.56
Large Dogs	51 – 90	8.85 ± 1.39
Giant Dogs	> 90	7.46 ± 1.94
Cats		11.88 ± 1.94

Table 3. Laboratory values from young and old Fox Terriers. (Data collected from 36 young and old Fox Terriers [1.8 *v* 11.5 years] and Labrador Retrievers [1.5 *v* 9.6 years]; n = 9 per age per breed.)

Unchanged	Decreased	Increased
Serum Chloride	Creatinine	Serum sodium
Total bilirubin	Albumin	Serum potassium
γ-Glutamyl-transferase	Serum calcium	Serum triglycerides
Alanine aminotransferase	Albumin/Globulin	Globulin
Cholesterol	Red blood cells	Polymorphonuclearcytes
Lactate dehydrogenase	Hemoglobin	Platelets
Magnesium	Hematocrit	
Blood urea nitrogen	Lymphocytes	
Blood urea nitrogen/creatinine		
Creatine kinase		
Eosinophils		

Table 4. Feline laboratory values in old age. (Data collected from 40 young and old cats [0.9 *v* 8.9 years].)

Unchanged	Decreased	Increased
Serum potassium	Alanine aminotransferase	Cholesterol
Polymorphonuclearcytes	Apartate aminotransferase	Globulin
Lymphocytes	Alkaline phosphatase	Monocytes
Eosinophils	Creatinine kinase	
Hematocrit	Albumin	
	Serum calcium	
	Serum phosphorus	
	Albumin/Globulin	
	White blood cells	
	Hemoglobin	

verified in the geriatric dog and cat. Therefore, aging results in a variety of physiological alterations that separate geriatric animals from young adults. Examination of these changes suggest that specific nutritional strategies can be developed to meet the changing needs of the aged.

Theories of Aging	A variety of theories of aging have been proposed over the years.[7] Some theories attribute the aging process to genetic controls. These theories include explanations such as codon restriction, somatic mutation, and gene regulation. Other theories explain aging as a gradual depression in certain physiological systems, such as the immune system or the neuroendocrine system. Still other theories state that aging is due to an accumulation of detrimental products such as lipofuscin or free radicals. None of these theories have completely explained the mammalian aging process, and it is generally thought that aging is a multifactorial phenomena including various aspects of these theories. It is interesting to note that while some of these theories are due to inevitable changes that are a result of physiological aging, others are a result of accumulative products over time. Therefore, anti-aging strategies should focus on both preventing accumulation of detrimental products as well as adjustment to inevitable physiological changes.

Several of these theories may interact with nutrient metabolism. For example, the immunological theory of aging states that certain aspects of aging may be a result of the dysregulation of the immune system as animals get older. The interaction between nutrition and the immune system has received much attention recently and nutrients such as vitamin E may aid the aging immune response.[8,9] Another example would be the free radical theory of aging which hypothesizes that the aging process results in an accumulation of free radicals which may cause intracellular damage leading to degenerative diseases associated with aging. The interaction between antioxidant nutrients and free radicals has also been an area of interest, and may play a role in the aging process. The association between these theories and nutrition emphasizes the need to consider optimal nutritional interventions in the geriatric patient.

Nutrient Absorption	When considering nutrition for a particular life stage, one must consider both nutrient absorption and nutrient utilization. The effect of age on intestinal absorption of nutrients has been examined in the dog.[10] In this study, nutrient balance experiments were conducted on young and old Beagles to determine any age-related changes in protein, fat, energy, vitamin or mineral absorption. It was demonstrated that there were no age-related changes in absorption of these nutrients. This same observation has been noted in other species as well and may be due to the ability of the gastrointestinal tract to compensate for small decreases in absorptive efficiency. Therefore, recommendations of age-related nutrient requirements may not be warranted on absorption deficiencies. It is important to note that this study demonstrated that there was an age-related decline in the immune system of these dogs. This observation further demonstrates that there may be changes in physiological systems that can influence nutritional needs of geriatric patients.

Nutrient Utilization	Although nutrient absorption may not change significantly with age, there are indications of age-related changes in nutrient utilization in geriatric populations.

Defining and understanding these alterations will help in designing specific diets to meet the needs of the older animal.

Protein. The influence of dietary protein on the geriatric dog and cat has been a widely debated area. For many years, it has been commonly believed that dietary protein contributes to chronic renal failure. However, recent research has demonstrated that high protein diets do not influence the incidence or progression of renal failure in dogs.[11-13] Therefore, the common practice of feeding low protein diets to geriatric dogs may not be necessary to prevent chronic renal failure during aging.

The issue of appropriate protein levels for geriatric individuals has been an area of debate for gerontologists. Some researchers have suggested that there is an increased dietary protein requirement in the geriatric animal. This statement comes from both nitrogen balance studies, as well as studies examining protein flux.[14] Also, it has been noted that lean body mass declines with age due to a loss of skeletal muscle protein resulting from decreased muscle protein synthesis. As a result, muscle mass accounts for less than 20% of the whole body protein in geriatric humans compared to 30% in young adults.[14]

An age-associated change in body composition has been observed in geriatric dogs. Thirty-six young and old Fox Terriers and Labrador Retrievers (Fox Terriers 1.8 *v* 11.5 years; Labrador Retrievers 1.5 *v* 9.6 years; n=9 per breed and age group) were maintained on a standard diet for 2 months. Body composition of the dogs was examined by Dual Energy X-ray Absorptiometry (DEXA). While there was no difference in body weight between the young and old dogs within each breed, there was an increase in the percent body fat and a decrease in the percent lean body mass (*Figure 2*). Interestingly, the percent change of lean body mass over time was greater for the Fox Terriers than the Labrador Retrievers (-20% *v* -6%). Thus, protein metabolism (i.e., maintenance of lean body mass) is affected by age as well as breed. The effect of levels of dietary protein on whole body protein turnover and how this influences the geriatric dog is reviewed elsewere in this proceedings.[15]

Glucose. It has been previously reported that the ability of older dogs to reach baseline glucose levels takes longer than their younger counterparts.[6,16] This observation has been noted with other species as well. Several theories have been proposed to explain the age-related intolerance to glucose. It has been proposed that this may be due to either a decline in the ability of insulin receptors to respond or an actual decrease in the number of receptors present.[17] Other theories have stated that it is due to a loss of hepatic sensitivity to insulin; reduced glycogenesis; in-creased glucagon levels, or a loss of lean body mass and increase in adipose tissue.[18] This suggests that considerations should be given to nutritional strategies that can alter glucose metabolism in geriatric animals.

Fatty Acids. Utilization of fatty acids may also be altered with age. Age-related alterations of omega-6 and omega-3 fatty acids have been reviewed by

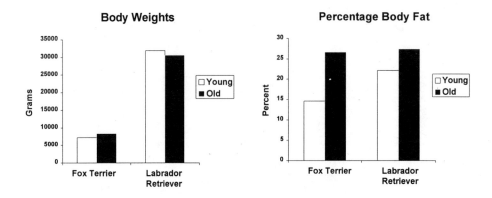

Body Weights

Percentage Body Fat

Percentage Lean Body Mass

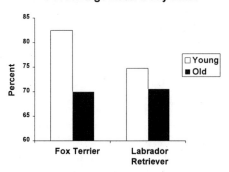

Figure 2. Effect of age on body weight, percentage body fat, and percentage lean body mass of Fox Terriers and Labrador Retrievers.

Turek.[19] It has also been demonstrated that the activity of various metabolic enzymes changes with age. One example is the decline in Δ6-desaturase activity and affinity in the rat and dog which contributes to slowing of desaturation of fatty acids with age.[20,21] Supplementation of fatty acids products of Δ6-desaturase (such as γ-linoleic acid) may bypass these age-related shifts in enzyme function.

Another example is age-related alterations in eicosanoid metabolism. Eicosanoids are a family of fatty acid metabolites derived from cellular membrane phospholipids. These eicosanoids have the potential to mediate physiological processes such as regulation of the immune system and inflammation. Some of these metabolites have been shown to increase with age. Increased production of PGE_2 has been demonstrated with cultures of adherent cells or spleen homogenates from old mice[22,23] and cultured mononuclear cells from old humans.[24] To determine if overall production or specific enzymatic products were increased with age, eicosanoid production was characterized in macrophages isolated from young and old mice.[25] It was found that macrophages from old mice produced increased levels of cyclooxygenase (PGE_2) and 5-lipoxygenase (LTB_4) products. In the case of the cyclooxygenase product PGE_2, this age-related increase is due to increased activity of the enzyme cyclooxygenase rather than age-related changes in substrate availability.[25,26] This is of particular interest since PGE_2 has been known to be a proinflammatory compound and has been demonstrated to be suppressive to the immune system.[27] Therefore, nutritional interventions that can influence the production of PGE_2, such as dietary omega-3 fatty acids or vitamin E, may be beneficial to the geriatric animal.

The age-associated decline of the immune system has been discussed elsewhere in this proceedings.[9,19] Several reports have demonstrated that the immune system of the dog declines with age. Laboratory studies have demonstrated a decline in mitogen stimulation, chemotaxis, and phagocytosis.[10,28,29] A recent longitudinal study has reported various clinical immunological parameters that change with age.[6] The results of this study are summarized in **Table 5**.

Immune System

Table 5. Age-related changes in clinical immunological parameters in the dog. Adapted from Strasser et al., 1993.[6]

Parameter	Young	Old
White blood cells 10^9/L	10.34 ± 0.38	8.37 ± 0.57
Immature neutrophil cells/μl	485 ± 33	275 ± 33
Mature neutrophil cells/μl	3374 ± 227	5712 ± 424
Immunoglobulin G (g/L)	23.80 ± 0.39	32.60 ± 0.44

To examine the effect of age on lymphocyte activation in different breeds, lymphocytes were isolated from 40 young and old Fox Terriers and Labrador Retrievers. These were stimulated with either Concanavalin A (Con A) or phytohemagglutinin (PHA) (T cell stimmulants) or pokeweed mitogen (B cell stimulant). Both breeds demonstrated an age-associated decline in their ability to respond to the different mitogens (**Figure 3**). It is interesting to note that similar to the body composition data, the degree of decline was greater for the Fox Terriers than the Labrador Retrievers (-216% *v* -114%; -292% *v* -106%; -234% *v* -102% Fox Terriers *v* Labrador Retrievers, ConA, PHA, and PWM, respectively). Together these data demonstrate that there is an age-related decline in immunity in dogs which may increase the susceptibility of the geriatric animal to infection.[16] However, this rate of age-related decline may be different between breeds. The potential exists to influence this rate of decline with nutrients that enhance the canine immune response such as vitamin E, or carotenoids.[9,29,30]

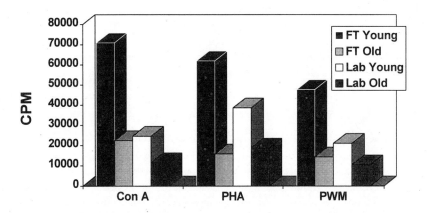

Figure 3. Effect of age and breed on T cell and B cell mitogen response. Blood was collected from 36 young and old Fox Terriers and Labrador Retrievers (n=9 per age per breed). 2.5 x 10⁶ cells were isolated from peripheral blood, incubated for 68 hours in the presence of Concanavalin A (Con A), phytohemagglutinin (PHA), and pokeweed mitogen (PWM), pulsed with [³H]-thymidine for 16 hours and harvested. Data is expressed as counts per minute (cpm) (Hayek and Kearns, unpublished data).

Conclusion

Accumulating data defining the physiology of the geriatric dog and cat demonstrate that specific nutritional formulations are warranted for the aging companion animal population. Nutritional strategies should be designed to delay the onset of age-associated physiological changes (i.e., decline in lean body mass and immune response) as well as compensate for age-dependent metabolic changes (i.e., changes in enzyme activities for fatty acid metabolism). Furthermore, one should think about nutrition for the aging animal before the signs of old age are evident. Nutritional formualtions incorporating moderate protein levels, antioxidant vitamin adjustments, and specific polyunsaturated fatty acids will help address many of these concerns. As data continues to be generated, further nutritional advances will provide guidance for further optimizing the health of geriatric dogs and cats.

References

1. Vercruyssen M, Graafmans JAM, Fozard JL, Bouman H, Rietsma J. Gerontechnology. In: Birren JE, ed. *Encyclopedia of Gerontology Age, Aging and the Aged*. New York: Academic Press, 1996; 593-604.

2. Timiras PS. Introduction: aging as a stage in the life cycle. In: Timiras PS, ed. *Physiological Basis of Aging and Geriatrics*. Boca Raton: CRC Press, 1994; 191-198.

3. Wise JK. The Veterinary Services Marketing for Companion Animals. Schaumburg, IL. *Am Vet Assoc* 1991.

4. Davies M. An introduction to geriatric veterinary medicine. In: Davies M, ed. *Canine and Feline Geriatrics*. Cambridge: Blackwell Science, 1996; 1-11.

5. Goldstein RT. Introduction and overview of geriatrics. In: Goldstein RT, Hoskins JD, eds. *Geriatrics and Gerontology of the Dog and Cat*. Philadelphia: W.B. Saunders Company, 1995.

6. Strasser A, Niedermuller H, Hofecker G, Laaber G. The effect of aging on laboratory values in the dog. *J Vet Med* 1993; 40:720-730.

7. Sharma R. Theories of aging. In: Timiras PS, ed. *Physiological Basis of Aging and Geriatrics*. Boca Raton: CRC Press, 1994; 37-46.

8. Meydani SN, Blumberg JB. Nutrition and immune function in the elderly. In: Munro HN, Danforrd DE, eds. *Human Nutrition: A Comprehensive Treatise*. Plenum Publishing Corporation, 1986; 61-86.

9. Meydani SN, Hayek MG, Wu D, Meydani M. Vitamin E and immune response in aged dogs. In: Reinhart GA, Carey DP, eds. *Recent Advances in Canine and Feline Nutrition, Vol. II: 1998 Iams Nutrition Symposium Proceedings*. Wilmington: Orange Frazer Press, 1998; 295-304.

10. Sheffy BE, Williams AJ, Zimmer JF, Ryan GD. Nutrition and metabolism of the geriatric dog. *Cornell Vet* 1985; 75:324-347.

11. Carey DP. Dietary protein and the kidney. In: Carey DP, Norton SA, Bolser SM, eds. *Recent Advances in Canine and Feline Nutritional Research: Proceedings of the 1996 Iams International Nutrition Symposium*. Wilmington: Orange Frazer Press, 1996; 117-122.

12. Finco DR, Brown SA, Crowell WA, Brown CA, Barsanti JA, Carey DP, Hirakawa DA. Effects of aging and dietary protein intake on uniphretomized geriatric dogs. *Am J Vet Res* 1994; 55:1282-1290.

13. Finco DR, Brown SA, Crowell WA. Effects of dietary protein and phosphorus on the kidneys of dogs. In: Carey DP, Norton SA, Bolser SM, eds. *Recent Advances in Canine and Feline Nutritional Research: Proceedings of the 1996 Iams International Nutrition Symposium*. Wilmington: Orange Frazer Press, 1996; 117-122.

14. Young VR, Gersovitz M, Munro HN. Human aging: protein and amino acid metabolism and implications for protein and amino acid requirements. In: Moment GB, ed. *Nutritional Approaches to Aging Research*. Boca Raton: CRC Press, Inc., 1982; 47-82.

15. Davenport GM, Williams CC, Cummins KA, Hayek MG. Protein metabolism and aging. In: Reinhart GA, Carey DP, eds. *Recent Advances in Canine and Feline Nutrition, Vol. II: 1998 Iams Nutrition Symposium Proceedings*. Wilmington: Orange Frazer Press, 1998; 363-378.

16. Mosier JE. Effect of aging on body systems in the dog. *Vet Clin N Am: Sm An Pract* 1989; 19:1-12.

17. Davis PJ, Davis FB. Endocrinology and aging. In: Reichel W, ed. *Clinical Aspects of Aging*. Baltimore: Williams and Williams, 1983; 396-410.

18. Timiras PS. The endocrine, pancreas and carbohydrate metabolism. In: Timiras PS, ed. *Physiological Basis of Aging and Geriatrics*. Boca Raton: CRC Press, 1994; 191-198.

19. Turek JJ, Hayek MG. Effect of omega-6:omega-3 fatty acid ratios on cytokine production in adult and geriatric dogs. In: Reinhart GA, Carey DP, eds. *Recent Advances in Canine and Feline Nutrition, Vol. II: 1998 Iams Nutrition Symposium Proceedings*. Wilmington: Orange Frazer Press, 1998; 305-324.

20. Biagi PL, Bordoni A, Hrelia S, Celadon M, Horrobin DF. Gamma-linoleic acid dietary supplementation can reverse the aging influence on rat liver microsome delta-6-desaturase activity. *Biochem Biophys Acta* 1991; 1083:187.

21. Reinhart GA, Vaughn DM, Hayek MG, Lauten S, Swaim SF. Effect of age on canine hepatic delta-6 and delta-5 desaturase activity. *J Anim Sci* 1997; 75(Suppl 1):227.

22. Rosenstein MM, Strausser HR. Macrophage induced T-cell mitogen suppression with age. *J Reticuloendothel Soc* 1980; 27:159-166.

23. Meydani SN, Meydani M, Verdon CP, Blumberg JB, Hayes KC. Vitamin E supplementation suppresses prostaglandin E$_2$ synthesis and enhances the immune response of aged mice. *Mech Ageing Dev* 1986; 34:191-201.

24. Meydani SN, Barklund MD, Lui S, Meydani M, Miller RA, Cannon J, Morrow F, Rocklin R, Blumberg JB. Vitamin E supplementation enhances cell-mediated immunity in healthy elderly. *Am J Clin Nutr* 1990; 52:557-563.

25. Hayek MG, Meydani SN, Meydani M, Blumberg JB. Age differences in eicosanoid production of mouse splenocytes: effects on mitogen-induced T-cell proliferation. *J Gerontol* 1994; 5:B197-B207.

26. Hayek MG, Wu D, Meydani SN. Age-associated changes in cyclooxygenase activity of splenocytes and macrophages from C57Bl/6 mice. *FASEB J* 1994; A4111.

27. Meydani SN, Hayek MG. Vitamin E and aging immune response. *Clinics in Geriatric Med* 1995; 1:567-576.

28. Greeley EH, Kealy RD, Ballman JM, Lawler DF, Segre M. The influnce of age on the canine immune system. *Vet Immunol Immunopath* 1996; 55:1-10.

29. Chew BP, Park JS, Wong TS, Weng B, Kim HW, Byrne KM, Hayek MG, Reinhart GA. Importance of β-carotene nutrition in the dog and cat: uptake and immunity. In: Reinhart GA, Carey DP, eds. *Recent Advances in Canine and Feline Nutrition, Vol. II: 1998 Iams Nutrition Symposium Proceedings.* Wilmington: Orange Frazer Press, 1998; 513-522.

30. Chew BP, Wong TS, Park JS, Weng BB, Cha N, Kim HW, Byrne KM, Hayek MG, Reinhart GA. Role of dietary lutein in the dog and cat. In: Reinhart GA, Carey DP, eds. *Recent Advances in Canine and Feline Nutrition, Vol. II: 1998 Iams Nutrition Symposium Proceedings.* Wilmington: Orange Frazer Press, 1998; 547-554.

Protein Metabolism and Aging

Gary M. Davenport, PhD
Associate Professor, Animal and Dairy Sciences
Auburn University, Alabama, USA
Currently: Research Nutritionist
Research and Development, The Iams Company, Lewisburg, Ohio, USA

Cathleen C. Williams, MS[a]; Keith A. Cummins, PhD[a];
Michael G. Hayek, PhD[b]
[a]Animal and Dairy Sciences, Auburn University, Alabama, USA
[b]Research and Development, The Iams Company, Lewisburg, Ohio, USA

Aging can be described as the sum of all physiological changes occurring in the body with the passage of time that ultimately result in functional impairment and death. These progressive and irreversible changes occur at the cellular and subcellular levels and express themselves through altered metabolic functions, body composition, and disease resistance. Although various external factors (disease, stress, malnutrition, lack of exercise, etc.) hasten these age-related changes, the population of geriatric humans and animals continues to increase rapidly. The rapid expansion of this elderly population can be attributed to improvements in the health status of individuals due to our increased knowledge and utilization of modern technologies in the diagnosis and treatment of metabolic disorders associated with aging. Research continues to focus on the nutritional status of the geriatric individual to ascertain the specific role of dietary nutrients in modulating the adverse effects of aging. The impact of dietary protein on the aging process has received considerable attention due to inherent relationships between protein turnover, body composition, and the aging process.

Introduction

Protein is required in the diet of humans and animals for a number of important reasons. Dietary protein provides essential, or indispensable, amino acids that are required by the body for protein synthesis during tissue growth and repair (**Table 1**). Essential amino acids must be provided in the diet because the body cannot synthesize them at a sufficient rate to meet tissue requirements. Dietary protein also supplies non-specific nitrogen (N) for the synthesis of nonessential, or dispensable, amino acids and other N-containing compounds in the body. In addition, dietary amino acids may be used as energy substrates resulting from their conversion to citric acid cycle intermediates and subsequent oxidation via intermediary metabolism. Certain amino acids are glucogenic or ketogenic, indicative of their use for glucose or fatty acid synthesis, respectively. The quantity of protein required in the diet reflects the summation of these various metabolic functions of

*Dietary
Protein
Requirements*

Table 1. Essential and nonessential amino acids for dogs and cats.

Essential Amino Acids		Nonessential Amino Acids	
Methionine	Arginine	Alanine	Asparagine
Threonine	Tryptophan	Aspartate	Cysteine
Histidine	Isoleucine	Glutamate	Glutamine
Leucine	Lysine	Glycine	Proline
Valine	Phenylalanine	Serine	Tyrosine
Taurine (cats only)			

individual amino acids. Therefore, optimizing the health and well-being of the animal requires the fulfillment of individual amino acid requirements by feeding sufficient quantities of protein in the diet.

Conflicting data exist regarding the quantity of protein and amino acids required by geriatric individuals compared with young-adults.[1] Some human studies indicate that protein requirements increase with age due to reduced food consumption and decreased efficiency of absorptive and metabolic processes. In contrast, others report lower requirements based on reduced rates of protein turnover, decreased muscle mass, and decreased physical activity in geriatric individuals. A similar controversy exists regarding the protein requirement of aging dogs. Historically, low protein diets have been recommended for geriatric dogs to minimize or prevent progressive renal failure. Despite any scientific evidence, this recommendation was based on the belief that catabolism of excess dietary protein and the subsequent excretion of metabolic waste was responsible for initiating progressive renal dysfunction in aging dogs.[2] However, research has demonstrated that feeding a high protein diet (34% protein) to uninephrectomized geriatric dogs for four years had no detrimental effect on renal function compared with an 18% protein diet.[3] Coincidentally, they reported that mortality rate during the four years was higher for dogs fed 18% protein compared with those fed 34% protein. To date, no evidence has been presented in humans or animals indicating that the quality or pattern of amino acids required in the diet is affected by aging.

Whole-body Protein Turnover and Aging

It is well-established in dogs, like humans and other animals, that body composition changes with advancing age. This change is reflected in the progressive reduction in lean body mass (muscle) with age while the percentage of body fat continually increases. Although a number of factors are involved in this age-related change in muscle mass, alterations in whole-body protein turnover are ultimately responsible for the loss. Whole-body protein turnover represents the continual replacement of individual proteins distributed throughout the body resulting from the combination of protein synthesis and degradation. The loss of body protein associated with aging occurs when protein degradation exceeds synthesis, thus producing negative N balance. Under ideal situations, N balance should be equal to or greater than zero in order to preserve body protein. If synthesis and degradation of body protein are equal in magnitude, then protein content of the body remains constant and N balance equals zero. Positive N balance occurs when body protein accumulates as the rate of protein synthesis exceeds the rate of protein degradation. Historically, a favorable N balance response to graded levels of dietary protein has been the principle factor used in establishing dietary protein requirements of humans and animals.

Measuring whole-body protein turnover in humans and animals requires the use of tracer amino acids labeled with ^{15}N, ^{14}C, ^{35}S or ^{3}H to estimate rates of protein synthesis and degradation. The flux of these tracer amino acids through the free amino acid pool can be used to calculate protein turnover. As shown in *Figure 1*, amino acids entering this metabolic pool are derived from dietary protein or from the breakdown of body protein, while exiting amino acids are destined for protein synthesis or degradation with the N component excreted primarily as urinary urea.[4] A widely used method for estimating amino acid flux and protein turnover involves the continuous oral administration of ^{15}N-glycine and the subsequent excretion of ^{15}N-urea in the urine.[5] It has been determined using this technique that rates of whole-body protein synthesis and degradation are lower in elderly individuals with the principle reduction occurring in skeletal muscle.[6] Furthermore, it has been estimated that muscle protein turnover accounts for 30% of the whole body protein turnover in young-adults but decreases to 20% in geriatric individuals.[7]

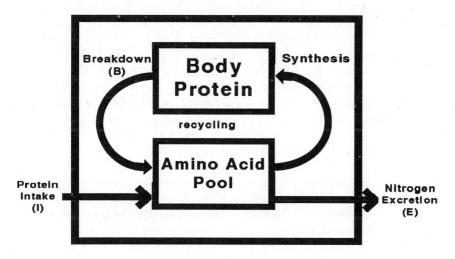

Figure 1. Amino acid flux (Q) through the metabolic pool is calculated as Q = I + B = E + S. Adapted from Munro, 1989.[4]

Skeletal muscle is highly vulnerable to the effects of aging based on the preferential loss of muscle compared to nonmuscular tissues such as the liver, heart, and digestive tract. The weight of internal organs in 70-year-old people is 9 to 18%

less than the same organs in young-adults, whereas skeletal muscle weighs 40% less. The progressive loss of muscle throughout adult life results in skeletal muscle comprising 27% of the body weight of elderly men compared to 45% in young-adult males.[8]

It has been suggested that loss of lean body mass resulting from lower rates of protein synthesis and degradation may diminish the body's ability to respond to physical trauma, infectious agents, or stress.[9] Decreased muscle protein reserves cannot provide sufficient quantities of amino acids needed for tissue repair and energy metabolism. Furthermore, it has been postulated that loss of lean body mass impairs the immune system and increases the susceptibility of elderly individuals to infectious organisms.[10] Consumption of a low protein diet by elderly women produced negative N balance due to loss of lean body mass which was accompanied by reduced immunocompetence.[11] In contrast, the consumption of a protein-adequate diet maintained N balance and lean body mass and enhanced immuno-competence. Reduced immunocompetence of protein-malnourished individuals has been attributed to impaired production and/or activity of various cytokines, such as interleukin-1 (IL-1β) and tumor necrosis factor (TNF-α).[12] These cytokines are immunomodulators that function to initiate and sustain an immune response when the body is challenged by an infectious organism.

Growth Hormone, IGF-I, and Dietary Protein

Reduced muscle mass in geriatric individuals has been attributed to decreased secretion of growth hormone from the anterior pituitary. In fact, growth hormone has been touted as an anti-aging hormone based on increased lean body mass, decreased adipose tissue, and increased bone density in elderly men administered biosynthetic growth hormone for 6 months.[13] The age-related reduction in growth hormone concentration results from decreased amplitude and duration of growth hormone pulses.[14] This altered secretory profile may be due to decreased numbers of pituitary somatotropes and/or decreased pituitary responsiveness to hypothalamic releasing hormones.[14,15] Regardless, it has been reported that mRNA levels for growth hormone in pituitary somatotropes are reduced 40% in elderly individuals compared to young-adults.[14]

Research has shown that growth hormone enhances muscle protein accretion due to its stimulatory effect on insulin-like growth factor-I (IGF-I). IGF-I is a hormone that mediates the biological effects of growth hormone in various tissues such as skeletal muscle and bone through its growth-promoting and insulin-like actions. In fact, the decline in growth hormone in geriatric individuals is paralleled by reduced IGF-I concentrations.[16] Furthermore, the addition of IGF-I to cultured skeletal muscle satellite cells directly increases the rate of protein synthesis while concurrently reducing protein degradation rates.[17] In contrast, the addition of physiological concentrations of growth hormone does not affect protein turnover in these cultured cells. Systemic infusion of IGF-I increases the rate of protein synthesis in muscle while reducing whole-body protein degradation.[18] These results suggest that the "anti-aging" effects of growth hormone on lean body tissue may be due to the anabolic responses associated with increased IGF-I secretion. Although many tissues have the capacity to bind growth hormone and synthesize IGF-I, the liver is the primary source of circulating concentrations of IGF-I.

A direct relationship between dietary protein intake and IGF-I has been demonstrated in growing animals.[19,20] Increasing the level of dietary protein increases hepatic IGF-I gene expression and circulating IGF-I concentrations, provided that energy intake is not limiting. As depicted in *Figure 2*, positive correlations exist between intestinal amino acid availability, hepatic IGF-I gene expression, serum IGF-I concentrations, and muscle protein accretion when increasing levels of dietary protein are consumed.[19] Supplementation of low protein diets with essential amino acids also increases IGF-I while supplementation with nonessential amino acids is ineffective.[21] Furthermore, IGF-I was reduced in rats fed a lysine-deficient diet while increased intestinal availability of arginine and ornithine enhanced growth hormone and IGF-I concentrations in growing animals.[22-25] This implies that IGF-I and its biological actions are affected by level and quality of protein in the diet.

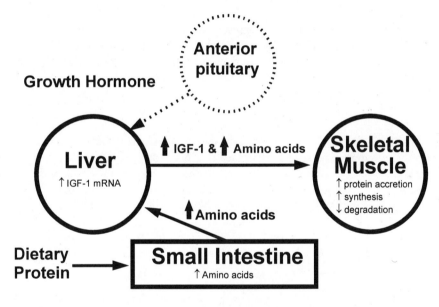

Figure 2. Relationship between intestinal amino acid availability and hormonal regulation of protein turnover in skeletal muscle.

Experimental Methods. The relationships that exist between protein intake, IGF-I, and body composition imply that increasing the dietary protein intake of geriatric dogs may prevent muscle wasting by supplying additional amino acids, thus decreasing the need to degrade skeletal muscle protein. These relationships have not been demonstrated in the dog. Therefore, an 8 week study was conducted to assess the effect of graded levels of dietary protein intake on whole-body protein turnover

Current Research

in geriatric and young-adult Beagles. Thirty-six female Beagles averaging 2 or 8 years of age were assigned to one of three isocaloric diets (gross energy = 4.4 kcal/g) containing 16, 24 or 32% crude protein. Chicken by-product meal was the principal source of protein in the experimental diets. All dogs were housed in individual stainless steel metabolism cages for the entire study. With the exception of a seven day collection period at the end of the study, each dog was allowed one hour of exercise daily in an indoor run. Whole-body N flux and rates of protein synthesis and degradation were estimated using ^{15}N-glycine administered orally as an initial flooding dose followed by continuous dosing every four hours for 48 hours.[26] Enrichment of ^{15}N was determined in the 36 hour urine sample using direct combustion of the sample and mass spectroscopy. A preliminary study indicated that urinary ^{15}N enrichment plateaued by 36 hours in these dogs signifying that steady state conditions had been established using this methodology.

N Balance and Protein Turnover. Feeding graded levels of dietary protein produced linear increases (P<0.05) in fecal and urinary N excretion. Furthermore, protein digestibility increased linearly (P<0.05) as dogs consumed more dietary protein. In contrast, N balance was similar for all treatments, averaging –0.5 g/d. The slightly negative N balance is typical of adults at maintenance that are in a state of N equilibrium. Furthermore, these values are not surprising considering that N balance was determined after these dogs had been fed their respective diets for seven weeks. Classical protein nutrition research has shown that positive N balance in adult dogs steadily falls to zero within 20 days as protein-depleted dogs are fed repletion diets containing different levels of dietary protein.[27] Protein concentration of the repletion diets did not affect the rate of protein repletion or the attainment of N equilibrium by day 20, but did alter the extent of protein repletion by altering size of body protein reserves. It was concluded that N equilibrium can be attained with long term feeding of either low or high protein diets once the size of the body protein reserve has been established.[27,28] Therefore, it can be implied from these historical data that body protein reserves in young-adult and geriatric Beagles would be affected by increased protein consumption considering N equilibrium had been achieved in these dogs. As a result, body protein reserves should have been greater in dogs fed 32% protein compared with those fed 16% protein despite the slightly negative N balance values.

Using ^{15}N-glycine as the tracer, it was determined that N flux in these dogs increased linearly (P<0.05) as dietary protein intake increased. Regression analysis revealed that N flux increased approximately 1% for every 1% increase in dietary protein consumed (r^2=0.96; y = 1.06x – 9.05). Other researchers have also reported significant positive correlations between N flux and protein intake in both adult and geriatric individuals using ^{15}N-glycine as the tracer.[29,30] These changes reflect the adaptive response of the body to alterations in dietary protein intake and whole-body protein status.

A quadratic response (P<0.05) to increased protein intake was noted for rates of whole-body protein synthesis and degradation (**Figure 3**). Dogs fed 32% protein had a 2-fold increase in whole-body protein turnover compared with dogs fed 16 and 24% protein. These differences in protein turnover coincide with larger body protein reserves that accompany increased consumption of dietary protein.[27,28] The slightly negative N balance of these dogs resulted in whole-body protein degradation rates that were 8.6, 7.6, and 2.5% greater than protein synthesis rates in dogs fed 16, 24, and 32% protein, respectively. These data demonstrate that increased consumption of dietary protein improved whole-body protein turnover based on smaller incremental differences between synthesis and degradation rates in dogs fed 32% compared with those fed 16 and 24% protein. These data are indicative of the dog's adaptive response to protein intake as those fed the low protein diets appear to be more dependent on tissue protein degradation to fulfill amino acid requirements than those fed the high protein diet. This dependency on tissue protein degradation would explain the smaller body protein reserves associated with dogs fed low protein diets.

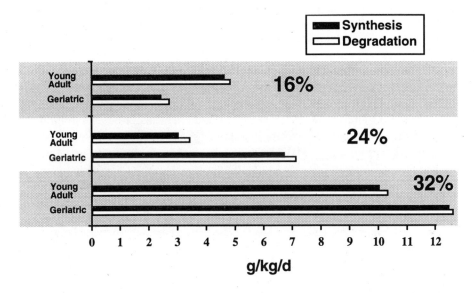

Figure 3. Rates of whole-body protein synthesis and degradation in young-adult and geriatric Beagles fed diets containing 16, 24 or 32% protein. Daily rates (g/d) are expressed per unit of body weight (kg).

A differential response to aging occurred within each level of dietary protein for rates of whole-body protein synthesis and degradation. In dogs fed 16% protein, synthesis and degradation rates were 48.4 and 43.2% lower for geriatric dogs compared with young-adult dogs, respectively. In contrast, synthesis and degradation rates were higher in the geriatric dogs compared with the young-adult dogs when fed diets containing 24 and 32% protein (128.1 and 115.5%; 25.1 and 24.7%, respectively). These age-dependent responses to dietary protein were reflected in relative changes in protein synthesis and degradation rates as young-adult and geriatric dogs consumed increasing levels of protein. Incremental increases in dietary protein resulted in higher synthesis and degradation rates in geriatric dogs as protein intake increased from 16 to 24% (184.0 and 159.5%, respectively) and from 24 to 32% (86.5 and 80.6%, respectively). In contrast, whole-body protein turnover in the young-adult dogs displayed a differential response to incremental increases in protein intake. Protein synthesis and degradation rates were 35.7 and 31.5% lower in young-adult dogs fed 24% compared with those fed 16% protein, respectively. However, increasing protein intake from 24 to 32% resulted in synthesis and degradation rates that were 240.0 and 212.1% higher in these young-adult dogs, respectively.

Serum Amino Acid Concentrations. The effect of dietary protein intake on serum amino acid concentrations were assessed by comparing changes in the molar percentages of individual essential amino acids in young-adult and geriatric dogs consuming increasing levels of dietary protein (**Figure 4**). Positive percentages for individual amino acids reflected higher concentrations with the increased level of dietary protein, indicating that amino acid supply exceeded protein synthetic utilization. In contrast, a negative percentage reflected reduced concentrations as protein consumption increased, implying greater utilization of the amino acid for synthetic or catabolic purposes.

Although incremental increases in dietary protein did not uniformly increase serum amino acid concentrations, tryptophan concentrations were reduced in all dogs as dietary protein increased. Differential responses to protein intake that were not age-dependent included lower lysine and phenylalanine concentrations in dogs fed 24% compared with 16% protein (panel A) and higher concentrations in those fed 32% protein (panel B). In contrast, histidine concentrations were higher in dogs fed 24% protein compared with 16% protein, but lower in dogs fed 32% protein. Responses of the remaining essential amino acids were both age- and protein-dependent as incremental increases in dietary protein resulted in higher arginine, threonine, and valine concentrations in geriatric dogs only. In contrast, serum methionine, isoleucine, and leucine concentrations were increased in the young-adult dogs with increasing levels of dietary protein.

A differential response to aging occurred within each level of dietary protein for the essential amino acids based on comparisons between young-adult and geriatric dogs fed 16, 24, and 32% protein (**Figure 5**). When compared with young-adult dogs, geriatric dogs fed 16% protein had higher methionine concentrations, but lower concentrations of threonine, arginine, and total amino acids (Panel A). Feeding the 24% protein diet resulted in higher methionine, threonine, leucine, and total essential amino acids in geriatric dogs compared with young-adult dogs, but lower isoleucine, arginine, and lysine concentrations (Panel B). Total essential amino acids were not affected by age in dogs fed 32% protein despite higher concentrations of tryptophan and threonine in the geriatric dogs (Panel C). Serum lysine concentrations were lower in geriatric dogs fed 32% protein compared with young-adult dogs fed the same diet.

The observed age-induced changes in total essential amino acids within each protein level corresponded to differences in rates of whole-body protein synthesis in these dogs. This relationship was illustrated by plotting age-dependent

Panel A
16% v 24%

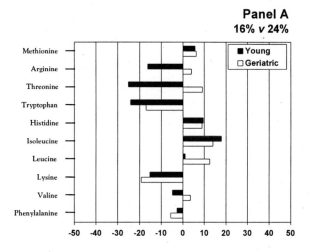

Panel B
24% v 32%

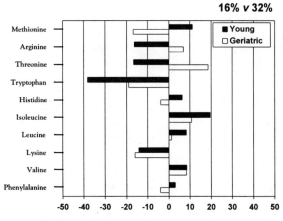

Panel C
16% v 32%

Figure 4. Changes in the molar percentages of circulating essential amino acids in young-adult and geriatric Beagles as dietary protein intake increased from 16 to 24% (panel A), 24 to 32% (panel B) and 16 to 32% (panel C). Individual values were calculated by expressing the amino acid concentration in the young-adult or geriatric dogs fed the higher protein level as a percentage of the amino acid concentration in the corresponding dogs fed the lower protein level.

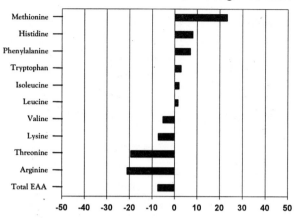

Panel A
16%: Young *v* Geriatric

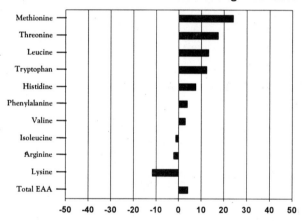

Panel B
24%: Young *v* Geriatric

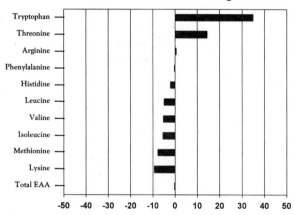

Panel C
32%: Young *v* Geriatric

Figure 5. Ranking of the relative changes in the molar percentages of circulating essential amino acids between young-adult and geriatric Beagles fed 16% protein (panel A), 24% protein (panel B), and 32% protein (panel C). Individual values were calculated by expressing the amino acid concentration in the geriatric dogs as a percentage of the amino acid concentration in the young-adult dogs within each level of dietary protein.

changes in whole-body protein synthesis rates against age-dependent changes in total essential amino acid concentrations for dogs fed 16, 24, and 32% protein (**Figure 6**). Plotting the differences between geriatric and young-adult dogs shows that every 1% increase in total essential amino acids corresponded to a 13.5% increase in the rate of whole-body protein synthesis ($r^2 = 0.984$; $y = 13.5x + 46.1$). The difference between geriatric and young-adult dogs was most noticeable when dogs were fed 24% protein. Geriatric dogs fed 24% protein had higher concentrations of total essential amino acids and greater rates of protein synthesis relative to the young-adult dogs indicating an improvement in whole-body protein status of the geriatric dogs. In contrast, feeding the low protein diet (16%) appeared to be more detrimental to geriatric dogs than young-adult dogs based on lower concentrations of total essential amino acids and reduced rates of protein synthesis. Age-related differences in whole-body protein status were minimal in dogs fed 32% protein due to the improved status of young-adult dogs fed the higher level of protein compared with those fed 24% protein.

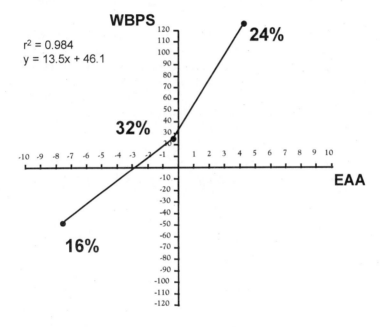

Figure 6. Relationship of age-dependent changes in whole-body protein synthesis (WBPS) rates to age-dependent changes in total essential amino acid (EAA) concentrations in Beagles fed 16, 24, and 32% protein. Individual values were calculated by expressing WBPS or EAA in geriatric dogs as a percentage of WBPS or EAA in young-adult dogs within each level of dietary protein.

Serum Hormones. Changes in amino acid concentrations and whole-body protein turnover reflected changes in serum IGF-I concentrations. Although serum IGF-I concentrations typically decline with age, IGF-I concentrations were 67% higher in geriatric dogs compared with young-adult dogs. This response was not affected by protein intake as IGF-I concentrations were 66, 87, and 49% higher in geriatric dogs than young-adult dogs when fed 16, 24, and 32% protein, respectively.

Western ligand blotting indicated that the pattern of IGF-I binding proteins (IGFBP) was similar to previous reports for canine serum.[31] IGFBP-3 (doublet bands of 43 and 39 kDa) was higher ($P<0.05$) in geriatric than young-adult dogs regardless of protein intake, while IGFBP-2 (37 kDa) and 28 and 24 kDa bands (IGFBP-1, IGFBP-4 and/or IGFBP-5) were not affected by age. When compared with young-adult dogs, total IGFBP was increased ($P<0.05$) in geriatric dogs fed 24 and 32% protein, while similar concentrations were observed for geriatric and young-adult dogs fed the low protein diet. IGFBP-2 was the only binding protein affected by dietary protein intake with lower ($P<0.05$) concentrations in dogs fed 16% protein compared with those fed 24 and 32% protein.

Serum insulin was not affected by dietary protein, while glucagon concentrations decreased linearly ($P<0.05$) with higher protein diets. The absence of an insulin response may be attributed to blood sampling immediately preceding the once daily offering of food when insulin levels are normally depressed.

Summary

These results demonstrate that feeding increased levels of dietary protein positively affected whole-body protein turnover in geriatric dogs based on increased amino acid flux through the metabolic pool. When all data were considered, it was determined that the dietary protein requirement of the geriatric dog was between 16 and 24%, while the requirement for the young-adult dog was between 24 and 32% protein. Similar conclusions regarding lower protein requirements have been reported in aging humans when whole-body protein turnover was used to establish requirements.[32] These data suggest that additional benefits may be provided to the geriatric dog if dietary protein levels exceed 24%. These results indicate that many commercial "senior" diets that are formulated to contain less than 20% protein may be inadequate for meeting the protein requirement of the geriatric dog. This problem may be further exacerbated if these diets are formulated using low-quality protein sources, such as vegetable-based protein sources rather than animal-based protein sources.

Increased levels of dietary protein have the potential to effectively increase or maintain muscle mass in geriatric individuals by supplying a continual source of essential amino acids that are required for tissue repair and immunocompetence. Increased amino acid utilization can be attributed to enhanced incorporation into tissue protein and/or increased amino acid catabolism and utilization of the resulting carbon-skeletons for energy, fat or glucose production. Shifting amino acid utilization from protein synthesis to these alternative functions may explain the inability of high protein diets to improve N balance despite positive changes in whole-body protein status. Amino acid utilization via these catabolic pathways requires removal of the amino-N group via deamination or transamination and subsequent disposal as urinary N which affects N balance determination.

More information is needed in this area to better understand the interrelationships that exist between nutrient intake, protein turnover, body composition, and health of the geriatric dog. It appears that increased dietary protein intake may enhance the health and well-being of the geriatric dog by increasing body protein reserves which prevents muscle wasting and delays the effects of aging. Although differences between whole-body protein synthesis and degradation rates and N balance were small, the accumulation of these changes over the life of the animal may have detrimental effects on their health and well-being due to the progressive reduction of skeletal muscle mass. Therefore, low protein diets may actually compromise the health of geriatric dogs due to their inability to maintain adequate lean body mass. Muscle wasting caused by feeding protein-inadequate diets may accelerate the aging process due to reduced body protein reserves, suppressed immunocompetence, and decreased resistance to various infectious organisms and stress. Therefore, a greater understanding of these relationships will be useful in the development of new diets and feeding strategies that prolong the health and well-being of our geriatric canine companions.

Acknowledgements

The authors acknowledge and appreciate the efforts of the following individuals associated with the Department of Animal and Dairy Sciences, Auburn University: Patricia Tyler, David McGee, Eric Altom, Tanya Schwab, Monnie Carol Powell, Suzanne Stilson, and Andrea Haman.

References

1. NRC (National Research Council). In: *Recommended Daily Allowances*, 10th Revised Ed. Washington DC: National Academy Press, 1989; 57-59.

2. Carey DP. Dietary protein and the kidney. In: Carey DP, Norton SA, Bolser SM, eds. *Recent Advances in Canine and Feline Nutritional Research: Proceedings of the 1996 Iams International Nutrition Symposium*. Wilmington: Orange Frazer Press, 1996; 117-121.

3. Finco DR, Brown SA, Crowell WA, Brown CA, Barsanti JA, Carey DP, Hirakawa DA. Effects of aging and dietary protein intake on uninephrectomized geriatric dogs. *Am J Vet Res* 1994, 55:1282-1290.

4. Munro HM. Protein nutriture and requirements of the elderly. In: Munro HM, Danford DE, eds. *Nutrition, Aging and the Elderly*. New York: Plenum Press, 1989; 153-181.

5. Picou D, Taylor-Roberts T. The measurement of total protein synthesis and catabolism and nitrogen turnover in infants in different nutritional states and receiving different amounts of dietary protein. *Clin Sci* 1969; 36:283-296.

6. Golden M, Waterlow J. Total protein synthesis in elderly people: A comparison of results with ^{15}N-glycine and ^{14}C-leucine. *Clin Sci Mole Med* 1977; 53:277-288.

7. Young V, Gersovitz M, Munro H. Human aging: Protein and amino acid metabolism and implications for protein and amino acid requirements. In: Moment G, ed. *Nutritional Approaches to Aging*. Boca Raton: CRC Press, 1982; 47-82.

8. Young VR. Impact of aging on protein metabolism. In: Armbrecht HJ, Prendergast JM, Coe RM, eds. *Nutritional Intervention of the Aging Process*. New York: Springer-Verlag, 1984; 27-47.

9. Uauy R, Winterer J, Bilmazes C, Haverberg L, Scrimshaw N, Munro H, Young V. The changing pattern of whole body protein metabolism in aging humans. *J Geront* 1978; 33:663-671.

10. Roubenoff R. Hormones, cytokines and body composition: Can lessons from illness be applied to aging? *J Nutr* 1983; 123:469-473.

11. Castenada C, Charnley J, Evans W, Crim M. Elderly women accomodate to a low-protein diet with losses of body cell mass, function and immune response. *Am J Clin Nutr* 1995; 62:30-39.

12. Simpson J, Hoffman-Goetz L. Nutritional deficiencies and immuno-regulatory cytokines. In: Cunningham-Rundles S, ed. *Nutrient Modulation of the Immune Response*. New York: Marcel Dekker, 1993; 31-45.

13. Rudman D, Feller A, Nagraj H, Gogans G, Lalitha P, Goldberg A, Schlenker R, Cohn L, Rudman I, Mattson D. Effect of human growth hormone in men over 60 years old. *N Engl J Med* 1990; 323:1-5.

14. Ceda G, Denti L, Hoffman AR, Ceresini G, Valenti G. Aging and pituitary responses to hypothalamic peptides. In: Segal HL, Rothstein M, Bergamini E, eds. *Protein Metabolism and Aging*. New York: Wiley-Liss, 1990; 335-344.

15. Sun YK, Xi YP, Fenoglio CM, Pushparaj N, O'Toole KM, Kledizik GS, Nette EG, King DW. The effect of age on the number of pituitary cells immunoreactive to growth hormone and prolactin. *Human Pathol* 1984; 15:169-180.

16. Rudman D, Kutner M, Rogers C, Lubin M, Fleming G, Bain R. Impaired growth hormone secretion in adult population. Relation to age and adiposity. *J Clin Invest* 1981; 67:1113-1369.

17. Harper J, Soar J, Buttery P. Changes in protein metabolism of ovine primary muscle cultures on treatment with growth hormone, insulin, IGF-I or epidermal growth factor. *J Endocrin* 1987; 112:87-96.

18. Lobley G. Species comparisons of tissue protein metabolism: Effects of age and hormonal action. *J Nutr* 1993; 123:337-343.

19. Davenport G, Cummins K, Mulvaney D. Abomasal nitrogen flow affects the relationship between dietary nitrogen and insulin-like growth factor-I in growing lambs. *J Nutr* 1995; 125:842-850.

20. Hays C, Davenport G, Osborn T, Mulvaney D. Effect of dietary protein and estradiol-17ß on growth and IGF-I in cattle during realimentation. *J Anim Sci* 1995; 73:589-597.

21. Clemmons D, Seeks M, Underwood, L. Supplemental essential amino acids augment the somatomedin-C/insulin-like growth factor I response to refeeding after fasting. *Metabolism* 1985; 34:391-398.

22. Cree T, Schalch D. Protein utilization in growth: Effect of lysine deficiency on serum growth hormone, somatomedins, total thyroxine (T4) and triiodothyronine, free T4 index and total corticosterone. *Endocrinology* 1985; 117:667-673.

23. Davenport G, Boling J, Schillo K. Growth and endocrine responses of lambs fed rumen-protected ornithine and arginine. *Small Rum Res* 1995; 17:229-236.

24. Davenport G, Boling J, Schillo K. Nitrogen metabolism and somatotropin secretion in beef heifers receiving abomasal arginine infusions. *J Anim Sci* 1990; 68:1683-1692.

25. Davenport G, Boling J, Schillo K, Aaron, D. Nitrogen metabolism and somatotropin secretion in lambs receiving arginine and ornithine via abomasal infusion. *J Anim Sci* 1990; 68:222-232.

26. Assimon S, Stein T. ¹⁵N-Glycine as a tracer to study protein metabolism *in vivo*. In: Nissen S, ed. *Modern Methods in Protein Nutrition and Metabolism*. San Diego: Academic Press Inc., 1992; 275-309.

27. Allison, J. The nutritive value of dietary proteins. In: Munro H, Allison J, eds. *Mammalian Protein Metabolism - Volume II*. New York: Academic Press Inc., 1964; 41-86.

28. Waterlow J. The assessment of protein nutrition and metabolism in the whole animal, with special reference to man. In: Munro H, ed. *Mammalian Protein Metabolism - Volume III*. New York: Academic Press Inc., 1969; 325-390.

29. Morais, JA, Gougeon R, Pencharz PB, Jones PJH, Ross R, Marliss EB. Whole-body protein turnover in the healthy elderly. *Am J Clin Nutr* 1997; 66:880-889.

30. Pannemans D, Wagenmakers A, Westerterp K, Schaafsma G, Halliday D. The effect of an increase of protein intake on whole-body protein turnover in elderly women is tracer dependent. *J Nutr* 1997; 127:1788-1794.

31. White ME, Hathaway MR, Dayton WR, Lepine AJ. The role of growth factors in canine and feline milk. In: Carey DP, Norton SA, Bolser SM, eds. *Recent Advances in Canine and Feline Nutritional Research: Proceedings of the 1996 Iams International Nutrition Symposium*. Wilmington: Orange Frazer Press, 1996; 89-98.

32. Milward DJ, Fereday A, Gibson N, Pacy PJ. Aging, protein requirements, and protein turnover. *Am J Clin Nutr* 1997; 66:774-786.

Renal Health

Clinical Assessment of Chronic Renal Failure

Daniel P. Carey, DVM
Director of Technical Communications, Research and Development
The Iams Company, Lewisburg, Ohio, USA

Introduction

Successful management of chronic renal failure requires not only an accurate diagnosis but also a clear description of the metabolic changes that are present. Although the laboratory criteria for diagnosis of clinically ill animals are fundamental, the manner of treatment is determined by our interpretation of those results. This paper will focus on the laboratory description of a chronic renal failure patient, which is not to minimize the significance of a complete history and physical examination. With an accurate diagnosis and knowledge of the specific functional losses, management of the patient can be more consistent and permit a more confident prognosis.

Although we often are unable to determine the cause of renal failure, the clinical and laboratory changes associated with the decompensating kidney are discernible. Even then, because renal failure is not an abrupt event, the marginal changes of many parameters and the variable pattern of changes make the early diagnosis of chronic renal failure a challenge in most practices. Indeed, it is generally agreed that detectable metabolic alterations do not appear until 75% of renal function is lost! At that time, the diagnosis is easy.[1] The insensitivity of typical measures to detect early changes of failure and the inadequacy of any one assay to provide total information makes the clinical assessment of failing kidneys a challenge.[2] Some tests are also influenced by treatment and may not always be indicative of real improvement in renal function.

Tests of renal function are conducted for one of two reasons:
- to diagnose renal health (whether normal or abnormal), and
- to monitor renal failure.

In either situation, the tests used may be the same and are simply interpreted against different standards. When evaluating renal health, reference normals from the diagnostic laboratory provide maximum or minimum results. When monitoring a patient, the individual's prior results become the reference point. It becomes very important for individual patients that repeated tests be run as part of a monitoring program. With the advent of treatments that can slow the progression of canine chronic renal failure, early identification of renal insufficiency assumes greater importance.

The tests available for diagnosing renal health are well known and included in most laboratory evaluations (*Table 1*). These tests are typically mixed into "panels" with other non-renal tests and are often viewed as separate results. For clarity, it is very useful to group the tests based on the renal function being assessed. This allows for a more complete understanding of renal functional losses and a more targeted approach to establishing management protocols for the patient.

The questions to be answered include:
- is renal disease present?
- how much renal function remains?
- are there extra-renal complications?
- what interventions are indicated?
- what is the prognosis?

Table 1. Renal function tests.

Glomerular Function	Tubular Function	Other
BUN Serum creatinine Clearance (iohexol, creatinine, inulin)	Urine specific gravity Fractional clearance	Serum bicarbonate Parathyroid hormone 1,25-cholecalciferol Serum ammonia Urine culture

As such, some cases are presented and are more or less routine. The clinical signs and laboratory tests are consistent with the history and the response to treatment is predictable. Many cases are more challenging than that, however. Often varying degrees of functional loss occur, creating questions in the clinician's mind as to adapting protocols for the difficult case. On the basis of results of individual tests, many of these cases are managed by evaluating blood urea nitrogen (BUN), serum creatinine, serum phosphorus, serum bicarbonate or total CO_2, hematocrit, urine specific gravity, systemic blood pressure, and hydration. A lack of urine concentrating ability is present in most dogs with diagnosed chronic renal failure, but may not be present in most cats. While this forms the basis for diagnosis and monitoring, there is value to understanding the basis for these assays.

For this approach, the kidney is considered in two regions: glomerulus and tubulointerstitium[3] (*Figure 1*). The tubules could be further subdivided into proximal tubules, loops of Henle and distal tubules, but for typical clinical situations, this increased precision is not necessary.

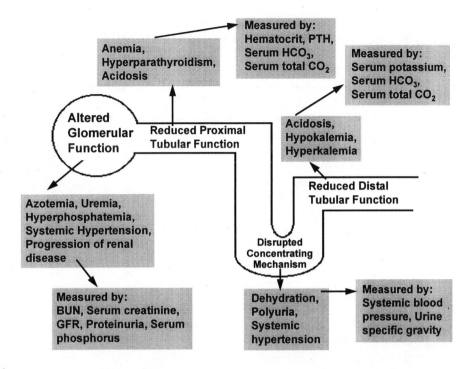

Figure 1. Consequences and measurement of nephron functional loss. Adapted from Brown et al., 1992.[5]

Glomerular Function. Glomerular function is a commonly measured renal parameter and is significantly related to renal functional mass.[4] Indeed, it is the reduction in glomerular filtration rate (GFR) that results in the accumulation of uremic toxins.[5] Any measurement that would provide information regarding GFR would then provide the earliest clue to declining renal function.[6] Consideration must be given, however, to the patient's condition, since pre- and post-renal factors can contribute greatly to abnormal test results. Routine tests such as BUN, serum creatinine, and urine protein are indicators of glomerular function. Attempts to actually measure GFR have been numerous. Successful endeavors involve expertise, equipment, and expense that are out of reach for most practicing veterinarians. Recent developments are promising, however; with support from diagnostic laboratories, an accurate, simple, reasonably priced method has become available.

Traditional research measurement of GFR involved determining creatinine or inulin clearance. Additional isotope-based clearance tests are also used in research or academic institutions.[1] Clearance is the volume of plasma that is filtered per minute per kilogram of body weight. Values from various laboratories are close, with a range between 2 and 5 ml/min/kg for endogenous creatinine clearance in dogs and cats. Endogenous creatinine clearance requires the timed collection of urine and the measurement of both serum and urine creatinine concentrations. Due to the low level of creatinine in both samples, non-creatinine chromagens can give

*Assessing
the Patient*

false readings. To correct for this, the exogenous creatinine clearance method requires creatinine to be given either by constant intravenous infusion or by single subcutaneous injection. The higher level of creatinine in both the serum and urine samples minimizes the effect of the non-creatinine chromagens.[7] Both the endogenous and exogenous creatinine clearance methods match the inulin clearance results and are accurate representations of GFR. Despite the accuracy and the absence of dietary effects, these clearance methods require restraint and either multiple urinary bladder catheterizations or an indwelling urinary catheter.

Efforts to develop a less complex and less expensive assessment of GFR have recently shown that the iodine-based radiographic contrast compound iohexol provides values comparable to both creatinine and inulin clearance.[8,9] A measured intravenous dose of 300mg I/kg (300 mg of actual iodine) is followed by blood samples at two, three, and four hours post-injection.[10] The serum from these samples is submitted to the Michigan State University Diagnostic Laboratory for iodine analysis. Results are reliable in both dogs and cats.[8,10]

The single-injection iohexol method for determining GFR allows repeated, non-invasive, outpatient monitoring of GFR. In one referral practice specializing in renal patients, this test has replaced the more cumbersome endogenous creatinine clearance method for determining GFR.[10] As awareness of this method spreads, the iohexol test should provide practitioners with a method of assessing GFR decreases early in non-azotemic, polyuric patients, as well as a means of monitoring the progression of disease in clinical cases.

Serum creatinine and BUN are included in most serum chemical profiles and used extensively by practitioners as their primary indicator of an animal's renal health. The objective behind reliance on these tests is to provide some indication of glomerular function.[4,11] The objective is valid since GFR is directly related to renal functional mass.[4] The challenge is that serum creatinine and BUN are imperfect measures of GFR. They are good screening tests and have been the most reliable methods for assessing glomerular function for years.[2,4] But it is well recognized that they are also insensitive, late indicators of renal functional loss[6] and do not provide indication of the magnitude of functional loss.[1]

The relationship between GFR and either BUN or serum creatinine is not linear.[4,6,12] Approximately 75% of renal function must be lost before the laboratory value increases above the normal range.[4,12] Once functional deficits are noted, small additional losses of function increase the BUN and serum creatinine more rapidly.

Urea is synthesized in the liver and excreted with glomerular filtrate. There is passive resorption in the proximal tubule which decreases its value as a measure of glomerular function. In dehydration, tubular flow is slowed and resorption increases, increasing the measured BUN.[4] This can occur despite adequate glomerular function otherwise. BUN is also not produced at a constant rate and is influenced by dietary protein intake.[13] Non-renal increases in BUN can be seen with gastrointestinal bleeding, hepatic insufficiency, increased catabolism (as in starvation or fever), and some drugs.[4] In addition to its insensitivity, BUN will decrease as dietary protein intake decreases. This can occur irrespective of an improvement in glomerular function. With all this aside, if non-renal variables are ruled out, BUN will increase above normal when about 75% of glomerular function is lost.[14]

Creatinine is produced at a constant rate by skeletal muscle and is excreted exclusively through the glomerulus. No tubular modification of the creatinine in the filtrate occurs.[4,11] As an indicator of glomerular filtration, serum creatinine can provide a reasonable estimate by noting the inverse (1/serum creatinine) of the result.[15] It is important to recall that serum creatinine is a function of skeletal muscle mass[7,16,17,18] and will decrease as muscle mass decreases. This should be considered in patients that lose muscle mass, whether from non-renal factors or from excessive dietary protein restriction. Decreases in serum creatinine must be evaluated accordingly.

Nonetheless, in practical situations with no change in non-renal factors, an increase in either BUN or serum creatinine suggests a decrease in renal glomerular function and is assumed to indicate a decline in patient condition.

Proteinuria can be physiologic or pathologic in origin. Exercise, seizures or fever can lead to transient increased urinary protein loss.[11] Non-renal diseases, such as hemoglobinuria, congestive heart failure, and urinary/genital tract inflammation, will cause pathologic increases. Both glomerular and, probably to a lesser degree, tubular lesions can cause persistent proteinuria that should be quantified. Initial indications of proteinuria come from screening tests using dipsticks. Results should be considered in relation to the urine specific gravity, since equal values on the dipstick have greatly different significance in dilute versus concentrated urine. Urinary sediment must be considered also. Indications of urinary or genital tract inflammation (inflammatory cells or bacteria) will increase the urine protein irrespective of renal condition.

Once identified as persistent, urinary protein losses can be quantified in stable patients.[11] Comparison of the urine protein and creatinine provides a rough idea of the degree of glomerular damage. Although either fasted or non-fasted urine samples can be assayed, dietary protein intake can cause an increase in urine protein loss without a change in GFR. The normal urine protein/creatinine ratio for both cats and dogs is less than 0.4. Anything above 1.0 is significant proteinuria.[4,11]

Clinical assessment of tubular function relies primarily on measurements of urine concentrating ability and fractional excretion.[4,11] As the kidney loses function, its ability to modify the glomerular filtrate and conserve water is also lost. This loss becomes measurable in dogs when approximately two-thirds of the nephrons are non-functional.[4] Cats often maintain concentrating ability despite a reduction in functional renal mass.[2,19] It is worth noting that concentrating ability can decrease before azotemia appears. The responsiveness of the distal tubule to antidiuretic hormone, the number of functional nephrons, and medullary hypertonicity deter-

Tubulointerstitial Function

mines the resultant urine concentration.[4] Patients presented with renal polyuria and polydipsia often already have dilute urine.

Urine specific gravity less than 1.030 in the dog and 1.035 in the cat is considered to indicate a loss of concentrating ability.[11,20] In the face of concurrent dehydration, these findings are significant. In the hydrated patient, hyposthenuria (1.013–1.029 in the dog or 1.013–1.034 in the cat) or isosthenuria (<1.013 in both species) can result from excess fluid intake and other medical conditions. In non-azotemic, hydrated, isosthenuric cases, a water deprivation test should be done to differentiate primary polydipsia from primary polyuria.

Fractional clearance is the ratio of the renal clearance of electrolytes, compared with that of creatinine. The test is based on the fact that creatinine filters through the glomerulus along with the other elements, but is not modified by the tubules. Secretion or resorption of electrolytes by the tubules changes the concentration in the urine and measurement provides an indication of tubular function.[4,11] Timed urine collection is not necessary, but simultaneous plasma and urine samples must be taken. The equation below provides the result as a percentage.

$$FC_X = 100(U_X P_{Cr})/(U_{Cr} P_X)$$

where FC_X = fractional clearance of electrolyte
          U_X = urine concentration of electrolyte
          P_{Cr} = plasma concentration of creatinine
          U_{Cr} = urine concentration of creatinine
          P_X = plasma concentration of electrolyte

Table 2 shows normal fractional clearance results for cats and dogs. The fractional clearance of sodium can also help differentiate pre-renal and renal azotemia.[4,11] Patients with pre-renal azotemia and volume depletion will show sodium retention and an FC_{Na} <1%. Renal parenchymal disease is characterized by a fractional clearance >1%.

Table 2. Normal fractional clearance values. Adapted from Dibartola, 1995.[4]

Fractional Clearance %	Dog	Cat
Sodium	<1	<1
Potassium	<20	<24
Chloride	<1	<1.3
Phosphorus	<39	<73

Acid-base balance depends upon ammoniagenesis in the proximal tubule consuming hydrogen ions and upon normal secretion/resorption of electrolytes in the distal tubule.[5] With failing ability to excrete H^+ and continued acid load from the diet, metabolic acidosis occurs. Serum electrolyte profiles of total CO_2 <15 mmol/L or bicarbonate <14 mEq/L are too low and require alkalinization therapy.[5,14]

Additional laboratory tests are available to both assess renal function and to influence the choice and degree of therapeutic intervention for renal patients. These include systemic blood pressure, hematocrit, serum phosphorus concentration, serum parathyroid hormone (PTH), calcium, potassium, activated vitamin D (1,25-dihydroxycholecalciferol or calcitriol), and blood ammonia. Radiographic evidence of small kidneys and ultrasound images of renal size, shape, and density are very useful tools for diagnosis, but are not frequently used to monitor renal patients in clinical settings.

Other Tests

Although systemic and intra-renal hypertension are not necessarily related, indirect measurement of systemic blood pressure is becoming more common. Over 50% of renal patients have systemic hypertension.[14] Because of the secondary renal, ocular, and cardiovascular effects of prolonged systemic hypertension, it should be controlled. Dogs with indirect blood pressure above 180/95 or cats above 200/145 are hypertense.

Although it cannot be measured clinically, intra-renal hypertension has been shown to be involved in the progression of renal failure.[21] Patients with diagnosed chronic renal failure should be assumed to have increased glomerular blood pressure.

Decreased renal production of erythropoietin will lead to decreased red blood cell production. Early changes may be minor or undetectable. Unfortunately, inappropriate dietary restrictions, blood losses or parasitism may compound the situation.[5] Hematocrits below 30% for dogs and 25% for cats should be treated.[14]

Gradually increasing serum phosphorus is common in renal failure and contributes to secondary renal damage via mineralization. Documentation of increased survival of renal patients when fed reduced phosphorus diets makes measurement and management of serum phosphorus important in slowing the progression of renal failure.[22] Whether PTH increases as a result of increased serum phosphorus or due to decreases in serum calcium and 1,25-dihydroxycholecalciferol is not clear. Much debate continues over the role of PTH as a uremic toxin, but regardless of the outcome, the expense of assaying for PTH makes it unlikely to be useful clinically. Further, as reported by Tetrick,[23] serum phosphorus can decrease without a concommitant decrease in serum PTH.

Serum calcium is often normal in renal patients but can go both below and above normal. If abnormal, the tendency is for lower values to appear as a result of increased serum phosphorus and the mass-ion effect. Decreased production of active vitamin D is also a factor. Increased calcium intake is commonly part of managing hyperphosphatemia. Additional vitamin D_3 intake is often indicated as well.

Serum potassium may be normal in canine chronic renal failure patients; cats frequently are hypokalemic. Urinary losses of potassium in polyuria can be high, contributing to hypokalemia.[3,14] Additionally, as acidosis develops, intercellular potassium will be driven intracellular, despite stable total body potassium. Adjustments to serum potassium must be cautiously made when simultaneously correcting acid-base balance.

Routine measurement of serum activated vitamin D or blood ammonia is unusual. These two tests can provide valuable information about the patient, but are either expensive or time-sensitive.

Monitoring the Patient

Managing a renal failure patient requires periodic reassessments.[3,14] The specific tests run and the frequency depend upon the patient and the client's willingness to support the effort. But, because renal failure is progressive and there are therapeutic options available to slow the rate of the progression of the disease, there is medical value in re-evaluating the patient's renal function regularly. Some testing, such as urine culture, does not directly involve the kidney but is surveillance for secondary complications found in renal patients.

Patients that are uremic need more frequent testing; the objective of management is to make them non-uremic. Once stable, maintenance testing can begin with frequencies dependent upon the patient's condition. *Table 3* contains recommendations for a minimum database and for scheduling.[3,14]

Table 3. Monitoring chronic renal failure. Adapted from Brown, 1997.[3]

	FREQUENCY	
Test	Uremic Patient	Non-uremic Patient
BUN	1–3 days	3–6 months
Serum creatinine	1–3 days	3–6 months
GFR		3–6 months
Systemic blood pressure	2–3 weeks	2–4 weeks*
Serum bicarbonate or total CO_2	1–3 days	3–6 months
Hematocrit		3–6 months
Serum phosphorus	1–3 days	3–6 months
Serum calcium	1–3 days	3–6 months**
Urinalysis		3–6 months
Urine culture		3–6 months
Serum electrolytes	1–3 days	3–6 months

* Once stabilized, recheck every 3-6 months
**Recheck every 2-4 weeks if on calcitriol

Urinary tract infection is more likely in the renal compromised patient.[3] Certainly ascending infection is to be avoided. Periodic urinalysis and examination for bacteria and inflammatory cells can give clues to current or impending problems. If in doubt, culture a properly collected urine sample.

Although not exactly "monitoring," attempts to diagnose loss of renal function in aging patients before clinical signs of polyuria/polydipsia or azotemia occur should be considered. With the advent of methods to slow the progression of the disease, early use of these tools has the potential to detect early changes permitting intervention that can change the rate of progression rather than waiting for overt clinical signs. With the increasing prevalence of renal disease in the aging animal (**Figure 2**),[20] routine monitoring of senior patients makes sense.

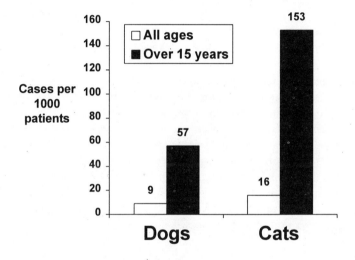

Figure 2. Chronic renal failure prevalence per 1,000 patients. Adapted from Tilley, 1997.[20]

It is generally accepted that renal failure progresses and that patients experience a decline in well-being. Nonetheless, the rate of progression is not constant and can be influenced and factors that contribute to clinical signs can be modified. The therapeutic objectives or goals for renal patients are:

Therapeutic Objectives

- Stabilize GFR
- Normophosphatemia
- Hematocrit above 30%
- Normal serum bicarbonate or total CO_2
- Normokalemia
- Reduce hypertension (both systemic and intra-renal)
- Avoid urinary tract infection
- Maintain nutritional status of patient

A stable GFR suggests stable glomerular function. Maintaining adequate dietary protein intake without aggravating azotemia would be beneficial. Reduced protein intake has been shown to decrease renal function.[24] Maintaining intake of an adequate amount of protein and the correct amounts of essential amino acids is key to maintaining the overall nutritional status of the patient as well. Adequate protein intake can be assured if innovative management, such as the Nitrogen Trap™,[25] is used. Although the measured total glomerular filtration rate might be maintained by increased single nephron GFR in the face of additional nephron losses, reduction in the glomerular pressure by increasing the intake of omega-3 fatty acids may slow progression.[21,26] A ratio of omega-6 to omega-3 fatty acids of 5:1 should have a positive effect on glomerular pressure.[26,27]

Correcting hyperphosphatemia by reducing dietary phosphorus intake to levels of 0.40% (1 gram per 1000 kcal ME) or lower may increase survival by slowing the progression of the disease.[3,22] Routine patient monitoring will show whether additional phosphorus restriction is needed via phosphate binders.[28]

With decreased renal production of erythropoetin, it becomes difficult for dogs with chronic renal disease to maintain their hematocrit. This can be compounded by inappropriate dietary protein restriction. Recombinant eryhropoeitin can be used, but there is risk of antibody production against both the exogenous erythropoetin as well as what endogenous erythropoetin is produced. The addition of anabolics, such as stanozolol, have recently been shown to improve nitrogen retention in a model of canine chronic renal failure,[29] but these drugs may have limited usefulness in correcting the decline in hematocrit.[3] Regardless, if the anabolics are used, adequate protein intake would be needed before any benefit from improved nitrogen retention could be expected.

Sodium bicarbonate is often used to correct for metabolic acidosis. In light of recent findings of the prevalence of both systemic and intra-renal hypertension in chronic renal failure, the addition of unnecessary sodium to the diet may be contraindicated.[3,14] Dietary potassium citrate is a viable alternative. In those patients who need alkalinization beyond that provided via diet, additional potassium citrate or potassium gluconate can be easily given.

Hypokalemia is typically managed by adding potassium to the diet.[3,20] This can be added to the food by the owner, but is more easily handled if the diet already contains the optimal amount. With persistent polyuria, or in some feline patients, additional potassium will be needed to maintain normokalemia.

Sustained systemic hypertension has negative effects that must be countered, but excessive reduction in blood pressure to the kidney can adversely affect renal blood flow. If normal blood pressure cannot be achieved, the goal should be to reduce systemic blood pressure by 25 to 50 mmHg.[3] While sodium restriction is often attempted, there are questions of its efficacy and there may be negative cardiovascular and renal effects to excessive sodium restriction. Reducing blood pressure is effective with pharmacologic antihypertensives such as angiotensin converting enzyme inhibitors.[20]

Urinary tract infections are not managed dietarily, but may occur with debilitated patients. Monitoring urine for other criteria will catch infections which should be treated thoroughly.

Clinicians must be aware of the potential negative effects of excessive nutrient restriction.[22,27] Additionally, laboratory parameters should be assessed in light of the effects of the consequences of dietary changes. For example, stable or reduced azotemia while maintaining muscle mass is preferable to a reduced azotemia with reduced muscle mass. Anorexia is to be avoided. Not only does general condition of the patient decrease, but this predisposes the patient to uremic crisis. Adequate total caloric intake and balanced nutrition must be assured.

With adequate monitoring and carefully planned pharmaceutical and nutritional management, patients can have reduced clinical signs and slowed progression of their renal failure.

References

1. Krawiec DR. Quantitative renal function tests in cats. *Comp Cont Educ Vet Prac* 1994; 16:1279-1284.

2. Brown SA. Treatment of hyperthyroidism and renal failure in cats. *Proc 15th ACVIM Forum*, 1997.

3. Brown SA. Chronic renal failure. In: Morgan RV, ed. *Handbook of Small Animal Practice*. Philadelphia: W.B. Saunders, 1997.

4. Dibartola SP. Clinical approach and laboratory evaluation of renal disease. In: Ettinger SJ, Feldman EC, eds. *Textbook of Veterinary Internal Medicine*. Philadelphia: W.B. Saunders, 1995.

5. Brown SA, Barsanti JA, Finco DR. Medical management of canine chronic renal failure. In: Kirk RW, ed. *Current Veterinary Therapy, XI*. Philadelphia: W.B. Saunders, 1992.

6. Brown SA. Evaluation of a single-injection method for estimating glomerular filtration rate in dogs with reduced renal function. *Am J Vet Res* 1994; 55:1470-1473.

7. Finco DR, Brown SA, Crowell WA, Barsanti JA. Exogenous creatinine clearance as a measure of glomerular filtration rate in dogs with reduced renal mass. *Am J Vet Res* 1991; 52:1029-1032.

8. Brown SA, Finco DR, Boudinot FD, Wright J, Taver SL, Cooper T. Evaluation of a single injection method, using iohexol, for estimating glomerular filtration rate in cats and dogs. *Am J Vet Res* 1996; 57:105-110.

9. Braselton WE, Stuart KJ, Kruger JM. Measurement of serum iohexol by determination of iodine with inductively coupled plasma-atomic absorption spectroscopy. *Clin Chem* 1997; 43:1429-1435.

10. Rumbeiha W. Personal communication, 1997.

11. Grauer GF. Introduction, assessment of renal function. In: Morgan RV, ed. *Handbook of Small Animal Practice.* Philadelphia: W.B. Saunders, 1997.

12. Chew DJ, Dibartola SP. *Manual of Small Animal Nephrology and Urology.* New York: Churchill Livingstone, 1986; 7.

13. Epstein ME, Barsanti JA, Finco DR, Cowgill LM. Postprandial changes in plasma urea nitrogen and plasma creatinine concentrations in dogs fed commercial diets. *J Am Anim Hosp Assoc* 1984; 20:779-782.

14. Birchard SJ, Sherding RG. Chronic renal failure. In: Birchard SJ, Sherding RG, eds. *Saunders Manual of Small Animal Practice.* Philadelphia: W.B. Saunders, 1994.

15. Finco DR, Brown SA, Vaden SL, Ferguson DC. Relationship between plasma creatinine concentration and glomerular filtration rate in dogs. *J Vet Pharmacol Ther* 1995; 18:418-421.

16. Pirlich M, Selberg O, Boker K, Schwarze M, Muller MJ. The creatinine approach to estimate muscle mass in patients with cirrhosis. *Hepatology* 1996; 24:1422-1427.

17. Wang ZM, Sun YG, Heymsfield SB. Urinary creatinine-skeletal muscle mass method: a prediction equation based on computerized axial tomography. *Biomed Environ Sci* 1996; 9:185-190.

18. Wang ZM, Gallagher D, Nelson ME, Matthews DE, Heymsfield SB. Total-body skeletal muscle mass: evaluation of 24-h urinary creatinine excretion by computerized axial tomography. *Am J Clin Nutr* 1996; 63:863-869.

19. Ross LA, Finco DR. Relationship of selected clinical renal function tests to glomerular filtration rate and renal blood flow in cats. *Am J Vet Res* 1981; 42:1704-1710.

20. Tilley LP, Smith FWK, Murray AC. Chronic renal failure. In: *The 5 Minute Veterinary Consult.* Baltimore: Williams & Wilkins, 1997.

21. Brown SA, Finco DR. Fatty acid supplementation and chronic renal disease. In: Carey DP, Norton SA, Bolser SM, eds. *Recent Advances in Canine and Feline Nutritional Research: Proceedings of the 1996 Iams International Nutrition Symposium.* Wilmington: Orange Frazer Press, 1996; 159-170.

22. Finco DR, Brown SA, Crowell WA. Effects of dietary protein and phosphorus on the kidneys of dogs. In: Carey DP, Norton SA, Bolser SM, eds. *Recent Advances in Canine and Feline Nutritional Research: Proceedings of the 1996 Iams International Nutrition Symposium.* Wilmington: Orange Frazer Press, 1996; 123-142.

23. Tetrick MA, Sunvold GD, Reinhart GA. Clinical experience with canine renal patients fed a diet containing a fermentable fiber blend. In: Reinhart GA, Carey DP, eds. *Recent Advances in Canine and Feline Nutrition, Vol. II: 1998 Iams Nutrition Symposium Proceedings.* Wilmington: Orange Frazer Press, 1998; 425-432.

24. Bovee KC, Kronfeld DS, Ramberg C, Goldschmidt M. Long-term measurement of renal function in partially nephrectomized dogs fed 56, 27, or 19% protein. *Invest Urol* 1979; 16:378-384.

25. Reinhart GA, Sunvold GD. New methods for managing canine chronic renal failure. In: Reinhart GA, Carey DP, eds. *Recent Advances in Canine and Feline Nutrition, Vol. II: 1998 Iams Nutrition Symposium Proceedings.* Wilmington: Orange Frazer Press, 1998; 395-404.

26. Brown SA. Managing chronic renal failure: the role of dietary polyunsaturated fatty acids. In: *New Concepts in Management of Renal Failure. Proc TNAVC*, 1998; 5-8.

27. Brown SA. Influence of dietary fatty acids on intrarenal hypertension. In: Reinhart GA, Carey DP, eds. *Recent Advances in Canine and Feline Nutrition, Vol. II: 1998 Iams Nutrition Symposium Proceedings*. Wilmington: Orange Frazer Press, 1998; 405-412.

28. Finco DR. Chronic renal failure: dietary protein and phosphorus. In: *New Concepts in Management of Renal Failure. Proc TNAVC* 1998; 9-10.

29. Cowan LA, McLaughlin R, Toll PW, Brown SA, Moore TI, Butine MD, Milliken G. Effect of stanozolol on body composition, nitrogen balance, and food consumption in castrated dogs with chronic renal failure. *J Am Vet Med Assoc* 1997; 15:719-722.

New Methods for Managing
Canine Chronic Renal Failure

Gregory A. Reinhart, PhD
Director of Strategic Research, Research and Development
The Iams Company, Lewisburg, Ohio, USA

Gregory D. Sunvold, PhD
Research and Development, The Iams Company, Lewisburg, Ohio, USA

Chronic renal failure is a common illness in companion animals and is characterized by an inability of the kidneys to perform their normal functions. Renal failure is defined as the sum effect of a wide range of diseases that results in the loss of 75% or more of the functional parenchyma of both kidneys (**Figure 1**). Renal failure can be the result of pre-renal factors, primary renal disease or post-renal factors. In chronic renal failure, this loss of function is progressive and irreversible. Chronic renal failure progression is associated with the following:

Introduction

- a gradual decline in glomerular filtration rate;
- an accumulation of metabolic byproducts;
- increased severity of histologic lesions; and
- development or worsening of clinical signs.

Laboratory abnormalities in canine chronic renal failure patients include an increase in the plasma concentrations of the products of protein metabolism, blood urea nitrogen, and creatinine. Blood urea nitrogen (BUN) and creatinine provide crude indications of glomerular filtration rate and are among the most commonly used renal function tests. Retention of urea, creatinine, and other nitrogen metabolites are associated with adverse clinical signs such as vomiting, anorexia, lethargy, pruritis, and tremors.

Although severe dietary protein restriction has been the cornerstone of traditional nutritional management of chronic renal failure, such restriction may have profound negative effects on overall animal well-being. Unnecessarily excessive restriction of protein puts many companion animals at risk of protein malnutrition. Very low protein diets also tend to have palatability problems in healthy dogs, with this problem being exacerbated in animals with chronic renal failure. However, there are situations in chronic renal failure patients in which high protein diets may be associated with adverse clinical signs. It is important to note that the relationship between protein intake and the progression of chronic kidney disease seen in rats

*Dietary
Protein
Restriction?*

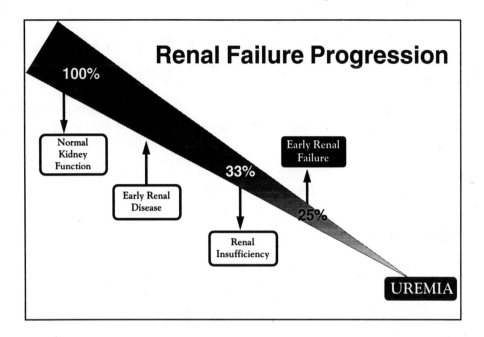

Figure 1. Progressive nature of chronic renal failure.

has not been found in dogs. Although no correlation has been shown between higher protein levels and the progression of kidney disease in dogs with experimental or natural renal failure, clinical signs associated with chronic renal failure should not be ignored. Because there is no evidence that feeding moderate protein diets relative to severely protein restricted diets contribute to progression of chronic renal failure in dogs or cats, the rationale for excessive protein restriction in these carnivorous species is even more questionable. Based on these findings, the most prudent dietary protein strategy is to match the level of protein restriction with the stage of disease progression. It should be cautioned that protein restriction must be viewed as a "nutritional balancing act". The benefits of protein restriction in helping manage azotemia must be weighed against the risks of amino acid deficiencies/protein malnutrition and resulting negative impact on requisite bodily functions. The goal is to feed an appropriate dietary protein level to maximize overall animal well-being. Due to these considerations, the optimal dietary approach is to provide proper protein nutrition without contributing to the accumulation of urea and creatinine in the blood.

Progressive Nutritional Strategies

      Recent discoveries in the nutritional management of the canine chronic renal failure patient allow for new alternatives to conventional low protein dietary regimens. New concepts in the nutritional management of canine chronic renal failure include:

- provide adequate amino acid nutrition to maintain requisite body function and avoid essential amino acid deficiencies and signs of protein malnutrition,

- diminish accumulation of nitrogenous waste products in blood by increasing fecal nitrogen excretion,
- provide dietary omega-3 fatty acids to decrease intrarenal blood pressure,
- reduce dietary phosphorus levels to slow progression of disease,
- provide a nutritional matrix that aids in the maintenance of acid-base balance,
- match the dietary protein level with the stage of the disease, and
- deliver these unique nutritional strategies in a product matrix that is palatable.

Dietary methods of increasing extrarenal nitrogen excretion have been identified, thereby reducing the reliance on the kidneys for urea and creatinine excretion. This in turn allows adequate protein to be fed to canine chronic renal failure patients without contributing to uremia and/or azotemia.

The reduced ability of the kidney to excrete nitrogenous protein catabolites is one of the major causes of both uremic signs and laboratory abnormalities in animals with renal failure. Methods that reduce protein catabolite levels in the body and/or allow for increased dietary protein intake without exacerbating uremia should be vigorously pursued. Specific nutritional programs allow for repartitioning of nitrogen excretion away from the kidney and into the feces by utilizing colonic fermentation. Canine renal patients may take advantage of a unique response that has been observed for years in dogs fed dietary fiber. It has been consistently noted that apparent protein digestibility is decreased when the canine diet contains fermentable fiber.[1-4] Apparent protein digestibility is the percentage of nitrogen that is excreted in the feces of an animal as a proportion of total ingested nitrogen. This evaluation method for protein availability assumes that dietary nitrogen is predominantly protein. It is termed "apparent" digestibility because a simple digestibility study, in which total dietary nutrient intake and fecal excretion are measured, gives no indication of the amount of dietary protein that is assimilated in the small intestine as amino acids or peptides, the amount of undigested "bypass" protein that reaches the colon, the quantity of nitrogen contained in sloughed intestinal cells and secreted enzymes that are excreted in the feces, or the amount of bacterial mass that is excreted in the feces.

Colonic Fermentation Provides An Alternative Nitrogen Excretion Route

Apparent protein digestibility values can be altered by dietary factors that increase non-dietary protein nitrogen excretion in the feces, increase endogenous protein excretion (sloughed colonocytes/enterocytes, enzymes) or increase the amount of undigested dietary protein that reaches the colon and is subsequently degraded (with the release of ammonia). Fermentable fiber is one known dietary factor that increases fecal nitrogen loss by stimulating bacterial growth and activity in the gut. The intestinal bacteria produce the enzyme urease which hydrolyzes urea to ammonia and carbon dioxide.[5-8] The ammonia generated by this process is readily incorporated into bacterial proteins which are then subsequently excreted in the

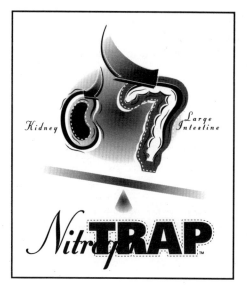

Figure 2. Schematic of Nitrogen Trap™ concept.

bacterial mass fraction of the feces.[6,9,10] This process of "nitrogen trapping" dietary protein metabolites into bacterial cells in the colon results in increased nitrogen excretion in the feces and less in the urine (*Figure 2*). This is the major contributing factor to the increased nitrogen excretion in the feces of dogs fed dietary fermentable fiber.

Nitrogen
Trapping

Scientific studies in dogs have demonstrated that incorporation of fermentable fiber in the diet decreases apparent nitrogen digestibility.[1-4] Further studies exploring the mechanism of this response observed that adding a blend of fermentable fiber to the diet of a dog resulted in increased colonic tissue weights and surface area,[11] increased colonic blood flow (delivering more nitrogenous catabolites in blood to the colon),[12] increased bacterial nitrogen excretion,[13] and increased overall fecal nitrogen excretion[13] (*Figure 3*).

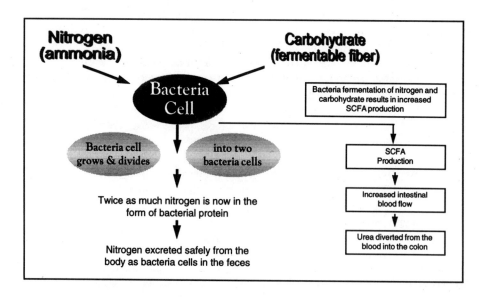

Figure 3. Factors contributing to increased nitrogen repartitioning into feces.

These factors allow for repartitioning of nitrogen excretion,[13] resulting in reduced reliance on the kidneys for nitrogen disposal (*Table 1*). Thus, repartitioning nitrogen excretion towards the fecal route allows

- more dietary protein to be fed without increasing the nitrogen excretion burden on the kidneys, and/or
- diminished blood levels of nitrogenous waste products.

Table 1. Canine nitrogen excretion repartitioning.

Fiber Type	Fecal N excretion, %	Urinary N excretion, %
Nonfermentable	17.2	82.8
Fermentable	23.0	77.0

The ability to repartition nitrogen loss from urinary to fecal excretion is possible without sacrificing nutrient availability or stool quality. To examine this, two diets were fed to 12 dogs in a switchback design. The diets were formulated to be isonitrogenous and isoenergetic and contained similar protein, fat, carbohydrate, mineral, and vitamin sources. Proximate analysis was similar between treatment diets, with both experimental formulas containing approximately 20.9% crude protein, 16.7% crude fat, 58.4% nitrogen free extract, and 4.6% ash on a dry matter basis. The diets differed in their fiber component, with one diet containing no supplemental fiber source (No Fiber) other than what was contained as indigenous constituents of other ingredients, while the other diet contained a blend of beet pulp, fructooligosaccharides, and gum arabic (Fermentable Fiber). The fiber sources in the fermentable fiber blend were chosen based on *in vitro* fermentation data.[4] The blend was designed to promote an elevated and sustained fermentation capacity throughout the intestinal tract of the dog. The *in vitro* fermentation data demonstrated that beet pulp has a slower and more sustained fermentation profile, fructooligosaccharides have a rapid and extensive fermentation profile, with gum arabic being intermediate in the rate and extent of fermentation. A combination of these three different fibers allows for early and sustained fermentation, without resulting in fermentation too rapidly and causing loose stools. Each diet was fed to all dogs for a 14 day period. Stool scores were excellent in both dietary groups and averaged 3.98 and 4.00 for the Fermentable Fiber and No Fiber diets, respectively (stool scores: 1=liquid; 2=soft, shapeless; 3=soft, with shape; 4=firm, well formed; 5=extremely dry). Apparent digestibility coefficients were excellent for both diets (*Table 2*).

Table 2. Apparent digestibility values for experimental diets differing in fiber source.

Apparent digestibility, %	No Fiber	Fermentable Fiber
Dry matter	91.0	87.6
Organic matter	93.4	89.6
Crude protein	91.3	88.2
Crude fat	93.7	93.5
Nitrogen free extract	95.3	91.7
Ash	41.9	45.7

As expected, the inclusion of a dietary fermentable fiber blend decreased dry matter and organic matter apparent digestibilities. This is a consistent response seen with the inclusion of many types of dietary fiber due to nonfermentable components being excreted in the feces and increasing overall dry matter and organic matter excretion.[1-4] Increased bacterial mass excretion also contributes to the decrease in dry matter and organic matter apparent digestibilities. Apparent fat digestibilities were very high for both diets and were not statistically different based on the presence or absence of a unique dietary fermentable fiber blend. Nitrogen free extract (NFE) apparent digestibility was higher for the fiber free diet, but both diets were excellent in their NFE apparent digestibility with values in excess of 91%. As expected, the inclusion of a fermentable fiber blend resulted in a decrease in apparent protein digestibility. This has been documented in previous studies[1-4] and is attributed to increased fecal bacterial nitrogen excretion.[13] It is unlikely that small intestinal protein digestion and/or absorption were drastically impaired in the small intestine and resulted in these changes in apparent protein digestibility. A study in ileal cannulated dogs did not demonstrate statistically significant differences in ileal digestibility of dietary protein when different fiber sources were fed.[14] Other investigators have reported that bacterial protein excretion is increased when a fermentable fiber blend is incorporated into the canine diet, with the increased fecal nitrogen loss attributed to increased bacterial protein loss in the feces and not to unassimilated dietary protein being excreted in the feces.[13]

A similar nitrogen trapping phenomenon has been demonstrated in rodents, humans, and swine in which dietary fermentable fiber repartitions nitrogen excretion into the feces. These findings are summarized in *Table 3*.

The human studies provide evidence that dietary fiber can increase fecal nitrogen excretion and lower serum concentrations of urea and other retained metabolites in chronic renal failure patients. The use of dietary fiber to increase fecal excretion of retained metabolites in chronic renal failure is suggested to be a

Table 3. References supporting nitrogen repartitioning in other species.

Species	↑ fecal N excretion	↑ bacterial N	↓ urinary N excretion	↓ BUN
Rodent	15,16,17,18	17	15,16,17,18,19	16,18,19
Human	20,21	20,21	21	20,21
Swine	22	n/a	22	n/a

beneficial adjunctive therapy.[20,21,23,24] In one study, human chronic renal failure patients had significantly lower serum urea nitrogen concentrations after ingesting a low protein diet supplemented with gum arabic than patients consuming a low protein diet containing no supplemental fiber or supplemental pectin. On average, the serum urea nitrogen concentrations were 12% lower after only 4 weeks of supplementation with gum arabic.[20] This was the first study to demonstrate that a statistically significant decrease in serum urea nitrogen concentration resulted during the same time period as a statistically significant increase in fecal nitrogen excretion in human chronic renal failure patients. This study also demonstrated that the bacterial fraction of the feces accounted for the majority of the increase in total stool dry weight and total fecal nitrogen content in these patients. Based on these findings, the authors concluded that colonic bacteria were largely responsible for the decrease in serum urea nitrogen.[20]

Rodent studies further substantiate the findings reported for the dog. Dietary fermentable fiber results in cecal hypertrophy, increased cecal absorptive mucosal area, and increased blood flow to the cecum. This allows for increased diffusion of urea from the blood into the cecal lumen. The presence of highly ureolytic bacteria in the cecum creates a urea concentration gradient that favors the net transfer of urea into the cecal lumen. The ammonia generated by bacterial urease is utilized for bacterial protein synthesis, thus trapping nitrogen for elimination in the feces. In one rodent study, it was observed that dietary oligosaccharides were the most effective in increasing the transfer of urea nitrogen from the blood into the large intestine.[19] The exact mechanism of this response was not clear, but the authors speculated that oligosaccharides may have favored the establishment of a highly ureolytic microflora. Fructooligosaccharides have been shown to alter fecal microbial populations in dogs,[25] but the effect on ureolytic bacteria *per se*, has not been determined.

Many nephrologists consider urea to be a minor uremic toxin or merely a marker of adequate dialysis. Regardless of its exact role, urea is associated with the symptomatology of chronic renal failure. Elevated BUN concentrations have been associated with adverse clinical signs that reduce the quality of life and contribute to morbidity. The involvement of urea, if any, in the mechanism of adverse effects on the patient requires clarification. Whether retained urea and other nitrogenous metabolites hasten the progression of chronic renal failure is debatable and also requires further delineation.

Despite the many unknowns associated with chronic renal failure morbidity and disease progression, it seems prudent to purposefully increase the excretion of protein metabolites into the feces as long as this can be accomplished without side effects. To date, the data generated in dogs suggests that this can be done safely, without side effects such as diarrhea, incontinence or excessive flatulence, and without compromising the delivery of essential nutrients to the host. Preliminary clinical impression studies have shown that appreciably greater dietary protein intakes can be provided to canine chronic renal failure patients with BUN and creatinine concentrations staying stable or declining.[26] In essence, adequate protein nutrition to meet essential amino acid requirements can be provided without contributing to uremia. It was also reported by the owners of these animals that the patients' overall attitude and activity level increased. Whether this is due to the diet supplying adequate protein nutrition, the reduction of BUN/creatinine or a combination of both is unknown.

Despite the lack of side effects in the dog, this approach should not be utilized in the cat without further study. Previous research has shown that feeding a highly fermentable fiber blend to cats severely depresses apparent protein digestibility (<60%) and apparent lipid digestibility (<40%).[27] This drastic depression in both protein and fat apparent digestibilities suggests that nutrient availability to the feline may be impaired. A diet that contains elevated levels of highly fermentable fiber could put the cat, an obligate carnivore, at high risk for nutritional deficiencies. For this reason, high levels of dietary fermentable fiber in the diet of cats are not recommended at this time.

Summary   Marked dietary protein restriction, although commonly used for dogs with chronic renal failure, can have deleterious effects and is unlikely to provide any benefit for animals that are not uremic. Proper nutritional balance is necessary to maintain normal bodily functions and to manage azotemia. An important goal of nutritional management in dogs with chronic renal failure should be to provide sufficient high quality protein to maintain nitrogen balance without exacerbating uremia. Including a blend of fermentable fiber sources in the diet may allow higher levels of protein to be fed to uremic dogs. The use of dietary fiber to increase fecal excretion of nitrogen metabolites may be beneficial dietary therapy in canine chronic renal failure patients.

Nitrogen Trap is a trademark of The Iams Company.

References   1. Fahey Jr GC, Merchen NR, Corbin JE, Hamilton AK, Serbe KA, Lewis SM, Hirakawa DA. Dietary fiber for dogs: I. Effects of graded levels of dietary beet pulp on nutrient intake, digestibility, metabolizable energy and digesta mean retention time. *J Anim Sci* 1990; 68:4221.

2. Fahey Jr GC, Merchen NR, Corbin JE, Hamilton AK, Serbe KA, Hirakawa DA. Dietary fiber for dogs: II. Iso-total dietary fiber (TDF) additions of divergent fiber sources to dog diets and their effects on nutrient intake, digestibility, metabolizable energy and digesta mean retention time. *J Anim Sci* 1990; 68:4221.

3. Fahey Jr GC, Merchen NR, Corbin JE, Hamilton AK, Bauer LL, Hirakawa DA. Dietary fiber for dogs: III. Effects of beet pulp and oat fiber additions to dog diets on nutrient intake, digestibility, metabolizable energy, and digesta mean retention time. *J Anim Sci* 1992; 70:1169.

4. Sunvold GD, Fahey Jr GC, Merchen NR, Titgemeyer EC, Bourquin LD, Bauer LL, Reinhart GA. Dietary fiber for dogs: IV. *In vitro* fermentation of selected fiber sources by dog fecal inoculum and *in vivo* digestion and metabolism of fiber-supplemented diets. *J Anim Sci* 1995; 73:1099-1109.

5. Brown CL, Hill MJ, Richards P. Bacterial ureases in uraemic men. *Lancet* 1971; 1:406-407.

6. Smith CJ, Bryant MP. Introduction to metabolic activity of intestinal bacteria. *Am J Clin Nutr* 1979; 32:149-157.

7. Walser M, Bodenlos LJ. Urea metabolism in man. *J Clin Invest* 1959; 38:1617-1627.

8. Vince A, Dawson AM, Park N, O'Grady F. Ammonia production by intestinal bacteria. *Gut* 1973; 14:171-177.

9. Takahashi M, Benno Y, Mitsuoka T. Utilization of ammonia nitrogen by intestinal bacteria isolated from pigs. *Appl Environ Microbiol* 1980; 39:30-35.

10. Wrong OM, Edmonds CJ, Chadwick VS. *The Large Intestine: Its Role in Mammalian Nutrition and Homeostasis*. New York: John Wiley & Sons, 1981; 133-155.

11. Hallman JE, Moxely RA, Reinhart GA, Wallace EA, Clemens ET. Cellulose, beet pulp and pectin/gum arabic effects on canine colonic microstructure and histopathology. *J Vet Clin Nutr* 1995; 2:137-142.

12. Howard MD, Kerley MS, Mann FA, Sunvold GD, Reinhart GA. Dietary fiber sources alter colonic blood flow and epithelial cell proliferation of dogs. *J Anim Sci* 1997; 75(Suppl. 1):170.

13. Howard MD, Sunvold GD, Reinhart GA, Kerley MS. Effect of fermentable fiber consumption by the dog on nitrogen balance and fecal microbial nitrogen excretion. *FASEB J* 1996; 10:A257.

14. Muir HE, Murray SM, Fahey Jr GC, Merchen NR, Reinhart GA. Nutrient digestion by ileal cannulated dogs as affected by dietary fibers with various fermentation characteristics. *J Anim Sci* 1996; 74:1641-1648.

15. Titens I, Livesey G, Eggum BO. Effects of the type and level of dietary fibre supplements on nitrogen retention and excretion patters. *Br J Nutr* 1996; 75:461-469.

16. Younes H, Rémésey C, Behr S, Demigné C. Fermentable carbohydrate exerts a urea-lowering effect in normal and nephrectomized rats. *Am J Physiol* 1997; 272:G515-G525.

17. Assimon SA, Stein TP. Digestible fiber (gum arabic), nitrogen excretion and urea cycling in rats. *Nutrition* 1994; 10:544-550.

18. Younes H, Garleb K, Behr S, Rémésy C, Demigné C. Fermentable fibers or oligosaccharides reduce urinary nitrogen excretion by increasing urea disposal in the rat cecum. *J Nutr* 1995; 125:1010-1016.

19. Rémésy C, Demigné C. Specific effects of fermentable carbohydrates on blood urea flux and ammonia absorption in the rat cecum. *J Nutr* 1989; 119:560-565.

20. Bliss DZ, Stein TP, Schleifer CR, Settle RG. Supplementation with gum arabic fiber increases fecal nitrogen excretion and lowers serum urea nitrogen concentration in chronic renal failure patients consuming a low-protein diet. *Am J Clin Nutr* 1996; 63:392-398.

21. Weber FL, Minco D, Fresard KM, Banwell JG. Effects of vegetable diets on nitrogen metabolism in cirrhotic subjects. *Gastroenterology* 1985; 89:538-544.

22. Canh TT, Verstegen MWA, Aarnnk AJA, Schrama JW. Influence of dietary factors on nitrogen repartitioning and composition of urine and feces of fattening pigs. *J Anim Sci* 1997; 75:700-706.

23. Yatzidis H, Koutsicos D, Digenis P. Oral locust bean gum therapy of uremia: favorable effect on biological abnormalities and hypertension. *Dialysis Transplant* 1980; 9:313-317.

24. Rampton DS, Cohen SL, Crammond V, Gibbons J, Lilburn MF, Rabet JY, Vince AJ, Wager JD, Wrong OM. Treatment of chronic renal failure with dietary fiber. *Clin Nephrol* 1984; 21:159-163.

25. Kearns RJ, Hayek MG, Sunvold GD. Microbial changes in aged dogs. In: Reinhart GA, Carey DP, eds. *Recent Advances in Canine and Feline Nutrition, Vol. II: 1998 Iams Nutrition Symposium Proceedings*. Wilmington: Orange Frazer Press, 1998; 337-352.

26. Tetrick MA, Sunvold GD, Reinhart GA. Clinical experience with canine renal patients fed a diet containing a fermentable fiber blend. In: Reinhart GA, Carey DP, eds. *Recent Advances in Canine and Feline Nutrition, Vol. II: 1998 Iams Nutrition Symposium Proceedings*. Wilmington: Orange Frazer Press, 1998; 425-432.

27. Sunvold GD, Fahey Jr GC, Merchen NR, Bourquin LD, Titgeyer EC, Bauer LL, Reinhart GA. Dietary fiber for cats: *In vitro* fermentation of selected fiber sources by cat fecal inoculum and *in vivo* utilization of diets containing selected fiber sources and their blends. *J Anim Sci* 1995; 73:2329-2339.

Influence of Dietary Fatty Acids on Intrarenal Hypertension

Scott A. Brown, VMD, PhD, DACVIM
Associate Professor, Department of Physiology and Pharmacology
College of Veterinary Medicine, University of Georgia, Athens, Georgia, USA

End-stage renal disease is a common cause of death in dogs and cats. Unfortunately, despite appropriate therapy for the primary cause of the disease, renal failure frequently is progressive, leading to terminal uremia.[1,2] This has at least two important consequences for a dog or cat with renal disease. First, the disease is inherently unstable and frequent re-evaluations and adjustments in therapy are required. Second, because of the tremendous cost and technical difficulty associated with therapy for end-stage uremia (i.e., dialytic therapy or renal transplantation), efforts designed to slow the rate of progression of renal disease are particularly important in veterinary medicine.

Once renal injury reaches a certain threshold, secondary factors not directly related to the primary renal disease process appear to be critical determinants of further renal injury. In particular, high intraglomerular vascular pressure develops as a normal response to renal disease, but causes secondary renal damage and self-perpetuation of renal failure. It is proposed that dietary omega-3 polyunsaturated fatty acid (ω-3 PUFA) supplementation will alter renal hemodynamics, lower intraglomerular pressure, and offer a novel therapy to slow the progression of renal disease in dogs.

Summary

Progression of Renal Disease

It has long been recognized that renal disease in human beings usually progresses, even if appropriate therapy eradicates the primary cause of the renal injury. In a landmark article in the *New England Journal of Medicine*,[3] Dr. Barry Brenner of Harvard University proposed that once a critical mass of renal tissue is destroyed, renal disease inevitably progresses to end-stage failure. This progression occurs in human beings suffering from post-streptococcal glomerulonephritis, acute cortical necrosis, and unilateral renal agenesis; all situations in which progressive destruction of renal tissue occurs in the absence of a primary disease process. Thus, once renal injury reaches a certain threshold, secondary factors appear to be the critical determinants of progressive renal injury.

The cause of self-perpetuating, progressive renal injury has been the focus of much attention in nephrology. A particular model of renal disease in rats, referred to as the remnant kidney model, was critical in elucidating the mechanism of this inherent progression. In this model, renal mass is reduced by uninephrectomy and infarction of a portion of the contralateral kidney. Following this reduction of renal mass, remaining (remnant) nephrons are initially normal and renal function is adequate to sustain the animal with only mild to moderate azotemia. However, over the ensuing months, remnant renal tissue develops structural lesions and many nephrons are ultimately destroyed in this process. As more and more nephrons are destroyed, renal function declines over time. As investigators studied this model of progressive renal disease with renal micropuncture techniques, it became apparent that high vascular pressure within the kidney, specifically within glomerular capillaries, played a pivotal role in this progression (*Figure 1*).[3-8] Further, manipulations that reduced the extent of glomerular hypertension were renoprotective in rats. These studies were criticized, though, because of concerns the results had limited applicability to nonrodent species.

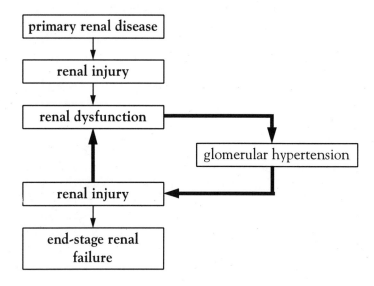

Figure 1. Self-perpetuating cycle of renal injury. Initially, the primary disease process destroys renal tissue. However, as a result of the renal response to the disease, secondary factors such as high intraglomerular vascular pressure develop and lead to a vicious cycle of progressive renal injury (dark lines). End-stage renal failure eventually develops as a consequence of this self-perpetuating cycle of renal damage.

Glomerular Hypertension and Progressive Renal Injury

Methods were recently developed that allow renal micropuncture techniques to be applied to the study of renal failure in dogs and cats. These studies have shown that dogs and cats with renal insufficiency exhibit glomerular hypertension (*Figure 2*).[9,10]

In an experimental study of diabetic dogs, therapy that reduced the extent of glomerular hypertension was shown to be renoprotective.[11,12] It was speculated that the favorable response to lowering glomerular pressure in diabetes would also be observed in other forms of chronic renal disease in dogs. If so, efforts to reduce the extent of glomerular hypertension could prove beneficial in all dogs with renal failure (**Figure 3**).

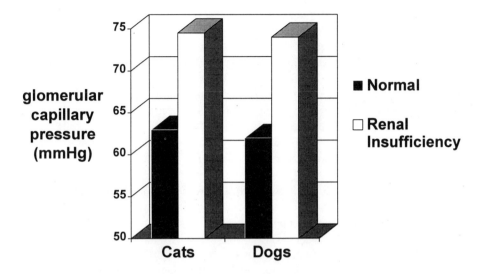

Figure 2. Recently, the application of micropuncture techniques to the study of intrarenal hemodynamics demonstrated that dogs and cats with renal insufficiency develop glomerular hypertension. This secondary factor may play an important role in progressive renal failure by causing hypertensive injury of renal tissue.

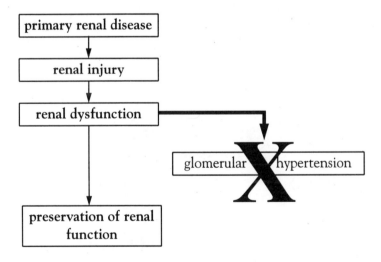

Figure 3. Nutritional or pharmacological therapeutic modalities that lower glomerular pressure may interrupt the self-perpetuating cycle of renal injury in dogs and cats with chronic renal failure, thereby serving a renoprotective function.

Fatty acids are generally categorized on the basis of number and location of carbon–carbon double bonds. Dietary fatty acids that contain no double bonds, such as palmitic acid, are referred to as saturated fatty acids. Animal fats, which contain predominantly saturated fatty acids, are often incorporated into feline diets because of availability, palatability, and as a source of arachidonic acid. In contrast, plant sources of fat contain high proportions of the polyunsaturated fatty acid, linoleic acid. Linoleic acid is referred to as an omega-6 polyunsaturated fatty acid (ω-6 PUFA) because the first carbon–carbon double bond occurs at the sixth carbon from the methyl group. In most mammals, including people and dogs, linoleic is readily converted to arachidonic acid, the immediate precursor of eicosanoids (i.e., prostaglandins and thromboxanes). An alternative source of PUFA is fish oils derived from fish feeding on plankton. These oils are rich in eicosapentaenoic acid and docosahexaenoic acid, which are omega-3 PUFA (ω-3 PUFA).

Thus, substantially different chemical forms of fatty acids are obtained when pet foods are supplemented with lipids obtained from animal fat, plant oil, or fish oil. These dietary fatty acids may affect renal function through effects on renal eicosanoid metabolism. Eicosanoids are compounds derived from PUFA within cell membranes and include prostaglandins, prostacyclin, leukotrienes, and thromboxanes. The usual precursor for eicosanoids is arachidonic acid. In dogs, people, and rats, arachidonic acid is derived from the elongation of PUFA linoleic acid, which comprises 50–80% of plant oils, or through dietary sources of animal fat which contain very small amounts of arachidonic acid. However, cats have limited hepatic $\Delta 6$ desaturase activity and thus cannot effectively convert linoleic to arachidonic acid and both are considered essential dietary fatty acids in cats.[13] It should be noted, however, that the activity of this enzyme in the feline kidney and the intrarenal capacity to convert linoleic to arachidonic acid have not been well studied.

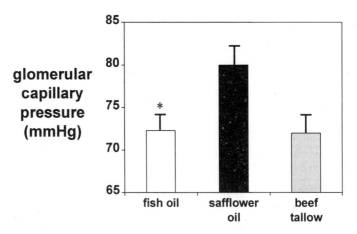

Figure 4. Results of preliminary studies in dogs in which dietary supplementation with menhaden fish oil led to a lowering of intraglomerular pressure compared to supplementation with safflower oil. This nutritional modification may prove to be beneficial to the long-term preservation of renal function.

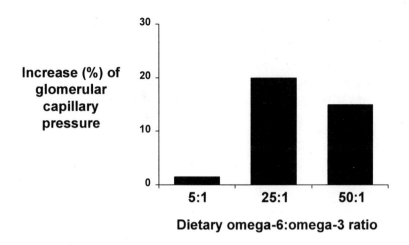

Figure 5. Mean increase in glomerular capillary pressure (%) in dogs with renal insufficiency fed a diet with an omega-6 to omega-3 fatty acid ratio of 5:1, 25:1, or 50:1.

The principal eicosanoids derived from the ω-3 polyunsaturated fatty acid, arachidonic acid, include prostaglandin E_2 (PGE_2), prostacyclin (PGI_2), and thromboxane A_2 (TxA_2). The vasodilatory eicosanoids, PGE_2 and PGI_2, increase renal blood flow and glomerular filtration rate (GFR). They also serve to promote, directly or indirectly, intrarenal inflammation. In contrast, renal TxA_2 has renal vasoconstrictor effects, with variable effects on GFR.

Cold water fish oils contain ω-3 PUFA which compete with arachidonic acid in the production of eicosanoids. Consequently, animals fed fish oil have a diminution of the 2-series of eicosanoids normally derived from arachidonic acid. Importantly, the eicosanoid derivatives of ω-3 polyunsaturated fatty acids are less potent than the usual arachidonic acid derivatives. In particular, thromboxanes derived from ω-3 PUFA have little vasoconstrictive effect.

Proponents of the importance of hemodynamic causes of progressive renal injury have proposed a link between production of the 2-series of prostaglandins and thromboxanes and progressive renal disease. This theory is based upon renal micropuncture studies suggesting that glomerular hypertension is dependent upon renal eicosanoids.[8] Manipulations that alter renal production of eicosanoids, such as dietary supplementation with fish oil, slow the progression of chronic renal disease in some studies of laboratory animals.[14-19]

In summary, as a potential therapy to slow the rate of progression of renal disease, dietary ω-3 PUFA supplementation is hypothesized to exert renoprotective effects by reducing the extent of glomerular hypertension, an effect seen in preliminary studies in dogs (**Figure 4**). A similar effect was observed with a dietary ratio of omega-6 to omega-3 fatty acids of 5:1 (**Figure 5**). Critically, long term studies have shown that a diet supplemented with menhaden fish oil will preserve renal function

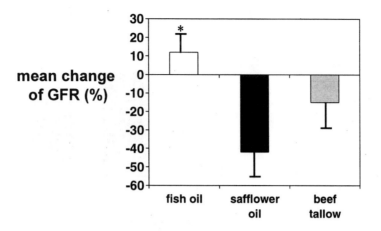

mean change
of GFR (%)

Figure 6. Changes in glomerular filtration rate over time in dogs with renal insufficiency fed a low fat diet enriched with beef tallow, menhaden fish oil, or safflower oil for 20 months, demonstrating a therapeutic advantage to dietary supplementation with the omega-3 fatty acid rich fish oil.

in dogs with induced renal failure (**Figure 6**), when compared to supplementation with safflower oil (a rich source of ω-6 polyunsaturated fatty acids) or a highly saturated fat-source (beef tallow). While further studies are needed to understand the mechanisms responsible for this protection, the use of diets supplemented with fish oil have become an important consideration in the therapy of chronic renal disease in dogs. Further, it is proposed that dietary ω-3 PUFA supplementation alters renal hemodynamics, lowers intraglomerular pressure, and may offer a novel approach to slow the progression of renal disease in dogs.

References

1. Polzin DJ, Osborne CA. Update: Conservative medical management of chronic renal failure. In: Kirk RW ed. *Current Veterinary Therapy IX*, Philadelphia: WB Saunders, 1986; 1167-1173.

2. DiBartola SP, Rutgers HC, Zack PM, Tarr MJ. Clinicopathological findings associated with chronic renal disease in cats: 74 cases. *J Am Vet Med Assoc* 1987; 190:1196-1202.

3. Brenner BM, Meyer TW, Hostetter TH. Dietary protein intake and the progressive nature of renal disease. *N Engl J Med* 1982; 307:652-659.

4. Barcelli U, Pollak V. Is there a role for polyunsaturated fatty acids in the prevention of renal disease and renal failure. *Nephron* 1985; 41:209-212.

5. Moorhead JF, Chan MK, Varghese Z. The role of abnormalities of lipid metabolism in the progression of renal disease. In: Mitch WE ed. *The Progressive Nature of Renal Disease*, New York: Churchill Livingstone, 1986; 133-148.

6. Purkerson ME, Hoffsten PE, Klahr S. Pathogenesis of the glomerulopathy associated with renal infarction in rats. *Kidney Int* 1976; 9:407-417.

7. Fries JWU, Sandstrom DJ, Meyer TW, Rennke HG. Glomerular hypertrophy and epithelial cell injury modulate progressive glomerulosclerosis in the rat. *Lab Invest* 1989; 60:205-218.

8. Nath KA, Chmielewski DH, Hostetter TH. Regulatory role of prostanoids in glomerular microcirculation of remnant nephrons. *Am J Physiol* 1987; 252:F829-F837.

9. Brown SA, Finco DR, Crowell WA, Choat DC, Navar LG. Single nephron adaptations to partial renal ablation in the dog. *Am J Physiol* 1990; 258:F495-F503.

10. Brown SA, Brown CA. Single-nephron adaptations to partial renal ablation in cats. *Am J Physiol* 1995; 269:R1002-R1008.

11. Brown SA, Walton C, Crawford P, Bakris G. Long-term effects of antihypertensive regimens on renal hemodynamics and proteinuria in diabetic dogs. *Kidney Int* 1993; 43:1210-1218.

12. Gaber L, Walton C, Brown S, Bakris GI. Effects of antihypertensive agents on the morphologic progression of diabetic nephropathy in dogs. *Kidney Int* 1994; 46:161-169.

13. *Nutrient Requirements of Cats*, National Research Council, National Academy Press, Washington, DC, 1986.

14. Brown S, Brown C, Finco D, Barsanti J, Crowell W. Long-term effects of dietary lipids on chronic renal disease in the dog. *Proc ACVIM*, 1996 (abstract); 750.

15. Brown S, Brown C, Finco D, Barsanti J, Crowell W. Hemodynamic effects of dietary lipids on chronic renal disease in the dog. *Proc ACVIM*, 1996 (abstract); 750.

16. Brown S, Crowell WA, Barsanti JA, White JV, and Finco DR. Beneficial effects of dietary mineral restriction in dogs with 15/16 nephrectomy. *J Am Soc Nephr* 1991; 1:1169-1179.

17. French SW, Yamanaka W, Ostred R. Dietary induced glomerulosclerosis in the guinea pig. *Arch Path* 1967; 83:204-210.

18. Heifets M, Morrissey JJ, Purkerson ML, Morrison AR, Klahr S. Effect of dietary lipids on renal function in rats with subtotal nephrectomy. *Kidney Int* 1987; 32:335-341.

19. Longhofer SL, Frisbie DD, Johnson HC, Culham CA, Cooley AJ, Schultz KT, Grauer GF. Effects of thromboxane synthetase inhibition on immune complex glomerulonephritis. *Am J Vet Res* 1991; 52:480-487.

Influence of Protein and Energy
in Cats with Renal Failure

Delmar R. Finco, DVM, PhD, DACVIM
Professor, Department of Physiology and Pharmacology
College of Veterinary Medicine, University of Georgia, Athens, Georgia, USA

Scott A. Brown, VMD, PhD, DACVIM[a]; Cathy A Brown, VMD, PhD[a];
Wayne A. Crowell, DVM, PhD[a]; Gregory D. Sunvold, PhD[b]; Tanya A Cooper[a]
[a]Department of Physiology and Pharmacology, College of Veterinary Medicine
University of Georgia, Athens, Georgia, USA
[b]Research and Development, The Iams Company, Lewisburg, Ohio, USA

Summary

The effects of protein and calorie restriction on progression of renal failure in cats with reduced renal function were evaluated. Contrary to a previous study, results did not demonstrate adverse effects of protein ingestion on glomerular mesangial matrix accumulation, even when amounts consumed were greater than previously shown to be injurious. Neither the glomerular filtration rate nor the degree of proteinuria was influenced by protein or calorie intake. This study demonstrated the development of minor nonglomerular renal lesions, which were significantly related to calorie, but not to protein ingestion.

It is concluded that restricting protein in cats with chronic renal dysfunction for renoprotective purposes is questionable, unless more convincing evidence of harmful effects is provided.

Introduction

Although renal failure seems to progress more slowly in cats than in dogs, primary renal failure is a common cause of death in both species. Slowing the rate of progression of renal failure may prolong the life span and increase the comfort of cats with renal failure.

The remnant kidney model has been used extensively to study progression of renal failure. With this model, renal mass is reduced surgically, usually by combining ligation of selected branches of the renal artery of one kidney with contralateral nephrectomy. In several species, marked reduction of renal mass is accompanied by development of renal lesions and progressive deterioration in renal function. Use of this model to study certain strains of rats revealed that dietary protein restriction decreased the severity of renal lesions and slowed progression of renal failure.[1]

The development of renal damage following reduction of renal mass has been attributed to glomerular capillary hypertension. Since ingestion of large

413

amounts of protein causes increased glomerular filtration rate (GFR) and intraglomerular pressure, a link between high protein intake and renal damage was formulated. However, low protein diets often are unpalatable, and caloric restriction that often accompanies protein restriction also has been found to have renal protective effects. Some investigators have provided evidence that beneficial effects previously attributed to protein restriction may actually be due to caloric restriction.[2]

Cats with remnant kidneys have intraglomerular hypertension, theoretically placing them at risk for glomerular injury.[3] In a study of cats in which chronic renal failure was induced by reduction of renal mass, a low protein diet resulted in milder renal lesions than a high protein diet.[4,5] However, in this study cats consumed less of the low protein diet, and thus they were deprived of calories and other nutrients as well. Although the cats fed the low protein diet had minimal renal lesions, they developed hypoalbuminemia, raising the question of whether protein malnutrition existed. Nevertheless, this study provided the first objective data suggesting that dietary protein intake could influence progression of renal failure in cats.

In 1982 phosphorus restriction in cats with induced renal failure was reported to be beneficial in decreasing both the degree of renal secondary hyperparathyroidism and the degree of renal mineralization.[6] Thus, as in other species, both protein restriction and phosphorus restriction have been advocated for management of renal failure in cats. However, the high dietary protein requirements of cats, compared to dogs, has made both protein and phosphorus restriction less applicable to cats, and with greater risk of protein malnutrition. In addition, the previous study demonstrating benefits from protein and calorie restriction did not separate the effects of protein from calories. Further studies were conducted in an attempt to clarify the protein and calorie issue.

Research
Protocol

Cats. Young adult female cats obtained from a commercial supplier were found healthy by physical examination, CBC, serum electrolyte and biochemical analysis (anion gap, albumin, alkaline phosphatase, alanine aminotransferase, bicarbonate, blood urea nitrogen [BUN], total calcium, chloride, creatinine, glucose, potassium, sodium, inorganic phosphorus, total protein), urinalysis and urine protein:creatinine (U P:C) determinations. Cats were housed in individual cages under conditions of controlled temperature, humidity, and light exposure.

Diets. Four experimental dry diets (A,B,C,D) were formulated so that cats would be provided with nutritionally adequate foods that differed only in the quantity of protein and calories that were ingested. Diets A and C (low calorie) were formulated to provide 56 Calories[a]/day/kg body weight as fed. Diets B and D were formulated to provide 75 Calories/day/kg body weight as fed. Diets A and B (low protein) were formulated to provide 5.0 g protein/day/kg body weight as fed and diets B and D were formulated to provide 9.3 g of protein/day/kg body weight as fed. Each diet was analyzed to determine actual concentration of components.

[a]1 Calorie=1 Kilocalorie

Model of Renal Failure. Renal mass in each cat was surgically reduced. Following surgery, all cats were fed diet A at a rate of 56 Calories/day/kg body weight, for a 2 month period in order to allow time for renal compensatory hypertrophy to occur.

Cat Groupings and Feeding Trials. After the 2 month period for renal hypertrophy, glomerular filtration rate (GFR) was determined in each cat using [14][C]-inulin as the marker for GFR,[6] and values (ml/min/kg body weight) were used to separate cats into four groups with equal mean GFR. Diets were randomly assigned to cat groups (diet A=Group A, diet B=Group B, diet C=Group C, diet D=Group D) and feeding trials were initiated. Food intake was measured daily, and cats were observed daily for signs of physical abnormalities. At bimonthly intervals after initiating feeding trials, blood biochemical analyses were repeated. At 4 month intervals GFR, urinalysis, and U P:C were measured.

Histologic and Morphometric Studies. After 12 month GFR measurements, cats were deeply anesthetized with sodium pentobarbital and the remnant kidney was quickly removed and perfused with fixative. For histologic study of kidneys, formalin-preserved blocks of both the right (nephrectomy) and the left (remnant) kidneys were imbedded in plastic, processed, and stained with H&E and PAS stains. Slides of kidney sections were viewed by three individuals without knowledge of the group of origin of the tissue. In PAS-stained slides, 25 outer cortical glomeruli from each cat were evaluated for mesangial matrix accumulation using the following scoring system: **0=normal, 1=mild, 2=moderate, 3=severe**. Groups were compared for mesangial matrix accumulation by analyzing absolute scores from remnant kidney sections and by analyzing the difference between remnant kidney scores and nephrectomy kidney scores on individual cats.

In remnant kidneys, H&E-stained slides were used to evaluate fibrosis, tubular morphology, and cellular infiltration. Tissues were scored for severity of lesion using the scale **0=normal, 1=mild, 2=moderate, and 3=severe**.

Statistical Analyses. Mean and SD values were computed. Analysis of variance (ANOVA) was used to determine differences between groups at each time of observation. Within groups, ANOVA was performed to determine if differences occurred with time. A paired t-test was used when a set of paired values was compared, and ANOVA, repeated measures was used to analyze mesangial matrix scores generated by 3 viewers. For determining significant differences, a $P \leq 0.05$ level of significance was chosen and Fishers test of least significant differences was used for post-hoc evaluations with multiple comparisons.

Clinical and Husbandry Observations. Twenty-six of 28 cats completed the study. One cat (Group D) abruptly developed uremia that was non-responsive to fluid therapy and was euthanatized during month 11 of the study. One cat (Group B) was found dead during month 10 following detection of leukocytosis and treat-

Results

ment with antibiotics; necropsy failed to establish cause of death. One cat (Group A) acutely developed severe azotemia and signs of uremia at month 3 but received fluid therapy, recovered, and completed the study. All other cats completed the study without major abnormalities in health. Data collected from all 28 cats were included in the analyses performed.

Body weight of cats decreased after surgery, during the 2 months while all received 56 Calories/day/kg body weight of diet A. At the time of separation into groups, body weight was similar among groups. During the 12 months of feeding trials that followed, body weight of Groups A and C remained stable. Body weight of Groups B and D increased soon after initiation of their 75 Calorie/day/kg diets, but Group B was unable to sustain its weight despite maintaining its food intake. At the conclusion of feeding trials, body weight of Group D was significantly greater than that of the other groups, but Groups A, B, and C did not differ from one another.

Food intake, and thus protein and calorie intake, remained relatively stable in each group throughout the study. Overall, protein intake expressed as a percent relative to diet A was 100, 98, 170, and 170% for groups A through D, respectively. Overall, caloric intake expressed as a percent relative to diet A was 100, 126, 95, and 122% for Groups A through D, respectively. Eating habits were evaluated subjectively throughout the study. In general cats receiving 56 Calories/day/kg (Groups A, C) ate their food immediately after it was available, whereas cats receiving 75 Calories/day/kg (Groups B and D) ate their food throughout the 24 hour feeding period.

Three cats in each group required sporadic treatment with potassium citrate or sodium bicarbonate in order to maintain plasma bicarbonate concentrations within the reference range. However, this treatment did not significantly affect K^+ or Na^+ intake by any group, nor did it cause any relevant difference in serum K^+ or Na^+ concentration between treated and untreated cats.

Renal Functions. The GFR was not significantly different between groups at the time that test diets were imposed and was not significantly different between groups at 4, 8, or 12 months (**Figure 1**). Within groups, GFR increased in Group D, after imposing diet D; the increase was significant at 4 months but not at 8 and 12 months. Plasma creatinine concentration was not significantly different between groups at any of the times tested, but a trend for higher values in groups A and B existed.

The U P:C values were not significantly different between groups for any of the times tested except at the time of separation of cats into groups (month 0) when Group A had a significantly greater U P:C than other groups. In each group a significant increase in U P:C occurred between presurgical values and values after 4, 8, and 12 months of feeding. However, mean values for each group at all times were within the reference range (0 to 0.3) for normal cats (**Figure 2**).

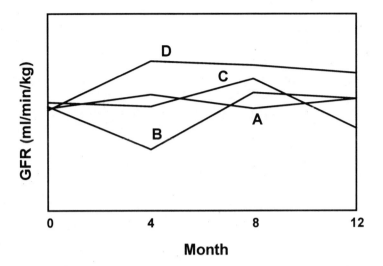

Figure 1.

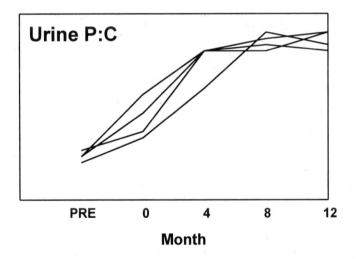

Figure 2.

Blood Biochemical Determinations. Cats had normal blood biochemical values prior to surgical reduction of renal mass, and groups did not differ in blood biochemical values once divided on the basis of GFR. Groups did not differ in anion gap, alkaline phosphatase, alanine aminotransferase, chloride, and glucose values at any of the time intervals after imposing diets. Serum K^+ concentration was normal, and not significantly different between groups for all times tested. Plasma bicarbonate concentration was not different between groups except at months 2 and 8 (data not shown), and were within the reference range (12–20 mM/l) for all groups at all time periods.

Groups varied at specific times in plasma albumin concentration; values were significantly higher in Groups C and D when differences existed. However, values in all groups were within the reference range for normal (2.6–3.7 g/dl) at all time periods (**Figure 3**). Overall values for BUN during the 12 months of dietary testing (expressed as a percent of diet A) were 100, 94, 146, and 130% for Groups A through D, respectively. Overall mean values for serum creatinine (expressed as a percent of diet A) were 100, 105, 85, and 95% for Groups A through D, respectively. The BUN:serum creatinine ratio was 25.2, 23.5, 45.1, and 35.3 for Groups A through D, respectively.

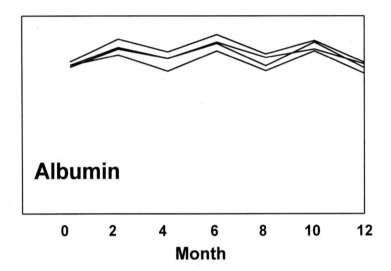

Figure 3.

Necropsy and Tissue Studies. Weights of right kidneys removed during nephrectomy were similar for Groups A, B, C, and D. At necropsy 14 months later, no significant gross lesions were noted in any cat except for remnant kidneys and lesions consistent with uremia in the cat euthanatized in Group D. Remnant kidney weights were similar among Groups A through C with Group D kidneys being significantly larger than the other groups.

Scoring of nephrectomized kidneys at time 0 revealed no difference between groups. Scoring of remnant kidneys at the termination of the experiment similarly revealed no significant differences between groups (**Figure 4**). Likewise, the change in mesangial matrix scores (remnant kidney minus nephrectomized kidney of each cat) was not significantly different between groups.

In remnant kidneys, fibrosis, tubular lesions, and cellular infiltrate were mild and uncommon. Nevertheless, a significant effect of calories on scores for cellular infiltrate and tubular lesions existed, and values approached significance for fibrosis (**Figure 5**). Protein intake did not affect scores for these nonglomerular lesions.

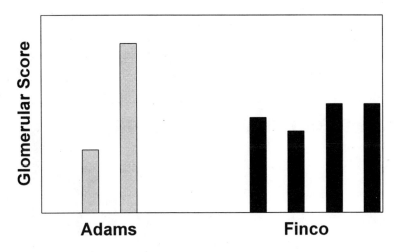

Figure 4.

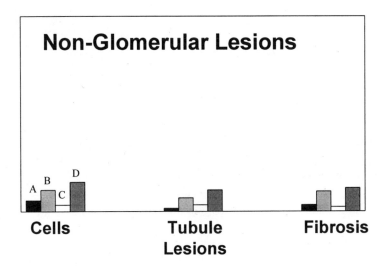

Figure 5.

A previous study reported that cats with reduced renal mass consuming 75 Calories and 6.8 g of protein/day/kg body weight developed severe renal lesions compared to cats with reduced renal mass consuming 56 Calories and 2.7 g of protein/day/kg body weight. Cats in the 75 Calorie, 6.8 g protein group had over 21% of glomeruli with adhesions, and a glomerulosclerosis score of 1.37 compared to 0.57% glomerular adhesions and a glomerulosclerosis score of 0.51 in the 56 Calorie, 2.7 g protein group. The present study was designed to distinguish the effects of protein from calories in the genesis of renal lesions.

Discussion

In contrast to the previous study, despite ingestion of considerably more protein (**Figure 6**), cats in our study had mild to minimal glomerular lesions. In our study, caloric intake influenced the severity of nonglomerular renal lesions, but protein intake did not.

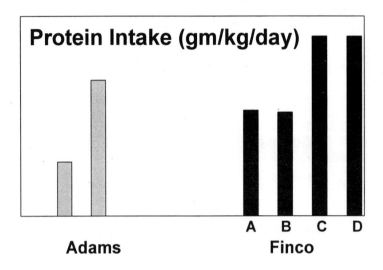

Figure 6.

Since strikingly different results were obtained from the two studies, the differences between the studies may explain the different results. Diets differed considerably in fat content (previous study = about 37%; our study = 12%), and in K⁺ content (about 0.4% v 0.8% in our study). Although both studies used diets with the same protein concentration to represent low (about 28%) and high (about 52%) protein diets, actual intake of protein was markedly different because of the effect of the fat on caloric density (**Figure 3**). Thus, Group A and Group B cats in the present study consumed approximately twice as much protein compared to cats fed 2.7 g/day/kg in the previous study, and Group C and Group D cats consumed approximately 30% more protein than cats fed 6.8 g/day/kg in the previous study. This higher protein intake in our study was reflected in BUN:serum creatinine ratios, which were higher than the previous study. Another difference between the present and previous study was body weight changes during the 12 months of feeding trials. In both studies, cats lost or only maintained body weight during the 2 months following surgical reduction of renal mass. After imposing the test diets, the high protein group in the previous study had over a 40% increase in body weight that was maintained for at least 6 months, while in the present study no group exceeded its presurgical weight during subsequent study.

The identification of differences between the two studies in intake of protein, K⁺, and fat warrant consideration of each as a potential cause of the difference in development of renal lesions. In addition, interactions between the factors should be considered.

Protein Intake. The present study does not support the hypothesis that the quantity of protein ingested is a significant factor in the development of renal lesions in cats with reduced renal mass. Cats in Groups C and D in the present study ingested considerably more protein than the high protein group in the previous study, without development of lesions of the magnitude as reported in the previous study. However, another factor to be considered is the source of protein. In our study, casein and soy protein were the major protein sources, while in the previous study pork liver and casein were protein sources. Studies in humans indicate that renal hemodynamic effects of protein differ depending in general on whether the protein is of animal or vegetable origin.[7-13] Since renal hemodynamic effects of protein are believed to be a mechanism for renal damage, it has been proposed that a vegan diet in humans may be beneficial in the prevention of glomerular sclerotic changes in health and disease.[14,15] Studies in rats with remnant kidneys demonstrated improved survival, less proteinuria, and milder renal lesions when fed soy protein, compared to casein.[16,17] Other studies in rats have suggested that protein source may affect serum lipid concentrations and lipid metabolism,[18,19] which also could affect the kidneys, as subsequently discussed. We are aware of no studies in either cats or dogs that address the issue of protein source as a relevant factor in the genesis of renal damage.

Dietary Potassium. In the previous study, hypokalemia and muscle weakness developed in 4 of 7 remnant kidney cats fed the high protein diet, which resolved after addition of K^+ to the diet. In another report, an association between hypokalemia and renal dysfunction in cats was identified.[20] Restriction of dietary K^+ caused hypokalemia and a transient reduction in GFR in normal cats, but renal tissues were not examined to determine if renal lesions developed.[21] At present it is well established that hypokalemia and renal dysfunction may be associated in cats, but the cause–effect relationship remains conjectural.[22] Epidemiologic studies in humans have demonstrated an inverse relationship between K^+ intake and hypertension. Potassium depletion induced by dietary K^+ restriction elevates blood pressure in both normal and hypertensive people.[23] The hypothesis that hypokalemia and K^+ depletion could cause renal damage to cats via hypertension apparently has not been tested.

Dietary Lipids. In both the previous study and the present one, poultry fat was used in the diets. Since there was a three-fold difference in fat between diets in the present study and those in the previous study, cats developing severe renal lesions had a substantially higher intake of fat. Alterations in serum lipid profiles are associated with renal disease in humans[24] and dogs,[25] including increases in total cholesterol, lower density lipoproteins, and triglycerides. Dietary lipids have been incriminated as a cause of renal damage in other species because of differences in unsaturated fatty acid composition of lipid sources, and the influence of these unsaturated fatty acids on generation of eicosanoids. Vasomotor, inflammatory, and platelet aggregating properties of the eicosanoids may affect several organs, including the kidneys. Studies of the relevance of dietary lipids in progression of renal failure in cats have not been reported.

Body Weight, Utilization of Calories. The difference between studies in weight gain by cats receiving 75 Calories/kg/day was remarkable. In our study Groups B and D cats failed to exceed presurgical weights, while a weight gain of over 40% occurred in cats in the previous study. A discrepancy in use of calories has been encountered in rodents pair-fed for caloric intake, and has been attributed to continuous versus sporadic food intake.[26] The same phenomenon of weight gain with sporadic versus continuous feeding probably occurs in cats as well, since body weight is maintained with less food intake by sporadic feeding compared to continuous feeding.[27] The metabolic differences that occur with sporadic feeding compared to continuous feeding do not seem well defined. However, such metabolic differences could play a role in the development of renal damage. It has been hypothesized that sporadic *v* continuous eating may affect renal hemodynamics.[1] Ironically, in considering the renal damage associated with protein intake, sporadic feeding has been hypothesized to be protective rather than harmful.[1] In the present study, Group C consumed its food abruptly, but Group D consumed its food over a longer period of time. Since both groups consumed 9 g of protein/day/kg, the effect of feeding pattern on renal damage does not seem to significant.

In the present study, non-glomerular renal lesions were minimal, but most were significantly greater as an effect of calories rather than protein intake. Recent studies have proposed that tubulointerstitial lesions may be significant in the development and progression of primary glomerular diseases.[28,29] Results of the present study suggest that caloric restriction should receive further attention as a factor in progression of renal failure in cats.

Interaction of Factors. In the previous study, intake of pork liver and poultry fat was shared by cats developing lesions and those that did not, suggesting that neither of these factors alone was responsible for the renal damage. It would require interaction of these factors with each other, or with hypokalemia or other factors, to explain the severity of the renal lesions in the previous study.

Other Nutritional Considerations

In the previous study, cats ingesting 2.7 g/day/kg body weight of protein had a significantly lower hematocrit and serum albumin concentration than cats ingesting 6.8 g/day/kg body weight. In the present study, albumin concentrations were maintained in the reference range for normal, albeit at some time periods values were significantly lower in cats of Groups A and B. Hematocrit values in the present study are difficult to interpret, since a small but significantly higher hematocrit existed in Group C compared to the other 3 groups. It is unclear whether the decreased serum albumin concentration found in the previous study was harmful, but it might represent generalized body protein depletion. Since results of the present study demonstrate that protein intake *per se* is not a risk factor for progression of renal lesions, the clinical practice of such severe protein restriction is questionable.

Cats in Group C initially gained weight after initiation of the feeding trial, but later lost weight and completed the study at the same weight level as cats getting the lower protein diets (Groups A, B). Group C cats had adequate protein for anabolism, but apparently the need for calories precluded optimal protein anabolism. The higher BUN:serum creatinine ratio in this Group C, compared to Group D, supports the theory that dietary protein catabolism was greater when calories were restricted.

References

1. Brenner BM, Meyer TW, Hostetter TH. Dietary protein intake and the progressive nature of kidney disease: The role of hemodynamically mediated glomerular injury in the pathogenesis of progressive glomerular sclerosis in aging, renal ablation, and instrinsic renal disease. *N Engl J Med* 1982; 307:652-659.

2. Tapp DC, Kobayaski S, Fernandes G, Venkatachalam MA. Protein restriction or calorie restriction? A critical assessment of the influence of selective calorie restriction in the progression of experimental renal disease. *Sem in Nephrol* 1989; 9:343-353.

3. Brown SA, Brown CA. Single-nephron adaptations to partial renal ablation in cats. *Am J Physiol* 1995; 269:R1002-R1008.

4. Adams LG, Polzin DJ, Osborne CA, O'Brien TD. Effects of dietary protein and calorie restriction in clinically normal cats and in cats with surgically induced chronic renal failure. *Am J Vet Res* 1993; 54:1653-1662.

5. Adams LG, Polzin DJ, Osborne CA, O'Brien TD, Hostetter TH. Influence of dietary protein/calorie intake on renal morphology and function in cats with 5/6 nephrectomy. *Lab Invest* 1994; 70:347-357.

6. Ross LA, Finco DR, Crowell WA. Effect of dietary phosphorus restriction on the kidneys of cats with reduced renal mass. *Am J Vet Res* 1982; 43:1023-1026.

7. Kontessis PS, Bossinakou I, Sarika L, Iliopoulou E, Papantoniou A, Trevisan R, Roussi D, Stipsanelli K, Grigorakis S, Souvatzoglou Z. Renal, metabolic, and hormonal responses to proteins of different origin in normotensive, nonproteinuric type I diabetic patients. *Diabetes Care* 1995; 18:1233-1240.

8. Pecis M, DeAzevedo MJ, Gross JL. Chicken and fish diet reduces glomerular hyperfiltration in IDDM patients. *Diabetes Care* 1994; 17:665-672.

9. Nakamura H, Takasawa M, Kasahara S, Tsuda A, Momotsu T, Ito S, Shibata A. Effects of acute protein loads of different sources on renal function of patients with diabetic nephropathy. *Tohoku J Exp Med* 1989; 159:153-162.

10. Dhaene M, Sabot J-P, Philippart Y, Doutrelepont JM, Vanherweghem JL. Effects of acute protein loads of different sources on glomerular filtration rate. *Kidney International* 1987; 32:S25-S28.

11. Nakamura H, Ito S, Ebe N, Shibata A. Renal effects of different types of protein in healthy volunteer subjects and diabetic patients. *Diabetic Care* 1993; 16:1071-1075.

12. Nakamura H, Yamazaki M, Chiba Y, Tani N, Momotsu T, Kamoi K, Ito S, Yamaji T, Shibata A. Acute loading with proteins from different sources in healthy volunteers and diabetic patients. *J Diabetic Complications* 1991; 5:140-142.

13. Kontessis P, Jones S, Dodds, R, Trevisan R, Nosadini R, Fioretto P, Borsato M, Sacerdoti D, Viberti G. Renal, metabolic and hormonal responses to ingestion of animal and vegetable proteins. *Kidney Int* 1990; 38:136-144.

14. Barsotti G, Morelli E, Cupisti A, Meola M, Dani L, Giovannetti S. A low-nitrogen, low-phosphorus vegan diet for patients with chronic renal failure. *Nephron* 1996; 74:390-394.

15. Wiseman MJ, Hunt R, Goodwin A, Gross JL, Keen H, Viberti GCl. Dietary composition and renal function in healthy subjects. *Nephron* 1987; 46:37-42.

16. Williams AJ, Baker F, Walls J. Effect of varying quantity and quality of dietary protein intake in experimental renal disease in rats. *Nephron* 1987; 46:83-90.

17. Williams AJ, Walls J. Metabolic consequences of differing protein diets in experimental renal disease. *Eur J of Clin Invest* 1987; 17:117-122.

18. Nagata Y, Ishiwaki N, Sugano M. Studies on the mechanism of antihyper-cholesterolemic action of soy protein and soy protein-type amino acid mixtures in relation to the casein counterparts in rats. *J Nutr* 1982; 112:1614-1625.

19. Vahouny GV, Chalcarz W, Satchithanandam S, Adamson I, Klurfeld DM, Kritchevsky D. Effect of soy protein and casein intake on intestinal absorption and lymphatic transport of cholesterol and oleic acid. *Am J Clin Nutr* 1984; 40:1156-1164.

20. Dow SW, Fettman MJ, LeCouteur RA, Hamar DW. Potassium depletion in cats: Renal and dietary influences. *J Am Vet Med Assoc* 1987; 191:1569-1575.

21. Dow SW, Fettman MJ, Smith KR, Hamar DW, Nagode LA, Refsal KR, Wilke WL. Effects of dietary acidification and potassium depletion on acid-base balance, mineral metabolism and renal function in adult cats. *J Nutr* 1990; 120:569-578.

22. Dow SW, Fettman MJ. Chronic renal disease and potassium depletion in cats. *Sem Vet Med Surg (Sm Anim)* 1992; 7:198-201.

23. Krishna GG. Role of potassium in the pathogenesis of hypertension. *Am J Med Sci* 1994; 307:S21-S25.

24. Moorhead JF, Chan MK, Varghese Z. The role of abnormalities of lipid metabolism in the progression of renal disease. In: Mitch WE, ed. *The Progressive Nature of Renal Disease*, New York: Churchill Livingstone, 1986:133.

25. Brown SA, Crowell WA, Barsanti JA, White JV, Finco DR. Beneficial effects of dietary mineral restriction in dogs with marked reduction of functional renal mass. *J Am Soc Nephrol* 1991; 1:1169-1179.

26. Cohn C, Joseph D. Caloric intake, weight loss and changes in body composition of rats as influenced by feeding frequency. *J Nutr* 1968; 96:94-100.

27. Finco DR, Adams DD, Crowell WA, Stattelman AJ, Brown SA, Barsanti JA. Food and water intake and urine composition in cats: Influence of continuous versus periodic feeding. *Am J Vet Res* 1986; 47:1638-1642.

28. D'Amico G, Ferrario F, Rastaldi MP. Tubulointerstitial damage in glomerular diseases: Its role in the progression of renal damage. *Am J Kidney Dis* 1995; 26:124-132.

29. Bohle A, Strutz F, Mller GA. On the pathogenesis of chronic renal failure in primary glomerulopathies: A view from the interstitium. *Exp Nephrol* 1994; 2:205-210.

Clinical Experience with Canine Renal Patients Fed a Diet Containing a Fermentable Fiber Blend

Mark A. Tetrick, DVM, PhD
Research Nutritionist, Research and Development
The Iams Company, Lewisburg, Ohio, USA

Gregory D. Sunvold, PhD; Gregory A. Reinhart, PhD
Researh and Development, The Iams Company, Lewisburg, Ohio, USA

Introduction

For decades, standard renal diets have been formulated with low levels of protein to slow progression of renal failure and to reduce azotemia. However, research in recent years has not supported an association between higher dietary protein levels and the progression of renal disease in dogs.[1-5] Drastic dietary protein restriction to reduce azotemia must be weighed against the detrimental effects on normal bodily functions (**Figure 1**). While lowering dietary protein may help reduce azotemia other factors such as the severity of the renal disease and the quality of dietary protein are involved.

If the amino acids provided by dietary protein more closely match the amino acid requirements of the dog, more amino acids from dietary protein will be incorporated in body protein. Greater incorporation of amino acids in body protein means fewer amino acids will be oxidized and ultimately excreted as urea. Improved protein quality can reduce the oxidation of amino acids and hence reduce the amount of waste nitrogen converted to urea at a given level of dietary protein.

The excretion route of waste nitrogen can be influenced by diet and may affect azotemia. Inclusion of fermentable fibers in the diet has been shown to alter urea and ammonia flux in the large intestine and cecum of rats[6-9] and humans.[10] These changes in flux shift some nitrogen excretion from urine to feces resulting in lower blood urea nitrogen (BUN).[7] This concept has been examined in normal dogs and shown to repartition nitrogen from urine to feces.[11] Interest has been heightened in the use of nitrogen repartitioning in clinical cases of canine renal failure. Can higher protein levels than provided by traditional renal diets be fed in conjunction with a fermentable fiber blend without exacerbating azotemia?

Objective

Document the clinical response of canine renal failure cases to either a low protein diet or a moderate protein diet containing a fermentable fiber blend.

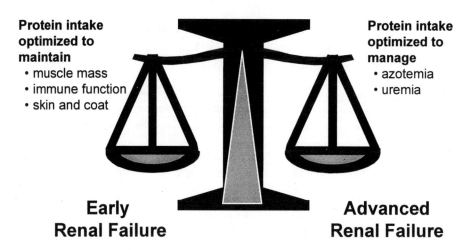

Protein intake optimized to maintain
• muscle mass
• immune function
• skin and coat

Protein intake optimized to manage
• azotemia
• uremia

Early Renal Failure

Advanced Renal Failure

Figure 1. Matching protein intake to the severity of renal failure.

Materials and Methods   Canine clinical cases in various stages of renal failure were recruited for 10 weeks of clinical monitoring. All of the dogs discussed here with previously diagnosed renal failure were fed a commercially prepared diet restricted in protein and phosphorus (Hill's® Prescription Diet® k/d®) for at least two weeks prior to gathering baseline information and laboratory analysis. Whole blood, serum, plasma, and urine samples were obtained and the following baseline laboratory analyses performed: blood chemistry panel, plasma ammonia, parathyroid hormone (intact) (PTH), hematology and urinalysis. Dogs were then switched over several days to renal diet 1 (Eukanuba Veterinary Diets® Nutritional Kidney Formula™ Early Stage) or renal diet 2 (Eukanuba Veterinary Diets Nutritional Kidney Formula Advanced Stage) according to the following guidelines. If BUN was between 30–65 and creatinine was between 1.5–2.5 mg/dL, dogs were transitioned to renal diet 1. Dogs with BUN >65 mg/dL and creatinine >2.5 mg/dL were transitioned to renal diet 2.

Rechecks consisting of a blood chemistry panel and urinalysis were conducted 2 and 5 weeks after the start of the transition to either renal diet 1 or renal diet 2. The 10 week recheck included the same sampling and laboratory work as the baseline. All sample analysis was performed by Labcorp, Columbus, Ohio, USA. Attending veterinarians and client owners completed questionnaires at the time the dog was enrolled and at each of the rechecks to monitor the status of each case.

Diet analysis is presented in **Table 1**. The analysis presented for the conventional renal diet is typical analysis of this product, not analysis of the specific lots fed to the animals in this study. The analysis presented for renal diet 1 and renal diet 2 is the analysis of the diets fed to this group of renal cases after the dietary switch from the conventional renal diet.

Table 1. Diet characteristics (dry matter basis)

	Typical Analysis Conventional Renal Diet	Analysis of Diet Fed	
		Renal Diet 1	Renal Diet 2
Crude Protein, %	14.2	21.1	17.5
Fat, %	19.6	14.3	13.0
Ash, %	3.3	5.8	4.2
Crude Fiber, %	1.1	3.0	2.7
Calcium, %	0.78	0.95	0.65
Phosphorus, %	0.31	0.45	0.29
omega-6:3 fatty acid ratio	22:1	4.4:1	5.6:1
% calories from protein	10.6	17.3	12.9
% calories from fat	38.7	31.1	29.4
% calories from carbohydrate	50.8	51.6	57.7

The conventional renal diet and renal diets 1 and 2 differ in the following ways. Renal diet 1 and 2 contain nearly 50% and 25% more protein than the conventional renal diet, respectively. Total fat content is reduced by ~30% in renal diets 1 and 2 relative to the conventional renal diet. The renal diets used in the trial have an adjusted omega 6:omega-3 fatty acid ratio of approximately 5:1 v 22:1 for the conventional renal diet. The phosphorus level of all the diets in this study were restricted. The conventional renal diet at 0.31% P falls between 0.45% P for renal diet 1 and 0.29% P for renal diet 2.

Case Studies

The results and case studies reported below are for dogs successfully completing the 10 week study at the time of this report. One dog that had serious complications at the start of the study was withdrawn by the owners within the first four weeks; the dog was subsequently euthanized.

Canine Renal Patients Transitioned to Renal Diet 1

Case 1. Dumas. Dumas is a male, neutered, 18-year-old, 20 pound, mixed breed with a one year history of renal failure. He had been fed the conventional renal diet since the renal failure was diagnosed. Results are summarized in **Table 2**.

At the time of the diet change, Dumas presented as a stabilized chronic renal failure case. After being switched to renal diet 1, BUN and creatinine declined slightly, despite the almost 50% increase in protein compared to the conventional renal diet. Although phosphorus level in renal diet 1 is higher than in the conventional diet, serum phosphorus levels dropped over the 10 weeks of observation from 5.9 to 4.3 mg/dL. This may indicate that phosphorus was more bioavailable in the previous diet. There was a corresponding drop in the PTH level from 246 to 182

Table 2. Patient "Dumas" summary of results.

| | Week | | | | Lab Normal |
	Initial	2	5	10	Range
BUN (mg/dL)	63	62	57	55	10-30
Creatinine (mg/dL)	2.3	2.6	2.2	2.1	0.5-1.5
Phosphorus, (mg/dL)	5.9	5.3	4.8	4.3	3.0-6.0
Triglycerides, (mg/dL)	48	82	65	41	0-160
NH_3 (mg/dL)	39	–	–	62	20-120
PTH (pg/mL)	246	–	–	182	16-136
Urine Specific Gravity	1.016	1.012	1.014	1.014	1.018-1.045
Urine Protein	trace	neg	neg	neg	neg
Hematocrit (%)	36.7	–	–	35.7	35-56
Hemoglobin (g/dL)	12.8	–	–	12.2	12-18

pg/mL, which may be a physiological response to the decreased serum phosphorus level. Dumas had a several month history of constipation on the conventional renal diet, which resolved on renal diet 1.

Case 2. Bessie. Bessie is a 12-year-old, 59 pound, spayed female Bassett Hound. Bessie had a one year history of mild azotemia and had been fed the conventional renal diet for 8 months prior to the switch to renal diet 1. Results are summarized in *Table 3*.

Blood urea nitrogen and creatinine remained stable following the change to renal diet 1. PTH increased despite an apparent decline in serum phosphorus levels. Triglyceride levels declined over the course of the study.

Table 3. Patient "Bessie" summary of results.

| | Week | | | | Lab Normal |
	Initial	2	5	10	Range
BUN (mg/dL)	37	42	36	37	10-30
Creatinine (mg/dL)	0.9	1.0	1.2	1.0	0.5-1.5
Phosphorus, (mg/dL)	5.1	5.1	4.2	3.7	3.0-6.0
Triglycerides, (mg/dL)	330	275	129	108	0-160
NH_3 (mg/dL)	161	–	–	96	20-120
PTH (pg/mL)	55	–	–	496	16-136
Urine Specific Gravity	1.012	1.015	1.012	1.012	1.018-1.045
Urine Protein	3+	3+	3+	3+	neg
Hematocrit (%)	45.7	–	–	46.9	35-56
Hemoglobin (g/dL)	17.5	–	–	15.0	12-18

In addition to the cases above, two additional cases switched to renal diet 1 did not show an increase in BUN, despite the nearly 50% increase in protein level, from 14 to 21%. Adequate protein to meet nutritional recommendations for adult maintenance was provided in these case studies without exacerbating azotemia. The effects of added fermentable fiber and a dietary amino acid profile that more closely matches the amino acid requirements of these patients may allow for higher protein intake without increases in BUN. Blood ammonia was monitored to examine the effect of the enhanced bacterial activity in the colon. For dogs fed renal diet 1, in two of three cases the blood ammonia declined. In the case of Dumas, the blood ammonia increased from 39 to 62 mg/dL, but was still well within the normal range. In a fourth case an initial sample was not obtained, however, blood ammonia after 10 weeks on renal diet 1 was 33 mg/dL.

Serum phosphorus concentrations declined in all cases after the change to renal diet 1. The response as measured by PTH levels was mixed and may indicate that more time is needed for changes in serum phosphorus to affect PTH levels. The trend appears to be toward lower triglycerides, which would follow from the lower percent of calories from fat and the lower n-6:n-3 fatty acid ratio in renal diet 1 and renal diet 2 compared to the conventional renal diet. In humans, supplementation with n-3 fatty acids has been associated with lowering triglycerides in diabetics[12] and non-diabetics.[13,14]

Acceptance of renal diet 1 relative to the conventional renal diet at 10 weeks was judged by the owners to be better in two cases and the same in one case (three out of four owners responding). Owners noted an improvement in the overall quality of their dog's coat in all three cases.

Case 3. Elle. Elle is a 4-year-old, spayed female, Labrador Retriever weighing 70 pounds. Elle had an acute onset of renal failure and was on the conventional renal diet for 2 weeks. Elle was transitioned to renal diet 2, based on initial BUN and creatinine concentrations. Lab results are summarized in *Table 4*.

Following the transition to renal diet 2, Elle's BUN, creatinine and phosphorus declined. With the acute nature of this case it is possible that there was some continued renal compensation during the course of the clinical monitoring. Overall, serum phosphorus levels declined. PTH levels were comparable at the beginning and end of 10 weeks.

Case 4. Peaches. Peaches is a 12-year-old, spayed female Cocker Spaniel. Peaches has a two year history of renal insufficiency and has been fed the conventional renal diet since that time. Though the initial BUN was just below the guideline of 65 mg/dL, the attending veterinarian transitioned Peaches to renal diet 2. Lab results are summarized in *Table 5*.

Table 4. Patient "Elle" summary of results.

| | Week | | | | Lab Normal Range |
	Initial	2	5	10	
BUN (mg/dL)	79	67	58	72	10-30
Creatinine (mg/dL)	8.8	7.2	6.2	6.8	0.5-1.5
Phosphorus, (mg/dL)	6.0	3.9	4.0	5.6	3.0-6.0
Triglycerides, (mg/dL)	470	75	131	31	0-160
NH$_3$ (mg/dL)	45	–	–	88	20-120
PTH (pg/mL)	237	–	–	230	16-136
Urine Specific Gravity	1.012	1.011	1.013	1.011	1.018-1.045
Urine Protein	1+	trace	1+	neg	neg
Hematocrit (%)	36.9	–	–	32.1	35-56
Hemoglobin (g/dL)	13.4	–	–	10.7	12-18

Blood urea nitrogen and creatinine remained fairly stable following the transition from the conventional renal diet to renal diet 2. Serum phosphorus levels were variable and PTH increased over the initial 10 weeks. The owner encouraged consumption of the previous renal diet and renal diet 2 by adding broth and green beans to the diets. On the questionnaire the owner noted continued feeding of table scraps which may have contributed to the variability in phosphorus levels. Although the owner in this case did not report feeding a vitamin/mineral supplement, it is important to note that supplementing renal diet 1 or 2 with four Nutritabs™, would increase total phosphorus intake by 40% and 62%, respectively.

Table 5. Patient "Peaches" summary of results.

| | Week | | | | Lab Normal Range |
	Initial	2	5	10	
BUN (mg/dL)	62	49	56	72	10-30
Creatinine (mg/dL)	1.5	1.5	1.5	1.2	0.5-1.5
Phosphorus, (mg/dL)	6.7	7.2	8.2	6.0	3.0-6.0
Triglycerides, (mg/dL)	112	101	98	203	0-160
NH$_3$ (mg/dL)	145	–	–	189	20-120
PTH (pg/mL)	319	–	–	650	16-136
Urine Specific Gravity	1.015	1.012	1.011	1.010	1.018-1.045
Urine Protein	3+	3+	3+	2+	neg
Hematocrit (%)	48.1	–	–	47.3	35-56
Hemoglobin (g/dL)	16.4	–	–	16.8	12-18

For the more advanced cases of renal failure converted to renal diet 2, BUN and creatinine concentrations were lower or comparable to the initial values over the 10 weeks following the transition from the conventional renal diet. Serum phosphorus concentrations declined and PTH remained stable in the case of Elle. In the second case, phosphorus concentrations declined between the initial and 10 week sample, but were more variable at the interim checks. The increased variability in serum phosphorus may have been related to the feeding of table scraps in the second case. Reducing phosphorus intake is important in slowing the progression of renal disease.

In Elle's case, triglycerides declined. Peaches' triglycerides were more variable, which may have been related to the feeding of table scraps. Blood ammonia levels increased but remained in the normal range for Elle. In the case of Peaches, the blood ammonia increased but was greater than the normal range initially. Peaches also had intermittently elevated alkaline phosphatase and ALT, which may indicate the involvement of some hepatic dysfunction in the elevated blood ammonia levels.

Acceptance of renal diet 2 relative to the previous diet was better in both cases, as judged by the owners at the end of 10 weeks. In most cases, the transition to full acceptance of the new diet took about 2 weeks. Both owners considered their dog's overall coat quality to be the same at 10 weeks as at the beginning of the study.

Summary of Cases Transitioned to Renal Diet 2

In this study, the cases of early renal failure transitioned to renal diet 1 were fed nearly 50% more dietary protein in the presence of a fermentable fiber blend without causing an increase in BUN concentrations. Dogs with more advanced renal disease and switched to renal diet 2 were fed approximately 25% more dietary protein, relative to the conventional renal diet, without increasing their BUN concentrations. In most cases, triglyceride levels were lower following the diet change, which would follow from the lower fat level and the increased amount of n-3 fatty acids in renal diets 1 and 2. While serum phosphorus decreased in most cases after the change in diet, longer term follow-up may be required to observe the expected changes in PTH. The study also highlights the importance of client education and owner compliance in reducing phosphorus intake, an important factor in the progression of renal disease.

Overall Conclusions

Eukanuba Veterinary Diets is a registered trademark of The Iams Company.
Nutritional Kidney Formula is a trademark of The Iams Company.
Hill's, Prescription Diet, and k/d are registered trademarks of Colgate-Palmolive Co. and used under license by Hill's Pet Nutrition, Inc.
Nutritabs is a registered trademark of the Upjohn Company.

1. Bovee KC, Kronfeld DS, Ramberg C, Goldschmidt M. Long-term measurement of renal function in partially nephrectomized dogs fed 56, 27, or 19% protein. *Investigative Urology* 1979; 16:378-384.

References

2. Brown SA, Finco DR, Crowell WA, Navar LG. Dietary protein intake and the glomerular adaptations to partial nephrectomy in dogs. *J Nutr* 1991; 121:S125-S127.

3. Finco DR, Brown SA, Crowell WA, Brown CA, Barsanti JA, Carey DP, Hirakawa DA. Effects of aging and dietary protein intake on uninephrectomized geriatric dogs. *Am J Vet Res* 1994; 55:1282-1290.

4. Finco DR, Brown SA, Crowell WA, Duncan RJ, Barsanti JA, Bennett SE. Effects of dietary phosphorus and protein in dogs with chronic renal failure. *Am J Vet Res* 1992; 53:2264-2271.

5. White JV, Finco DR, Crowell WA, Brown SA, Hirakawa DA. Effect of dietary protein on functional, morphological, and histologic changes of the kidney during compensatory renal growth in dogs. *Am J Vet Res* 1991; 52:1357-1365.

6. Assimon SA, Stein TP. Digestible fiber (gum arabic), nitrogen excretion and urea recycling in rats. *Nutrition* 1994; 10:544-550.

7. Rémésy C, Demigné C. Specific effects of fermentable carbohydrates on blood urea flux and ammonia absorption in the rat cecum. *J Nutr* 1989; 119:560-565.

8. Younes H, Garleb K, Behr S, Rémésy C, Demigné C. Fermentable fibers or oligosaccharides reduce urinary nitrogen excretion by increasing urea disposal in the rat cecum. *J Nutr* 1995; 125:1010-1016.

9. Younes H, Demigné C, Behr SR, Garleb KA, Rémésy C. A blend of dietary fibers increases urea disposal in the large intestine and lowers urinary nitrogen excretion in rats fed a low protein diet. *Nutritional Biochemistry* 1996; 7:474-480.

10. Bliss DZ, Stein TP, Schleifer CR, Settle RG. Supplementation with gum arabic fiber increases fecal nitrogen excretion and lowers serum urea nitrogen concentration in chronic renal failure patients consuming a low-protein diet. *Am J Clin Nutr* 1996; 63:392-398.

11. Howard MD, Sunvold GD, Reinhart GA, Kerley MS. Effect of fermentable fiber consumption by the dog on nitrogen balance and fecal microbial nitrogen excretion. *FASEB J* 1996; 10:A257.

12. Berry EM. Dietary fatty acids in the management of diabetes mellitus. *Am J Clin Nutr* 1997; 66:991S-997S.

13. Mackness MI, Bhatnagar D, Durrington PN, Prais H, Haynes B, Morgan J, Borthwick L. Effects of a new fish oil concentrate on plasma lipids and lipoproteins in patients with hypertriglyceridaemia. *Eur J Clin Nutr* 1994; 48:859-865.

14. Harris WS. Fish oils and plasma lipid and lipoprotein metabolism. *J Lipid Res* 1989; 30:785-807.

Gastrointestinal Health

Clinical Diagnosis of
Canine Small Intestinal Disease

David A. Williams, MA, VetMB, PhD, DACVIM
Professor and Head, Department of Small Animal Medicine and Surgery
College of Veterinary Medicine
Texas A&M University, College Station, Texas, USA

The specific diagnosis of small intestinal disease in dogs is difficult. Histologic examination of small intestinal biopsies allows documentation of a few specific infectious or neoplastic enteropathies. In most patients morphologic abnormalities are mild and nonspecific however, and many affected dogs have normal-appearing intestinal biopsies even though functional disease is present.[1] Further complicating this is the difficulty of associating morphologic and functional findings with relatively specific diagnoses, such as dietary sensitivity or idiopathic small intestinal bacterial overgrowth. Specific diagnosis of well-defined enteropathies similar to celiac sprue (gluten-sensitive enteropathy), tropical sprue, or Whipple's disease in human patients cannot presently be routinely made in canine patients.

Introduction

Despite these major limitations to current knowledge of canine gastroenterology, clinical research has allowed progress to be made in the recognition and definition of canine intestinal disease. As in human patients, the intestinal defects in patients with enteropathies can be broken down into pre-mucosal, mucosal, and post-mucosal components (**Table 1**), and the severity of dysfunction in proximal and distal small intestine can be assessed. Recognition of defects in these locations can facilitate effective management of patients with small intestinal disease even when specific enteropathies cannot be identified.

Traditional tests to evaluate suspected malabsorption in dogs include microscopic examination of feces for the presence of undigested food, several methods that indirectly assess fat or sugar absorption, and assay of pancreatic enzyme activities in feces. Many of these tests have found limited application because of their unreliability (lack of sensitivity or specificity),[2] practical constraints, or expense. Several new tests have recently been shown to be diagnostically highly reliable and technically feasible in the majority of veterinary practices. Markedly subnormal serum trypsin-like immunoreactivity (TLI) in patients with signs compatible with diseases of the small intestine (vomiting, diarrhea, weight loss, polyphagia, anorexia) identifies individuals with exocrine pancreatic insufficiency. Conversely, by a process of elimination, normal serum TLI concentration strongly incriminates underlying small intestinal disease as the cause of clinical signs.

Table 1. Pathophysiologic mechanisms of malabsorption.

PHASE OF ABSORPTIVE PROCESS	PATHOPHYSIOLOGIC MECHANISM (EXAMPLE OF DISEASE PROCESS)

Premucosal (luminal)	• Defective substrate hydrolysis
	  – Enzyme deficiency (exocrine pancreatic insufficiency)
	  – Enzyme inactivation (gastric acid hypersecretion)
	  – Rapid intestinal transit (hyperthyroidism)
	• Defective solubilization of fat
	  – Decreased bile salt secretion (biliary obstruction)
	  – Bile salt deconjugation (bacterial overgrowth)
	  – Bile salt loss (resection or disease of terminal ileum)
	  – Impaired release of pancreatic secretogogue (severe small intestinal disease)
	• Intrinsic factor deficiency (exocrine pancreatic insufficiency)
	• Bacterial competition for cobalamin (bacterial overgrowth)

Mucosal	• Brush border enzyme deficiency
	  – Congenital defects (enteropeptidase, lactase – man)
	  – Acquired defect secondary to diffuse enteropathies
	• Brush border transport deficiency
	  – Selective defects (inherited selective cobalamin malabsorption)
	  – Generalized defects (inflammatory bowel diseases, infectious enteropathies, dietary sensitivities, villous atrophy, intestinal resection)
	• Enterocyte processing defects (abetalipoproteinemia – man)
	• Disruption of lamina propria

Postmucosal (hemolymphatic)	• Lymphatic obstruction
	  – Primary lymphangiectasia
	  – Secondary (acquired) lymphatic obstruction (neoplasia, infiltrative infectious or inflammatory disease)
	• Vascular failure (intestinal ischemia, intestinal vasculitis, portal hypertension)

Once normal exocrine pancreatic function has been documented, serum cobalamin and folate concentrations and breath hydrogen concentration[3] provide specific information about intestinal absorptive function. Fecal α_1-protease inhibitor (α_1-PI) concentration provides a useful marker for protein-losing enteropathy in dogs,[4] while inert sugar absorption tests assess intestinal permeability (barrier function)[5,6] and the serum concentration of unconjugated bile acids helps identify dogs with small intestinal bacterial overgrowth.[7]

Each of these methods examines a different aspect of intestinal function, and none is perfect or superior to all of the others. Several approaches are required to examine absorptive capacity, intestinal permeability, and enteric protein loss, as well as to identify pre-mucosal, mucosal, and post-mucosal contributory factors. Clearly it is rarely practical to perform all available tests, and not all of these aspects of intestinal function are likely to be abnormal in all patients with small intestinal disease. Nonetheless, selective application of a few of the more modern tests facilitates diagnosis and management of a high proportion of canine patients with small intestinal disease. Test results can establish with certainty in some cases that small intestinal disease is present, that there is malabsorption of one or more nutrients, that there is overgrowth of bacteria in the upper small intestine, that there is protein-losing enteropathy, or that intestinal permeability is abnormally high. In this review, advantages and limitations of the more commonly applied of these diagnostic methods will be discussed in reference to a series of questions that can be used to define and characterize enteropathies in individual patients.

Tests of Fat and Xylose Absorption. Indirect tests of fat absorption (qualitative fecal fat test, plasma turbidity test) are generally accepted to be unreliable, while quantitative tests based on assay of fecal fat output are expensive and very insensitive tests for small intestinal disease.[8] The xylose absorption test is also expensive and inconvenient to perform, and also has poor sensitivity for identifying patients with intestinal disease.[8-10] These tests are now rarely used, largely because of the emergence of more sensitive, specific, economical, and practical tests that reflect carbohydrate and vitamin absorption.

Is There Malabsorption?

Serum Cobalamin Assay. Cobalamin is a water-soluble vitamin (vitamin B_{12}) plentiful in canine diets. Dietary deficiency is highly improbable, and it is very difficult to induce cobalamin deficiency in most species. Studies of cobalamin absorption in normal dogs show that the mechanisms involved are similar to those in human beings.[11] Acid and pepsins (proteolytic enzymes) in gastric juice release cobalamin from dietary protein. At the acid pH in the stomach, the free vitamin is bound by proteins called R proteins that are probably secreted in saliva and gastric juice. R protein-bound cobalamin then passes into the duodenum where pancreatic proteolytic enzymes degrade the R protein and thereby release cobalamin.[12] At the neutral pH in the small intestine, free cobalamin binds to intrinsic factor, a protein secreted predominantly in the pancreatic juice of dogs.[11] Absorption of cobalamin bound to intrinsic factor finally occurs by way of specific receptors located in the distal small intestine.[13,14]

Cobalamin malabsorption results in a subnormal serum concentration only when malabsorption is severe enough and has been present long enough to deplete body reserves. In human beings, cobalamin malabsorption occurs in association with atrophic gastritis or gastric resection, chronic exocrine pancreatic insufficiency, duodenal bacterial overgrowth, and ileal disease or ileal resection.[15] Rare causes of malabsorption in humans include failure to synthesize intrinsic factor, synthesis of nonfunctional intrinsic factor, and selective defects in ileal absorption.[15] In dogs, subnormal serum cobalamin concentrations may occur in association with small intestinal disease, exocrine pancreatic insufficiency, small intestinal bacterial overgrowth, and inherited selective defects in cobalamin absorption. Pancreatic intrinsic factor presumably maintains cobalamin absorption in dogs with gastric disease, in contrast to the situation in human beings.

Cobalamin malabsorption associated with small intestinal disease may be due to pathology specific to the intrinsic factor-cobalamin receptors in the distal small intestine. Disease localized exclusively in the ileum is probably uncommon in dogs, however, and ileal dysfunction is more frequently associated with generalized disease affecting additional segments of the intestinal tract. Ileal resection causes cobalamin malabsorption in human beings and probably does so in dogs too. Cobalamin deficiency has recently been described in Giant Schnauzers and Border Collies with selective cobalamin malabsorption.[16-18]

Bacterial overgrowth in the proximal small intestine causes cobalamin malabsorption due to competition for the vitamin by the abnormally high numbers of bacteria.[9,19] While bacteria are the ultimate source of all naturally available cobalamin, many species of bacteria present in the intestine, particularly obligate anaerobes, are dependent on exogenous cobalamin. So competition for this vitamin by large numbers of bacteria can lead to a reduction in serum concentrations.

Cobalamin malabsorption is common in canine exocrine pancreatic insufficiency and can arise by several mechanisms including failure of pancreatic enzymes to liberate cobalamin from binding by R proteins, failure of the pancreas to secrete intrinsic factor, failure of intrinsic factor to bind cobalamin due to abnormally acidic pH in the intestine secondary to impaired pancreatic-bicarbonate secretion, and competition for available cobalamin by intestinal microflora in those dogs with coexisting small intestinal bacterial overgrowth.[20,21] Whatever the mechanism, serum cobalamin concentrations are often subnormal in dogs with exocrine pancreatic insufficiency, even after otherwise effective treatment.

Serum cobalamin can be assayed by a variety of bioassay or competitive-binding assay methods. Bioassays are more technically demanding, however, and have to a large extent been superseded by competitive-binding assays. Results can vary considerably between different laboratories because different test methods are used. It is also very important to note that stable cobalamin-binding proteins in the serum of some veterinary species may interfere with some commonly-used methods that are reliable for assay of cobalamin in serum from human beings. Assays should therefore be validated for use in individual veterinary species.[22] Reported normal serum cobalamin concentrations determined by *Euglena viridis* assay in dogs are 200 to 400 ng/L.[1] Whole blood cobalamin concentrations determined by *Ochromonas malhamensis* protozoa bioassay are 135 to 950 ng/L in dogs.[23] Normal canine serum concentrations determined by competitive-binding assay in the author's laboratory are greater than 160 ng/L.

In human patients with gastrointestinal diseases, severe cobalamin deficiency resulting from malabsorption eventually causes megaloblastic anemia and neurologic disease. Anorexia and poor growth have been described in young Giant Schnauzers and Border Collies with selective cobalamin malabsorption.[16-18] Hematologic abnormalities in these dogs include a moderate nonregenerative normocytic anemia with marked anisocytosis, only occasional megaloblasts, and moderate poikilocytosis as well as a neutropenia with occasional hypersegmented neutrophils, in contrast to the macrocytic anemia seen in human beings. Clinical signs due to cobalamin deficiency have not yet been described in dogs with other gastrointestinal diseases, even when serum concentrations are severely subnormal. However, some patients with idiopathic inflammatory bowel disease and villous atrophy do not respond well to therapy with glucocorticoids and/or antibiotics until subnormal serum cobalamin concentrations are corrected. Cobalamin deficiency has also been reported to cause villous atrophy and secondary malabsorption of folate, fat and xylose in human beings.[24]

Serum Folate Assay. Folate is a water-soluble vitamin that, like cobalamin, is plentiful in canine diets so nutritional deficiency is unlikely. Dietary folate is usually present in a poorly absorbed form because of conjugation with several glutamate residues to form folate polyglutamates. Folate conjugase, an enzyme located in the brush border of the jejunal mucosa, removes all but one residue before mucosal uptake. Specific folate carriers located only in the proximal small intestine then transport folate monoglutamate into mucosal cells. The canine distal small intestine has little ability to absorb folate.[25,26]

As with cobalamin, malabsorption results in a subnormal serum concentration of folate only when the defect in absorption is sufficiently severe and has been present long enough to deplete body reserves. Folate malabsorption does occur, however, and canine small intestinal disease is sometimes associated with subnormal serum folate concentrations.[19] In dogs, as in human patients, a subnormal serum folate concentration in the face of normal dietary intake reflects disease involving the proximal small intestine. Disease restricted to the middle or distal segments of the small intestine does not impair folate absorption. While various drugs, including phenytoin and sulfasalazine, impair folate absorption in humans, there is no evidence that this is a problem in dogs.[27]

Serum folate concentrations can increase in dogs with bacterial overgrowth as a result of folate synthesis by the abnormal microflora.[25,26] Overgrowth must be present in the proximal small bowel for serum folate concentrations to increase; changes in the microflora distal to the site of absorption will have no effect.

Dogs with exocrine pancreatic insufficiency often have elevated serum folate concentrations, which probably reflect associated bacterial overgrowth.[20,28] Impaired pancreatic bicarbonate secretion can also enhance folate absorption by decreasing the pH in the proximal small intestine. Folate absorption is optimal at a mildly acidic pH, and minimal reductions in intraluminal pH promote uptake.

Folate, like cobalamin, can be assayed using a variety of bioassays and competitive-binding assays. As with serum cobalamin, serum folate values may vary considerably with different methods and laboratories. Published normal canine serum and plasma concentrations determined by *Lactobacillus casei* bioassay are 4.8 to 13.0 μg/L[19] and 4.0 to 26.0 μg/L,[23] respectively. Normal canine serum concentrations determined by competitive-binding assay in the author's laboratory range from 4.7 to 9.0 μg/L. Erythrocyte folate concentrations are much greater than in serum, and assay of hemolyzed samples may indicate misleadingly increased values or mask subnormal values.

Clinical Application of Serum Cobalamin and Folate Assays

It is apparent that both small intestinal and exocrine pancreatic diseases may affect serum cobalamin and folate concentrations. Results of assays can therefore only be interpreted in light of knowledge of the status of pancreatic function, as provided by the result of a serum TLI assay. Even prolonged anorexia does not appear to lead to depletion of serum cobalamin or folate concentration, but oral folate supplementation (unlikely) or parenteral cobalamin administration will increase serum concentrations. Preferably, both cobalamin and folate should be assayed because interpretation is most useful when results are considered together. Markedly increased concentrations of both vitamins, for example, may reflect supplementation before sampling. Interpretation of folate concentration alone in such instances could mistakenly indicate bacterial overgrowth. Since commercial competitive binding assays for cobalamin and folate are usually combination dual-isotope kits, most diagnostic laboratories do not offer individual assays of cobalamin or folate alone. Finally, commercially available assay methods use a variety of different technologies and have been designed to assay vitamins in serum from human beings; some methods are known not to be valid in veterinary species so it is important to verify that your laboratory is using an appropriate method.

Decreased serum concentrations of both cobalamin and folate are a relatively uncommon finding and suggest severe, long-standing disease affecting the entire small intestine. Such decreased concentrations have been observed in association with a canine enteropathy resembling chronic tropical sprue in human beings.[29]

Reduction in serum folate accompanied by normal cobalamin concentrations is consistent with dysfunction localized predominantly in the upper small intestine. These changes often accompany wheat-sensitive enteropathy in Irish Setters, but they are not a consistent finding with the disease.[30]

Serum folate and cobalamin concentrations may also provide evidence for the presence of bacterial overgrowth in the proximal small intestine of dogs. Decreased serum cobalamin concentration accompanied by increased serum folate concentration in a dog with normal exocrine pancreatic function are highly suggestive of bacterial overgrowth. These characteristic changes have led to the identification of an antibiotic-responsive enteropathy associated with bacterial overgrowth in German Shepherd Dogs. Bacterial overgrowth can also occur in other breeds, either as a primary enteropathy or as a secondary complication of other gastrointestinal disorders. The prevalence of bacterial overgrowth in dogs is unknown, but it has probably been under-diagnosed in the past. Diagnosis is difficult because histologic examination of intestinal biopsies from affected dogs reveals minimal, if any, morphologic changes. Furthermore, documentation of overgrowth by quantitative bacteriologic culture of intestinal aspirates is technically difficult, time consuming, and expensive.[1,31] Unfortunately, only a small proportion of affected dogs exhibits both subnormal serum cobalamin and increased serum folate concentrations. Normal test results are also observed in some dogs with this diagnosis.

Breath Hydrogen Test. Results of a breath hydrogen test may be abnormal either when there is a carbohydrate malabsorption or when there is small intestine bacterial overgrowth; it is more sensitive than the xylose absorption test for detection of these abnormalities.[3,32,33] Mammalian cells do not metabolize carbohydrate to generate hydrogen, but many bacteria in the gut lumen do. Some of this hydrogen is absorbed into the blood stream and subsequently excreted in breath. The normal minimal output of hydrogen in breath can increase either as a result of carbohydrate malabsorption, in which case more substrate passes to the lower bowel and is fermented, or as a result of abnormal proliferation of bacteria in the upper small bowel, in which case dietary carbohydrate is metabolized by bacteria competing with the host for available nutrients. In animals with a normal bowel transit time, carbohydrate malassimilation, and no small intestinal bacterial overgrowth, the rise in breath hydrogen begins four to six hours after eating. If bacteria have overgrown the small bowel, increased breath hydrogen excretion is detected within one to two hours of eating. This early peak is more readily identified after oral administration of a readily fermentable sugar, such as lactulose.

The fraction of hydrogen in single samples of dog breath correlates with total hydrogen excretion, so data from single time points can be evaluated in clinical studies.[34] In a group of dogs with carbohydrate malabsorption due to chronic small intestinal disease fasting expired hydrogen concentration (mean ± SE) was 5.3 ± 1.3 ppm, and increased to a peak of 72.2 ± 18 ppm seven hours after feeding.[3] While there is variation between dogs on a given diet, the results from a given dog seem quite reproducible within narrow limits from day to day.[35]

Expired air is easily collected using an anesthetic induction mask, a non-rebreathing valve, and a 1-liter latex bag. Samples are collected hourly for up to eight hours after feeding a carbohydrate-containing diet. A sample of expired air is withdrawn from the latex bag through a three-way sampling valve into a syringe. Syringes are capped by a three-way valve and can be stored at room temperature for at least 12 hours without significant loss of hydrogen (hydrogen is lost at the rate of approximately 5% per day from new syringes). Hydrogen in the gas samples is assayed using thermal conductivity gas chromatography or hydrogen-sensitive electrochemical cells.

The breath hydrogen test is potentially a very practical technique. Even though multiple samples may be drawn, the sampling time is very brief and the sampling procedure very well tolerated by most dogs and cats. Hydrogen assay methodology is available at many human hospitals, and the sampling equipment is relatively inexpensive. The test has the potential to differentiate between dogs with bacterial overgrowth and those with carbohydrate malabsorption. Unfortunately, as yet insufficient data are available to assess the test's value for diagnosis of small intestinal disease; preliminary results suggest that the method represents a significant advance in sensitivity, certainly over xylose absorption testing and probably over assay of serum cobalamin and folate. Breath hydrogen testing in dogs after oral sugar (xylose, lactulose, others) administration shows promise for having a high sensitivity and a high specificity for small intestinal bacterial overgrowth.

Is There Protein-Losing Enteropathy?	*Fecal α_1-protease Inhibitor.* Studies in human patients have shown that assay of fecal α_1-PI provides a reliable marker for the diagnosis of protein-losing enteropathy.[36-39] Protein-losing enteropathy occurs when there is excessive loss of plasma and intercellular fluid into the lumen of the gastrointestinal tract as a result of mucosal ulceration, lymphatic obstruction, or mucosal inflammation (**Table 2**).[40] These protein-rich fluids contain albumin and other proteins, including α_1-PI. Most such proteins, including albumin, are readily hydrolyzed by digestive proteases and so are not lost into feces in immunologically intact forms. However, α_1-PI is resistant to degradation by digestive proteases by virtue of its inhibitory activity, and so passes down the gastrointestinal tract essentially undegraded. It can then be detected in fecal extracts using a species-specific immunologic assay.

Canine α_1-PI has recently been purified and characterized,[41] and a species-specific immunoassay has been shown to be valid for measurement of concentrations in both serum and fecal extracts;† the assay appears to be as useful as the classic radiolabeled albumin test for the diagnosis of canine protein-losing enteropathy.[4] The test can reveal the presence of excessive loss of protein into the gastrointestinal tract before the concentration of albumin in serum becomes subnormal.

Is There Small Intestinal Bacterial Overgrowth (SIBO)?	Small intestinal bacterial overgrowth (SIBO) describes the proliferation of abnormal numbers of bacteria in the lumen of the upper small intestine.[40] The abnormal microflora usually includes species that are normal inhabitants of that area, but may also include species not normally present in upper small intestine. Normal physiologic processes, including secretion of gastric acid, intestinal propulsive movements, and secretion of antibacterial factors in pancreatic juice function to regulate bacterial numbers within the small intestine. Gastric acid kills many ingested bacteria and inhibits seeding of the duodenum with microbes. Even when acid secretion is inhibited, however, if intestinal motility is normal then the cleansing action of normal intestinal motility effectively limits bacterial proliferation. In contrast, even when acid secretion is normal, if intestinal propulsive activity is disrupted, then SIBO develops. Subsequently, factors such as host malnutrition may be important in favoring persistence of the abnormal microflora by affecting factors such as local immunity and mucus secretion.[40]

---

†This assay is presently only available through Dr. David A. Williams, GI Lab, Department of Small Animal Medicine and Surgery, College of Veterinary Medicine, College Station TX 77843-4474. Telephone 409 862 2861, Fax 409 862 2864, E-mail - gilab@cvm.tamu.edu

Table 2. Some disorders associated with protein-losing gastroenteropathy

Gastrointestinal Ulceration	– Gastric carcinoma and lymphoma – Ulcerative gastritis / enteritis – Chronic foreign body – Intussusception – Parasitic gastroenteritis (hook-, whip-worms) – Intestinal neoplasia – Drugs/toxins
Gastrointestinal Inflammation	– Lymphocytic-plasmacytic gastritis / enteritis – Eosinophilic gastritis / enteritis – Granulomatous enteritis – Histoplasmosis – Phycomycosis – Acute viral / bacterial enteritis
Disorders of Intestinal Hemolymphatic System	– Primary intestinal lymphangiectasia – Neoplastic lymphatic infiltration – Granulomatous lymphatic infiltration – Congestive heart failure – Vasculitis
Disorders Without Ulceration or Inflammation	– Small intestinal bacterial overgrowth – Systemic lupus erythematosus – Gastrointestinal parasitism (giardiasis) – Portal hypertension

When SIBO develops, the factors that determine what species of bacteria subsequently proliferate and to what total population are less well understood, but complex interactions between bacteria within the gut lumen are certainly important. These microbial interactions include competition for available nutrients, alteration of intraluminal pH or redox potential, production of toxic metabolites, enzyme sharing, and transfer of antibiotic resistance.[40]

In human beings SIBO most commonly occurs when there are abnormalities that result in impairment of normal motility. This most commonly occurs with anatomic changes such as may occur with obstruction secondary to gastrointestinal neoplasms or after surgical manipulations such as bypass operations, and with functional motor changes secondary to diseases such as diabetic autonomic neuropathy or idiopathic pseudo-obstruction; similar circumstances can clearly arise in veterinary patients.[42] In dogs, SIBO has been documented as an idiopathic abnormality in patients with gastrointestinal signs,[9] in association with exocrine pancreatic insufficiency[20] and degenerative myelopathy,[43] and also as a subclinical finding in apparently healthy beagles[44] and German Shepherd dogs.[45] In a university referral practice setting in the United Kingdom, about 50% of cases with chronic small intestinal disease were shown to have associated SIBO.[33]

The gold standard for diagnosis of SIBO is a properly collected and appropriately cultured aspirate from the proximal small intestine. The aspirate should be collected by peroral intubation or direct needle puncture under anaerobic conditions, and diluted serially to allow quantitative culture on a variety of selective media.[40] This is technically difficult, time-consuming and expensive, and rarely feasible outside of referral settings. Even this approach may miss SIBO in some individuals due to pockets of overgrowth distal to the point of sampling.

Numerous non-invasive, indirect laboratory tests have been evaluated for the diagnosis of SIBO in human beings, including assay of serum cobalamin and folate, assay of serum unconjugated bile acids or urinary indican (or other products of bacterial metabolism within the intestine), and a variety of breath tests (^{14}C-xylose, ^{14}C-bile acid, lactulose-hydrogen, glucose-hydrogen) designed to detect microbial activity within the upper small intestine.[40] Of these, the various breath tests, particularly the ^{14}C-xylose breath test, appear to be the most sensitive and specific, but while technically feasible are generally not available in veterinary practice. Intestinal permeability was increased in beagles with SIBO compared to those without SIBO, and was particularly elevated in dogs with anaerobic over-growth.[44] However, increased intestinal permeability is not a specific abnormality associated only with SIBO.[5]

Assays of serum cobalamin and folate appear to be the most helpful aids to diagnose SIBO in the dog presently available for use by veterinarians in general practice, although they undoubtedly have limited sensitivity (that is, many affected dogs do not have abnormal test results). If pancreatic function is normal (that is, serum trypsin-like immunoreactivity, TLI, is normal) then finding a decreased serum cobalamin or increased serum folate is supportive of SIBO. If both of these abnor-malities are found, then this is strong evidence in support of SIBO, but this combi-nation is rarely encountered. In patients with SIBO, elevated folate alone is seen in about 50% of cases, and decreased cobalamin alone in about 25% of cases.

In the future, assay of unconjugated bile acids in serum may provide evidence as to the presence of SIBO.[7] In normal patients serum bile acids are largely conjugated (the form of bile acids specifically absorbed in the ileum) but when there is SIBO the intraluminal bacteria may deconjugate the bile acids allowing them to be non-specifically absorbed along the small intestine. Unconjugated bile acids may be detected both in duodenal aspirates and serum of human and canine patients with SIBO.[7,40] At present, availability of this diagnostic approach is limited by technical complexities associated with selective assay of unconjugated bile acids.

Is Intestinal Permeability (Barrier Function) Abnormal?

While the intestinal tract is traditionally thought of as being a specialized absorptive surface, it also serves an important role as a barrier to keep unwanted substances from being absorbed to any great extent. This barrier function not only excludes large molecules, but also small molecules the size of mono- and disaccha-rides. Nonetheless, there is background absorption of such small molecules. Inert (essentially non-metabolized) monosaccharides such as rhamnose, and the hexitol mannitol (molecular weights approximately 150) for which no brush border transport mechanisms exist, apparently diffuse across the intestinal mucosa, probably through transcellular aqueous pores.[5] In contrast, [51]Chromium-labeled ethylenediaminetetraacetate (^{51}Cr-EDTA) and larger inert disaccharides such as cellobiose or lactulose (molecular weights approximately 300) cannot traverse these pores, but can cross the gut in small amounts by means of leakage through the tight junctions.[5] When these molecules enter the blood they undergo rapid glomerular filtration and are excreted in urine. Thus absorption from the gut is reflected in urinary sugar output.

In many intestinal diseases it appears that the tight junctions become more leaky, thereby increasing passive absorption through the intercellular route, while at the same time the surface area of the brush border membrane decreases, thereby decreasing absorption through the transcellular route. If absorption through the two routes is expressed as a ratio, this ratio tends to depart even further from normal than the change through either route evaluated alone, thereby increasing the sensitivity of the tests.[5] Expressing the ratio of passive absorption of two marker molecules has the additional advantage of correcting for errors potentially caused by bacterial degradation within the gut lumen, and variations in gastric emptying. It would be difficult to account for these effects if changes in only a single marker molecule were evaluated.

At present, tests of gastrointestinal permeability have application primarily in research centers. Published reports indicate that this approach offers good sensitivity and specificity for diagnosis of small intestinal disease in the dog. It is likely that increased availability of newer analytical methods for sugars in specialist laboratories will facilitate use of tests of intestinal permeability in veterinary patients in the future.

Are There Intestinal Morphologic Abnormalities?

Duodenoscopy and/or abdominal surgery is required in some patients to establish the cause of intestinal disease, and in some patients for its treatment. The rapidity with which a clinician must resort to exploratory celiotomy for diagnosis is largely a reflection of the diagnostic equipment and financial resources available. Celiotomy optimizes visual inspection and palpation of the small intestine and other abdominal organs. Indications for celiotomy include rapid progressive decline in the condition of a patient with abdominal disease, suspected gastrointestinal perforation, and the need for multiple organ or full-thickness biopsies. Celiotomy is required for the diagnosis of intestinal lesions out of reach of the endoscope, as well as for definitive diagnosis of post-mucosal changes associated with lymphangiectasia.[40] Biopsies of the intestine should be taken even when it appears grossly normal.

Conclusion

It is important to emphasize that in many dogs with chronic small intestinal disease there are minimal histologic abnormalities.[46] Thus examination of intestinal biopsies will not always provide definitive diagnostic information, even when disease is present, so patient evaluation should usually include evaluation of intestinal function using one or more of the above approaches. Histologic examination of intestinal biopsies allows many infectious, neoplastic and severe inflammatory enteropathies to be identified or eliminated with a high degree of confidence however, allowing a more rational approach to patient management based on the results of function tests.

References

1. Batt RM. New approaches to malabsorption in dogs. *Comp Cont Ed Prac Vet* 1986; 8:783-795.

2. Handelman CT, Blue J. Laboratory data: Read beyond the numbers. *Comp Cont Ed Prac Vet* 1983; 5:687-694.

3. Washabau RJ, Strombeck DR, Buffington CA, Harrold D. Use of pulmonary hydrogen gas execretion to detect carbohydrate malabsorption in dogs. *JAVMA* 1986; 189:674-679.

4. Melgarejo T, Tamayo A, Williams DA. Fecal $alpha_1$-protease inhibitor (α_1-PI) for the diagnosis of canine protein-losing enteropathy. *J Vet Int Med* 1997; 11:115.

5. Hall EJ, Batt RM. Differential sugar absorption for the assessment of canine intestinal permeability: the celobiose/mannitol test in gluten-sensitive enteropathy of Irish setters. *Res Vet Sci* 1991; 51:83-87.

6. Rutgers HC, Batt RM, Hall EJ, Sorensen SH, Proud FJ. Intestinal permeability testing in dogs with diet-responsive intestinal disease. *J Sm Anim Pract* 1995; 36:295-301.

7. Melgarejo T, Williams DA, Setchell KD, O'Connell N. Serum total unconjugated bile acids (TUBA) in dogs with small intestinal bacterial overgrowth. *J Vet Int Med* 1997; 11:114.

8. Batt RM, Mann LC. Specificity of the BT-PABA test for the diagnosis of exocrine pancreatic insufficiency in the dog. *Vet Rec* 1981; 108:303-307.

9. Batt RM, Needham JR, Carter MW. Bacterial overgrowth associated with a naturally occurring enteropathy in the German Shepherd dog. *Res Vet Sci* 1983; 35:42-46.

10. Batt RM, McLean L. Comparison of the biochemical changes in the jejunal mucosa of dogs with aerobic and anaerobic bacterial overgrowth. *Gastroenterology* 1987; 93:986-993.

11. Batt RM, Horadagoda NU, McLean L, Morton DB, Simpson KW. Identification and characterization of a pancreatic intrinsic factor in the dog. *Am J Physiol* 1989; 256:G517-G523.

12. Herzlich B, Herbert V. The role of the pancreas in cobalamin (vitamin B12) absorption. *Am J Gastro* 1984; 79:489-493.

13. Marcoullis G, Rothenberg SP. Intrinsic factor-mediated intestinal absorption of cobalamin in the dog. *Am J Physiol* 1981; 241:G294-299.

14. Levine JS, Allen RH, Alpers DH, Seetharam B. Immunocytochemical localization of the intrinsic factor-cobalamin receptor in dog-ileum: Distribution of intracellular receptor during cell maturation. *J Cell Biol* 1984; 98:1111-1118.

15. Lindenbaum J. Malabsorption of vitamin B12 and folate. *Curr Concepts Nutr* 1980; 9:105-123.

16. Fyfe JC, Ramanujam KS, Ramaswamy K, Patterson DF, Seetharam B. Defective brush-border expression of intrinsic factor-cobalamin receptor in canine inherited intestinal cobalamin malabsorption. *J Biol Chem* 1991; 266:4489-4494.

17. Fyfe JC, Jezyk PF, Giger U, Patterson DF. Inherited selective malabsorption of vitamin B12 in giant schnauzers. *JAAHA* 1989; 50:533-539.

18. Outerbridge CA, Myers SL, Giger U. Hereditary cobalamin deficiency in Collie dogs. *J Vet Int Med* 1996; 10:(Abstract).

19. Batt RM, Morgan JO. Role of serum folate and vitamin B12 concentrations in the differentiation of small intestinal abnormalities in the dog. *Res Vet Sci* 1982; 32:17-22.

20. Williams DA, Batt RM, McLean L. Bacterial overgrowth in the duodenum of dogs with exocrine pancreatic insufficiency. *JAVMA* 1987; 191:201-206.

21. Westermarck E, Myllys V, Aho M. Effect of treatment on the jejunal and colonic bacterial flora of dogs with exocrine pancreatic insufficiency. *Pancreas* 1993; 8:559-562.

22. Batt RM, McLean L, Rutgers HC, Hall EJ. Validation of a radioassay for the determination of serum folate and cobalamin concentrations in dogs. *J Sm Anim Pract* 1991; 32:221-224.

23. Baker H, Schor SM, Murphy BD, DeAngelis B, Feingold S, Frank O. Blood vitamin and choline concentrations in health domestic cats, dogs and horses. *Am J Vet Res* 1986; 47:1468-1471.

24. Arvanitakis C. Functional and morphological abnormalities of the small intestinal mucosa in pernicious anemia — a prospective study. *Acta Hepato-Gastroenterol* 1978; 25:313-318.

25. Bernstein LH, Gutstein S, Efron G, Wager G. Experimental production of elevated serum folate in dogs with intestinal blind loops II. Nature of bacterially produced folate coenzymes in blind loop fluid. *Am J Clin Nutr* 1975; 28:925-929.

26. Bernstein LH, Gutstein S, Efron G, Wager G. Experimental production of elevated serum folate in dogs with intestinal blind loops: Relationship of serum levels to location of the blind loop. *Gastroenterol* 1972; 63:815-819.

27. Bunch SE, Easley JR, Cullen JM. Hematologic values and plasma and tissue folate concentrations in dogs given phenytoin on a long-term basis. *Am J Vet Res* 1990; 51:1865-1868.

28. Westermarck E, Myllys V, Aho M. Intestinal bacterial overgrowth in dogs with exocrine pancreatic insufficiency: Effect of enzyme replacement and antibiotic therapy. *J Vet Int Med* 1991; 5:131.

29. Batt RM, Bush BM, Peters TJ. Subcellular biochemical studies of a naturally occurring enteropathy in the dog resembling chronic tropical sprue in human beings. *Am J Vet Res* 1983; 44:1492-1496.

30. Batt RM, Carter MW, McLean L. Morphological and biochemical studies of a naturally occurring enteropathy in the Irish setter dog: a comparison with coeliac disease in man. *Res Vet Sci* 1984; 37:339-346.

31. King CE, Toskes PP. Small intestine bacterial overgrowth. *Gastroenterol* 1979; 76:1035-1055.

32. Washabau RJ, Strombeck DR, Buffington CA, Harrold D. Evaluation of intestinal carbohydrate malabsorption in the dog by pulmonary hydrogen gas excretion. *Am J Vet Res* 1986; 47:1402-1406.

33. Rutgers HC, Lamport A, Simpson KW, Elwood CE, Batt RM. Bacterial overgrowth in dogs with chronic intestinal disease. *J Vet Int Med* 1993; 7:133.

34. Ludlow CL, Bruyette DS, Davenport DJ, Lieth DE. Relationship between breath hydrogen fraction and calculated breath hydrogen excretion in healthy dogs. *J Vet Int Med* 1994; 8:152.

35. Ludlow CL, Bruyette DS, Davenport DJ, Lieth DE. Daily and individual variation of breath hydrogen excretion in healthy dogs. *J Vet Int Med* 1994; 8:150.

36. Mizon C, Becuwe C, Balduyck M, Colombel JF, Cortot A, Mizon J, Degand P. Qualitative study of fecal α_1-proteinase inhibitor in normal subjects and patients with Crohn's disease. *Clin Chem* 1988; 34:2268-2270.

37. Karbach U, Ewe K, Bodenstein H. Alpha1-antitrypsin, a reliable endogenous marker for intestinal protein loss and its application in patients with Crohn's disease. *Gut* 1983; 24:718-723.

38. Crossley JR, Elliott RB. Simple method for diagnosing protein-losing enteropathies. *Br Med J* 1977; 1:428-429.

39. Bernier JJ, Florent CH, Desmazures CH, Aymes C, L'Hirondel C. Diagnosis of protein-losing enteropathy by gastro-intestinal clearance of alpha$_1$-antitrypsin. *Lancet* 1978; 2:763-764.

40. Williams DA. Malabsorption, small intestinal bacterial overgrowth, and protein-losing enteropathy. In: Guilford WG, Center SA, Strombeck DR, Williams DA, Meyer DJ, eds. *Small Animal Gastroenterology*. 3 Ed. Philadelphia: W.B. Saunders, 1996; 367-380.

41. Melgarejo T, Williams DA, Griffith G. Isolation and characterization of α_1-protease inhibitor from canine plasma. *Am J Vet Res* 1996; 57:258-263.

42. Leib MS. Stagnant loop syndrome in the dog and cat. *Semin Vet Med Surg* 1987; 2:257-265.

43. Williams DA, Batt RM, Sharp NJH. Degenerative myelopathy in German Shepherd dogs: an association with mucosal biochemical changes and bacterial overgrowth in the small intestine. *Clin Sci* 1984; 66:25.

44. Batt RM, Hall EJ, McLean L, Simpson KW. Small intestinal bacterial overgrowth and enhanced intestinal permeability in healthy Beagles. *Am J Vet Res* 1992; 53:1935-1940.

45. Willard MD, Simpson RB, Fossum TW, Cohen ND, Delles EK, Kolp DL, Carey DP, Reinhart GA. Characterization of naturally developing small intestinal bacterial overgrowth in 16 German Shepherd Dogs. *Am Vet Med Assoc* 1994; 204:1201-1206.

46. Batt RM, Hall EJ. Veterinary gastroenterology: chronic enteropathies in the dog. In: Pounder R, ed. *Recent Advances in Gastroenterology*. London: Churchill Livingstone, 1988; 131-152.

Fermentable Fiber and the
Gastrointestinal Tract Ecosystem

Randal K. Buddington, PhD
Professor, Department of Biological Sciences
Mississippi State University, Mississippi State, Mississippi, USA

Gregory D. Sunvold, PhD
Research and Development, The Iams Company, Lewisburg, Ohio, USA

Dietary fibers, particularly fermentable forms, are well recognized as playing an important role in health. This has been attributed in large part to changes in bacterial populations present in the gastrointestinal tract (GIT). Even though dogs, and particularly cats, are considered carnivores, they too apparently derive health benefits when fed diets containing fermentable fibers. These findings are relatively new and contrary to earlier thoughts that fiber fermentation was not important for cats and dogs. However, the types, amounts, and proportions of different fermentable fibers that promote optimal health of the cat and dog (GIT) have yet to be defined. This will not be an easy task as the role of fiber in promoting GIT health is a complex issue, involving interactions between the bacteria and several variables, many of which are not yet well understood for cats and dogs, as well as other species.

Introduction

Several groups of bacteria present in the GIT are considered beneficial. These include the bifidobacteria, lactobacilli, more recently the eubacteria, and there will probably be other groups added to the list.[1] A common characteristic shared among these groups is the capacity to ferment fibers, and they are considered to be more effective at doing so than pathogenic and putrefactive species. This enhanced ability has encouraged the use of fermentable fibers as a means to selectively encourage beneficial bacteria and thereby reduce the proportion of detrimental groups. Other purported benefits of having higher densities of beneficial bacteria include a reduction in cancer risk, improved serum lipid profiles, immunopotentiation, and better stool characteristics and defecation patterns. Furthermore, the short chain fatty acids produced by bacterial fermentation are rapidly absorbed and utilized by the host.[2]

This contribution seeks to provide readers with an understanding about the influence of fermentable fiber on the gastrointestinal tract of cats and dogs. It extends information presented in a previous review.[3] To accomplish this objective it is first necessary to describe the GIT as a complex ecosystem that is sensitive to internal and external factors and how it can be studied, and perhaps better understood, by applying the principles of ecology. A subsequent section describes the specific influences of fermentable fiber on GIT bacteria, as elucidated by *in vitro* and *in vivo* studies with companion animals. This review is concluded with the implications and perspectives of the findings reported to date about the influences of fermentable fibers on the GIT of cats and dogs.

Fermentable Fibers	Dietary fiber is a general term that is used to describe the portion of the food resistant to hydrolysis by the digestive secretions of vertebrates. Historically, dietary fiber has been considered to primarily consist of lignin, cellulose, hemicellulose, and pectin. However, recent interest has focused on other components such as resistant starch and oligosaccharides. The sources of dietary fiber vary widely and include trees (α-cellulose), plant extracts (i.e., gum arabic), tuber extracts (i.e., beet pulp from sugar beets, fructooligosaccharides from inulin), fruit extracts (i.e., citrus pectin), seaweed (i.e., kelp, carrageenan), and husks from nuts (i.e., peanut hulls).

Chemically, dietary fiber can be classified based on solubility in water. Although fructooligosaccharides and other similar types of complex carbohydrates have traditionally not been considered as fibers, they do meet the necessary criteria, and are now accepted by some as forms of dietary fiber. From a biological perspective, dietary fiber can also be separated based on whether they can be utilized by the GIT bacteria. Forms that are utilized by the bacteria are considered to be fermentable and appear to have great relevance in improving animal health. Recent evidence has suggested a role of fermentable fibers in beneficially modifying the population of intestinal bacteria,[4] possibly enhancing gut immunity,[5] improving oral glucose tolerance,[6] and repartitioning of nitrogenous waste excretion.[7] As presented in a later section, fermentable fibers vary as to which bacteria are able to utilize them as substrates, the degree of utilization, and the products of fermentation. Further impacts of the fermentability aspect of fiber will be discussed in the context of how this is important to canine health.

The Gastrointestinal Tract Ecosystem	Ecologists have been modeling the interactions of organisms with their physical, chemical, and biological environments for many decades. It is proposed that many of the same principles can, and perhaps should, be applied to better understand the GIT and the potential health benefits of adding fermentable fibers to the diet.

Ecosystems are considered to consist of two basic components. An abiotic component includes the physical and chemical features of the environment, whereas a biotic component consists of all the living organisms residing in the space defined by the ecosystem. Interactions between and within each of the two components are important determinants of the structure and functions of ecosystems.

The use of an analogy may serve as an appropriate way to simplify the complexity of the GIT ecosystem. Specifically, in many ways the GIT ecosystem is like a river that begins as a fast flowing stream and ends as a slow moving river. Similarly, the GIT includes several distinct segments, beginning with the stomach, a small intestine with rapid movement of digesta, and a colon with longer residence times. Each region of the GIT, like the different segments of the river, has distinct abiotic characteristics. These include the physical features associated with the mucosal architecture, the rate of digesta flow caused by peristalsis, and chemical characteristics, such as pH, electrolyte and nutrient concentrations, and digestive secretions. Even within a region there is variation. For example, there is a proximal to distal gradient in the small intestine with respect to physical and chemical characteristics, and the rate of flow for the digesta (declining from proximal to distal). The gradient results in the presence of different habitats along the length of the small intestine. There are also differences between the bacteria associated with the lumenal contents and the mucosa, much like in a stream the organisms that live in the water column are different from those that are on or in the stream bed. The large intestine and associated cecum provide another set of habitats that differ from those in the small intestine.

The continuum of habitats along the GIT ecosystem make it very difficult to use fecal samples to evaluate conditions and processes occurring in the different regions of the GIT. Similarly, ecologists are unable to fully understand mountain streams based on samples that are collected where rivers drain into oceans. Although this analogy may be an oversimplification, it does highlight the problems clinicians and investigators face when only fecal samples are available for analysis.

Physical and Chemical Features of the GIT Ecosystem

The GIT ecosystem of adult humans includes over 400 known species of bacteria, and this number is increasing as our abilities to culture and identify bacteria improve. Historically, the majority of attention has been focused on pathogenic groups. Although beneficial forms have been recognized for nearly 100 years, only until relatively recently have they received a comparable level of interest.[1] It needs to be emphasized that in addition to bacteria, the biotic component of the GIT includes yeast, fungi, viruses, spirochaetes, protozoa, and various other single and multicellular organisms. This contribution will be restricted to the bacteria, mainly because there is very little known for the other organisms, not because they are considered unimportant.

Although the bacteria resident in GIT of the cat and dog are not as well characterized as those of humans, it is likely the numbers of different species will be comparable to those of humans and other mammals. The available data show there are distinct quantitative and qualitative differences between bacterial populations present in the different GIT regions of both cats and dogs[8] (unpublished data). The densities and relative proportions of various bacteria present in a region are partly determined by factors, such as pH, motility, concentrations and profiles of nutrients

Bacteria in the GIT Ecosystem of Cats and Dogs

from the diet as well as secretions from the pancreas, gall bladder, and alimentary canal (e.g., stomach and intestine), enteric immune functions, composition of the glycocalyx, and binding sites on the membranes of the cells lining the GIT.[9] Therefore, each region and habitat along the GIT has a characteristic assemblage of bacterial species. Similar to other mammals, densities of bacteria in the GIT of cats and dogs increase from less than 10^{3-4}/g wet weight in the acidic stomach to over 10^{10} in the colon. Aerotolerant forms dominate the bacteria in the upper bowel, whereas they are less abundant in the anoxic colon, which compared to the small intestine has a higher redox potential, lower concentrations of dietary nutrients, and different chemical conditions. In addition to regional variation, bacterial assemblages in the same GIT region of different animals are often quite different, and even more so for comparisons between species.

Ecosystems are sensitive to slight changes and differences in the abiotic components. Therefore it is not surprising that differences in GIT physical and chemical characteristics that appear to be slight and not significant, can have a profound effect on the populations of bacteria. In a similar manner, adjacent streams may differ only slightly in physical and chemical characteristics, but will have different assemblages of organisms. Corresponding with this, the changes in GIT characteristics during development and variation between individuals are reflected by different assemblages of bacteria.

Activities of and interactions between bacteria are other important determinants of the characteristics of bacterial populations. For example, the depletion of oxygen and production of metabolites by aerobic and facultative anaerobic bacteria alter the chemical features of the ecosystem allowing obligate anaerobes to proliferate. This process, whereby one set of organisms modifies the environment, thereby enhancing the proliferation of other organisms, is known as facilitation. Competition for nutrients and attachment sites can also influence which species dominate. More recently it has been shown that certain GIT bacteria produce metabolites and other chemicals that suppress the growth of other species,[10,11] a process called inhibition. Of particular relevance is the ability of lactic acid bacteria (e.g., bifidobacteria and lactobacilli) to inhibit the growth of certain pathogenic and putrefactive bacteria.

The interactions between bacteria appear to be especially important after birth, particularly the process of facilitation. The first bacteria to enter and colonize the GIT are thought to alter the environment allowing other groups to proliferate. As a consequence, the GIT microbiota goes through a series of successional stages that eventually culminate in the adult microbiota.[12] The final assemblage reflects tolerance of the constituent species for existing physical and chemical conditions, competitive interactions, and inhibitory influences. It is clear that many of the same events that have been well documented for developing terrestrial and aquatic ecosystems can be applied to the GIT.

The microbiota of adults is often considered to be stable. However, there is increasing evidence that although total densities of bacteria may remain constant, the relative proportions of the different species can and do change in response to fluctuations in internal and external factors.

In addition to influencing the structural and functional characteristics of the GIT, diet can directly affect the resident bacteria. In a similar manner, adding different amounts and types of nutrients to streams will cause varying influences on the balances between species. A recent review highlights how the microbial ecology of the GIT can be modulated by diet.[13] The GIT bacteria of cats and dogs is also influenced by levels and types of macronutrients.[14] The following reviews results from the two basic approaches that have been used to examine the fermentation of fibers by the GIT bacteria of cats and dogs. Readers are referred to previous reports.[3, 15]

Mixed culture systems have proven effective for studying the fermentation of different types and sources of fiber. This approach provides the benefits of being a rapid, non-invasive way to inexpensively assess whether certain types or sources of fiber can be fermented. Furthermore, comparisons with data from concurrent *in vivo* studies indicate *in vitro* studies can be used to reasonably predict fiber digestion in intact organisms.

In a series of four papers, Sunvold and coworkers used fecal samples from cats, dogs, and other species as sources of mixed cultures.[16-19] The objective was to simulate *in vivo* conditions in the colonic environment. Fermentation characteristics were based on the disappearance of the fiber from culture media and the resulting concentrations and ratios of short chain fatty acids (SCFA). Four points need to be highlighted from this collection of studies.

First, a variety of fiber sources can be fermented by the colonic bacteria of cats and dogs. There is wide variation in how well different fibers were fermented by the fecal bacteria, with differences between cats and dogs (***Figure 1***). Even among closely related fibers there can be variation in the ability to support fermentation as well as the resulting metabolic products.

Second, the authors demonstrated that it is possible to design blends of fiber sources to yield specific proportions of SCFA. They describe how this could be used to influence the nutrition and health of the host. Specifically, the three main SCFA produced by fermentation of fiber are preferentially used as metabolic substrates by different tissues; butyrate by colonocytes, propionate by liver, and acetate by the peripheral tissues. Additional information regarding specific proportions of SCFA that provide the most benefits is discussed elsewhere in this publication by Drackley et al.

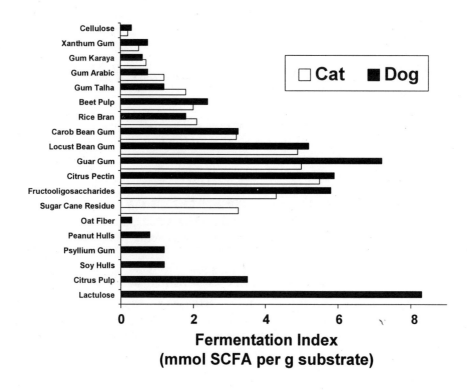

Figure 1. Fermentation indices for mixed cultures of cat and dog fecal flora incubated with different types and sources of fiber. From references 16, 17, 18.

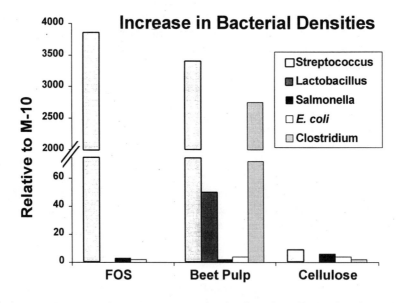

Figure 2. Growth of monocultures of streptococcus, lactobacillus, salmonella, *E. coli*, and clostridium in a minimal growth medium with 1% fructooligosaccharides, beet pulp, and cellulose. Values represent the peak bacterial densities (cfu/ml) relative to those in M-10 alone.

Third, although fecal bacteria from the various species had the capacities to ferment fiber, the metabolic processes varied widely among the animals. This was evident by the differences in proportions of SCFA that were produced when fecal bacteria from the various species fermented the same substrate. This is explained by the differences between animals with respect to the types of bacteria present in the fecal samples. The investigators also noted a high level of individual variation, and how this can limit the ability to apply results obtained from a single donor to a population.

Fourth, the diet fed to the animals prior to collecting the stool samples influences the intensity and characteristics of the fermentation processes. Although diet-related changes in the assemblage of bacterial populations are well documented, it also needs to be considered that existing species are likely to adapt their metabolic processes to match changes in diet composition. The influence of diet on *in vitro* activities of the GIT bacteria has been reported in dogs fed different sources of protein.[20] Not only did species composition respond to the levels and types of protein, the proteolytic activity of the bacteria was directly related to levels of protein. This latter study contrasts with those of Sunvold and coworkers in that samples were obtained from the ileum using fistulated dogs. Because the cats and dogs used in the Sunvold studies were fed different diets and fiber sources, it is difficult to make relevant comparisons about the fermentative capacities of the two species.

Mixed cultures do provide valuable information, however, they do not yield insights about the abilities of individual species to ferment different fibers. A recent study (Buddington, Williams, and Sunvold, unpublished data) isolated six species of bacteria from the stool of an adult dog and measured growth rates of monocultures in the presence of five different types and sources of fiber. A minimal nutrient broth (M-10) served as a negative control, and to suspend the different fibers. As seen in **Figure 2**, growth rates varied between species when cultured on the different substrates. These findings, though preliminary, suggest that when selecting certain types and sources of fibers, one should consider the relative abilities of both beneficial and detrimental bacteria to use the fiber as a substrate. Although not included in the figure, canine mucosa served as an excellent growth medium for all of the groups of bacteria studied, except the streptococcus. Finally, there is a need to extend these studies to 1) include other species of bacteria, 2) determine the abilities of the GIT bacteria of cats and dogs to adapt metabolic processes for utilization of different substrates, and 3) elucidate any competitive, inhibitory, and facilitative interactions between species that are co-cultured.

There have been only a few *in vivo* studies of the effects of diet or fiber on the GIT of cats and dogs, and the complex interactions that occur between the GIT of the host, the resident bacteria, and dietary inputs can make it difficult to interpret results. For example, because SCFA are absorbed so rapidly, concentrations and profiles of SCFA (Buddington, Williams and Sunvold, unpublished data) measured

In Vivo
Studies

in fecal samples, or even in lumenal contents, do not adequately reflect bacterial fermentation. Despite this and other limitations of studies using intact animals, results from *in vivo* studies have provided valuable information.

Bacterial densities and relative proportions are stable in ileal chyme when dogs are fed mixed diets that are prepared with different components, but have balanced nutrient profiles.[14] Diets that are not balanced nutritionally do disturb the bacterial populations. However, this is known only for the bacteria that can be recovered from the ileal chyme. Information regarding the effect of diet on the adherent populations is relatively limited.[21]

Of the numerous substances known to be 'bifidogenic', only two purified forms have been investigated in feeding studies with cats and dogs. Terada and coworkers[22] evaluated the effect of lactosucrose (sucrose conjugated with lactose) in dogs. Similar to results with humans, there was an increase in the fecal densities of lactic acid bacteria. There was a concurrent decline in *Clostridium perfringens* and fecal concentrations of ammonia and metabolites characteristic of putrefaction. Although not quantified, the authors noted a decrease in the offensive odors of the stool samples when the dogs were fed the lactosucrose.

A subsequent report by the Terada group[23] used the same protocols to study cats fed a diet with lactosucrose. Interestingly, the responses were of greater magnitude and more groups were affected compared to the dogs. The reasons for the differences with the dog were not presented, but could be related to the longer time food remains in the GIT of cats compared to dogs (Sunvold, unpublished data). This would permit more fermentation, and thus enhance the opportunity for facilitative and inhibitory interactions among the different groups of bacteria.

A recent study by the present authors compared two groups of adult beagles that were fed diets with different sources of fiber.[24] One diet contained cellulose as a nonfermentable fiber, whereas the second diet had a combination of beet pulp and fructooligosaccharides (FOS) as sources of fermentable fiber. Because FOS is fermented more quickly than beet pulp, these two sources of fermentable fiber were predicted to differ in their site of primary fermentation.

The two groups of dogs had similar densities of anaerobes and aerobes in stool samples, but dogs fed the diet with fermentable fiber tended to have fewer Enterobacteriaceae and clostridia and more lactobacilli and streptococci than those fed the diet with cellulose. Another interesting observation was that dogs fed the fermentable fiber had small intestines that were longer and heavier, and had more mucosa and absorptive surface area. Although colonic responses were not measured, previous investigations have reported beneficial effects of fermentable fiber on the colonic mucosa.[25,26] Also, even though the levels and types of protein and other carbohydrates did not differ between the two diets, rates of carrier-mediated transport for glucose and the amino acid proline were higher in dogs fed the diet with fermentable fiber. As a consequence of the combination of increased dimensions and higher transport rates per unit intestine, dogs fed the diet with fermentable fiber would have had markedly higher capacities to absorb nutrients. The trophic and functional influences of fiber in the small intestine may be restricted to highly fermentable forms, as mucosal responses were not seen in dogs fed wheat bran, which is poorly fermented.[27]

The studies with dogs show that fermentable fibers can cause changes in the structural and functional characteristics of the GIT. The signaling pathway(s) for these changes are as yet unknown. A possibility is that the fermentation of the beet pulp and FOS resulted in higher concentrations and different proportions of SCFA. These would be rapidly absorbed by the colon of dogs,[28] and could stimulate the release of hormones, such as GLP-1 (glucagon-like peptide 1), that are known to induce intestinal growth and increase digestive functions.[29]

Adding fermentable fiber to the diet is likely to influence other GIT functions.[26] Fatty acids and other metabolites produced by bacterial fermentation can enhance the absorption of ions and water. There is also circumstantial evidence that suggests the changes in the microbiota induced by fermentable fiber induces immunopotentiation.[21] Preliminary information reported by Fields et al.[30] lends support to this hypothesis.

In light of the above, it is obvious that adding fermentable fiber to the diet should improve the health status of cats and dogs. This possibility has been evaluated in German Shepherd Dogs that suffered small intestinal bacterial overgrowth (SIBO) due to enteric immune deficiencies.[31] Dogs fed a diet with FOS added at a level of 1% for about 50 days had lower bacterial densities in the contents and mucosa of the proximal small intestine. The authors emphasized two other points. First, if at all possible, collection of intestinal samples should be by laparotomy instead of endoscopy to avoid the increased risk of bacterial contamination. Second, like other investigators, the authors observed wide variation between animals which complicated statistical analysis and may obscure clinical differences.

Conclusions and Perspectives

All studies performed to date are consistent in showing that adding fermentable fiber to the diets of cats and dogs results in changes in the GIT bacteria that are perceived as beneficial. A few studies have shown these responses are accompanied by changes in the structural and functional characteristics of the GIT. Further work is needed to characterize the mechanisms and signals causing the changes and to understand the health relations.

SIBO is often considered as the cause of gastrointestinal distress, and may be more prevalent than thought.[32] The mucosa in the proximal small intestine of dogs suffering from SIBO exhibits structural damage and changes in the physical and chemical features of the brush border membrane[9] and has higher permeability to macromolecules.[33] Conventional diets and supplements to treat dogs with exocrine pancreatic insufficiency and SIBO have not proven effective at reducing the bacterial population,[32,34] and clinicians are relegated to using antibiotics. However, this can lead to secondary effects that can be partly attributed to the antibiotics disturbing other bacterial components of the GIT ecosytem. Therefore, the reduction of bacterial densities when dogs suffering from SIBO are fed a diet with FOS is of profound clinical interest, and there is a need to determine the specific ways FOS and other fermentable fibers can provide a nutritional means to control the bacteria.

Diarrhea, regardless of cause, perturbs the GIT ecosystem, much in the same manner as a flood in a stream. By selectively encouraging the proliferation and faster recovery of beneficial bacteria, fermentable fiber may reduce the risk of invasion or reinfection by pathogens. Furthermore, the increased dimensions and absorptive capacities of the small intestine in dogs fed a diet with fermentable fiber will improve the absorption of nutrients, ions, and water.

In vivo studies need to take several factors into consideration. Environmental conditions are known to influence bacterial populations in dogs,[8,35] and these could affect responses to diet. Where to obtain samples and the implications will remain problematic. Obviously, it is not possible to collect samples from all habitats in the GIT ecosystem, and even if this was possible, it would be impractical to identify and enumerate all of the organisms. Following the lead of ecologists, there is a need to identify indicator species that can be used to infer responses to diet and fermentable fiber.

Finally, the GIT of dogs and cats has several diverse environments that contribute foundationally to host animal health. Assessment of the impact of fermentable fibers on the GIT has resulted in new insights as to their role in maintaining animal health and influencing disease. Additional information about this complex and dynamic ecosystem and the responses to diet will provide valuable insights regarding how fiber can be used to improve the well-being of cats and dogs.

Acknowledgements   The authors would like to thank Carol and Carron Williams and Ken Jackson for providing data for *in vitro* fermentation of several subtrates by bacteria isolated from the feces of dogs.

References   1. Gibson GR, Roberfroid MB. Dietary modulation of the human colonic microbiota: Introducing the concept of prebiotics. *J Nutr* 1995; 125:1401-1412.

2. Stevens CE. Physiological implications of microbial digestion in the large intestines of mammals: relation to dietary factors. *Am J Clin Nutr* 1978; 31:S161-S168.

3. Sunvold GD. Dietary fiber for dogs and cats: An historical perspective. In: Carey DP, Norton SA, Bolser SM, eds. *Recent Advances in Canine and Feline Nutritional Research: Proceedings of the 1996 Iams International Nutritional Symposium.* Wilmington: Orange Frazer Press, 1996; 3-14.

4. Sparkes AH, Papasouliotis K, Sunvold G, Werrett G, Gruffydd-Jones EA, Egan K, Gruffydd-Jones TJ, Reinhart G. The effect of dietary supplementation with fructo-oligosaccharides on the faecal flora of healthy cats. *Am J Vet Res* 1998; in press.

5. Field CJ, Goruk S, McBurney MI, Hayek MG, Sunvold GD. Feeding fermentable fiber alters the function and composition of gut associated lymphoid tissue (GALT). *FASEB J* 1997; 11:A650(Abstr.).

6. Massimino SS, Field CJ, McBurney MI, Sunvold GD, Hayek MG. Fermentable dietary fiber improves glucose tolerance but not immune function in dogs. *FASEB J* 1997; 11:A650(Abstr.).

7. Howard MD, Sunvold GD, Reinhart GA, Kerley MS. Effect of fermentable fiber consumption by the dog on nitrogen balance and fecal microbial nitrogen excretion. *FASEB J* 1996; 10:A257.

8. Davis CP, Cleven D, Balish E, Yale CE. Bacterial association in the gastrointestinal tract of beagle dogs. *Appl Env Micro* 1977; 34:194-206.

9. Batt RM, McLean L. Comparison of the biochemical changes in the jejunal mucosa of dogs with aerobic and anaerobic bacterial overgrowth. *Gastroenterol* 1987; 93:986-993.

10. Gibson GR, Wang X. Inhibitory effects of bifidobacteria on other colonic bacteria. *J Appl Bacteriol* 1994; 77:412-420.

11. Wang X, Gibson GR. Effects of the *in vitro* fermentation of oligofructose and inulin by bacteria growing in the human large intestine. *J Appl Bacteriol* 1993; 75:373-380.

12. Swords WE, Wu CC, Champlin FR, Buddington RK. Postnatal changes in selected bacterial groups of the pig colonic microflora. *Biol Neonate* 1993; 63:191.

13. Collins MD, Gibson GR. Nutritional modulation of microbial ecology. *Am J Clin Nutr* 1998: (in press).

14. Zentek J. Influence of diet composition on the microbial activity in the gastro-intestinal tract of dogs. II. Effects on the microflora in the ileum chyme. *J Anim Physiol Anim Nutr* 1995; 74:53-61.

15. Clemens ET. Dietary fiber and colonic morphology. In: Carey DP, Norton SA, Bolser SM, eds. *Recent Advances in Canine and Feline Nutritional Research: Proceedings of the 1996 Iams International Nutritional Symposium.* Wilmington: Orange Frazer Press, 1996; 25-32.

16. Sunvold GD, Fahey Jr GC, Merchen NR, Titgemeyer EC, Bourquin LD, Bauer LL, Reinhart GA. Dietary fiber for dogs: IV. *In vitro* fermentation of selected fiber sources by dog fecal inoculum and *in vivo* digestion and metabolism of fiber-supplemented diets. *J Anim Sci* 1995a; 73:1099-1109.

17. Sunvold GD, Fahey Jr GC, Merchen NR, Bourquin LD, Titgemeyer EC, Bauer LL, Reinhart GA. Dietary fiber for cats: *in vitro* fermentation of selected fiber sources by cat fecal inoculum and *in vivo* utilization of diets containing selected fiber sources and their blends. *J Anim Sci* 1995b; 73:2329-2339.

18. Sunvold GD, Fahey GC, Merchen NR, Reinhart GA. *In vitro* fermentation of selected fibrous substrates by dog and cat fecal inoculum: Influence of diet composition on substrate organic matter disappearance and short-chain fatty acid production. *J Anim Sci* 1995c; 73:1110-1122.

19. Howard MD, Gordon DT, Garleb KA, Kerley MS. Dietary fructooligo-saccharide, xylooligosaccharide and gum arabic have variable effects on cecal and colonic microbiota and epithelial cell proliferation in mice and rats. *J Nutr* 1995; 125:2604.

20. Zentek J. Influence of diet composition on the microbial activity in the gastro-intestinal tract of dogs. III. *In vitro* studies on the metabolic activities of the small-intestinal microflora. *J Anim Physiol Anim Nutr* 1995; 74:62-73.

21. Ueda K. Immunity provided by colonized enteric bacteria. Bifido Microflora 1976; 5:67-72.

22. Terada A, Hara K, Oishi T, Matsui S, Mitsuoka T, Nakajyo S, Fujimori I, Hara K. Effect of dietary lactosucrose on faecal flora and faecal metabolites of dogs. *Microbial Ecol Health Dis* 1992; 5:87-92.

23. Terada A, Hara H, Kato S, Kimura T, Fujimori I, Hara K, Maruyama T, Mitsuoka T. Effect of lactosucrose (4^G-β-D-galactosylsucrose) on fecal flora and fecal putrefactive products of cats. *J Vet Mid Sci* 1993; 55:291-295.

24. Buddington RK, Buddington KK, Sunvold GD. The influence of ferment-able fiber on the small intestine of the dog: Intestinal dimensions and transport of glucose and proline. *Am J Vet Res.* 1998; Submitted.

25. Hallman JE, Moxley RA, Reinhart GA, Wallace EA, Clemens ET. Cellu-lose, beet pulp, and pectin/gum arabic effects on canine colonic microstructure and histopathology. *Vet Clin Nutr* 1995; 2:137-142.

26. Kerley MS. Physiological response to short chain fatty acid production in the intestine. In: Carey DP, Norton SA, Bolser SM, eds. *Recent Advances in Canine and Feline Nutritional Research: Proceedings of the 1996 Iams International Nutritional Symposium*. Wilmington: Orange Frazer Press, 1996; 33-39.

27. Stock-Damge C, Aprahamian M, Raul F, Humbert W, Bouchet P. Effects of wheat bran on the exocrine pancreas and the small intestinal mucosa in the dog. *J Nutr* 1984; 114:1076-1082.

28. Herschel DA, Argenzio RA, Southworth M, Stevens CE. Absorption of volatile fatty acid, Na, and H2O by the colon of the dog. *Am J Vet Res* 1981; 42:1118-1124.

29. Walsh JH. Gastrointestinal hormones. In: Johnson LR, ed. *Physiology of the Gastrointestinal Tract*, 3rd Ed. New York: Raven Press, 1994; 1-128.

30. Field CJ Goruk S McBurney MI, Hayek MG, Sunvold GD. Feeding fermentable fiber alters the function and composition of gut associated lyphoid tissue (GALT). *FASEB J* 1997; 11:A650.

31. Willard MD, Simpson RB, Delles EK, Cohen ND, Fossum TW, Kolp D, Reinhart G. Effects of dietary supplementation of fructo-oligosaccharides on small intestinal bacterial overgrowth in dogs. *Am J Vet Res* 1994; 55:654-658.

32. Westermarck E, Myllys V, Aho M. Effect of treatment on the jejunal and colonic bacterial flora of dogs with exocrine pancreatic insufficiency. *Pancreas* 1993; 8: 559-562.

33. Morris TH, Sorensen SH, Turkington J, Batt RM. Diarrhoea and increased intestinal permeability in laboratory beagles associated with proximal small intesti-nal bacterial overgrowth. *Lab Anim* 1994; 28:313-319.

34. Westermarck E, Siltanen, Maijala R. Small intestinal bacterial overgrowth in seven dogs with gastrointestinal signs. *Acta Vet Scand* 1993; 34:311-314.

35. Balish E, Cleven D, Brown J, Yale CE. Nose, throat, and fecal flora of beagle dogs housed in "locked" or "open" environments. *Appl Env Micro* 1977; 34:207-221.

Energetic Substrates for Intestinal Cells

James K. Drackley, PhD
Associate Professor, Department of Animal Sciences
University of Illinois, Urbana, Illinois, USA

A. Denise Beaulieu, PhD[a]; Gregory D. Sunvold, PhD[b]
[a]University of Illinois, Urbana, Illinois, USA
[b]Research and Development, The Iams Company, Lewisburg, Ohio, USA

Maintenance of small intestinal function and health is of obvious *Introduction* importance to the well-being of domestic animals, given the importance of the small intestine as the route of entry for nutrients into the body. The large intestine (cecum and colon) typically receives less attention and is usually thought of only as a waste processing center. The importance of the scavenging functions of the large intestine should not be underestimated, however, for this portion of the tract plays a vital role in regulation of whole-body electrolyte and water balance, in disposal of metabolic wastes and toxins, and in recovery of usable energy from undigested nutrients. In addition, both the small and large intestines serve as a barrier to entry of microbial pathogens. In concert with the gut-associated immune cells, this barrier function serves as the first line of defense of the animal against microbial and toxic insult.

To carry out these diverse functions, the tissues of the intestinal tract display a high rate of metabolic activity. Tissues of the portal-drained viscera may account for 20 to 35% of whole-body energy expenditure in sheep and pigs at rest.[1] Indeed, the contributions of the gastrointestinal tract and total skeletal mass to overall heat production (metabolic rate) may be essentially equal, despite five- to fifteen-fold differences in contributions to total body mass.[1] Much of the greater rate of heat production by intestinal tissues is accounted for by very high fractional rates of protein synthesis in the intestinal mucosa, which are 5 to 10 times greater than synthetic rates in skeletal muscle.[1] Although the intestinal tract constitutes a smaller proportion of body weight in dogs than in sheep or pigs,[2] understanding energy utilization by epithelial cells of the small and large intestines still is important both for quantifying maintenance energy requirements and for maintaining gut health of dogs.

Lower gut health of dogs is a major concern for dog owners, especially as adult dogs move into old age. Increasing evidence in the medical literature links consumption of certain fermentable fibers to decreased incidence of colon cancer and other diseases.[3,4] Fermentation of fiber in the large intestine produces short chain fatty acids (SCFA), principally acetate, propionate, and butyrate. The SCFA are absorbed into colonic epithelial cells and either metabolized or transported into the blood. Butyrate, in particular, has been shown to be an important metabolic fuel for colonocytes from rats[5-7] and pigs.[8] In addition to supplying energy, butyrate exerts direct trophic effects on colonic cells. Butyrate stimulates proliferation of normal epithelial cells while inhibiting growth and proliferation of neoplastic colonocytes.[9,10] Little is known about metabolism of the SCFA that are produced through fermentation in the dog colon, or about substrate utilization by cells of the large or small intestines in dogs. Such knowledge should be useful as dietary strategies are developed to better maintain gut health and to promote longevity.

Metabolism in Small Intestinal Epithelial Cells

Early *in vivo* experiments with rats demonstrated that the small intestine utilized primarily glutamine and the ketone bodies as respiratory fuels.[11] Utilization of respiratory fuels also has been studied in isolated epithelial cells from the small intestine of a variety of species, including rats,[7,12-15] chickens,[12] pigs,[16] and humans.[17] These experiments have shown that the epithelial cells of the small intestinal mucosa (enterocytes) utilize glutamine, glucose, and the ketone bodies (acetoacetate and β-hydroxybutyrate) as respiratory substrates. Glutamine generally is the major fuel during the fed state, with the ketone bodies becoming more important during fasting. Glutamine is utilized by a variety of actively proliferating cells, such as those in the intestinal mucosa and the immune system, for synthesis of nucleic acids as well as an oxidative fuel.[18] *In vivo* experiments have shown that much of the glutamine that is taken up is incompletely metabolized, with release of alanine or lactate (among others) as partial oxidation products.[12,17]

Enterocytes from rats also oxidized SCFA, with an apparent affinity of acetate > propionate > butyrate.[7] Availability of the SCFA to enterocytes from arterial blood generally would be limited, and thus the SCFA have been considered to be of minor importance as fuels for the small intestine.[13]

Metabolism in Large Intestinal Epithelial Cells

The mucosa of the large intestine functions within an inseparable relationship with the resident bacterial population within the cecum and colon. Epithelial cells isolated from the colon (colonocytes) readily oxidize the SCFA that are produced from microbial fermentation in the lumen of the large intestine.[7,8,14] In addition to luminal SCFA, colonic cells also receive energetic substrates from arterial blood, including glucose, glutamine, ketone bodies, and acetate. Most research has demonstrated that butyrate is the primary respiratory fuel for colonocytes. Roediger[19] found that 70-75% of oxygen consumption by isolated colonocytes was attributable to butyrate oxidation. In colonocytes from rats, butyrate and acetate significantly depressed the oxidation of glucose and glutamine; oxidation of butyrate was unaffected by glucose or glutamine.[5,7] In addition to complete oxidation to CO_2, a portion of butyrate may be converted to ketone bodies, as demonstrated in colonocytes from rats[5] and pigs.[8] That the presence of SCFA from gut fermentation has important effects on colonic epithelial cell metabolism is demonstrated by observations of altered metabolic characteristics of colonocytes isolated from germ-free rats.[20]

The importance of butyrate as a metabolic fuel for colonocytes and its regulatory actions on cell proliferation has stimulated substantial interest in the role of butyrate availability and metabolism in diseases of the large intestine, such as ulcerative colitis.[9] Impaired oxidation of butyrate has been shown to occur during models of ulcerative colitis.[21] More recent work[22] has implicated increased luminal sulfides as a factor that inhibits oxidation of butyrate and other fatty acids. Butyrate enema therapy is used in treatment of ulcerative colitis.[23] Butyrate therapy was effective in stimulating tissue repair in a model of ulcerative colitis,[24] but did not improve barrier function after acid-induced injury.[25] Diets containing fermentable fiber, which are expected to increase availability of butyrate through large intestinal fermentation, have been shown to alter metabolic characteristics of colonocytes in both rats[14,26] and pigs.[8]

Alteration of fiber sources in dog food can cause marked changes in production and profiles of the SCFA produced from fermentation. For example, beet pulp is more fermentable than cellulose[27] and produces a greater proportion of butyrate in the SCFA products.[28] As a result, the colonic mucosa of dogs fed diets containing beet pulp should be exposed to different amounts and profiles of SCFA, compared with dogs fed diets containing less fermentable fiber. A diet containing beet pulp increased colonic weight and resulted in lower indices of colonic mucosal disturbance in dogs than diets containing cellulose.[29] Beet pulp-containing diets also tended to change the ratio of mucosal oxygen consumption to DNA content.[30] In determining whether such changes will be beneficial to the health of dogs, it is necessary to know the extent that butyrate, as well as other potential fuels, are utilized by colonocytes from dogs.

Fuel Utilization by Canine Intestinal Cells

A series of experiments were conducted to define metabolism of energetic substrates by mucosal epithelial cells isolated from the small intestine and large intestine of dogs.[31] Intestinal tissues were obtained from five purpose-bred dogs. Small intestinal epithelial cells (enterocytes) were isolated from the mid-jejunum and large intestinal epithelial cells (colonocytes) were isolated from the colon, using procedures adapted from Fleming et al.[7,13] For comparison, enterocytes and colonocytes were prepared from Sprague-Dawley rats fed either a commercial rat chow or fed the same food as the dogs (Eukanuba® Adult Maintenance Formula). Rats were fed each diet for at least 14 days before experiments were conducted.

After isolation, cells were incubated in Krebs-Henseleit buffer supplemented with various energetic substrates. Oxygen consumption of the cells, a measure of overall metabolic rate, was determined using an oxygen electrode and a biological oxygen monitor. Rates of substrate oxidation were determined by incubating the cells with ^{14}C-labeled substrates and collecting the $^{14}CO_2$ evolved.[32] Mean rates (plus or minus standard errors) are expressed as nanomoles of substrate metabolized per milligram of cell dry matter (DM). Cells were incubated with individual substrates to determine the maximal rate of oxidation of that substrate, and also were incubated in combination with other substrates to determine the extent to which the presence of alternate fuels altered the oxidation of the radio-labelled substrate.

The rate of oxygen consumption did not differ between enterocytes and colonocytes in the dogs (*Figure 1*). In contrast, colonocytes from rats consumed oxygen about 2.2 times faster than enterocytes (data not shown). Our data for rats indicating a higher rate of metabolism in colonocytes than in enterocytes were similar to data reported previously by others.[7,14] Rates of oxygen consumption by canine colonocytes were greater when the cells were incubated with a combination of glucose (5 mM), glutamine (1 mM), and SCFA (butyrate, propionate, and acetate, each at 5 mM) than when the cells were incubated with 5 mM butyrate, 5 mM glucose, or 5 mM glutamine individually (*Figure 1*). This could indicate that the combination of multiple substrates better supported metabolic activities in the cells than the individual substrates.

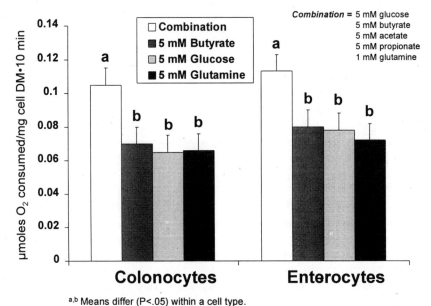

a,b Means differ (P<.05) within a cell type.
No differences between cell type within a substrate.

Figure 1. Canine colonocyte and enterocyte oxygen consumption.

Canine colonic cells readily oxidized butyrate, propionate, glucose, and glutamine. Oxidation of acetate could not be detected reliably because of extremely high background counts for acetate. In the absence of alternate substrates, rates of oxidation were greatest for the SCFA propionate and butyrate, followed by glutamine and glucose. Although propionate had the greatest oxidation rate when it was the only exogenous substrate supplied to the colonic cells, its oxidation was inhibited by 96% when the media also contained the mixture of butyrate, acetate, glutamine, and glucose (*Figure 2*). Butyrate oxidation was not affected by glucose or β-hydroxybutyrate (data not shown), or by a mixture of propionate, acetate, glutamine, and glucose (*Figure 2*). No production of ketone bodies from butyrate could be detected either by enzymatic procedures or by radio-HPLC methodology. Glucose appears to be an obligatory fuel for canine colonocytes because of its substantial rate of oxidation and the fact that its oxidation was not depressed significantly by the presence of butyrate or glutamine (data not shown), or by the mixture of SCFA plus glutamine (*Figure 2*). Oxidation of glutamine was decreased by 18% in the presence of butyrate alone and 45% by glucose alone (data not shown); glutamine oxidation was decreased 60% by the combination of SCFA plus glucose (*Figure 2*).

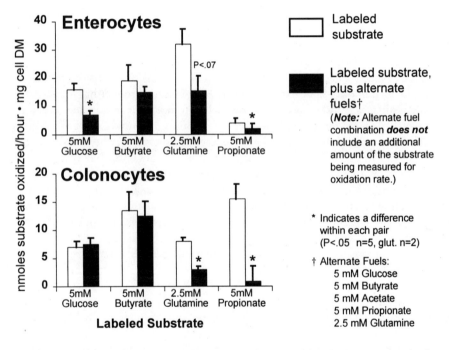

Figure 2. Effect of the availability of alternate fuels on substrate oxidation by canine intestinal cells.

Extrapolating *in vitro* results from isolated colonocytes to the *in vivo* situation in dogs suggests that luminal butyrate would be a major fuel because of its substantial production by colonic microbes[27,28] and the fact that its oxidation was not suppressed by alternate fuels. Results also indicate that glucose absorbed from arterial blood would likely be an important fuel source. Low concentrations of glutamine in arterial blood probably preclude it as a major fuel source for colonocytes under most situations. Some propionate might be utilized because it is produced from fermentation in greater amounts than butyrate,[27,28] but the marked inhibition of propionate oxidation in the presence of alternate fuels suggests that the majority of propionate is not metabolized within the colonic tissue. Other possible substrates for colonocytes that were not evaluated directly in our experiments include acetate and acetoacetate.

Jejunal enterocytes from the dogs readily oxidized glutamine, glucose, and butyrate. Enterocytes also oxidized propionate, but at a much slower rate. Glutamine oxidation was not affected significantly by butyrate but was decreased 34% by glucose (data not shown) and 48% by the mixture of SCFA plus glucose (*Figure 2*). Oxidation of glucose was decreased 21% by glutamine and 35% by butyrate (data not shown), and was decreased 54% when the incubation medium also contained the mixture of SCFA plus glutamine (*Figure 2*).

It was interesting to observe the relatively high rate of butyrate oxidation by enterocytes isolated from the mid-jejunum (*Figure 2*). Furthermore, oxidation of butyrate by these cells was not decreased significantly by glucose, glutamine, or β-hydroxybutyrate alone (data not shown), or by a mixture of SCFA plus glucose and glutamine (*Figure 2*). These findings contrast with data from rats, in which the rate of oxidation of butyrate was much lower than oxidation rates of glucose or glutamine.[7] Based on data largely obtained from rats, dogma states that epithelial cells of the jejunum would be exposed to very little butyrate from either the serosal or luminal surfaces. While this dogma also appears to hold true in dogs fed cereal-based diets,[33] dogs fed meat-based diets had substantial concentrations of SCFA in the mid-section of the jejunum.[33] Therefore, the high rate of butyrate oxidation in canine enterocytes may be physiologically important, because dogs have evolved as primarily carnivorous animals. As a result, their enterocytes may be more highly adapted to utilize butyrate that would be produced in the small intestine when the animals consume a meat-based diet. During cereal-based dietary regimes, glutamine and glucose presumably would be the major fuels for enterocytes in dogs, similar to the situation in other species.[7,12,16] Possible *in vivo* contributions of acetate and ketone bodies to respiratory metabolism in canine enterocytes were not assessed in this experiment.

When direct comparisons of substrate oxidation rates were made between canine colonocytes and canine jejunal enterocytes, rates were generally higher in enterocytes than in colonocytes, although in most instances the differences between tissues for a particular combination of substrates did not achieve statistical significance because of the relatively low number of observations. In the absence of alternate substrates, glucose oxidation was significantly greater in enterocytes than in colonocytes, whereas propionate oxidation was greater in colonocytes than in enterocytes. When all observations with each labeled substrate were combined within tissues, oxidation rates of butyrate, glucose, and glutamine were significantly greater ($P<.01$) for enterocytes than for colonocytes.

As mentioned earlier, we conducted parallel experiments with rats fed either a standard rat chow or the same diet as the dogs received. These experiments were intended to allow comparison of the results with published results from other

researchers and to determine if rats could be a suitable model for intestinal metabolism in dogs. Oxidation rates and patterns of substrate utilization in the rats generally corresponded to results reported by others. In enterocytes from chow-fed rats,
oxidation rates were greatest for glutamine, intermediate for glucose, and lowest for
butyrate. Oxidation of glutamine was not decreased by the presence of glucose, but
oxidation of glucose was decreased by about 47% when glutamine was added to the
medium, indicating that glutamine was the primary fuel for rat enterocytes as shown
previously by others.[7,13] Enterocytes from rats fed dog food showed the same pattern
of responses to substrates as those from chow-fed rats, although oxidation rates
tended to be lower for glutamine and glucose.

Colonocytes isolated from chow-fed rats oxidized butyrate at a rate about
4.5 times greater than the rate of glucose oxidation. Glucose did not significantly
depress butyrate oxidation, but addition of butyrate decreased glucose oxidation by
about 25%. Colonocytes from rats fed dog food oxidized butyrate and glucose at
lower rates than the cells from chow-fed rats. The depression of glucose oxidation by
butyrate tended ($P<.10$) to be less in colonocytes from rats fed dog food than in
those from chow-fed rats, similar to the situation in the canine colonocytes. Surprisingly, intestinal cells isolated from rats fed dog food had greater rates of oxygen
consumption than the cells isolated from chow-fed rats, despite the lower rates of
substrate oxidation for cells from rats fed dog food. This suggests that oxidation rates
for other substrates not measured in this experiment may have been enhanced by
the dog food diet.

Reasons for the dietary-induced differences between rats fed chow and
those fed dog food are not clear. The diets differed in many ways, including greater
energy density (4.86 *v* 4.01 kcal gross energy/g), protein content (26.2 *v* 22.2%),
and fiber type and content, but the greatest difference was in fat content (16.9 *v*
5.4%). Rats fed the dog food had lower food intake and energy intake but improved
feed efficiency than rats fed chow. Daily fecal output was greater for the chow-fed
rats, and empty wet weights of cecum and colon were greater for the chow-fed rats.
Concentrations of acetate and propionate in colonic contents were similar between
dog food and chow-fed rats, but the concentration of butyrate was nearly doubled in
rats fed chow. Because of these dietary-induced differences in colonic butyrate
availability in rats, it would be of interest to determine the effects of enhancing
butyrate availability on colonocyte metabolism in dogs.

This data indicate that species differences in intestinal fuel metabolism
likely exist between dogs and rats. Overall, feeding the dog food to rats resulted in
rates and patterns of substrate metabolism in enterocytes and colonocytes that were
more similar to those of the dogs than were cells from chow-fed rats. Additionally,
dietary effects on relative capacities for fuel utilization in intestinal cells may be
more pronounced than previously realized.

Implications   In general, the data for enterocytes and colonocytes from dogs agree with previously documented patterns of substrate utilization in rats and other species. In canine colonocytes, butyrate was a major fuel, although the cells appeared to have an obligate utilization of glucose in contrast to other species. Jejunal enterocytes oxidized glutamine and butyrate at high rates, although glucose also appeared to be an important fuel. As shown by differences in magnitude of responses between cells from rats fed dog food and those from chow-fed rats, the comparison of species differences between dogs and rats may be confounded to some degree by differences in the type of diet fed.

References   1. Reeds PJ, Burrin DG, Davis TA, Fiorotto ML. Postnatal growth of gut and muscle: competitors or collaborators. *Proc Nutr Soc* 1993; 52:57-67.

2. Argenzio RA. Introduction to gastrointestinal function. In: Swenson MJ, ed. *Dukes' Physiology of Domestic Animals, 10th edition*. Ithaca: Cornell Univ Press, 1984; 262-277.

3. Jacobs LR. Relationship between dietary fiber and cancer: metabolic, physiologic, and cellular mechanisms. *Proc Soc Exp Biol Med* 1986; 299-310.

4. McIntyre A, Gibson PR, Young GP. Butyrate production from dietary fibre and protection against large bowel cancer in a rat model. *Gut* 1993; 34:386-391.

5. Roediger WEW. Utilization of nutrients by isolated epithelial cells of the rat colon. *Gastroenterology* 1982; 83:424-429.

6. Ardawi MSM, Newsholme EA. Fuel utilization in colonocytes of the rat. *Biochem J* 1985; 231:713-719.

7. Fleming SE, Fitch MD, DeVries S, Liu ML, Kight C. Nutrient utilization by cells isolated from rat jejunum, cecum, and colon. *J Nutr* 1991; 121:869-878.

8. Darcy-Vrillon B, Morel MT, Cherbuy C, Bernard F, Posho L, Blachier F, Meslin JC, Duée PH. Metabolic characteristics of pig colonocytes after adaptation to a high fiber diet. *J Nutr* 1993; 123:234-243.

9. Hague A, Butt AJ, Paraskeva C. The role of butyrate in human colonic epithelial cells: an energy source or inducer of differentiation and apoptosis? *Proc Nutr Soc* 1996; 55:937-943.

10. Velázquez OC, Lederer HM, Rombeau JL. Butyrate and the colonocyte. Implications for neoplasia. *Dig Dis Sci* 1996; 41:727-739.

11. Windmueller HG, Spaeth AE. Identification of ketone bodies and glutamine as the major respiratory fuels *in vivo* for postabsorptive rat small intestine. *J Biol Chem* 1978; 253:69-76.

12. Watford M, Lund P, Krebs HA. Isolation and metabolic characteristics of rat and chicken enterocytes. *Biochem J* 1979; 178:589-596.

13. Kight CE, Fleming SE. Nutrient oxidation by rat intestinal epithelial cells is concentration dependent. *J Nutr* 1993; 123:867-882.

14. Marsman KE, McBurney MI. Dietary fiber increases oxidative metabolism in colonocytes but not in distal small intestinal enterocytes isolated from rats. *J Nutr* 1995; 125:273-282.

15. Colomb V, Darcy-Vrillon B, Jobert A, Guihot G, Morel MT, Corriol O, Ricour C, Duée PH. Parenteral nutrition modifies glucose and glutamine metabolism in rat isolated enterocytes. *Gastroenterology* 1997; 112:429-436.

16. Posho L, Darcy-Vrillon B, Blachier F, Duée PH. The contribution of glucose and glutamine to energy metabolism in newborn pig enterocytes. *J Nutr Biochem* 1994; 5:284-290.

17. Ashy AA, Ardawi MSM. Glucose, glutamine, and ketone-body metabolism in human enterocytes. *Metabolism* 1988; 37:602-609.

18. Abumrad NN, Kim S, Molina PE. Regulation of gut glutamine metabolism: role of hormones and cytokines. *Proc Nutr Soc* 1995; 54:525-533.

19. Roediger WEW. Role of anaerobic bacteria in the metabolic welfare of the colonic mucosa in man. *Gut* 1980; 21:793-798.

20. Cherbuy C, Darcy-Vrillon B, Morel MT, Pégorier JP, Duée PH. Effect of germfree state on the capacities of isolated rat colonocytes to metabolize n-butyrate, glucose, and glutamine. *Gastroenterology* 1995; 109:1890-1899.

21. Roediger WEW, Nance S. Selective reduction of fatty acid oxidation in colonocytes: correlation with ulcerative colitis. *Lipids* 1990; 25:646-652.

22. Moore JWE, Babidge W, Millard S, Roediger WEW. Effect of sulphide on short-chain acyl-CoA metabolism in rat colonocytes. *Gut* 1997; 41:77-81.

23. Scheppach W, Sommer H, Kirchner T, Paganelli GM, Bartram P, Christl S, Richter F, Dusel G, Kasper H. Effect of butyrate enemas on the colonic mucosa in distal ulcerative colitis. *Gastroenterology* 1992; 103:51-56.

24. Butzner JD, Parmar R, Bell CJ, Dalal V. Butyrate enema therapy stimulates mucosal repair in experimental colitis in the rat. *Gut* 1996; 38:568-573.

25. Scheppach W, Dusel G, Kuhn T, Loges C, Karch H, Bartram HP, Richter F, Christl SU, Kasper H. Effect of L-glutamine and n-butyrate on the restitution of rat colonic mucosa after acid induced injury. *Gut* 1996; 38:878-885.

26. Marsman KE, McBurney MI. Dietary fiber and short-chain fatty acids affect cell proliferation and protein synthesis in isolated rat colonocytes. *J Nutr* 1996; 126:1429-1437.

27. Sunvold GD, Fahey Jr GC, Merchen NR, Reinhart GA. *In vitro* fermentation of selected fibrous substrates by dog and cat fecal inoculum: Influence of diet composition on substrate organic matter disappearance and short-chain fatty acid production. *J Anim Sci* 1995; 73:1110-1122.

28. Sunvold GD, Fahey Jr GC, Merchen NR, Titgemeyer EC, Bourquin LD, Bauer LL, Reinhart GA. Dietary fiber for dogs: IV. In vitro fermentation of selected fiber sources by dog fecal inoculum and *in vivo* digestion and metabolism of fiber-supplemented diets. *J Anim Sci* 1995; 73:1099-1109.

29. Hallman JE, Moxley RA, Reinhart GA, Wallace EA, Clemens ET. Cellulose, beet pulp, and pectin/gum arabic effects on canine colonic microstructure and histopathology. *Vet Clin Nutr* 1995; 2:137-142.

30. Hallman JE, Reinhart GA, Wallace EA, Milliken A, Clemens ET. Colonic mucosal tissue energetics and electrolyte transport in dogs fed cellulose, beet pulp or pectin/gum arabic as their primary fiber source. *Nutr Res* 1996; 16:303-313.

31. Beaulieu AD, Drackley JK, Emmert LS, Overton TR, Sunvold GD. Metabolic fuel utilization by canine and murine intestinal cells. *FASEB J* 1997; 11:A612.

32. Cremin Jr JD, Drackley JK, Grum DE, Hansen LR, Fahey Jr GC. Effects of reduced phenolic acids on metabolism of propionate and palmitate in bovine liver tissue *in vitro*. *J Dairy Sci* 1994; 77:3608-3617.

33. Banta CA, Clemens ET, Krinsky MM, Sheffy BE. Sites of organic acid production and patterns of digesta movement in the gastrointestinal tract of dogs. *J Nutr* 1979; 109:1592-1600.

Characterization of the Intestinal Flora of the Cat and Its Potential for Modification

T. J. Gruffydd-Jones, BVetMed, PhD, MRCVS
Reader, Small Animal Medicine and Director of The Feline Centre
Department of Clinical Veterinary Science
University of Bristol, Bristol, United Kingdom

K. Papasouliotis, DVM, PhD, MRCVS;
A. H. Sparkes, BVetMed, PhD, MRCVS
The Feline Centre, Department of Clinical Veterinary Science,
University of Bristol, Bristol, United Kingdom

Introduction

A major focus of interest in feline gastroenterology centers on the bacterial flora of the intestinal tract. It has been suggested that the normal flora of the intestinal tract of the cat, particularly of the small intestine, is unusual both quantitatively, in terms of high numbers of organisms compared to most species, and possibly also qualitatively, for example in having a high proportion of *Clostridial* species. This has potential relevance to both normal function and dysfunction of the intestinal tract.

Assessment of Small Intestinal Bacterial Flora in Cats

Bacteriological investigation of samples obtained endoscopically from the upper small intestine has been regarded as the "gold standard" for diagnosing small intestine bacterial overgrowth (SIBO) and for assessing changes in the gut flora. However, this technique suffers from a number of potential problems. There is potential for contamination either with oral flora[1] or through improper preparation or use of the endoscope, although this risk can be minimized through careful use of good technique. This approach is also very dependent on good bacteriological support, particularly for handling and isolating anaerobic organisms.

Collection of intestinal juice by endoscopy is limited to the upper small intestine. The bacterial flora in this portion of the duodenum may not reflect disturbances in the more distal ileum. Indeed, if the large bowel is the source of bacteria involved in inducing SIBO, any changes in bacterial flora in the small intestine might be expected to occur earlier and to be more severe in the more distal part.

The most appropriate method of sampling the bacterial flora is an additional point of controversy. Intestinal juice is most often used for bacteriological studies, but there is a view that mucosal biopsies or brushings may be preferable since they are more representative of the bacterial flora associated with the mucosal surface, which may be more important.[2] Fasting the animal is necessary in the preparation of cats for the anesthesia required for endoscopy, but this too may influence the bacterial flora.[3]

Indirect methods have also been developed for assessing the intestinal flora dependent largely on administering substrates and assessing their utilization by the bacterial flora. This is the basis for the use of breath tests (e.g., the breath hydrogen test) which were developed for use in cats[4] and which can be utilized to assess changes in the intestinal bacterial flora. This approach has some advantages in that potentially it allows the whole of the small intestine to be assessed. However, there are inherent disadvantages with such methods. Utilization of the substrate may be affected by qualitative changes in the flora and whether the bacteria present are able to utilize the substrates used.[5] It may also be difficult to separate what corresponds to activity within the small and large intestine.

Assessing
Normal Small
Intestinal Flora
of Cats

Establishing methods for assessing the small intestinal bacterial flora of cats is an important research area. This is an essential prerequisite for defining the intestinal flora. In addition, convenient, relatively non-invasive, reliable methods are required for both clinical investigations and for research studies, necessitating repetitive assessment of the flora.

Endoscopic aspiration of intestinal juice from the proximal small intestine is the most convenient, relatively non-invasive method for obtaining suitable samples to assess the bacterial flora. Initial studies have been aimed at establishing how reliable this method is. This technique suffers from a number of potential problems; attempts have been made to address the question of how important these problems are.

The potential problem of contamination with oral bacteria during endoscopy has been investigated by comparing the results of culture of intestinal juice obtained simultaneously by endoscopic aspiration and by direct needle aspiration from the same site. No significant differences comparing either quantitative or qualitative results have been found[6] (Gruffydd-Jones and Sparkes, unpublished results).

Collection of undiluted aspirates via endoscopy can be difficult in some cats, but is usually possible with perseverance. Even a very small quantity may be adequate and is preferable to a diluted sample. Not surprisingly, significantly lower numbers of organisms were recovered from diluted endoscopic aspirates ($10^{4.3}$ cfu/ml) compared with undiluted aspirates collected at the same time ($10^{5.5}$ cfu/ml). A brief study comparing the results for endoscopic aspirates with those for mucosal brushes was conducted; preliminary results suggest that the two techniques give similar yields (Papasouliotis, Gruffydd-Jones, Sparkes; unpublished results). This contrasts with results of a study in dogs[2] in which significantly fewer bacteria were isolated from aspirates compared to mucosal biopsies. There were also notable qualitative differences in the bacteria isolated in this study. However, some studies in man have shown higher isolation rates from aspirates compared to mucosal samples.[7] Results of the study reported herein did not suggest that mucosal brush samples offer any advantage over aspirates.

The question arises as to whether bacteria isolated from the duodenum reflect bacteria located in the more distal small intestine. This question was addressed by comparing cultures of intestinal juice collected simultaneously from the duodenum and ileum. Significantly higher numbers of bacteria, particularly aerobes, were found in the ileum; noticeable qualitative differences also existed.[8] While the anaerobic flora was similar at both sites with Clostridia predominating, *Pasteurella* spp. were the most common aerobes found in the duodenum, while *Enterococci* and *E. coli* were most often isolated from the ileum. This is presumed to reflect the source of bacteria with the duodenal flora being derived mainly from the oral flora, while the ileal flora largely reflects the colonic bacteria. Clearly duodenal aspirates may not necessarily provide an accurate indication of the flora lower down the small intestine in normal cats. It is uncertain whether this would also apply to cats with SIBO, although it would appear likely.

Within the limitations discussed above, a clearer idea of the upper small intestinal bacterial flora for cats using bacteriological techniques is now available. These results are based on 83 samples of endoscopically aspirated, undiluted intestinal juice collected from the upper duodenum of healthy cats[8,9] (Papasoulitis, Gruffydd-Jones, Sparkes; unpublished results). The median total bacterial count has ranged from $10^{5.8}$ cfu/ml up to $10^{7.9}$. The median aerobic bacterial count has been $10^{5.6}$ cfu/ml with an upper range up to $10^{7.7}$ cfu/ml and for anaerobes a median of $10^{5.0}$ cfu/ml with values up to $10^{7.8}$ in individual cats. No organisms were isolated from one sample and just anaerobes from a further three samples. *Table 1* shows that these figures correspond closely with the few previous reports for cats.

Normal Small Intestinal Bacterial Flora of Cats

Table 1. Previously reported bacterial numbers in the small intestine of cats.

	Total Bacteria cfu/ml	Total Aerobes cfu/ml	Total Anaerobes cfu/ml
Williams-Smith (1965)[10]	Median $10^{5.7}$	$10^{4.2}$	$10^{5.7}$
Johnston et al (1993)[13]	Median $10^{6.2}$	$10^{5.9}$	$10^{5.6}$
	Range ($10^{5.3}$–$10^{8.2}$)	Range ($10^{4.7}$–$10^{7.7}$)	Range ($10^{4.8}$–$10^{8.0}$)

The bacterial numbers are much higher than those reported in many other species, including man. Indeed a total bacterial count in excess of 10^5 cfu/ml has been used as a criteria for small intestinal bacterial overgrowth in dogs and man. However, other studies have found much higher numbers of bacteria in dogs, numbers that are, in fact, comparable to those reported for cats.[10,11,12] Based on these figures, the total bacterial count for duodenal aspirates should be in excess of $10^{7.0}$–$10^{8.0}$ cfu/ml to be considered indicative of SIBO in cats. The relatively high numbers of bacteria in the small intestine may simply be a feature of carnivores.

There are certainly important qualitative differences in the small intestinal bacterial flora. *Table 2* indicates the organisms most frequently isolated from endoscopic duodenal aspirates in cats at The Feline Centre, University of Bristol. There are notable differences in comparison with other species. *Clostridium perfringens* is the most consistently isolated anaerobe from cats, yet it is rarely isolated from humans and is considered significant if found at this site. Clostridia are also frequently found in the small intestinal flora of healthy dogs and, therefore, this too is probably a feature of carnivores.

Table 2. Frequency of isolation of bacteria from endoscopically collected aspirates of duodenal juice in normal cats[8,9] (Papasouliotis, Gruffydd-Jones, Sparkes; unpublished results).

Aerobes	% Isolation	Anaerobes	% Isolation
Pasteurella spp.	87	*Clostridia* spp.	98
Streptococcus spp.	72	(mainly perfringens)	
Gram negative rods	53	*Bacteroides* spp.	58
Enterococcus spp.	43	(mainly fragilis)	
E. coli	41	*Fusobacterium* spp.	24
Staphylococcus spp.	36	Gram positive cocci	14
Neisseria spp.	25	Gram positive rods	14
Diptheroids	17	*Eubacterium* spp.	13
Pseudomonas spp.	17	*Peptostreptococcus* spp.	8
Weeksella spp.	13		
Xanthomonas spp.	12		
Moraxella spp.	12		
Enterobacter, Flavobacter, Lactobacillus	<10		

The consistency of the duodenal flora over time in cats has been evaluated by culture of repeated endoscopic aspirates. Marked variability of the bacterial flora was found, with total bacterial counts varying by as much as $10^{2.0}$ to $10^{6.3}$ cfu/ml over a 12 week period. Repeat sampling of dogs maintained on the same diet showed a similar variability in numbers of organisms isolated.[2]

Diet may be a factor in influencing the gut flora. It has been suggested that this may be important in explaining the higher dietary requirement of taurine of cats fed on canned diets compared with dry diets (discussed later). Although no studies have been reported which have been specifically aimed at assessing the influence of diet on the bacterial flora of the gut in cats, results of studies of cats receiving a dry diet are very similar to those previously reported for two different studies of cats receiving canned diets.[6,9]

Clearly there are some unusual features of the intestinal bacteria flora of cats compared to some other species. However, these features may simply reflect that the cat is a carnivore. They should not be considered as unusual for cats and indeed, the balance of the bacterial flora is likely to have evolved in a manner most beneficial to this species. Nevertheless, these unusual features may have some potential relevance in certain situations.

Small intestinal bacterial overgrowth is a well-recognized syndrome in humans and now in dogs. Does SIBO occur in cats either as a primary problem or associated with other intestinal disorders, such as inflammatory bowel disease? Characterization of the normal small intestinal bacterial flora of cats is clearly essential for establishing a diagnosis of SIBO. This is particularly important if relatively high numbers of small intestinal bacteria are normally found in this species.

Small Intestinal Bacterial Overgrowth (SIBO)

Inflammatory bowel disease is recognized as an important cause of chronic gastrointestinal signs in cats, typically causing signs of weight loss, vomiting, and diarrhea. This is now the most common form of intestinal disease diagnosed at The Feline Centre, University of Bristol. Many questions about this syndrome remain unanswered. The syndrome has not yet been well characterized and the underlying pathogenesis is not known, although the cellular infiltration is thought to reflect an aberrant immune response. It is speculated that dietary antigens may play a role in this abnormal immune response, either as a primary underlying etiological factor, or possibly through perpetuating damage following an initial insult induced by some other factor. The suspicion of dietary antigen involvement in the pathogensis is based largely on the perceived beneficial role of the use of restricted protein diets in some cases. It is also suggested that an abnormal response to bacterial antigens may also play a role in the pathogenesis of IBD. Small intestinal bacterial overgrowth is reported in some cases of canine IBD[14] although it is not clear whether this is a cause of the IBD or a consequence. Furthermore, the criteria that have been used for defining SIBO in dogs are arguable. Nevertheless, interest is currently focused on the possible link between development of an inflammatory response and breakdown of tolerance to normal bacterial flora in the pathogenesis of IBD in man.[15,16] Although there are important differences in IBD in humans and small animals, similarities do exist and a common etiopathogenesis may be present in some cases.

Pathogenesis of Inflammatory Bowel Disease (IBD)

Studies undertaken to develop an intestinal permeability test in cats have shown that the intestine of the cat appears to be particularly permeable to lactulose (used as large molecular weight probes) compared to other species.[17] This suggests that the tight junctions in the small intestine of the cat are particularly weak and may permit large molecules to permeate through the paracellular route more readily than in other species. This could be a consequence of the high numbers of bacteria which constitute the normal flora since it has been shown that bacterial peptides may increase intestinal permeability[18] and changes in permeability have been reported in dogs with SIBO.[19] Whether or not increased intestinal permeability plays a role in the pathogenesis of IBD is still a point of contention.[20]

Relevance of Intestinal Bacterial Flora to Nutritional Requirements of Cats

The importance of taurine as a nutritional requirement for cats is now well-established. It is also well-recognized that higher concentrations of taurine are required in canned diets compared to dry diets to meet the requirements of cats. Administration of antibiotics reduces fecal loss of taurine; this is believed to result from reduced bacterial deconjugation of bile acids in the intestine.[21] It is postulated that increased bacterial degradation of taurine is the explanation for the higher taurine requirement for canned diets and that this may be associated with the formation of Maillard products in such diets. It is not known whether quantitative or qualitative differences in the intestinal bacterial flora occur depending on the type of diet and whether this may contribute to the differences in requirements through altering metabolism of taurine within the gut. However, striking differences in duodenal flora of cats fed dry diets compared with canned diets have not been observed to date.

Maintenance of the Normal Intestinal Flora

Maintenance of an optimal balance of bacteria which constitutes the normal flora of the intestinal tract may have a number of benefits.

1. *Protection from infection.* There is now overwhelming evidence to support the concept of a balanced intestinal microflora contributing to protection against infection with specific enteropathogens through the phenomenon of "competitive exclusion".[22] A balanced microflora may also help to protect against SIBO and factors which compromise the flora, such as administration of antibiotics.

2. *The importance of intestinal flora* in altering nutrient availability (e.g., taurine) has been described earlier. In addition, the bacterial flora may provide an important input to metabolic needs locally through the fermentation products of bacterial activiting acting as fuel substrates for colonic cells.

Potential for Manipulating the Intestinal Flora

The concept of using probiotics has been long recognized, although there is controversy over their effectiveness. The suggested rationale for the use of probiotics is based on attempting to colonize the intestinal bacterial tract with live organisms, most commonly *Lactobacilli* given by mouth. This may be considered beneficial in situations in which the intestinal flora may be compromised (e.g., following antibiotic treatment or enteric infection) which may become important in perpetuation of enteric dysfunction. However, there is little convincing evidence that probiotics are effective. It is questionable whether organisms administered orally are able to survive or are capable of colonizing the intestinal tract.

A more attractive concept is the use of prebiotics. This approach is based on including non-digestible food ingredients within the diet which alter intestinal bacterial flora.[23] Some of the bacteria which represent part of the normal bacterial flora are considered to be largely beneficial, particularly *Bifidobacteria*, *Lactobacilli*, and *Eubacteria*.[23] Their beneficial effect may be achieved in a number of ways. Their metabolic products may serve as a direct energy source for intestinal cells, and they may help to suppress potentially harmful bacteria within the intestine, particularly through lowering the pH. Other bacteria are considered to be potentially harmful. These consist largely of toxin producers such as *Clostridial* species, *E. coli*, and *staphylococci*. Prebiotics serve as substrates to encourage growth of beneficial bacteria, thus inhibiting potentially harmful organisms. A number of non-digestible food substances have been considered as potential prebiotics, but oligosaccharides particularly fulfill the criteria required of a successful prebiotic. Oligosaccharides have been shown to have a beneficial effect on the colonic flora in man.[23] In addition they have been shown to be fermented into short chain fatty acids by fecal cultures derived from cats *in vitro*[24] and potentially to modify the bacterial flora of the upper small intestine in German Shepherd Dogs with evidence of SIBO.[25] Oligosaccharides are therefore potentially attractive candidates as prebiotics for use in cats to manipulate the intestinal flora in a beneficial manner.

An experiment was conducted to assess the effect of dietary inclusion of fructooligosaccharides (FOS) on the intestinal flora of healthy cats. Addition of 0.75% FOS to the diet had a significant effect on the fecal flora. *Lactobacilli* (**Figure 1**) were increased in number while there was a reduction in *Clostridium perfringens* (**Figure 2**) and *E. coli* (**Figure 3**).[26] It was not possible to assess the effect on *Bifidobacteria* because, in contrast to a previous study,[27] *Bifidobacteria* were isolated from only a small proportion of fecal samples. However, no significant effect was

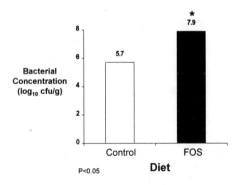

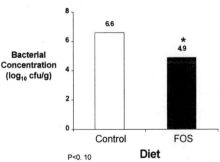

Figure 1. Dietary FOS increases *Lactobacilli* in the feline large intestine. From Sparkes et al., 1998.[26]

Figure 2. Dietary FOS decreases *Clostridium perfringens* in the feline large intestine. From Sparkes et al., 1998.[26]

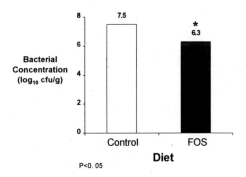

P<0. 05

Figure 3. Dietary FOS decreases *E. coli* in the feline large intestine. From Sparkes et al., 1998.[26]

noted on the duodenal bacterial flora. Nevertheless, it is possible that changes may have been induced which were masked by the marked intra-individual variability in bacterial numbers recovered from duodenal aspirates evident from repeated assessment while cats received a constant diet. Furthermore, significant effects on the duodenal flora may perhaps be achieved by inclusion of higher levels of FOS. These results suggest that oligosaccharides have a potential for manipulating the intestinal bacterial flora of cats. Further work is necessary to explore the potential benefits which may be derived from this effect.

References

1. Knutson NG, McKee J, Welsh JD, Griffiths WJ, Flournoy DJ. Endoscopic cultures of the proximal gastrointestinal tract. *Gastro Endoscopy* 1982; 28:12-14.

2. Delles EK, Willard MD, Simpson RB, Fossum TW, Slater M, Kolp D, Lees GE, Helman R, Reinhart G. Comparison of species and numbers of bacteria in concurrently cultured samples of proximal small intestinal fluid and endoscopically obtained duodenal mucosa in dogs with intestinal bacterial overgrowth. *Am J Vet Res* 1994; 55:957-964.

3. Drasar BS, Shiner M, McLeod GM. Studies on the intestinal flora. 1. The bacterial flora of the gastrointestinal tract in healthy and achlorhydric persons. *Gastroenterology* 1969; 56:71-79.

4. Muir P, Gruffydd-Jones TJ, Cripps PJ, Papasouliotis K, Brown PJ. Breath hydrogen excretion after oral administration of xylose to cats. *J Sm Anim Pract* 1994; 35:86-92.

5. Strocchi A, Corazza G, Ellis CJ, Gasbarrini G, Levitt MD. Detection of malabsorption of low doses of carbohydrate: accuracy of various breath H_2 criteria. *Gastroenterology* 1993; 105:1404.

6. Papasouliotis K, Sparkes AH, Werrett G, Egan K, Gruffydd-Jones EAD, Gruffydd-Jones TJ. An assessment of the bacterial flora of the proximal small intestine in healthy cats, and the effect of sampling method. *Am J Vet Res* 1998; 59:(In press).

7. Plant AG, Gorback SL, Nahas L, Weinstein L, Spanknebel G, Levitan R. The microbial flora of human small intestinal mucosa and fluids. *Gastroenterology* 1967; 53:868-873.

8. Papasouliotis K, Sparkes AH, Gruffydd-Jones TJ, Cripps PJ, Werrett G, Clarke C, Gruffydd-Jones EAD. A comparison of the bacterial flora of the duodenum and ileum in cats. *Proc Brit Sm Anim Vet Assoc Congress* 1996; 24.

9. Sparkes AH, Papasouliotis K, Sunvold G, Werrett G, Clarke C, Jones M, Gruffydd-Jones TJ, Reinhart G. The bacterial flora in the proximal small intestine of healthy cats, and the effect of dietary supplementation with fructo-oligosaccharides. *Am J Vet Res* 1998; 59:(In press).

10. Williams-Smith. Observations on the flora of the alimentary tract of animals and factors affecting its comparison. *J Path Bact* 1965; 89:95.

11. Simpson KW, Batt RM, Jones D, Morton DB. Effects of exocrin pancreatic insufficiency and replacement therapy on the bacterial flora of the duodenum in dogs. *Am J Vet Res* 1990; 51:203-206.

12. Benno Y, Nakas H, Uchida K, Mitsuioka T. Impact of advances in age on the gastrointestinal microflora of Beagle dogs. *J Med Vet Sci* 1992; 54:703-706.

13. Johnston K, Lamport A, Batt RM. Unexpected bacterial flora in the proximal small intestine of normal cats. *Vet Rec* 1993; 132:362-363.

14. Rutgers HC, Batt RM, Elwood CM, Lamport A. Small intestinal bacterial overgrowth in dogs with chronic intestinal disease. *J Amer Vet Med Assoc* 1995; 206:187-193.

15. Duchmann R, Kaiser I, Hermann E, Mayet W, Ewe K, Meyer Zum Büschenfelde K-H. Tolerance exists towards resident intestinal flora but is broken in active inflamatory bowel disease (IBD). *Clin Exp Immunol* 1995; 102:448-455.

16. MacDonald TT. Breakdown of tolerance to the intestinal flora in inflammatory bowel disease (IBD). *Clin Exp Immunol* 1995; 102:445-447.

17. Papasouliotis K, Gruffydd-Jones TJ, Sparkes AH, Cripps PJ, Millard WG. Lactulose and mannitol as probe markers for *in vivo* assessment of passive intestinal permeability in healthy cats. *Am J Vet Res* 1993; 54:840-844.

18. Von Ritter C, Sekizuka E, Grisham MB, Granger DN. The chemotactic peptide N formyl methionyl-loucyl-phenylalanine increases mucosal permeability in the distal ileum of the rat. *Gastroenterology* 1988; 95:651-656.

19. Rutgers HC, Batt RJ, Proud FJ, Sorensen SH, Elwood CM, Petrie G, Matthewman LA, Forster-van Hijfte MA, Boswood A, Entwistle M, Fensome RH. Intestinal permeability and function in dogs with small intestinal bacterial overgrowth. *J Sm Anim Pract* 1996; 37:428-434.

20. Bjaranson I, MacPherson A, Hollander D. Intestinal permeability: an overview. *Gastroenterology* 1995; 108:1566-1581.

21. Kim SW, Rogers QR, Morris JC. Maillard reaction products in purified diets induce taurine depletion in cats which is reversed by antibiotics. *J Nutr* 1996; 126:195-201.

22. Snoeyenbos GH. Role of native intestinal microflora in protection against pathogens. *Proc Ann Meeting US Animal Health Assoc* 1979; 83:388-393.

23. Gibson GR, Roberfroid MB. Dietary modulation of the human colonic microbiota: introducing the concept of prebiotics. *J Nutr* 1995; 125:1401-1412.

24. Sunvold GD, Fahey GC, Merchen NR, Reinhart GA. *In vitro* fermentation of selected fibrous substrates by dog and cat fecal inoculum: influence of diet composition on substrate organic matter disappearance and short chain fatty acid production. *J Anim Sci* 1995; 78:1110-1122.

25. Willard MD, Simpson RB, Delles EK, Cohen ND, Fossum TW, Kolp D, Reinhart G. Effects of dietary supplementation of fructo-oligosacchardies on small intestinal bacterial overgrowth in dogs. *Am J Vet Res* 1994; 55:654-659.

26. Sparkes AH, Papasouliotis K, Sunvold G, Werrett G, Gruffydd-Jones EA, Egan K, Gruffydd-Jones TJ, Reinhart G. The effect of dietary supplementation with fructo-oligosaccharides on the faecal flora of healthy cats. *Am J Vet Res* 1998; 59:(in press).

27. Itoh K, Mitsuoka T, Maejima K, Hiraga C, Nakano K. Comparison of faecal flora of cats based on different housing conditions with special reference to Bifidobacerium. *Lab Anim* 1984; 18:280-284.

Summary and Application of Present Knowledge in Gastrointestinal Health

Gregory D. Sunvold, PhD
Research Nutritionist, Research and Development
The Iams Company, Lewisburg, Ohio, USA

Gregory A. Reinhart, PhD
Research and Development, The Iams Company, Lewisburg, Ohio, USA

Introduction

Providing a complete and balanced diet to dogs and cats is necessary to support life, maintain health, and promote long-term well being. Nutrients in the diet are not only important for health maintenance after absorption, but can also significantly influence the health of the gastrointestinal tract. Research in recent years has shown that the amount and type of dietary fiber that is provided in dog and cat diets significantly affect the functioning and health of the intestine and is relevant to the treatment of certain intestinal diseases. Attention to fiber in the diet may also be important when formulating pet foods for geriatric animals and for those with disorders such as diabetes mellitus or chronic renal disease.

Categorization of Dietary Fiber

Dietary fiber is plant material that resists digestion by the endogenous enzymes of the gastrointestinal tract, but is fermented to varying degrees by microorganisms present in the distal small intestine and colon. The major components of dietary fiber include the carbohydrates, cellulose, hemicellulose, pectin, gums and mucilages, and the phenyl propane polymer, lignin. Additionally, unique carbohydrate substances such as fructooligosaccharides (FOS) and lactulose are classified as fiber because they behave similarly in the gastrointestinal tract.[1]

Fibers can be classified according to their botanical source, solubility and viscosity characteristics, or the degree to which they are fermented by intestinal bacteria. Because the fermentability of a fiber provides direct evidence of its effects within an animal's gastrointestinal tract, this classification scheme is of greatest practical use in pet nutrition. The degree of fermentation of a fiber depends on the species of animal, the type of fiber that is present in the diet, gastrointestinal transit time, the types of bacterial populations that are present, and the health status of the gastrointestinal tract. *In vitro* and *in vivo* studies with dogs and cats have resulted in the identification of three major categories of fiber for these species. These include fibers that are poorly fermentable, moderately fermentable and highly fermentable.[2,3,4] Examples of poorly fermentable fibers for dogs and cats are cellulose, peanut hulls, and oat fiber. Moderately fermentable sources include beet pulp, citrus pulp, gum arabic, gum talha, and carob bean gum. Some highly fermentable sources are citrus pectin, lactulose, fructooligosaccharides, and guar gum. A second related characteristic of fiber is the amount and type of short chain fatty acids (SCFA) that are produced during fermentation by gut microbes. The SCFA, which include acetate, propionate, and butyrate, are a major end product of bacterial fermentation and are important contributors to many documented benefits of fiber. In general, fibers with low fermentability produce minimal SCFAs. Fibers with very high fermentability, on the other hand, produce high amounts of SCFA, but may cause undesirable side effects of loose stools, excess gas, or diarrhea.

Maintenance Role of Dietary Fiber in the Healthy Gastrointestinal Tract

There are several ways in which dietary fiber influences the health and functioning of the gastrointestinal tract. These include physical effects, effects of SCFA, and fiber's impact upon intestinal bacteria populations (**Figure 1**). All of these effects are dependent upon the specific type of fiber that is incorporated into the diet.

Physical Effects. A well established effect of dietary fiber is its influence upon the rate of passage of digesta through the intestinal tract. In dogs, moderately fermentable fibers such as beet pulp result in a shorter intestinal transit time.[2] In contrast, diets containing a fiber blend that includes nonfermentable fiber such as cellulose have longer transit times. These results are important to companion animal nutritionists because they do not support the commonly held belief that insoluble or nonfermentable fiber invariably results in increased rates of passage. A related theory about fiber is that its inclusion in a diet causes increased feelings of satiety and decreased intake of calories. This effect is presumed to be due to the physical bulk of fiber and its diluting effect on caloric density. However, studies of dogs that were fed diets with increasing levels of beet pulp found that dogs compensated for the dilution of calories by increasing intake of dry matter. As a result, they maintained a relatively constant caloric intake.[5,6]

The type and amount of fiber can significantly affect a diet's digestibility. This may reflect the influence that fiber has upon transit time as well as the ability of certain types of fiber to sequester nutrients and affect contact with intestinal enzymes or with the absorptive surface of the intestine. For example, recent studies of the use of soy oligosaccharides in pet foods found that diets containing the least amount of soy oligosaccharides had improved apparent nutrient digestibility.[7] In addition, fermentable fibers may alter the amount of nitrogen that appears in the feces by promoting intestinal bacterial growth and the subsequent excretion of increased bacterial mass in fecal matter.[8] In general, diets containing moderately fermentable fiber sources maintain nutrient digestibility in dogs and cats, but feeding diets containing high levels of highly fermentable fiber sources may negatively impact nutrient and dry matter digestibilities.[9]

Stool quality can be significantly affected by dietary fiber. The production of liquid feces, diarrhea, or constipation are all undesirable in companion animals.

Gregory D. Sunvold

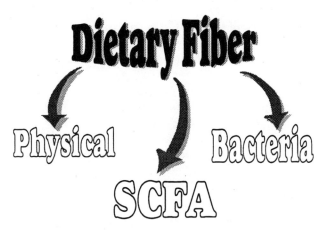

Figure 1. Physiological effects of dietary fiber.

Optimal stool quality is defined as feces that are of an adequate firmness to prevent
diarrhea, but soft enough to prevent constipation. These characteristics are usually
found when the feces are approximately 25-35% dry matter (65-75% moisture).
Feeding highly fermentable fibers (pectin, carob bean gum, locust bean gum, and
gum talha) results in liquid, unformed stools and undesirable gas production in dogs
and cats.[2,9] In contrast, fiber sources that are low in fermentability cause decreased
defecation frequency, decreased fecal moisture content, and the production of hard,
dry feces. Inclusion of a moderately fermentable fiber (i.e., beet pulp) in dog and cat
diets results in moist, well-formed stools. These results indicate that moderately
fermentable fibers provide the physical benefits of bulk and tactile stimulation
within the gastrointestinal tract that facilitates the production of well-formed stools.

SCFA Effects. The SCFA that are produced from the fermentation of fiber
provide a number of benefits to the gastrointestinal tract. The enterocytes and
colonocytes of the large intestine are active cells that have a high turnover rate and
rely on SCFA to provide a significant proportion of their energy requirements.
Fermentation of beet pulp by dog and cat fecal microflora results in the production
of a relatively high proportion of butyrate, which is a preferred energy source of
colonocytes.[3,4]

In addition to "feeding the gut", the SCFA produced from the fermentation
of fiber positively influence the histopathology of the intestinal mucosa.[10] Dogs that
were fed diets containing moderately fermentable fiber had increased colon weights,
mucosal surface area, and mucosal hypertrophy compared with dogs fed a diet
containing a nonfermentable fiber source.[10,11,12] This increase appears to be due to a
greater ratio of mucosal surface area to colonic mass and is indicative of increased
absorptive potential. Dogs fed a cellulose-containing diet had smaller or denser
mucosal cells, lower cellular metabolism, and a higher proportion of cells with
cryptitis. Exfoliation, which is representative of increased cell turnover, is seen to
the greatest degree when dogs are fed highly fermentable fibers. Increased mucous
distension was also noted in dogs fed highly fermentable fiber. These data show that

there are disparate effects of fermentable and nonfermentable fiber sources on colonic microstructure and function. Feeding dogs and cats diets containing moderately fermentable fibers avoids these extreme effects.

The SCFA produced from fiber fermentation are also important for maintaining normal absorptive function of the intestine. An early study showed that sodium and SCFA absorption in the colon of dogs accounted for virtually all osmotic absorption of water.[13] Other effects of SCFA include the enhancement of gut motility and influences on the growth of certain types of intestinal microbes (see following discussion).[14,15]

Intestinal Bacteria Effects. Dietary fiber has the potential to modify the number and the species of bacteria that are present in the intestinal tract. The intestines of dogs and cats contain several genera and species of aerobic and anaerobic bacteria.[16,17,18] Typically, these bacteria are categorized into beneficial and harmful/pathogenic species. Beneficial bacteria inhibit the proliferation of harmful species, stimulate immune function, aid in digestion or absorption of food, and synthesize vitamins. Pathogenic species of bacteria may cause harm to the host animal by producing toxins, carcinogens or putrefactive compounds.[19] It has been demonstrated that the source of fiber that a dog is fed directly influences the composition of intestinal bacteria populations or the enzymatic activity of existing populations.[3]

Fructooligosaccharides (FOS) are naturally occurring carbohydrates that are not digested by the enzymes of the gastrointestinal tract, but may be metabolized by bacterial species. For this reason, they are classified with dietary fiber. Species of bacteria differ in their ability to use FOS as an energy source, and intestinal bacterial populations are affected by the presence of these compounds. Studies of humans that were fed diets containing FOS have shown that FOS is fermented minimally in the small intestine, but undergoes almost complete fermentation in the colon.[20,21] In dogs, fecal bacteria are capable of fermenting FOS and a related novel fiber, lactulose, to a greater degree than the nonfermentable fiber, cellulose.[2,9] Eating a diet containing FOS or related types of fibers significantly increases the number of beneficial bacteria in the colon of dogs and humans.[22-25] In humans, the promotion of beneficial bacterial populations has resulted in decreased intestinal illness and suppressed the growth of harmful bacteria. Similarly, feeding diets containing FOS decreases intestinal infections with *Salmonella*, *Clostridium difficile* or *Escherichia coli* in chickens, hamsters and piglets.[26,27] These studies indicate that FOS can be used as a dietary component that promotes a healthy intestinal environment by maintaining optimal populations of beneficial microflora and decreasing populations of harmful bacteria.

Immune Function and Cellular Growth. There is recent evidence that feeding fermentable fiber may improve immune functioning of the intestinal mucosa.[28] Specifically, incorporation of fermentable fiber into the diet of dogs for 14 days favorably altered the proportion of T cells in gut-associated lymphoid tissue and increased T cell mitogen responses. There is additional evidence that the consumption of fermentable fibers such as FOS result in increased colonic blood flow and may reduce the incidence of colonic neoplastic growth.[29]

In dogs and cats, intestinal disease typically is manifested as acute or chronic diarrhea, constipation, vomiting, and associated behavioral changes. Several common intestinal disorders in companion animals include small intestinal bacteria overgrowth (SIBO), pathogen overgrowth, and inflammatory disorders. New knowledge about the benefits of dietary fiber to the intestinal tract and the various ways in which fiber manifests these effects have led to the use of certain types of fiber in the treatment of intestinal disease.

Diarrhea. Because the type of fiber in the diet influences the amount of water that is retained in feces, modifying dietary fiber is often an effective means of treating or managing diarrhea in dogs and cats. Feeding moderately fermentable fibers such as beet pulp and rice bran result in stools that have optimal form and consistency, but which still contain a relatively high amount of moisture (65% or greater).[2,9] In contrast, poorly fermented fiber sources such as cellulose result in low water content in feces and the production of dry and hard stools. Excessive amounts of highly fermentable fibers are contraindicated for use in animals with diarrhea because of their tendency to produce loose stools or diarrhea. An added problem with the use of highly fermentable fibers is that they do not provide appreciable bulk to the intestine and have been shown to contribute to mucous distension and epithelial exfoliation in the colon.[10]

Inflammatory Bowel Disease and Colitis. The inflammatory diseases that involve the bowel in dogs are referred to collectively as inflammatory bowel disease (IBD). These are generally named for the type of inflammatory cell that predominates in the intestinal mucosa, the area of the intestine that is affected, or the underlying cause, if it is known. Colitis is a general term for a condition that describes irritation or inflammation of the large intestine.

There is evidence suggesting that chronic intestinal disorders such as inflammatory bowel disease and ulcerative colitis may be influenced by fermentable fiber and SCFA status in the intestine. The provision of specific bowel nutrients, including SCFA, has been shown to protect intestinal tissue and promote restoration of normal intestinal function in several animal models. For example, a study with humans found that ulcerative colitis is characterized by diminished rates of oxidation of the SCFA butyrate in the large intestine, and that providing a supplemental source of butyrate to the colon results in a reduction in inflammation.[30,31] Nutritional intervention that promotes mucosal growth, provides energy substrates for enterocytes, and minimizes cryptitis and mucous distension may be of benefit to dogs and cats that are diagnosed with inflammatory intestinal disorders. Fibers that are demonstrated to have moderate fermentability in the canine and feline intestinal tract can provide the gut with adequate amounts of SCFA needed for recovery.

Therefore, types of dietary fiber that yield a high concentration of butyrate may have beneficial effects for diseases of the large intestine.

Small Intestinal Bacterial Overgrowth. Small intestinal bacterial overgrowth (SIBO) is a relatively common and clinically important cause of small intestinal disease in dogs. It is seen in greater prevalence in German Shepherd Dogs and there is evidence that an inherited IgA-deficiency may be involved in this breed.[32] Typical signs include chronic, intermittent diarrhea for which an underlying cause cannot be determined.[33] Diagnosis of SIBO is typically based upon culturing >10^5 total or >10^4 anaerobic colony-forming units (CFU) of bacteria per ml of duodenal juice obtained endoscopically in fasted dogs.[33] Coliforms, staphylococci, enterococci, clostridium and bacteroides are reported to be the most predominant species of bacteria in dogs diagnosed with SIBO.[33] Asymptomatic SIBO has also been reported in cats.[34]

Current treatment of SIBO involves removing the cause, if it is known, and/or antibiotic therapy. While antibiotics are often utilized in the treatment and management of SIBO, there is a risk of indiscriminately killing both pathogenic and beneficial bacteria. The resulting "ecological void" favors proliferation of opportunistic pathogens that are resistant to the antibiotic. In addition, maintaining populations of beneficial bacteria in the intestine appear to be important for improving nutrient availability and immune function, and preventing the overgrowth of harmful bacterial populations.

Clinical trials designed to test the efficacy of FOS-containing diets in treating SIBO in dogs found that when dogs with SIBO were fed a diet containing 1% FOS for a period of 45 days, intestinal fluid and mucosal samples had significantly fewer aerobic/facultative anaerobic bacterial CFU, compared with those of a control group.[35] These results indicate that the incorporation of FOS into diets for animals with SIBO may be efficacious in promoting the growth of desirable bacterial populations and inhibiting the growth of pathogenic bacterial populations.

Pathogen Overgrowth and Taurine Utilization. The effect of FOS supplementation on taurine status in cats has been evaluated recently.[37] Results indicated that taurine synthesis and degradation were increased with no change in whole-body taurine balance or whole-blood taurine concentration in domestic short-hair cats fed a commercial canned food. Researchers indicated no intestinally-related disease in these cats.

Intestinal disease in cats may result in pathogen overgrowth that may manifest itself as a single problem or occur as a component of several forms of intestinal disease. Two important pathogens in companion animal medicine are Clostridium perfringens and Escherichia coli.[38,39] The ability of these pathogens to utilize taurine has been recently investigated and may be an important consideration when treating feline intestinal disease.[40] Results indicate that certain beneficial intestinal bacteria, such as lactobacilli, cannot utilize taurine or taurocholic acids, while some harmful bacteria, such as salmonella, are capable of utilizing these compounds. The metabolism of taurine and taurocholic acid by intestinal bacteria renders it unavailable to the host animal. Since diets containing FOS promote the intestinal proliferation of beneficial bacteria (e.g., lactobacilli) and decrease the growth of harmful bacteria such as *Clostridium perfringens*, taurine status during pathogen overgrowth may actually improve with FOS supplementation.[35,36] Another way in which FOS may be effective against pathogenic bacteria is through the production of certain fermentation end-products. Use of the *in vitro* fermentation technique has indicated that FOS produces a significant amount of lactate, whereas most other fiber sources do not (Sunvold and Reinhart, unpublished results). These results are intriguing in light of results published by Hinton and Hume.[15] These researchers evaluated the growth of *Salmonella typhimurium* in culture media. When acetate, propionate or butyrate was added to the media containing *S. typhimurium*, growth of the bacteria was not inhibited. However, when acetate, propionate or butyrate was added in combination with lactate to the media containing *S. typhimurium*, growth of this pathogen was virtually eliminated. It can be implied from these data that providing a dietary source of FOS may be helpful in promoting a healthy intestinal environment and improving taurine availability and utilization in cats.

Carbohydrate Source and Intestinal Disease

A related component to dietary fiber, carbohydrate, may also be an important factor to consider in the treatment of intestinal disease. Animals with intestinal disease may digest and assimilate carbohydrate less efficiently than healthy animals. This may be due to increased rate of gastric emptying, reduced secretion of intestinal enzymes, changes in the absorptive capacity of the gut, or overgrowth of bacterial populations in portions of the small intestine. For example, dogs with exocrine pancreatic insufficiency (EPI) have a decreased ability to digest carbohydrate due to deficiency of the pancreatic enzyme, amylase.[40] In other types of disease such as SIBO, protein-losing enteropathy, and IBD, changes to the intestinal brush border cause impaired digestion of starch and oligosaccharides and compromised absorption of monosaccharides.[42] Abnormal digestion of starch in the small intestine allows it to be available for fermentation in the large intestine. Large intestinal fermentation of undigested starch is undesirable as it can disrupt normal fermentation patterns.

Starch is the principle form of carbohydrate that is included in commercial dog foods. The digestibility of starch is influenced by its botanical source, the physical size and form of the starch granules, effects of food processing (for example gelatinization), and the presence of other interfering or enhancing dietary components. Recent studies have shown that different carbohydrate sources produce variable amounts and types of fermentation gas when exposed to intestinal microbes.[43,44] *In vitro* fermentation studies with canine fecal flora have shown that there are marked differences between the amount and rate of hydrogen gas that is produced from the fermentation of wheat, potato, corn or rice starch.[45]

The type of starch that is included in dog foods may have important implications for dogs with intestinal disease. Breath hydrogen studies can be used to test the degree of malabsorption of dietary carbohydrate because hydrogen gas that is expelled in the breath is derived primarily from the microbial fermentation of carbohydrates in the colon. Therefore, the amount of hydrogen exhaled is a reflection of the amount of dietary carbohydrate that escapes digestion in the small intestine and travels to the large intestine where it is fermented.[46] When dogs with EPI or mild IBD were fed diets containing different carbohydrate sources, the dogs with EPI had a greater degree of carbohydrate malabsorption than those diagnosed with IBD, based upon post-prandial breath hydrogen concentrations.[45] Differences in malabsorption between carbohydrate sources were not detectable using breath hydrogen tests because of large variability between individual dogs. These data indicate that dogs with intestinal disease have varying capacities to digest and assimilate specific carbohydrate sources. It may be important for clinicians to observe a dog's response to a carbohydrate source when treating intestinal disease and to change to an alternate source if the dog does not respond well to a particular type of starch.

In addition to the type of carbohydrate that is fed, the size of the starch granules, commonly called the grind size, may also be important. Dogs that were fed cooked whole or blended (ground in food processor) rice digested and absorbed blended rice more completely than whole rice, as determined by breath hydrogen concentration.[47] This difference is probably attributable to reduced food particle size or structural damage to the starch granules as a result of blending. Light microscopy showed that the blended rice had a decreased proportion of intact starch granules and an increased proportion of exuded starch compared with the whole rice. The smaller particles are believed to be more accessible to intestinal enzymes and more rapidly hydrolyzed and assimilated in the small intestine. These results are in agreement with studies of the effect of grain size on starch digestion in humans.[48,49,50]

In contrast to the results with rice, cooked chopped (kernels cut in half) or blended (ground in food processor) corn were assimilated to the same degree when fed to dogs.[47] Because cooked corn is a carbohydrate that is already highly digestible to dogs, it is likely that the effect of particle size and mechanical disruption may not be an important consideration. Light microscopy showed that the blended and chopped corn meals contained similar proportions of intact granules and exuded (i.e., dispersed) starch, indicating that cooking alone causes sufficient starch disruption. Because breath hydrogen levels rose at a faster rate in dogs fed blended corn compared with those fed chopped corn, blended corn may have either a faster rate of passage or faster fermentability than chopped corn. The findings that particle size of rice affects assimilation, and that particle size of corn affects gastrointestinal time or degree of fermentation indicate that the source and form of carbohydrate should be considered when formulating diets for dogs with intestinal disease.

In addition to effects upon gastrointestinal health, dietary fiber may also be an important nutrient to consider when formulating diets for geriatric dogs and cats, and for pets with various diseases and/or conditions (***Figure 2***). The number and incidence of intestinal bacterial species changes with advancing age in many species. In humans, the number of bifidobacteria decrease with advancing age, while numbers of *Clostridium perfringens*, enterobacteria, streptococci, and lactobacilli increase.[51] Similar changes have been reported in elderly dogs.[52] While there were no significant differences between microbial populations of the stomach, duodenum, jejunum or ileum of young and old dogs, the bacteria found in the large intestines of elderly dogs had significantly different microflora populations. Elderly dogs had lower numbers of bacteroides, eubacteria, peptostreptococci, bifidobacteria, lactobacilli and staphylococci, and higher numbers of *Clostridium perfringens* and streptococci than young dogs. Modifying dietary fiber with advancing age may be helpful in maintaining beneficial populations of intestinal bacteria such as bifidobacteria and lactobacilli and inhibiting growth of harmful populations such as *Clostridium perfringens*. Further studies that examine the effects of different fibers on bacterial populations in older dogs are warranted.

Other Potential Applications of Fiber Technology

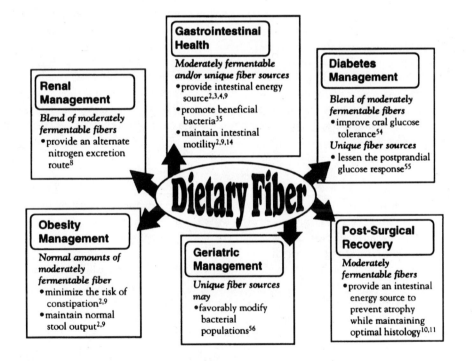

Figure 2. The role of dietary fiber on various diseases and life conditions.

Dietary fiber may also be helpful in the management of other diseases and conditions. Studies using rat models have shown that the provision of a blend of fibers that include FOS as the prominent type of fiber caused reductions in plasma urea and maximized gut nitrogen excretion concentration when added to a reduced protein diet.[53] These results may have implications for the use of dietary fibers in the clinical management of dogs with chronic renal disease. Another recent study examined the effects of fermentable and nonfermentable fibers on glucose tolerance in healthy adult dogs.[54] The results of oral glucose tolerance tests conducted 2 weeks after the introduction of the diets showed that dogs consuming diets containing fermentable fiber had significantly lower glucose response curves compared to dogs fed diets that contain nonfermentable fiber. Results reported elsewhere in this proceedings (see chapter by Nelson and Sunvold) indicate that a viscous fiber source may be important in slowing the postprandial glucose response to a meal.[55] These results provide preliminary evidence for the use of certain types of fiber in the dietary management of diabetes. Research with dogs and cats has demonstrated that a moderately fermentable fiber source, beet pulp, results in a moisturizing effect on the feces without excessive fecal output.[2,9] Therefore, weight loss diets formulated with normal amounts of beet pulp can help prevent constipation and excessive fecal output associated with many weight loss products containing excessive amounts of nonfermentable fibers (e.g., cellulose, peanut hulls) and thereby help maintain owner compliance. Research on dogs fed diets with or without a source of fermentable fiber has indicated that intestinal weights are increased and optional intestinal histology is achieved when the moderately fermentable fiber beet pulp is consumed.[10,11] Therefore, feeding a source of moderately fermentable fiber before and after surgery can help maintain a source of energy to intestinal cells and thus lessen the associated gut atrophy. Fructooligosaccharides may be a useful fiber source in favorably modifying the population of gut intestinal bacteria in geriatric dogs (see chapter by Kearns et al.).[56]

Summary   Given the diverse physiological effects of different fibers, the formulation of diets for healthy dogs and cats and for animals with intestinal disease must incorporate appropriate levels and sources of this nutrient. Feeding moderately fermentable fiber to healthy animals provides physical benefits, SCFA benefits, and can positively influence intestinal microbial populations. Both beet pulp and rice bran are appropriate for inclusion in diets for dogs and cats. Because different fiber sources and the SCFA patterns that they produce have varied effects on the host animal, the selection of appropriate fibers is important for the treatment of intestinal disease. The nutritional objective in choosing dietary fibers should be to select those that predispose the colonization of beneficial indigenous microflora and promote sufficient SCFA production for intestinal epithelial recovery. The source and form of carbohydrate that is included in the diet may be of equal importance for animals with intestinal disease.

Recent evidence indicates that dietary fiber may have uses beyond its normal role of maintaining intestinal health. Specifically, certain dietary fibers may be a useful tool in managing various diseases (e.g., diabetes, renal disease) or life conditions (e.g., geriatric animals).

The authors gratefully acknowledge Linda P. Case, MS for assistance in technical writing of this manuscript.

Acknowledgements

References

1. Brown DH. Applications of fructooligosaccharides in human foods. In: Carey DP, Norton SA, Bolser SM eds. *Recent Advances in Canine and Feline Nutritional Research: Proceedings of the Iams International Nutrition Symposium*, Wilmington: Orange Frazer Press, 1996; 41-44.

2. Sunvold GD, Fahey Jr GC, Merchen NR, Titgemeyer EC, Bourquin LD, Bauer LL, Reinhart GA. Dietary fiber for dogs: IV. *In vitro* fermentation of selected fiber sources by dog fecal inoculum and *in vivo* digestion and metabolism of fiber-supplemented diets. *J Anim Sci* 1995; 73:1099-1119.

3. Sunvold GD, Fahey Jr GC, Merchen NR, Reinhart GA. *In vitro* fermentation of selected fibrous substrates by dog and cat fecal inoculum: Influence of diet composition on substrate organic matter disappearance and short-chain fatty acid production. *J Anim Sci* 1995; 73:1110-1122.

4. Sunvold GD, Hussein HS, Fahey Jr GC, Merchen NR, Reinhart GA. *In vitro* fermentation of Solca Floc®, beet pulp, citrus pulp, and citrus pectin using fecal inoculum from cats, dogs, horses, humans, and pigs and ruminal fluid from cattle. *J Anim Sci* 1995; 73:3639-3648.

5. Fahey Jr GC, Merchen NR, Corbin JE, Hamilton AK, Serbe KA, Lewis SM, Hirakawa DA. Dietary fiber for dogs: I.Effects of graded levels of dietary beet pulp on nutrient intake, digestibility, metabolizable energy and digesta mean retention time. *J Anim Sci* 1990; 68:4221-4228.

6. Fahey Jr GC, Merchen NR, Corbin JE, Hamilton AK, Serbe KA, Hirakawa DA. Dietary fiber for dogs: II. Iso-total dietary fiber (TDF) additions of divergent fiber sources to dog diets and their effects on nutrient intake, digestibility, metabolizable energy and digesta mean retention time. *J Anim Sci* 1990; 68:4229-4235.

7. Wiernusz CJ, Shields Jr RG, Van Vilerbergen DJ, Kigin PD, Ballard R. Canine nutrient digestibility and stool quality evaluation of canned diets containing various soy protein supplements. *Vet Clin Nutr* 1995; 2:49-56.

8. Howard MD, Sunvold GD, Reinhart GA, Kerley MS. Effect of fermentable fiber consumption by the dog on nitrogen balance and fecal microbial nitrogen excretion. *FASEB J* 1996; 10:A257.

9. Sunvold GD, Fahey Jr GC, Merchen NR, Bourquin LD, Titgemeyer EC, Bauer LL, Reinhart GA. Dietary fiber for cats: *In vitro* fermentation of selected fiber sources by cat fecal inoculum and *in vivo* utilization of diets containing selected fiber sources and their blends. *J Anim Sci* 1995; 73:2329-2339.

10. Hallman JE, Moxley RA, Reinhart GA, Wallace GA, Clemens ET. Cellulose, beet pulp, and pectin/gum arabic effects on canine microstructure and histopathology. *Vet Clin Nutr* 1995; 2:137-142.

11. Hallman JE, Reinhart GA, Wallace EA, Milliken A, Clemens ET. Colonic mucosal tissue energetics and electrolyte transport in dogs fed cellulose, beet pulp or pectin/gum arabic as their primary fiber source. *Nutr Res* 1996; 16:303-313.

12. Clemens ET. Dietary fiber and colonic morphology. In: Carey DP, Norton SA, Bolser SM, eds. *Recent Advances in Canine and Feline Nutritional Research: Proceedings of the 1996 Iams International Nutrition Symposium*. Wilmington: Orange Frazer Press, 1996; 25-32.

13. Herschel DA, Agrenzio RA, Southworth M, Stevens CE. Absorption of volatile fatty acid, Na, and H_2O by the colon of the dog. *Amer J Vet Res* 1981; 42:1118-1124.

14. Kamath PS, Hoepfner MT, Philips SF. Short-chain fatty acids stimulate motility of the canine ileum. *Amer J Physiol* 1987; 253:G427.

15. Hinton Jr A, Hume ME. Synergism of lactate and succinate as metabolites utilized by Veillonella to inhibit the growth of *Salmonella typhimurium* and *Salmonella eteriitidis in vitro*. *Avian Dis* 1995; 39:309-316.

16. Terada A, Hara H, Kato S, Kimura T, Fujimori I, Hara K, Maruyama T, Mitsuoka T. Effects of lactosucrose (4-beta-D-galactosylsucrose) on fecal flora and fecal putrefactive product of cats. *J Vet Med Sci* 1993; 55:291-295.

17. Terada A, Tara H, Oishi T, Matsui S, Mitsuoka T, Nakajyo S, Fujimori I, Hara K. Effect of dietary lactosucrose on faecal flora and faecal metabolites of dogs. *Microb Ecol Health Dis* 1992; 5:87-92.

18. Balish E, Cleven D, Brown J, Yale CE. Nose, throat, and fecal flora of beagle dogs housed in locked or open environments. *Appl Environ Micro* 1977; 34:207.

19. Gibson GR, Roberfroid MB. Dietary modulation of the human colonic microbiota: Introducing the concept of prebiotics. *J Nutr* 1995; 125:1401.

20. Alles MS, Hautvast JGA, Nagengast FM, Hartemink R. Fate of fructooligosaccharides in the human intestine. *Br J Nutr* 1996; 76:211-221.

21. Molis C, Flourie B, Ouarne F, Gailing MF. Digestion, excretion, and energy value of fructooligosaccharides in healthy humans. *Am J Clin Nutr* 1996; 64:324-328.

22. Williams CH, Witherely SA, Buddington RK. Influence of dietary neosugar on selected bacterial groups of the human faecal microbiota. *Microbial Ecol Health Dis* 1994; 7:91.

23. Mitsuoka T, Hidaka H, Eida T. Effect of fructooligosaccharides on intestinal microflora. *Die Nahrung* 1987; 31:927.

24. Okazaki M, Fujikawa S, Matumoto N. Effect of xylooligosaccharide on the growth of bifidobacteria. *Bifidobact Microflora* 1990; 9:77.

25. Ogata M. Use of neosugar in pets. *Proc 3rd Neosugar Conf* Tokyo, Japan 1986; 1-16.

26. Bailey JS, Blankenship LC, Cox NA. Effect of fructooligosaccharide on Salmonella colonization of the chicken intestine. *Poult Sci* 1991; 70:2433-2438.

27. Kerley MS, Sunvold GS. Physiological response to short chain fatty acid production in the intestine. In: Carey DP, Norton SA, Bolser SM, eds. *Recent Advances in Canine and Feline Nutritional Research: Proceedings of the 1996 Iams International Nutrition Symposium*. Wilmington: Orange Frazer Press, 1996; 33-39.

28. Field CJ, Goruk S, McBurney MI, Hayek MG, Sunvold GD. Feeding fermentable fiber alters the function and composition of gut associated lymphoid

tissue (GALT). *FASEB J* 1997; 11:A650.

29. Howard MD, Kerley MS, Mann FA, Sunvold GD, Reinhart GA. Dietary fiber sources alter colonic blood flow and epithelial cell proliferation of dogs. *J Anim Sci* 1997; 75(suppl):170.

30. Chapman MAS, Grahn MF, Boyle MA, Hutton M, Rogers J, Williams NS. Butyrate oxidation is impaired in the colonic mucosa of suffers of quiescent ulcerative colitis. *Gut* 1994; 35:73.

31. Scheppach WH, Sommer T, Kirchner GM, Paglanelli P, Bartman S, Christl F, Richter G, Dasel G, Kasper H. Effect of butyrate enemas on the colonic mucosa in distal ulcerative colitis. *Gastroent* 1992; 103:51-56.

32. Willard MD, Simpson RB, Fossum TW, Cohen ND, Delles EK, Kolp D, Carey DP, Reinhart GA. Characterization of naturally developing small intestinal bacterial overgrowth in 16 German shepherd dogs. *JAVMA* 1994; 204:1201-1206.

33. Rutgers HC, Batt RM, Elwood CM, Lamport A. Small intestinal bacterial overgrowth in dogs with chronic intestinal disease. *J Am Vet Med Assoc* 1995; 206:187-193.

34. Johnston K, Lamport A, Batt RM. An unexpected bacterial flora in the proximal small intestine of normal cats. *Vet Rec* 1993; 132: 362-363.

35. Willard MD, Simpson RB, Delles EK, Cohen ND, Fossum TW, Kolp D, Reinhart G. Effects of dietary supplementation of fructo-oligosaccharides on small intestinal bacterial overgrowth in dogs. *Am J Vet Res* 1994; 55:654-659.

36. Sparkes AH, Papsouliotis K, Sunvold G, Werrett G, Gruffydd-Jones EA, Eagn K, Gruffydd-Jones TJ, Reinhart G. The effect of dietary supplementation with fructo-oligosaccharides on the faecal flora of healthy cats. *Am J Vet Res* 1998; 59:(In press).

37. Ballèvre O, Johnston KL, Batt RM. Role of gut flora in cat taurine metabolism: A stable isotope approach. *Proc 7th ESVIM*; Lyon, France. Sept. 11-13, 1997; 171.

38. Twedt DC. Clostridium perfringens associated diarrhea in dogs. *Proc ACVIM* 1993; 11:121-125.

39. Batt RM, Rutgers HC, Sancak AA. Enteric bacteria: Friend or foe? *J Small Anim Pract* 1996; 37:261-267.

40. Kearns RJ, Sunvold GD. Microbial degradation of taurine and taurocholic acid. *Proc ACVIM* 1996; 14:774.

41. Hill FWG. Malabsorption syndrome in the dog: A study of 38 cases. *J Small Anim Pract* 1972; 13:575-594.

42. Williams DA. Malabsorption, small intestinal bacterial overgrowth, and protein-losing enteropathy. In: Guilford WG, Center SA, Strombeck DR, Williams DA, Myer DJ eds. *Strombeck's Small Animal Gastroenterology*, Philadelphia: WB Saunders, 1996; 367-380.

43. Christl SU, Murgatroyd PR, Gibson GR, Cummings JH. Production, metabolism, and excretion of hyrdogen in the large intestine. *Gastroent* 1990; 102:1269-1277.

44. Grubler B, Ingwersen M, Meyer H, Schunemann C. *In vitro* investigations on gas formation from ileum and colon chyme in dogs. In: *Nutrition, Malnutrition and Dietetics in the Dog and Cat*. 1990; 34-36.

45. Bissett SA. A comparison of wheat, potato, corn and rice assimilation in dogs with diarrhoea using breath hydrogen tests. M.S. Thesis, 1997; Massey University, New Zealand.

46. Levitt MD, Donaldson RM. Use of respiratory hyrdogen (H_2) excretion to detect carbohydrate malabsorption. *J Lab Clin Med* 1970; 75:937-945.

47. Bissett SA, Guilford WG, Lawoko CR, Sunvold GD. Effect of food particle size on carbohydrate assimilation assessed by breath hydrogen testing in dogs. *Vet Clin Nutr* 1997; 4:82-88.

48. Snow P, O'Dea K. Factors affecting the rate of hydrolysis of starch in food. *Am J Clin Nutr* 1981; 34:2721-2727.

49. O'Dea K, Snow P, Nestel P. Rate of starch hydrolysis *in vitro* as a predictor of metabolic responses to complex carbohydrates *in vivo*. *Am J Clin Nutr* 1982; 34:1991-1993.

50. Levitt MD, Hirsh P, Fetzer CA. H_2 excretion after ingestion of complex carbohydrates. *Gastroent* 1987; 92:383-389.

51. Benno Y, Mitsuoka T. Effect of diet and aging on human fecal microflora. *Bifidobacteria Microflora* 1991; 10:89-96.

52. Benno Y, Nakao H, Uchida K, Mitsuoka T. Impact of the advances in age on the gastrointestinal microflora of beagle dogs. *J Vet Med Sci* 1992; 54:703-706.

53. Younes H, Demigne C, Behr SR, Garleb KA, Remesy C. Dietary fiber decreases urinary nitrogen excretion and blood urea in rats fed a low protein diet. *FASEB J* 1996; 10:A257.

54. Massimino SP, Field CJ, McBurney MI, Sunvold GD, Hayek MG. Fermentable dietary fiber improves glucose tolerance but not immune function in dogs. *FASEB J* 1997; 11:A650.

55. Nelson RW, Sunvold GD. Effect of carboxymethylcellulose on postprandial glycemic response in healthy dogs. Reinhart GA, Carey DP, eds. *Recent Advances in Canine and Feline Nutrition, Vol. II: 1998 Iams Nutrition Symposium Proceedings*, Wilmington: Orange Frazer Press, 1998; 97-102.

56. Kearns RJ, Hayek MG, Sunvold GD. Microbial changes in aged dogs. Reinhart GA, Carey DP, eds. *Recent Advances in Canine and Feline Nutrition, Vol. II: 1998 Iams Nutrition Symposium Proceedings*, Wilmington: Orange Frazer Press, 1998; 337-352.

Immunology

Interaction Between Nutrition and Immune Response: Implications for Canine and Feline Health

Michael G. Hayek, PhD
Research Nutritionist, Research and Development
The Iams Company, Lewisburg, Ohio, USA

The interaction between nutrition and the immune response has been an area of intensive research over the past three decades. In the late 1950's Schimshaw[1] first suggested the existence of a bi-directional interaction among nutrition, immune response and infectious disease. Subsequently, it was recognized that malnourished individuals were at increased risk for infection.[2] Recently, studies have demonstrated that deficiencies of most micronutrients result in impaired host defense.[3-6] On the other hand, others have demonstrated that supplementation of certain nutrients beyond accepted requirements may improve certain indices of the immune response. This raises the possibility of designing specific nutritional interventions for improvement of immune function and overall health in companion animals.

Introduction

The immune system is an interactive network of cells, proteins, and signaling agents designed to provide protection to the host from environmental pathogens, parasites, malignant cells, allergens, and toxins (**Figure 1**).[7] The immune system can be divided into two interactive parts: innate or antigen-nonspecific and adaptive or antigen-specific.[8,9] The innate component of the immune system includes protective barriers such as the skin, gastrointestinal tract, and lung as well as humoral components such as lysozyme, complement system, and phagocytic cells.[9-11] The innate system is considered to be the first line of defense for the host.

Immune System Overview

Adaptive immunity can be further divided into cell mediated and humoral immunity. Humoral immunity includes the production of antibodies or immunoglobulins from B cells. There are five different immunoglobulin isotypes (IgG, IgA, IgM, IgD, and IgE) consisting of different subclasses within these isotypes. These antibodies can work in concert with the complement system to rid the body of invading antigens.[7,12]

The cellular portion of the immune system includes the interaction of bone marrow derived macrophages and B cells as well as thymus derived T cells. T cells can be further divided into subsets based on cell surface protein expression.[10-12] These subsets include the CD4+ or T helper (Th) cells and the CD8+ or T cytotoxic/suppresser cells. T helper can be further classified based on the cytokines that they produce. T helper 1 (Th1) cells secrete Interleukin (IL)-2 and are important in

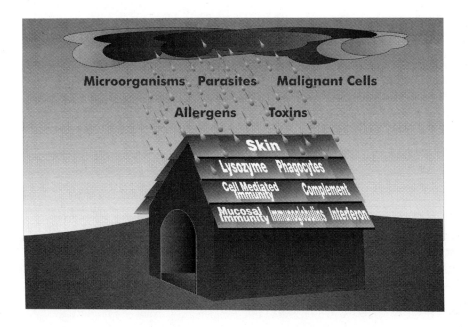

Figure 1. Protective compartments of the immune system. Adapted from Chandra, 1983.[7]

bacterial responses while T helper 2 (Th2) cells secrete IL-4, Interferon (INF)-γ and are important in parasite infections.[13] CD8+ cells may either play a role as a killer cell that will assist in a response to a viral antigen or may play a suppresser role with B cells to regulate the immune response. Another set of cells that do not contain either CD4+ or CD8+ makers but play an important role is the Natural Killer Cells (NK cells). NK cells can help rid the host of tumor cells in the body. A summary of these cells and functions is presented in *Table 1*.

Cells of the immune system utilize hormone-like substances to communicate intracellularly. These protein mediators have been classified by different names based upon their cellular origin. Lymphocyte derived mediators that are capable of

Table 1. Cells of the immune system.

Cell Type	Function
Macrophage	Phagocytosis and antigen presentation to T cells
B cells	Antibody production
T helper 1 cells (CD4+)	Activation of B cells (bacterial response)
T helper 2 cells (CD4+)	Activation of B cells (parasite response)
T cytotoxic/suppresser cells (CD8+)	Regulation of CMI, viral clearance
Natural Killer Cells	Attack tumor or virus containing cell

regulating growth and mobility of leukocytes were collectively called lymphokines.[14] It was then discovered that nonlymphoid cells can also produce these lymphokines, thus the name cytokine was suggested.[15] Another name used to describe most mediators is interleukins, a term that refers to their basic property of serving as communication vehicles between different leukocytes.[16] The major cytokines, cells of origin and functions are listed in *Table 2*.

Table 2. Major cytokines involved in immune regulation.

Cytokine	Source	Function
Interleukin-1	Macrophages	Proinflammation, stimulate production of prostaglandins and other cytokines.
Interleukin-2	Th cells	T cell and B cell growth, activates NK cells and lymphokine activated killer (LAK) cells.
Interleukin-3	T cells	Colony stimulating factor for hemopoietic cells.
Interleukin-4	Th cells; mast cells	B cell and T cell growth factor; stimulate IgE production
Interleukin-5	Th cells and mast cells	B cell and eosinophil growth differentiation factor
Interleukin-6	Endothelial cells; fibroblasts; macrophages; T cells	B cell differentiation factor; stimulates acute phase protein production from hepatocytes
Interleukin-7	Bone marrow stromal cells	Stem cell differentiation to B cells
Interleukin-8	Macrophages and endothelial cells	T cell and neutrophil chemotactic factor
Interleukin-9	T cells	T cell growth factor
Interleukin-10	Th 2 cells	Cytokine synthesis inhibitory factor
Interleukin-11	Bone marrow cells	Hematopoetic factor; B cell growth factor
Interleukin-12	T cells	T cell; NK cells and LAK cell activation
Interleukin-13	Activated T cells	Inhibits inflammatory cytokine production
Interleukin-14	Dendritic cells; T cells and B cells	Enhance proliferation of B cells
Interleukin-15	T cells; monocytes	Enhances T cell proliferation
Interferon-α	Macrophages and B cells	Prevent viral replication, stimulate NK cells, induce MHC class I cells
Interferon-β	Fibroblasts	Prevent viral replication
Interferon-γ	T cells, NK cells	Prevent viral replication, activate monocytes, increase expression MHC class I and II
Tumor necrosis factor-α	Macrophages, T,B and NK cells	Mediate inflammation, wound healing, remodeling of tissue, induce fever
Tumor necrosis factor-β	Actvated lymphocytes	Kill tumor cells, stimulate fibroblast proliferation

A variety of tests have been developed to assess immunological status or function. These include *in vivo* tests such as delayed type hypersensitivity, titer response to vaccine, antibody response to a protein challenge, and circulating lymphocyte concentrations. *In vitro* tests include response of lymphocytes to mitogen compounds, cytokine production, phagocytic function (particle uptake and bacterial killing), natural killer cell activity, and cytotoxic T cell activity. No single test or group of tests are perfect for evaluating immunological assessment. However, a combination of *in vitro* and *in vivo* indices should provide a useful indication of immune status within an individual.

Nutrient Effects on the Immune Response

As mentioned previously, reports have demonstrated that deficiency of most nutrients will result in impaired host defense. A review of the literature on micronutrient deficiencies is beyond the scope of this paper and the reader is referred to the following reviews.[5,6] Several nutrients, when supplemented beyond established requirements, have been shown to positively modulate the immune system (*Tables 3* and *4*). The effect of supplemental β-carotene, lutien, fermentable fiber, and chromium on canine or feline immune response will be reviewed by Chew,[17,18] Field,[19] and Spears,[20] respectively.

Certain physiological or environmental states can weaken particular aspects of the immune system leaving the host at risk for infection (*Figure 2*). It is within these physiological states that nutritional intervention could have great potential. The potential interaction between nutrition and the geriatric patient has been reviewed by Meydani.[21] Two other examples of clinical conditions which could benefit from nutritional intervention include viral infections and critical care patients.

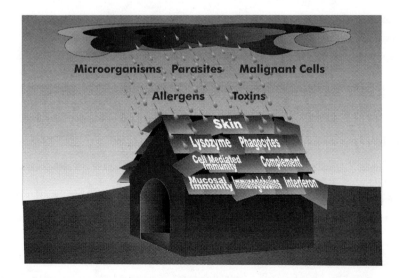

Figure 2. Physiological states that weaken certain aspects of the immune system and place the host in health risk situations. Adapted from Chandra, 1983.[7]

Table 3. Vitamins demonstrated to have immuno-enhancing properties above recognized required intakes.

Vitamin	Species	Effect
Thiamin	Human	Increase neutrophil motility[22]
Vitamin B6	Human	Increase lymphocyte proliferation in elderly subjects[23]
	Human	Maintenance of immune function in the elderly[24]
Vitamin C	Human	Increase neutrophil motility and lymphocyte proliferation[25]
	Human	Increase lymphocyte proliferation and DTH[26]
	Human	Increase lymphocyte proliferation and DTH[27]
	Human	Increase serum IgG, IgM and complement in elderly women[28]
	Human	Reduce severity of viral infections[29,30]
Vitamin E	Rodent	Increase T cell mitogenesis[31]
	Rodent	Increase T helper cell function[32]
	Rodent	Increase B cell mitogenesis[31]
	Rodent	Increase antibody titer[33]
	Rodent	Increase plaque forming cells[31]
	Rodent	Increase IL-2 production[34]
	Rodent	Increase delayed type hypersensitivity[34]
	Rodent	Increase natural killer cell activity[35]
	Rodent	Decrease live influenza pulmonary titers[36]
	Chicken	Increase antibody titer[37]
	Chicken	Increase plaque-forming cells[33]
	Calves	Increase lymphocyte proliferation[38]
	Pigs	Increase lymphocyte proliferation[39]
	Sheep	Increase antibody titer[40]
	Human	Increase polymorphonuclear cell phagocytosis[41]
	Human	Increase T cell mitogenesis[42]
	Human	Increase IL-2 production[42]
	Human	Increase DTH[42]
β-carotene	Rodent	Increase IL-2 recceptor expression[43]
	Rodent	Increase proliferation of cytotoxic T cells[44]
	Cattle	Increase lymphocyte proliferation[45,46]
	Pigs	Increase lymphocyte proliferation[46]
	Human	Increase percent Th, NK, and IL-2R[47]
	Human	Increase NK cell activity[48]
	Human	Increase DTH response[48]
	Human	Increase Th cell number[49]

Table 4. Minerals demonstrated to have immuno-enhancing properties at levels above recognized required intakes.

Mineral	Species	Effect
Zinc	Rodent	Increased T cell and macrophage function resistance to *Candida albicans* and virus infection[50]
	Human	Increased # circulating T cells, DTH, antibody titer response[51]
Selenium	Sheep	Increased T cell mitogen response[52]
	Rodent	Increase NK cell activity[53]
	Rodent	Increase T cell mitogen response[55]
	Rodent	Increased expression of IL-2 receptors[56]
	Human	Increased NK cell activity[54]
Chromium	Cattle	Increase antibody production[57-62]
	Cattle	Increase T cell mitogen response[59,60]

Several lines of evidence suggest that there is an interaction between antioxidant status of the host and viral infection. Experimental infection with influenza in mice has been demonstrated to result in decreasing the concentration of vitamin E, vitamin C, and glutathione.[63] Experimentally infected mice also had higher stimulated lung superoxide production, as well as higher xanthine oxidase activity.[64] Human immunodeficiency virus (HIV) infected individuals also demonstrate changes in tocopherol, ascorbic acid, carotenoids, selenium, and glutathione as well as having elevated hydroperoxides and malondialdehyde in their plasma.[65] Both lines of evidence suggest that the viral infection alters the oxidant/antioxidant balance in the host.

Evidence suggests that these viruses may be more virulent in a proxidant environment. Receptor binding of influenza requires the cleavage of the surface glycoprotein HA0 to the peptide HA1 or HA2 converting the virus from a non-infectious to an infectious form. Cleavage of HA0 glycoprotein requires extracellular proteases that are present in pulmonary surfactant.[66] As a protective mechanism anti-proteases are present to prevent this cleavage, but reactive oxygen species (ROS) are capable of inactivating them. *In vitro* tests have also demonstrated that that oxidative stress increases the replication of HIV.[65]

Utilizing an experimental Coxsackievirus B3 (CV3) model, Beck and coworkers demonstrated an increased viral pathology when the virus was infected in selenium or vitamin E deficient mice compared to nutritionally adequate controls.[67] In subsequent studies this group observed that the non-infectious phenotype of the virus was altered to the infectious phenotype when passed through vitamin E or selenium deficient mice but not altered when passed through nutritionally adequate mice. Taken together this data demonstrates that viral infections alter the antioxidant/oxidant status of the host and that a pro-oxidant environment is favorable for viral infection.

The aging process is associated with a decrease in antioxidant defense status which results in increased free radical formation and lipid peroxidation. This would suggest that the geriatric patient provides an ideal environment for viral infection and antioxidant supplementaion should reduce lung viral titers in infected animals. To test this hypothesis Hayek and coworkers[36] fed young and old mice either 30 or 500 ppm vitamin E. These mice were infected with influenza virus and lung viral titers were measured 0, 5, and 7 days postinfection. Vitamin E supplementation decreased pulmonary live viral titers in both age groups but the decrease was 25-fold in old animals *v* 15-fold in young animals. This suggests that the oxidant status of the animals will influence viral infection outcome.

The critical care/trauma patient provides an excellent crosstalk between nutrient metabolism and immune response. A systemic inflammatory reaction results in the stimulation of the immune system which in turn triggers the production of certain cytokines. Three cytokines that have been demonstrated to be elevated during critical care are IL-1, IL-6 and tumor necrosis factor (TNF)-α.[68]

Recent research efforts have demonstrated that the above mentioned cytokines have an interactive role with the metabolism of mammalian hosts. For instance, both IL-1 and TNF-α have been demonstrated to cause anorexia when injected into laboratory animals.[69-71] Also, IL-1 and TNF-α have been shown to be mediators of fever in laboratory animals.[72] This can affect energy expenditure since injections of recombinant (r)IL-1 and rTNF-α act synergistically to increase resting energy expenditure.[73]

Recent reports have also demonstrated that these cytokines affect metabolism of specific nutrients. Hypoglycemia is induced by injections of rIL-1 and rTNF-α into laboratory rats.[74,75] This is due to increased utilization of glucose in macrophage rich tissues such as spleen, intestine, liver, skin, and kidney as well as increased skeletal muscle glucose uptake and oxidation to lactate.[75] Although the mechanism for increased glucose utilization induced by these cytokines has not been completely delineated, it has been proposed that TNF-α exerts its effect through increased glucose transporters on the cell membrane[76] while IL-1 has been proposed to increase the rate of alanine transport into hepatocytes resulting in increased oxygen consumption and gluconeogenesis from alanine,[77] as well as to attenuate the induction of phosphoenolpyruvate carboxykinase (PEPCK) caused by fasting.[78] In either case, the net result is decreased blood glucose. This hypoglycemia has been demonstrated in the septic dog[79,80] and cat.[81-86]

Hyperlipidemia has also been shown to be induced by TNF-α and IL-1. Mechanisms proposed for this phenomena include inhibition of lipoprotein lipase activity,[85] inhibition of the activities of acetyl CoA carboxylase and fatty acid synthetase,[88] increased hepatic triglyceride synthesis,[89] and increased cholesterol synthesis due to increased 3-hydroxy-3-methylglutaryl (HMG) CoA reductase activity.[91] Protein metabolism is also affected by increased levels of these cytokines. Muscle wasting is often noted in critical care patients thus placing the animal in negative nitrogen balance. The amino acids that are released from the septic patient are utilized for synthesis of acute phase proteins in the liver, oxidized for energy, used as gluconeogenic substrates, and used for protein synthesis in leukocytes to support clonal expansion and secretion of immunoglobulins and regulatory proteins.[91] Both IL-1 and TNF-α have been implicated, causing muscle wasting through protein degradation.[69, 93-95] The IL-1 mechanism may be mediated through increase PGE_2 production[95] while TNF-α may be working in conjunction with other cytokines and hormones.[94]

Lastly, the cytokines increased during sepsis have been demonstrated to affect plasma concentrations of certain minerals. These include increased copper levels due to ceruloplasmin,[69,96] decreased zinc levels due to increased production of metallothionein,[97,98] and decreased iron concentration due to the release of apolactoferrin by granulocytes.[99,100]

The potential exists to modulate cytokine production through nutrition. Several studies have demonstrated that IL-1, IL-6, and TNF-α production can be modulated with fish oil supplementation.[101] However, it should be noted that fish oil supplementation may lead to depression of other indices of cell-mediated immunity.[101-105] In humans it has been demonstrated that the negative effects of fish oil supplementation may be negated by tocopherol supplementation.[103] In primates it has been demonstrated that when proper tocopherol levels are considered, marine oil derived omega-3 fatty acids may actually enhance T cell function, while plant derived n-3's have no effect.[106] Studies examining the n-6:n-3 ratios in dogs have demonstrated that ratios as low as 5:1 have no suppressive effect on neutrophil function or DTH.[107] However, ratios as low as 1.4:1 have been shown to depress DTH in geriatric Beagles.[105] The optimal ratio for modulating cytokine production and not effecting CMI in critical care patients needs to be determined.

Summary   These data demonstrate that certain nutrients have the potential to up-regulate the immune system. In several species this positive interaction can enhance overall health during certain physiological states. Further research is needed to define how nutritional interventions can aid the canine and feline immune system during immunocompromised situations.

References   1. Schrimshaw NS, Taylor CE, Gordon JE. Interaction of nutrition and infection. *Am J Med Sci* 1959; 237:367-403.

2. Chandra RK. Immunocompetence in undernutrition. *J Pediatr* 1972; 81:1194-1200.

3. Keush GT, Wilson, CS, Waksal SD. Nutrition, host defenses, and lymphoid system. *Arch Host Def Mech* 1983; 2:275-359.

4. Chandra S, Chandra RK. Nutrition and immune response outcome. *Prog Food Nutr Soc* 1986; 10:1-65.

5. Beisel WR. Single nutrients and immunity. *Am J Clin Nutr* 1982; 35(Supp):417-468.

6. Hwang D. Essential fatty acids and immune response. *FASEB J* 1989; 3:2052-2061.

7. Chandra RK. Basic immunology and its application to nutritional problems. In: Forse RA, Bell S, Blackburn GL, Kabbash LG, eds. *Diet, Nutrition and Immunity*. Boca Raton: CRC Press, Inc., 1994.

8. Brostoff J, Scanding GK, Male D, Roitt IM. *Clinincal Immunology*. London: Grower Medical Publishing, 1991.

9. Chandra RK, ed. *Primary and Secondary Immunodeficiency Disorders*. Edinburgh: Churchill Livingstin, 1983.

10. Nossal GLV. The basic components of the immune system. *New Engl J Med* 1987; 316:1320.

11. Goodman JW. The immune response. In: Stites DP, Terr A, eds. *Basic and Clinical Immunology*. East Norwalk: Appleton and Lange, 1991; 34-44.

12. Cruse JM, Lewi RE. *Illustrated Dictionary of Immunology*. Boca Raton: CRC Press, Inc., 1995.

13. Scott P, Kaufmann HE. The role of T-cell subsets and cytokines in the regulation of infection. *Immunology Today* 1991; 12:346-348.

14. Dumonde DC, Wolstencroft RA, Panayi GS, Matthew M, Morley J, Howson WT. Lymphokines: non-antibody mediators of cellular immunity generated by lymphocyte activation. *Nature* 1969; 224:38-42.

15. Cohen S, David J, Feldman M, Glade PR, Mayer M, Oppenheim JJ, Papermaster BW, Pick E, Pierce CW. Current state of studies of mediators of cellular immunity: a progress report. *Cell Immunol* 1977; 33:233-244.

16. Meydani SN. Dietary modulation of cytokine production and biological functions. *Nutr Rev* 1990; 48:361-369.

17. Chew BP, Park JS, Wong TS, Weng B, Kim HW, Byrne KM, Hayek MG, Reinhart GA. Importance of β-carotene nutrition in the dog and cat: uptake and immunity. In: Reinhart GA, Carey DP, eds. *Recent Advances in Canine and Feline Nutrition, Vol. II: 1998 Iams Nutrition Symposium Proceedings.* Wilmington: Orange Frazer Press, 1998; 513-522.

18. Chew BP, Wong TS, Park JS, Weng BB, Cha N, Kim HW, Byrne KM, Hayek MG, Reinhart GA. Role of dietary lutein in the dog and cat. In: Reinhart GA, Carey DP, eds. *Recent Advances in Canine and Feline Nutrition, Vol. II: 1998 Iams Nutrition Symposium Proceedings.* Wilmington: Orange Frazer Press, 1998; 547-554.

19. Field CJ, McBurney MI, Hayek MG, Sunvold GD. Interaction of fiber fermentation and immunology of the gastrointestinal tract. In: Reinhart GA, Carey DP, eds. *Recent Advances in Canine and Feline Nutrition, Vol. II: 1998 Iams Nutrition Symposium Proceedings.* Wilmington: Orange Frazer Press, 1998; 523-532.

20. Spears JW, Brown Jr TT, Hayek MG, Sunvold GD. Effect of dietary chromium on the canine immune response. In: Reinhart GA, Carey DP, eds. *Recent Advances in Canine and Feline Nutrition, Vol. II: 1998 Iams Nutrition Symposium Proceedings.* Wilmington: Orange Frazer Press, 1998; 555-564.

21. Meydani SN, Hayek MG, Wu D, Meydani M. Vitamin E and immune response in aged dogs. In: Reinhart GA, Carey DP, eds. *Recent Advances in Canine and Feline Nutrition, Vol. II: 1998 Iams Nutrition Symposium Proceedings.* Wilmington: Orange Frazer Press, 1998; 295-304.

22. Jones PT, Anderson R. Oxidative inhibition of polymorphonuclear leukocyte motility mediated by the peroxidase/H2O2 halide system: studies on the reversible nature of the inhibition and mechanism of protection of migratory responsiveness by ascorbate, levaminsole, thiamin, and cysteine. *Int J Immunopharmacol* 1983; 5:377.

23. Talbott MC, Miller LT, Kervliet NI. Pyridoxine supplementation: effect on lymphocyte response in elderly persons. *Am J Clin Nutr* 1987; 46:659-664.

24. Meydani SN, Ribaya-Mercado JD, Russell RM, Sahyoun N, Morrow RD, Gershoff SN. Vitamin B6 deficiency impairs interleukin-2 production and lymphocyte proliferation in elderly adults. *Am J Clin Nutr* 1991; 53:1275-1280.

25. Anderson R, Oosthuighen R, Maritz R, Theron A, Van Rensburg AJ. The effect of increasing weekly doses of ascorbate on certain cellular and humoral immune functions in normal volunteers. *Am J Clin Nutr* 1980; 33:71-76.

26. Keenes B, Dumont I, Brohee D, Hubert C, Neve P. Effect of vitamin C supplementation on cell-mediated immunity in old people. *Gerontology* 1983; 29:305-310.

27. Panush RS, Delafuente JC, Katz P, Johnson J. Modulation of certain immunologic responses by vitamin C. III. Potentiation of *in vivo* and *in vitro* lymphocyte responses. *Int J Vit Nutr Res* 1982; 23:35-47.

28. Ziemlanski S, Wartanowicz M, Kios A. Raczka A, Klos M. The effect of ascorbic acid and alpha-tocopherol supplementation on serum proteins and immunoglobulin concentrations in the elderly. *Nutr Int* 1986; 2:1.

29. Siegel BV. Vitamin C and the immune response in health and disease. In: Klurfeld DM, ed. *Nutrition and Immunity*. New York: Plenum Press, 1993; 167-196.

30. Anderson R, Smith MJ, Joone GK, Van Staden AM. Vitamin C and cellular immune functions. *Ann NY Acad Sci* 1990; 587:34.

31. Corwin LM, Schloss J. Influence of vitamin E on the mitogenic response of murine lymphocytes. *J Nutr* 1980; 110:916-923.

32. Tanaka J, Fuyiwara H, Torisu M. Vitamin E and immune response: Enhancement of T-helper activity by dietary supplementation of vitamin E in mice. *Immunol* 1979; 38:727-734.

33. Tengerdy RP, Heinzerling RH, Methias MM. Effect of vitamin E on disease resistance and immune reponse. In: de Dune C, Hayaishi O, eds. *Tocopherol, Oxygen and Biomembranes*. 1978; 191-200.

34. Meydani SN, Meydani M, Verdon CP, Shapiro AC, Blumberg JB, Hayes KC. Vitamin E supplementation suppresses prostaglandin E2 synthesis and enhances the immune reponse of aged mice. *Mech Ageing Dev* 1986; 34:191-201.

35. Moriguchi S, Kobayashi N, Kishino Y. High dietary intakes of vitamin E and cellular immune functions in rats. *J Nutr* 1990; 120:1096-1102.

36. Hayek MG, Taylor SF, Bender BS, Han SN, Meydani M, Smith DE, Eghtesada S, Meydani SN. Vitamin E supplementation decreases lung virus titers in mice infected with influenza. *J Infect Dis* 1997; 176:273-276.

37. Tengerdy RP, Lactera NG. Vitamin E adjuvant formulations in mice. *Vaccine* 1991; 9:204-206.

38. Reddy PG, Morill JL, Minocha HC, Morill MB, Dayton AB, Frey RA. Effects of supplemental vitamin E on the immune system of calves. *J Dairy Sci* 1985; 69:164-171.

39. Larsen HJ, Tollersrud S. Effect of dietary vitamin E and selenium on the phytohaemagglutin response in pig lymphocytes. *Am J Vet Sci* 1981; 31:301-305.

40. Afzal M, Tengerdy RP, Ellis RP, Kimberling CV, Morris CJ. Protection of rams against epididymitis by a *B. Ovis*-vitamin E vaccine. *Vet Immunol and Immunopath* 1984; 7:293-304.

41. Baehner RL, Boxer LA, Allen JM, Davis J. Autooxidation as a basis for altered function of polymorphonuclear leukocytes. *Blood* 1977; 50:327-335.

42. Meydani SN, Barlund PM, Lui S, Meydani M, Miller RA, Cannon JG, Morrow FD, Rocklin R, Blumberg JB. Vitamin E supplementation enhances cell-mediated immunity in healthy elderly subjects. *Am J Clin Nutr* 1990; 52:557-563.

43. Prabahla RH, Maxey V, Hicks MJ, Watson RR. Enhancement of the expression of activation markers of human peripheral blood mononuclear cells by *in vitro* culture with retinoids and carotenoids. *J Leuk Biol* 1989; 45:249.

44. Seifter E, Rettara G, Padawer J, Levenson SM. Moloney murine sarcoma virus tumors in CBA/J mice: Chemopreventative and chemotheraputic actions of supplemental beta-carotene. *J Natl Cancer Inst* 1982; 68:835.

45. Daniel LR, Chew BP, Tanaka TS, Tjoelker LW. *In vitro* effects of β-carotene and vitamin A on peripartum bovine peripheral blood mononuclear cell proliferation. *J Dairy Sci* 1991; 74:911.

46. Michal JJ, Heiman LR, Wong TS, Chew BP. Modulatory effects of dietary β-carotene on blood and mammary leukocyte function in periparturient dairy cows. *J Dairy Sci* 1994; 77:1408.

47. Watson RR, Prabhala RH, Pleiza PM, Alberts DS. Effect of beta-carotene on lymphocyte subpopulations in elderly humans: Evidence for a dose response relationship. *Am J Clin Nutr* 1991; 53:90-94.

48. Santos M, Meydani SN, Leka L, Wu D, Fotouhi N, Meydani M, Hennekens CH, Gaziano JM. Elderly male natural killer cell activity is enhanced by β-carotene supplementation. *FASEB J* 1995:A441.

49. Alexander M, Newmark H, Miller R. Oral beta-carotene can increase number of OKT4+ cells in human blood. *Immunol Lett* 1985; 9:221.

50. Singh KP, Zaidi SIA, Raisuddin S, Saxena AK, Murthy RC, Ray PK. Effect of zinc on immune function and host reistance against infection and tumor challenge. *Immunopharm Immunotox* 1992; 14:813-840.

51. Duchateau J, Delepesse G, Vrijens R, Collet H. Beneficial effects of oral zinc supplementation on the immune response of old people. *Am J Med* 1981; 70:1001-1004.

52. Larson HJ. Effect of selenium on lymphocyte responses to mitogens. *Res Vet Sci* 1988; 45:11-15.

53. Talcott PA, Exon JH, Koller LD. Attraction of natural killer cell-mediated cytotoxicity in rats treated with selenium, diethylnitrosamine and ethylnitrosourea. *Cancer Lett* 1984; 23:313-319.

54. Dimitrov NV, Charamella LJ, Meyer CJ, Stowe HD, Ku PK, Ulrey DE. Modulation of natural killer cell activity by selenium in humans. *J Nutr Growth Cancer* 1986; 3:193.

55. Kiremidjian-Schumacher L, Roy M, Wishe HI, Cohen MW, Stotzky G. Selenium and immune cell functions. I. Effect of lymphocyte proliferation and production of interleukin 1 and interleukin 2. *PSEBM* 1990; 193:136-142.

56. Roy M, Kiremidjian-Schumacher L, Wishe HI, Cohen MW, Stotzky G. Effect of selenium on the expression of high affinity interleukin 2 receptors. *PSEBM* 1992; 200:36-43.

57. Burton JL, Mallard BA, Mowat DN. Effects of supplemental chromium on immune responses of periparturient and early lactation cows. *J Anim Sci* 1993; 71:1532.

58. Burton JL, Malard BA, Mowat DN. Effects of supplemental chromium on responses of newly weaned beef calves to IBR/PI$_3$ vaccination. *Can J Vet Res* 1994; 58:148.

59. Chang X, Mowat DN. Supplemental chromium for stressed and growing feeder calves. *J Anim Sci* 1992; 70:559.

60. Kegley EB, Spears JW. Immune response, glucose metabolism, and performance of stressed feeder calves fed inorganic and organic chromium. *J Anim Sci* 1995; 73:2721.

61. Moonsie-Shageer S, Mowat DN. Effects of level of supplemental chromium on performance, serum constituents, and immune status of stressed feeder calves. *J Anim Sci* 1993; 71:232.

62. Chang X, Mallard BA, Mowat DN. Proliferation of peripheral blood lymphocytes of feeder calves in response to chromium. *Nutr Res* 1994; 14:851.

63. Hennet T, Peterhans E, Stocker R. Alterations in antioxidant defences in lung and liver of mice infected with influenza A virus. *J Gen Virol* 1992; 73:39-46.

64. Peterhans E. Oxidants and antioxidants in viral disease:disease mechanisms and metabolic regulation. *J Nutr* 1997; 127: 962S-965S.

65. Droge W, Eck HP, Mihm S. Oxidant-antioxidant status in human immuno-deficiency virus infection. In: Packard L, ed. *Oxygen Radicals in Biological Systems.* San Diego: Academic Press, 1994; 594-601.

66. Kido H, Sakai K, Kishino Y, Tashiro M. Pulmonary surfactant is a potential endogenous inhibitor of proteolytic activation of Sedai and influenza A virus. *FEBS Lett* 1993; 322:115-119.

67. Beck MA. Increased virulence of coxsackievirus B3 in mice due to vitamin E or selenium deficiency. *J Nutr* 1997; 127:966S-970S.

68. Casey LC, Balk BA, Bone RC. Plasma cytokine and endotoxin levels correlate with survival in patients with the sepsis syndrome. *Ann Intern Med* 1993; 119:771-778.

69. Klasing KC, Laurin DE, Peng RK, Fry DM. Immunologically mediated growth depression in chicks: influence of feed intake, corticosterone and interleukin-1. *J Nutr* 1987; 117:1629-1637.

70. McMarthy DO, Kluger MG, Vander AJ. Effect of centrally administered interleukin-1 and endotoxin on food intake of fasted rats. *Physiol Behav* 1985; 745-749.

71. Cerami A, Ikeda Y, Le Trang N, Hotez PJ, Beutler B. Weight loss associated with an endotoxin-induced mediator from peritoneal macrophages: the role of cachetin (tumor necrosis factor). *Immunol Lett* 1985; 11:173-177.

72. Blatteis CM, Shibata M, Dinarello C. Comparison of the central nervous sytem effects of recombinant(R) interleukin-1$_{beta}$(IL-1), rInterferon$_{alpha2}$ (INF) and rTumor necrosis factor$_{alpha}$ (TNF). *J Leukocyte Biol* 1987; 42:560.

73. Flores E, Drabik M, Bisrtian BR, Istan N, Dinarello CA, Blackburn GL. Synergistic effect of human recombinant mediators during the acute phase reaction. *Clin Res* 1987; 35:384A(abs).

74. Del Ray A, Besedovsky H. Interleukin 1 affects glucose homeostasis. *Am J Physiol* 1987; 253:R794-R798.

75. Meszaros K, Lang CH, Bagby GJ, Spitzer JJ. Tumor necrosis factor increases *in vivo* glucose utilization of macrophage-rich tissues. *Biochem Biophys Res Commun* 1987; 149:1-6.

76. Lee MD, Zentella A, Pekala PH, Cerami A. Effect of endotoxin-induced monokines on glucose metabolism in the muscle cell line L6. *Proc Natl Acad Sci* 1987; 84:2590-2594.

77. Roh MS, Moldawer LL, Ekman LG, Dinarella CA, Bistrian BR, Jeevandam M, Brennan MF. Stimulatory effect of interleukin-1 upon hepatic metabolism. *Metabolism* 1986; 35:419-424.

78. Hill MR, Sitth RD, McCallum RE. Interleukin 1: a regulatory role in glucocorticiod-regulated hepatic metabolism. *J Immunol* 1986; 137:858-862.

79. Breitschwerdt EB, Loar AS, Hribernik TN, McGrath RK. Hypoglycemia in four dogs with sepsis. *J Am Vet Med Assoc* 1981; 178:1072-1076.

80. Hardie EM, Barsanti JA. Treatment of canine actinomycosis. *J Am Vet Med Assoc* 1982; 180:537-541.

81. Paratt JR, Strrgess RM. The effect of indomethacin on the cardiovascular and metabolic responses to *E. coli* endotoxin in the cat. *Br Pharmacol* 1974; 50:177-183.

82. Hinshaw LB, Peyton MD, Archer LT, Black MR, Coalson JJ, Greenfield LJ. Prevention of death in endotoxic shock by glucose adminstration. *Surg Gynecol Obstet* 1974; 136:897-859.

83. Archer LT. Hypoglycemia in conscious dogs in live *Eschericia coli* septicemia. *Circ Shock* 1976; 3:93-106.

84. Postel J, Schoerb PR. Metabolic effects of experimental bacteriemia. *Ann Surg* 1978; 185:475-480.

85. Berk JL, Hagen JF, Beyer WH, Gerber MJ. Hypoglycemia of shock. *Ann Surg* 1970; 171:400-408.

86. Manny J, Rabinovici N, Manny N. Effect of glucose-insulin-potassium on survival in experimental endotoxic shock. *Surg Gynecol Obstet* 1978; 147:405-409.

87. Beutler B, Cerami A. Cachectin tumor necrosis factor: an endogenous mediator of shock and inflammation. *Immunol Res* 1986; 5:281-293.

88. Pekala PH, Kawakami M, Angus CW, Lane MD, Cerami A. Selective inhibition of synthesis of enzymes for *de novo* fatty acid biosynthesis by an endotoxin-induced mediator from exudate cells. *Proc Natl Acad Sci* 1983; 80:2743-2747.

89. Feingold KR, Grunfeild C. Tumor necrosis factor-alpha stimulates hepatic lipogenesis in the rat *in vivo. J Clin Invest* 1986; 184-190.

90. Klasing KC. Influence of stress on protein metabolism. In: Moberg GP, ed. *Animal Stress*. American Physiological Society, USA, 1985; 269-280.

91. Yang RS, Moldawer LL, Sakamoto A, Keenana RA, Matthews DE, Young VR, Wannemacher Jr RW, Blackburn GW, Bristrian BR. Leukocyte endogenous mediator alters protein dynamics in rats. *Metabolism* 1983; 308:654-660.

92. Klasing KC. Nutritional aspects of leukocyte cytokines. *J Nutr* 1988; 118:1436-1446.

93. Baracos V, Rodemann HP, Dinarello CA, Goldberg AL. Stimulation of muscle protein degradation and prostaglandin E2 release by leukocytic pyrogen (interleukin-1). *N Engl J Med* 1983; 308:553-558.

94. Tracey KJ, Wei H, Manogue KR, Fong Y, Hesse DG, Nguyen HT, Kuo GC, Beultler B, Contran RS, Cerami A, Lowry SF. Cachectin/tumor necrosis factor induces cachexia, anemia, and inflammaton. *J Exp Med* 1988; 167:1211-1227.

95. Goldberg AL, Baracos V, Rodermann P, Waxman L, Dinarello CA. Control of protein degradation in muscle by prostaglandins, Ca^{2+} and leukocytic pyrogen (interleukin-1). *Fed Proc* 1987; 43:1301-1306.

96. Barber EF, Cousins RJ. Interleukin 1- Stimulated induction of ceruloplasmin synthesis in normal and copper-deficient rats. *J Nutr* 1988; 118:375-381.

97. DilSilvestro RA, Cousins RJ. Glucocorticoid independent mediation of interleukin-1 induced changes in serum zinc and liver metallothionein levels. *Life Sci* 1984; 35:2113-2118.

98. Klasing KC. Effect of inflammatory agents and interleukin 1 on iron and zinc metabolism. *Am J Physiol* 1984; 247:R901-R904.

99. Goldblum SE, Cohen DA, Jay M, McClain CJ. Interleukin 1 induced depression of iron and zinc: role of granulocytes and lactoferrin. *Am J Physiol* 1987; 252:E27-E32.

100. Tanaka T, Araki E, Nitta K, Tateno M. Recombinant human tumor necrosis factor depresses serum iron in mice. *J Biol Res Mod* 1987; 6:484-488.

101. Meydani, SN, Endres S, Woods MN, Goldin BR, Soo C, Morrill-Labrode A, Dinarello CA, Gorbach SL. Oral (n-3) fatty acid supplementation suppresses cytokine production and lymphocyte proliferation: comparison between young and old women. *J Nutr* 1991; 121:547-555.

102. Meydani SN, Lichenstein AH, Cornwall S, Meydani M, Goldin BR, Rasmussen H, Dinarello CA, Schaefer EJ. Immunological effects of national cholesterol education panel step-2 diets with and without fish-derived n-3 fatty acid enrichment. *J Clin Invest* 1993; 92:105-113.

103. Kramer TR, Schoene N, Douglass LW, Judd JT, Ballard-Barbash R, Taylor PR, Bhagavan HN, Nair PP. Increased vitamin E restores fish-oil induced suppressed blastogenesis of mitogen stimulated T lymphocytes. *Am J Clin Nutr* 1991; 54:896-902.

104. Santoli D, Zurier RB. Prostaglandin E precursor fatty acids inhibit human IL-2 production by a prostaglandin E-dependent mechanism. *Immunol* 1989; 143:1303-1309.

105. Wander RC, Hall JA, Gradin JL, Du SH, Jewell DE. The ratio of dietary (n-6) to (n-3) fatty acids influences immune system function, eicosanoid metabolism, lipid peroxidation and vitamin E status in aged dogs. *J Nutr* 1997; 127:1198-1205.

106. Wu D, Meydani SN, Meydani M, Hayek MG, Huth P, Nicolosi RJ. Immunologic effects of marine- and plant-derived n-3 polyunsaturated fatty acids in nonhuman primates. *Am J Clin Nutr* 1996; 63:273-280.

107. Vaughn DM, Reinhart GA, Swaim SF, Lauten SD, Garner CA, Boudreaux MK, Spano JS, Hoffman CE, Conner B. Evaluation of effects of dietary n-6 to n-3 fatty acid ratios on leukotriene B synthesis in dog skin and neutrophils. *Vet Derm* 1994; 54:163-173.

Importance of β-Carotene Nutrition in the Dog and Cat: Uptake and Immunity

Boon P. Chew, PhD
Professor, Department of Animal Sciences
Washington State University, Pullman, Washington, USA

Jean Soon Park, MS[a]; Teri S. Wong, BS[a]; Brian Weng, BS[a];
Hong Wook Kim, MS[a]; Katherine M. Byrne, DVM, PhD[a];
Michael G. Hayek, PhD[b]; Gregory A. Reinhart, PhD[b]
[a]Department of Animal Sciences, Washington State University,
Pullman, Washington, USA
[b]Research and Development, The Iams Company, Lewisburg, Ohio, USA

Introduction

Carotenoids are naturally-occurring plant pigments which are absorbed in varying degrees by different species. Common carotenoids include β-carotene, lutein, lycopene, zeaxanthin, and astaxanthin. These carotenoids are known to play important roles in modulating immunity and promoting health in humans and animals.[1-4] In vitro and in vivo studies have shown β-carotene to increase the number of T-helper cells,[5,6] IL-2 receptor expression on natural killer cells,[6] lymphocyte proliferation,[6-8] and humoral response.[9,10] Enhanced immune function in mice supplemented with β-carotene and other carotenoids has also been reported recently.[7] β-Carotene also modulates nonspecific cellular host defense including the bactericidal ability of blood neutrophils.[8,11]

In spite of the available data on the importance of β-carotene on immunity and health, little is known about the absorption or role of β-carotene in dogs and cats. Early studies have reported trace amounts, if any, of carotene in the blood, liver, and milk of dogs[12] and others have reported low to moderate concentrations of β-carotene in the blood.[13-16] Similarly, exotic canids do not have detectable blood carotene whereas exotic felids have high concentrations of β-carotene in the blood.[17] Therefore, a systematic approach in studying the absorption and immunomodulatory action of dietary β-carotene in dogs and cats was undertaken.

Role of β-Carotene in Dogs

β-Carotene Uptake. The uptake of oral β-carotene by blood plasma and leukocytes was studied in mature female Beagle dogs (18 months of age, 8–9 kg body weight). In experiment 1, dogs were fed once orally with 0, 50, 100 or 200 mg of β-carotene and blood sampled at 0, 3, 6, 9, 12, 15, 18, 21, and 24 hours after dosing. Concentrations of plasma β-carotene increased in a dose-dependent manner (**Figure 1**). Peak concentrations were observed at six hours and blood β-carotene

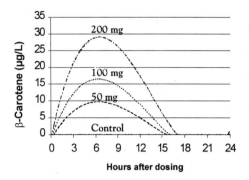

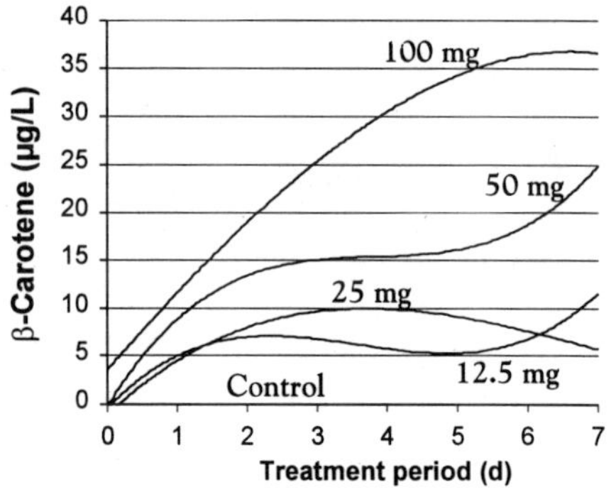

Figure 1. Changes in concentrations of plasma β-carotene in dogs given a single oral dose of 0, 50, 100 or 200 mg of β-carotene.

Figure 2. Changes in concentrations of plasma β-carotene in dogs given repeated oral doses of 0, 12.5, 25, 50 or 100 mg of β-carotene (day 0 = prior to first dose; day 7 = 24 hours after last dose).

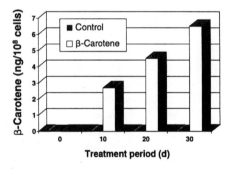

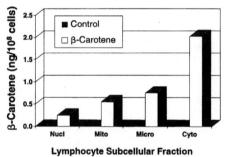

Figure 3. Uptake of β-carotene by blood lymphocytes from dogs fed β-carotene daily for 30 days. β-Carotene values represent means of samples pooled across supplemented treatments.

Figure 4. Uptake of β-carotene by the nuclei (Nucl), mitochondria (Mito), microsomes (Micro), and cystol (Cyto) of blood lymphocytes daily for 30 days. β-Carotene values represent means of samples pooled across supplemented treatments.

declined rapidly thereafter. The half-life of plasma β-carotene was three to four hours. In experiment 2, dogs were dosed daily for seven consecutive days with 0, 12.5, 25, 50 or 100 mg β-carotene. Blood was sampled once daily at six hours after each dosing. There was a dose-dependent increase in circulating β-carotene with the daily supplementation of β-carotene (**Figure 2**). Concentrations of plasma β-carotene after the last dose was generally 2.5- to 4-fold higher than that observed after one dose. Experiment 3 was designed to study the uptake of β-carotene by blood leukocytes. Dogs were fed 0, 50 or 100 mg of β-carotene daily for 30 days. Blood lymphocytes (**Figure 3**) obtained on days 10, 20, and 30 showed significant uptake of β-carotene in β-carotene-supplemented dogs only. Also, there was significant uptake of β-carotene into the cytosol, mitochondria, microsomes, and nuclei (**Figure 4**). The highest accumulation of β-carotene in both leukocytes was observed in the cytosol. Blood neutrophils also take up significant amounts of

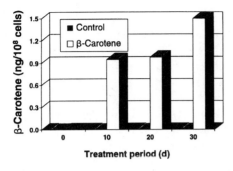

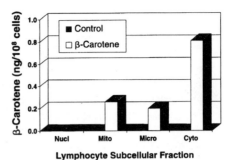

Figure 5. Uptake of dietary β-carotene by blood neutrophils from dogs fed β-carotene daily for 30 days. β-Carotene values represent means of samples pooled across supplemented treatments.

Figure 6. Uptake of β-carotene by the nuclei (Nucl), mitochondria (Mito), microsomes (Micro), and cystol (Cyto) of blood neutrophils from dogs fed β-carotene daily for 30 days. β-Carotene values represent means of samples pooled across supplemented treatments.

β-carotene (**Figure 5**) and distribute into the cytosol, mitochondria, microsomes but not the nuclei (**Figure 6**). Again, the cytosol contain the highest concentration of β-carotene. In summary, the dog is able to absorb significant amounts of dietary β-carotene. Furthermore, peripheral blood lymphocytes and neutrophils take up significant amounts of β-carotene into their subcellular organelles.

The present systematic study on the uptake of β-carotene by dogs contradicts earlier studies. Previous studies reported either trace amounts, if any, of carotene in the blood, liver, and milk of dogs[18] or low to moderate concentrations of β-carotene in the blood.[13-16] Similarly, exotic canids do not have detectable blood carotene.[17] Studies on other species have reported significant uptake of β-carotene by the bovine,[2] porcine,[19,20] and human[21] blood and lymphocytes. Bovine and porcine lymphocytes also take up significant amounts of β-carotene into their subcellular organelles.[19,20,22]

In summary, the dog is able to absorb significant amounts of dietary β-carotene. Furthermore, peripheral blood lymphocytes and neutrophils take up significant amounts of β-carotene into their subcellular organelles. The significance of these observations as it relates to immune modulation in the dog is studied next.

β-Carotene on Immunity. The objective is to study the role of dietary β-carotene in enhancing the cell-mediated and humoral immune systems of the dog. Female Beagles (4 to 5 months old) were supplemented daily with 0, 25, 50 or 100 mg of β-carotene. The following parameters were assessed in all the animals or in their peripheral blood lymphocytes: 1) delayed-type hypersensitivity (DTH) against PHA (nonspecific immunity) and a polyvalent vaccine (Vanguard 5, Smith/Klein/Pfizer) (specific immunity), 2) lymphocyte proliferation, 3) lymphocyte populations, and 4) immunoglobulins (Ig).

β-Carotene supplementation increased plasma β-carotene concentrations in a dose-dependent manner (*Figure 7*) but did not influence plasma retinol or α-tocopherol. These changes generally reflected the DTH response to both the specific (vaccine) and non-specific (PHA) antigens (*Figure 8*). The greatest response to PHA challenge was observed in dogs fed 50 mg of β-carotene whereas dogs fed either 20 or 50 mg of β-carotene showed significantly higher DTH response to the vaccine. Delayed type hypersensitivity is strictly a cellular reaction involving T cells and macrophages without involving an antibody component. Antigen-presenting cells (e.g., macrophages) present the antigen or allergen to T cells that become activated and release lymphokines. These lymphokines activate macrophages and cause them to become voracious killers of the foreign invaders. Therefore, the data show a heightened cell-mediated response in dogs fed β-carotene.

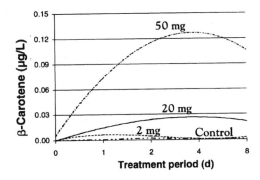

Figure 7. Changes in concentrations of plasma β-carotene in dogs fed 0, 2, 20 or 50 mg of β-carotene daily for 8 weeks.

β-Carotene feeding also produced significant changes in lymphocyte subsets. Compared to controls, dogs fed 20 or 50 mg of β-carotene had an elevated population of CD4[+] cells (week 8) (*Table 1*) and CD5[+] cells (week 2). Dogs fed 20 mg of β-carotene also had elevated population of CD8[+] cells (weeks 2 and 4). The T cells can be classified according to the expression of CD4 membrane molecules. The CD4 functions as an adhesion molecule and as a co-signaling co-receptor. It plays a role in T cell activation. The CD4[+] T lymphocytes recognize antigen in association with the class II MHC molecules and largely function as helper cells. The increase in T helper cell population in this study can explain the corresponding increase in DTH response in dogs fed 20 to 50 mg of β-carotene.

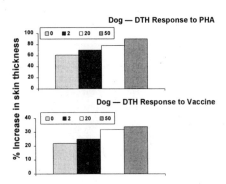

Figure 8. Forty-eight hour DTH response in dogs fed 0, 2, 20 or 50 mg of β-carotene daily for 7 weeks.

Table 1. Changes in lymphocyte CD4$^+$ subset in dogs fed 0,2,20 or 50 mg of β-carotene daily.

Treatment (mg β-carotene/d)	Feeding period (wk)			
	0	**2**	**4**	**8**
0	38.48	32.8	33.98	30.08
2	38.07	32.54	35.51	30.23
20	39.32	32.57	34.98	37.35
50	37.74	36.08	41.25	37.42

Concentrations of IgG, IgM and total Ig (**Figure 9**) increased significantly in dogs fed β-carotene 1 week after dietary supplementation. Increases in Ig were dose-dependent for dogs fed 0 to 20 mg of β-carotene. The highest level of β-carotene (50 mg) did not produce a further increase. Dogs fed 20 mg of β-carotene consistently had the greatest antibody response for both Ig. One of the major functions of the immune system is the production of antibodies which circulate freely to protect the body against foreign materials. Antibodies serve to neutralize toxins, immobilize certain microorganisms, neutralize viral activity, agglutinate microorganisms or antigen particles, and precipitate soluble antigens.

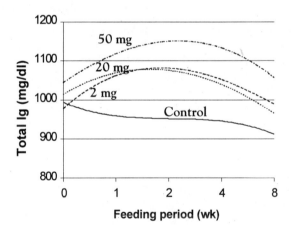

Figure 9. Changes in plasma total Ig in dogs fed 0, 2, 20 or 50 mg of β-carotene daily for 8 weeks.

β-Carotene feeding did not influence mitogen-induced lymphocyte blastogenesis and IL-2 production. Lymphocytes are involved in cell-mediated immunity. Upon recognizing an antigen, lymphocytes will divide rapidly, thereby cloning themselves in preparation for combating a potential invasion. In humoral immune response, IL-2 stimulates both T helper cells and B cells to proliferate in response to antigens. It is required for the clonal expansion of antigen- or mitogen-activated T cells. In cell-mediated immune response, IL-2 activates natural killer cells, stimulates thymocyte proliferation and induces cytotoxic T cell activity. It is surprising that these two immune parameters were not influenced by β-carotene feeding, whereas numerous others were.

No data are available on the effect of dietary β-carotene on immunity in dogs. However, studies in other species have shown that β-carotene supplementation can modulate immunity and promote health.[1-4] *In vivo*, β-carotene increased the number of T-helper cells in humans[5] and mice,[6] increased IL-2 receptor expression on natural killer cells,[23] enhanced the proliferation and induction of cytotoxic T cells,[6] and stimulated lymphocyte proliferation in cattle,[8,24] pigs,[25] and mice.[7] Carotenoids also stimulated humoral response in humans and in mice[9,10] and the bactericidal ability of blood neutrophils in the bovine.[8,11]

Summary

It has been demonstrated for the first time that the dog absorbs a significant amount of β-carotene from the diet and transfers the β-carotene into the subcellular organelles of immune cells and phagocytes. In these cells, β-carotene seems to enhance the immune system of the dog through enhanced cell-mediated immune responses (DTH response, shift in lymphocyte subsets) and humoral response (IgG and IgM production). Therefore, supplemental β-carotene promotes the immune health of dogs. This will likely translate into improved overall health of these dogs.

Role of
β-Carotene
in Cats

β-Carotene Uptake. Three experiments were conducted to study the uptake of oral β-carotene by blood plasma and leukocytes in the domestic cat. In experiment 1, mature female Tabby cats (7 to 8 months of age) were given once perorally 0, 10, 20 or 50 mg of β-carotene and blood sampled at 0, 12, 24, 30, 36, 42, 48, and 72 hours after dosing. Concentrations of plasma β-carotene increased in a dose-dependent manner (**Figure 10**). Peak concentrations were observed at 12 to 24 hours and declined subsequently. The half-life of plasma β-carotene was 12 to 24 hours. In experiment 2, cats were dosed daily for six consecutive days with 0, 1, 2, 5 or 10 mg of β-carotene. Blood was sampled once daily at 12 hours after each dosing. Daily dosing of cats with β-carotene for six days resulted in a dose-dependent increase in circulating β-carotene (**Figure 11**). The concentration of plasma β-carotene after the last dose was generally 1.5- to 2-fold higher than that observed after one dose. Experiment 3 was designed to study the uptake of β-carotene by blood lymphocytes. Cats were fed 0, 5 or 10 mg of β-carotene daily for 14 days. Blood lymphocytes were obtained on days 7 and 14 to determine β-carotene content in whole lymphocytes and in subcellular fractions. Blood lymphocytes take up significant amounts of β-carotene by day 7 of feeding (**Figure 12**). Furthermore, β-carotene was observed to accumulate in the mitochondria (40 to 52%), microsomes (20 to 35%), cytosol (15 to 34%), and nuclei (1.5 to 6%) by day 7 of feeding (**Figure 13**). Therefore, the domestic cat is able to absorb dietary β-carotene. Furthermore, peripheral blood lymphocytes take up significant amounts of β-carotene into their subcellular organelles.

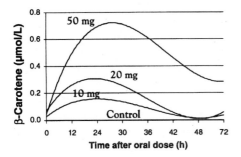

Figure 10. Changes in concentrations of plasma β-carotene in cats given a single oral dose of 0, 10, 20 or 50 mg of β-carotene.

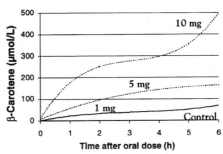

Figure 11. Changes in concentrations of plasma β-carotene in cats fed 0, 1, 5 or 10 mg of β-carotene orally for six days.

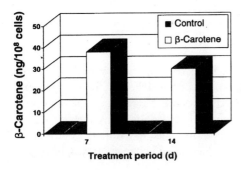

Figure 12. Uptake of dietary β-carotene by blood lymphocytes obtained from cats supplemented orally with β-carotene daily for 14 days. β-carotene was undetectable in unsupplemented cats. β-Carotene values represent means of samples pooled across supplemented treatments.

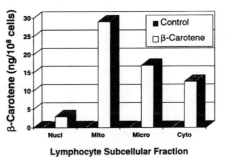

Figure 13. Blood lymphocyte uptake of dietary β-carotene by the nuclei (Nucl), mitochondria (Mito), microsomes (Micro), and cystol (Cyto) in cats fed β-carotene daily for seven days. β-Carotene values represent means of samples pooled across supplemented treatments.

Results from this study suggest that the domestic cat readily absorbs dietary β-carotene. These findings disagree with earlier reports that indicated domestic cats are unable to absorb oral β-carotene.[18,26] Only one recent study indicated the presence of β-carotene in the blood of domestic cats.[13] In fact, the cat absorbs β-carotene more efficiently than the dog. Hence, the ability of the domestic cat to absorb β-carotene is in a way similar to exotic felids (jaguars, bobcats) which have high concentrations of blood β-carotene in spite of being fed diets low in the carotenoid.[17] Cats do not possess the necessary intestinal enzyme to convert β-carotene to vitamin A.[20] This has been suggested by some researchers as an explanation for the presence of high concentrations of β-carotene in the general circulation.[17] However, it is very unlikely that this physiological difference has direct bearing on the cat's ability to absorb β-carotene because pigs and rodents have very low concentrations of β-carotene, yet humans have high concentrations even though they all possess intestinal β-carotene cleavage enzymes. Thus, the ability of cats to absorb dietary β-carotene as demonstrated in this study is more likely due to the presence of a β-carotene transport mechanism in the intestinal mucosa. These results are in agreement with others who showed significant uptake of β-carotene by bovine,[2] porcine,[19,20] and human[8] lymphocytes. Furthermore, significant uptake of β-carotene by subcellular lymphocyte fractions similarly have been reported in the bovine and porcine.[20,22]

In conclusion, these studies provide the first available evidence that the domestic Tabby cat is able to absorb dietary β-carotene. Furthermore, circulating β-carotene is significantly absorbed by peripheral blood lymphocytes and distributed into the various subcellular organelles, notably the mitochondria. It is tempting to postulate that the β-carotene in the lymphocyte subcellular organelles may serve to protect the lymphocytes from oxygen free radical attack, or directly regulate nuclear events. If indeed this is the case, then one can expect enhanced immune function and improved health in cats fed adequate amounts of β-carotene. This possibility is therefore investigated in the next study on the role of dietary β-carotene in modulating immunity in cats.

β-Carotene on Immunity. The role of dietary β-carotene in stimulating both cell-mediated and humoral immunity in the cat was studied. Female Tabby cats were supplemented daily with 0, 0.4, 2 or 10 mg of β-carotene. Several immune responses were measured including IgG production, lymphoblastogenesis, delayed-type hypersensitivity response to a polyvalent vaccine (modified live rhinotracheitis and calici viruses) and to concanavalin A, IL-2 production and changes in lymphocyte subsets.

β-Carotene supplementation produced a dose-dependent increase in plasma β-carotene concentrations (**Figure 14**) but had no influence on plasma retinol and α-tocopherol. However, β-carotene supplementation did not significantly influence lymphocyte proliferation, DTH response or the production of IgG and IL-2. Its effect on other immune measures is presently unknown.

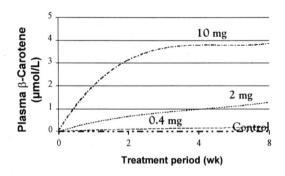

Figure 14. Changes in concentrations of plasma β-carotene in cats fed 0, 0.4, 2 or 10 mg of β-carotene daily for 8 weeks.

Summary. Even though β-carotene supplementation can enhance immunity in the dog and in other species,[1-4] it does not seem to significantly influence immunity in the cat, as measured by lymphocyte proliferation, DTH response or the production of IgG and IL-2. It has been demonstrated for the first time that cats absorb a significant amount of β-carotene from the diet and transfer the β-carotene into the subcellular organelles of lymphocytes. However, it does not seem to influence immune defense. This does not rule out the possibility that other carotenoids (other than β-carotene) may enhance the immune system in the cat. Also, β-carotene may enhance other aspects of immune defense or may play other physiological roles, including reproduction.

From the standpoint of companion animal nutrition, it is exciting to observe that both the domestic dog and cat absorb β-carotene from the diet and transfer the compound into important subcellular components of immune cells. Consequently, absorbed β-carotene may play an important role in the health of these animals. Indeed, β-carotene enhances several different aspects of cell-mediated and humoral immunity, at least in the dog. From these findings, it is proposed that β-carotene be included in the diets of cats and dogs, especially the latter, in order to optimize health.

Overall Summary

References

1. Chew BP. Vitamin A and ß-carotene on host defense. Symposium: Immune function: Relationship of nutrition and disease control. *J Dairy Sci* 1987; 70:2732-2743.

2. Chew BP. Role of carotenoids in the immune response. Symposium on "Antioxidants, Immune Response and Animal Function." *J Dairy Sci* 1993; 76:2804-2811.

3. Chew BP. Antioxidant vitamins affect food animal immunity and health. Conference: Beyond deficiency: New views of vitamins in ruminant nutrition and health. *J Nutr* 1995; 125:1804S-1808S.

4. Chew BP. The influence of vitamins on reproduction in pigs. In: Garnsworthy PC, Cole D, eds. *Recent Advances in Animal Nutrition*. Nottingham: Nottingham University Press, 1995; 223-239.

5. Alexander M, Newmark H, Miller RG. Oral β-carotene can increase the number of OKT4+ cells in human blood. *Immunol Lett* 1985; 9:221-224.

6. Seifter E, Rettara G, Padawer J, Levenson SM. Moloney murine sarcoma virus tumors in CBA/J mice: Chemopreventive and chemotherapeutic actions of supplemental beta-carotene. *J Natl Cancer Inst* 1982; 68:835-840.

7. Chew BP, Wong MW, Wong TS. Effects of dietary β-carotene, canthaxanthin and astaxanthin on lymphocyte function in mice. *FASEB J* 1995; 9:A441.

8. Michal JJ, Heirman LR, Wong TS, Chew BP. Modulatory effects of dietary β-carotene on blood and mammary leukocyte function in periparturient dairy cows. *J Dairy Sci* 1994; 77:1408-1421.

9. Jyonouchi H, Sun S, Gross M. Effects of carotenoids on *in vitro* immunoglobulin production by human peripheral blood mononuclear cells: Astaxanthin, a carotenoid without vitamin A activity, enhances *in vitro* immunoglobulin production in response to a T-dependent stimulant and antigen. *Nutr Cancer* 1995; 23:171-183.

10. Jyonouchi H, Zhang L, Gross M, Tomita Y. Immunomodulating actions of carotenoids: Enhancement of *in vivo* and *in vitro* antibody production to T-dependent antigens. *Nutr Cancer* 1994; 21:47-58.

11. Tjoelker LW, Chew BP, Tanaka TS, Daniel LR. Effects of dietary vitamin A and β-carotene on polymorphonuclear leukocyte and lymphocyte function in dairy cows during the early dry period. *J Dairy Sci* 1990; 73:1017-1022.

12. Goodwin TW. Mammalian carotenoids. In: Goodwin TW, ed. *The Comparative Biochemistry of the Carotenoids*. London: Chapman and Hall Ltd, 1952; 229-269.

13. Baker H, Schor SM, Murphy BD. Blood vitamin and choline concentrations in healthy domestic cats, dogs and horses. *Am J Vet Res* 1986; 47:1468-1471.

14. Frohring WO. Vitamin A requirements of growing puppies. *Proc Soc Exp Biol Med* 1935; 33:280-282.

15. Steenbock H, Nelson EM, Hart EB. Fat soluble vitamine. IX. The incidence of an opthalamic reaction in dog fed a fat soluble vitamine deficient diet. *Am J Physiol* 1921; 58:14-19.

16. Turner RG. Effect of prolonged feeding of raw carrots on vitamin content of liver and kidneys in the dog. *Proc Soc Exp Biol Med* 1934; 31:866-868.

17. Slifka K, Crissey S, Stacewicz-Sapuntzakis M, Bowen P. A survey of serum carotenoids in captive exotic animals. *FASEB J* 1994; 8:A191.

18. Goodwin TW. Metabolism, nutrition and function of carotenoids. *Ann Rev Nutr* 1986; 6:273-297.

19. Chew BP, Wong TS, Michal JJ, Standaert FE, Heirman LR. Kinetic characteristics of β-carotene uptake after an injection of β-carotene in pigs. *J Anim Sci* 1991; 69:4883-4891.

20. Chew BP, Wong TS, Michal JJ, Standaert FE, Heirman LR. Subcellular distribution of β-carotene, retinol and α-tocopherol in porcine lymphocytes after a single injection of β-carotene. *J Anim Sci* 1991b; 69:4892-4897.

21. Mathews-Roth MM. Carotenoids in the leukocytes of carotenemic and non-carotenemic individuals. *Clin Chem* 1978; 24:700-701.

22. Chew BP, Wong TS, Michal JJ. Uptake of orally administered β-carotene by blood plasma, leukocytes, and lipoproteins in calves. *J Anim Sci* 1993; 71:730-739.

23. Prabhala RH, Maxey V, Hicks MJ, Watson RR. Enhancement of the expression of activation markers of human peripheral blood mononuclear cells by *in vitro* culture with retinoids and carotenoids. *J Leuk Biol* 1989; 45:249-254.

24. Daniel LR, Chew BP, Tanaka TS, Tjoelker LW. *In vitro* effects of β-carotene and vitamin A on peripartum bovine peripheral blood mononuclear cell proliferation. *J Dairy Sci* 1991; 74:911-915.

25. Hoskinson CD, Chew BP, Wong TS. Effects of β-carotene (BC) and vitamin A (VA) on mitogen-induced lymphocyte proliferation in the pig *in vivo*. *FASEB J* 1989; 3:A663.

26. Ahmad, B. The fate of carotene after absorption in the animal organism. *Biochem J* 1931; 25:1195-1204.

Interaction of Fiber Fermentation and Immunology of the Gastrointestinal Tract

Catherine J. Field, PhD
Associate Professor, Department of Agricultural, Food and Nutritional Sciences
University of Alberta, Edmonton, Alberta, Canada

Michael I. McBurney, PhD[a];
Michael G. Hayek, PhD[b]; Gregory D. Sunvold, PhD[b]
[a]Department of Agricultural, Food and Nutritional Sciences,
University of Alberta, Edmonton, Alberta, Canada;
[b]Research and Development, The Iams Company, Lewisburg, Ohio, USA

The gastrointestinal tract constantly encounters enormous antigenic stimuli in the form of both food and microbes. It is critical that protective immune responses are made to potential pathogens and equally important that hypersensitivity responses to dietary antigens are minimized. There are numerous very important non-immunological barrier defenses in the gut. These include: the anatomy of the gut (intact microvillus and tight junctions between cells), peristalsis and mucus which make it difficult for bacteria/virus to attach or enter cells, the low pH of gastric secretions and the digestive and bactericidal enzymes secreted by the stomach, pancreas, and epithelial cells that inhibit the attachment and growth of bacteria.[1]

Introduction

Despite the non-immunological barriers in the gut, under normal circumstances, small amounts of immune-active antigen cross the epithelium. The intestine is protected by an extensive immune system that make it the largest immune organ in the body.[2-3] Although there is little anatomical data available, it is often stated that the gut associated lymphoid tissue (GALT) represents approximately 40% of an immune animal's effector cells,[2] 80% of the body's immunological secreting cells,[4] and accounts for as much as 25% of mucosal mass.[2] GALT is composed of the cells residing in the lamina propria regions of the gut, those interspersed between epithelial cells (intraepithelial lymphocytes; IEL), and cells residing in organized lymphatic tissue such as Peyer's Patches and mesenteric lymph nodes.[3,5] These immunocompetent cells distributed throughout the intestine are critical in maintaining the mucosal barrier.[6] The integrity of the immune barrier in the gut is essential for optimal host defense and maintenance of the normal internal intestinal milieu.

The Gut-Associated Immune System

It has been clearly demonstrated that nutritional status and specific nutrients in the diet can modulate immune function.[7-9] Alterations in GALT function have been observed with protein-calorie malnutrition, vitamin A deficiency and glutamine deprivation.[9-10] Nutrients and their digestion products are in direct contact with GALT and it has been suggested that the presence of food in the small intestine is necessary for adequate function and development of GALT.[11]

The effect of plant fibers and their fermentation products on the structure and function of the gut is well known.[12,13] However, less is known about the role of fiber on immune function. Recently it was reported that feeding a diet high in fermentable fiber increased cytokine production by mesenteric lymph node cells.[14] This observation suggests an immunostimulatory effect of fermentable fiber, or its fermentation products, on the gut. In support of this we have demonstrated that adding the end products of fiber fermentation, short chain fatty acids, to total parenteral nutrition improved parameters of host immune defense after gastrointestinal resection.[15]

The role of fiber and their fermentation products (short chain fatty acids) is of current interest in maintaining intestinal health in companion animals.[16-18] As little is known about the effect of fiber on immune function, a study was conducted to determine the role of fiber type, in this case fermentability, on the composition and function of GALT in dogs. Sixteen adult mongrel dogs (23 ± 2 kg) were randomly assigned to receive one of two diets, differing in fiber source and fermentability, for 2 weeks. The experimental diets were designed to be isonitrogenous, isoenergetic (providing approximately 4,650 kcal/kg) and made to provide similar amounts of total dietary fiber (6% w/w) but differing in fiber fermentability (*Table 1*). After feeding the diets for 2 weeks, the dogs were anesthetized and several mesenteric lymph nodes removed. In addition a 1 m segment of jejunum was removed beginning 10 cm distal to the Ligament of Treitz, and immune cells from the Peyer's patches, lamina propria and intraepithelial regions of the gut were isolated.

Mesenteric Lymph Nodes. Although not always included as part of GALT, the mesenteric lymph nodes are composed of immune cells leaving and entering the gut and those that are part of peripheral circulation.[5] Most mature lymphocytes are found to recirculate continuously between blood and lymphoid organs. This does not appear to be a random process and is a special feature of GALT. Cells drain to the intestinal lymphatics after differentiation in Peyer's patches and pass through mesenteric lymph nodes on route to the thoracic duct and then again on route back to the lamina propria regions of the gut.[5]

The ability of cells to incorporate [^{3}H]-thymidine *in vitro* in response to mitogens is a frequently used assay to estimate cell-mediated immunity.[19] Of all the cell types in GALT studied, the response to mitogens by immune cells from mesen-

Table 1. Ingredient composition of the diets (g/kg diet as mixed).

Nutrient	Nonfermentable Cellulose[1]	Fermentable Fiber Blend[2]
Chicken by product meal	460	460
Fish Meal	120	120
Egg	40	40
Chicken digest	25	25
Chicken fat	160	160
Menhaden oil	3	3
Pregelled starch	110	80
Iams vitamin premix[3]	3.2	3.2
Iams mineral premix[4]	2.4	2.4
Potassium chloride	2.1	2.2
Calcium chloride	1.1	1.9
Choline chloride	0	1.1
Sodium chloride	0.3	0.3
Cellulose	70	0
Beet pulp	0	60
Fructooligosaccharide powder	0	15
Gum arabic	0	20

[1] Dietary fiber cellulose yields an *in vitro* fermentability of 9 mmol SCFA/kg organic matter

[2] Dietary fiber blend yields an *in vitro* fermentability of 229 mmol SCFA/kg organic matter

[3] Proprietary vitamin premix provided the following per kg diet: 25 KIU vitamin A, 124 IU vitamin E, 1561 IU vitamin D3, 14 mg thiamin, 59 mg riboflavin, 90 mg niacin, 32 mg d-pantothenic acid, 10 mg pyridoxine, 0.6 mg biotin, 1.9 mg folic acid, 2,067 mg choline, 23 mg inositol, 0.31 µg vitamin B12

[4] Proprietary mineral premix provided the following per kg diet: 41 mg manganese, 217 mg zinc, 168 mg iron, 47 mg copper, 4 mg iodine, 0.08 mg magnesium, 4.8 mg sulfur, 0.62 mg selenium.

teric lymph nodes were most affected by dietary fiber. Feeding the fermentable fiber blend diet, as compared to the nonfermentable cellulose diet, resulted in a significantly higher response to all tested mitogens: Concanavalin A (Con A), Phytohemaglutinin (PHA), Pokeweed mitogen (PWM) and the combination of Phorbol Myristate Acetate (PMA) plus Ionomycin (Iono, **Figure 1**). The response by mesenteric lymphocytes to the T cell mitogens Con A and PHA was 100% higher in cells from dogs fed the fermentable fiber blend diet. Feeding the fermentable fiber blend diet increased the proportion of CD4+ T cells in mesenteric lymph nodes which may have contributed to their higher response. An increase in the proportion of CD4+ cells is often associated with an increase in the response to mitogens.[20-22]

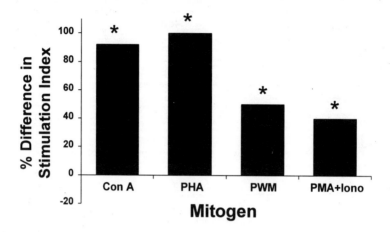

Figure 1. Bars represent the % difference in [³H]-thymidine incorporation by mesenteric lymph node cells from dogs fed the fermentable fiber blend diet as a % of the response by dogs fed the nonfermentable cellulose diet. * indicates that the response is significantly (P<0.05) different from the low fiber group.

The results of this study suggest that feeding fermentable fiber increases the ability of cells to respond to immune challenges in this important lymphoid site. Recently it was reported that feeding fermentable fiber to rats enhanced the production of IFN-γ by mesenteric lymph node lymphocytes stimulated by Con A.[14] This suggests that feeding fermentable fibers may promote a Th1 type response which would favor stimulation of the innate immune system.

Peyer's Patches. The classical mucosal defense in the gut is the production of IgA. Microfold/membranous (M) cells that overlay the Peyer's patches at the interface with the lumen are specially designed to take up antigens (peptides) by endocytosis.[23] In the epithelium overlying Peyer's patches are goblet cells that enable intestinal content to reach the M cell.[23] Thus M cells serve as a portal of entry for selected pathogens and potential dietary antigens to the cells residing in the Peyer's patches. Peyer's patches are the site of antigen priming that provides the basis for IgA secretion into the gut. The Peyer's patches are densely populated with lymphocytes (primarily mature CD4+ T cells and B cells).[24] Antigens are processed and presented directly to T and B lymphocytes residing in Peyer's patches, or are transferred to the 'professional' antigen-presenting cells such as macrophages, Langerhans cells or dendritic cells.[5] Presentation of antigen induces lymphocyte activation and proliferation. Proliferation results in T cells (primarily CD4+) producing cytokines that include interleukin (IL)-4, IL-5, IL-6 and transforming growth factor (TGF-β) that stimulate B cells to differentiate to plasma cells with the ability to produce IgA.[2]

Feeding a diet high in fermentable fibers resulted in a lower (60%) T cell mitogen response (estimated by the incorporation of [³H]-thymidine) by Peyer's patches lymphocytes, as compared to feeding a diet low in fermentable fibers (*Figure 2*). These results suggest a lower T cell response in stimulated cells from dogs fed the fermentable fiber blend diet. Regulation of B cell function in Peyer's patches is dependent on the balance between the cytokines produced by Th1 and Th2 CD4⁺ T cells.[25] In the current study, the proportion of CD8⁺ (T suppressor/cytotoxic) cells was significantly higher in dogs fed the high fermentable diet. This may have contributed to the lower T cell response.

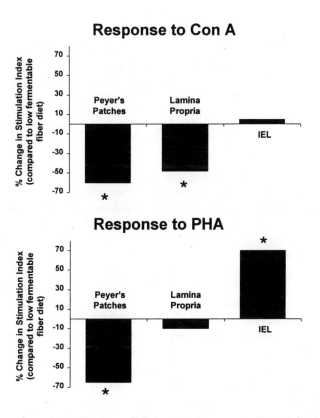

Figure 2. Bars represent the % difference in [³H]-thymidine incorporation by gut derived immune cells from dogs fed the fermentable fiber blend diet as a % of the response by dogs fed the nonfermentable cellulose diet. * indicates that the response is significantly (P<0.05) different from the low fiber group.

Lamina Propria. Plasma cells, originating in the Peyer's patches, return to the gut from the periphery to reside in the lamina propria region.[5] This is a poorly understood process of specific homing that involves a number of specialized adhesion molecules and is a special feature of GALT.[26] B cells in the lamina propria primarily secrete IgA as compared to those in peripheral circulation which primarily produce IgG and IgM. The secretory component of sIgA originates as a transmembrane protein found on the basal and lateral plasma membrane of luminal epithelial cells.

IgA is one of the most important defense factors in the mucosal immune system. Dogs that are unable to produce IgA demonstrate increased susceptibility to intestinal infections.[27, 28] Secretory IgA, unlike other immunoglobulins, does not fix complement, opsonize bacteria nor is it efficient in killing microorganisms. The unique actions of secretory IgA are beneficial since they prevent the initiation of inflammatory responses. The role of sIgA in the gut is to inhibit the attachment and penetration of bacteria and toxins in the lumen, bind undigested protein to prevent absorption, and increase time for digestive enzymes to work and to increase mucus secretion.[2]

In the current study, increasing the amount of fermentable fiber in the diet of dogs significantly decreased [³H]-thymidine incorporation by immune cells from the lamina propria of the gut after stimulation with Con A (*Figure 2*). The amount of fermentable fiber did not significantly alter the proportion of B cells in this predominantly B tissue but did result in a significantly higher proportion of CD8⁺ cells and a lower CD4/CD8 T cell ratio. Further studies are required to determine the effect of feeding fermentable fiber on the balance between Th1 and Th2 cytokines and IgA secretion in both the lamina propria and Peyer's patches regions of the gut.

Intraepithelial Lymphocytes. Although the immune cells in Peyer's patches are important in the initial contact of food and bacterial antigen in the gut, the number is small in relation to the total mucosal surface. In contrast there is an average of 1 intraepithelial T cell for every 6-10 epithelial cells, making IEL the largest immunocompetent cell pool in the body.[29] Although IEL line both the small and large intestine from the crypt base to the villus tip, their exact biological function in the mucosal immune system is not known. IEL are situated in a central location for host defense against numerous orally encountered foreign antigens. They are in continuous contact with luminal antigen through the epithelial layer and are likely involved in several aspects of mucosal immune defense. It has been suggested that they may be the first compartment of the immune system that responds to gut-derived antigens (both pathogens and dietary antigens).[2] Phenotypically they are quite different from immune cells elsewhere in the body, suggesting a specific biological function. IEL are comprised primarily of CD8⁺ cells. This suggests that IEL cells may be functional suppressor cells and permits an explanation for processes such as oral tolerance.[5] Indeed the epithelial cells in the gut may be involved in selectively activating the CD8⁺ IEL.[30]

Although they express the CD3 T cell marker, IEL have low expression of CD5, CD6, LFA-1, and VLA-4 markers seen on peripheral T cells. Few of these cells express regular activation markers such as CD25 (IL-2 receptor) or CD71 (transferrin receptor).[31] In some species there are a number of CD4⁺CD8⁺ (double positive)T cells, cells that are usually only seen during maturation in the thymus.[32] In the present study, we did not find these double positive cells in the IEL of adult dogs. NK cytotoxic activity has been demonstrated against some target cell lines, but not against others. In the dog we demonstrated that canine IEL have cytotoxic

Natural Killer Cell Activity of IEL

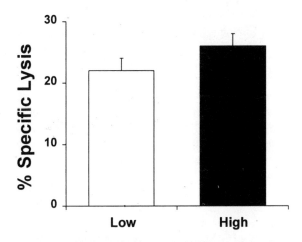

Fermentable Fiber Content of Diet

Figure 3. Bars represent the % specific lysis against canine NK sensitive cells (CTAC) at an effector: target ratio of 100:1. There was no significant effect of fermentable fiber on the response.

activity against a canine NK sensitive cell line (CTAC; *Figure 3*). The physiological importance of this cytotoxic activity has not been established, but is suggested to provide an important first line defense against invasion by enteric pathogens or the elimination of transformed (pre-carcinogenic) epithelial stem cells.[31] The fermentability of fiber in the diet did not significantly affect this activity (*Figure 3*).

Canine IEL are large and granular and respond well to mitogen stimulation. Adding fermentable fiber to the diet increased the [³H]-thymidine response to the T cell mitogen PHA (*Figure 2*). IEL from dogs fed the high fermentable fiber diet contained a higher proportion of CD8⁺ cells (the major lymphocyte subset in this region of the gut). The physiological significance of these changes is not known, but may be important in IEL immunosurveillance against bacterial invasion.[33] The majority of IEL cells (CD8⁺) produce IL-5 and TNF-γ,[31] two cytokines believed to be involved in oral tolerance.[34] Oral tolerance describes a state of hyporesponsiveness following exposure to a previously fed antigen.[5]

During the last 20 years there has been increased interest in IEL, not only as a component of GALT, but also the possible role in disease states both within and outside the gastrointestinal tract. Specific cells from regions of GALT (primarily IEL) have been suggested to be involved in autoimmune diseases, inflammatory bowel disease, and food allergies.[4] Further work is needed to determine the role of fiber fermentability not only in healthy animals but also in disease states.

Conclusions   GALT is a unique and important part of the canine immune system located in an organ that is chronically exposed to antigens. Adding fermentable plant fibers to the diet of dogs changed the composition and function of the immune cells in GALT. More specifically, feeding fermentable fiber produced a higher mitogen response in the predominantly T cell tissues (mesenteric lymph nodes and IEL) and a lower response in cells isolated from the area involved in B cell mediated functions (Peyer's patches and lamina propria). The role of reduced T cell function in the areas involved in IgA secretion is not known, however, it may be important to have a higher response in dogs fed the low fermentable fiber diet. Low fiber diets have been shown to increase the permeability of the gastrointestinal tract, making the animal more susceptible to bacterial translocation.[35] Further work is needed to identify the physiological consequences of diet-induced changes in the composition and function of GALT.

Acknowledgements   The authors would like to acknowledge the excellent technical help of S. Goruk and the assistance of S. Massimino in conducting this study.

References   1. Insoft RM, Sanderson IR, Walker WA. Development of immune function in the intestine and its role in neonatal diseases. *Ped Clin North Amer* 1996; 43:551-571.

2. McKay DM, Perdue MH. Intestinal epithelial function: the case for immunophysiological regulation. *Dig Dis Sci* 1993; 38:1377-1387.

3. Jalkanen S. Lymphocyte homing into the gut. *Immunopath* 1990; 12:153-164.

4. Brandtzaeg P, Halstensen TS, Kett K, Krajci P, Kvale D, Rognum TO, Scott H, Sollid LM. Immunobiology and immunopathology of human gut mucosa: humoral immunity and intraepithelial lymphocytes. *Gastro* 1989; 97:1562-1584.

5. Weiner HL. Oral tolerance: immune mechanisms and treatment of autoimmune diseases. *Immunol Today* 1997; 18:335-343.

6. Ruthlein J, Heinze G, Auer IO. Anti-CD2 and anti-CD3 induced T cell cytotoxicity of human intraepithelial and lamina propria lymphocytes. *Gut* 1992; 33:1626-1632.

7. Bowers RH. Nutrition and immune function. *Nutr Clin Pract*, 1990; 5:189-195.

8. Cerra FB. Nutrient modulation of inflammatory and immune function. *Am J Surgery* 1991; 161:230-234.

9. Spaeth G, Gottwald T, Werner H, Haas W, Holmer M. Glutamine peptide does not improve gut barrier function and mucosal immunity in total parenteral nutrition. *JPEN* 1997; 17:317-323.

10. Langkamp-Henken B, Glezer JA and Kudsk KA, Immunologic structure and function of the gastrointestinal tract. *Nutr Clin Pract* 1992; 7:100-108.

11. Ferguson A, Parrott DMV. The effect of antigen deprivation on thymus-dependent and thymus-independent lymphocytes in the small intestine of the

mouse. *Clin Exper Immunol* 1972; 12:477-482.

12. Mortensen PB, Clausen MR. Short-chain fatty acids in the human colon: relation to gastrointestinal health and disease. *Scand J Gastroenterol* 1996; 216:132-148.

13. McBurney MI. The gut: central organ in nutrient requirements and metabolism. *Can J Physiol Pharm* 1994; 72:260-265.

14. Lim BO, Yamada K, Nonaka M, Kuramoto Y, Hung P, Sugano M. Dietary fiber modulates indices of intestinal immune function in rats. *J Nutr* 1997; 127:663-667.

15. Pratt VC, Tappenden KA, McBurney MI, Field CJ. Short-chain fatty acid-supplemented total parenteral nutrition improves nonspecific immunity after intestinal resection in rats. *JPEN* 1996; 20:264-271.

16. Sunvold GD. Dietary fiber for dogs and cats: an historical perspective. In: Carey D, Norton SA, Bolser SM, eds. *Recent Advances in Canine and Feline Nutritional Research: Proceedings of the 1996 Iams International Nutrition Symposium.* Wilmington: Orange Frazer Press, 1996; 3-14.

17. Willard MD. Effects of dietary fructooligosaccharide (FOS) supplementation on canine small intestinal bacterial populations. In: Carey D, Norton SA, Bolser SM, eds. *Recent Advances in Canine and Feline Nutritional Research: Proceedings of the 1996 Iams International Nutrition Symposium.* Wilmington: Orange Frazer Press, 1996; 45-52.

18. Clemens ET. Dietary fiber and colonic morphology. In: Carey D, Norton SA, Bolser SM, eds. *Recent Advances in Canine and Feline Nutritional Research: Proceedings of the 1996 Iams International Nutrition Symposium.* Wilmington: Orange Frazer Press, 1996; 15-25.

19. Field CJ. Using immunological techniques to determine the effect of nutrition on T-cell function. *Can J Physiol Pharm* 1996; 74:769-777.

20. Hansbrough JF, Bender EM, Zapata-Sirvent R, Anderson J. Altered helper and supressor lymphoctye populations in surgical patients. *Amer J Surgery* 1984; 148:303-307.

21. Alexander JW. Specific nutrients and the immune response. *Nutr* 1995; 11:229-232.

22. Hendricks KM, Duggan C, Gallagner L, Carlin AC, Richardson DS, Collier SB, Simpson W, Lo C. Malnutrition in hospitalized pediatric patients: current prevalence. *Arch Ped Adol Med* 1995; 149:1118-1122.

23. Trier JS. Structure and function of intestinal M cells. *Gastrol Clin N Amer,* 1991; 20:531-547.

24. Hogenesch H, Felsburg PJ. Development and functional characterization of T cell lines from canine Peyer's patches. *Vet Immunol Immunopath* 1989; 23:29-39.

25. McGhee JR, Strober W, Fujihashi K, Kiyono H. T cell cytokine regulation of mucosal natibody responses with emphasis on intraepithelial lymphocytes helper function. In: Kiyono H, McGhee JR, eds. *Advances in Host Defense Mechanisms.* Birmingham: Raven Press, 1993; 1-20.

26. Farstad IN, Halstensen TS, Kvalel D, Fausa O, Brandtzaeg P. Expression of VLA-4 and L-selectin in human gut-associated lymphoid tissue (GALT). *Adv Exp Med Biol* 1995; 371A:91-96.

27. Whitbread TJ, Batt RM, Garthwaite G. Relative deficiency of serum IgA in the German Shepherd Dog: a breed abnormality. *Res Vet Sci* 1984; 37:350-352.

28. Felsburg PJ, Glickman LT, Shofer F, Kirkpatrick CE, HogenEsch H. Clinical, immunologic and epidemiologic characteristics of canine slective IgA deficiency. *Adv Exp Biol Med* 1987; 216:1461-1470.

29. Macdonald TT, Spencer J. Ontogeny of the gut-associated lymphoid system in man. *Acta Ped* 1994; 83(supplement):3-5.

30. Kaiserlian D, Vidal K. Antigen presentation by intestinal epithelial cells. *Immunol Today* 1993; 14:144.

31. Yamamoto M, Fujihashi K, Beagley KW, McGhee JR, Kiyono H. Cytokine synthesis by intestinal intraeipithelial lymphocytes. *J Immunol* 1993; 150:106-114.

32. Ebert EC, Roberts AI. Pitfalls in the characterization of small intestinal lymphocytes. *J Immunol Meth* 1995; 178:219-227.

33. Kuhnlein P, Park JH, Herrmann T, Elbe A, Hunig T. Identification and characterization of rat gamma/delta T lymphocytes in peripheral lymphoid organs, small intestine, and skin with a monoclonal antibody to a constant determinant of the gamma/delta T cell receptor. *J Immunol* 1994; 153:979-986.

34. Trejdosiewicz LK. Intestinal intraepithelial lymphocytes and lympho-epithelial interactions in the human gastrointestinal mucosa. *Immunol Lett* 1992; 32:13-20.

35. Mao Y, Kasravi B, Nobaek S, Wang LQ, Adawi D, Roos G, Stenram U, Molin G, Bengmark S, Jeppsson B. Pectin-supplemented enteral diet reduces the severity of methotrexate induced enterocolitis in rats. *Scand J Gastroenterol* 1996; 31:558-567.

Efficacy of a Nutrient Dense Diet for Maintenance of Canine Patients Receiving Radiation Therapy

Glenna E. Mauldin, DVM, MS, DACVIM
Assistant Professor of Veterinary Oncology, Department of Veterinary Clinical Sciences
School of Veterinary Medicine, Louisiana State University, Baton Rouge, Louisiana, USA

Introduction

Protein calorie malnutrition (PCM) is the pathophysiologic state that results when intake of protein and calories is inadequate.[1] PCM occurs only rarely in the general human population of the industrialized world. However, PCM is commonly diagnosed among hospitalized patients in these countries.[1,2] Approximately fifty percent of surgical patients in the United States have clinically detectable PCM,[3] and the syndrome is even more prevalent in critically ill intensive care unit patients. It is widely accepted that nutritional support of malnourished human patients must be undertaken before a favorable response to appropriate therapy for primary disease processes can be expected.[1]

Veterinarians are now increasingly aware that PCM also occurs with comparable frequency among their patients, and supportive alimentation is necessary to prevent the associated increase in morbidity and mortality.[4] This chapter will describe a recently completed study examining the efficacy of a nutrient dense diet in preventing PCM in canine patients receiving radiation therapy. As background, the clinically relevant pathophysiologic aspects of PCM will be reviewed, with discussion of the tumor-bearing state. Methods enabling the clinical identification of small animal veterinary patients with special nutritional requirements will also be presented.

Complicated Starvation

Healthy dogs are well adapted to survive extended periods of uncomplicated starvation.[5-11] In the short term, a source of glucose is maintained for use by obligate glycolytic tissues; in the long term, conservation of lean body mass is promoted through the use of fat derived fuels instead of glucose.[12,13] However, the adaptations to a protein and calorie deficit are significantly compromised with the superimposition on the starved state of insults such as severe trauma, sepsis, neoplasia, or extensive thermal burns.[13] Critically ill patients are commonly anorexic, and the term "complicated starvation" is used to describe this combination of serious illness and inadequate food intake. Complicated starvation has been most extensively studied in man, but clinical work and the results of investigations using the dog as a model suggest that many analogous changes occur in the canine patient.[4]

The classic physiologic response to injury consists of three phases. The initial hypometabolic "ebb" or shock phase is followed by a "flow" phase, during which there is a relative increase in metabolic rate. In a patient without food intake, the flow phase is characterized by significant catabolism of body energy and protein reserves to allow healing and fuel other metabolic processes. These losses are restored and recovery occurs during the convalescent phase. This phase is strongly anabolic and is characterized by an increased food intake, which is necessary to support ongoing tissue synthesis and repair.[14]

The flow phase, with its high demand for protein and energy, is the period when optimal nutrition is most critical.[14] In contrast to the reduced metabolic rate typical of uncomplicated starvation,[12] a patient who is severely stressed or injured has a relative increase in metabolic rate which is proportional to the severity of their injury.[13-15] All major organ systems are involved.[13] This response is initiated via spinal pathway input into the central nervous system or elaboration of endogenous cytokines[13,14] and mediated by a variety of hormonal changes. Acutely, marked elevations in plasma catecholamine, cortisol, ACTH, glucagon and growth hormone concentrations are seen.[13,14,16-18] Insulin levels are decreased, often in spite of significant hyperglycemia.[13,14,19]

Proteolysis proceeds at an accelerated rate during complicated starvation,[20,21] due to a decrease in protein synthesis relative to protein catabolism.[22-24] In a stressed, starved patient whose previous nutritional status is normal, rates of both protein synthesis and breakdown are increased as compared with either the normal situation or uncomplicated starvation, but synthesis is increased less. The result is a net increase in protein breakdown.[13,14,22-24] It is important to recognize that the amino acids released through this catabolism of protein must not only satisfy normal requirements for protein turnover, they must also meet the special needs of various tissues in the stressed state. Hepatic glycogen stores are depleted early in complicated starvation, and amino acids provide alternative gluconeogenic precursors for obligate glycolytic tissue.[13] Injured tissue is included in this category and can significantly increase the amount of glucose required.[14] The ketoacids resulting from the transamination of the branch chain amino acids in skeletal muscle are among the preferred glucogenic substrates of the liver during complicated starvation and are consumed at an increased rate.[25,26] There is also increased utilization of the amino acid glutamine. Glutamine is a major substrate for renal ammonia production and for renal and hepatic gluconeogenesis during stress and is a primary respiratory fuel for the gastrointestinal mucosa and cells of the immune system.[14,27] Finally, requirements for acute phase reactants, white blood cells, clotting factors, and cell proliferation for wound healing are elevated during complicated starvation as well, due to infection and injury.[28]

All of these diverse and increased requirements for both amino acids and glucose mean lean body mass is catabolized at an increased rate and cannot be spared by adipose reserves as it would be in uncomplicated starvation.[4,13,14] When there is pre-existing starvation or an extended period of stress, it becomes impossible for the body to continue to protect high priority protein pools such as circulating protein or vital hepatic enzyme systems from breakdown.[29] Cardiac, pulmonary, gastrointestinal, and immune function are all seriously compromised. If catabolism continues without either resolution of the underlying injury or provision of exogenous energy and protein, the patient will quickly deteriorate and death will ensue.[13-15]

Researchers studying dogs hospitalized in an intensive care unit were recently able to confirm high rates of urinary nitrogen loss, a reflection of accelerated protein catabolism in these patients. Loss of lean tissue among anorectic dogs in this study was over 200 grams per day.[30] High protein intake is necessary to offset this type of deficit, and critically ill dogs and cats may require as many as 30 to 50% of their total daily calories as protein.[4] This is especially true in the cat; the potentially increased protein requirements of illness are superimposed on an unusually high basal protein requirement in this species,[31] making effective conservation of lean body mass virtually impossible.

PCM has long been associated with neoplastic disease; "cancer cachexia" is the unique form of PCM which occurs in both human and veterinary cancer patients. The presence of weight loss in the patient with malignant disease is of critical importance because it is an independent determinant of prognosis.[32-34] Therefore, frequent revaluation of nutritional status followed by prompt nutritional intervention whenever indicated is essential for optimal management of the tumor-bearing patient.

Neoplastic Disease

The relationship between the tumor-bearing state and weight loss has been an area of intense study for many years. Research has revealed that unique biochemical alterations are often present in patients with cancer, in addition to many of the abnormalities associated with complicated starvation as described above. Direct effects of the tumor itself, substances elaborated by it, as well as the host hormone and cytokine response to the presence of neoplastic disease, are probably all involved in the pathogenesis of these changes.[35-38] Ultimately, the biochemical abnormalities observed are thought to cause inefficient energy utilization by the host[39-41] and weight loss in the form of both lean body mass and adipose stores is the end result.[15,42,43]

Abnormalities considered characteristic of the tumor-bearing state have been documented in the intermediary metabolism of carbohydrates, proteins, and lipids in human cancer patients,[15,35,42-55] rodents bearing implanted tumors,[56-68] and dogs with naturally occurring neoplastic disease.[69-76] Many specific perturbations have been described, but two related groups of alterations seem to offer the best potential for routine nutritional intervention. First, tumor cells are incapable of significant fat oxidation or aerobic glycolysis, and must derive energy through anaerobic glycolysis.[41,43,60] Glucose consumed by tumor glycolysis is obviously unavailable to the host and, furthermore, host hepatocytes are forced to use host energy stores to resynthesize glucose from the lactate produced.[57,58,60] A diet low in highly digestible carbohydrate and relatively high in fat is currently recommended as a possible way to limit excessive energy utilization by the tumor, while still providing an efficient source of fuel for host tissues. A second group of alterations centers around the high metabolic activity and rapid growth that characterize many tumor cells. Accelerated catabolism of host lean body mass beyond that normally seen with PCM may be required in order to provide a constant supply of amino acids for these functions. Mobilized amino acids are used for various anabolic processes within the tumor cell, as well as being converted through gluconeogenesis to glucose and utilized by the tumor for energy.[41,43,50] Thus, adequate quantities of high biologic value protein should be present in diets fed to tumor-bearing patients in order to maintain host nitrogen balance.

The futile cycling and alteration in flux through various metabolic pathways described above should theoretically increase the energy expenditure of the tumor-bearing host. Many studies have described the measurement of energy expenditure by indirect calorimetry in human and veterinary cancer patients as well as rodent models.[44-47,51,56,74,75] Unfortunately, the results of these studies are variable and do not necessarily confirm increased energy loss. Energy expenditure varies with tumor type and stage of disease. It is apparently increased in some studies, unchanged in others, and actually decreased in still others. Variation in the manifestations of cancer cachexia between tumor types or even individuals with the same tumor may explain some of these discrepancies, but several additional points should also be considered. First, indirect calorimetry is a sensitive and complex technique. Results may vary between investigators and be difficult to consistently reproduce. Secondly, authors disagree regarding the most appropriate study subjects and controls for energy expenditure studies. Many studies describe energy expenditure in tumor-bearing subjects prior to any weight loss at all. Some investigators compare cachectic cancer patients to young, healthy, weight stable controls, while others argue that the only suitable comparison is between weight losing cancer patients and weight losing patients with non-malignant disease. Finally, interpretation of results is complicated in small animal veterinary patients, because the true energy requirements of even healthy dogs and cats are controversial. Further work in this area is obviously required.

Nutritional
Assessment

The systematic collection and integration of clinical information evaluating a patient's protein and energy status is called nutritional assessment.[1] Nutritional assessment has several important functions. It determines the etiology and severity of existing PCM as well as predicting which patients are at greatest risk for the future development of PCM and its related complications. Nutritional assessment identifies those patients requiring immediate nutritional intervention. Finally, it also permits the clinician to gauge the effectiveness of nutritional support as instituted.[1]

A detailed diet history and physical examination comprise the initial components of a complete nutritional assessment. The diet history should be as thorough as possible. The patient's current diet should be exactly and quantitatively defined with regard to content, amount, frequency, and method of feeding. The owner should be questioned specifically regarding any medications or nutritional supplements being administered. It is also important to remember that the primary or underlying illness may have prompted a significant alteration in what is being fed, and how and when it is being offered. Information regarding a patient's diet prior to the onset of illness may provide the clinician with critical insights into current nutritional status.[4]

A careful physical examination is the next step in nutritional assessment. Few specific clinical syndromes are associated with malnutrition in small animal patients, although the central retinal degeneration and dilated cardiomyopathy associated with taurine deficiency in the cat are examples. More commonly the signs of malnutrition are nonspecific, and the clinician must preserve an increased index of suspicion in order to identify affected patients. Physical examination of the cat or dog suffering from PCM may reveal one or more abnormalities including muscle wasting, pallor, poor hair coat, cranial organomegaly, evidence of chronic infections, lymphadenopathy, or peripheral edema.[77]

In human patients, lean body mass and body fat stores are evaluated through anthropometric measurements such as triceps skinfold thickness and midarm circumference.[1] Further study will be necessary to determine if these techniques will be useful in veterinary patients, but adapting them for use in small animals may be difficult because of the large variation in body size and conformation among different breeds. However, consistent use of a standardized body condition scoring system can provide the practicing veterinarian with comparable information regarding lean body mass and adipose stores. Body condition scoring systems generally utilize a five or nine point scale, where each point corresponds to a particular body condition with defined criteria. Studies show that there is good correlation between body condition scoring and actual body composition in canine and feline patients.[78]

Several hematologic and biochemical parameters which are readily accessible to the veterinarian can also be utilized as markers of nutritional status, although they are relatively insensitive. PCM may result in anemia and decreased total lymphocyte counts in some patients.[77] Animals suffering from serious PCM may also have decreased serum albumin concentrations.[77] However, because the serum half life of albumin is relatively long (approximately eight days in the dog),[79] an extended period of malnutrition is necessary before concentrations fall below the normal range. In human patients, serum proteins with shorter half lives, such as transferrin or fibrinogen, have been shown to provide a more accurate assessment of protein status.[1]

Another serum protein that has been extensively investigated in human patients as a biochemical marker of nutritional status is insulin-like growth factor-I, or IGF-I. IGF-I is a low molecular weight peptide hormone that stimulates bone and cartilage formation,[80] and also has an insulin-like effect.[81-84] IGF-I is produced primarily by the liver in response to growth hormone, and has a half life of approximately 15 hours in man. There is a strong correlation between serum concentrations of IGF-I, energy intake, and nitrogen balance; IGF-I falls by 60 to 70% in healthy human volunteers after a five day fast, and then rapidly returns to baseline with reinstitution of normal food intake.[85] Serum IGF-I concentrations are significantly decreased and accurately reflect suboptimal nutritional status in elderly human patients with PCM,[85] children with cystic fibrosis,[86] adult patients undergoing continuous ambulatory peritoneal dialysis[87] or hemodialysis,[88] and children with marasmus or kwashiorkor.[89] Serum IGF-I concentrations can also be utilized to accurately predict those patients most likely to experience serious complications during hospitalization.[85] It is intriguing to speculate that short half life serum proteins such as IGF-I, transferrin, and fibrinogen will also be useful markers of nutritional status in critically ill or stressed veterinary patients, but additional work will be necessary to prove this hypothesis.

Another potential biochemical marker of nutritional status is the muscle specific enzyme creatine kinase. As already described, skeletal muscle is rapidly catabolized to provide amino acids for many purposes during illness and PCM. Interestingly, hospitalized human surgical patients in negative nitrogen and energy balance have high serum concentrations of creatine kinase. These concentrations decrease after institution of nutritional support.[90] Recent work has shown that serum creatine kinase concentrations also increase rapidly in the cat during anorexia and decrease dramatically after initiation of supportive alimentation.[91] The median serum creatine kinase concentration was over ten times higher among the anorectic cats in this study than in normal controls, but decreased significantly after 48 hours of nutritional support delivered through a nasoesophageal tube. Further study will be required to determine if serum creatine kinase concentrations are a similarly useful marker of nutritional status in the dog.

Recent Studies   The ability of a standardized calorie dense, highly digestible diet to maintain tumor-bearing dogs receiving radiation therapy was recently investigated at the Radiation Therapy Unit of the Donaldson-Atwood Cancer Clinic in New York. It was hypothesized that the test diet would be more effective in preventing PCM and maintaining lean body mass in these highly stressed patients than the current nutritional standard of care. The study was also designed to provide clinically useful data on methods of nutritional assessment in the dog, as well as evaluating the potential benefit of high fat diets in tumor-bearing animals.

Any dog receiving definitive radiation therapy for neoplastic disease was eligible for entry into the study. Depending on the type of tumor being treated, a definitive course of radiation therapy consisted of 18 to 21 three Gy treatment fractions. Therapy was administered over 42 to 49 days, and each treatment was delivered under general anesthesia after an overnight fast. A total of 50 study subjects were identified prior to initiation of radiation therapy and enrolled in the study. All owners signed an informed consent release.

Initial diagnostics for clinical and nutritional assessment included the following: a complete nutritional history; body weight; mid-triceps skinfold thickness; complete blood count and differential; serum biochemical profile; serum transferrin, fibrinogen, and IGF-I concentrations; and, serum creatine kinase concentration. After baseline testing was completed, dogs were stratified by disease category and performance score[92] and randomized to receive one of two nutritional treatments. Dogs in one group received the test diet, while dogs in the other group continued to receive their regular diets as fed by their owners. The guaranteed analysis of the test diet, as supplied by the manufacturer,[a] was as follows:

Crude Protein not less than ---------------- 35.0%
Crude Fat not less than -------------------- 25.0%
Crude Fiber not more than ------------------ 4.0%
Moisture not more than --------------------- 10.0%

Dogs that were randomized to receive the test diet were allowed a one week period of gradual adaptation to the new diet. Caloric intake necessary for maintenance of body weight at entry into the test diet group was estimated using the equation:[93]

$$MER = 132(BW_{kg})^{3/4}$$

Study subjects were monitored closely throughout the course of radiation therapy. All owners filled out detailed diet history forms. These forms recorded daily food intake, appetite, and the presence or absence of vomiting or diarrhea. All dogs were weighed three times weekly, prior to each radiation treatment. A mid-triceps skinfold thickness measurement, as well as a complete blood count, serum biochemical profile, serum transferrin, fibrinogen, an IGF-I concentration, and a serum creatine kinase concentration were performed weekly during therapy.

Data from this study, while not yet fully analyzed, has already provided encouraging results. The high fat test diet was palatable and well tolerated, and gastrointestinal upset was very uncommon. Dogs consuming the test diet are, so far, less likely to lose weight than dogs in the control group, although this difference has not yet reached statistical significance (P<0.08, **Figure 1**). Dogs in the test diet group have gained a median of 4% of their initial body weight over the course of their radiation therapy (range, loss of 4.89% to gain of 9.74%), while dogs in the control group have lost a median of 0.54% of their initial body weight during radiation therapy (range, loss of 11.79% to gain of 14.05%).

There is also biochemical evidence that dogs consuming the test diet have more optimal nutritional status. Blood urea nitrogen concentrations (BUN), while still well within the normal range, are higher in dogs consuming the test diet after the second week of radiation therapy (P<0.03, **Figure 2**). This most likely reflects a more consistent protein intake. Dogs in the test diet group have a median week 5 BUN of 18.9 mg/dL (range, 8.6 to 27.3), while dogs in the control group have a

[a] The Iams Company, Dayton OH, 45414

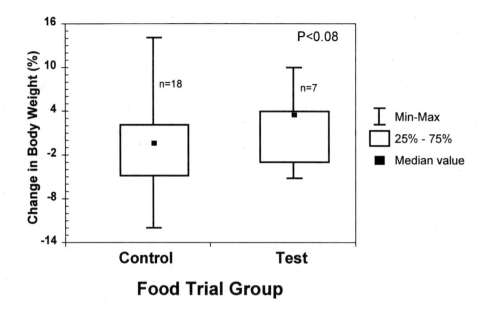

Figure 1. Change in body weight through radiation therapy, expressed as a percentage of initial body weight. The box in the box plot extends from the 25th to the 75th percentile. The small square contained within the box is the median. The error bars represent observed range between minimum and maximum values.

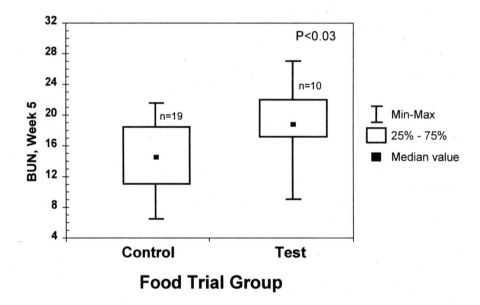

Figure 2. Week 5 blood urea nitrogen concentration, in mg/dL. The box in the box plot extends from the 25th to the 75th percentile. The small square contained within the box is the median. The error bars represent observed range between minimum and maximum values.

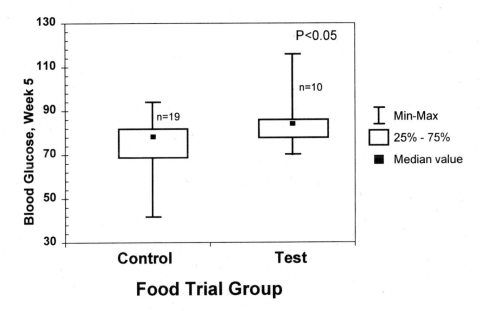

Figure 3. Week 5 blood glucose concentration, in mg/dL. The box in the box plot extends from the 25th to the 75th percentile. The small square contained within the box is the median. The error bars represent observed range between minimum and maximum values.

median week 5 BUN of 14.5 mg/dL (range, 6.4 to 21.3). By week 5 of radiation therapy, dogs eating the test diet also exhibit improved ability to maintain normoglycemia after an overnight fast (P<0.05, *Figure 3*). Dogs in the test diet group have a median week 5 blood glucose concentration of 84 mg/dL (range, 70 to 116), while dogs in the control group have a median week 5 blood glucose concentration of 79 mg/dL (range, 42 to 94).

Definitive conclusions must obviously await analysis of all data collected, but at this time it does appear that the highly digestible and energy dense test diet was more effective in maintaining nutritional status among the dogs in this study.

References

1. Daley BJ, Bistrian BR. Nutritional assessment. In: Zaloga GP, ed. *Nutrition in Critical Care*, St. Louis: Mosby-Year Book, Inc., 1994; 9-33.

2. Lemonnier D, Acher S, Boukaiba N, Flament C, Doucet C, Piau A, Chappuis P. Discrepancy between anthropometry and biochemistry in the assessment of the nutritional status of the elderly. *Eur J Clin Nutr* 1991; 45:281-286.

3. Bistrian BR, Blackburn GL, Hallowell E, Heddle R. Protein status of general surgical patients. *J Am Med Assoc* 1974; 230:858-860.

4. Donoghue SD. Nutritional support of hospitalized patients. *Vet Clin N Amer* 1989; 19:475-495.

5. Lemieux G, Plante GE. The effect of starvation in the normal dog including the dalmation coach hound. *Metabolism* 1968; 17:620-630.

6. Brady LJ, Armstrong MK, Muiruri KL, Romsos DR, Bergen WG, Leveille GA. Influence of prolonged fasting in the dog on glucose turnover and blood metabolites. *J Nutr* 1977; 107:1053-1061.

7. DeBruijne JJ. Biochemical observations during total starvation in dogs. *Inter J Obesity* 1979; 3:239-247.

8. Cowan JS, Vranic M, Wrenshall GA. Nutritional conditions affecting the rate of glucose production in fed and fasting female dogs. *Metabolism* 1965; 14:468-470.

9. Steele R, Winkler B, Rathgeb I, Bjerknes C, Altszuler N. Plasma glucose and free fatty acid metabolism in normal and long-fasted dogs. *Am J Physiol* 1968; 214:313-319.

10. Davis MA, Williams PE, Cherrington AD. Net hepatic lactate balance following mixed meal feeding in the four-day fasted conscious dog. *Metabolism* 1987; 36:856-862.

11. Lewis LD. Obesity in the dog. *J Am Anim Hosp Assoc* 1978; 14:402-409.

12. Cahill GF. Starvation in man. *N Engl J Med* 1970; 282:668-675.

13. Meguid MM, Collier MD, Howard LJ. Uncomplicated and stressed starvation. *Surg Clin N Amer* 1981; 61:529-543.

14. Editorial. Nutrition and the metabolic response to injury. *Lancet* 1989; 1:995-997.

15. Brennan MF. Uncomplicated starvation versus cancer cachexia. *Cancer Res* 1977; 37:2359-2364.

16. Lilly MP, Engeland WC, Gann DS. Adrenal medullary responses to repeated hemorrhage in conscious dogs. *Am J Physiol* 1986; 251:R1193-R1199.

17. Lilly MP, Engeland WC, Gann DS. Pituitary-adrenal responses to repeated small hemorrhage in conscious dogs. *Am J Physiol* 1986; 251:R1200-R1207.

18. DeMaria EJ, Lilly MP, Gann DS. Potentiated hormonal responses in a model of traumatic injury. *J Surg Res* 1987; 43:45-51.

19. Black PR, Brooks DC, Bessey PQ, Wolfe RR, Wilmore DW. Mechanisms of insulin resistance following injury. *Ann Surg* 1982; 196:420-435.

20. Clowes GHA, George BC, Villee CA, Saravis CA. Muscle proteolysis induced by a circulating peptide in patients with sepsis or trauma. *N Engl J Med* 1983; 308:545-552.

21. Baracos V, Rodemann HP, Dinarello CA, Goldberg AL. Stimulation of muscle protein degradation and prostaglandin E_2 release by leukocytic pyrogen (interleukin-1). *N Engl J Med* 1983; 308:553-558.

22. Long CL, Jeevanandam M, Kim BM, Kinney JM. Whole body protein synthesis and catabolism in septic man. *Am J Clin Nutr* 1977; 30:1340-1344.

23. Yamamori H, Tashiro T, Mashima Y, Okui K. Effects of severity of surgical trauma on whole body protein turnover in patients receiving total parenteral nutrition. *J Parent Ent Nutr* 1987; 11:454-457.

24. Wolfe BM, Chock GP. Protein metabolism in surgical patients. *Surg Clin N Amer* 1981; 61:509-518.

25. Groves AC, Woolf LI, Duff JH, Finley RJ. Metabolism of branched-chain amino acids in dogs with *Escherichia coli* endotoxin shock. *Surgery* 1983; 93:273-278.

26. Yeaman SJ. The 2-oxo acid dehydrogenase complexes: recent advances.

Biochem J 1989; 257:625-632.

27. Watford M. Does glutamine regulate skeletal muscle protein turnover? *TIBS* 1989; 14:1-2.

28. Askanazi J, Mathews D, Rothkopf M. Patterns of fuel utilization during parenteral nutrition. *Surg Clin N Amer* 1986; 66:1091-1103.

29. Stein TP, Buzby GP. Protein metabolism in surgical patients. *Surg Clin N Amer* 1981; 61:519-527.

30. Michel KE, King LG, Ostro E. Measurement of urinary urea nitrogen content as an estimate of the amount of total urinary nitrogen loss in dogs in intensive care units. *J Am Vet Med Assoc* 1997; 210:356-359.

31. Rogers QR, Morris JG. Protein and amino acid nutrition of the cat. *Amer Anim Hosp Proc* 1983; 333-336.

32. DeWys WD. Weight loss and nutritional abnormalities in cancer patients: incidence, severity and significance. *Clinics in Oncology* 1986; 5:251-261.

33. DeWys WD, Begg C, Lavin PT, Band PR, Bennett JM, Bertino JR, Cohen MH, Douglass HO, Engstrom PF, Ezdinli EZ, Horton J, Johnson GJ, Moertel CG, Oken MM, Perlia C, Rosenbaum C, Silverstein MN, Skeel RT, Sponzo RW, Tormey DC. Prognostic effect of weight loss prior to chemotherapy in cancer patients. *Am J Med* 1980; 69:491-497.

34. Hickman DM, Miller RA, Rombeau JL, Twomey PL, Frey CF. Serum albumin and body weight as predictors of postoperative course in colorectal cancer. *J Parent Ent Nutr* 1980; 4:314-316.

35. Burt ME, Aoki TT, Gorschboth CM, Brennan MF. Peripheral tissue metabolism in cancer-bearing man. *Ann Surg* 1983; 198:685-691.

36. Beutler B, Greenwald D, Hulmes JD, Chang M, Pan YCE, Mathison J, Ulevitch R, Cerami A. Identity of tumour necrosis factor and the macrophage secreted factor cachectin. *Nature* 1985; 316:552-554.

37. Oliff A, Defeo-Jones D, Boyer M, Martinez D, Kiefer D, Vuocolo G, Wolfe A, Socher S. Tumors secreting human TNF/cachectin induce cachexia in mice. *Cell* 1987; 50:555-563.

38. Norton JA, Moley JF, Green MV, Carson RE, Morrison SD. Parabiotic transfer of cancer anorexia/cachexia in male rats. *Cancer Res* 1985; 45:5547-5552.

39. Theologides A. The anorexia-cachexia syndrome: a new hypothesis. *Ann NY Acad Sci* 1974; 230:14-22.

40. Brennan MF. Total parenteral nutrition in the cancer patient. *N Engl J Med* 1981; 305:375-382.

41. DeWys WD. Pathophysiology of cancer cachexia: current understanding and areas for future research. *Cancer Res* 1982; 42(Suppl):721s-726s.

42. Kern JA, Norton JA. Cancer cachexia. *J Parent Ent Nutr* 1988; 12:286-298.

43. Heber D, Byerley LO, Chi J, Grosvenor M, Bergman RN, Coleman M, Chlebowski RT. Pathophysiology of malnutrition in the adult cancer patient. *Cancer* 1986; 58:1867-1873.

44. Lerebours E, Tilly H, Rimbert A, Delarue J, Piguet H, Colin R. Change in energy and protein status during chemotherapy in patients with acute leukemia. *Cancer* 1988; 61:2412-2417

45. Arbeit JM, Lees DE, Corsey R, Brennan MF. Resting energy expenditure in controls and cancer patients with localize and diffuse disease. *Ann Surg* 1984; 199:292-298.

46. Dempsey DT, Feurer ID, Knox LS, Crosby LO, Buzby GP, Mullen JL. Energy expenditure in malnourished gastrointestinal cancer patients. *Cancer* 1984; 53:1265-1273.

47. Dempsey DT, Knox LS, Mullen JL, Miller C, Feurer ID, Buzby GP. Energy expenditure in malnourished patients with colorectal cancer. *Arch Surg* 1986; 121:789-795.

48. Norton JA, Maher M, Wesley R, White D, Brennan MF. Glucose intolerance in sarcoma patients. *Cancer* 1984; 54:3022-3027.

49. Holroyde CP, Skutches CL, Boden G, Reichard GA. Glucose metabolism in cachectic patients with colorectal cancer. *Cancer Res* 1984; 44:5910-5913.

50. Norton JA, Burt ME, Brennan MF. *In vivo* utilization of substrate by human sarcoma-bearing limbs. *Cancer* 1980; 45:2934-2939.

51. Eden E, Ekman L, Bennegard K, Lindmark L, Lundholm K. Whole-body tyrosine flux in relation to energy expenditure in weight-losing cancer patients. *Metabolism* 1984; 33:1020-1027.

52. Norton JA, Stein TP, Brennan MF. Whole body protein synthesis and turnover in normal man and malnourished patients with and without known cancer. *Ann Surg* 1981; 194:123-128.

53. Lundholm K, Karlberg I, Schersten T. Albumin and hepatic protein synthesis in patients with early cancer. *Cancer* 1980; 46:71-76.

54. Alexopoulos CG, Blatsios B, Avgerinos A. Serum lipids and lipoprotein disorders in cancer patients. *Cancer* 1987; 60:3065-3070.

55. Eden E, Edstrom S, Bennegard K, Lindmark L, Lundholm K. Glycerol dynamics in weight-losing cancer patients. *Surgery* 1985; 97:176-184.

56. Popp MB, Brennan MF, Morrison SD. Resting and activity energy expenditure during total parenteral nutrition in rats with methylcholanthrene-induced sarcoma. *Cancer* 1982; 49:1212-1220.

57. Burt ME, Lowry SF, Gorschboth C, Brennan MF. Metabolic alterations in a noncachectic animal tumor system. *Cancer* 1981; 47:2138-2146.

58. Singh J, Grigor MR, Thompson MP. Glucose homeostasis in rats bearing a transplantable sarcoma. *Cancer Res* 1980; 40:1699-1706.

59. Arbeit JM, Burt ME, Rubinstein LV, Gorschboth C, Brennan MF. Glucose metabolism and the percentage of glucose derived from alanine: non-tumor-bearing rats. *Cancer Res* 1982; 42:4936-4942.

60. Roh MS, Ekman L, Jeevanandam M, Brennan MF. Gluconeogenesis in tumor-influenced hepatocytes. *Surgery* 1984; 96:427-433.

61. Inculet RI, Peacock JL, Gorschboth CM, Norton JA. Gluconeogenesis in the tumor-influenced rat hepatocyte: importance of tumor burden, insulin and glucagon. *J Natl Cancer Inst* 1987; 79:1039-1046.

62. Alexander HR, DePippo P, Rao S, Burt ME. Substrate alterations in a sarcoma-bearing rat model: effect of tumor growth and resection. *J Surg Res* 1990; 48:471-475.

63. Lowry SF, Foster DM, Norton JA, Berman M, Brennan MF. Glucose disposal and gluconeogenesis from alanine in tumor-bearing Fischer 344 rats. *J Natl Cancer Inst* 1981; 66:653-658.

64. Norton JA, Shamberger R, Stein TP, Milne GWA, Brennan MF. The influence of tumor-bearing on protein metabolism in the rat. *J Surg Res* 1981; 30:456-462.

65. Warren RS, Jeevanandam M, Brennan MF. Protein synthesis in the tumor-influenced hepatocyte. *Surgery* 1985; 98:275-281.

66. Warren RS, Jeevanandam M, Brennan MF. Comparison of hepatic protein synthesis *in vivo* versus *in vitro* in the tumor-bearing rat. *J Surg Res* 1987; 42:43-50.

67. Younes RN, Vydelingum NA, Noguchi Y, Brennan MF. Lipid kinetic alteration in tumor-bearing rats: reversal by tumor excision. *J Surg Res* 1990; 48:324-328.

68. Noguchi Y, Vydelingum NA, Younes RN, Fried SK, Brennan MF. Tumor-induced alteration in tissue lipoprotein lipase activity and mRNA levels. *Cancer Res* 1991; 51:863-869.

69. Vail DM, Ogilvie GK, Wheeler SL, Fettman MJ, Johnston SD, Hegstad RL. Alterations in carbohydrate metabolism in canine lymphoma. *J Vet Int Med* 1990; 4:8-11.

70. Ogilvie GK, Vail DM, Wheeler SL, Ford RB, Czarnecki GL. Alterations in fat and protein metabolism in dogs with cancer. *Proc 8th Annual Vet Cancer Soc* 1988; 31.

71. Ogilvie GK, Ford RB, Vail DM, Walters LM, Salman MD, Babineau C, Fettman MJ. Alterations in lipoprotein profiles in dogs with lymphoma. *J Vet Int Med* 1994; 8:62-66.

72. Noonan M, Mauldin GE, Mauldin GN. Serum lactate concentrations in 120 hospitalized dogs. *Proc 13th Annual Vet Cancer Soc* 1993; 130.

73. Ogilvie GK, Vail DM, Wheeler SL, Fettman MJ, Salman MD, Johnston SD, Hegstad RL. Effects of chemotherapy and remission on carbohydrate metabolism in dogs with lymphoma. *Cancer* 1992; 69:233-238.

74. Ogilvie GK, Walters LM, Fettman MJ, Hand MS, Salman MD, Wheeler SL. Energy expenditure in dogs with lymphoma fed two specialized diets. *Cancer* 1993; 71:3146-3152.

75. Ogilvie GK, Walters LM, Salman MD, Fettman MJ. Resting energy expenditure in dogs with nonhematopoietic malignancies before and after excision of tumors. *Am J Vet Res* 1996; 57:1463-1467.

76. Ogilvie GK, Walters L, Salman MD, Fettman MJ, Johnston SD, Hegstad RL. Alterations in carbohydrate metabolism in dogs with nonhematopoietic malignancy. *Am J Vet Res* 1997; 58:277-281.

77. Lewis LD, Morris ML, Hand MS. Anorexia, inanition and critical care nutrition. In: *Small Animal Clinical Nutrition*, 3rd edition. Topeka: Mark Morris Associates, 1987; 5-1–5-43.

78. LaFlamme DP, Kealy RD, Schmidt DA. Estimation of body fat by body condition score. *J Vet Int Med* 1994; 8:154.

79. Dixon FJ, Maurer PH, Deichmiller MP. Half-lives of homologous serum albumins in several species. *Proc Soc Exp Biol Med* 1953; 83:287-288.

80. Rogachefsky RA, Dean DD, Howell DS, Altman RD. Treatment of canine osteoarthritis with insulin-like growth factor-I (IGF-I) and sodium pentosan polysulfate. *Osteoarthritis Cartilage* 1993; 1:105-114.

81. Sakurai Y, Zhang X, Wolfe RR. Insulin-like growth factor-I and insulin reduce leucine flux and oxidation in conscious tumor necrosis factor-infused dogs. *Surgery* 1995; 117:305-313.

82. Valentini L, Holzenbein T, Winkler S, Sautner T, Ollenschlager G, Hortnagl H, Karner J, Roth E. Acute effects of insulin-like growth factor I on interorgan glucose and lactate flux in protein-catabolic dogs. *J Surg Res* 1995; 59:606-613.

83. Umpleby AM, Shojaee-Moradie F, Thomason MJ, Kelly JM, Skottner A, Sonksen PH, Jones RH. Effects of insulin-like growth factor-I (IGF-I), insulin and combined IGF-I-insulin infusions on protein metabolism in dogs. *Eur J Clin Invest* 1994; 24:337-344.

84. Shojaee-Moradie F, Umpleby AM, Thomason MJ, Jackson NC, Boroujerdi MA, Sonksen PH, Skottner A, Jones RH. A comparison of the effects of insulin-like growth factor-I, insulin and combined infusions of insulin and insulin-like growth factor-I on glucose metabolism in dogs. *Eur J Clin Invest* 1995; 25:920-928.

85. Sullivan DH, Carter WJ. Insulin-like growth factor I as an indicator of protein-energy undernutrition among metabolically stable hospitalized elderly. *J Am Coll Nutr* 1994; 13:184-191.

86. Laursen EM, Juul A, Lanng S, Hoiby N, Koch C, Muller J, Skakkebaek NE. Diminished concentrations of insulin-like growth factor I in cystic fibrosis. *Arch Dis Child* 1995; 72:494-497.

87. Jacob V, Marchant PR, Wild G, Brown CB, Moorhead PJ, El Nahas AM. Nutritional profile of continuous ambulatory peritoneal dialysis patients. *Nephron* 1995; 71:16-22.

88. Parker TF, Wingard RL, Husni L, Ikizler A, Parker RA, Hakim RM. Effect of the membrane biocompatibility on nutritional parameters in chronic hemodialysis patients. *Kidney Int* 1996; 49:551-556.

89. Zamboni G, Dufillot D, Antoniazzi F, Valentini R, Gendrel D, Tato L. Growth hormone-binding proteins and insulin-like growth-factor binding proteins in protein-energy malnutrition, before and after nutritional rehabilitation. *Pediatr Res* 1996; 39:410-414.

90. Antonas KN, Curtas MS, Meguid MM. Use of serum CPK-MM to monitor response to nutritional intervention in catabolic surgical patients. *J Surg Res* 1987; 42:219-226.

91. Fascetti AJ, Mauldin GE, Mauldin GN. Correlation between serum creatine kinase activities and anorexia in cats. *J Vet Int Med* 1997; 11:9-13.

92. Burk RL, Mauldin GN. Use of a performance scale in small animal radiation therapy. *Vet Radiol* 1992; 33:388-391.

93. National Research Council. *Nutrient Requirements of Dogs.* Washington: National Academy Press, 1985.

The Role of Dietary Lutein in the Dog and Cat

Boon P. Chew, PhD
Professor, Department of Animal Sciences
Washington State University, Pullman, Washington, USA

Teri S. Wong, BS[a]; Jean Soon Park, MS[a]; Brian B. Weng, BS[a];
Nani Cha, BS[a]; Hong Wook Kim, MS[a]; Katherine M. Byrne, DVM, PhD[a];
Michael G. Hayek, PhD[b]; Gregory A. Reinhart, PhD[b]
[a]Department of Animal Sciences,
Washington State University, Pullman, Washington, USA;
[b]Research and Development, The Iams Company, Lewisburg, Ohio, USA

Introduction

Several naturally occurring carotenoids have been reported to play important roles in regulating immunity.[1-4] However, most studies have concentrated on β-carotene. Recent studies have reported the importance of other carotenoids, notably astaxanthin, lycopene, and canthaxanthin, in regulating immune function and disease etiology. For instance, canthaxanthin prevented chemical-induced carcinogenesis in mice[5] while α-carotene inhibited human neuroblastoma cell proliferation.[6] Canthaxanthin increased lymphocyte proliferation in rats[7] and enhanced the production of tumor necrosis factor (TNF) by macrophages in hamsters.[8] Astaxanthin and β-carotene increased *ex vivo* antibody reponse of mouse splenocytes to T-dependent antigens.[9]

Little is known concerning the possible physiologic function of lutein, a major blood carotenoid in some species (human, chicken). It has been recently reported that dietary lutein decreased mammary tumor incidence, tumor growth, and shortened tumor latency in mice challenges with a transplantable murine mammary tumor cell line.[10,11] Astaxanthin and canthaxanthin also possess inhibitory effect against mammary tumor growth in mice.[12] Dietary lutein also enhanced lymphocyte proliferation in mouse splenocytes.[10] Chew et al.[13] similarly reported enhanced mitogen-induced blastogenesis in mice fed astaxanthin, β-carotene, and canthaxanthin. Splenocytes from mice injected peritoneally with lutein, astaxanthin, and β-carotene had enhanced antibody response to T-dependent antigens.[9] Therefore, carotenoids including lutein possess immuno-modulatory activities and may be important in disease etiology. Similar studies on the uptake and possible physiological action of lutein in dogs and cats are not available. This paper will systematically investigate the kinetic uptake of dietary lutein in blood and in leukocytes of dogs and cats. Furthermore, the importance of lutein in modulating immune function will be studied.

Lutein Uptake in Dogs. Two experiments were conducted to study the kinetic characteristics of lutein uptake in dogs given lutein orally. Experiment 1 was designed to study the changes in concentrations of lutein in plasma in dogs given a single oral dose of lutein. Mature female Beagles were given once perorally 0, 10, 20 or 40 mg of lutein. Blood was obtained 0, 3, 6, 9, 12, 15, 18, and 24 hours post-dosing. Plasma lutein increased rapidly and in a dose-dependent manner within three hours post-dosing (**Figure 1**). Concentrations generally remained high thereafter and decreased to pre-treatment levels by 24 hours. The half-life of plasma lutein was approximately 20 hours. In experiment 2, repeated daily doses of 0, 10, 20 or 40 mg of lutein were administered and blood obtained daily. On day 7 and 14 blood also was obtained for the isolation of peripheral blood lymphocytes and neutrophils for the quantification of lutein content in whole blood cells and in subcellular fractions. Plasma lutein continued to increase for 2 to 5 days and generally reached steady-state by day 6 (**Figure 2**). There was no difference in uptake in dogs fed 10 and 20 mg of lutein while dogs fed 40 mg had higher plasma lutein concentrations. Peak concentrations in dogs fed 40 mg of lutein were approximately 7-fold of that after a single dose. The uptake of lutein by peripheral blood lymphocytes after 7 or 14 days of feeding reflected that observed in plasma (**Figure 3**). Dogs given lutein had elevated concentrations of lutein, with dogs fed 40 mg of lutein showing the highest lutein uptake. Lutein concentrations on day 14 were 4- to 5-fold higher than on day 7. In the lymphocytes, lutein was taken up by all subcellular fractions (**Figure 4**), with concentrations averaging 10-fold higher on day 14 as compared to day 7. Concentrations were lowest in the nuclear fraction and were similar in the mitochondria, microsome, and cytosol. Blood neutrophils also showed significant uptake of lutein (**Figure 5**), albeit at a lower level than that for lymphocytes. Maximal concentrations were observed by day 7. In the neutrophils, lutein was taken up by all subcellular fractions at almost similar rates (**Figure 6**). Concentrations of lutein in the subcellular fractions were 4- to 10-fold higher on day 14 compared to day 7. Dietary lutein did not influence plasma retinol or α-tocopherol concentrations.

This study shows for the first time, that the dog is able to absorb lutein from the diet and transfers the lutein into the subcellular fractions of both lymphocytes and neutrophils. No studies are available to date for comparison. However, earlier studies have generally reported either trace[14] to moderate[15-18] concentrations of β-carotene in the blood. Similarly, exotic canids do not have detectable blood carotene.[19] The bovine,[20] porcine,[21,22] and human[23] blood and lymphocytes take up significant amounts of β-carotene into their subcellular organelles[21,22] although not much is known concerning lutein uptake.

In summary, the dog absorbs significant amounts of lutein from the diet. The circulating lutein is subsequently taken up by peripheral blood lymphocytes and neutrophils and transferred into all subcellular organelles. Therefore, how absorbed lutein modulates immunity in the dog is studied.

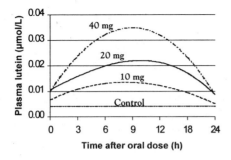

Figure 1. Changes in concentrations of plasma lutein in dogs given a single oral dose of 0, 10, 20 or 40 mg of lutein.

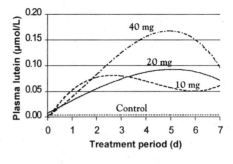

Figure 2. Changes in concentrations of plasma lutein in dogs given daily oral doses of 0, 10, 20 or 40 mg of lutein.

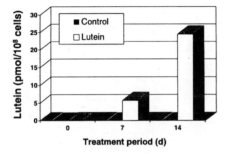

Figure 3. Uptake of dietary lutein by blood lymphocytes from dogs fed lutein daily for 7 or 14 days. Lutein values represent means of samples pooled across supplemented treatments.

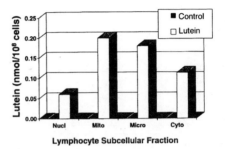

Figure 4. Uptake of dietary lutein by the nuclei (Nucl), mitochondria (Mito), microsomes (Micro) and cytosol (Cyto) of blood lymphocytes from dogs fed lutein daily for 14 days. Lutein values represent means of samples pooled across supplemented treatments.

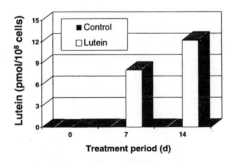

Figure 5. Uptake of dietary lutein by blood neutrophils from dogs fed lutein daily for 7 or 14 days. Lutein values represent means of samples pooled across supplemented treatments.

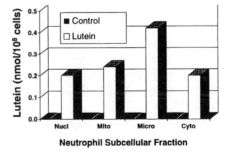

Figure 6. Uptake of dietary lutein by the nuclei (Nucl), mitochondria (Mito), microsomes (Micro) and cytosol (Cyto) of blood neutrophils from dogs fed lutein daily for 14 days. Lutein values represent means of samples pooled across supplemented treatments.

Lutein Uptake in Cats. Mature female short hair Tabby cats were used to study lutein uptake in plasma and in blood lymphocytes and neutrophils. In experiment 1, cats were given a single oral dose of 0, 2, 5 or 10 mg lutein and blood sampled at 0, 3, 6, 9, 12, and 24 hours post-dosing. Concentrations of plasma lutein increased in a dose-related manner throughout the study period (***Figure 7***). Maximal concentrations were observed at six hours in all lutein-fed cats. The half-life of plasma lutein was approximately 20 hours and is thus similar to that observed in dogs. Adjusted for body weight, the peak concentration of plasma lutein in cats averaged about 3-fold higher than in dogs. In experiment 2, repeated doses of 0, 2, 5 or 10 mg of lutein was given. Again, plasma concentrations increased in a dose-dependent manner throughout the 7 day feeding period (***Figure 8***). Plasma lutein in lutein-fed cats decreased rapidly after the last dose of lutein was given on day 7. Lutein feeding did not influence plasma retinol or α-tocopherol.

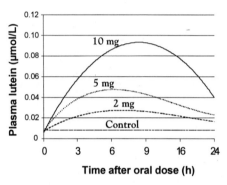 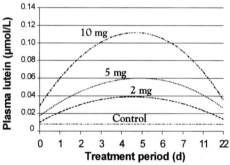

Figure 7. Changes in concentrations of plasma lutein in cats given a single oral dose of 0, 2, 5 or 10 mg of lutein.

Figure 8. Changes in concentrations of plasma lutein in cats given daily oral doses of 0, 2, 5 or 10 mg of lutein.

Therefore, cats absorb significant amounts of lutein from the diet and transfer the circulating lutein to peripheral blood lymphocytes and neutrophils. How absorbed lutein modulates immunity in the cat is presently not known. However, it is known that cats are able to absorb β-carotene[24] and similarly transfer the β-carotene to blood leukocytes.

Lutein on Immunity in Dogs

A study was designed to examine the role of dietary lutein in modulating both cell-mediated and humoral immunity in dogs. Female Beagles (4 to 5 months old) were supplemented daily with 0, 5, 10 or 20 mg of lutein for 12 weeks. The immune parameters measured included delayed-type hypersensitivity (DTH) response against PHA, a nonspecific antigen, and a polyvalent vaccine (Vanguard 5, Smith Klein/Pfizer), a specific antigen.

Lutein supplementation increased plasma lutein concentrations in a dose-dependent mannner. These changes generally reflected the DTH response to both the specific (vaccine) and non-specific (PHA) antigens (***Figure 9***). At 6 weeks of

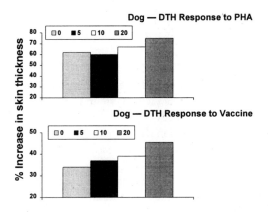

Figure 9. Forty-eight hour DTH response in dogs fed 0, 5, 10 or 20 mg of lutein daily for 6 weeks.

lutein feeding, DTH response to both PHA and the vaccine was dose-dependent. The dose-dependent DTH response was most evident at 24 hours post-injection for PHA, but was distinct at all periods for the vaccine. The DTH response to the vaccine remained high through 72 hours post-injection, whereas the response to PHA decreased after the first 24 hours. Delayed type hypersensitivity is a cellular reaction involving T cells and macrophages but does not involve an antibody component. Upon presentation of an antigen or allergen by antigen-presenting cells (e.g., macrophages), T cells become activated and release lymphokines. These lymphokines activate macrophages and cause them to become voracious killers of the foreign invaders. Therefore, this data show heightened cell-mediated response in dogs fed lutein. In a similar study, dogs fed β-carotene also showed enhanced dose-related DTH response.[25] Data on other immune responses are not available at the present time.

Other studies on the immuno-modulatory action of lutein are presently unavailable. However, studies in other species with other carotenoids have generally shown enhanced immune response to carotenoid supplementation.[1-3] For instance, enhanced DTH response, Ig production, and CD4⁺ lymphocyte population was observed in dogs fed β-carotene.[26] Also, β-carotene increased the number of T helper cells in human[27] and mice,[28] increased IL-2 receptor expression on natural killer cells,[29] enhanced the proliferation and induction of cytotoxic T cells,[28] and stimulated lymphocyte proliferation in cattle,[30,31]pigs,[32] and mice.[13] Carotenoids also stimulated humoral response in humans and in mice[9,33] and bactericidal ability of blood neutrophils in the bovine.[30,34]

These studies represent the first report on the uptake of dietary lutein by the blood and circulating leukocytes in dogs and cats. Furthermore, this increase in lutein is associated with a heightened cell-mediated immune response as evident from an increased DTH response (and likely in other immune parameters) in lutein-supplemented dogs. No data is presently available on the immuno-modulatory

Overall
Summary

effects of dietary lutein in cats. Therefore, supplemental lutein promotes the immune health of dogs and will likely improve their overall health.

References

1. Chew BP. Antioxidant vitamins affect food animal immunity and health. Conference: Beyond deficiency: New views of vitamins in ruminant nutrition and health. *J Nutr* 1995; 125:1804S-1808S.

2. Chew BP. Role of carotenoids in the immune response. Symposium on "Antioxidants, Immune Response and Animal Function." *J Dairy Sci* 1993; 76:2804-2811.

3. Chew BP. Vitamin A and β-carotene on host defense. Symposium: Immune function: Relationship of nutrition and disease control. *J Dairy Sci* 1987; 70:2732-2743.

4. Chew BP. Importance of antioxidant vitamins in immunity and health in animals. *Anim Feed Sci Tech* 1996; 59:103-114.

5. Santamaria L, Bianchi A, Arnaboldi A, Andreoni L, Bermond P. Dietary carotenoids block photocarcinogenic enhancement by benzo (a)pyrene and inhibit its carcinogenesis in the dark. *Experientia* 1983; 39:1043-1045.

6. Murakoshi M, Takayasu J, Kimura O, Kohmura E, Nishino H, Iwashima A, Okuzumi J, Sakai T, Sugimoto T, Imanishi J. Inhibitory effects of α-carotene on proliferation of the human neuroblastoma cell line GOTO. *J Natl Cancer Inst* 1989; 81:1649-1652.

7. Bendich A, Shapiro SS. Effect of β-carotene and canthaxanthin on the immune responses of the rat. *J Nutr* 1986; 116:2254-2262.

8. Shklar G, Schwartz J. Tumor necrosis factor in experimental cancer regression with alpha-tocopherol, beta-carotene, canthaxanthin and algae extract. *Eur J Cancer Clin Oncol* 1988; 24:839-850.

9. Jyonouchi H, Zhang L, Gross M, Tomita Y. Immunomodulating actions of carotenoids: Enhancement of *in vivo* and *in vitro* antibody production to T-dependent antigens. *Nutr Cancer* 1994; 21:47-58.

10. Chew BP, Wong MW, Wong TS. Effects of lutein from marigold extract on immunity and growth of mammary tumors in mice. *Anticancer Res* 1996; 17:3689-3694.

11. Park JS, Chew BP, Wong TS. Effect of dietary lutein on growth of mammary tumor in BALB/c mice. *FASEB J* 1997; 10:A447.

12. Wong TS, Chew BP, Wong MW. Effect of dietary β-carotene, canthaxanthin and astaxanthin on growth of mammary tumors in mice. *FASEB J* 1995; 9:A459.

13. Chew BP, Wong MW, Wong TS. Effects of dietary β-carotene, canthaxanthin and astaxanthin on lymphocyte function in mice. *FASEB J* 1995; 9:A441.

14. Goodwin TW. In: Goodwin TW, ed. *Mammalian Carotenoids in the Comparative Biochemistry of the Carotenoids.* London: Chapman and Hall Ltd., 1952; 229-269.

15. Baker H, Schor SM, Murphy BD. Blood vitamin and choline concentrations in healthy domestic cats, dogs and horses. *Am J Vet Res* 1986; 47:1468-1471.

16. Frohring WO. Vitamin A requirements of growing puppies. *Proc Soc Exp Biol Med* 1935; 33:280-282.

17. Steenbock H, Nelson EM, Hart EB. Fat soluble vitamins. IX. The incidence of an opthalamic reaction in dog fed a fat soluble vitamin deficient diet. *Am J Physiol* 1921; 58:14-19.

18. Turner RG. Effect of prolonged feeding of raw carrots on vitamin content of liver and kidneys in the dog. *Proc Soc Exp Biol Med* 1934; 31:866-868.

19. Slifka K, Crissey S, Stacewicz-Sapuntzakis M, Bowen P. A survey of serum carotenoids in captive exotic animals. *FASEB J* 1994; 8:A191.

20. Chew BP, Wong TS, Michal JJ. Uptake of orally administered β-carotene by blood plasma, leukocytes, and lipoproteins in calves. *J Anim Sci* 1993; 71:730-739.

21. Chew BP, Wong TS, Michal JJ, Standaert FE, Heirman LR. Kinetic characteristics of β-carotene uptake after an injection of β-carotene in pigs. *J Anim Sci* 1991; 69:4883-4891.

22. Chew BP, Wong TS, Michal JJ, Standaert FE, Heirman LR. Subcellular distribution of β-carotene, retinol and α-tocopherol in porcine lymphocytes after a single injection of β-carotene. *J Anim Sci* 1991; 69:4892-4897.

23. Mathews-Roth MM. Carotenoids in the leukocytes of carotenemic and non-carotenemic individuals. *Clin Chem* 1978; 24:700-701.

24. Chew BP, Weng BC, Park JS, Wong TS, Combs RL, Hayek MG, Reinhart GA. Uptake of β-carotene by plasma and lymphocytes in cats. *FASEB J* 1997; 10:A447.

25. Chew BP, Park JS, Wong TS, Weng BC, Kim HW, Byne KM, Hayek MG, Reinhart GA. Role of dietary β-carotene in modulating cell-mediated and humoral immune resonse in dogs. *FASEB J* 1998; submitted.

26. Weng BC, Chew BP, Park JS, Wong TS, Combs RL, Hayek MG, Reinhart GA. β-carotene uptake by blood plasma and leukocytes in dogs. *FASEB J* 1997; 10:A447.

27. Alexander M, Newmark H, Miller RG. Oral β-carotene can increase the number of OKT4+ cells in human blood. *Immunol Lett* 1985; 9:221-224.

28. Seifter E, Rettara G, Padawer J, Levenson SM. Moloney murine sarcoma virus tumors in CBA/J mice: Chemopreventive and chemotherapeutic actions of supplemental β-carotene. *J Natl Cancer Inst* 1982; 68:835-840.

29. Prabhala RH, Maxey V, Hicks MJ, Watson RR. Enhancement of the expression of activation markers of human peripheral blood mononuclear cells by *in vitro* culture with retinoids and carotenoids. *J Leuk Biol* 1989; 45:249-254.

30. Michal JJ, Heirman LR, Wong TS, Chew BP. Modulatory effects of dietary β-carotene on blood and mammary leukocyte function in periparturient dairy cows. *J Dairy Sci* 1994; 77:1408-1421.

31. Daniel LR, Chew BP, Tanaka TS, Tjoelker LW. *In vitro* effects of β-carotene and vitamin A on peripartum bovine peripheral blood mononuclear cell proliferation. *J Dairy Sci* 1991; 74:911-915.

32. Hoskinson CD, Chew BP, Wong TS. Effects of β-carotene (BC) and vitamin A (VA) on mitogen-induced lymphocyte proliferation in the pig *in vivo*. *FASEB J* 1989; 3:A663.

33. Jyonouchi H, Sun S, Gross M. Effects of carotenoids on *in vitro* immunoglobulin production by human peripheral blood mononuclear cells: Astaxanthin, a carotenoid without vitamin A activity, enhances *in vitro* immunoglobulin production in response to a T-dependent stimulant and antigen. *Nutr Cancer* 1995; 23:171-183.

34. Tjoelker LW, Chew BP, Tanaka TS, Daniel LR. Effects of dietary vitamin A and β-carotene on polymorphonuclear leukocyte and lymphocyte function in dairy cows during the early dry period. *J Dairy Sci* 1990; 73:1017-1022.

Effect of Dietary Chromium on the Canine Immune Response

Jerry W. Spears, PhD
Professor, Department of Animal Science
North Carolina State University, Raleigh, North Carolina, USA

Talmage T. Brown, Jr., DVM, PhD[a];
Michael G. Hayek, PhD[b]; Gregory D. Sunvold, PhD[b]
[a]Department of Veterinary Microbiology, Pathology and Parasitology,
North Carolina State University, Raleigh, North Carolina, USA;
[b]Research and Development, The Iams Company, Lewisburg, Ohio, USA

Introduction

Animals are dependent on an efficient host defense system for eliminating potential disease causing organisms. Nutrition plays a major role in maximizing immunity and disease resistance. A number of different nutrients have been shown to affect immune functions. Increased incidence or severity of certain diseases has also been associated with deficiencies of certain nutrients. Dietary requirements of some minerals and vitamins for maximum immune response may be higher than for growth or other measures of nutrient adequacy.

Chromium (Cr) was shown to be essential for normal glucose metabolism in 1959 and subsequent research indicated that chromium potentiated insulin function.[1] Early studies indicated that Cr supplementation increased longevity in rats[2] and male mice.[3] Furthermore, Cr addition to diets reduced mortality during pregnancy in guinea pigs[4] and following an epidemic of pneumonia in rats.[2] More recently Cr has been shown to affect immunity and disease susceptibility in cattle.[5-6] This paper will review the role of Cr in immunology and disease resistance and describe research examining the effect of dietary Cr on immune response in dogs.

Chromium and Nonspecific Immunity

Phagocytosis and killing of infectious microorganisms are important functions of nonspecific cellular immune effectors such as macrophages, monocytes, and neutrophils. When foreign materials, such as disease causing organisms, enter the body they are first subjected to phagocytic cells that serve to bind, ingest, and destroy foreign material.

The effect of Cr on the ability of phagocytic cells to ingest and kill microorganisms has received little attention. Preincubation of leukocyte with Cr from children with insulin dependent diabetes improved chemotaxis.[7] It is known that insulin dependent diabetes impairs chemotaxis of leukocytes. However, neutrophils

555

isolated from dairy cows supplemented with 0.5 ppm of Cr (amino acid chelate) and control cows had a similar ability to phagocytize fluorescent beads.[8] The addition of high Cr yeast to calf diets did not affect the ability of neutrophils to kill *Staphylococcus aureus*.[9]

Chromium and Humoral Immunity	The humoral immune system produces antibodies against substances that are foreign to the body. Antibody production against a specific antigen involves a coordinated interaction between antigen presenting cells (macrophages) and T and B lymphocytes with differentiation of B lymphocytes into antibody-secreting plasma cells.

Dietary Cr effects on humoral immunity have been evaluated by measuring specific antibody production following administration of either a foreign protein or a vaccine. Dairy cows supplemented with 0.5 ppm of Cr from an amino acid chelate had greater primary and secondary antibody responses to ovalbumin than control cows.[6] The primary injection of ovalbumin was given 2 weeks prior to parturition and the secondary injection was administered 2 weeks postpartum. In this same experiment, cows were also injected with human red blood cells, and Cr did not affect antibody response to this antigen. In calves that had been stressed, due to shipping and feed restriction, Cr supplementation from high Cr yeast increased primary but not secondary antibody responses to human red blood cells.[5] In contrast, Kegley et al.[10] reported that Cr supplementation from a Cr nicotinic acid complex did not affect antibody response to porcine red blood cell immunization in stressed cattle. Similarly, in young calves fed milk diets neither Cr chloride or Cr nicotinic acid complex enhanced specific antibody responses to porcine red blood cells.[11]

van Heugten and Spears[12] evaluated antibody responses to sheep red blood cells and ovalbumin in weanling pigs fed diets supplemented with 0 or 0.2 ppm of Cr from different sources (Cr chloride, Cr nicotinic acid complex, Cr picolinate). Antibody response to sheep red blood cells tended to be increased by Cr nicotinic acid, but not by Cr chloride or Cr picolinate. Pigs supplemented with Cr nicotinic acid complex or Cr picolinate showed lower antibody responses to ovalbumin than control or Cr chloride supplemented pigs.

Supplemental Cr, as an amino acid chelate, increased antibody titers to bovine rhinotracheitis virus but not to parainfluenza virus type 3 following immunization using a commercial vaccine.[13] Chang[14] also observed that antibody titer responses to Cr supplementation were antigen-dependent and variable in cattle. Following vaccination, Cr supplementation enhanced antibody titers to bovine viral diarrhea but not to infectious bovine rhinotracheitis, parainfluenza-3, bovine respiratory syncytial virus or *Pasteurella hemolytica*.

The primary effectors of cell-mediated immune responses are T lymphocytes. A subpopulation of T lymphocytes is involved in cell-mediated immunity as helper cells to facilitate recognition of antigens by T and B cells and aid in production of antibodies. Suppressor T cells attenuate functional activity of other T cells, B cells, and macrophages, thereby providing a negative control in immune responsiveness.

A number of studies have investigated the effect of dietary Cr on the ability of isolated lymphocytes to proliferate in response to mitogen stimulation. Lymphocytes isolated from dairy cows supplemented with a Cr amino acid chelate from 6 weeks prepartum through 16 weeks postpartum had increased blastogenic responses to concanavalin A (Con A) stimulation.[6] Chromium addition to the diet prevented a decrease in blastogenic response that was observed in control cows 2 weeks prepartum. The addition of blood serum from Cr-supplemented cows to cultures of lymphocytes isolated from control cows also increased Con A-induced lymphocyte blastogenesis.[15] The enhanced blastogenesis observed did not appear to be related to concentrations of insulin or other hormones present in serum from Cr-supplemented cows. Direct addition of Cr from either a Cr amino acid chelate or Cr chloride to lymphocytes obtained from non-Cr-supplemented cattle also increased blastogenic response to Con A stimulation.[8, 16]

In stressed calves, Cr supplementation, from an amino acid chelate, increased Con A-induced lymphocyte blastogenesis in calves showing signs of morbidity, but not in calves with normal body temperatures and no visual signs of sickness.[16] In contrast, Cr supplementation did not affect blastogenic responses of lymphocytes obtained from calves following inoculation with bovine herpesvirus-1.[9] Other studies in cattle have reported no effect of Cr supplementation on phytohemagglutinin (PHA) or pokeweed mitogen (PWM) stimulated lymphocyte blastogenesis.[11,17] Lymphocyte blastogenic responses to PHA and PWM were increased nine days after the initiation of Cr supplementation in weanling pigs fed Cr chloride or Cr picolinate.[12] However, lymphocyte stimulation was not affected by dietary Cr on day 34 of the study.

Lymphocytes produce a number of cytokines in response to mitogen stimulation that are involved in the regulation of a number of host defense mechanisms. Burton et al.[18] compared cytokine production from mononuclear cells obtained from Cr-supplemented and control cows. Following stimulation with Con A, mononuclear cells from Cr-supplemented cows produced lower concentrations of interleukin-2, interferon-γ, and tumor necrosis factor-α than cells from control cows.

Effects of Cr on cell-mediated immunity have also been evaluated *in vivo* by measuring inflammatory responses following percutaneous application of dinitrochlorobenzene or intradermal injection of PHA. In stressed calves that had been sensitized to dinitrochlorobenzene, Cr supplementation did not affect response to dinitrochlorobenzene application.[5,10] Supplementation of either Cr chloride or a Cr nicotinic acid complex increased inflammatory responses to intradermal injection of PHA in young calves fed milk.[11] The Cr nicotinic acid complex gave a slightly greater skin thickness response than Cr chloride.

Interaction Between Chromium, Stress, and Disease

Various types of stress increase urinary losses of Cr and this may lead to Cr deficiency.[19] Studies with cattle that had been stressed due to shipping indicate that Cr supplementation may alleviate effects of stress on animal performance and health. Incidence of respiratory disease is frequently high in stressed calves. Chromium supplementation of stressed calves has reduced morbidity following shipping.[5,20,21] In other studies with stressed calves, Cr supplementation has not affected incidence of disease.[22-24] Wright et al.[25] reported no effect of Cr supplementation on morbidity, but Cr-supplemented calves that required treatment had fewer relapses than control calves during a 28 day period following shipping. Chromium addition to diets of stressed calves has also improved, or at least tended to improve, rate of body weight gain in some studies.[5,20,25]

Recently, Cr picolinate supplementation of dairy cows during the last 9 weeks of pregnancy reduced incidence of retained placenta after parturition from 56 to 16%.[26] In another study, supplementing dairy cows with a Cr amino acid chelate did not affect reproductive or mammary gland health status.[8]

Studies have also evaluated the effects of dietary Cr on physiological responses of calves to an experimental disease challenge.[9-11] Chromium has been supplemented for 49 to 75 days prior to disease challenge in these studies. Kegley et al.[11] inoculated young calves, fed milk diets, intranasally with infectious bovine rhinotracheitis virus followed by *Pasteurella hemolytica*, intratracheally, five days later. Calves supplemented with 0.4 ppm of a Cr nicotinic acid complex or inorganic Cr chloride tended to have lower body temperatures at certain time points following the viral and bacterial challenges than control calves. Supplementing calves with 0.4 ppm of Cr (Cr nicotinic acid complex) for 56 days prior to shipping did not affect body temperature or feed intake responses to an intranasal infectious bovine rhinotracheitis viral challenge.[10] However, Cr supplementation did increase body weight gain after the disease challenge. Rectal temperature responses were also not affected by Cr supplementation (high Cr yeast) in calves inoculated with bovine herpesvirus-1.[9]

Stress results in elevated blood concentrations of cortisol which is known to depress immune functions.[27] Chromium supplementation in cattle has decreased serum cortisol concentrations in some studies,[5,20,24] but not in others.[10,17,21] When serial blood samples were obtained from jugular cannulated calves at 4 hour intervals for 6 days, Cr supplementation (high Cr yeast) did not affect serum cortisol concentrations.[9]

Experiment 1. This study was conducted to determine the effects of dietary Cr on cell-mediated and humoral immune response in dogs. Twenty-four female Beagle dogs, 2 to 3 years of age, were used in this study. All dogs were fed the control diet for 14 days before being stratified by weight and randomly assigned to diets containing 0, 0.15 or 0.30 ppm of supplemental Cr.[28] Chromium was supplied in the form of Cr tripicolinate. Dogs were offered 250 grams of treatment diet once daily in the morning from stainless steel feeders. Dogs were housed individually in 2.7 m x 1.3 m pens in an environmentally controlled room and allowed outdoors to exercise with their treatment group at least once daily.

Humoral immunity was determined by measuring specific antibody responses following intramuscular injection of 1 ml of a 20% solution of sheep red blood cells (RBC). The RBC were injected on day 88 of the study and blood samples were collected on days 0, 7, 14, and 21 post injection for antibody titer determination. Hemagglutination titers to sheep RBC were determined using a mercaptoethanol-phosphate buffered saline microtitration procedure.[29]

In vitro cell-mediated immunity was assessed using a lymphocyte blastogenesis assay.[30] Approximately 10 ml of blood was collected from each dog in heparinized tubes via venipuncture for isolation of mononuclear cells. Blood mononuclear cells were isolated by gradient centrifugation and plated in 96-well plates at a concentration of 2 x 10^6 cells/ml. Phytohemagglutinin, Con A, and PWM were used as mitogens at concentrations of 10, 5, and 5 μg/ml, respectively. Cells were incubated at 37° C in 5% CO_2 atmosphere for 48 hours. Cultures were then pulsed with 0.1μ Ci of methyl [^{3}H]-thymidine and incubated for an additional 18 hours. Uptake of [^{3}H]-thymidine was used as a measure of lymphocyte blastogenesis. Lymphocyte blastogenesis was measured prior to initiation of dietary treatments and after dogs were fed the treatment diets for 94 days. Initial values obtained when all dogs were consuming the control diet were used as a covariate when data were analyzed statistically.

Cell-mediated immunity also was measured *in vivo* by determining the inflammatory response of dogs to an intradermal injection of PHA. Each dog was injected with 150 μg of PHA in 0.1 ml of phosphate buffered saline in the skin outside the rear flank muscles. The injection site was shaved with surgical clippers and skinfold thickness was measured at 0, 4, 24, and 48 hours after injection using micrometric calipers.

All dogs responded to sheep RBC immunization (**Table 1**). Peak antibody titers against sheep RBC were observed by day 14 following injection. Chromium supplementation did not affect antibody titer responses. Immunoglobulin G and IgM subclasses also were not affected by dietary Cr (data not shown).

The results of the mitogen-induced lymphocyte blastogenesis assay are shown in **Table 2**. Uptake of labeled thymidine was low in unstimulated cultures,

Table 1. Effect of dietary chromium on antibody response to sheep red blood cells in experiment 1. Antibody titers are expressed as log, of the reciprocal of the highest serum dilution causing agglutination of sheep red blood cells.

Day*	Dietary Chromium (ppm)			
	Control	0.15	0.30	SEM
0	0.38	0.56	0.25	0.17
7	1.88	1.00	1.44	0.48
14	1.88	1.88	1.94	0.11
21	1.81	1.71	1.81	0.17

* Day post injection of sheep red blood cells.

Table 2. Effect of dietary chromium on mitogen-induced lymphocyte blastogenesis in experiment 1. Values are expressed as cpm x 10^3.

	Dietary Chromium (ppm)			
	Control	0.15	0.30	SEM
Unstimulated	0.85	1.33	1.17	0.24
Stimulated				
PHA	27.5	35.7	38.3	8.5
Con A	43.8	54.0	52.4	9.3
PWM	26.7	36.4	36.6	7.3

but as expected, was greatly increased by addition of either mitogen. Numerically, blastogenic response to mitogen stimulation was higher for lymphocytes isolated from Cr-supplemented dogs. However, dietary Cr did not significantly affect lymphocyte blastogenic responses to either of the mitogens tested. Different mitogens were used because PHA and Con A stimulate predominantly T-lymphocytes, whereas PWM is a T-dependent B cell mitogen.

Dietary Cr also did not affect *in vivo* cell-mediated immunity based on skinfold thickness response to an intradermal injection of PHA (**Table 3**). Maximal inflammatory response to PHA was observed at the 24 hour measurement and by 48 hours post injection, skin thickness had decreased.

Experiment 2. This study evaluated the effect of Cr picolinate addition to lymphocytes, isolated from dogs, on mitogen stimulation.[28] Blood was obtained from 24 dogs fed a diet containing no supplemental Cr. Chromium, as Cr picolinate, was added to lymphocytes from each dog prior to the initial 48 hour incubation to provide either 0 or 0.45 ppm of Cr in the culture medium. Lymphocytes were stimulated with Con A and PWM.

Table 3. Effect of dietary chromium on *in vivo* cell-mediated immune response to PHA in experiment 1. Values are expressed as skinfold thickness (mm) at the injection site.

Time*	Dietary Chromium (ppm)			
	Control	0.15	0.30	SEM
4 hours	4.51	5.02	4.68	0.24
24 hours	5.87	5.84	6.14	0.36
48 hours	5.48	5.76	5.51	0.29

* Hours after intradermal injection of PHA.

Addition of 0.45 ppm of Cr to lymphocytes in the blastogenesis assay neither enhanced nor depressed blastogenic response (*Table 4*). In contrast, Cr addition to lymphocytes, isolated from cattle, increased blastogenic responses to stimulation with Con A.[8,16] In these studies, Cr was added to lymphocyte cultures in the form of Cr chloride or a Cr amino acid chelate. Failure of Cr addition to stimulate mitogen-induced blastogenesis in the present study could relate to the form of Cr added or species differences between dogs and cattle.

Table 4. Effect of chromium addition to lymphocyte cultures on mitogen-induced blastogenesis in experiment 2. Values are expressed as cpm x 10^3.

	Added Chromium (ppm)		
	0	0.45	SEM
Con A	20.6	23.4	4.3
PWM	17.1	15.1	4.1

Summary and Perspectives

Supplementation of Cr has increased cell-mediated and humoral immune response in cattle. Consistent with findings of enhanced immunity, Cr supplementation has also decreased the incidence of stress related diseases in cattle. However, responses in immunity and disease resistance to Cr supplementation have been variable, suggesting that dietary or physiological factors affect immunological responses to dietary Cr. Variable responses to Cr may relate to differences in available Cr content of basal diets. Little is known regarding bioavailability of Cr from feed ingredients. Since Cr and stress appear to be interrelated, the degree and type of stress may be important determinants of whether Cr supplementation enhances immune response.

In the present study with dogs, the addition of 0.15 or 0.30 ppm of Cr to a control diet did not affect cell-mediated or humoral immune response. The control diet contained approximately 0.70 ppm of Cr and this level may have provided adequate bioavailable Cr to maximize immune function. Dogs in the present study were exposed to minimal stress and this may at least partly explain the lack of response to increasing dietary Cr.

Recently, immune responses were compared in young (mean age of 2.4 years), middle age (mean of 5.8 years), and old dogs (mean of 9.1 years).[31] This study indicated that lymphocytes from old dogs were less responsive to mitogen stimulation than lymphocytes from young or middle age dogs. Dogs used in the present study were only 2 to 3 years of age. If older dogs had been used, perhaps Cr supplementation would have improved immune response. Furthermore, providing small quantities of a bioavailable Cr source such as Cr picolinate may prevent age-related immunosuppression and increase longevity.

References

1. Offenbacher EG, Pi-Sunyer FX, Stoecker BJ. Chromium. In: O'Dell BL, Sunde RA, eds. *Handbook of Nutritionally Essential Mineral Elements.* New York: Marcel Dekker Inc., 1997; 389-412.

2. Schroeder HA, Balassa JJ, Vinton Jr WH. Chromium, cadmium, and lead in rats: effects on life span, tumors, and tissue levels. *J Nutr* 1965; 86:51-66.

3. Schroeder HA, Vinton Jr WH, Balassa JJ. Effect of chromium, cadmium and other trace metals on the growth and survival of mice. *J Nutr* 1963; 80:39-47.

4. Preston AM, Dowdy RP, Preston MA, Freeman JN. Effect of dietary chromium on glucose tolerance and serum cholesterol in guinea pigs. *J Nutr* 1976; 106:1391-1397.

5. Moonsie-Shageer S, Mowat DN. Effect of level of supplemental chromium on performance, serum constituents, and immune status of stressed feeder calves. *J Anim Sci* 1993; 71:232-238.

6. Burton JL, Mallard BA, Mowat DN. Effects of supplemental chromium on immune responses of periparturient and early lactation dairy cows. *J Anim Sci* 1993; 71:1532-1539.

7. Hambidge KM, Martinez B, Jones JA, Boyle CE, Hathaway WE, O'Brien D. Correction of impaired chemotaxis of polymorphonuclear leukocytes from patients with diabetes mellitus by incubating with trivalent chromium *in vitro. Pediatr Res* 1972; 6:133(abstr).

8. Chang X, Mallard BA, Mowat DN. Effects of chromium on health status, blood neutrophil phagocytosis, and *in vitro* lymphocyte blastogenesis of dairy cows. *Vet Immunol Immunopathol* 1996; 52:37-52.

9. Arthington JD, Corah LR, Minton JE, Elsasser TH, Blecha F. Supplemental dietary chromium does not influence ACTH, cortisol, or immune responses in young calves inoculated with Bovine Herpesvirus-1. *J Anim Sci* 1997; 75:217-223.

10. Kegley EB, Spears JW, Brown Jr TT. Effect of shipping and chromium supplementation on performance, immune response, and disease resistance of steers. *J Anim Sci* 1997; 75:1956-1964.

11. Kegley EB, Spears JW, Brown Jr TT. Immune response and disease resistance of calves fed chromium nicotinic acid complex or chromium chloride. *J Dairy Sci* 1996; 79:1278-1283.

12. van Heugten E, Spears JW. Immune response and growth of stressed weanling pigs fed diets supplemented with organic or inorganic forms of chromium. *J Anim Sci* 1997; 75:409-416.

13. Burton JL, Mallard BA, Mowat DN. Effects of supplemental chromium on antibody responses of newly weaned feedlot calves to immunization with infectious bovine rhinotracheitis and parainfluenza 3 virus. *Can J Vet Res* 1994; 58:148-151.

14. Chang X. Effects of chromium on performance, health status, and immune response in cattle. PhD Dissertation. University of Guelph, Guelph, Canada. 1994.

15. Burton JL, Nonnecke BJ, Elsasser TH, Mallard BA, Yang WZ, Mowat DN. Immunomodulatory activity of blood serum from chromium-supplemented periparturient dairy cows. *Vet Immunol Immunopathol* 1995; 49:29-38.

16. Chang X, Mallard BA, Mowat DN. Proliferation of peripheral blood lymphocytes of feeder calves in response to chromium. *Nutr Res* 1994; 14:851-864.

17. Kegley EB, Spears JW. Immune response, glucose metabolism, and performance of stressed feeder calves fed inorganic or organic chromium. *J Anim Sci* 1995; 73:2721-2726.

18. Burton JL, Nonnecke BJ, Dubeski PL, Elsasser TH, Mallard BA. Effects of supplemental chromium on production of cytokines by mitogen-stimulated bovine peripheral blood mononuclear cells. *J Dairy Sci* 1996; 79:2237-2246.

19. Anderson RA. Stress effects on chromium nutrition of humans and farm animals. In: *Biotechnology in the Feed Industry*; Proceedings of the Alltech 10th Annual Symposium. Nottingham; University Press 1994; 267-274.

20. Mowat DN, Chang X, Yang WZ. Chelated chromium for stressed feeder calves. *Can J Anim Sci* 1993; 73:49-55.

21. Lindell SA, Brandt Jr RT, Milton JE, Blecha F, Stokka GL, Milton CT. Supplemental Cr and revaccination effects on performance and health of newly weaned calves. *J Anim Sci* 1994; 72(Suppl. 1):133(abstr).

22. Chang X, Mowat DN, Mallard BA. Supplemental chromium and niacin for stressed feeder calves. *Can J Anim Sci* 1995; 75:351-358.

23. Mathison GW, Engstrom DF. Chromium and protein supplements for growing-finishing beef steers fed barley-based diets. *Can J Anim Sci* 1995; 75:549-558.

24. Chang X, Mowat DN. Supplemental chromium for stressed and growing feeder calves. *J Anim Sci* 1992; 70:559-565.

25. Wright AG, Mowat DN, Mallard BA. Supplemental chromium and bovine respiratory disease vaccines for stressed feed calves. *Can J Anim Sci* 1994; 74:287-295.

26. Vallalobos-F JA, Romero-R C, Tarrago-C MR, Rosado A. Supplementation with chromium picolinate reduces the incidence of placental retention in dairy cows. *Can J Anim Sci* 1997; 77:329-330.

27. Kelley KW. Stress and immune function; A bibliographic review. *Ann Rech Vet* 1980; 11:445-459.

28. Keeling KL. Effect of chromium picolinate on glucose metabolism and immune response in dogs. MS Thesis. North Carolina State University, Raleigh. 1997.

29. Wegmann NTT, Smithies O. A simple hemagglutination system requiring small amounts of red cells and antibodies. *Transfusion* 1966; 6:67-72.

30. Lessard M, Yang WC, Elliott GS, Deslauriers N, Grisson GJ, Van Vleet JF, Schultz RD. Suppressive effect of serum from pigs and dogs fed a diet deficient in vitamin E and selenium on lymphocyte proliferation. *Vet Res* 1993; 24:291-303.

31. Greeley EH, Kealy RD, Ballam JM, Lawler DF, Segre M. The influence of age on the canine immune system. *Vet Immunol Immunopathol* 1996; 55:1-10.